MANAGERIAL ACCOUNTING

MANAGERIAL ACCOUNTING

FIRST EDITION

JOHN G. HELMKAMP
Indiana University

JOHN WILEY & SONS
NEW YORK   CHICHESTER   BRISBANE   TORONTO   SINGAPORE

Library of Congress Cataloging in Publication Data:

Helmkamp, John G.
  Managerial accounting.

  Bibliography: p.
  Includes index.
  1. Managerial accounting. I. Title.
HF5635.H45 1987   658.1′511   86-29021
ISBN 0-471-88910-5

Printed in the United States of America

10 9 8 7 6 5 4 3 2

Managerial Accounting

ACCOUNTING TEXTBOOKS FROM JOHN WILEY & SONS

Arpan and Radebaugh: INTERNATIONAL ACCOUNTING AND MULTINATIONAL ENTERPRISES, 2nd

Burch and Grudnitski: INFORMATION SYSTEMS: THEORY AND PRACTICE, 4th

DeCoster and Schafer: MANAGEMENT ACCOUNTING: A DECISION EMPHASIS, 3rd

Defliese et al.: MONTGOMERY'S AUDITING, Second College Edition

Delaney and Gleim: CPA EXAMINATION REVIEW—AUDITING

Delaney and Gleim: CPA EXAMINATION REVIEW—BUSINESS LAW

Delaney and Gleim: CPA EXAMINATION REVIEW—THEORY AND PRACTICE

Delaney et al.: GAAP: INTERPRETATION AND APPLICATION ANNUAL

Gleim and Delaney: CPA EXAMINATION REVIEW Volume I OUTLINES AND STUDY GUIDE

Gleim and Delaney: CPA EXAMINATION REVIEW Volume II PROBLEMS AND SOLUTIONS

Gross and Jablonsky: PRINCIPLES OF ACCOUNTING AND FINANCIAL REPORTING FOR NONPROFIT ORGANIZATIONS, 3rd

Guy: INTRODUCTION TO STATISTICAL SAMPLING IN AUDITING, 2nd

Haried, Imdieke, and Smith: ADVANCED ACCOUNTING, 3rd

Helmkamp, Imdieke, and Smith: PRINCIPLES OF ACCOUNTING, 2nd

Imdieke and Smith: FINANCIAL ACCOUNTING

Kam: ACCOUNTING THEORY

Kell and Ziegler: MODERN AUDITING, 3rd

Kieso and Weygandt: INTERMEDIATE ACCOUNTING, 5th

Moscove and Simkin: ACCOUNTING INFORMATION SYSTEMS, 3rd

Ramanathan: MANAGEMENT CONTROL IN NONPROFIT ORGANIZATIONS, TEXT AND CASES

Romney, Cherrington, and Hansen: CASEBOOK IN ACCOUNTING INFORMATION SYSTEMS

Sardinas, Burch, and Asebrook: EDP AUDITING: A PRIMER

Schroeder, McCullers, and Clark: ACCOUNTING THEORY, 3rd

Taylor and Glezen: AUDITING: Integrated Concepts and Procedures, 3rd

Taylor, Glezen, and Ehrenreich: CASE STUDY IN AUDITING, 3rd

Weygandt, Kieso, and Kell: ACCOUNTING PRINCIPLES

Wilkinson: ACCOUNTING AND INFORMATION SYSTEMS, 2nd

PREFACE

The complexities of today's business world make managerial accounting an absolute necessity for all types of managers. Every business organization must attempt to acquire and utilize its scarce resources in the best ways. Managers of retailing businesses, manufacturing operations, service firms, and not-for-profit organizations share this important responsibility. To do so, the managers need reliable managerial accounting information to anticipate the future and monitor the activities of their businesses. As a business expands in size and complexity, so does the need for managerial accounting information as responsibilities are assigned to more people.

The objective of this textbook is to explain how managerial accounting information is used by managers in various types of business organizations. The emphasis is on the development, interpretation, and application of managerial accounting information for planning activities, controlling operations, and making decisions. The approach taken in writing the book is a balance between the concepts and procedures associated with managerial accounting.

The book is designed for a one-term course in managerial accounting, to be used by students who have completed at least one term of financial accounting. The author has attempted to write the book with a lively and user-friendly style. References to a variety of businesses are included throughout the text to assist the student in understanding how the managerial accounting topics can be applied in the real world. The breadth and depth of the coverage should make the book useful and understandable for accounting majors and other students alike.

ORGANIZATION

This textbook is based on a logically developed, building-block process that covers the entire spectrum of managerial accounting. Five parts are involved, presented as follows:

PART	TITLE
1	Introduction to managerial accounting
2	Developing a cost data base for managerial accounting
3	Use of managerial accounting for decision making with a planning focus
4	Use of managerial accounting for decision making with a control focus
5	Consideration of specialized managerial accounting topics

Part 1 contains Chapter 1, which introduces the use of managerial accounting in a business organization. Of special interest in the chapter is a case study in which a business identifies the different kinds of managerial accounting information required to manage the operation. Part 2 consists of Chapters 2 through 5, and covers the development of the cost data base needed for managerial accounting. In Chapter 2, students are introduced to cost classifications, concepts, and uses. In Chapters 3 and 4, job order costing systems and process costing systems are described as the two types of product costing. Chapter 5 discusses how cost behavior is evaluated and translated into an income statement with a contribution margin format.

With an understanding of the cost data base, students are prepared to proceed to Part 3, which covers the use of managerial accounting for decision making with a planning focus in Chapters 6 through 9. Chapter 6 describes how cost-volume-profit relationships are developed as an extension of cost behavior analysis and used for managerial accounting purposes. In Chapter 7, decision making based on relevant information is discussed. Chapter 8 covers financial and operating budgeting, and Chapter 9 describes the use of capital budgeting techniques.

The use of managerial accounting for decision making with a control focus is presented in Part 4 (Chapters 10 through 13). Chapter 10 covers standard costs for direct materials and direct labor, with an emphasis on what management should do with significant cost variances. The same approach is taken for flexible budgets and standard manufacturing overhead costs in Chapter 11. In Chapter 12, profit variance analysis in general is considered, with the focus on profit variances from selling prices, sales volume, sales mix, and costs. The final chapter in Part 4, Chapter 13, describes how to account for decentralized operations with a responsibility accounting approach.

The final phase of the book, Part 5, contains four chapters, each of which discuss a specialized managerial accounting topic. Chapter 14 presents a more detailed coverage of cost allocation than the basic concepts of that topic introduced in Chapter 3. Chapter 15 integrates quantitative methods with managerial accounting applications. The author has chosen to include a chapter on quantitative methods instead of presenting the related topics in separate chapters because some instructors prefer to cover them separately or not at all. However, Chapter 15 is divided into parts so the quantitative methods can be considered at the same time the most closely related managerial accounting topics are taught in earlier chapters for those instructors who prefer that approach. For example, the following coverage can be used effectively:

PART IN CHAPTER 15	SUBJECT AREA	PRESENTED ALONG WITH
I	Decision making under uncertainty	Decision making in Chapter 7
II	Statistical cost control	Variance significance in Chapter 10
III	Inventory management	Budgeting in Chapter 8
IV	Linear programming	Decision making in Chapter 7
V	PERT	Budgeting in Chapter 8

The final two chapters in Part 5 of the book cover the analysis of financial statements and accounting for changing prices (Chapter 16) as well as the statement of cash flows (Chapter 17). The five parts represent a pedagogically sound sequence for a complete development of the subject of managerial accounting. At the same time, the organization enables an instructor to select topics and depth of coverage in different sequences without negatively affecting the continuity of the teaching process.

BASIC FEATURES OF THE BOOK

1. Each chapter begins with a concise description (overview) of the chapter and a list of the learning objectives involved. The learning objectives are also repeated in the margins of the text next to the relevant subject material to assist students through the chapters.

2. A glossary of key terms is presented at the end of each chapter. Each definition is keyed to a page within the chapter where the term is identified in boldface color. In addition, the index at the back of the text uses boldface color type to refer users to the end-of-chapter glossary definitions.

3. Discussion questions are included in every chapter to emphasize major points.

4. Exercises covering the most important topics in the chapters are presented in compact form.

5. Problems are included in each chapter for more comprehensive homework assignments.

6. Over 850 discussion questions, exercises, and problems are used to cover the various managerial accounting topics. All of the end-of-chapter materials have been classroom tested and carefully checked for accuracy and clarity.

7. Each exercise and problem has a brief description of the topic(s) covered. The intent is to focus the student's attention on the main considerations being addressed.

8. Illustrations of and references to real-world applications are presented throughout the text to show the students how managerial accounting is used.

9. A comprehensive discussion of the time value of money is presented in Appendix A at the end of the text.

10. Flow charts, graphs, illustrations, lists, and sentence breaks have been used extensively as visual or verbal aids to enhance student understanding and interest.

11. A complete package of supplementary materials are available to support the use of the book. Included are:

  a. An instructor's manual
  b. Overhead transparencies
  c. Check figures
  d. Test bank
  e. Computerized test bank
  f. Study guide
  g. Working papers
  h. Computerized spreadsheet exercises

ACKNOWLEDGMENTS

Any textbook is the product of numerous people whose efforts, ideas, and suggestions make the author's job manageable. I am indebted to many people for their assistance in making this book a reality. Of prime importance, the following professors reviewed the manuscript and made valuable suggestions concerning the organization and content of the book: Hobart Adams, University of Akron; Gordon Chapman, Eastern Washington University; Wallace Leese, California State University—Chico; Pat Mckenzie, Arizona State University; Steve Rowley, University of Minnesota—Duluth; and Doug Rusth, Portland State University.

I particularly appreciate the perseverance and contributions of a managerial accounting class at Indiana University, in which the manuscript was used for testing and improvement purposes. Other students at Indiana University who provided a variety of important inputs to the book are Peggy Andersen, Roy Elkes, Susan Probost, Jean Price, Rick Schrimper, Beth Taylor, and Craig Watson. I am especially thankful for the use of a limited number of relevant questions from previous Certificate in Management Accounting (CMA) examinations and the Uniform Certified Public Accountant (CPA) examinations.

Finally, I would be remiss not to express a special thanks to the many fine people on the John Wiley & Sons staff who gave so much of themselves to this book. Of particular importance, Lucille Sutton started the project and Dave Anthony made it all happen. In addition, Edward Burke was instrumental in guiding the book through the production process. As always, any errors or omissions are the sole responsibility of the author. Any suggestions for improving the book are always welcome.

John G. Helmkamp
Indiana University

ABOUT THE AUTHOR

John G. Helmkamp, DBA, CPA is Chairperson/Professor of Accounting in the School of Business at Indiana University. He received a doctorate in accounting from Indiana University, an MBA degree from Indiana University, and a BS degree from Purdue University. He formerly was a professional baseball player in the Los Angeles Dodgers organization and has worked in both public accounting and industry. Professor Helmkamp has published articles in *The Accounting Review, Journal of Information Science, Managerial Planning,* and other professional journals. He has taught undergraduate and graduate accounting courses at Arizona State University, Purdue University, and Indiana University. He also was the Chairperson of the accounting department at Arizona State University. In addition, Professor Helmkamp has developed and taught a variety of managerial accounting courses offered both nationally and internationally in executive development programs. He is a member of the American Institute of Certified Public Accountants, American Accounting Association, Financial Executives Institute, the Indiana CPA Society, Beta Gamma Sigma, and Beta Alpha Psi. Professor Helmkamp is also active as a consulting CPA and is listed in *Who's Who in America.* He is also a co-author of *Principles of Accounting,* a textbook published by John Wiley & Sons.

CHAPTER OUTLINE

CONTENTS

CHAPTER 16
ANALYSIS OF FINANCIAL STATEMENTS AND ACCOUNTING FOR CHANGING PRICES

CHAPTER 17
STATEMENT OF CASH FLOWS   670

PART 1

INTRODUCTION TO MANAGERIAL ACCOUNTING

1

MANAGERIAL ACCOUNTING: AN OVERVIEW

CHAPTER OVERVIEW AND OBJECTIVES

This chapter describes the role of managerial accounting in a business organization. After studying the chapter, you should be able to:

1. Understand how important it is for managers to obtain and use their organizations' resources in the best possible way.
2. Describe the similarities and differences between managerial and financial accounting.
3. Recognize the most significant characteristics of managerial accounting information.
4. Explain the importance of organizational considerations for management.
5. Realize why a major goal of every organization is to achieve satisfactory financial results by being efficient and effective.
6. Describe how the management process with a decision-making focus is used for planning, organizing, directing, and controlling.
7. Trace the basic concepts of management and managerial accounting through a case study.
8. Define the role of a controller in an organization.
9. Evaluate how the combination of a microcomputer and an electronic spreadsheet is used in managerial accounting.

INTRODUCTION

**Objective 1:
Obtaining and
using resources in
the best way**

Managers working for the IBM Corporation, American Airlines, a local hospital, the Coca-Cola Company, a campus pizza parlor, the Federal Bureau of Investigation, and the Tampa chapter of United Way have an important common objective: They must make good decisions to obtain and use their organizations' resources—including people, money, inventory, real estate, investments, technology, and equipment—in the best possible way. This is the most fundamental business principle in use today. Every organization's resources are in limited supply, but the demand for them is unlimited. This is true for a merchandising business, a manufacturer, a service firm, a governmental agency, a utility, or a not-for-profit organization. The resource decisions of most businesses are made with the primary goal of earning a satisfactory profit as an important measure of financial success. Even not-for-profit groups such as a fraternal organization must be certain that their expenses do not exceed their revenues for an extended period.

Management decisions concerning the acquisition and use of resources provide answers to such questions as:

- What products or services should be sold?
- Where should they be sold?
- What are the responsibilities of each management position?
- Who should be hired to fill these positions?
- How much does it cost to produce a product or offer a service?
- What is the most profitable combination of products or services?
- What will happen to profits if selling prices are increased or decreased?
- How much operating capacity is needed in the form of people, funds, inventory, and fixed assets?
- How should the organization finance its various activities?

Good management decision making is highly dependent on good information. Where does this information come from in a typical organization? Think back to your first course in financial accounting. You learned that a great deal of information is made available to the managers of a business in the general purpose financial statements prepared for the firm. But, as we will see later, general purpose financial statements have limited usefulness to managers. Managerial accounting is an important branch of accounting that provides the information needed by managers to determine how resources should be obtained and used in any type of business—large or small. Managerial accounting builds on the principles you learned in financial accounting to satisfy the internal reporting needs of managers.

In this book, we will use terms such as "business" and "firm" as general references for all types of economic entities, including not-for-profit organizations. Although our primary concern is with profit-seeking firms, many of the concepts and procedures developed here are also applicable to not-for-profit organizations such as a sorority, university, governmental agency, or hospital. Specific references to these applications will be made throughout the book. Our study of managerial accounting begins by comparing it to financial accounting.

MANAGERIAL ACCOUNTING: A COMPARISON WITH FINANCIAL ACCOUNTING

SIMILARITIES BETWEEN MANAGERIAL AND FINANCIAL ACCOUNTING

Although the emphasis is different, both managerial and financial accounting involve three types of functions:

1. *Recordkeeping* that is concerned with selecting, measuring, and accumulating data concerning business transactions;

Objective 2: Comparing managerial and financial accounting

2. *Performance evaluation* that directs an interested party's attention to important features of a firm based on reports that classify and summarize the financial results of operating a business or a part of the business for a particular time period;

3. *Decision making* that is performed by a wide variety of interested parties (both external and internal to the firm) who must choose between alternative courses of action regarding the business's future.

Financial accounting and managerial accounting are alike in two other ways. First, they are both founded on the principle of stewardship, which simply means that a firm (or a part of a firm) must account for its financial and operating performance to all parties having an economic interest in it. However, financial accounting is concerned primarily with the firm's entire operation, whereas managerial accounting divides the business into well-defined responsibility units to provide more detailed stewardship reporting. Second, both financial and managerial accounting information should be developed within the same general accounting system. The cost of maintaining two separate systems would be excessive, if not prohibitive, because of the duplication of such items as a chart of accounts, journals, ledgers, bookkeeping, and computer time.

DIFFERENCES BETWEEN MANAGERIAL AND FINANCIAL ACCOUNTING

There are several important differences between the two types of accounting. These differences must be understood to realize how each type of accounting is used properly by a business. They are summarized in Figure 1-1.

User Orientation

Managers need more comprehensive and detailed information than that contained in the general purpose financial statements reported to external parties. Managers are deeply involved with day-to-day operations and need information to *plan* for the future, *organize* resources, *direct* activities, and *control* performance. In turn, the management process of planning, organizing, directing, and controlling (all discussed later in this chapter) is the central theme of managerial accounting. The accounting information needed by management would be meaningless to external parties such as stockholders who do not actively participate in the company's daily affairs.

Figure 1-1
Financial Accounting versus Managerial Accounting

Comparative Bases	Financial Accounting	Managerial Accounting
User orientation	External users	Internal users
Freedom of choice	Mandatory	Complete freedom
Time frame	Historical	Futuristic
Restrictive standards	Generally accepted accounting principles	None
Accounting entity	Mainly firm as a whole	Mainly firm's segments
Reporting frequency	Well-defined schedule	Whenever needed
Degree of precision	Objectivity principle	More subjective
Other disciplines	Little use	Used often

Freedom of Choice

Financial accounting must be performed to satisfy the requirements of various external parties such as the Securities and Exchange Commission (SEC) and the Internal Revenue Service (IRS). In contrast, management alone must decide how much and what kind of information it requires. The benefits of management reports must be compared continually with their costs to assure that they are cost-effective.

Time Frame

The emphasis of managerial accounting is on the future, whereas financial accounting is concerned primarily with reporting what has happened in the past. In managerial accounting applications, past performance evaluations are used mainly as benchmarks for predicting the future. Such environmental changes as economic conditions, technology, competition, product life cycles, and social responsibility can quickly invalidate historical data.

Restrictive Standards

Managerial accounting is more flexible than financial accounting; external reporting with financial accounting must be restricted by tight accounting standards because of the typical separation of management and ownership. Generally accepted accounting principles (GAAP) dictate what can be done in financial accounting to protect the interests of external parties who do not have access to a firm's accounting records. Managerial accounting focuses on usefulness to managers and may involve departures from conventional GAAP methods of accounting such as inventory costing, income determination, and cost allocations.

Accounting Entity

Managerial accounting generally divides the firm's total operation into well-defined segments. It does not follow the accounting entity concept used in external reporting for the firm as a whole. Performance reports are prepared for such segments as departments, divisions, offices, plants, product lines, and sales territories. Although many large companies must report externally on the summarized financial performance of their major lines of business, the reports prepared for internal purposes are much more detailed and are personalized to the managers who are responsible for the operating results.[1]

Reporting Frequency

The reporting frequency with managerial accounting also is subject to management's choice in contrast to the time period assumption of financial accounting. Special reports on an infrequent basis as needed or frequently prepared reports covering short time periods (e.g., daily) may be used. For management purposes, the need for information is the key factor.

[1] For financial reporting purposes, diversified companies operating in several industries must disclose certain financial information by segments of the business to comply with Financial Accounting Standards No. 14, "Financial Reporting for Segments of a Business Enterprise."

Degree of Precision

Objectivity or verifiability is a major consideration in financial accounting to assure that the information is free from any personal bias on the part of the persons responsible for the financial statements. Since managerial accounting is concerned more with the future than the past and does not affect external parties, objectivity is not as important as it is with financial accounting; the result often is the use of less precise information with managerial accounting.

Many management decisions have to be made quickly so managers simply cannot wait until complete and verifiable information is available. They must act on the basis of good estimates and projections instead of waiting for better information. In other words, managerial accounting often requires a trade-off between the benefits of immediate action versus the cost of a delay for more precise information.

For example, a sales manager who has to price a product for a new customer today will base the price on projections of the costs required to produce the product instead of waiting for the accounting department to perform a more sophisticated study of historical cost data for similar products that will take a week. Otherwise, the sale may be lost. This does not mean that managerial accounting is merely a "guessing game," because every effort must be made to use only valid information. Nevertheless, the uncertainties of the future make some degree of subjectivity (personal opinion) inevitable, thus reducing the precision of the information involved.

Other Disciplines

In contrast to financial accounting, which basically is a self-contained subject, managerial accounting is wide open in the way it uses other disciplines to obtain the information needed by management. Economics (micro and macro), finance, management, mathematics, marketing, decision science, statistics, and behavioral science are integrated with managerial accounting techniques whenever necessary. The integration of these disciplines can be seen in this book.

CHARACTERISTICS OF USEFUL MANAGERIAL ACCOUNTING INFORMATION

Objective 3: Important characteristics of managerial accounting information

Although the two terms "data" and "information" are often used synonymously, a useful distinction between them can be made. Data are recorded facts; information is data that have been processed in some prescribed manner so they are more useful to a potential user. For example, sales data are collected chronologically on invoices, processed through an accounting system, and reported as sales information (revenue) on the income statement. If managerial accounting information is to be valuable to management, it should possess these characteristics:

1. Relevance
2. Accuracy
3. Timeliness
4. Understandability
5. Cost-effectiveness

Relevance is a key factor because of the flexible nature of managerial accounting information that can take any form management chooses. In this age of the computer, an endless stream of information is available to management, so we need a way to determine which information should be considered and which can be ignored. This choice is made on the basis of relevance. What is relevant in one use of managerial accounting information may be irrelevant in another. To be relevant to a manager, information must make a difference in a decision being considered. If certain information can be ignored because it has no bearing on the outcome of the decision, that information is irrelevant for that decision. Thus, the various functions performed by managers in a particular business and their related information needs must be carefully analyzed when the accounting system is developed to assure that relevant information will be available.

To illustrate the concept of relevance, assume that you are planning a trip and are comparing the cost of driving versus the cost of flying. Would the annual automobile insurance premium you pay be relevant to the decision? The answer is no because the premium will be the same whether you drive or fly. Thus, it can be ignored in the decision. However, the cost of automobile insurance is relevant if you are going to purchase a new car and the two models you are considering have significantly different insurance rates. In this case, the amounts of the insurance premiums will influence your decision because of the difference in operating costs for the two vehicles.

Even though much of the time managerial accounting is based on estimates and projections, information must be as *accurate* as possible if it is to have value. Sound judgment and experience should underlie any development of subjective data. All available relevant information should be considered and evaluated for accuracy, although this often must be done quickly because of the time constraints discussed earlier for many management decisions. At times, a range of values is considered when the accuracy of a single measure is questionable. For example, a sales manager may forecast next year's sales within a range of $1.5 to $2 million instead of identifying a single amount because of too many uncertainties. In any case, management should take all steps possible to use the most accurate information available.

Timeliness is important because management usually operates in a changing environment. The concept of timeliness simply means that information should be as current as possible because old information may not be representative of present or future conditions. If a report is issued months after the related performance, the information will have lost much of its value as a result of subsequent activity.

The accounting information also must be *understandable*. Typically, users of the information are not trained accountants, so any preoccupation with technical jargon will adversely affect the use of the information. Finally, managerial accounting information must be *cost-effective*. This means it must pass a cost-benefit test in each application. As we mentioned earlier, vast quantities of information can be developed with the computer systems in operation today. The information available in a given business is limited only by the imagination and capability of the firm's management and its managerial accounting staff. However, information costs money and its value must exceed its cost. In most cases, the ultimate measure of the benefits of the information is the quality of the decision making based on it.

A basic understanding of what managers do and the organizational structure in which they operate must be developed before management's information requirements can be considered in more detail. That is the next topic for discussion.

ORGANIZATIONAL CONSIDERATIONS FOR MANAGEMENT

Objective 4: Organizational considerations for management

The most basic form of economic enterprise is a one-person business. Its management and information needs are not as complex as those of a large organization because all decision-making responsibilities for such functions as purchasing, selling, production, accounting, and financing rest with the individual owner. Aside from the hot dog vendor or the summer lemonade stand, this simple situation seldom exists today. Where it does exist, it normally will be found only during the initial stage of the business firm's life cycle. As soon as the first employee is hired, a division of labor occurs, responsibility for performance is shared, and an organization begins to develop. An **organization** is defined as a group of people with the following characteristics:

1. They have a common purpose.
2. There is a well-defined division of labor.
3. The parts of the organization are integrated with an information based decision-making system.
4. The group has continuity through time.

In other words, an organization must have a *common purpose* (e.g., produce and sell certain products with acceptable profits), must *organize its human resources* to accomplish the common purpose, must have *information* that indicates how well the members of the group are working together toward the common purpose, and must *operate continuously* over a period of time. These same characteristics must exist for all organizations, including a bank, a professional baseball team, a manufacturing firm, an airline, a charitable organization, or a governmental agency.

By definition, a well-organized business is properly arranged, orderly, and integrated so the different segments of the organization work for *common goals.* In contrast, a disorganized firm is characterized by disorder, confusion, and segments that work *independently* of each other for *different goals.* Managerial accounting is needed to make sure a business is well organized. As an organization grows in size and complexity, authority and responsibility for performance are delegated to a number of people. Consequently, the role of management becomes increasingly important. Profit-seeking and not-for-profit organizations alike must accept this fact.

MANAGEMENT PROCESS: A PERSPECTIVE

Who are the managers we are concerned with in this book and what do they do? Unfortunately, we must deal with generalities in answering these questions because the titles and responsibilities of managers are innumerable, depending on their qualifications as well as the nature and size of the organizations in which they work. By definition, a **manager** is a person who is involved with planning, organizing, directing, and controlling an organization's human and physical resources to achieve its stated goals. In this role, a manager works with other people and must coordinate their efforts.

Large organizations classify managers as being part of top management, middle management, or lower management. The amount of authority and decision-making responsibilities decrease as we move from higher to lower management levels. The president of the Coca-Cola Company is part of the firm's top management, the manager of the company's bottling plant located in New York is part of middle management, and a production supervisor in that plant is part of lower management. In a small business such as a local drug store, the pharmacist who owns the store may be the only manager with a wide range of job assignments involving purchasing, accounting, marketing, personnel, and financing.

The structure and direction of an organization are provided by its management process. A successful financial performance will be highly dependent on the capability of management. For example, Henry Ford started an automobile manufacturing firm in 1903. By 1920, he had built one of the largest and most financially successful manufacturing operations in the world. His achievements resulted primarily from engineering innovations involving mass production, central assembly, and interchangeable parts. However, during the late 1920s, the organization experienced serious financial problems because Ford was unwilling to hire competent managers. He believed that all any business needed was an owner who made every decision and some assistants who carried out orders. His firm simply outgrew this management philosophy.

At the other extreme was Alfred P. Sloan, Jr. In 1923, Sloan became president of a company that actually was a collection of small automobile firms that, individually, had been unable to compete with Ford. Sloan believed that the automobile business had become too complicated for decision making by one person. He relinquished the operating authority for the divisions of the organization to a number of managers. A managerial accounting system was developed to measure and compare actual performance versus the goals of the firm. Through the combination of motivation and opportunity, Sloan successfully obtained the cooperation of people who were too individualistic to be managed in the Ford fashion, but who would accept policy making through an orderly management process. As you may have guessed, Sloan's company is now known as General Motors Corporation. In recent years, a number of Japanese companies have used a modern version of Sloan's participative management to achieve remarkable success in the automotive industry.

ROLE OF MANAGEMENT IN AN ORGANIZATION

A major goal of every organization is to achieve satisfactory financial results. What is considered satisfactory depends on the nature of the organization. At one end of the spectrum, the management of a business firm such as General Motors Corporation is accountable to its owners—the shareholders—for adequate profits as indicators of a successful operation. The shareholders have invested money in the business, and they expect a good return on their investment. At the other extreme, the financial performance of a not-for-profit organization, such as a local United Way, consists of (1) raising enough money to fund its future activities and (2) spending that amount of money wisely. Every organization, whether profit-making or not, must accept the fact that its resources are limited and must be conserved if a satisfactory financial performance is to be achieved. Such factors as inflation, technological change, competition, government regulation, high interest rates, increased energy costs, and declining productivity have an adverse effect on most business firms' financial performance.

If a business is to be financially successful, management must be both efficient and effective. **Efficiency** means maintaining a satisfactory relationship between a firm's resource inputs and its outputs of products or services (e.g., the number of labor hours required to produce a product). **Effectiveness** refers to how well a firm attains its goals (e.g., the number of products sold compared

Objective 5: Goal of achieving satisfactory financial results

Figure 1-2

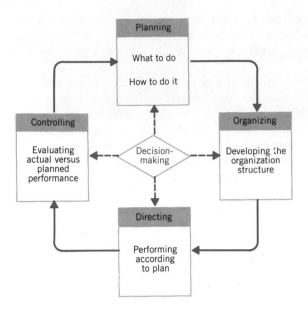

Objective 6:
Role of the management process

with the number planned). The efficiency and effectiveness performances of the management process diagrammed in Figure 1-2 are essential to the overall success of any business. It is important to note that these management functions are not always as sequentially dependent as Figure 1-2 may suggest since they often are performed concurrently and constantly interact with each other.

Planning

A successful business prepares for the future by carefully setting financial and nonfinancial goals with the **planning** function. Examples of financial goals are earning a profit margin of 12%, increasing the return on shareholders' investment to 22%, and obtaining 20% of total industry sales. Nonfinancial goals include introducing the best new products in the industry, improving employee job satisfaction, and maintaining good public standing by being socially responsible. Goal setting is the initial phase of management by objective.

Management by objective means that the managers responsible for the performance of the various segments of the firm will have the opportunity to participate both in setting goals and in fulfilling them. Management must decide what action the firm should take in the future in order to achieve its goals. Alternative courses of action are identified, their probable results are evaluated, and the course of action that appears best for the achievement of the firm's goals is selected. Thus, planning is intended to help management anticipate future events rather than react to actual circumstances once they are known.

Much of managerial planning is concerned with the efficiency and effectiveness of future operations. *Long-term planning* (often called strategic planning) for a period such as the next five to ten years is mainly performed by the top management of a business. For example, top management must anticipate what the firm's customers will buy in several years because it takes time and costs money to research, develop, produce, and market new products or services. *Short-term planning* (often called operational planning) is needed to implement the goals established during long-term planning. It is primarily performed by middle and lower management. For example, a firm must plan how much it wants to spend to promote new products once they are available.

Organizing

Plans are only words and numbers on paper until they are implemented. The **organizing** function provides the structure or capacity within which management will work to achieve its plans. The organizing function identifies the work to be done to achieve the firm's goals and the relationships between the tasks to be performed. Important steps involved in organizing are:

1. The firm is divided into segments (such as departments, divisions, plants, and offices) to take advantage of the specialization of skills and abilities.
2. The right people are hired, trained, and assigned to specific jobs.
3. Well-defined lines of authority and responsibility are established.
4. Sources of operating resources (such as materials, utilities, and advertising) are selected, physical facilities (land, buildings, machinery, and equipment) are obtained, and financing commitments are arranged to fund the operation.

Directing

This function deals with the day-to-day management of the firm. Actions, decision making, communication, and leadership are combined in the **directing** function to carry out the planned activities within the organizational structure. Problems are solved, questions are answered, disagreements are resolved, and the various operating segments are coordinated.

Controlling

Performance evaluation is an essential managerial step needed to identify problem areas and reward good results. **Controlling** with managerial accounting is defined as the comparison of actual results to the planned performance and the correction of any significant differences, whenever possible. Management must be sure that the actual results achieved by the firm and each of its segments compare favorably with the goals established during the planning function. If managers are to be held accountable for their performance, they should know where and why actual results differ from planned results. Control is based on the concept of management by exception.

Management by exception recognizes that (1) management time is a scarce resource and (2) the attention of a manager should be directed toward performance that deviates significantly from the related plan. Even significantly favorable deviations must be considered because the planned performance may have been too easy to attain. For example, actual sales that are higher than those planned may be the result of a sales forecast that was too low to begin with.

Performance evaluation reports are issued periodically to inform management of any significant variations from the expected results. Managers may take two types of action in evaluating deviations from the planned performance: (1) The preferred type is *corrective action* to improve the efficiency or effectiveness of future operations. For example, in response to sales that were lower than expected, management may increase its advertising or put more pressure on the sales force. (2) Another type of management action is an *adaptive response,* which is only appropriate when the plan itself is considered unrealistic. Consequently, the related targets for the future are revised. For example, further examination might show that the lower sales noted earlier are acceptable because changes in the market have made the original sales target impossible to attain.

Decision Making

Competent decision making is at the core of each management function discussed above. A wide range of decisions must be made. Top management is primarily concerned with strategic (long-term) decisions concerning the firm's environment, including such factors as economic conditions, social responsibility, technological developments, and market considerations. For example, General Motors Corporation's top management made the strategic decision to significantly reduce the size of its automobiles during the late 1970s and early 1980s to have more fuel-efficient vehicles. Middle and lower-level management is mainly engaged in operating decisions needed for the day-to-day performance of a business. Operating decisions deal with such functions as product pricing, selecting the amount of inventory to have available, product cost analysis, equipment replacement evaluation, and advertising media selection.

Management **decision making,** regardless of the level within the organization or the time dimension involved, is concerned with the selection between alternatives. Many managerial decisions are made continually. For example, managers must decide daily what products to produce, how many products are needed, and what prices should be charged for the products. Other decisions are made infrequently. Examples include whether to build a new plant, enter a new marketing territory, or add a new product line.

All managerial decisions have one thing in common—*the need for reliable information.* This information can be either historical or a reflection of management's expectations about the future. It can be objective or subjective. It can come from either internal or external sources, and much of it is provided by managerial accounting. One of a successful manager's most important assets is the ability to (1) identify the important alternatives involved in a given decision, (2) collect accurate information, and (3) make a decision based on an assortment of quantifiable and subjective information.

ANALOGY WITH OUR PERSONAL LIVES

We use these same managerial functions and the decision-making process in our personal lives—often without even realizing it. Consider this example: Spring semester break is coming soon, and you want to take a vacation. You must *plan* the trip before doing anything else. Do you want to go skiing or to a beach? How much money do you have to spend? How much time do you have? Once you have determined the general destination, you must then make other decisions. Where will you stay? How will you get there? Who will go with you? When will you leave? Who will pick up your mail and water the plants in your room?

Once your plans are finalized, you must then *organize* for the trip. Assuming you have decided to drive, you must make sure your car is mechanically sound, full of fuel, and properly loaded. You must pack your clothes and personal items. You must arrange for the funds you will need during the trip. You must obtain any maps needed to reach your destination and leave a phone number where you can be reached in case of an emergency.

While en route, you will *direct* your attention each day toward deciding when and where to stop for fuel, rest, food, and lodging. In addition, you will choose how fast to drive, when to switch drivers, and the amount of sight-seeing you will do. Certain *control* checks will be made to assure that you arrive at your destination safely and on time. You may refer to a map periodically, observe road signs, check your fuel gauge, watch the speedometer (or set the cruise control), listen to weather reports, and be on the alert for police radar (or use a radar detection device) if you choose to exceed the speed limit. Note that some of these considerations do not fit exclusively in only one of the four functions—planning, organizing, directing, or controlling. However, you need all four functions to have a successful trip.

CASE STUDY—JOHNSON AUTOMOTIVE INC.

OVERVIEW OF THE COMPANY

To help you develop a perspective concerning the managerial accounting needs of management, let's consider the following case. Kevin Johnson has owned and managed a franchised automobile dealership that has sold and serviced a domestic line of vehicles in a small midwestern town for five years. His company, Johnson Automotive Inc., is organized into four departments: new cars, used cars, service, and parts, as diagrammed in Figure 1-3. The firm has a bookkeeper who maintains a general ledger and prepares financial statements for Kevin Johnson, the firm's major suppliers, and two local banks.

Objective 7: Considering management and managerial accounting concepts

At the end of each year, the company's certified public accountant (CPA), Linda Flora, uses the same information to prepare the corporate tax returns. For the last three years, Linda has been advising Kevin that his firm should expand upon these basic uses of financial accounting information by developing managerial accounting information. Profits have been declining during the three-year period because of lower industry sales, an increase in the market share of imported automobiles, and a weak local economy.

Kevin Johnson asked the bookkeeper to prepare income statements that show a comparison of the current year's profit performance to that of the previous year and is alarmed at the results, shown in Figure 1-4. The firm has never prepared a budget (a quantitative plan of action discussed in Chapter 8) to forecast the profit performance of the future, so the comparison of a current year to the previous year is the only information available for controlling profits.

INITIAL CONSIDERATION OF MANAGERIAL ACCOUNTING INFORMATION

Kevin Johnson decided to have a meeting with the CPA, the bookkeeper, and the firm's department managers to evaluate ways to improve the company's profit performance. He began the meeting by asking two key questions: (1)

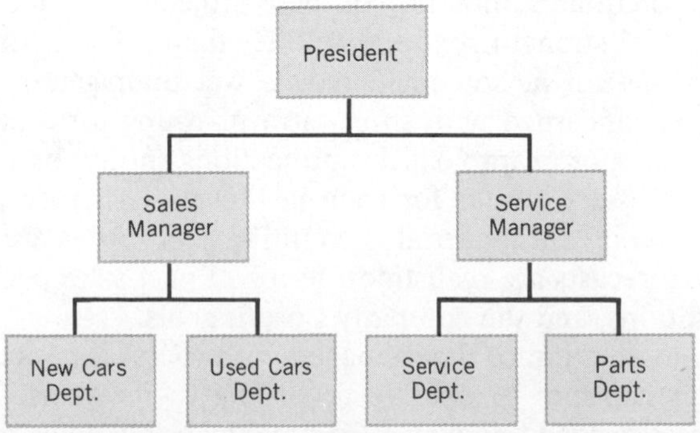

Figure 1-3
Organization Chart Johnson Automotive Inc.

Figure 1-4
Johnson Automotive Inc. Income Statements Current Year and Previous Year

	Current Year	Previous Year
Sales	$8,328,352	$8,568,540
Cost of goods sold	7,909,614	7,852,710
Gross profit	418,738	715,830
Operating expenses	348,572	541,557
Net income	$ 70,166	$ 174,273

What caused the decline in net income from the previous year to the current year? and (2) What kind of managerial accounting information should be developed for the firm's management process? Linda Flora addressed the first question by noting that profit is a function of four interacting variables:

1. Selling prices charged for products and services
2. Sales volume of products and services
3. Sales mix of products and services
4. Costs

She also said that a good managerial accounting system should produce information that will measure the impact of each of these key variables. Evaluations such as the following should be made regularly:

- Are *selling prices* high enough to sustain desired profits?
- Is the firm selling enough *units* (e.g., automobiles and service jobs)?
- Does the firm have the most profitable *sales mix* (proportion of new cars, used cars, service jobs, and parts sold)?
- Are the firm's *costs* within acceptable control limits?

Linda responded to Kevin's second question by suggesting that managerial accounting information is essential to management in planning for the future, organizing resources, directing operations, and controlling performance. Kevin asked Linda to elaborate on the uses of managerial accounting information in the dealership and to give some examples. Linda began by explaining that planning must take place from top management to lower management if the business is to prepare for the future with well-defined goals that it wants to accomplish. As the company's president, Kevin Johnson should be involved with long-term planning that defines the firm's overall strategies. An example would be determining the automotive products and services that are likely to be demanded by the local community five years from now and how much of the resulting sales volume the firm would like to achieve.

Linda went on to explain that managerial accounting information is needed to evaluate the potential profitability of these projected products and services as well as the financial strength required to offer them. The addition of a foreign import product line might be considered. Lower management (e.g., the firm's sales manager) is concerned with short-term planning for a period such as the next calendar year. For example, sales projections should be made by the sales manager to define sales quotas for each new car salesperson and for the sales department as a whole. Managerial accounting procedures are needed to make sure these sales forecasts are realistic in terms of past sales performance, future economic conditions, and the company's profit goals.

The organizing function of the management process is concerned with developing the firm's capacity to operate according to its plans. The human and physical resources needed to achieve the organizational goals must be identified and acquired. Managerial accounting is used in many ways during the organizing function. For example, the service department manager must carefully evaluate a guaranteed minimum salary required to hire a new mechanic compared with the revenue expected from the person's efforts. The service department manager also needs reliable cost information to evaluate the potential profitability of buying or leasing electronic equipment used to analyze automotive mechanical problems. In addition, the sales manager can use managerial accounting information to find the most cost-effective way to arrange automobile floor plan financing and to advertise through various media such as newspaper, radio, or television.

The directing phase of management provides the leadership and motivation of the people within the organization to make sure they work toward the goals established during the planning function. Managerial accounting procedures are required to ensure that all managers participate in goal setting, to provide the communication of the firm's goals to everyone, and to furnish feedback with which the various managers can evaluate how well they are doing. If mistakes are made or problems develop, they should be revealed quickly so they can be corrected during the control phase of management.

For example, a bid price from the service manager for repairs to a wrecked car that has been accepted by an insurance company must be communicated to the person doing the work so the job can be done profitably. The president reminding the sales manager how much money is available for advertising, the sales manager complimenting a salesperson on a profitable sale, and the service manager congratulating a mechanic for suggesting a way to improve the service department's efficiency are other examples of the use of managerial accounting in the directing function.

Finally, managerial accounting information is needed for control purposes. Control is concerned with evaluating the company's performance to ensure that what is being accomplished is compatible with the goals established during the planning function. For example, the monthly expenses of each department are compared with carefully prepared budgeted amounts to evaluate how efficiently the firm is using its resources. Managerial accounting provides this control information in a way that identifies the various managers responsible for the related segment's spending performances.

Linda Flora concluded by suggesting to Kevin that the group should evaluate the work performed by each manager in his or her area of responsibility and develop a list of the most important kinds of accounting information needed to manage the operation. Kevin agreed, and, after a critical analysis of every management function and a thorough discussion (involving the managers themselves) of the associated accounting information needs, the group compiled a list of the 20 most important managerial accounting information needs of Johnson Automotive Inc. The list, as shown below, should be beneficial to you for two reasons. First, it gives you examples of the different kinds of managerial accounting information needed to manage a business. Second, it serves as a general frame of reference for you to use later as we develop certain concepts and procedures in this book.

LIST OF MANAGERIAL ACCOUNTING INFORMATION NEEDED

1. Information concerning cost concepts and definitions that can be used consistently throughout the organization.

2. Information about the cost of buying and selling inventory as well as performing services.
3. Information identifying an efficient amount of resources (such as inventory, labor, and overhead) needed to operate the business.
4. Information measuring how well costs are being controlled in each department.
5. Information defining a profit plan acceptable to management.
6. Information about why planned profits are not achieved.
7. Information showing how effectively managers are achieving the goals of their segments of the business as they relate to those of the firm as a whole.
8. Information about sales demand for the products and services at different selling prices.
9. Information concerning the relationship of sales demand and marketing effort.
10. Information regarding the total costs needed to operate specific segments of the business when all costs incurred by and for the segments are considered.
11. Information communicated among the various managers to coordinate efforts toward common goals.
12. Information providing the basis for a reliable income statement that can be used to predict the future financial performance and evaluate actual operating results.
13. Information about how costs will fluctuate as the volume of business changes and what result this will have on profits.
14. Information with which managers can evaluate alternative courses of action such as equipment replacement, product or service line profitability, and the basis for rewarding employees.
15. Information concerning the evaluation of future capital expenditures and the assignment of scarce resources within the firm.
16. Information about the sources and uses of funds needed to support the operation.
17. Information regarding the pricing of all interdepartmental transfers of products or services.
18. Information that will monitor the financial and operating progress of the company over time, including statistics measuring such items as profitability, liquidity, and solvency.
19. Information about payroll costs, indicating not only how much each employee was paid but also the person's work performance.
20. Information about current economic trends and how they affect the relationship of the firm's capacity to do business and the demand for its products and services.

MANAGERIAL ACCOUNTING IN AN ORGANIZATION

ROLE OF THE CONTROLLER

Objective 8: Role of a controller

When a firm such as Johnson Automotive Inc. commits itself to managerial accounting, the position of **controller** usually is created, and a person with the appropriate credentials and experience is hired as the chief accountant who is responsible for the organization's entire accounting function. The specific responsibilities of a controller vary significantly from firm to firm, depending on such factors as the *size* of the organization, the *nature* of the operation, *management information needs,* and *top management's commitment to accounting applications.* There are, however, some general comments that can be made about the typical controller. Most important for our purposes, the controller is an integral part of the management team with the dual functions of providing information and participating actively in the management process diagrammed in Figure 1-2.

A statement by the National Association of Accountants states that managerial accountants should provide information needed for:(1)planning,evaluating, and controlling operations for all levels of management; (2) safeguarding the organization's assets; and (3) communicating with interested parties outside the organization such as shareholders and regulatory bodies.[2] Participation in the management process includes assisting in decision making and helping to coordinate the efforts of the entire organization as a unified whole. All these functions would be performed by the typical controller.

AUTHORITY OF THE CONTROLLER

The title "controller" is somewhat of a misnomer because the person does not actually control anyone or anything outside the accounting function. Most organizations are **decentralized** so that the work is divided into specialized units, enabling the organizations to accomplish more than they otherwise could. Decision making usually is better since the managers of the decentralized segments are closest to the day-to-day activities and can control them more effectively. An abbreviated example of an **organizational chart** for a decentralized organization is shown in Figure 1-5 to illustrate the specialized functions used by a typical business.

Figure 1-5
Partial Organizational Chart John Wiley and Sons, Inc.

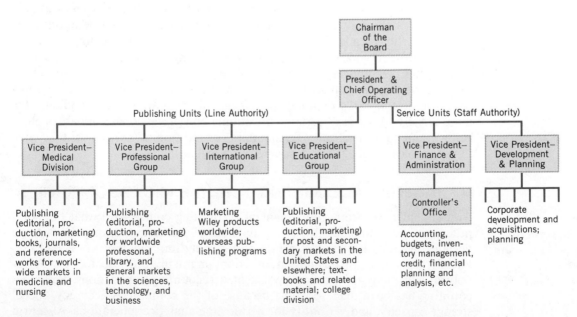

[2] National Association of Accountants, "Statements on Management Accounting (1B)," June 17, 1982, p. 2.

In the development of a decentralized organization, management must carefully distinguish between **line authority** and **staff authority**. The managers with line authority are in charge of the activities representing the firm's revenue-generating segments such as the production and marketing functions of a manufacturing operation. Staff functions provide support to the line segments and include such activities as accounting, personnel, legal, maintenance, quality control, and engineering. As such, the staff personnel, including the controller, work with line managers in an advisory capacity by providing information and consultation.

In a large corporation, the controller usually has several assistant controllers, each with assigned responsibility for various accounting applications. The separation of duties is needed to cope with the increasing specialization and complexities of accounting, which are often more than one person can master. Represented in a large controller's department are specialists in such areas as budgeting, financial reporting, strategic planning, cost accounting, taxation, financial statement analysis, internal auditing, electronic data processing, operations research, and management information systems.

CERTIFICATE IN MANAGEMENT ACCOUNTING (CMA)

Since 1972, expertise in managerial accounting has been recognized with the **Certificate in Management Accounting (CMA).** The National Association of Accountants sponsors the Institute of Certified Management Accountants (ICMA), which offers the program leading to the CMA designation. The purposes of the program are: (1) to recognize management accounting as a profession; (2) to promote high educational standards for a managerial accountant; and (3) to develop an objective means of measuring a person's knowledge and competence in the area of managerial accounting. The CMA designation is widely recognized as evidence of a holder's knowledge and ability to become an important member of a firm's management team.

To qualify for the CMA designation, a person must pass a rigorous written examination consisting of the following five parts: (1) economics and business finance; (2) organization and behavior (including ethical considerations); (3) public reporting standards, auditing, and taxes; (4) internal reporting and analysis; and (5) decision analysis (including modeling and information systems). Each part is taken during a three-and-a-half hour period, and the entire examination lasts two-and-a-half days. The breadth of the examination topics indicates the diverse skills required in managerial accounting. The candidate for the CMA also must meet certain educational and professional standards before being granted the certificate. To maintain certification, a CMA must take continuing professional education courses on a regular basis.

MANAGERIAL ACCOUNTING AND THE MICROCOMPUTER

**Objective 9:
Using a micro-
computer and an
electronic
spreadsheet**

You should recall from your financial accounting course work that the computer has had a dramatic impact on the field of accounting during the last two decades. A computer enables a firm to not only improve the way it had previously accounted for business transactions manually but also to become involved with many new, more sophisticated accounting applications. Better accounting has been made possible because of the computer's accuracy, speed, storage capacity, and versatility for performing analytical operations. As a firm grows in size and complexity, the volume of paperwork from business transactions increases significantly. At some point, the cost, inaccuracy, and time delays of a manual accounting system force a business to evaluate the benefits of using a computer for its financial and managerial accounting needs.

In recent years, managerial accounting has been influenced in a very exciting and innovative way by the combination of a microcomputer and an electronic spreadsheet program. As the name suggests, a **microcomputer** (also called a personal computer or a home computer) is a small computer that can fit on the top of an ordinary desk. However, it is fully operational in the sense of total computing capabilities with a microprocessor contained on a single silicon chip as its central processing unit. A microcomputer not only can perform the same basic functions as a large, expensive computer but is also much more accessible for a manager because it can be used at the manager's desk as a self-contained unit. In addition, a microcomputer can be purchased for a fraction of the cost of a large computer and its operation is much easier to learn. Popular models of microcomputers are the IBM Personal Computer (which is being used for word processing to write this book), Apple Macintosh, and COMPAQ Portable Computer.

Although a microcomputer can be used to perform all accounting functions —including accounts receivable, accounts payable, payroll, inventory control, budgeting, product costing, and general ledger—an important development for managerial accounting has been the electronic spreadsheet. An **electronic spreadsheet** is a versatile computer program that can be used to perform numerous types of financial analysis on a microcomputer. Spreadsheet analysis can be applied to a wide range of managerial accounting functions to help managers make better business decisions. A spreadsheet program provides a matrix display of cells organized into rows and columns that can be used effectively for managerial accounting to electronically manipulate data and predict the impact of future actions.

This program permits a manager to perform calculations, using formulas or rules, that would be impossible manually because of the time required. For example, the impact on profits over the next 10 years of an annual sales increase of 8% combined with an annual manufacturing cost increase of 6% and selling expense increase of 5% can be quickly evaluated during a management meeting.

Popular names of electronic spreadsheets used today are VisiCalc, Super-Calc^4, and Lotus 1-2-3. These spreadsheets provide the means of electronically utilizing most of the managerial accounting techniques developed in this book. Examples include budgeting, sales forecasting, cash flow projections, product costing, cost-volume-profit analysis, variance analysis, standard cost accounting, capital budgeting, relevant cost analysis, and financial statement analysis. Once you understand the concepts and procedures associated with managerial accounting topics, you can easily develop electronic spreadsheets that will enable you to quickly perform the calculations involved, thus eliminating time-consuming manual computations. Detailed instructions that explain how the electronic spreadsheets can be developed are presented in the user's guides accompanying specific spread- sheet programs (e.g., SuperCalc^4).

SUMMARY

Managerial accounting provides the accounting information required by management to plan its future, organize resources, direct activities, and control performance. The goal of achieving a satisfactory financial performance is at the core of managerial accounting. Since every type of organization must be certain that resources are obtained and used in the best way, managerial accounting is universally applicable. Managerial accounting builds on the principles of financial accounting, and the two subjects are similar in that they both involve the same three functions (recordkeeping, performance evaluation, and decision making) characteristic of accounting in general. Financial and managerial accounting are concerned with the stewardship principle and should be developed within the same general accounting system. The major differences between the two subjects relate to their user orientation, freedom of choice, time frame, restrictive standards, accounting entity, reporting frequency, degree of precision, and use of other disciplines.

The most important characteristics of good managerial accounting information are its relevance, accuracy, timeliness, understandability, and cost-effectiveness. The nature of an organization and the role of management must be considered carefully in applying managerial accounting in the organization. Management provides the structure and direction for an organization with its planning, organizing, directing, and controlling functions. Each of these functions requires decision making based on reliable information.

The controller is the chief accountant for the typical organization and is an integral part of the management team, providing information and assisting in decision making. The controller has staff authority while performing in an advisory capacity. In a large decentralized organization, the controllership function typically is divided into such accounting specialties as budgeting, financial reporting, strategic planning, managerial accounting, taxation, financial statement analysis, and internal auditing.

The Certificate in Management Accounting (CMA) is evidence not only of the diverse skills needed in managerial accounting but also of the subject's recognition as a field of professional study. The combination of a microcomputer and an electronic spreadsheet enables managers to perform managerial accounting functions much more effectively than they could manually. An electronic spreadsheet computer program provides the capability to rapidly manipulate data and predict the impact of future actions.

GLOSSARY

CERTIFICATE IN MANAGEMENT ACCOUNTING (CMA). A designation awarded to a person who has demonstrated a specified amount of competence in managerial accounting (p. 18).

CONTROLLER. The chief accountant responsible for an organization's accounting function with the dual responsibilities of providing information and participating in the management process (p. 16).

CONTROLLING. The management function concerned with making sure that actual results agree with those planned (p. 11).

DECENTRALIZATION. Dividing an organization into specialized units so decision-making authority and responsibility are spread throughout the organization (p. 17).

DECISION MAKING. Making a choice among alternative courses of action (p. 12).

DIRECTING. The management function that provides the leadership and motivation needed to carry out an organization's plans (p. 11).

EFFECTIVENESS. A measure of how well a firm attains its goals (p. 9).

EFFICIENCY. Maintaining a satisfactory relationship between a firm's resource inputs and its outputs of products or services (p. 9).

ELECTRONIC SPREADSHEET. A versatile problem-solving computer program used to electronically manipulate data and predict the impact of future actions (p. 19).

FINANCIAL ACCOUNTING. A branch of accounting that provides information for external sources such as creditors, stockholders, and governmental agencies (p. 5).

LINE AUTHORITY. The right to give orders and direct the activities representing the organization's main missions such as production and marketing in a manufacturing firm (p. 18).

MANAGEMENT BY EXCEPTION. The concentration on performance results that deviate significantly from those expected (p. 11).

MANAGEMENT BY OBJECTIVE. The process by which management goals are developed by various managers and performance is evaluated to determine if the goals are achieved (p. 10).

MANAGERIAL ACCOUNTING. A branch of accounting that provides information needed by managers to perform the various management functions (p. 3).

MANAGERS The persons within an organization with the authority and responsibility to perform planning, organizing, directing, and controlling functions (p. 8).

MICROCOMPUTER. A small but fully operational computer that uses a microprocessor contained on a single silicon chip as its central processing unit (p. 19).

ORGANIZATION. A group of people who share common goals with a well-defined division of labor, are integrated by an information based decision-making system, and have continuity over time (p. 8).

ORGANIZATIONAL CHART. A graphic display of the structure within which an organization's activities are performed and managed (p. 17).

ORGANIZING. The management function used to provide the structure or capacity needed by a firm to operate and achieve organizational goals (p. 11).

PLANNING. The management function used to decide what action the organization should take in the future and how it should be accomplished (p. 10).

STAFF AUTHORITY. The right to support line managers with advice and assistance in some specialized area such as accounting (p. 18).

DISCUSSION QUESTIONS

1. What do managers of all organizations have in common?
2. How is information developed in the typical organization to satisfy the needs of managers?
3. Identify the major similarities between financial accounting and managerial accounting.
4. What are the basic differences between financial accounting and managerial accounting?
5. Differentiate between recordkeeping accounting, performance-evaluation

accounting, and decision-making accounting. Where does the data required for each come from?

6. What are the characteristics of good managerial accounting information?

7. Assume that you are the president of a small bank. Explain why your bank is an organization and why managerial accounting is required in any organization.

8. What are the basic steps of the management process? Do these steps change as we move from higher to lower management in the typical organization?

9. Distinguish between efficiency and effectiveness measurements. Which of the two concepts is being measured in the following:
   a. Departmental sales salaries required to attain July sales in a retail store.
   b. Actual July sales compared with those planned by a retail store.
   c. Labor costs needed to perform laboratory tests during May in a medical clinic.
   d. New car sales for an automobile dealership in August were 52 units. The sales manager had forecast 58 units.
   e. The labor cost per tax return prepared by a CPA firm.

10. A university football team is an organization. How are such managerial considerations as goals, management functions, and the role of information important to the success of the team?

11. Explain why good decision making is highly dependent on reliable information.

12. Identify how a decision you have made in recent months can be structured within the management process discussed in this chapter.

13. Assume that you are the president of a retail business that operates four stores selling and renting video equipment. Give examples of several kinds of managerial accounting information you would like to have to manage the company.

14. Why do the controller and his or her staff have to understand the firm's organizational structure and the role of each manager?

15. You recently overheard the following comment: "The way our company's controller operates we ought to make him the president because he wants to be involved in every decision anyway." Is this true of a correct use of a controller's position?

16. It has been said that the controller is both a line executive and a staff executive. Do you agree? Why?

17. What are some of the causes of disagreement between line and staff managers?

18. What is the Certificate in Management Accounting (CMA)?

19. How does a microcomputer assist in the preparation and use of managerial accounting information?

20. What is an electronic spreadsheet? Give examples of managerial accounting applications that are greatly facilitated with an electronic spreadsheet.

EXERCISES

Exercise 1-1 **Use of Managerial Accounting Information**

The management of the Merrill Corporation, a new company that will produce plumbing supplies, is trying to determine the firm's managerial accounting needs.

Required:

A. Identify and explain the most important characteristics of managerial accounting information.

B. Determine whether the following information would be used primarily for recordkeeping, performance evaluation, or decision making.

    1. Information about expenses contained in a subsidiary ledger.

    2. Information comparing the cost of leasing equipment versus financing it at a bank.

    3. Information about the cost of producing a component needed for manufacturing or purchasing it.

    4. Information concerning the profitability of a particular department.

    5. Information about how well costs are controlled in the sales department.

Exercise 1-2   Comparing Financial Accounting with Managerial Accounting

You recently overheard a conversation between the controller of a business and one of its engineers. In response to a description of the firm's accounting capabilities by the controller, the engineer replied: "To me, accounting is accounting. I don't see why any differentiation is necessary concerning financial and managerial accounting."

Required:

A. Identify the major differences between financial and managerial accounting.

B. Why would the engineer be concerned primarily with managerial accounting? Would that person ever be interested in financial accounting?

Exercise 1-3   Financial Accounting versus Managerial Accounting

Listed below are several accounting functions performed by the SMC Company. Indicate whether each activity is financial accounting or managerial accounting.

A. A monthly report on the profit performance of a new plant is sent to the bank that funded the project.

B. The marketing manager receives a monthly report concerning the advertising costs for each product line.

C. A consolidated federal income tax return is prepared for a large company.

D. A company's annual report is prepared and sent to interested parties.

E. Each regional sales manager is sent a report showing the actual earnings performance of the operation compared with the expected results.

F. A company's independent CPA firm requests detailed product cost information during the annual audit.

G. Monthly payroll costs are summarized and related to specific work performances.

H. A detailed analysis of the cost of purchasing or leasing computer equipment is prepared.

Exercise 1-4   Evaluating Types of Accounting Information

Listed below are several types of accounting information. Identify the primary function involved with each type of information (recordkeeping, performance evaluation, or decision making):

A. The detailed description of a new product line's profitability.
B. Journal entries for year-end accruals.
C. A report concerning the profit results of a production department.
D. The payroll register for the engineering department.
E. A report showing why the marketing department did not achieve its sales quotas.
F. Data regarding the costs and capabilities of three similar machines when only one of them will be purchased by an automobile factory.

Exercise 1-5 Evaluating Types of Managerial Accounting Information

The Midwest Transportation Company operates a number of bus terminals throughout the midwest with its central headquarters located in Indianapolis. Each terminal has a limited number of personnel and a computerized ticket processing capability that is linked with the central office.

Required:
Identify the general types of managerial accounting information needed by each bus terminal manager and the managers operating in the central office for recordkeeping, performance evaluations, and decision making.

Exercise 1-6 Management Functions and Managerial Accounting Information

Indicate whether each of the following managerial accounting items would be used primarily for planning, organizing, directing, or controlling:

A. A sales forecast of consumer demand for a particular product line.
B. A personnel report showing the number of new accountants needed by a CPA firm during the next year.
C. A memo from a sales manager to a sales representative explaining how a personnel issue should be resolved.
D. A report showing the differences between the forecast sales of various product lines and those sales actually achieved.
E. A projection of net incomes for different sales levels.

Exercise 1-7 Evaluating Management Functions

Determine whether the following management functions are primarily involved with planning, organizing, directing, or controlling:

A. The engineering department of a manufacturing firm predicting the type of vehicle the public will want five years from now.
B. Comparing actual financial results with those expected for an accounting period.
C. Allocating resources to four product lines for an upcoming operating period.
D. A plant manager answering questions raised by five department managers about a new bonus compensation plan recently adopted by the firm.
E. Combining separate goals of the segments of a business into overall firm goals.
F. Combining budgets of individual segments of a business into an overall firm budget.
G. Evaluating the last quarter's financial performance of a sales territory.

Exercise 1-8   Developing an Organizational Chart

Prepare a partial organizational chart based on the following positions occupied within the Grannit Company:

A. Vice president of sales
B. Controller
C. Vice president of production
D. President
E. Western plant manager
F. Eastern plant manager
G. Western region sales manager
H. Eastern region sales manager
 I. Financial accounting department manager
J. Managerial accounting department manager

Exercise 1-9   Time Focus for Decision Making

Listed below are several decision-making activities. Indicate whether each is a long- or short-term decision. Justify your answer.

A. A plant manager is evaluating the feasibility of purchasing a new piece of equipment to take advantage of advanced technology that offers substantial cost savings.
B. A manufacturing firm is evaluating the profitability of a proposed plant expansion.
C. A marketing manager is trying to decide which products should be listed in the firm's advertising campaign.
D. A plant manager is trying to decide whether to hire a maintenance crew or obtain maintenance services from an outside source.
E. Facing a significant decline in the company's cash balance, the board of directors is evaluating whether a quarterly dividend should be paid and, if so, how much it should be.
F. The demand for the products produced at a firm's midwestern plant has declined significantly. The president is evaluating whether the plant should be closed or a new product should be added.
G. A firm's top management is trying to determine the scope and direction of the research and development program.
H. A retailing firm is considering a price decrease for certain products to meet competition.

Exercise 1-10   Role of a Controller

At a recent management meeting, the vice president of production presented a proposal concerning a capacity expansion program. The firm's controller questioned the financial ramifications of the proposal, given a recent decline in the profitability of the products involved. The vice president of production became very disturbed and said, "I don't have to listen to you. You may not like the proposal but you don't make decisions and only the president can rule against my plans."

Required:

Is the vice president correct? What is the responsibility of the controller in a situation like this?

PART 2

DEVELOPING A COST DATA BASE FOR MANAGERIAL ACCOUNTING

2

COST CLASSIFICATIONS, CONCEPTS, AND USES

CHAPTER OVERVIEW AND OBJECTIVES

This chapter describes how cost information is developed in a business. After studying this chapter, you should be able to:

1. Explain why cost information is so important to managers.
2. Recognize why there are different costs for different purposes.
3. Determine how costs are classified by business function.
4. Distinguish between product and period costs and give examples of each one.
5. Explain the difference between direct and indirect costs and provide examples of each type.
6. Distinguish between manufacturing and nonmanufacturing firms and understand their accounting differences.
7. Describe the three manufacturing cost elements and give examples of each one.
8. Identify the three inventory accounts maintained by a manufacturing firm and explain how each is used in the balance sheet and income statement.
9. Prepare a manufacturing firm's income statement and related cost of goods manufactured statement in proper form.
10. Explain the limitations of periodic inventory control in a manufacturing firm and why a perpetual system usually is needed.
11. Classify costs by their cost behavior and give examples of variable and fixed costs.
12. Distinguish between controllable and uncontrollable costs and give examples of each type.
13. Compare relevant and irrelevant costs and provide examples of each type.

IMPORTANCE OF COST INFORMATION

We learned in Chapter 1 that managers in every type of business must be accountable for acquiring and utilizing scarce resources efficiently and effectively. In doing so, the managers must be certain that the revenues of a given period exceed all the costs charged to the period (e.g., cost of goods sold, operating expenses, and taxes) by an amount consistent with their firm's profit goals. As a result, the term "cost" has a special importance for financial reporting purposes. Managers of every organization need much more detailed cost information than the summarized cost results reported in financial statements in order to carry out their managerial responsibilities. Consequently, an awareness of costs on the basis of their treatment in the financial statements is only a small part of management's overall concern for the diverse subject of costs. To manage a business efficiently and effectively, managers must frequently answer the question "What does it cost?" Examples are:

Objective 1:
Importance of cost information

- What does it cost to produce a desk in a furniture manufacturing business?
- What does it cost a utility to provide electrical service in a rural area?
- What does it cost a university to play a home football game?
- What does it cost a bank to offer a credit card service?
- What does it cost a sporting goods store to operate a golf equipment department?
- What does it cost the government to provide a food stamps program for the needy?

Management must accurately answer such questions if the organization involved is to achieve its financial goals. Many different kinds of costs are involved in the questions listed above so the various managers must be able to identify the specific costs that affect the decisions being evaluated. Cost information is used by managers for five general purposes:

1. *Inventory valuation*—Management must know which costs to include in the firm's inventories.
2. *Income determination*—Management needs to know the costs to be deducted from revenues in the income statement to determine the profit of a period.
3. *Financial planning*—Management requires cost information to plan for the future with desired financial goals.
4. *Controlling operations*—Management requires information regarding actual cost results compared with those costs expected.
5. *Decision making*—Management often must evaluate the costs associated with alternative courses of action from which the best option is selected.

Different types of costs are necessary to provide the cost information managers need for these five purposes, as we will see next.

DIFFERENT COST CLASSIFICATIONS FOR DIFFERENT PURPOSES

Two of the most frequently used terms in a managerial accountant's vocabulary are "cost" and "expense." The distinction between the two terms and the many ways costs are defined are extremely important in managerial accounting. Although these terms often are used synonymously for the sake of conve-

Objective 2:
Using different costs for different purposes

nience, there is a technical difference between them. A **cost** is an economic sacrifice of resources (e.g., cash) made in exchange for a product or service (e.g., inventory), whereas an **expense** is an expired cost (e.g., inventory that is sold).

In general, as long as a cost has future benefit, it is an asset reported on the balance sheet. The cost expires when it no longer has future benefit, which normally occurs when the cost is consumed in the production of revenue. Then, the cost becomes an expense that is deducted on the income statement. For example, a firm may pay cash for an annual insurance policy for liability protection. The amount of the payment is a cost, which is treated as a monthly expense as the firm uses the insurance.

Managerial accountants use several modifiers to identify specific meanings of cost because they are concerned about how one definition of cost is suitable for a given purpose while another is meaningless. Examples include *product cost, period cost, direct cost, indirect cost, variable cost, fixed cost, controllable cost, uncontrollable cost, relevant cost,* and *irrelevant cost.* Before we can choose meaningfully from the different types of cost, we have to identify the purpose for which we want the information.

For example, how much does it cost to operate your automobile? By itself, that question is too ambiguous to have a definite answer. If you want to know the cost of driving to campus tomorrow because your gas tank and wallet are almost empty, the price of gasoline may be your only concern. But if you are evaluating the cost of driving the car during the entire time you own it, you must consider additional costs (e.g., maintenance, insurance, license plates, taxes, and depreciation). The important point is that *different costs* will be applicable for *different purposes.* The same principle applies to business decisions because managers must evaluate the purpose for which they want cost information before they can choose the correct type of cost.

COST CLASSIFICATION BY BUSINESS FUNCTION

Objective 3: Classifying costs by business function

Costs are required in all types of organizations—service, merchandising, and manufacturing—to obtain revenues. The specific cost items incurred by a given organization and the way they are classified will depend on the business functions performed by the firm. As we move from a service organization such as a real estate office to a manufacturing firm, the business functions involved and their costs become more complex. A basic way to classify costs in a particular organization is by the business function to which they relate. This classification is used both for evaluating how managers have used their functions' resources and for financial reporting.

A **manufacturing firm** is generally the most complex type of business for accounting purposes because it involves a manufacturing (or production) function, a selling function, and an administrative function. In turn, an important way to classify costs for such a business is into manufacturing, selling, and administrative categories. The production function distinguishes a manufacturing firm from service and merchandising operations, which offer services or buy and sell inventory without producing products. Since it is the most complete type of business, we will mainly concentrate on a manufacturing type of operation to illustrate cost classification by business function and describe other cost considerations in this chapter. An important point, however, is that many of the same concepts apply to nonmanufacturing organizations as well.

Manufacturing costs will include all costs needed to acquire basic materials from a supplier and convert them into finished products that are salable in a different form. Selling costs are all costs incurred to market the finished products, including advertising, sales salaries, and transportation charges to deliver the products to customers. Administrative costs are all costs needed for the general management of the organization and include executive salaries, accounting services, and office supplies. The next step is to determine which costs should be inventoried as assets on the balance sheet and which should be deducted from revenue on the income statement.

PRODUCT AND PERIOD COSTS

Accrual accounting does not permit all costs to be expensed against revenues on the income statement of the period in which the costs are initially recorded. The terms "product cost" and "period cost" (also called inventoriable cost and noninventoriable cost) are important in the development of an income statement for either a merchandising firm or a manufacturing firm. A proper matching of revenues and expenses must be based on a well-defined distinction between the product and period costs. As we mentioned earlier, the *period in which the benefit of any cost is received is the period in which the cost should be deducted as an expense.* The separation of product costs from period costs provides the basis for determining which costs to include in the cost of inventory as well as when the various costs should be deducted as expenses in the income statement.

Objective 4: Comparing product costs and period costs

Product costs are those costs incurred to have inventory that is ready for sale. They are inventoried as assets until the products are sold (note that this is the period of time during which the costs benefit the business because the related inventory is available for sale). At the point of sale, the product costs have been consumed in the production of revenue so they no longer can benefit the business and are expensed in the income statement of the period. **Period costs** are identified with a specific time interval since they are not required to have a salable product. Consequently, they are not inventoried and are charged as expenses to a period according to the matching principle you learned in financial accounting. An example of a period cost is a sales commission that is expensed when it is earned by a sales representative.

The flows of product costs and period costs through the financial statements can be shown schematically as:

	Balance Sheet	Income Statement
	Current assets:	Sales
Product costs (as incurred) ───▶	Inventory ───▶ (as sold)	Cost of goods sold
		Gross profit
Period costs (as incurred) ─────────────────▶		Operating expenses
		Net income

Product costs for a merchandising firm consist only of its purchase costs because the inventory purchased is ready for resale. The purchase costs are kept in an inventory account until they are matched against revenue as cost of goods sold according to an acceptable flow assumption such as first in, first out (FIFO) or last in, first out (LIFO). All other costs, including salaries and wages, are charged to a specific period as selling or administrative expenses (collectively called operating expenses). A service firm such as a medical clinic or an insurance agency will not have product costs since it does not maintain an inventory for resale. As a result, all costs are period costs because they are expensed with accrual accounting in specific periods as they are incurred.

In a manufacturing firm, all manufacturing cost elements needed to produce a salable product are treated as product costs. They are inventoried as assets on the balance sheet until the products are sold. Then, they are transferred as expenses to the cost of goods sold section of the income statement. The nonproduct or period costs chargeable to a specific period are classified as either selling or administrative expenses according to their functional nature and are expensed on that period's income statement because they are not incurred to produce a salable product. For example, advertising expenses and the president's salary would be treated as period costs—classified separately as selling expenses and administrative expenses, respectively. Before considering the three manufacturing cost elements needed to produce salable inventory (direct materials, direct labor, and manufacturing overhead) that are treated as product costs, we need to introduce two more cost classifications, direct costs and indirect costs.

DIRECT AND INDIRECT COSTS

Objective 5: Comparing direct costs and indirect costs

The terms "direct" and "indirect" by themselves have no real significance. They must be related to some cost objective to be useful to management. A **cost objective** is defined as any activity for which separate cost measurement is performed. For inventory valuation in a manufacturing firm, the cost objective is the product or products being produced. However, a number of cost objectives are used in managerial accounting with a specific selection depending on the nature of the business and management's intentions. Examples are a check processing service performed by a bank, prescriptions filled by a pharmacy, tax returns prepared by an accounting firm, a trip taken for an away game by a professional football team, license applications processed by a governmental agency, patients treated by a medical clinic, and a health foods department operated by a grocery store. Note that in some of these cases the cost objective is measured by the performance output (e.g., the tax returns prepared), while in others it relates to the operation of a segment of the organization (e.g., the health foods department).

The same concept applies in a manufacturing firm where the terms "direct cost" and "indirect cost" can be related to either the products produced or the operation of a department. Once a specific cost objective is identified, these terms can be put to use effectively. They are important to us now because they provide the basis for classifying and accounting for manufacturing costs. Direct costs are treated one way, indirect costs another. A **direct cost** can be traced to a specific cost objective because it is incurred solely for the benefit of the single cost objective. In contrast, an **indirect cost** is incurred for multiple cost objectives, so it is a **common cost**.

Since an indirect cost cannot be traced to the individual cost objectives involved, it can be assigned to them only on some allocation basis. This means that the indirect costs are apportioned among the various cost objectives that jointly benefit from the costs. For example, the rent on a building occupied by several departments often is allocated to the departments on the basis of the square feet used. For product costing in a manufacturing firm, those costs that are easily identified as being part of the product are classified as direct costs. All other manufacturing costs are indirect or common for the products produced.

MANUFACTURING VERSUS
NONMANUFACTURING FIRMS — A CLOSER LOOK

ILLUSTRATION OF A MANUFACTURING OPERATION

To help you visualize what manufacturing is all about, let's consider the simplified production flow used by Designer Jeans, Inc., a maker of high-quality jeans, shown below. The company has two production departments, Cutting and Sewing. Skilled labor and a highly automated production process are combined to make each pair of jeans that is sold to a retail store. Raw materials (primarily denim) are purchased from an outside supplier, kept in the Storeroom Department, and issued as needed to the Cutting Department. In the Cutting Department, each pair of jeans is cut to an appropriate size and then transferred to the Sewing Department, where the product is finished through an elaborate sewing process.

Objective 6:
Accounting differences for manufacturing and nonmanufacturing firms

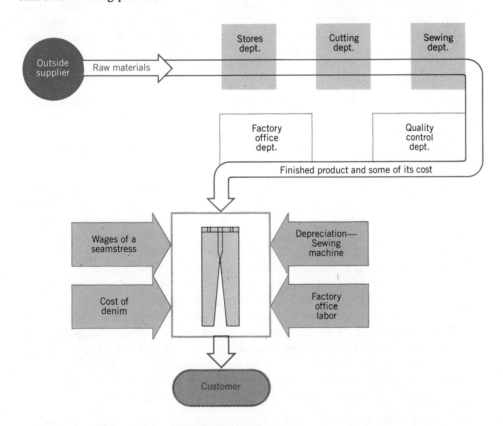

Management of Designer Jeans, Inc. will require a great deal of cost information about the production operation to (1) value inventory, (2) determine net income, (3) plan future profits, (4) control costs in the operation, and (5) make decisions such as what price to charge for the jeans and what kind of equipment to use. Note that production occurs in only the two production departments (Cutting and Sewing), although the company operates five departments in the manufacturing process. The other three departments — Storeroom, Factory Office, and Quality Control — are called service departments because they support the two production departments. For example, the Quality Control Department inspects the finished products to make sure they meet the firm's quality standards, and the Factory Office performs accounting, payroll, and personnel services. The managers of the service departments have staff authority as defined in Chapter 1. Note also that the selling and administrative functions are not part of the manufacturing process. As a result, the related selling and administrative expenses are not needed to produce a salable pair of jeans so they are accounted for as period costs, not product costs.

MANUFACTURING COST ELEMENTS

Objective 7: Three manufacturing cost elements

Manufacturing firms need three manufacturing cost elements to produce finished products during the production operation:

1. **Direct materials**—The raw materials directly traceable as an integral part of a finished product are called direct materials. The aluminum used for an automobile, the plastic used for a hair dryer, the crude oil used for gasoline, the steel used for a golf club, and the silicon chip used for a microcomputer are some examples of direct materials. In the Designer Jeans, Inc. illustration, the denim used to produce a pair of jeans is classified as direct materials.

   Since direct materials physically become part of a finished product, they can be traced to the product or, in some situations, to batches of products. Direct materials do not include such miscellaneous items as lubricants, glue, screws, or bolts that are treated as indirect materials and included in manufacturing overhead. It may be impossible or uneconomical to trace such items to the products.

2. **Direct labor**—The compensation paid to employees whose time and effort can be traced to the products is classified as direct labor. As long as the employees perform tasks that can be identified specifically with the conversion of raw materials to finished goods, the labor is a direct cost. Examples are the wages paid to welders on an automobile assembly line. In the Designer Jeans, Inc. case, the seamstress's wages are direct labor.

   The direct labor also becomes part of the finished product, so it can be traced to a product or batches of products. Other labor is required to support the production process but will not be traceable to finished products. The wages or salaries paid to janitors, maintenance people, production supervisors, cafeteria workers, medical staff, and material handlers are classified as indirect labor and included in manufacturing overhead. The combination of direct materials and direct labor is referred to as **prime costs** because these costs are such an integral part of the total product costs.

3. **Manufacturing overhead**—All manufacturing costs except direct materials and direct labor are included in manufacturing overhead. Manufacturing overhead may also be referred to as indirect manufacturing cost, factory overhead, or factory burden. Manufacturing overhead includes such cost items as:
   1. Indirect materials
   2. Indirect labor
   3. Maintenance
   4. Utilities
   5. Rent

6. Insurance
7. Depreciation
8. Property taxes
9. Payroll taxes

For example, depreciation on the sewing machines is treated as manufacturing overhead by Designer Jeans, Inc. Some of the items classified as manufacturing overhead may also be incurred for the selling and administrative functions. For example, when the same building is used for manufacturing, selling, and administrative functions, building occupancy costs such as depreciation, utilities, and insurance are common costs for all three functions. Only the portion required for the production operation should be considered manufacturing overhead so the total common costs must be apportioned among the three functions. Again, this division is based on the need for a distinction between product and period costs. The cost items needed for the selling and administrative functions will not be inventoried. Instead, they will be treated as period costs. The combination of direct labor and manufacturing overhead is called **conversion costs** since these are the costs needed to convert direct materials into a salable product.

COST FLOWS OF MANUFACTURING
AND NONMANUFACTURING FIRMS

The flow of costs through the production function introduces some important accounting differences between a manufacturing operation and a merchandising business that buys goods ready for resale or a service entity that does not have any inventory. As products flow through the production operation, the three manufacturing cost elements—direct materials, direct labor, and manufacturing overhead—are incurred to convert raw materials into finished products. The cost flow associated with the production operation causes more complicated inventory valuation problems than those experienced by nonmanufacturing businesses. For example, compare the inventory cost flows of a merchandising business and a manufacturing firm, as shown in Figure 2-1. Three different inventory accounts must be maintained by a manufacturing firm: raw materials, work in process, and finished goods. At the end of any accounting period, the balance in each of these three inventory accounts will be reported as a current asset on the balance sheet. In contrast, a merchandising firm uses a single inventory account. A proper matching of revenues and expenses will depend on the accuracy with which the costs of the three inventories are accumulated throughout the production operation. Costs are transferred from raw materials to work in process to finished goods and ultimately to cost of goods sold. The following is a description of the three types of inventory for a manufacturing firm:

Objective 8: Three types of inventories for a manufacturing firm

1. **Raw materials**—The costs of the basic materials and parts that have been purchased and are available for future conversion into salable products of a different form are classified as raw materials. Examples include the silicon chips, plastic, steel, and electronic components used to manufacture microcomputers.
2. **Work in process**—Inventory that is partially finished but requires further processing before it can be sold is called work in process inventory. All the microcomputers placed into production on an assembly line but unfin-

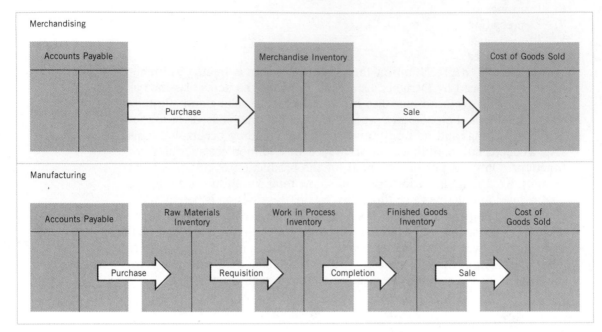

Figure 2-1
Merchandising and Manufacturing Firms' Inventory Cost Flows

ished at the end of an accounting period are treated as work in process inventory.

3. **Finished goods** — The total cost assigned during the production operation to all products fully manufactured and ready for sale is classified as finished goods inventory. The microcomputers that have been completed and will be delivered later to retail stores are identified as finished goods inventory.

The inventory cost flow of a manufacturing firm, illustrated in Figure 2-1, can be expanded to the more complete manufacturing cost flow shown in Figure 2-2.

COST OF GOODS SOLD

The major income statement difference between accounting for a merchandising firm and accounting for a manufacturing operation is the calculation of cost of goods sold. Remember from financial accounting that a merchandising firm calculates cost of goods sold as follows:

$$\begin{array}{c} \text{Beginning merchandise} \\ \text{inventory} \end{array} + \begin{array}{c} \text{Purchases of} \\ \text{merchandise} \end{array} - \begin{array}{c} \text{Ending merchandise} \\ \text{inventory} \end{array} = \begin{array}{c} \text{Cost} \\ \text{of goods} \\ \text{sold} \end{array}$$

In contrast, a manufacturing operation determines cost of goods sold in this way:

$$\begin{array}{c} \text{Beginning finished} \\ \text{goods inventory} \end{array} + \begin{array}{c} \text{Cost of goods} \\ \text{manufactured} \end{array} - \begin{array}{c} \text{Ending finished} \\ \text{goods inventory} \end{array} = \begin{array}{c} \text{Cost} \\ \text{of goods} \\ \text{sold} \end{array}$$

At a glance, the two cost of goods sold calculations may appear to be the same, but the production flow associated with manufacturing makes them dif-

Figure 2-2
Manufacturing
Cost Flow

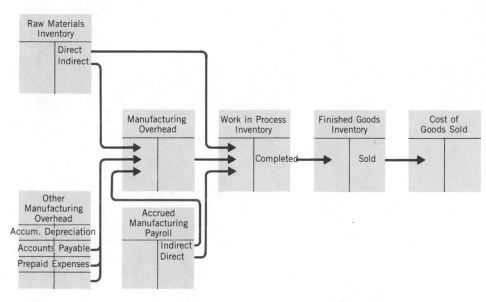

ferent. The cost of goods manufactured in a manufacturing firm results from the conversion of raw materials to finished goods. It replaces the purchases of merchandise in a merchandising enterprise. This difference carries forward to the development of an income statement.

COMPARISON OF INCOME STATEMENTS
OF MERCHANDISING AND MANUFACTURING FIRMS

In Figure 2-3, the cost of goods sold calculation is shown as the difference between income statements prepared for merchandising and manufacturing firms. Sales revenue, selling expenses, administrative expenses, and income taxes are treated the same, as can be seen in Figure 2-3. The merchandising firm's cost of goods sold consists of the costs incurred to purchase the inventory sold from a supplier. In contrast, the cost of goods sold for a manufacturing firm includes the manufacturing cost elements assigned as product costs to the inventory that was sold. Again, we see that the cost of goods manufactured in the manufacturing firm's income statement replaces the purchases of the merchandising business. The next step is to determine what constitutes the cost of goods manufactured.

**Objective 9:
Preparing an income statement for a manufacturing firm**

COST OF GOODS MANUFACTURED STATEMENT

The cost of goods manufactured can be computed as:

$$\begin{array}{c}\text{Cost}\\\text{of goods}\\\text{manufactured}\end{array} = \begin{array}{c}\text{Direct}\\\text{materials}\end{array} + \begin{array}{c}\text{Direct}\\\text{labor}\end{array} + \begin{array}{c}\text{Manufacturing}\\\text{overhead}\end{array} + \begin{array}{c}\text{Beginning}\\\text{work in}\\\text{process}\\\text{inventory}\end{array} - \begin{array}{c}\text{Ending}\\\text{work in}\\\text{process}\\\text{inventory}\end{array}$$

A **cost of goods manufactured statement** is prepared to show the supporting calculations for the cost of goods manufactured reported on the income state-

A MERCHANDISING FIRM Income Statement Year Ended December 31, 1987			A MANUFACTURING FIRM Income Statement Year Ended December 31, 1987		
Sales		$1,200,000	Sales		$1,200,000
Cost of goods sold:			Cost of goods sold:		
Beginning merchandise inventory	$ 180,000		Beginning finished goods inventory	$ 180,000	
Purchases of merchandise	852,000		Cost of goods manufactured (Figure 2-4)	852,000	
Goods available for sale	1,032,000		Goods available for sale	1,032,000	
Ending merchandise inventory	192,000		Ending finished goods inventory	192,000	
Cost of goods sold		840,000	Cost of goods sold		840,000
Gross profit		360,000	Gross profit		360,000
Operating expenses:			Operating expenses:		
Selling expenses	132,000		Selling expenses	132,000	
Administrative expenses	144,000		Administrative expenses	144,000	
Total operating expenses		276,000	Total operating expenses		276,000
Net income before taxes		84,000	Net income before taxes		84,000
Income taxes		19,200	Income taxes		19,200
Net income		$ 64,800	Net income		$ 64,800

Figure 2-3
Comparison of Income Statements

ment. In Figure 2-3, the cost of goods manufactured amounts to $852,000. The purpose of the supporting statement shown in Figure 2-4 is to provide a detailed explanation of that total. The sum of the direct materials, direct labor, and manufacturing overhead represents the manufacturing costs of the period.

The direct materials used ($170,400) are computed by adding the purchases of the period ($169,200) to the beginning raw materials inventory ($57,600) and subtracting the ending raw materials inventory ($56,400). Note that the presentation of the direct materials used is basically the same as the cost of the goods sold on the income statement of the merchandising business. The direct labor ($426,000) and the manufacturing overhead ($249,600) would be recorded in the accounting system during the period. Consequently, the total manufacturing costs for the period are $846,000.

The individual manufacturing overhead items are listed and totaled on the statement if they are not too numerous. When a large number of accounts are involved, they may be shown on a separate schedule to keep the cost of goods manufactured statement from being too lengthy.

The beginning work in process inventory of $42,000 represents costs that have been incurred in the previous period. These costs are added to the manufacturing costs of the current period. Since the ending work in process of $36,000 consists of costs associated with products that will be finished later, it must be subtracted to compute the cost of goods manufactured for the period. The cost of goods manufactured ($852,000) represents the manufacturing cost elements assigned to the products that have been completed and transferred to finished goods inventory during the period. This figure is carried to the income statement in Figure 2-3.

Figure 2-4
Cost of Goods
Manufactured
Statement

A MANUFACTURING FIRM Cost of Goods Manufactured Statement Year Ended December 31, 1987		
Direct materials:		
Beginning raw materials	$ 57,600	
Purchases (net)	169,200	
Raw materials available for production	226,800	
Ending raw materials	56,400	
Direct materials used		170,400
Direct labor		426,000
Manufacturing overhead:		
Indirect labor	67,200	
Supplies	6,000	
Utilities	50,400	
Rent	27,120	
Insurance	21,600	
Payroll taxes	34,080	
Depreciation	38,400	
Miscellaneous	4,800	
Total manufacturing overhead		249,600
Manufacturing costs for the period		846,000
Beginning work in process		42,000
Total work in process		888,000
Ending work in process		36,000
Cost of goods manufactured		$852,000

PERIODIC VERSUS PERPETUAL INVENTORY CONTROL

In financial accounting, you learned that a merchandising firm must decide between a periodic or a perpetual inventory system. The same decision must be made by a manufacturing business. However, the very nature of the production operation makes a periodic inventory system impractical except for small manufacturing firms with a single product or a few similar products. Even then, the results may be inadequate to satisfy the product cost information needs of management. With a periodic system, cost information is only available at the end of an accounting period after physical inventories have been taken for raw materials, work in process, and finished goods. A periodic system is not sufficient in most cases because management needs the information for decisions that must be made regularly throughout the period. As we will see in the next two chapters, perpetual inventory control is achieved with a product costing system based on either job order costing or process costing. These product costing systems provide management with information that is timely, accurate, and detailed.

Objective 10:
Need for perpetual inventory in a manufacturing firm

OTHER COST CLASSIFICATIONS

Thus far, we have been primarily concerned with the cost concepts and classifications needed to value inventories and determine net income. Managers also require other cost information to plan and control operations as well as to make decisions. Among the additional important cost classifications used in the management process are variable and fixed, controllable and uncontrollable, and relevant and irrelevant. We will consider each of these types of costs next and others later in our coverage of managerial accounting.

VARIABLE AND FIXED COSTS

Objective 11: Comparing variable and fixed costs

Managers often must evaluate the effect of changes in sales or production volume on the profits of the firm. To do so, the managers must be able to predict what will happen to costs when the level of business activity changes. Each cost is classified by its **cost behavior,** which is the measure of how the total amount of the cost changes as the level of business activity changes. Our primary concern at this point is the cost behavior of manufacturing costs, although the same basic concepts can be applied to selling and administrative expenses.

Variable Cost

A **variable cost** fluctuates in total amount proportionately with some measure of business activity such as units produced or direct labor hours worked. Direct materials cost, direct labor cost, and a limited number of manufacturing overhead items (such as supplies, utilities, and maintenance) are variable costs. For example, if a $20 silicon chip is used to produce a microcomputer, the total cost of the chips increases and decreases proportionately with the number of computers produced, as illustrated below:

Microcomputers Produced	Cost of a Chip	Total Direct Materials
1	$20	$ 20
10	20	200
100	20	2,000
1,000	20	20,000

Note that the cost per silicon chip is constant but the total direct materials change with the level of production.

Fixed Cost

A **fixed cost** remains constant in total amount over a wide range of business activity for a given period. In a manufacturing operation, a fixed cost is the same regardless of the amount produced. Many of the manufacturing overhead items are fixed costs. Examples are depreciation, rent, property taxes, and supervisory salaries. As manufacturing operations become more and more automated, including using robots instead of labor, their cost structures are increasingly fixed because of high depreciation charges. Although a fixed cost remains constant in total amount regardless of the level of activity, it will have a unit cost that varies inversely with volume. For example, a $1,000 monthly depreciation charge for equipment used to produce microcomputers will be constant for all production levels but will change as a unit cost as follows:

Microcomputers Produced	Monthly Depreciation	Depreciation Per Unit
1	$1,000	$1,000
10	1,000	100
100	1,000	10
1,000	1,000	1

CONTROLLABLE AND UNCONTROLLABLE COSTS

Another important way to classify costs is on the basis of managerial influence, which is the extent to which a given manager can control a particular cost. This classification determines the costs for which specific managers should be held responsible. Since every cost must be authorized by a responsible manager, all costs are controllable at some level of an organization at some point in time. Note the two important characteristics of controllability, "level of organization" and "point in time." In determining whether a particular cost is controllable, we must consider both characteristics concurrently.

Top management has the broad authority to make decisions that commit the organization to certain costs for long time periods. For example, the decision may be made to build a new plant that will result in additional costs such as depreciation, property taxes, labor, and maintenance. As time passes, many of these costs will benefit the operations for which lower level managers are responsible. However, such costs as depreciation and property taxes are only controllable at the time the decision to build the new plant is made and only then by top management. In general, as the time period shortens and we move downward through an organization, fewer and fewer costs can be considered controllable.

As a result of the two characteristics of controllability, a **controllable cost** is one that a given manager can regulate or influence during a particular time period. In contrast, an **uncontrollable cost** is beyond the influence of the manager because he or she cannot authorize it. For example, consider the service department of an automobile dealership such as Johnson Automotive Inc., discussed in Chapter 1. The service manager can influence the mechanics' labor by controlling such factors as efficiency, idle time, overtime, the number of employees, and work scheduling. Consequently, the related labor cost is controllable by the service manager. However, the rent paid on the building occupied by the entire firm is uncontrollable by the service manager. As such, the service manager *should not* be held responsible for the amount of rent expense charged to his or her department.

**Objective 12:
Evaluating
controllable and
uncontrollable
costs**

RELEVANT AND IRRELEVANT COSTS

We learned in Chapter 1 that relevance is one of the most important qualities of good managerial accounting information. If we extend this concept to the subject of cost, we will find relevance to be very useful for managerial decision making. A **relevant cost** is a future expected cost that will differ depending on the alternative selected in a specific situation. Because of the difference, it will have a bearing on the decision, whereas an **irrelevant cost** will not since it will be the same for all alternatives.

For example, if management is deciding which of two machines to purchase, direct materials cost may or may not be relevant. If the same direct materials cost of $12 per pound is required with either machine, the cost is irrelevant. However, if one machine can be operated with direct materials costing only $10 per pound, whereas the other machine requires a higher quality material that costs $12 per pound, a relevant cost is involved. Well-defined distinctions between relevant and irrelevant costs are important for good managerial decision making so managers will not waste their time considering costs that will be the same regardless of the alternative selected.

**Objective 13:
Separating
relevant and
irrelevant costs**

SUMMARY

"What does it cost?" is a question that must be asked continually in a business as management uses cost information for (1) inventory valuation, (2) income determination, (3) financial planning, (4) controlling operations, and (5) decision making. The many different types of costs must be understood by managers so they can select the correct ones for different situations. The theme "different costs for different purposes" is a fundamental part of managerial accounting. This theme means that the purpose for which we want the cost information must be identified carefully before we select from the many types of costs. Examples of cost classifications are product cost, period cost, direct cost, indirect cost, variable cost, fixed cost, controllable cost, uncontrollable cost, relevant cost, and irrelevant cost. Most of the different types of costs are applicable in all forms of business—manufacturing, merchandising, and service.

A manufacturing firm is the most complex form of business because it is involved with production, selling, and administrative functions. The production function creates the need for more sophisticated accounting treatment than that required by nonmanufacturing businesses. The product costs of a manufacturer are more complicated than those of a merchandising firm because they consist of all costs needed to convert raw materials into a salable product. Consequently, both direct and indirect costs (direct materials, direct labor, and manufacturing overhead) are involved. A flow of these three manufacturing cost elements is associated with the physical flow of products through the production process. Three different inventory accounts—raw materials, work in process, and finished goods—must be maintained by a manufacturer.

The major difference beween the income statements of a manufacturer and a merchandiser is the calculation of cost of goods sold. In effect, the cost of goods manufactured replaces the purchases of a merchandiser because of the conversion of raw materials into finished goods. The cost of goods manufactured for a period is equal to the manufacturing costs of the period plus or minus the change in work in process inventory.

Most manufacturing firms require perpetual inventory control because product cost information is needed by management on a regular basis, not just at the end of an accounting period. Either a job order costing system or a process costing system can be used for the perpetual inventory control.

Managers need more cost information than that required to value inventory and determine net income. A cost classification based on cost behavior is often used to evaluate how costs will change for different levels of business activity. A variable cost will fluctuate in total amount proportionately with the level of business activity. In contrast, a fixed cost remains constant in total amount over a wide range of business activity. Controllable costs are especially important to management in evaluating financial performance results, and relevant costs are used extensively in making decisions.

As a final step in our introduction of the many meanings of cost, let's see if we can apply what we have learned in this chapter to the Designer Jeans, Inc. illustration introduced earlier as follows:

> **Product costs** are the costs assigned to the jeans produced. The direct materials, direct labor, and manufacturing overhead incurred to produce jeans are treated as product costs. Therefore, they are inventoried as assets until the jeans are sold.

Period costs are the selling and administrative expenses charged to the period in which they are incurred instead of to the jeans manufactured. Examples are the sales manager's salary and depreciation on the company president's automobile.

Direct costs are the costs traceable to a specific cost objective such as the jeans produced or the operation of the Cutting Department. The denim materials and cutting labor identified as an integral part of a pair of jeans are direct costs for the finished product.

Indirect costs are incurred for more than one cost objective so they are common costs. For example, the depreciation on a sewing machine and the salary paid to the manager of the Quality Control Department are indirect costs for the jeans. Note, however, that the two items are direct costs if the cost objectives are the Sewing Department and the Quality Control Department, respectively.

Variable costs fluctuate proportionately in total amount with some measure of business activity such as the number of pairs of jeans produced. The cost of denim and the cutting labor are examples of variable costs.

Fixed costs remain constant in total amount regardless of the level of business activity. The depreciation on a sewing machine is a fixed cost if the straight-line depreciation method is used.

Controllable costs can be regulated or influenced at a given level of management during a specific time period. The manager of the Sewing Department would be responsible for the direct materials and direct labor used in her department because both items are controllable.

Uncontrollable costs cannot be regulated or influenced at a given level of management during a specific time period. The depreciation on a particular sewing machine is uncontrollable by the Sewing Department manager once the machine has been purchased.

Relevant costs are future expected costs that will differ in a decision depending on the alternative selected. For example, if two new sewing machines are being evaluated and the cost of thread for each machine is significantly different, that cost is relevant.

Irrelevant costs are the same regardless of the alternative chosen in a given decision. If the two new machines above require the same thread cost in the production of a pair of jeans, the cost of thread is irrelevant.

GLOSSARY

COMMON COST. A cost incurred for the benefit of more than one cost objective (p. 32).

CONTROLLABLE COST. A cost that can be regulated or influenced at a particular level of management during a specified time period (p. 41).

CONVERSION COSTS. The total of the direct labor and manufacturing overhead required to produce products (p. 35).

COST. An economic sacrifice made in exchange for a product or service (p. 30).

COST BEHAVIOR. The measure of how a cost will react to changes in the level of business activity. Examples are variable costs and fixed costs (p. 40).

COST OBJECTIVE. An activity for which separate cost measurement is performed. Examples are a department, a product, or an office (p. 32).

COST OF GOODS MANUFACTURED STATEMENT. A detailed accounting of the manufacturing cost performance reported on the income statement of a manufacturing firm (p. 37).

DIRECT COST. A cost that can be traced to a specific cost objective (p. 32).

DIRECT LABOR. Represents the wages paid to employees whose time and effort can be traced to finished products (p. 34).

DIRECT MATERIALS. The raw materials that can be identified as being an integral part of finished products (p. 34).

EXPENSE. A cost that has expired and thus is charged to the income statement because it no longer has future benefit (p. 30).

FINISHED GOODS. The cost of the products that have been manufactured completely and are ready for sale (p. 36).

FIXED COST. A cost that will remain constant in total amount over a wide range of business activity for a given period (p. 40).

INDIRECT COST. A cost incurred for the common benefit of multiple cost objectives (p. 32).

IRRELEVANT COST. A cost that will be the same in a decision-making situation regardless of the alternative selected (p. 41).

MANUFACTURING FIRM. A business that converts raw materials into finished goods (p. 30).

MANUFACTURING OVERHEAD. All manufacturing costs except direct materials and direct labor required in the production operation (p. 34).

PERIOD (NONINVENTORIABLE) COST. Cost charged to the income statement of the time period in which it is incurred rather than being inventoried as a product cost (p. 31).

PRIME COSTS. The total of the direct materials and the direct labor needed to produce products (p. 34).

PRODUCT COST (INVENTORIABLE COST). Cost inventoried as an asset and charged to the income statement when the related product is sold (p. 31).

RAW MATERIALS. Represent the cost of the basic materials and parts that have been purchased by a manufacturing firm and are available for conversion into salable products (p. 35).

RELEVANT COST. An expected future cost that will differ between alternatives in a decision-making situation (p. 41).

UNCONTROLLABLE COST. A cost that cannot be regulated or influenced at a particular level of management during a specified time period (p. 41).

VARIABLE COST. A cost that will vary in total amount proportionately with some measure of business activity (p. 40).

WORK IN PROCESS. The inventory that has been partially converted into finished products (p. 35).

DISCUSSION QUESTIONS

1. Why is the question "What does it cost" so difficult to answer in the typical business?
2. What are the major ways managers use cost information?

3. Differentiate between a cost and an expense. What is meant by the saying, "There are different costs for different purposes?"
4. Why are costs often classified by business function?
5. Distinguish between a manufacturing firm and a merchandising firm.
6. Distinguish between product and period costs. Identify which of the following is a product cost and which is a period cost:
    a. Indirect materials
    b. Depreciation — manufacturing equipment
    c. Gas heat — sales office
    d. President's salary
    e. Direct labor
    f. Insurance — factory
    g. Sales manager's salary
    h. Production supervisor's salary
    i. Depreciaton — president's car
7. How do we know which costs should be treated as product costs in a manufacturing firm?
8. Distinguish between direct and indirect costs. What must each be related to before the terms "direct" and "indirect" have meaning?
9. What is a cost objective? Identify an example of a cost objective from the business world and one from your personal life.
10. Define the following terms: direct materials, direct labor, manufacturing overhead, indirect materials, indirect labor, conversion costs, and prime costs.
11. What are the three manufacturing cost elements? Which of the nine items in question 6 would be classified as a manufacturing cost and what cost element would they represent?
12. Explain the basic differences between the inventories of a manufacturing firm and those of a merchandising operation. What is the effect of these differences on the income statements of the two types of business?
13. What is the basic difference between cost of goods sold in a manufacturing firm versus that of a merchandising operation?
14. Explain the fundamental difference between:
    a. Manufacturing costs for the period
    b. Cost of goods manufactured
    c. Cost of goods sold
15. The Ansek Company incurred the following manufacturing costs during the year:

Direct materials	$210,000
Direct labor	525,000
Manufacturing overhead	315,000

    a. Assume that the company had no work in process inventory at the beginning or end of the year. How much was the firm's cost of goods manufactured?
    b. Assume instead that the company had a work in process inventory of $30,000 at the beginning of the year but none at the end of the year. How much was the firm's cost of goods manufactured?
    c. Assume instead that the company had a work in process inventory of $30,000 at the beginning of the year and $60,000 at the end of the year. How much was the firm's cost of goods manufactured?

16. During the previous year, the cost of raw materials used by a manufacturing firm was $120,000. The raw materials inventory decreased by $13,500 during the year. What was the cost of raw materials purchased?

17. What is the basic problem with using periodic inventory control in a manufacturing operation? How does perpetual inventory control solve this problem?

18. Explain the basic difference between a variable cost and a fixed cost. On the basis of their most likely cost behavior, how would each of the items in question 6 be classified (fixed or variable)?

19. "Fixed costs are really variable because the more a firm produces, the less they become." Do you agree? Explain.

20. Distinguish between controllable costs and uncontrollable costs.

21. The Easy-Accounting Company evaluates the performance of its manufacturing operation by considering controllable costs only. All direct costs are classified as being controllable and all indirect costs are considered uncontrollable. Do you agree with this approach?

22. Differentiate between relevant costs and irrelevant costs. Why is this comparison important to management?

EXERCISES

Exercise 2-1 Distinguishing Between Costs and Expenses
Indicate which of the following is a *cost* and which is an *expense*:

A. Cash payment of $12,000 for a new business automobile.
B. Purchase of a three-year liability insurance policy for $3,600.
C. Cash payment of $98 for advertising in a local newspaper.
D. Annual depreciation of $3,000 recorded on a business automobile.
E. One month's usage of the insurance policy mentioned in item B.

Exercise 2-2 Identifying Product or Period Costs
Classify the following items as being either *product costs* or *period costs*:

A. Salaries of workers handling inventories during the production process.
B. Advertising expenses.
C. Depreciation on an airplane used by the firm's president.
D. Plant manager's salary.
E. Lease payments on manufacturing equipment.
F. Lease payments on automobiles used by sales representatives.
G. Depreciation on manufacturing equipment.
H. Rent on a factory building.
I. Clean-up materials used by production workers at the end of a day.
J. Social security payments for production workers.

Exercise 2-3 Evaluating Cost Classifications
Identify the most likely correct answer for each of the following costs as a *product* or *period* cost and as a *variable* or *fixed* cost with respect to level of activity:

Product   Period   Variable   Fixed

1. Manufacturing utilities
2. Manufacturing supplies
3. Direct materials
4. President's salary
5. Depreciation on manufacturing equipment
6. Manufacturing rent
7. Sales office utilities
8. Depreciation on sales office equipment
9. Nails used in production
10. Maintenance contract on manufacturing equipment

Exercise 2-4 Income Statement for a Manufacturing Firm

Listed below are selected financial data from the 1987 accounting records of the CSB Company:

Cost of goods manufactured	$305,000
Ending finished goods inventory	55,000
Sales	510,000
Beginning finished goods inventory	45,000
Selling and administrative expenses	105,000

Required:
Prepare an income statement for 1987.

Exercise 2-5 Cost of Goods Manufactured Statement

Listed below are selected financial data from the 1987 accounting records of the Johnson Manufacturing Corporation:

Beginning raw materials inventory	$ 69,120
Ending raw materials inventory	67,680
Beginning work in process inventory	50,400
Direct labor cost	511,200
Manufacturing overhead	299,520
Ending work in process inventory	43,200
Purchases of raw materials	203,040

Required:
Prepare a cost of goods manufactured statement for 1987.

Exercise 2-6 Determining Beginning Work in Process Inventory

The information below is taken from the accounting records of the Able Company for the year ended December 31, 1987.

Manufacturing overhead (62.5% of direct labor cost)	$108,000
Raw materials inventory, January 1, 1987	18,000
Cost of goods manufactured	490,800
Raw materials inventory, December 31, 1987	24,000
Work in process inventory, December 31, 1987	54,000
Raw materials purchased in 1987	237,600

Required:
Use a cost of goods manufactured statement format to determine the cost of the work in process inventory on January 1, 1987.

Exercise 2-7 Manufacturing Accounting with Missing Data

For each company, fill in the missing data. Each company is independent of the others.

Income Statements

	Company X	Company Y	Company Z
Sales	$106,000	?	$122,000
Finished goods, beginning inventory	14,000	?	30,000
Cost of goods manufactured	38,000	80,000	?
Finished goods, ending inventory	?	36,000	42,000
Cost of goods sold	40,000	74,000	?
Gross profit	?	88,000	?
Operating expenses	30,000	?	46,000
Net income	?	50,000	?
Work in process, beginning inventory	?	21,000	24,000
Direct labor cost	14,000	30,000	42,000
Raw materials used	13,000	18,000	34,000
Manufacturing overhead	16,000	24,000	30,000
Work in process, ending inventory	18,000	?	60,000

Exercise 2-8 Evaluating Basic Cost Behavior

The Southern Boat Company produces ski boats that are sold to marinas located throughout the United States. A boat contains a dual battery system that is purchased from an outside supplier at $150 for each system. The boat manufacturing process involves a computerized robotics system that initially cost the firm $1,500,000. The equipment is depreciated on a straight-line basis over a 10-year life. No residual value is expected for the equipment at the end of the 10 years.

Required:

A. What are the unit and total costs of the dual battery systems for 10 boats, 100 boats, 1,000 boats, and 10,000 boats?
B. What is the depreciation charge per boat if 1,000 boats per year are produced? For 10,000 boats per year?
C. What kind of cost behavior is involved in part A and part B?

Exercise 2-9 Evaluating the Use of Raw Materials

The Toledo Tool Company produces and sells high-quality automotive tool sets. Each set of tools is contained in a wooden carrying case that is purchased from an outside supplier. The wooden carrying cases are held as raw materials inventory until they are placed into production and combined with the related tool sets. The firm's accountant has provided the following information for the month of July:

1. Beginning raw materials inventory included 1,900 wooden cases at a cost of $85,500.
2. The company purchased 4,000 additional cases at $45 each.
3. A total of 4,400 cases were transferred into production.
4. 300 cases were given for promotional purposes to managers of prospective retail outlets.

Of the cases placed into production, 65% were combined with tool sets that were completed and transferred to finished goods inventory. Of the cases transferred to finished goods inventory during July, 70% had been sold by month-end. There was no beginning inventory of wooden cases in finished goods inventory or in work in process inventory.

Required:
Determine the cost of the wooden cases that would be included in the following accounts as of July 31:

A. Raw materials inventory
B. Work in process inventory
C. Finished goods inventory
D. Selling expense
E. Cost of goods sold

Exercise 2-10 Different Costs for Different Purposes

We have noted that there are different costs for different purposes in this chapter. Included in the discussion have been the following terms:

Product cost

Period cost

Direct cost

Indirect cost

Variable cost

Fixed cost

Required:
Choose the term or terms above that best describe the cost involved with each of the following situations:

A. The paper used to produce this textbook is a _____ on the income statement. It also is a _____ in terms of cost behavior.
B. Depreciation for printing equipment used for this book is a _____ on the income statement. If it is computed using the straight-line method, it is classified as a _____ in terms of cost behavior.
C. A commission paid to the sales representative who sold this book is a _____ on the income statement.
D. Depreciation for the automobile used by the sales representative is a _____ on the income statement. In terms of cost behavior, it is a _____ .
E. A _____ is also called an inventoriable cost because this type of cost is treated as an asset on the balance sheet unless the related item is sold.

Exercise 2-11 Different Cost Classifications

The Seawell Manufacturing Company incurred the following costs during the past year:

1. Indirect labor
2. Depreciation—sales equipment
3. Property taxes—sales office
4. Direct labor
5. Indirect materials
6. Direct materials
7. President's salary
8. Payroll taxes—plant workers
9. Plant insurance
10. Finished goods inventory insurance
11. Utilities—manufacturing
12. Rent—president's office

Required:

For each of the costs listed above, indicate whether it should be listed as a:

A. Product or period cost
B. Fixed or variable cost

PROBLEMS

Problem 2-1 Cost of Goods Manufactured Statement

The Webster Manufacturing Company recorded the following data during 1987:

Raw materials purchased		$ 350,000
Inventories – January 1, 1987:		
Raw materials	$ 70,000	
Work in process	240,000	
Finished goods	50,000	
Direct labor cost		1,260,000
Manufacturing overhead (80% fixed)		900,000
Selling expenses (all fixed)		600,000
Administrative expenses (all fixed)		$ 462,000
Sales		7,500 units at $648 per unit
Inventories – December 31, 1987:		
Raw materials	$ 60,000	
Work in process	120,000	
Finished goods	50,000	

Required:

A. Prepare a cost of goods manufactured statement for 1987.
B. What is the firm's net income for 1987?
C. Divide the manufacturing costs for 1987 into their variable and fixed components.

Problem 2-2 Developing an Income Statement for a Manufacturing Firm

The Peat Company recorded the following data during 1987:

Sales	$600,000
Raw materials purchased	72,000
Selling and administrative expenses	96,000
Direct labor cost	118,000
Beginnng raw materials inventory	12,000
Ending raw materials inventory	10,000
Plant depreciation	108,000
Plant utilities	6,500
Indirect labor	8,800
Insurance – plant	3,000
Beginning work in process inventory	57,000
Ending work in process inventory	59,000
Beginning finished goods inventory	25,000
Ending finished goods inventory	22,000
Maintenance – plant	4,700

Required:

A. Prepare a cost of goods manufactured statement for 1987.

B. Prepare an income statement for 1987.
C. Assume 4,000 units were manufactured during 1987. What was the unit cost of plant depreciation if the straight-line depreciation method is used? Would the unit depreciation cost change if 6,000 units were produced?

Problem 2-3 Fundamentals of Manufacturing Accounting

During 1987, the Cain Manufacturing Company incurred the following costs in connection with its production activities:

Plant utilities	$ 36,600
Indirect labor	51,600
Raw material purchases	210,000
Direct labor	156,000
Depreciation on plant equipment	28,800
Plant rent	30,000
Supplies used in production	15,600
Repairs to plant equipment	32,400

The beginning and ending inventories were:

	Beginning Inventory	Ending Inventory
Raw materials	$26,400	$22,800
Work in process	44,400	50,400
Finished goods	51,600	42,000

Required:
A. Calculate the relationship between direct labor costs and manufacturing overhead costs.
B. Prepare a cost of goods manufactured statement for the year ended December 31, 1987.

Problem 2-4 Fundamentals of Manufacturing Accounting

The following costs were incurred by the Cohen Corporation in its manufacturing activities during 1987:

Plant insurance	$ 24,000
Direct labor	144,000
Raw material purchases	183,600
Plant utilities	51,600
Repairs to plant equipment	20,400
Indirect labor	64,800
Plant supplies	40,800

The beginning and ending inventories were:

	Beginning Inventory	Ending Inventory
Raw materials	$32,400	$28,800
Work in process	49,200	54,000
Finished goods	39,600	37,200

Required:
A. Calculate the relationship between direct labor costs and manufacturing overhead costs.

B. Prepare a cost of goods manufactured statement for the year ended December 31, 1987.

Problem 2-5 Determining Cost of Goods Sold

The treasurer of the Hoagie Company has accumulated cost data concerning the company's 1987 manufacturing performance. The beginning inventories included raw materials ($192,200), work in process ($128,000), and finished goods ($236,000). The company's direct labor costs were $1,353,600 and its total cost of goods manufactured was $4,820,000 for the year. Overhead costs are assigned to work in process inventory and finished goods inventory using the relationship between direct labor costs and manufacturing overhead costs. The ending inventories include the following costs:

	Raw Materials	Work in Process	Finished Goods
Raw materials	$176,000	$44,000	$ 60,000
Direct labor	–0–	44,800	52,800
Manufacturing overhead	–0–	?	79,200
Total ending inventory	$176,000	?	$192,000

Required:
Prepare a schedule showing the cost of goods sold for 1987.

Problem 2-6 Determining Cost of Goods Sold

The Wayward Manufacturing Corporation incurred labor costs of $453,600, and its total cost of goods manufactured was $1,380,000 during 1987. The company assigns manufacturing overhead costs to work in process inventory on the basis of direct labor costs. The beginning inventories included raw materials ($90,000), work in process ($99,600), and finished goods ($150,000). The ending inventories include the following costs:

	Raw Materials	Work in Process	Finished Goods
Raw materials	$96,000	$ 34,020	$49,860
Direct labor	–0–	30,600	49,800
Manufacturing overhead	–0–	39,780	?
Total ending inventory	$96,000	$104,400	?

Required:
Prepare a schedule showing the cost of goods sold for 1987.

Problem 2-7 Manufacturing Income Statement

The following amounts and accounts were taken from the records of the Weber Manufacturing Company:

Advertising	$ 126,000
Bad debt expense	33,000
Depreciation – plant machinery	45,000

Depreciation – office equipment	18,000
Direct labor cost	759,000
Plant utilities	32,100
Plant rent	234,000
Plant supplies	150,000
Finished goods inventory, 1/1/87	276,000
Finished goods inventory, 12/31/87	255,000
Indirect labor cost	186,000
Machinery repairs	42,000
Sales and administrative office	63,000
Officers' salaries	462,000
Property taxes – plant equipment	18,000
Property taxes – office equipment	39,000
Purchase discounts on raw materials	36,000
Raw materials inventory, 1/1/87	132,000
Raw materials inventory, 12/31/87	159,000
Raw materials purchases	1,350,000
Sales	3,753,000
Sales returns	66,000
Sales commissions	120,000
Work in process inventory, 1/1/87	51,000
Work in process inventory, 12/31/87	63,000

Required:

Prepare an income statement and a cost of goods manufactured statement for the year ended December 31, 1987.

Problem 2-8   Manufacturing Income Statement

The Toronto Manufacturing Company, Inc. has compiled the following amounts and accounts for the preparation of the annual financial statements:

Work in process inventory, 1/1/87	$ 32,400
Raw materials inventory, 1/1/87	42,000
Finished goods inventory, 1/1/87	90,000
Indirect labor cost	80,400
Sales commissions	165,168
Sales	1,376,400
Raw materials purchases	432,000
Freight-in	18,000
Purchase discounts on raw materials	8,400
Plant rent	20,640
Advertising	30,000
Finished goods inventory, 12/31/87	81,600
Sales returns	19,200
Factory supplies	41,400
Depreciation – office equipment	59,400
Raw materials inventory, 12/31/87	46,800
Direct labor	236,400
Plant utilities	16,440
Officers' salaries	188,640
Work in process inventory, 12/31/87	37,920
Plant insurance	10,920
Depreciation – plant equipment	19,320

Required:

Prepare an income statement and a cost of goods manufactured statement for the year ended December 31, 1987.

Problem 2-9 Manufacturing Accounting with Missing Data

Income statement data for the Daily Corporation for four years are presented below.

Income Statements

	1984	1985	1986	1987
Sales	?	?	$230,000	$225,000
Finished goods, beginning inventory	32,500	?	?	?
Work in process, beginning inventory	10,000	?	?	7,500
Raw materials used	44,500	47,500	30,000	42,500
Direct labor cost	?	52,500	40,000	27,500
Manufacturing overhead	47,500	?	37,500	30,000
Work in process, ending inventory	15,000	?	?	?
Cost of goods manufactured	?	?	112,500	95,000
Finished goods, ending inventory	42,500	?	?	11,500
Cost of goods sold	145,500	144,500	121,000	?
Gross profit	137,500	?	?	105,000
Operating expenses	42,500	37,500	?	25,000
Net income	?	$ 90,000	$ 60,000	?

Required:

Fill in the missing information. (Hint: 1987 data provide information required to find 1986 unknowns.)

Problem 2-10 Correcting a Manufacturing Income Statement

The treasurer of the Top Notch Manufacturing Company hired his niece, who had just completed her first accounting course, as summer help in the accounting department. Her first assignment was to prepare an income statement for the month of May. Applying the knowledge she had acquired in Financial Accounting, she prepared the following statement.

TOP NOTCH MANUFACTURING COMPANY
Income Statement
Month Ended May 31, 1987

Sales	$986,000
Operating expenses:	
Raw material purchases	194,000
Rent	124,000
Depreciation	30,000
Utilities	60,000
Direct labor	250,000
Indirect labor	46,000
Office Salaries	62,000
Selling and administrative expenses	94,000
Total operating expenses	860,000
Net income	$126,000

The treasurer has decided to prepare a correct income statement and has gathered the following data:

1. The beginning and ending inventories of raw materials were $42,000 and $48,000, respectively.
2. Three of the expenses listed on his niece's income statement were applicable to the manufacturing operations as well as the selling and administrative functions. The percentages applicable to each are as follows:

	Manufacturing	**Selling and Administrative**
Rent	65%	35%
Depreciation	75%	25%
Utilities	60%	40%

3. The work in process and finished goods inventories were:

	May 1	**May 31**
Work in process	$74,000	$70,000
Finished goods	58,000	62,000

Required:
Prepare a corrected income statement for the month of May.

Problem 2-11 Correcting a Manufacturing Income Statement

Mr. Parker has offered to perform accounting services for the manufacturing company his nephew has organized. Using his financial accounting textbook, he has prepared the following income statement.

DOLLY MANUFACTURING COMPANY
Income Statement
Month Ended July 31, 1987

Sales	$54,000
Operating expenses:	
Raw material purchases	26,400
Rent	2,400
Depreciation	1,800
Insurance	1,080
Direct labor	14,400
Indirect labor	2,160
Selling and administrative	3,720
Total operating expenses	51,960
Net income	$ 2,040

The nephew does not like the results above and has accumulated the following data in order to prepare a corrected income statement.

	Beginning Inventory	Ending Inventory
Raw materials	$2,400	$3,000
Work in process	5,160	5,640
Finished goods	2,160	2,520

Three of the expenses listed on the income statement benefit the manufacturing operations as well as the selling and administrative functions. The percentages applicable to each are:

	Manufacturing	Selling and Administrative
Rent	70%	30%
Depreciation	80%	20%
Insurance	62%	38%

Required:

Prepare a corrected income statement for the month of July.

Problem 2-12 Income Statement with Incomplete Data

The Beta Corporation experienced a fire on December 31, 1987. The fire destroyed a significant portion of the firm's accounting records, and the controller is currently trying to prepare a reliable income statement for 1987. She has gathered the following information from various sources:

1. Sales $300,000
2. Beginning inventories for 1987:
   Work in process $20,000
   Finished goods   45,000
3. Raw materials inventories are not maintained by the firm as materials are purchased as needed for production.
4. Manufacturing overhead cost is three times as much as direct labor cost.
5. Direct materials used in production are one half as much as direct labor cost.
6. The firm's gross profit percentage is 38% of sales.
7. Selling and administrative expenses are $80,000 each year.
8. The work in process inventory increased $5,000 during 1987.
9. The finished goods inventory decreased by an unknown amount during 1987.
10. Direct labor cost amounting to $40,000 was recorded in 1987.

Required:

Prepare the income statement and cost of goods manufactured statement for the firm's 1987 performance based on the data above.

Problem 2-13 Cost of Goods Manufactured Statement

The Hill Company produces one product. The following data were taken from the firm's accounting records for the year ended December 31, 1987:

Total manufacturing costs (direct materials, direct labor, and
  manufacturing overhead) for the year $2,000,000

Manufacturing overhead was 250% of direct labor cost and was 60% of the total manufacturing costs for the year

Cost of goods manufactured for 1987 $1,940,000

Beginning work in process inventory on January 1 was 80% of the ending work in process inventory on December 31.

Required:
Prepare a cost of goods manufactured statement for the year ended December 31, 1987.

Problem 2-14 Cost Classifications
The All-Wood Company produces office desks with matching chairs. The firm has the capacity and the sales orders for 5,000 sets (a desk and a chair) each year. Annual costs if 5,000 sets are produced and sold are:

Advertising	$ 18,000
Property taxes–plant	4,000
Insurance–plant	7,500
Materials used for sets	225,000
Depreciation–plant	350,000
Depreciation–office equipment	6,000
General office supplies	3,000
Utilities–plant	18,000
President's salary	75,000
Plant labor needed to produce the sets	400,000
Supervisory labor–plant	60,000
General office salaries	32,000

Required:
A. Prepare an answer sheet with the following set-up:

				Product	
Cost	Variable	Fixed	Period	Direct	Indirect

Classify in the most likely ways each cost item listed above under the proper heading.
B. What is the total cost required to produce one set at the 5,000 set level?
C. Suppose production declines to 4,000 sets. What effect, if any, will this have on the cost of producing one set?

3

JOB ORDER COSTING SYSTEMS

CHAPTER OVERVIEW AND OBJECTIVES

This chapter presents an introduction to product costing and describes the essential features of a job order costing system. After studying this chapter, you should be able to:

1. Recognize why product costing is so important to managers of a manufacturing firm.
2. Distinguish between job order costing and process costing as well as identify industries that use each type of system.
3. Trace the flow of transactions through a job order costing system.
4. Identify the role of a job order cost sheet.
5. Explain how materials are accounted for in a job order costing system.
6. Explain how labor is accounted for in a job order costing system.
7. Describe the problems associated with accounting for manufacturing overhead and why cost allocation is necessary.
8. Compute a predetermined overhead rate and account for manufacturing overhead in a job order costing system.
9. Explain why manufacturing overhead is often overapplied or underapplied during a given accounting period and what to do with the amount involved.
10. Realize how the percentage-of-completion method is used to recognize revenue for long-term jobs (Appendix to the chapter).

NEED FOR A PRODUCT COSTING SYSTEM

**Objective 1:
Importance of
product costing**

As noted previously, managers need reliable cost information for inventory valuation, income determination, financial planning, controlling operations, and decision making. A manufacturing firm's production operation and related cost flow make accounting for such firms quite complex. Product costs are an essential part of the total cost information required to manage a manufacturing firm. Many management decisions—such as establishing selling prices, deciding what products to produce, selecting marketing strategies for the products, computing the cost of goods sold, and evaluating the profitability of a product line—can only be made effectively if managers know the cost of producing specific products or batches of products. Consequently, in addition to developing information about the total cost of goods manufactured (as covered in Chapter 2), managerial accounting must provide a systematic way to (1) accumulate the manufacturing costs perpetually as production takes place and (2) assign the total costs to the products so that unit costs of the different products can be computed. The combination of these two steps is called **product costing.**

CHOICE BETWEEN JOB ORDER COSTING AND PROCESS COSTING

The two types of product costing systems available to management are job order costing and process costing. The choice between the two systems depends on the nature of the production operation involved. Some firms use both types of product costing because job order costing works best for certain products and process costing for others.

Objective 2: Job order costing versus process costing

Generally, when products are produced as separately identifiable units or groups of units, a **job order costing system** should be used. Since the output of a firm using job order costing is heterogeneous, costs are accumulated per job and unit costs are computed for each job completed. A **job** may be a single product or a batch of identical products. For example, a publishing firm such as the one producing this textbook can identify the specific costs—including writing, editing, reviewing, class testing, and printing—for each publishing project. These costs can then be assigned to the number of books printed to determine the unit cost per book. Job order costing is also used by the shipbuilding, furniture, heavy machinery, and commercial printing industries.

Products manufactured on a continuous or homogeneous basis cannot be separated realistically, so job order costing will not be effective and a **process costing system** should be used. A firm producing paint that is sold to retail stores cannot differentiate between the identical units that continuously flow through the production process. Thus, it would be impossible to determine the cost of any particular gallon of paint when it is finished. The chemical, brewing, oil refining, and candy industries are examples of other industries needing process costing. All of these industries have continuous production processes and homogeneous production output.

With process costing (discussed more completely in Chapter 4), costs are accumulated within the segments of the firm doing the work (e.g., a department) for a given period such as a month. The total costs accumulated are then assigned to the number of units produced during the period. Product costing with either system is, in essence, an averaging procedure. However, job order costing usually produces a more accurate unit cost than one computed with process costing.

Although the emphasis of this chapter is on job order costing in a manufacturing operation, basically the same type of costing system is also used by many nonmanufacturing businesses such as construction firms, hospitals, repair shops, law firms, banks, and movie producing companies. These businesses use job order costing for **activity costing,** which is the determination of the costs involved with an activity such as a service, program, or project, instead of products. Examples are a hospital costing a particular blood test in the laboratory, a bank costing a promotional campaign for new money market accounts, a video service center costing the repair of a video recorder, and a construction company costing a building project.

JOB ORDER COSTING FLOWS

Objective 3:
Job order costing flows

Job order costing is most appropriate when products are manufactured according to customers' orders or specifications and the identity of each job must be kept separate. A manufacturing operation using job order costing must have a well-defined beginning and completion time for each of its jobs. An illustration of the cost flows found in a typical job order costing situation (that you should refer to as you study this chapter) is shown in Figure 3-1. Job order costing is used to value a manufacturing firm's work in process inventory and finished goods inventory as well as to control costs and determine each job's profitability. Remember that perpetual inventory control takes place with job order costing, so the cost results are available to management on a current basis instead of only at the end of an accounting period. With job order costing, the emphasis of the accounting is on the costs of the individual jobs being produced instead of being on the costs of the departments or other segments of the manufacturing operation doing the work.

A job is entered into production as a unique project to be accounted for, and the costs incurred for the job are accumulated during the various phases of production. At the point of completion, the cost of the job can be determined by totaling all the costs accumulated during its production life. The job costs are then used to calculate cost of goods sold when part or all of the job is sold to a customer. For example, the total costs incurred in publishing this book were

Figure 3-1
Job Order Costing Flow

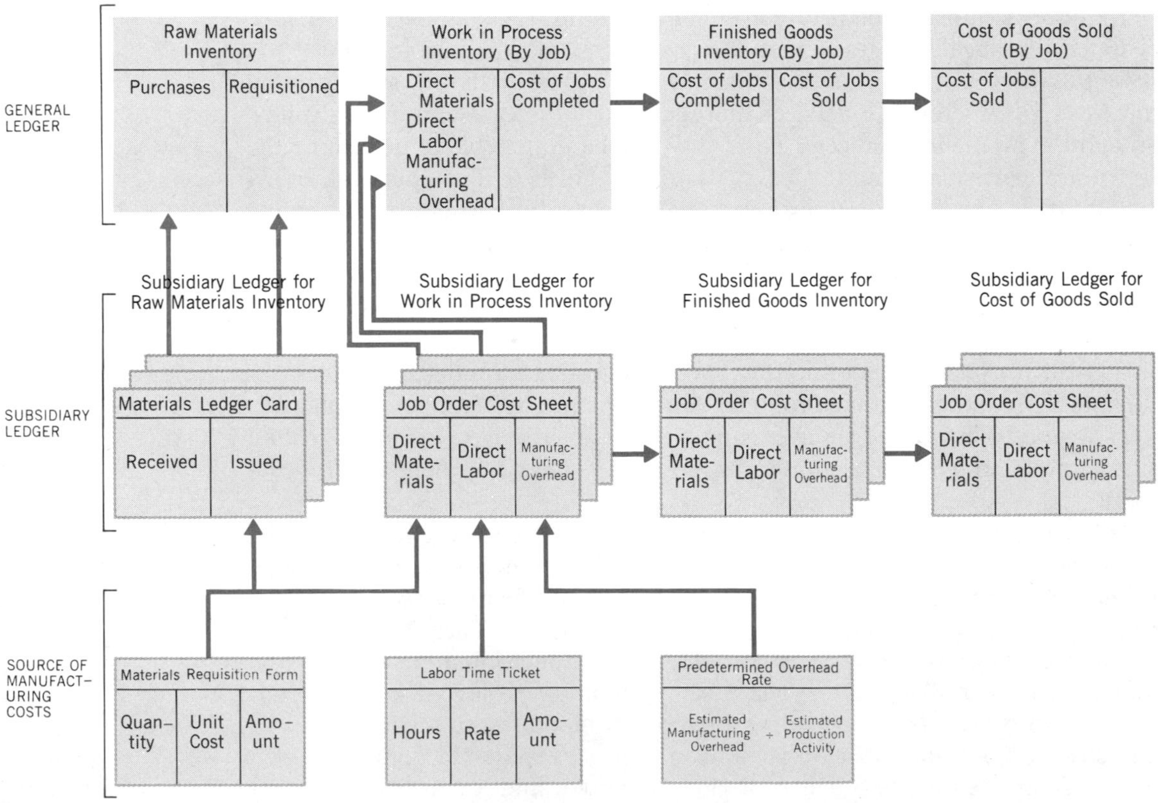

charged to a specific account number so the publisher could determine the actual cost of producing each of the copies sold to bookstores around the country.

All manufacturing cost elements — direct materials, direct labor, and manufacturing overhead — required to produce a completed job are charged to a job as it passes through the production operation, as shown in Figure 3-1. To do so, these costs are debited to the Work in Process Inventory account as the job is being produced. When the job is finished, the costs accumulated for the job at that point are totaled and debited to Finished Goods Inventory with an equal credit to Work in Process Inventory. When the product(s) accounted for in the job are sold, their costs are debited to the Cost of Goods Sold account and credited to Finished Goods Inventory. In this way, the cost of the inventory is matched with the related sales revenue.

CONTROL DOCUMENT — JOB ORDER COST SHEET

A control document called a **job order cost sheet** is used to: (1) accumulate production costs in a job order costing system and (2) report the results to management. This control document has two basic purposes. It provides an itemized listing of all direct materials, direct labor, and manufacturing overhead charged to a job, and it serves as a subsidiary ledger during and after the manufacturing operation. (Remember from financial accounting that a subsidiary ledger is the detailed accounting of a balance of a control account maintained in the general ledger.) Although management chooses the specific format of a job order cost sheet to coincide with the firm's own operating conditions, some basic information should be collected in every case, as illustrated in Figure 3-2.

Objective 4:
Use of a job order cost sheet

Figure 3-2
Job Order Cost Sheet

Job No. __197__

JOB ORDER COST SHEET
GREER MANUFACTURING COMPANY

Customer __Toronto Office Supply__
Product __D-99__   Quantity __200__
Date Started __1/17__   Date Finished __1/29__

Labor			Materials			Manufacturing Overhead		
Date	Reference	Amount	Date	Reference	Amount	Direct Labor Hours		1,890
1/17	17-46	$ 2,688	1/17	1060	$ 8,400	Overhead Rate		$9
1/18	18-45	2,688	1/20	1098	2,100	Overhead Applied		$17,010
1/19	19-42	2,688	Total		$10,500			
1/20	20-48	2,688				Summary		
1/21	21-46	2,688						
1/24	24-45	1,680				Direct Labor		$15,120
Total		$15,120				Direct Materials		10,500
						Manuf. Overhead		17,010
						Total Cost		42,630
						Unit Cost		$ 213.15

A control number is assigned to each job entered into production to keep the various jobs separate for accounting purposes and is recorded on the job order cost sheet (197 in Figure 3-2). Many firms use computer assisted job order costing systems in which the cost sheets are prepared by the computer according to instructions specified in a computer program.

Information about the customer requesting the related product or products (if the customer is known at this point) and the product description is also recorded before the cost sheet is filed in the work in process subsidiary ledger. The cost sheet in Figure 3-2 indicates that the Greer Manufacturing Company, which produces office furniture, started Job 197 on January 17 and finished it on January 29. Two hundred office desks were produced for the customer, Toronto Office Supply. After all labor, materials, and manufacturing overhead costs are added up, the cost of the desks to Greer Manufacturing Company is $42,630. Thus, the cost to produce each desk is $213.15 ($42,630/200).

The subsidiary ledger of job order cost sheets is controlled by the Work in Process Inventory account while production takes place. The reference columns of a cost sheet refer to various source documents (business forms) used to record the direct costs assigned to the job (e.g., labor time tickets used for the direct labor needed for the job, as shown later in the chapter). The direct materials cost incurred for a job is shown in the materials column of the cost sheet. The direct labor cost incurred to convert raw materials to finished goods is charged to a job in the labor column of the cost sheet, and an appropriate amount of manufacturing overhead also is recorded.

The manufacturing costs recorded on the job order cost sheets also are charged periodically to the Work in Process Inventory account. At the end of each accounting period (e.g., a month), the sum of the costs shown on the cost sheets assigned to unfinished jobs should equal the balance in the Work in Process Inventory account after all accounting work is done.

We now turn our attention to the more important accounting procedures needed to perform job order costing. The Greer Manufacturing Company's January, 1987 operating performance will be used to explain the various accounting steps.

ACCOUNTING FOR MATERIALS

Objective 5:
Job order costing
for materials

Effective perpetual inventory control of the flow of raw materials requires several accounting records and procedures similar to those used for merchandise inventory. A purchasing cycle involving the preparation and use of purchase requisition forms, purchase order forms, and receiving reports is used to control the raw materials acquired for production. The purchase cost is debited to Raw Materials Inventory and credited to either Accounts Payable or Cash, depending on the credit terms involved. Materials ledger cards such as the one presented in Figure 3-3 are maintained for each type of materials used and serve as the subsidiary ledger for the Raw Materials Inventory account. The ledger cards provide perpetual inventory control with columns for receipts, issues, and a current balance of the inventory involved. The receipt of 360 units of the materials at a cost of $10,080 was recorded on January 10.

All raw materials are kept in a storeroom under the supervision of a storeroom manager. The materials are issued to work in process inventory when a

Figure 3-3
Materials Ledger Card

MATERIALS LEDGER CARD
Item _____Rx-9_____

		Received			Issued			Balance		
Date	Reference	Quantity	Unit Cost	Total Cost	Quantity	Unit Cost	Total Cost	Quantity	Unit Cost	Total Cost
1/10		360	$28	$10,080				360	$28	$10,080
1/17					300	$28	$8,400	60	$28	$ 1,680

Figure 3-4
Materials Requisition Form

MATERIALS REQUISITION FORM   Number _____1060_____
Job Number _____197_____   Date _____1/17_____
Overhead Account _____
Authorized by _____JGH_____

Description	Quantity	Unit Cost	Amount
Rx-9	300	$28	$8,400

properly prepared and authorized materials requisition form such as the one shown in Figure 3-4 is received by the storeroom. The materials requisition form is authorized by the manager responsible for the production work being performed. Computer software packages are available to facilitate perpetual raw materials inventory control with a computer. The form identifies the specific materials required and shows the job or manufacturing overhead account to which it is to be charged as direct materials (a job) or indirect materials (manufacturing overhead). Figure 3-4 shows that 300 units of a specific type of raw materials were charged to Job 197 at a total cost of $8,400 on January 17.

In Figure 3-3, the $8,400 of direct materials requisitioned for Job 197 has been deducted in the issued column to maintain a current balance of the inventory available. The cost of the total raw materials requisitioned must also be debited to the control accounts established for Work in Process Inventory and Manufacturing Overhead. We assume for illustrative purposes that Greer Manufacturing Company makes all journal entries to the general ledger accounts at the end of each month, although most firms record them as the transactions take place during the month. The entries in the ledger cards should be made perpetually throughout the period so current balances are available. If the company purchased raw materials amounting to $59,500 in January, including the

$10,080 for the materials added to the ledger card in Figure 3-3, the following journal entry is required (the journal entries required in this illustration are numbered for later reference):

(1)

Jan.	31	Raw Materials Inventory	59,500	
		Accounts Payable		59,500
		To record raw materials purchased in January.		

Six jobs, including Job 197, were worked on during the month and each would have a separate job order cost sheet. However, we will only consider the specific detail of the cost breakdowns for Job 197 in this illustration. As we observed in Figure 3-2, raw materials totaling $10,500 were requisitioned for Job 197 during January. Assume that the raw materials requisitioned for the other five jobs totaled $40,670 and that the amount charged to manufacturing overhead was $2,352. Remember that all indirect materials are part of manufacturing overhead (e.g., the nuts and bolts types of inventory). The following journal entry is necessary to record the raw materials requisitioned (total direct materials for the six jobs are $51,170, or $10,500 + $40,670):

(2)

Jan.	31	Work in Process Inventory	51,170	
		Manufacturing Overhead	2,352	
		Raw Materials Inventory		53,522
		To record direct and indirect materials requisitioned in January (including direct materials of $10,500 for Job 197).		

ACCOUNTING FOR LABOR

Objective 6:
Job order costing for labor

A significant amount of recordkeeping is required to accurately separate and account for direct and indirect labor costs. The direct labor cost is traced to specific jobs, while indirect labor is charged to manufacturing overhead. Indirect labor can consist of many different items, depending on how management wants to treat certain labor related costs, given its own operating circumstances. Examples of indirect labor costs include salaries or wages paid to employees whose time cannot be traced to jobs (such as supervisors, janitors, maintenance people, and material handlers), idle time, and overtime premiums.

IDLE TIME AS A MANUFACTURING OVERHEAD COST

The actual dollar amount paid to production workers often will exceed the direct labor costs because the workers are not always working productively (they are being paid but are not engaged in revenue-producing activities). The difference is accounted for as **idle time** (also called **down time**) and is caused by such factors as production scheduling problems, machine breakdowns, lack of work, and materials shortages. Unlike raw materials, the "unused labor" cannot be inventoried so it is charged to manufacturing overhead as long as the amount involved is normal for a particular firm. The normal amount of idle time varies between companies and industries, given their operating conditions. A certain amount of idle time is inevitable in any manufacturing operation because the production process does not always function perfectly. The cost associated with the normal amount of idle time should be charged to all jobs through manufacturing overhead. Any abnormal amount of idle time should be charged as an expense of the current period.

OVERTIME PREMIUM AS A MANUFACTURING OVERHEAD COST

An **overtime premium** is the amount paid to an employee above his or her regular hourly rate for every hour worked in excess of 40 hours a week. For example, assume a worker regularly earning $8 per hour works five hours of overtime. If the overtime rate is one and one half times the regular wage rate, the premium is $4 per hour or a total of $20 (5 hours × $4).

To avoid inconsistent product costing between jobs, the overtime premiums paid to employees working in the manufacturing operation are usually accounted for as manufacturing overhead even if the overtime hours can be traced to a specific job. To illustrate, assume that Job X, which takes four hours, is started and finished in the morning. Job Y, which also takes four hours, is started late in the afternoon and finished after the regular workday is over at overtime labor rates. Both jobs would be costed using regular labor rates, and the overtime premium required for Job Y would be charged to manufacturing overhead.

Initially, this approach may not seem logical since both regular and overtime hours could be charged to Job Y. Consider, however, that a firm's management decides how many regular labor hours should be available for the jobs expected to be worked on during a period. Overtime hours are required whenever the labor requirements of all the jobs performed exceed the regular hours available because the level of production activity is greater than that expected. Thus, no single job really causes the need for overtime even though it may be the one worked on during overtime hours.

Instead, the overtime is required because the level of production activity in general is higher than the firm's capacity to satisfy it during regular working hours. If the level of production activity were lower, the jobs requiring overtime could be worked on during regular hours. This line of reasoning is the justification for charging direct labor at regular hourly rates to the jobs and overtime premiums to manufacturing overhead. When the manufacturing overhead is charged to each job, it will include a component for the total cost of overtime that is incurred because a firm does not have the capacity to produce everything during regular work hours. Some firms deviate from this approach by charging the overtime premium incurred for jobs that are accepted on a rush order basis to the jobs themselves instead of to manufacturing overhead.

USE OF A TIME REPORTING SYSTEM FOR LABOR

A time reporting system consisting of (1) labor time tickets, (2) time cards, and (3) a payroll register is used to accumulate labor costs with job order costing. Many firms account for labor with an electronic data processing system, and computer software is readily available for this purpose. A **labor time ticket** (see Figures 3-5 and 3-6) is needed to record the time spent by each employee on a specific job or manufacturing overhead assignment (e.g., idle time is an overhead assignment). A **time card** (see Figure 3-7) is necessary to control the total

Figure 3-5
Labor Time Ticket

LABOR TIME TICKET

Employee Name	W. Burns		Number	17-18	
Employee Number	18		Date	1/17	
Work Performed	Assembly		Job Number	197	
Approved by	JGH		Overhead Account		

Time Started	Time Stopped	Hours	Rate	Amount
7:00	11:00	4	$8	$32
12:00	3:00	3	$8	$24
Total Cost				$56

Figure 3-6
Labor Time Ticket

LABOR TIME TICKET

Employee Name	W. Burns		Number	17-18A	
Employee Number	18		Date	1/17	
Work Performed	Idle		Job Number		
Approved by	JGH		Overhead Account	Indir Labor	

Time Started	Time Stopped	Hours	Rate	Amount
3:00	4:00	1	$8	$8

Figure 3-7
Time Card

TIME CARD

Employee Name	W. Burns	Employee Number	18
Department	Production	Week Ending	1/21

	Morning		Afternoon		Overtime		Total Hours
	In	Out	In	Out	In	Out	
1/17	6:58	11:00	12:00	4:03			8
1/18	6:59	11:01	12:00	4:01			8
1/19	6:55	11:05	12:00	4:05			8
1/20	6:59	11:02	12:00	4:00			8
1/21	7:00	11:00	11:59	4:01			8

Regular Hours	40	Wage Rate	$8	$320
Overtime Hours		Wage Rate		0
		Gross Earnings	$320	

daily labor hours. Each employee clocks in when work begins and clocks out for lunch and at the end of each day. A **payroll register** (see Figure 3-8) is a detailed listing of a firm's payroll for a given period and is usually classified on a departmental basis. Collectively, the three documents provide both total payroll accounting and a breakdown of how the labor time was spent. As such, they represent important internal control documents needed to effectively

| Payroll Register
Production Department | | | | | | | | | January |
| Gross Earnings | | | | | | Deductions | | | |
Employee	Hours	Regular	Overtime	Total	FICA Tax	Fed. Tax	State Tax	Union Dues	Net Earnings
R. Andrews	160	1,280		1,280	92	196	26	48	918
W. Burns	160	1,280		1,280	92	144	26	40	978
L. Davis	170	1,280	120	1,400	100	160	28	48	1,064
D. Warren	160	1,280		1,280	92	196	26	52	914
M. Worth	166	1,280	72	1,352	97	120	27	50	1,058
J. Young	160	1,280		1,280	92	168	26	44	950
Totals	8,397	66,568	912	67,480	4,825	8,435	1,350	2,300	50,570

Figure 3-8
Production Department Payroll Register

manage the labor performance. The labor time tickets are prepared daily under the supervision of the manager responsible for the work activity. Each labor hour recorded on the time tickets is multiplied by the related worker's wage rate, and the total labor cost is charged either to a job as direct labor or to manufacturing overhead as indirect labor. In many manufacturing operations, a computer will perform the clerical functions needed to process the time tickets, which are coded for computerized processing.

During the day, a time ticket is prepared each time an employee changes from one job or overhead assignment to another. For example, employee W. Burns, accounted for in Figures 3-5 and 3-6, spent seven hours on Job 197 and was idle one hour on January 17. At the end of each day, the costs on the labor time tickets are classified as either direct or indirect labor. Based on the time cards accumulated during January, Greer Manufacturing Company incurred a total manufacturing payroll cost of $67,480 during January. The labor time tickets indicate that the firm's direct labor cost was $58,800 (including $15,120 for Job 197) and the indirect labor amounted to $8,680 (a combination of supervisory salaries, janitorial wages, idle time, and overtime premiums). The following journal entry is required (payroll taxes are ignored):

(3)

Jan.	31	Work in Process Inventory	58,800	
		Manufacturing Overhead	8,680	
		Wages Payable		67,480
		To record the direct and indirect labor cost for		
		January (including direct labor cost of $15,120		
		for Job 197).		

ACCOUNTING FOR MANUFACTURING OVERHEAD

Objective 7: Problems with manufacturing overhead

Accounting for the direct manufacturing costs by jobs is relatively straightforward because these costs can be traced to the different jobs with a materials requisition system or a labor time reporting system. Accounting for manufacturing overhead is more complicated for three reasons. *First,* several costs, such as rent, depreciation, electronic data processing, insurance, and property taxes, often are common costs incurred partly for the manufacturing operation and partly for selling and administrative functions.

In other words, they are costs needed for all three business activities and cannot easily be isolated for any specific part of the business. Since a portion of the common costs are needed for the production of products, they must somehow be identified and assigned to the manufacturing operation as a cost objective separate from the selling and administrative functions. This is accomplished with **cost allocation,** which is the assignment of a common cost to one or more cost objectives in proportion to a reasonable measure of the anticipated benefits from the cost. Cost allocation will be discussed more completely in Chapter 14. Here, our main concern is how it affects product costing. Remember that only the manufacturing costs are inventoried as product costs. Therefore, we need a rational and systematic way to separate the portion of the common costs that are treated as product costs (manufacturing overhead) from those that are period costs (selling and administrative expenses).

Second, manufacturing overhead is incurred in both production and service departments, although products are only worked on in production departments. Service departments provide support to the production departments with such activities as maintenance, quality control, purchasing, cost accounting, inventory storage, and engineering. If these departments did not exist, the production departments would have to acquire the related services from outside sources or provide the services themselves. Consequently, service department costs will be direct costs for the service departments but indirect for the production departments; they must be assigned to the production departments so they can be included in the cost of the jobs. Cost allocation is also used to distribute service department costs to the various production departments.

Finally, the indirect nature of manufacturing overhead (e.g., depreciation on equipment) prevents it from being traced to the products in the same manner as the direct costs. It would be impossible to trace a small portion of the depreciation cost to each of thousands of products produced with the equipment during a particular time period. Nevertheless, such items as indirect labor, rent, property taxes, depreciation, insurance, and utilities are indispensable for the production operation because manufacturing could not take place without them. A manufacturing firm has to develop a reliable method with which the manufacturing overhead costs can be allocated to the products as a substitute for the tracing procedures discussed earlier for the direct manufacturing costs. The firm does this by applying the manufacturing overhead costs to production on some basis that closely relates the costs incurred with the work performed. In other words, the basis should essentially reflect the way the work performance causes the need for manufacturing overhead. Applying the overhead costs in this manner is a form of cost allocation because the costs that are indirect to the products are allocated to the products instead of being traced directly to them.

In summary, all direct or indirect manufacturing overhead costs needed to operate a production department are either: (1) charged directly to the department as a cost objective or (2) assigned to the department with cost allocation procedures. The total manufacturing overhead costs accumulated for the departments of a manufacturing operation with the two approaches are then applied to the products to determine the full cost of producing them. The manufacturing overhead costing process is shown schematically as follows:

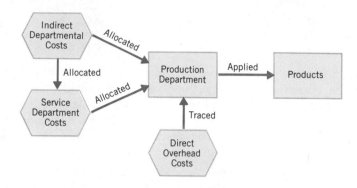

FUNDAMENTALS OF COST ALLOCATION

Remember that our main concern with cost allocation here is the way it affects product costing. Cost allocation requires the selection of a realistic cause and effect relationship for assigning indirect costs to cost objectives (e.g., production departments) as a measure of the benefits received from the costs. Examples of cost allocations include:

1. Building rent allocated on the basis of the relative amount of floor space occupied by several production departments.

2. Telephone expense allocated on the basis of the number of telephones used.

3. Health insurance for employees allocated on the basis of departmental payrolls.

Unfortunately, the cause and effect relationships between specific indirect costs and cost objectives are only approximations in most cases because direct measurement is impossible. Logical allocation bases are established as substitutes for direct measurements of the cause and effect relationships for overhead costs. Although the allocation bases should be selected carefully, they are usually somewhat arbitrary and can lead to misleading results for managerial decision-making purposes if they are not used correctly, as discussed in Chapter 14.

To illustrate the fundamentals of cost allocation, we will continue to use the Greer Manufacturing Company case. Assume that the firm operates *five* departments: *Production, Storeroom, Quality Control, Sales,* and *Administrative.* The first three departments are involved with manufacturing, although products are only worked on in the Production Department. The Storeroom Department and Quality Control Department are service departments that support the Production Department. The accounting records of the Greer Manufacturing Company indicate that the following overhead costs were budgeted for 1987:

Department	Budgeted Direct Department Overhead Costs
Storeroom	$ 96,000
Quality Control	58,000
Production	296,000
Sales	110,000
Administrative	93,000
Total	$653,000
Building Occupancy Costs (common to all departments)	$360,000

How can the total overhead costs required to directly and indirectly operate each of the manufacturing departments be determined? How can the total amount of manufacturing overhead needed to produce products be calculated and applied to the products? These are two important questions involved with product costing that must be answered with cost allocation procedures, as shown in the following discussion.

The five departments occupy the same building, which has 100,000 square feet of usable space. The five departments should share the total costs involved with maintaining the building based on an estimate of the benefits they receive from the costs. Building occupancy costs (e.g., rent, utilities, property taxes, insurance, and cleaning) are charged to the various departments on the basis of the relative amount of space they occupy, as an estimate of the benefits the departments receive. During 1987, the departments will occupy floor space in the building and be assigned their share of the $360,000 of building occupancy costs as follows:

Department	Square Feet Occupied	% of Total	Allocated Cost $360,000 × % of Total
Storeroom	20,000	20	$ 72,000
Quality Control	5,000	5	18,000
Production	60,000	60	216,000
Sales	10,000	10	36,000
Administrative	5,000	5	18,000
Total	100,000	100	$360,000

The building occupancy costs are allocated to the five departments on the basis of their relative square feet, or 20%, 5%, 60%, 10%, and 5%, respectively. These cost allocation results, combined with the budgeted direct departmental overhead cost for 1987, give us the total overhead costs (both direct and indirect) for the departments shown next.

Department	Direct Department Overhead Cost	Allocated Department Overhead Cost	Total Costs
Storeroom	$ 96,000	$ 72,000	$ 168,000
Quality Control	58,000	18,000	76,000
Production	296,000	216,000	512,000
Sales	110,000	36,000	146,000
Administrative	93,000	18,000	111,000
Total	$653,000	$360,000	$1,013,000

Next, we must allocate the total manufacturing overhead costs assigned directly or indirectly to the two service departments to the production department. The Sales Department and the Administrative Department would not be assigned any service department overhead costs because they are not involved with manufacturing and, thus, are not supported by the two service departments. In addition, the total overhead costs of the Sales Department ($146,000) and the Administrative Department ($111,000) would not be applied to the products produced because these costs are not required to have finished jobs ready for sale. We have only included the Sales Department and Administrative Department in this illustration to show the complete impact of allocating common costs such as building occupancy costs.

Since Greer Manufacturing Company has only one production department, we simply allocate the overhead costs of the two service departments [Storeroom Department ($168,000) and the Quality Control Department ($76,000)] to the Production Department. After the allocation process is completed, the total costs directly or indirectly assigned to the Production Department are $756,000 ($512,000 from the schedule above plus the $168,000 and $76,000). The $756,000 represents the total estimated manufacturing overhead required by the Production Department during 1987. Next, we must determine how to apply the $756,000 of manufacturing overhead costs budgeted for the Production Department to the Work in Process Inventory for product costing purposes.

APPLICATION OF MANUFACTURING OVERHEAD TO JOBS

Remember that manufacturing overhead cannot be traced to the products produced because it is always indirect to the products as cost objectives. Instead, the **application of manufacturing overhead** to jobs must be applied to jobs on the basis of some production activity measure that *can* be directly related to the jobs. Examples of production activity measures used are direct labor hours, direct labor cost, machine hours, or units produced.

The choice of a production activity measure depends on which one will provide the best causal relationship between it and manufacturing overhead; that is, the amount of production activity required for a job will determine the amount of manufacturing overhead needed. If a manufacturing operation is labor intensive, direct labor hours or direct labor costs typically are used. In contrast, machine hours are more appropriate for a highly automated company because so much of the overhead is the result of operating the equipment.

In the Greer Manufacturing Company illustration, the Production Department will apply manufacturing overhead amounting to $756,000 to the jobs worked on during 1987. *Note that this is not the actual amount of manufacturing overhead incurred.* The actual overhead costs for 1987 are not known until the end of the year. Management needs product cost information concerning the various jobs on a perpetual basis during the year and cannot wait until the end of an accounting period to determine how much manufacturing overhead to charge to the jobs produced. Postponing the final job costing for manufacturing overhead until the end of an accounting period would defeat the purpose of perpetual inventory control with a job costing system. With current information, management can use the product costs to establish selling prices for the jobs, evaluate the jobs' profitability, and make other key production and marketing decisions.

Problems with Fluctuating Production Costs or Activity

Using actual manufacturing overhead costs and actual production activity also can cause another problem: fluctuations in either the amount of manufacturing overhead or the level of production activity between short time periods (such as months) will produce inconsistent product costing results. To illustrate, assume that a highly automated video game manufacturing company has a monthly depreciation charge of $125,000, which must be included in the total cost of producing a game. Production activity is seasonal—only 10,000 games are produced in January while 100,000 are manufactured in September for Christmas sales. If actual manufacturing overhead and actual production activity are used, the depreciation charged to each game would be $12.25 in January and $1.25 in September.

Thus, despite the fact that the products and the manufacturing operation are the same from month to month, in months of high production, the unit cost would be low while in months of low production the unit cost would be high. Even if a firm has stable production from month to month, some manufacturing overhead costs will change seasonally and cause potential distortions. An example is the monthly heat bill of a New England plant, which will be low in the summer and high in the winter.

USE OF A PREDETERMINED OVERHEAD RATE

**Objective 8:
Using a predetermined overhead rate**

To avoid the accounting problems involved with actual manufacturing overhead and actual production activity, a predetermined overhead rate is used to apply manufacturing overhead cost to the jobs as they are worked on. A **predetermined overhead rate** is computed with the following formula:

$$\frac{\text{Estimated manufacturing overhead for the period}}{\text{Estimated level of production activity for the period}} = \frac{\text{Predetermined}}{\text{overhead rate}}$$

For now, we will assume that an annual period is long enough to avoid the problems mentioned earlier with fluctuating costs or production activity, even when estimates are used. In Chapter 11, we consider the most appropriate time period for the determination of a predetermined overhead rate in more depth. The predetermined overhead rate is calculated at the beginning of each year by dividing the estimated manufacturing overhead for the year by the estimated production activity for the same period.

Assume that Greer Manufacturing Company estimates that 84,000 direct labor hours is the expected level of production activity for 1987 (the total estimated manufacturing overhead is $756,000). Using the predetermined overhead rate formula, the 1987 rate is:

$$\frac{\$756,000}{84,000 \text{ direct labor hours}} = \$9 \text{ per direct labor hour}$$

The $9 rate is charged to a job for each direct labor hour recorded for the job. Thus, if a given job requires 300 direct labor hours, manufacturing overhead totaling $2,700 (300 hours × $9) would be applied to the job. If the different jobs worked on during 1987 require exactly 84,000 direct labor hours, a total manufacturing overhead cost of $756,000 will be applied to the jobs. Since both the numerator and the denominator of the predetermined overhead rate formula are based on *estimates,* it is likely that the overhead applied to jobs during 1987 will differ from the actual amount of overhead incurred. The result is a *variance* that must be accounted for as we will see later in this chapter.

RECORDING MANUFACTURING OVERHEAD

We can see in the job order cost sheet prepared for Job 197 (Figure 3-2) that a total of 1,890 direct labor hours were required to complete the job. In addition, the manufacturing overhead applied is $17,010 (or 1,890 hours times $9, as shown in the last column of Figure 3-2). Remember that each job will have a separate job order cost sheet, so the same approach will be used for each job. Once the manufacturing overhead charged to the various job order cost sheets is determined, the amounts would be totaled and recorded in the Work in Process Inventory account. To charge the applied manufacturing overhead to the Work in Process Inventory account, Greer Manufacturing Company would make the following journal entry (we assume that the payroll records and job cost sheets indicate that a total of 7,350 direct labor hours were worked in January, including the 1,890 hours recorded for Job 197):

(4)

Jan.	31	Work in Process Inventory	66,150	
		Manufacturing Overhead		66,150
		To record manufacturing overhead applied		
		during January on the basis of 7,350 hours at		
		$9 per hour for all jobs, or $66,150 (including		
		$17,010 for Job 197, or 1,890 hours × $9).		

The applied manufacturing overhead is *credited* to the Manufacturing Overhead account. The actual manufacturing overhead incurred is *debited* to the same account and to subsidiary ledger accounts established for individual overhead items. Examples of such overhead items include building occupancy costs, Storeroom Department costs, Quality Control Department costs, depreciation, utilities, insurance, indirect materials, and indirect labor. Greer Manufacturing Company already has recorded $2,352 for indirect materials and $8,680 for indirect labor. Additional manufacturing overhead charges for January are:

Building occupancy costs	$18,000
Storeroom Department costs	14,000
Quality Control Department costs	6,333
Depreciation	10,200
Electricity	3,667
Insurance	2,518
Total	$54,718

The following journal entry is made by Greer Manufacturing Company to record the additional manufacturing overhead charges shown above:

(5)

Jan.	31	Manufacturing Overhead	54,718	
		Building Occupancy Costs		18,000
		Storeroom Department Costs		14,000
		Quality Control Department Costs		6,333
		Accumulated Depreciation		10,200
		Accrued Expenses		6,185
		To record additional manufacturing overhead for		
		January.		

The total actual manufacturing overhead for January is $65,750 (indirect materials of $2,352 plus indirect labor of $8,680 plus the unrecorded items above totaling $54,718).

OVERAPPLIED AND UNDERAPPLIED MANUFACTURING OVERHEAD

Objective 9:
Comparing actual
and applied
manufacturing
overhead

The use of the single manufacturing overhead account makes it easy to compare the amount of overhead actually incurred with the amount applied to the Work in Process Inventory. We can show the results of the previous accounting in the Manufacturing Overhead account (in T account form), as follows:

Manufacturing Overhead

Jan. 31	Indirect materials	2,352	Jan. 31	Applied overhead	66,150
	Indirect labor	8,680			
	Other overhead	54,718			
			Jan. 31	Balance	400

Remember that the Greer Manufacturing Company used a predetermined overhead rate because management could not wait to determine the actual manufacturing overhead and production results when the job order costing was performed. In addition, the firm wanted to spread cost or production differences from month to month over a longer period of time. Since the predetermined overhead rate is based on estimates, instead of actual amounts, we would expect a difference between the debit and credit sides of the Manufacturing Overhead account as the actual costs and production results vary from those planned. As such, the actual manufacturing overhead and the applied manufacturing overhead are seldom equal at the end of any given accounting period.

If the applied amount exceeds the actual costs, the Manufacturing Overhead account will have a credit balance so the overhead will be **overapplied.** This means that more overhead is charged to the Work in Process Inventory than is actually incurred. When the amount applied is less than the actual costs, a debit balance will exist and manufacturing overhead will be **underapplied.**

In the Greer Manufacturing Company example, manufacturing overhead is overapplied by $400, since $66,150 was applied to the jobs but only $65,750 actually was incurred. Ideally, the estimates used for the predetermined overhead rate will be accurate and any balance will be small—particularly at the end of an annual period.

One of three alternative treatments of overapplied/underapplied manufacturing overhead at the end of an accounting period is selected, depending on the amount and timing involved:

1. The difference is carried forward on the balance sheet to the next period (only used for interim reporting).
2. The difference is closed out to Cost of Goods Sold.
3. The difference is prorated between the Work in Process Inventory, Finished Goods Inventory, and Cost of Goods Sold for the period.

On an interim basis (e.g., monthly or quarterly), any balance in the manufacturing overhead account is often carried forward on the balance sheet from month to month as an asset (underapplied) or a liability (overapplied). The basic reason for this treatment is that management expects the difference to reverse in a future period. An underapplied balance is an asset because more overhead has been incurred than the amount applied to Work in Process Inventory, so the difference is similar to a prepaid expense. In contrast, an overapplied balance is shown as a liability because that amount has not actually been incurred even though it has been inventoried.

At the end of the year, any over- or underapplied manufacturing overhead can be subtracted from (overapplied) or added to (underapplied) the annual Cost of Goods Sold to balance or equalize the actual and applied amounts if the difference is relatively small. Alternatively, the difference may be disposed of by prorating it among the ending Work in Process Inventory, ending Finished Goods Inventory, and annual Cost of Goods Sold. The proration approach is the most accurate treatment because the overhead is assigned where it would have been if the predetermined overhead rate had been correct to begin with. In many cases, however, this proration is impractical because of the accounting time and problems involved. When the amount of over- or underapplied manufacturing overhead is significant (large compared with the actual amount of manufacturing overhead), generally accepted accounting principles require that the proration approach be used for financial reporting. As a result, management may also choose the proration method for internal reporting.

Proration Between Accounts at the End of the Year

To illustrate the basic principles involved with proration, assume that a given firm ended an accounting period with the following account balances:

Account	Ending Balance	Percent of Total
Work in Process Inventory	$ 60,000	10
Finished Goods Inventory	120,000	20
Cost of Goods Sold	420,000	70
Total	$600,000	100

Assume also that the company's manufacturing overhead is underapplied by $32,000 for the period; we would prorate this difference and *increase* the three accounts as follows:

Work in Process Inventory — $60,000 + (.10) $32,000 = $63,200
Finished Goods Inventory — $120,000 + (.20) $32,000 = $126,400
Cost of Goods Sold   — $420,000 + (.70) $32,000 = $442,400

If the manufacturing overhead had been overapplied by $32,000, these same prorated amounts would have been subtracted from the three account balances. While this proration may seem simple enough, significant problems are typically involved in actual cases because the over- or underapplied overhead must also be assigned to the individual jobs included in each of the three accounts. These problems increase substantially as the number of jobs increase. Consequently, the adjustment usually is made only to Cost of Goods Sold as long as the over- or underapplied amount is insignificant because it is easy to do and reasonably accurate.

Adjustment of Cost of Goods Sold at the End of the Year

At the end of January, Greer Manufacturing Company's $400 credit balance in the Manufacturing Overhead account would most likely be shown as a liability on the balance sheet because interim reporting is involved. If the same relatively small $400 overapplied balance exists at the end of the year, the $400 would be credited to the annual Cost of Goods Sold, thereby reducing it. In contrast, an underapplied balance of $400 would be added to the Cost of Goods Sold for the period by debiting that account. To illustrate, the following journal entry would be made by Greer Manufacturing Company to close out an overapplied balance of $400 to Cost of Goods Sold at the end of 1987:

Dec.	31	Manufacturing Overhead	400	
		Cost of Goods Sold		400
		To eliminate overapplied manufacturing overhead for the year, thereby reducing cost of goods sold.		

If the manufacturing overhead was underapplied by $400 at the end of 1987, the following journal entry would be made to increase the annual cost of goods sold:

Dec.	31	Cost of Goods Sold	400	
		Manufacturing Overhead		400
		To eliminate underapplied manufacturing overhead for the year, thereby increasing cost of goods sold.		

The result of both entries is a Manufacturing Overhead account with a balance of zero (actual overhead is equal to applied overhead) and an adjusted cost of goods sold for the period.

ACCOUNTING FOR THE COMPLETION OF A JOB

Since Greer Manufacturing Company only operates one production department, it uses a single Work in Process Inventory account. In firms with more than one production department, separate Work in Process Inventory accounts are maintained for the various production departments; the accumulated costs follow the physical flow of jobs by being transferred from one department to the next through the departmental Work in Process Inventory accounts.

When a job is completed, the costs accumulated on its job order cost sheet are totaled and transferred from the final production department's Work in Process Inventory to the Finished Goods Inventory. The costs accumulated up to this point consist of all direct and indirect costs required to produce the salable product(s). Since Job 197 was produced for a customer's order, it will be shipped as soon as possible to Toronto Office Supply, the customer that ordered the products. The total costs accumulated for Job 197 amounted to $42,630—$10,500 for direct materials, $15,120 for direct labor, and $17,010 for manufacturing overhead. Greer Manufacturing Company will make the following journal entry to record the completed job:

(6)

Jan.	31	Finished Goods Inventory	42,630	
		Work in Process Inventory		42,630
		To record the completion of Job 197 and transfer it to Finished Goods Inventory.		

ACCOUNTING FOR THE SALE OF A JOB

Since perpetual inventory costs are maintained with job order costing, each job's cost of goods sold can easily be matched with the revenue from the job at the point of sale. To do so, the total cost of the products sold is transferred from the Finished Goods Inventory account to the Cost of Goods Sold account. If the entire job is sold to one customer, as in the case of the Greer Manufacturing Company, the total costs from the job order cost sheet are charged to Cost of Goods Sold and matched against the revenue earned. Whenever only part of a job is sold to a given customer, the unit cost of each product included in the job is multiplied by the number of products sold to determine how much cost should be transferred from Finished Goods Inventory to Cost of Goods Sold.

Each of the 200 desks produced in Job 197 by Greer Manufacturing Company costs $213.15 ($42,630/200 desks). To illustrate the partial sale of a job, assume that 10 of the desks had been sold to one customer; the cost of goods sold involved would have been $2,131.50 ($213.15 × 10 desks). Since the company actually sold the entire job to one customer, Toronto Office Supply, we do not have to differentiate between the cost of desks sold and those left in the Finished Goods Inventory. The entire cost of the job, $42,630, is charged to Cost of Goods Sold when the desks are shipped to the customer. If Job 197 is sold to Toronto Office Supply on credit for $67,776, the transaction would be recorded as follows:

(7)

Jan.	31	Accounts Receivable	67,776	
		Sales		67,776
		Cost of Goods Sold	42,630	
		Finished Goods Inventory		42,630
		To record the sale of Job 197.		

The job order cost sheet for Job 197 would be transferred from the finished goods subsidiary ledger to the cost of goods sold subsidiary ledger as the final step in the job order costing flow. Note that the difference between the selling price of Job 197 ($67,776) and the cost of goods sold ($42,630) is the job's gross profit ($25,146).

SUMMARY OF JOB ORDER COSTING FLOW

Let's summarize the discussion of the job order costing flow of Greer Manufacturing Company by tracing the various transactions involved through the appropriate T accounts to see their interrelationships. The numbers (1) through (7) refer to the journal entries recorded earlier in the chapter to start with the purchase of raw materials and end with a job at the point of sale. The only entries shown here are those used in the illustration. Additional entries would be required for a complete accounting for the company during January. For example, the building occupancy costs and the service department costs would have to be initially recorded with debit entries before they are distributed to the Manufacturing Overhead account.

Accounts Receivable	
(7) 67,776	

Raw Materials Inventory	
(1) 59,500	(2) 53,522

Work in Process Inventory	
(2) 51,170	(6) 42,630
(3) 58,800	
(4) 66,150	

Finished Goods Inventory	
(6) 42,630	(7) 42,630

Manufacturing Overhead	
(2) 2,352	(4) 66,150
(3) 8,680	
(5) 54,718	

Building Occupancy Costs	
	(5) 18,000

Storeroom Department Costs	
(5) 14,000	

Quality Control Department Costs	
(5) 6,333	

Cost of Goods Sold	
(7) 42,630	

Accounts Payable	
	(1) 59,500

Wages Payable	
	(3) 67,480

Accrued Expenses	
	(5) 6,185

Sales	
	(7) 67,776

Accumulated Depreciation	
	(5) 10,200

Transactions:
(1) Raw materials purchased
(2) Direct and indirect materials requisitioned
(3) Direct and indirect labor performance
(4) Manufacturing overhead applied
(5) Actual manufacturing overhead in addition to indirect materials and labor
(6) Completion of Job 197
(7) Sale of Job 197

SUMMARY

Managers need reliable product cost information for such actions as *setting selling prices, deciding what products to produce, selecting marketing strategies for products, computing cost of goods sold,* and *evaluating the firm's profit performance.* Two methods are available for product costing, job order costing and process costing. Job order costing is used whenever products are produced as separately identifiable units or groups of units. In contrast, process costing is employed whenever homogeneous products are manufactured with a continuous production flow. Many nonmanufacturing firms apply product costing procedures to accumulate activity costs, such as an accounting firm determining the total cost of performing an audit of a client's financial records.

A job order cost sheet is the control document in a job order costing system and has two purposes: (1) it provides an itemized listing of the direct materials, direct labor, and manufacturing overhead assigned to a job; and (2) it is a subsidiary ledger during and after the manufacturing operation. Direct and indirect manufacturing costs are treated differently in job order costing. The direct costs are traced to the products as production takes place, whereas manufacturing overhead is applied to the products on the basis of some production activity measure. The basic accounting steps required in job order costing are:

1. Direct materials costs are accumulated with a materials requisition system.
2. Direct labor costs are recorded with a time reporting system.
3. Manufacturing overhead is applied to the products with a predetermined overhead rate.

The predetermined overhead rate is computed as a fraction, the numerator of which is the estimated manufacturing overhead for a given period and the denominator is the estimated level of production activity for the same period. The predetermined overhead rate is multiplied by the actual amount incurred for the production activity measure to apply the manufacturing overhead to the Work in Process Inventory. Production activity measures used for a predetermined overhead rate include direct labor hours, direct labor cost, machine hours, and units produced.

Any difference between the manufacturing overhead actually incurred and the amount applied to the products must be disposed of at the end of an accounting period, using one of three options: (1) carrying the difference forward on the balance sheet (interim reporting only); (2) closing the difference to Cost of Goods Sold; or (3) prorating the difference among the ending Work in Process Inventory, ending Finished Goods Inventory, and Cost of Goods Sold. The choice among the three options depends on the amount of the difference and the time of the year.

When a job is completed, it is transferred to Finished Goods Inventory. At the point of sale, the total costs accumulated are charged to Cost of Goods Sold and credited to Finished Goods Inventory to complete the perpetual accounting. The cost of goods sold is matched with the revenue from the job to determine the gross profit involved.

APPENDIX: ACCOUNTING FOR LONG-TERM PROJECTS

Many firms using job order costing have a common accounting problem that was not discussed in the Greer Manufacturing Company illustration. Since Job 197 was started and finished in January, 1987, its revenue, costs, and resulting income (in the form of gross profit) would be reported on the 1987 income statement. As long as Greer Manufacturing Company has a short production cycle, the firm can report its income performance based on the revenue realization principle of accounting. This principle specifies that revenue is recognized when (1) the earning process is complete or virtually complete and (2) an exchange has taken place. Since Greer Manufacturing Company completed the job for Toronto Office Supply and exchanged one asset (finished goods inventory) for another (an account receivable), both conditions were satisfied.

Objective 10:
Need for the percentage-of-completion method

The recognition of revenue is not as easy for a firm undertaking manufacturing or construction projects that extend over more than one annual accounting period. While the job order costing concepts and procedures discussed in this chapter can be used to accumulate the costs of long-term projects, a revenue recognition method different from the one shown for Job 197 usually is needed to provide meaningful information about the earning process.

COMPLETED-CONTRACT METHOD
VERSUS PERCENTAGE-OF-COMPLETION METHOD

A choice must be made between the completed-contract method and the percentage-of-completion method for the recognition of revenue from projects involving long-term contracts. As the name suggests, the completed-contract method recognizes revenue only in the year in which the project is finished, so income statements prepared for prior years of the project's life will not provide any information about its performance. This presents an obvious problem for management which needs reliable information to monitor the progress of the projects and evaluate their potential profitability. If the income performance is not reported to management until the project is finished, it will be too late to do anything about unsatisfactory results.

In contrast, the percentage-of-completion method recognizes revenue in proportion to the progress made on a project, so information about the revenue from the project and the costs required to earn the revenue is available on a timely basis. These two accounting methods are not acceptable alternatives for the same circumstances. The percentage-of-completion method should always be used when the selling price in the long-term contract is fixed, the terms of the agreement are enforceable, and estimates of the progress toward completion are dependable. Let's see how the percentage-of-completion method can be used in the shipbuilding industry.

In a recent annual report, Tenneco, Inc., a large industrial conglomerate company with a subsidiary that builds ships, showed revenue from shipbuilding of $733 million on the income statement and a Shipbuilding in Progress Inventory account of $178 million on the balance sheet. The company explained the accounting involved in the following footnote:

Newport News Shipbuilding and Dry Dock Company (Newport), a subsidiary, reports profits on its long-term shipbuilding contracts on the percentage-of-completion method of accounting, determined on the basis of costs incurred to date to estimated final costs. Newport reports losses on such contracts when first estimated. The performance of such contracts may extend over several years; therefore, periodic reviews of estimated final revenues and costs are necessary during the term of the contracts. Final contract settlements and periodic reviews may result in revisions to estimated final contract profits or losses which have the effect of including cumulative adjustments of income in the period in which the revisions are made.

We can see from this explanation that income (in the form of gross profit) is reported with the percentage-of-completion method by comparing the actual costs incurred on a job with the estimated final costs needed to finish the job. Consequently, a proportionate amount of gross profit is reported each year the job is worked on. Any anticipated loss should be recognized immediately.

To illustrate the computations involved, assume that the Atlantic Shipbuilding Company, a hypothetical firm, has signed a contract to build a cargo vessel for a marine transport firm at a cost of $10 million during the next three years. The company estimates that it will cost $9 million to build the ship, so a gross profit of $1 million is expected at the beginning of the project. The actual costs incurred and the gross profit recognized each year are:

Year	1	2	3
Actual costs to date (1)	$3,150,000	$6,516,000	$9,150,000
Estimated total costs (2)	9,000,000	9,050,000	9,150,000
% complete (1)/(2) = (3)	35	72	100
Estimated total gross profit (4)	1,000,000	950,000	850,000
Gross profit to date (3) × (4)	350,000	684,000	850,000
Previous gross profit recognized	(–0–)	(350,000)	(684,000)
Annual gross profit recognized	$ 350,000	$ 334,000	$ 166,000

As shown above, the percentage-of-completion method assumes that the degree of completion can be determined by comparing costs actually incurred with management's best estimate of the total costs needed to complete the project. Obviously, the accuracy with which the costs are accumulated with a job order costing system will have a significant bearing on the reliability of the revenue recognition results. In year 1, the actual costs were 35% of the estimated total costs so 35% of the $1 million estimated gross profit for the job is recognized. Note that the estimated total costs have been increased in year 2 by $50,000 over the original estimate, thereby decreasing the estimated gross profit to $950,000.

The actual costs for years 1 and 2 are $6,516,000, or 72% of the $9,050,000 revised estimated total costs. The amount of gross profit recognized in year 2 is 72% of the $950,000 estimated gross profit, or $684,000, less the $350,000 recognized in year 1. As a result, a gross profit of $334,000 is included in the income statement for year 2. The same approach is taken in the final year of the project (year 3) when the actual costs for the entire project are determined to be $9,150,000. Once the actual gross profit is known ($10,000,000 − $9,150,000 = $850,000), we simply subtract the gross profit previously recognized in years 1 and 2 ($684,000) from $850,000 to determine the final amount for year 3, or $166,000. The costs incurred each year plus the gross profit recognized equal the revenue reported by Atlantic Shipbuilding Company. For example, revenue of $3,500,000, costs of $3,150,000, and a gross profit of $350,000 would be reported in year 1. The use of the percentage-of-completion method enables the Atlantic Shipbuilding Company to effectively match revenue and the costs required to earn it.

GLOSSARY

ACTIVITY COSTING. Concepts and procedures used by a firm to accumulate the costs of a nonmanufacturing activity such as a service, program, or project (p. 59).

COST ALLOCATION. The assignment of a common cost to one or more cost objectives in proportion to some reasonable measure of the anticipated benefits from the cost (p. 68).

IDLE (DOWN) TIME. Unproductive labor time that is costed as manufacturing overhead (p. 64).

JOB. A product or group of products being produced when job order costing is used (p. 59).

JOB ORDER COSTING SYSTEM. A product costing system with which costs are accumulated for jobs as the work is performed (p. 59).

JOB ORDER COST SHEET. The control document used with job order costing to provide both a detailed listing of the manufacturing costs incurred during the production of a job and a subsidiary ledger accounting (p. 61).

LABOR TIME TICKET. A record of how much time an employee spends on a job or an overhead assignment (p. 65).

MATERIALS LEDGER CARD. A form representing a subsidiary ledger for each type of raw materials used in the production process that provides a perpetual accounting of the purchases and requisitions of the materials (p. 62).

MATERIALS REQUISITION FORM. A record of the amount of raw materials requisitioned from the storeroom for a job or as indirect materials (p. 63).

OVERAPPLIED MANUFACTURING OVERHEAD. The excess of the manufacturing overhead applied to Work in Process with a predetermined overhead rate over the actual manufacturing overhead incurred (p. 74).

OVERHEAD APPLICATION. The use of a predetermined overhead rate to charge manufacturing overhead to Work in Process as a job is worked on (p. 71).

OVERTIME PREMIUM. Amount paid to an employee above his or her regular hourly wage for every hour worked in excess of 40 hours a week (p. 65).

PAYROLL REGISTER. A detailed listing of a firm's payroll, usually on a departmental basis, for a given period (p. 66).

PREDETERMINED OVERHEAD RATE. A rate used to apply manufacturing overhead to Work in Process that is computed by dividing the estimated manufacturing overhead for a period by the estimated production activity (p. 72).

PROCESS COSTING SYSTEM. A product costing system used with a continuous production process and homogeneous products (p. 59).

PRODUCT COSTING. Concepts and procedures used to accumulate the manufacturing costs needed to produce products (p. 59).

TIME CARD. A document used to control the hours worked each day by an employee (p. 65).

UNDERAPPLIED MANUFACTURING OVERHEAD. The excess of the actual manufacturing overhead incurred during a particular period over the manufacturing overhead applied to Work in Process (p. 74).

DISCUSSION QUESTIONS

1. Why is it essential for management to be able to assign the total costs collected during the manufacturing process to the products produced in an accurate manner?
2. How are perpetual inventories maintained with job order costing?
3. Distinguish between job order costing and process costing.
4. What type of manufacturing firm is likely to use job order costing? Give some examples.
5. Is job order costing ever appropriate for nonmanufacturing firms? Explain.
6. What is a job order cost sheet?
7. What are the main purposes of a job order cost sheet?
8. Identify the business documents required to account for materials in a job order costing system. For direct labor.

9. Distinguish between a materials ledger card and a materials requisition form used in a job order costing system.

10. Compare a labor time ticket, a labor time card, and a payroll register used in a job order costing system.

11. What are the major complications involved with manufacturing overhead?

12. Why are some manufacturing overhead costs the result of a firm incurring so-called common costs?

13. Distinguish between service departments and producing departments in a manufacturing operation. What are the product costing ramifications of the service departments' costs? Give some examples of service departments.

14. What are the two most important cost objectives in defining direct and indirect costs in a manufacturing firm?

15. What is meant by cost allocation? How is it used in a job order costing system?

16. What is a predetermined overhead rate and why is it used in most manufacturing companies?

17. "It seems to me that it is sheer nonsense to use estimates of manufacturing overhead and production activity instead of actual amounts to charge overhead to jobs. This is just another example of how accountants over complicate everything." Do you agree? Explain.

18. The Lincoln Manufacturing Company applies manufacturing overhead to jobs on the basis of 60% of direct labor cost. Job 432 has been charged with $12,600 of direct labor cost and $9,300 of direct materials. If 100 units were produced in Job 432, what is the cost per unit?

19. What is underapplied manufacturing overhead? Overapplied manufacturing overhead? How would each be treated at the end of an accounting period?

20. Will a firm using job order costing know what the cost of goods sold is for a given job when it is sold or must additional calculations be made?

21. What are the revenue-realization ramifications of long-term projects? (Appendix)

22. Explain why the percentage-of-completion method provides the best measure of profit results with most long-term projects. Why is the completed-contract method typically an inferior method of revenue realization? (Appendix)

EXERCISES

Exercise 3-1   Basic Job Order Costing

Ernie's Garage employs four mechanics. Ernie has signed a contract with a local car rental agency to change the oil, replace the oil filter, and lubricate 165 cars over a four-day period. The wage rate and hours for each mechanic are as follows:

Mechanic	Hourly Wage	Hours/Day				
		1	2	3	4	Total
1	$14.00	8.0	8.0	8.0	8.0	32.0
2	8.00	9.0	8.5	7.0	8.5	33.0
3	12.00	9.5	8.0	8.0	8.5	34.0
4	10.00	7.0	9.5	8.25	8.0	32.75

Each mechanic is paid at an overtime rate of 1.5 times the hourly wage for each hour over eight that is worked on any given day. Due to an oil filter stockout, each mechanic was idle for 1.5 hours on day four.

Required:
Calculate the amount to be paid to each mechanic for the four-day period. Give the journal entries to record direct and indirect labor. Assume that Ernie withholds no taxes or union dues from wages. Assign indirect labor to a Garage Overhead account.

Exercise 3-2 Job Order Costing Procedures

Paul Frazier Inc. produces disposable food containers. This company uses a job order cost system. The firm's managerial accountant compiled the following information:

1. Purchased raw materials on account, $95,000.
2. Issued raw materials to production, $80,000 (95% direct, remainder indirect).
3. Direct labor cost incurred, $70,000.
4. Indirect labor cost incurred, $15,000.
5. Other manufacturing overhead costs incurred are paid, $40,000, and depreciation expense for production equipment is $45,000.
6. Manufacturing overhead applied to jobs on the basis of $9 per direct labor hour. There were 12,000 direct labor hours for the period.
7. Jobs amounting to $225,000 were completed.
8. Jobs costing $200,000 were shipped to customers. Paul Frazier Inc. uses a 30% markup on cost rate. These orders were sold on account.

Required:
Give the journal entries for the transactions above. If work in process inventory had a balance of $7,000 at the beginning of the period, what is the ending balance for work in process inventory? What is the ending balance for manufacturing overhead?

Exercise 3-3 Basic Cost Allocation

B.J. Manufacturing Company expects to incur building occupancy costs of $425,000 during the year. Each of the departments shown below occupies the following square footage:

Department	Square Feet Occupied
Machining	30,000
Storeroom	12,000
Assembly	24,000
Sales	36,000
Administrative	18,000
Total	120,000

Required:
Based on square feet occupied, what share of the building occupancy costs should be allocated to each department? How much of the total cost would be classified as product costs?

Exercise 3-4 Computing Predetermined Overhead Rates

Estimated manufacturing overhead and production activity levels for four different firms are presented on following page.

	Company			
	L	**M**	**N**	**O**
Manufacturing overhead	$1,187,200	$6,182,400	$5,672,400	$2,870,600
Direct labor cost	500,000	672,000	432,000	762,000
Machine hours	100,000	643,000	652,000	247,000
Direct labor hours	212,000	572,000	364,000	463,000

Each company uses the following to calculate its predetermined overhead rate:

Company	**Basis**
L	Direct labor hours
M	Direct labor cost
N	Machine hours
O	Direct labor hours

Required:
Compute the predetermined overhead rate for each company.

Exercise 3-5 Operating a Job Order Costing System
The following account appears in the general ledger after only part of the transactions have been completed for the month of January. This is the first month of the firm's fiscal year.

Work in Process Inventory

Bal. 1-1-87	12,500
Direct materials	39,200
Direct labor	55,000

Manufacturing overhead is applied at the rate of 75% of direct labor costs. The actual manufacturing overhead incurred in January was $40,600. Jobs completed during the month totaled $85,000.

Required:
A. Prepare journal entries to:
   1. Record the application of Manufacturing Overhead to production during January.
   2. Record jobs completed.
B. 1. What is the balance of the Manufacturing Overhead account on January 31?
   2. Was manufacturing overhead overapplied or underapplied?
   3. What was the cost of unfinished jobs on January 31?

Exercise 3-6 Preparing a Job Order Cost Sheet
The BSB Company manufactures high-quality speedboats using fiberglass, fabrics, wood, and steel. The boats are produced to fill specific orders placed by customers and involve top-quality craftsmanship and strict quality control. A job order cost system is used to accumulate the costs incurred for each boat. Job 1169 was performed to produce a boat for a customer in the Midwest. Direct costs are traced to each job, and manufacturing overhead is applied on the basis of 75% of direct labor cost. During June, 1987, the following cost data are recorded for Job 1169:

Direct materials requisitioned:

Date	Requisition Number	Amount
6/1	11487	$2,640
6/10	12501	3,810
6/17	13419	1,860

Direct labor recorded:

Date	Time Ticket Number	Amount
6/1	866	$ 865
6/2	882	962
6/3	901	1,624
6/10	1061	842
6/11	1111	967
6/17	1270	1,100

Required:
Prepare a job order cost sheet for Job 1169.

Exercise 3-7 Job Order Costing Transactions

The Curry Manufacturing Company uses a job order cost system. During July, 1987, the following transactions took place:

1. Raw materials costing $86,000 were purchased.
2. Raw materials amounting to $78,500 were requisitioned to the jobs performed.
3. Direct labor cost of $114,500 was recorded. Indirect labor cost amounted to $8,600.
4. Other actual manufacturing overhead costs totaled $138,525.
5. Manufacturing overhead is applied to work in process on the basis of 125% of direct labor cost.
6. Jobs with total costs of $335,625 were completed during the month.
7. Jobs with total costs of $320,225 were sold to customers at a markup of 32% above cost.

Required:
A. Prepare all journal entries required to record the July transactions. Assume the credit entry for actual manufacturing overhead (other than indirect labor) is to accounts payable.
B. Assuming the beginning work in process inventory balance was $10,600, what is the ending balance?

Exercise 3-8 Job Order Costing Procedures

Job order cost data for Jobs 1–10 are shown on the next page. The costs were incurred by the Cardinal Company during May and June, the firm's first two months of operations.

Job Order No.	Costs as of June 1	June Production Costs
1	$5,040	
2	4,440	
3	3,120	
4	2,280	$ 960
5	2,640	2,520
6		4,440
7		5,532
8		1,848
9		1,548
10		948

Jobs 1–3 were completed in May.
Jobs 4–7 were completed in June.
Jobs 8–10 were incomplete as of June 30.
Jobs 1, 3, 5, 7 were sold during June.

Required:
Calculate the following costs:

A. Work in process, June 1.
B. Work in process, June 30.
C. Finished goods, June 1.
D. Finished goods, June 30.
E. Cost of goods sold for June.

Exercise 3-9   Job Order Costing Procedures

The Hammer Furniture Company utilizes a job order cost system. The May cost and operating data were as follows:

Raw materials purchased	$228,800
Direct labor cost	236,800
Raw materials issued for production	212,800
Actual manufacturing overhead incurred	177,600
(Included is depreciation of $17,600)	
Cost of goods manufactured	609,600
Machine hours	43,200
Sales on account	672,000

The company applies manufacturing overhead to production at a rate of $4 per machine hour. The beginning raw materials inventory was $25,600; the beginning work in process inventory was $43,200. The beginning and ending finished goods inventories were $64,000 and $83,200, respectively.

Required:
A. Prepare journal entries to record the May transactions.
B. Was manufacturing overhead overapplied or underapplied for the month of May?
C. Calculate the ending balances of raw materials and work in process. (Hint: Prepare T accounts for the inventory accounts.)

Exercise 3-10   Use of Predetermined Overhead Rates

The estimated cost and operating data for two manufacturing companies are presented on following page.

	Company	
	X	**Y**
Units produced	31,200	20,400
Manufacturing overhead	$ 84,240	$175,032
Direct labor hours	50,400	67,320
Direct labor cost	228,000	302,880

Company X applied overhead on the basis of units of production while Company Y uses direct labor hours. During the past year, Company X actually produced 28,800 units and incurred overhead costs of $75,600. Company Y's actual overhead costs were $180,120 and 68,400 direct labor hours were used.

Required:
A. Calculate the predetermined overhead rate of each company.
B. Determine whether manufacturing overhead was overapplied or underapplied for each company.

Exercise 3-11 Evaluating Problems with Fluctuating Unit Costs

The Patch Toy Company produces a single product that is sold to retail stores throughout the country. The demand for the toy is very seasonal, with high retail sales in the summer months and just before Christmas. Joe Patch, the president of the company, is concerned about the variation in unit costs from quarter to quarter and wants to know whether there is a better way to determine unit product costs than the method currently being used. Unit costs are computed quarterly by dividing the total manufacturing costs for a quarter by the units produced during the quarter. The company's estimated costs and production, by quarter, for the next year are:

	First Quarter	Second Quarter	Third Quarter	Fourth Quarter
Direct materials	$ 24,000	$ 48,000	$ 24,000	$ 96,000
Direct labor	48,000	96,000	48,000	192,000
Variable manufacturing overhead	14,400	28,800	14,400	57,600
Fixed manufacturing overhead	192,000	192,000	192,000	192,000
Total manufacturing costs	$278,400	$364,800	$278,400	$537,600
Units produced	12,000	24,000	12,000	48,000
Unit cost	$ 23.20	$ 15.20	$ 23.20	$ 11.20

Required:
What suggestions would you make to Mr. Patch to improve the way the firm computes unit costs?

Exercise 3-12 Manufacturing Overhead and Job Order Costing

The King Manufacturing Company produces high-quality furniture on a job order basis. Two jobs were started and finished as the firm's only production during March. Manufacturing overhead is applied with a rate of $7 per direct labor hour. The following cost data were recorded during the month:

	Job 675	**Job 676**
Direct materials	$ 20,125	$16,050
Direct labor		
Cost	48,000	21,600
Hours	6,000	2,700
Selling price	$143,163	$67,860

Actual manufacturing overhead for the month totaled $66,700.

Required:
A. Was the manufacturing overhead overapplied or underapplied during the month?
B. What was the gross profit for each job?

Exercise 3-13 Indirect Operating Expense Allocation

The Rapps Clothing Store operates three selling departments. Certain indirect operating expenses are allocated to the selling departments as follows:

Expense	**Amount**	**Basis of Allocation**
Personnel department	$28,800	Payroll
Building rent	43,200	Square feet of floor space
Advertising	72,000	Sales
Insurance on inventory	18,000	Amount of inventory

The following information is obtained from store records for 1987:

	Dept. A	**Dept. B**	**Dept. C**
Payroll	$100,800	$ 72,000	$115,200
Square feet of floor space	3,600	4,608	6,192
Sales	$270,000	$225,000	$405,000
Amount of inventory	63,000	48,600	68,400

Required:
Prepare a schedule allocating the indirect operating expenses to the three selling departments.

Exercise 3-14 Use of Predetermined Overhead Rates

Estimated cost and operating data for two companies during 1987 are shown below:

	Company A	**Company B**
Units of production expected	12,000	11,000
Machine hours	65,000	13,200
Direct labor hours	16,500	22,000
Direct labor cost	$132,000	$198,000
Manufacturing overhead cost	260,000	66,000

Predetermined overhead rates are computed on the following bases in the two companies:

Company	**Basis Used**
A	Machine hours
B	Direct labor hours

Required:
A. Determine the predetermined overhead rate for each company.
B. Assume that three jobs are worked on during 1987 in Company A. Machine hours recorded by job are: Job 610, 28,000 hours; Job 611, 17,000 hours; and Job 612, 18,000 hours. How much overhead will the company apply to work in process? If actual overhead costs are $258,400 for 1987, will manufacturing overhead be over- or underapplied? By how much?

Exercise 3-15 Job Order Costing and Overhead Application

The Pace Company began operations in January, 1987. The following transactions were recorded in the Work in Process Inventory account during January.

Work in Process Inventory

Direct materials	25,000	Finished goods	168,000
Direct labor	70,000		
Manufactured overhead	91,000		

The Pace Company uses a job order cost system and applies manufacturing overhead to work in process on the basis of direct labor cost. At the end of January, Job 160 was the only one left in process. Direct labor cost totaling $6,500 has been charged to Job 160.

Required:
A. Compute the predetermined overhead rate used during January.
B. Complete the following job cost sheet for Job 160 as of January 31, 1987.

Job Cost Sheet — Job 160

Direct materials	$_____
Direct labor	_____
Manufacturing overhead cost	_____
Total	$_____

Exercise 3-16 Percentage-of-Completion Method — Appendix

Stern Construction Company signed a contract to construct a dam on the Mississippi River for $19,200,000. The project is expected to take four years to complete at an estimated cost of $14,400,000. Actual costs incurred each year were:

Year	Costs Incurred
1	$ 2,880,000
2	4,032,000
3	4,320,000
4	3,312,000
Total	$14,544,000

Assume that the estimated total cost of the project remained at $14,400,000 through the end of the third year.

Required:
Determine the amount of gross profit that should be recognized each year with the percentage-of-completion method.

PROBLEMS

Problem 3-1 Job Order Costing Flows

Selected amounts for the Indiana Company are shown below. Some of the amounts for the debits and credits for the month of March are missing. They are designated by a capital letter. The company operates a job order costing system.

Accounts Receivable

March 1	Balance	37,250	Collections		42,750
	Sales	A			
31	Balance	38,000			

Raw Materials Inventory

March 1	Balance	7,800	Requisitions		B
	Purchases	12,500			
31	Balance	5,850			

Work in Process Inventory

March 1	Balance	7,400	Jobs completed		E
	Raw materials	C			
	Direct labor	21,500			
	Overhead	D			
31	Balance	7,500			

Finished Goods Inventory

March 1	Balance	19,750	Cost of goods sold		G
	Jobs completed	F			
31	Balance	17,900			

Manufacturing Overhead

March 1	Balance	100	March 31	Applied manufacturing overhead	H
	Cost incurred	16,200			

Cost of Goods Sold

I	

Sales

	J

Manufacturing overhead is applied at the rate of 75% of direct labor cost. Of the raw materials requisitioned in March, $600 were issued for indirect use. All sales are made on account.

Required:

Determine the correct amounts for each missing item (A–J).

Problem 3-2 Job Order Costing Procedures

The Poor Company operates a job order cost system and applies manufacturing overhead costs on the basis of direct labor cost. Manufacturing overhead costs for 1987 are estimated to be $109,250. Direct labor costs are expected to be $115,000. The Poor Company uses a 45% markup rate on total cost for all sales. Inventory balances are:

	January 1, 1987	December 31, 1987
Raw materials	$ 80,000	$ 83,000
Work in process	95,000	97,000
Finished goods	107,000	117,000

The actual costs incurred were:

Raw materials purchases	$160,000
Direct labor cost	112,000
Manufacturing overhead:	
Indirect labor	50,000
Building occupancy cost	12,000
Maintenance	1,200
Overtime premium	3,300
Insurance	4,600
Production manager's salary	25,000
Property tax	2,400
Depreciation	16,000

Required:
A. Show the necessary calculations for the predetermined overhead rate that the Poor Company should use.
B. Was manufacturing overhead overapplied or underapplied? By what amount? Explain why this occurred.
C. Prepare a schedule of cost of goods manufactured for 1987.
D. If a certain job required $4,700 in materials and $2,300 in direct labor, what would the Poor Company charge for the sale of this job?

Problem 3-3 Job Order Costing for Specific Jobs

During the month of February, the Scott Company started Jobs 67, 68, 69, and 70. Job 66 was started in January, and was in process with direct materials cost of $30,000, direct labor cost of $12,000, and applied manufacturing overhead of $9,000 as of February 1.

Direct materials issued during February:

Job	
67	$42,000
68	51,000
69	27,000
70	19,000

Direct labor cost during February:

Job	
66	$ 7,000
67	20,000
68	42,000
69	28,000
70	10,000

Manufacturing overhead is applied at 75% of direct labor cost. Jobs 66, 67, 68, and 70 were completed and sold during February.

Required:
A. Determine the cost of each job.
B. Determine the amount of cost of goods sold for February.
C. What was the total cost of direct materials requisitioned in February and transferred to work in process?
D. What was the work in process inventory on February 28?

Problem 3-4 Job Order Costing Procedures

The Superior Products Company uses a job order cost system. Cost and operating data for 1987 are as follows:

1. Total payroll incurred – $97,200, of which $25,200 was indirect labor and the remainder direct.
2. Raw materials purchased – $102,000.
3. Raw materials issued to production – $106,800; $10,800 of these materials were indirect.
4. Manufacturing overhead is applied at 140% of direct labor cost.
5. Manufacturing overhead costs actually incurred:

Utilities	$14,400
Rent	28,800
Supplies	13,200
Insurance	8,400
Miscellaneous	12,000

6. Manufacturing equipment depreciation – $9,600.
7. Jobs completed and transferred to finished goods inventory — $174,000.
8. Jobs with a cost of $168,000 were sold for $261,600 on account.
9. The beginning inventories for 1987 were: raw materials – $10,800; work in process – $24,000; and finished goods – $6,000.

Required:
A. Prepare the journal entries to record the transactions.
B. Calculate the ending balances in raw materials inventory, work in process inventory, and finished goods inventory.
C. Was manufacturing overhead underapplied or overapplied for 1987?

Problem 3-5 Job Order Costing Procedures

The controller of the Sells Company has asked you to journalize the following transactions, which took place during May, 1987. The company uses a job order cost system.

1. Raw materials purchased – $18,000.
2. Total payroll included $21,600 for direct labor and $4,800 for indirect labor.
3. Manufacturing overhead is applied on the basis of 125% of direct labor cost.
4. Raw materials issued to production – $16,800 direct materials and $2,400 indirect materials.
5. Actual manufacturing overhead incurred:

Rent	$3,240
Supplies	3,600
Insurance	3,000
Utilities	5,040

6. Manufacturing equipment depreciation – $4,200.
7. Jobs completed and transferred to finished goods – $63,720.
8. Jobs with a cost of $62,400 were sold for $78,000.
9. The beginning inventories included:

Raw materials	$4,200
Work in process	6,720
Finished goods	5,760

Required:
A. Prepare the journal entries to record the transactions during May.
B. Calculate the ending balances in work in process, raw materials, and finished goods. (Hint: Prepare T accounts.)
C. Was manufacturing overhead underapplied or overapplied in May, 1987?

Problem 3-6   Journal Entries for Job Order Costing

The Jonathon Company uses a job order cost system. On January 1, 1987, Jobs 63 and 64 were in process with costs of $12,000 and $15,000, respectively. During January, the following transactions took place:

1. Manufacturing payroll of $50,330 was incurred. Each factory worker earns $7 per hour. Ignore income taxes and other payroll deductions.
2. The labor cost was distributed as follows:

Job 63	$10,500
Job 64	11,900
Job 65	12,950
Job 66	10,780
Indirect labor	4,200

3. Raw materials requisitioned were charged to the following:

Job 63	$18,000
Job 64	20,500
Job 65	22,000
Job 66	19,500
Indirect materials	6,500

4. Additional manufacturing overhead costs incurred and paid during the month – $4,100.
5. Manufacturing overhead is applied at $2.10 per direct labor hour.
6. Jobs 63, 64, and 65 were completed and transferred to finished goods.
7. Jobs 63 and 65 were sold at cost plus 40%.

Required:
Prepare the journal entries needed to record the January transactions.

Problem 3-7   Journal Entries for Job Order Costing

The Wentworth Company accounts for its manufacturing costs using a job order cost system and has provided the following production data for part of its performance during the month of June:

1. Job order number 503 was in process as of June 1 with costs of $8,500.
2. Raw materials requisitioned were charged to the following jobs:

Job 503	$7,000
Job 504	6,500
Job 505	9,500
Indirect materials	3,500

3. Manufacturing payroll of $24,375 was paid. Each worker earns $7.50 per hour. Ignore income taxes and other payroll deductions.
4. The manufacturing payroll was distributed as follows:

Job 503	$6,900
Job 504	8,100
Job 505	7,350
Indirect labor	2,025

5. Additional manufacturing overhead costs incurred and paid during the month were $4,300.
6. Manufacturing overhead is applied at $3.35 per direct labor hour.
7. Jobs 503 and 504 were completed and transferred to finished goods.
8. Job 503 was sold at its cost plus 50%.

Required:
A. Prepare the journal entries to record the transactions.
B. What is the cost of each job finished during June?
C. What is the cost of each job left in work in process inventory at the end of the month?
D. Was manufacturing overhead over- or underapplied during June?

Problem 3-8   Job Order Costing and an Income Statement

The Laverty Company had the following inventory balances on January 1, 1987:

Raw materials	$16,000
Work in process	10,000
Finished goods	50,000

During 1987, the firm recorded these transactions:

1. Raw materials amounting to $110,000 were purchased on account.
2. $100,000 of raw materials were requisitioned to production—$90,000 direct and $10,000 indirect.
3. Payroll expenses during 1987 were:

Direct labor, manufacturing (44,000 hours)	$352,000
Indirect labor, manufacturing	18,000
Sales representative salaries	30,000
Administrative salaries	45,000

4. Plant utility expenses were $26,000.
5. Plant insurance expense was $14,500.
6. Advertising expense was $15,000.
7. $5,000 of depreciation expense was recorded on plant equipment.
8. $30,000 of depreciation expense was recorded on the factory building.
9. Other manufacturing overhead was $16,000.
10. Other selling and administrative expenses were $18,000.
11. Manufacturing overhead was applied to work in process using a predetermined overhead rate of $2.82 per direct labor hour.
12. Jobs completed and transferred to finished goods were $553,500.
13. Finished goods totaling $563,500 were sold at a markup of 40% above cost.

Required:
A. Prepare journal entries to record the 1987 transactions.

B. Prepare a journal entry to close any balance in the manufacturing overhead account to cost of goods sold.

C. Prepare an income statement for 1987.

Problem 3-9 Job Order Costing and Overhead Rates

Johnson Company uses a job order costing system. The company applies manufacturing overhead to jobs with a predetermined overhead rate. The predetermined overhead rate in Department X is based on machine hours, and the rate in Department Y is based on direct labor cost. At the beginning of 1987, the company's controller prepared the following estimates for the year:

	Department X	Department Y
Direct labor hours	18,000	32,000
Machine hours	60,000	14,000
Direct labor cost	$144,000	$288,000
Manufacturing overhead cost	210,000	374,400

Job 415 was started in production on September 1 and completed on October 15. The firm's cost records show the following information for the job:

	Department X	Department Y
Direct labor hours	30	50
Machine hours	110	15
Materials requisitioned	$360	$310
Direct labor cost	240	450

Required:

A. Determine the predetermined overhead rate that should be used during 1987 in Department X. Compute the rate that should be used in Department Y.

B. Compute the total overhead cost applied to Job 415.

C. What would be the total cost of Job 415? If the job contained 10 units of product, what would be the cost per unit?

D. At the end of 1987, the records of the Johnson Company show the following actual cost and operating data for all jobs performed during the year:

	Department X	Department Y
Direct labor hours	18,500	34,000
Machine hours	59,000	11,500
Direct labor cost	$148,000	$307,000
Manufacturing overhead cost	209,000	376,000

How much underapplied or overapplied overhead cost was incurred in each department during 1987?

Problem 3-10 Job Order Costing and Overhead Analysis

The Perry Company uses a job order cost system that includes the application of a predetermined overhead rate based on direct labor hours. For 1987, the predetermined overhead rate was $3.50 (estimated manufacturing overhead of $122,500 divided by estimated 35,000 direct labor hours). During 1987, Job 708 required $1,600 of raw materials and 116 direct labor hours at $8.25 per hour. The job contained 100 units of product.

Required:

A. Prepare the journal entries needed to record the costs for Job 708.

B. Prepare the journal entry required to transfer Job 708 to finished goods.

C. What was the unit cost of each product produced in Job 708?

D. Assume that the firm incurred 33,800 actual direct labor hours and manufacturing overhead cost of $121,900 in 1987. How much over- or underapplied manufacturing overhead was involved? Prepare the journal entry required to close the manufacturing overhead balance to cost of goods sold.

Problem 3-11   Alternative Treatment of Over- or Underapplied Manufacturing Overhead

The MBAH Corporation operates a job order cost system. A predetermined overhead rate based on direct labor hours is used to apply manufacturing overhead to the jobs. Estimated cost and operating data for 1987 are shown below:

Estimated direct labor hours	50,000
Estimated manufacturing overhead	$300,000

At the end of 1987, the firm's accounting records include the following actual cost and operating data:

Direct labor hours	45,000
Direct labor cost	$365,000
Manufacturing overhead	290,000
Raw materials inventory	14,000
Work in process inventory	50,000
Finished goods inventory	150,000
Cost of goods sold	800,000

Required:

A. What was the firm's predetermined overhead rate for 1987?

B. Determine the over- or underapplied manufacturing overhead for 1987.

C. If the company closes any over- or underapplied overhead to cost of goods sold, what was the actual cost of goods sold for 1987?

D. Prorate any over- or underapplied overhead to the appropriate inventory accounts and cost of goods sold.

E. What would be the difference in the firm's net income between C and D above?

Problem 3-12   Analysis of Job Order Cost Flows with T Accounts

Summarized ledger accounts for the Burnell Company's 1987 operating performance are shown below:

Raw Materials Inventory

1/1 Bal.	16,000	1987 Credits	?
1987 Debits	60,000		
12/31 Bal.	10,000		

Work in Process Inventory

1/1 Bal.	26,000	1987 Credits	336,000
Materials	60,000		
Labor	90,000		
Overhead	180,000		
12/31 Bal.	?		

Finished Goods Inventory

1/1 Bal.	38,000	1987 Credits	?
1987 Debits	?		
12/31 Bal.	42,000		

Cost of Goods Sold

1987 Debits	?

Manufacturing Overhead

1987 Debits	190,000	1987 Credits	?

Wages Payable

1987 Debits	94,000	1/1 Bal.	3,000
		1987 Credits	93,000
		12/31 Bal.	2,000

Required:

A. Find the correct amounts for each of the unknowns in the T accounts shown above.

B. What was the actual manufacturing overhead cost for 1987?

C. How much of the actual manufacturing overhead cost was for indirect materials? For indirect labor?

D. What was the cost of goods manufactured for 1987?

E. What was the cost of goods sold for 1987?

F. Assuming manufacturing overhead cost is applied on the basis of direct labor cost, what was the predetermined overhead rate?

G. Was manufacturing overhead over- or underapplied during 1987? By how much?

Problem 3-13 Basic Cost Allocation Procedures

The Bock Department Store operates four departments, A–D, at its Toronto location. In order to prepare a departmental income statement, the store's bookkeeper allocates indirect costs with the following predetermined allocation bases:

Indirect Cost	Allocation Base	Total Amount
Rent	Relative amount of square footage	$16,000
Personnel Department	Number of employees	24,000
Insurance	Value of inventory	11,200
Utilities	Square footage	6,400

The bookkeeper has also provided the following data concerning the four departments:

	Dept. A	Dept. B	Dept. C	Dept. D
Square footage	1,400	600	800	1,200
Number of employees	10	8	12	10
Value of inventory	$24,000	$30,000	$12,000	$14,000

Required:

Prepare a schedule allocating the indirect costs to the four departments.

Problem 3-14 Cost Allocation and Predetermined Overhead Rates

The Gift Company has asked you to develop predetermined rates for applying indirect manufacturing costs in its two producing departments—Machining and Finishing. The following estimated data have been collected for 1987:

Direct labor cost—Machining, $120,000; Finishing, $60,000.
Floor space occupied—Factory Office, 10%; Machining, 60%; Finishing, 30%.
Manufacturing overhead costs directly traceable to departments:

Factory Office	$ 49,200	
Machining Department	110,400	
Finishing Department	63,600	$223,200

Indirect overhead costs common for departments:

Building occupancy	$ 12,000

It has been determined that Factory Office costs should be allocated to the other departments on the basis of direct labor cost. Building occupancy costs should be allocated to the three departments on the basis of floor space occupied.

The Machining Department operates on a 40-hour week. There are five machines in the department and management estimates that each machine will be idle for a total of 160 hours a year for vacations, holidays, and repairs.

Required:

A. Compute a predetermined overhead rate based on machine hours for the Machining Department.
B. Compute a predetermined overhead rate based on direct labor cost for the Finishing Department.

Problem 3-15 Job Order Costing and Percentage-of-Completion Method — Appendix

The Conner Construction Company uses a combination of job order costing and the percentage-of-completion method to account for its projects. On July 1, 1987, the firm entered into a fixed-price contract to build a large office building. The company's chief engineer estimates that it would take 2½ years to complete the project. The total contract price is $5 million with estimated costs of $3.5 million. Estimated percentage-of-completion, accumulated contract costs incurred, and estimated costs to complete the contract were as follows:

	1987 As of December 31	1988 As of December 31	1989 As of December 31
Actual costs incurred	$1,400,000	$2,450,000	$3,550,000
Estimated costs to complete	2,100,000	1,050,000	–0–

Required:

Determine the firm's gross profit for each of the years 1987, 1988, and 1989.

4

PROCESS COSTING SYSTEMS

CHAPTER OVERVIEW AND OBJECTIVES

This chapter continues the discussion of product costing with a coverage of process costing systems. After studying this chapter, you should be able to:

1. Describe how process costing is used by manufacturing and nonmanufacturing firms.
2. Identify a processing center.
3. Explain how products and costs flow through a production process and know the accounting procedures needed to accumulate costs perpetually.
4. Calculate unit costs for products produced in a process costing operation.
5. Determine equivalent units of production.
6. Prepare a cost of production report.
7. Recognize how the weighted-average method and the FIFO method are used with a beginning work in process inventory.
8. Compute equivalent units of production with the weighted-average and FIFO methods.
9. Interpret cost of production reports prepared with the weighted-average method and the FIFO method.
10. Evaluate how costs incurred in a preceding department are treated in a cost of production report.
11. Prepare the journal entries needed to record the production costs, the transfer of products, and the sale of products with process costing.
12. Compare job order costing with process costing.

USE OF PROCESS COSTING

**Objective 1:
Use of process costing**

When homogeneous products are produced in a continuous flow without definite beginning and ending points, job order costing is not feasible and a **process costing system** should be used. Manufacturing firms operate continuous production flows for two basic reasons:

1. A continuous process may be the only way to produce certain products such as chemicals, paint, and soft drinks which, by their very nature, con-

sist of homogeneous units. One unit of output (such as a gallon) cannot be separated from another.

2. Many firms use mass production techniques to manufacture standardized products in order to achieve better productivity and higher profits. For example, a large refinery is a highly automated process that must be operated nonstop to make the extensive capital investment involved profitable.

By producing large quantities of a product according to the firm's own specifications rather than those of each individual customer, a company often can lower the cost of one unit of product because the rate of production increases faster than costs do. Other examples of firms with homogeneous products are plastics, wine, rubber, and pharmaceuticals. Essentially the same process costing concepts and procedures applied in this chapter to product costing can be utilized to accumulate costs for a wide range of nonmanufacturing activities. Examples are mail sorting in a post office, food preparation in a fast-food restaurant, check processing in a bank, and tax returns processed by the Internal Revenue Service (IRS).

BASIC STEPS REQUIRED WITH PROCESS COSTING

The development and operation of a process costing system involves several essential steps that will be explained in this chapter. These steps can be summarized as:

1. Identifying the continuous production flow used to manufacture the homogeneous products, including the specific processing centers that do the work and the relationships between the centers.
2. Determining the time period for which the process costs will be accumulated and reported to management.
3. Accumulating the manufacturing costs—materials, labor, and overhead—incurred to produce the products in specific processing centers for the time period chosen in step 2.
4. Calculating the equivalent units as production output for each processing center for the reporting period, taking into consideration an inventory flow assumption if a beginning work in process inventory is involved.
5. Computing the unit cost of each product produced by each processing center using the costs accumulated (step 3) and the equivalent units as production output (step 4).
6. Preparing a cost of production report for each processing center's performance during the reporting period.

PRODUCTION FLOWS AND COST FLOWS WITH PROCESS COSTING

In a process costing operation, the homogeneous products move from one **processing center** to the next until they are finally completed. Each processing center incurs manufacturing costs to perform its part of the total work required for finished products and transfers its production output to the next phase of the process. Thus, the cost flow follows the production flow and the first step in a process costing application is to identify the processing centers involved and the relationships between them. The number of processing centers used depends on the type of products involved. Some products may require only one

Objective 2: Identifying a processing center

**Objective 3:
Impact of
processing cost
flow on accounting**

processing center whereas others will require several centers. In every case, however, the focal point of process costing is the processing center(s) in which the work is performed instead of the products being produced as it is with job order costing. A processing center can be a department, a work station, an assembly line, a product line, or a division. Regardless of what they are called, all processing centers must have two essential characteristics: (1) only one type of product is produced by the center; and (2) the same kind and amount of work must be performed on all units passing through the center.

To illustrate a process costing flow, consider the Southeastern Chemical Company's manufacturing operation that is summarized in Figure 4-1. We will use the firm's production and cost flows later in this chapter to explain process costing. The company operates two departments, *Blending* and *Finishing,* to produce gallon quantities of a single type of product, Aqua-bright, used for swimming pool maintenance. Since the firm's homogeneous products flow continuously through the process from the Blending Department to the Finishing Department and then to Finished Goods Inventory, it is impossible to differentiate between units of production output.

An important point to recognize in Figure 4-1 is that the flow of costs is *cumulative.* This means that the manufacturing costs accumulated in the Blending Department are transferred along with the related products being produced to the Finishing Department. After the Finishing Department completes its work, the costs recorded in that department are added to those transferred from the Blending Department to determine the cost of the finished goods inventory. As a result, the production output of the Blending Department becomes the production input of the Finishing Department, which is an example of a sequential product flow. In any sequential product flow, production starts in the

Figure 4-1
Southeastern Chemical Company Process Costing Flows

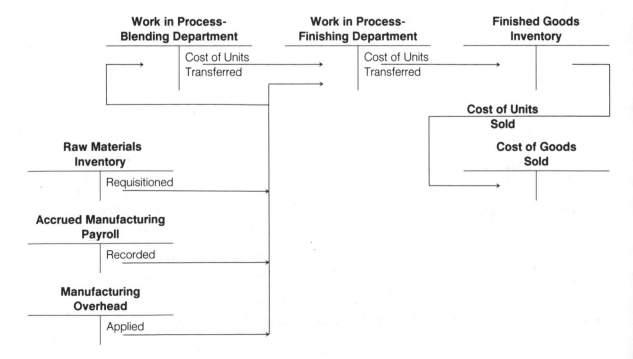

first processing center and flows through every processing center with each succeeding center dependent on the preceding work performance.

A second type of product flow used in some process costing situations is a **parallel product flow,** illustrated in Figure 4-2. In a parallel product flow, certain phases of the work are performed concurrently and then are combined for further processing or completion. Not all products are worked on in every processing center, but the cumulative effect of the cost flow must be accounted for to determine unit costs of the finished products.

ACCUMULATING MANUFACTURING COSTS WITH A PROCESS COSTING SYSTEM

The accounting records required with process costing are similar to those discussed in the previous chapter for job order costing—with one important difference. In our discussion of job order costing, we pointed out that manufacturing costs usually are collected on a departmental basis and then traced or applied as direct or indirect costs to the jobs. The recordkeeping required for process costing is *simpler* than that needed for job order costing because the manufacturing costs are accumulated for each processing center but are not reassigned to individual products as jobs.

Direct materials, direct labor, and manufacturing overhead are recorded in a Work in Process Inventory account established for each processing center. Job order cost sheets are not used to provide the detail of the amount in the Work in Process Inventory account because of the homogeneous nature of the products. In the Southeastern Chemical Company case, the manufacturing costs incurred by the Blending Department and by the Finishing Department would be recorded in separate departmental Work in Process Inventory accounts. Raw materials issued to production are recorded on materials requisition forms and charged to the processing center requesting them (e.g., the Blending Department). Consequently, the accounting for materials in process costing is essentially the same as it is in job order costing without the identification of specific uses of the materials by the processing center.

Additional recordkeeping savings are achieved in accounting for labor in process costing. In most cases, the employees work in only one processing center, so the labor time reporting system only has to identify the processing center involved, not the specific activities performed. For example, a departmentalized payroll register may provide all the information required to account

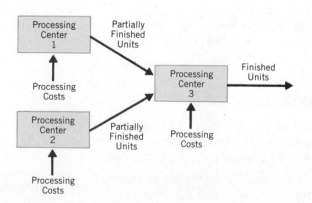

Figure 4-2
Parallel Product
Flow

for the labor costs of the Blending Department without the detail of labor time tickets.

Another important feature of process costing is that the distinction between direct and indirect costs (materials and labor) needed in job order costing *is not necessary* because the cost objective changes from a job to a processing center. All materials and labor costs incurred are charged directly to a specific processing center, such as the Blending Department. Thus, no distinction between the costs directly related to products and those treated as manufacturing overhead is necessary. For example, the wages of a Blending Department employee who works on the products and the salary of the department supervisor will be treated the same way—as direct department costs. Remember that they would have to be separated in job order costing because of the difference between the direct and indirect costs for the individual jobs.

Manufacturing overhead usually is applied in each processing center on the basis of a predetermined overhead rate, calculated in the same manner as it is in job order costing. For example, a predetermined overhead rate is determined for the Blending Department by dividing the department's estimated manufacturing overhead for a relatively long period such as a year by the estimated level of production activity. A separate calculation is necessary for the Finishing Department's predetermined overhead rate because of the need to account for each processing center's costs individually. Any difference between actual and applied manufacturing overhead is computed and accounted for in the same way it is with job order costing.

If the amount of manufacturing overhead and the level of production activity both are relatively constant between short time periods such as months, actual manufacturing overhead may even be used for costing purposes instead of a predetermined overhead rate. This simplifies product costing with process costing even further because the actual manufacturing overhead incurred in a given processing center during a particular period is charged to the center's Work in Process Inventory account and later included in the unit cost of the homogeneous products produced. Since the production process is continuous with homogeneous output, each product requires essentially the same amount of production effort, including the amount of manufacturing overhead. In contrast, many of the jobs in a job order costing system are different and require varying amounts of production effort, including manufacturing overhead.

However, if the amount of manufacturing overhead or level of production activity fluctuates from period to period (e.g., between months) with process costing, the actual manufacturing overhead should not be used for the same reason we identified in job order costing (the problem with volatile unit product costs). Instead, manufacturing overhead should be applied with a predetermined overhead rate to absorb the differences in cost or production activity between short periods over the production results of longer periods.

DETERMINING UNIT COSTS

Objective 4: Calculating unit costs with process costing

The production output in a process costing system usually is measured in such units as gallons, pounds, liters, tons, barrels, or square feet. In general, process costing produces an **average unit cost** computed as:

$$\frac{\text{Total processing center costs for a period}}{\text{Total processing center output for a period}} = \text{Average unit cost}$$

This deceptively simple computation often becomes more complicated because:

1. Since the process is continuous, beginning and ending work in process inventories usually exist. These unfinished inventories cannot be added to the denominator of the fraction shown above as whole units. Costs will have been incurred for any partially completed units that are part of the processing center's output despite the fact they are not in a finished form. For example, it is likely that the Blending Department of the Southeastern Chemical Company will begin and end a particular period with work in process inventory.

2. The individual cost elements won't always be incurred uniformly during the production process. For example, conversion costs (direct labor and manufacturing overhead) typically are consumed continuously in the production process, whereas raw materials are added at specific points in the process (e.g., the Finishing Department may incur conversion costs throughout its production cycle but add materials at the very end). Consequently, a work in process inventory may be at different stages of completion for different cost elements.

3. In most situations, multiple processing centers operate in a sequential or parallel relationship with each other. The costs and production output transferred between centers must be accounted for in the unit cost computation.

EQUIVALENT UNITS OF PRODUCTION

In a process costing system, any unfinished work must be accounted for along with the finished units. Thus, production output usually cannot be expressed entirely in terms of physical or whole units (those finished). Unfinished work in process inventory on hand at the end of a period requires additional work and costs in the next period. Beginning work in process inventory will include work and costs incurred in a previous period, and additional processing will be required to complete the products involved. The partially finished units cannot be equated with whole units because their form obviously is not the same.

Objective 5: Computing equivalent units of production

Equivalent units of production (or simply equivalent units), used to overcome this problem of unfinished products, represent the number of units that would have been produced if all the work and costs had been applied to completed units. In other words, *any partially processed inventories must be restated to the equivalent number of finished units they would represent before they are combined with the completed units.* For example, 2,000 units that are 25% finished are the equivalent of 500 units that are 100% completed. Since no additional work is required for the finished units, they automatically become equivalent units of production. Consequently, the equivalent units of production for a particular period are a measure of how many whole units of production are represented by the units finished plus the units partially completed.

To visualize how equivalent units are used as a measure of production output, refer to Figure 4-3. The Roundball Company produces basketballs with a continuous production process. The firm began the current period with four basketballs that were 75% finished. During the current period, 10 basketballs were started and finished. At the end of the period, two basketballs were left in work in process, 50% completed.

To determine the equivalent units of production for the current period, we have to take into account the work that is performed to complete the beginning

Figure 4-3
The Roundball
Company
—Equivalent
Units of Production
with Beginning
and Ending
Inventories

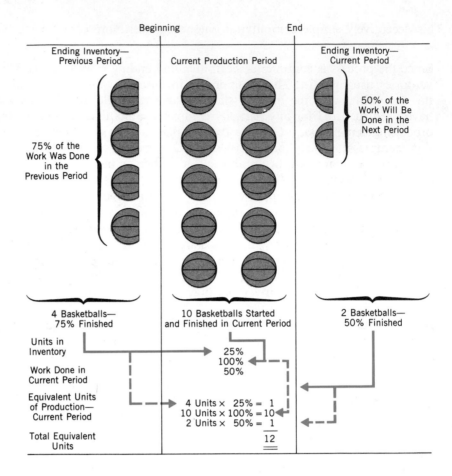

inventory, the work required for the basketballs started and finished during the period, and the work done on the units in the ending inventory. Since the units in the beginning inventory were 75% finished when the current period began, 25% additional work is needed to complete them, so they represent one equivalent unit of production for the current period (4 basketballs × 25%). The 10 basketballs started and finished during the period are all equivalent units of production since they are completed. Finally, the two units in the ending inventory are only 50% finished so they represent one equivalent unit of production (2 basketballs × 50%). Thus, the total equivalent units of production for the current period are 12 (1 + 10 + 1).

The overall stage of completion for the ending work in process inventory can only be estimated in most cases; it really is an average because some of the units in process may not have reached that point while others may be beyond it. The stage of completion for each manufacturing cost element (raw materials, direct labor, and manufacturing overhead) must be evaluated separately in the calculation of equivalent units, except in a rare case where all manufacturing costs are incurred uniformly. To do so, it is helpful to visualize the production process as a continuum ranging from 0% completion to 100% completion, as shown below:

Production Process

Inputs → ———————————————————————— Outputs →

0% 10% 20% 30% 40% 50% 60% 70% 80% 90% 100%
% of Completion for Each Manufacturing Cost Element

The calculation of equivalent units of production for each cost element must take into consideration where the work in process inventory is on the continuum as far as the particular cost element is concerned. That is, how complete is the work in process inventory in terms of that cost element? Since a wide range of outcomes is possible depending on the operating conditions of different firms and how they incur costs, we will consider typical cases only.

The same concepts and procedures are applicable even in unusual situations, however, because two general rules can be followed in all cases:

1. When a particular manufacturing cost element is incurred continuously, its equivalent units of production are proportional to the stage of completion.
2. When a manufacturing cost element is added to production at a specific point in the process, its equivalent units of production are the number of units that are at or past that point.

As stated earlier, conversion costs normally are incurred evenly throughout the production process, whereas raw materials are added at specific points in the process. To illustrate how equivalent units of production are computed, assume that a particular firm adds Material A at the beginning of the production process and Material B at the end of the process. Assume too that conversion costs (direct labor and manufacturing overhead) are incurred continuously throughout the production process. The firm's operating results for a given month show the following:

1. There is no work in process inventory at the beginning of the month.
2. 100,000 units are entered into production during the month.
3. 90,000 units are finished during the month.
4. 10,000 units are left in the work in process inventory at the end of the month, 40% finished as far as conversion costs are concerned.

Referring to the continuum again, we can observe that the ending work in process inventory is 40% converted, Material A is added before the estimated stage of completion, and Material B is added after it.

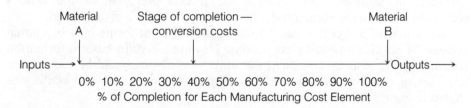

The equivalent units of production for the conversion costs would be 94,000 (90,000 units completed plus 40% of the 10,000 units unfinished). The equivalent units for Material A would be 100,000 because the stage of completion for Material A is 100% (no more of that material is needed). Finally, the equivalent units for Material B would be 90,000 (the number finished) because Material B would only be added to the finished products. Since the ending work in process inventory is only 40% completed, it would not contain any Material B.

COMPUTING UNIT COSTS WITH EQUIVALENT UNITS

Earlier, we noted that a unit cost with process costing is calculated with a fraction, the numerator of which is the costs incurred by a processing center for a period and the denominator of which is the processing center's production output of the period. Equivalent units of production are used in the denominator as the measure of production output. A unit cost must be computed *separately* for each of the manufacturing cost elements when different equivalent units are involved. To illustrate how unit costs are computed with the equivalent units for the conversion costs, Material A, and Material B above, assume that the same firm incurred the following costs for the equivalent units of production:

Conversion costs	$310,200
Material A	180,000
Material B	34,200

The unit cost for each of the three cost elements is:

Conversion costs $\dfrac{\$310,200}{94,000} = \$3.30$ per unit

Material A $\dfrac{\$180,000}{100,000} = \$1.80$ per unit

Material B $\dfrac{\$34,200}{90,000} = \$.38$ per unit

Thus, the total unit cost of each product produced is $5.48 ($3.30 + $1.80 + $.38). We could also divide the conversion costs into their direct labor and manufacturing overhead components and determine the unit costs of each category.

CONTROL DOCUMENT — COST OF PRODUCTION REPORT

Objective 6:
Use of a cost of
production report

A **cost of production report** serves as the control document in a process costing system like a job order cost sheet does in job order costing. It is used to account for the costs charged to a processing center during a specified time period and provides management with a complete description of the production activity that took place, including the unit product costs that resulted. The report usually is prepared on a monthly basis, although a shorter or longer period may be chosen if the benefits exceed the costs. When multiple processing centers are operated, management can combine the reports prepared for the various centers to evaluate the entire production performance for a given period.

The format of a report is not standard, and different forms may be chosen because of specific operating conditions. However, certain basic information concerning the costs incurred and the units worked on should be included in any cost of production report. A cost of production report such as the one shown in Figure 4-4 has three sections:

1. **Physical flow section:** Shows the physical flow of production through a processing center. Included are the number of production units for which a processing center is responsible, their stage of completion, where they are at the end of the period, and the equivalent units of production involved with the physical flow. This section provides a check to make sure that the number of units worked on during a period (the units to be accounted for) are

actually accounted for (e.g., the number of units finished and those in process at the end of the period).

2. **Costs to be accounted for section:** Identifies the amounts accumulated for each manufacturing cost element (e.g., raw materials) within the processing center during the period, the equivalent units of production for each cost element, and the unit costs computed for the various cost elements. By adding together the unit costs for the various cost elements, we can determine the total cost of producing one unit in the processing center.

3. **Costs accounted for section:** Indicates what happened to the manufacturing cost elements for which the processing center is responsible in terms of finished units and those left in process at the end of the period.

A cost of production report can be prepared using the following steps:

1. Trace the physical flow of units for a processing center's production activities and account for all units worked on during the period.
2. Identify the amount of cost incurred for each manufacturing cost element used in the production process. Total the various costs to determine the total costs to be accounted for.
3. Calculate the equivalent units of production for each manufacturing cost element.
4. Divide the costs accumulated for each cost element by the related equivalent units and sum the resulting quotients to determine the cost of producing one unit of product.
5. Distribute the total costs to be accounted for between the finished products and the ending work in process inventory. The unit cost computed in step 4 is multiplied times the number of units completed to value the finished products transferred from the processing center. Each manufacturing cost element in the ending work in process inventory is costed separately by multiplying its unit cost by the equivalent units of production.
6. Check to make sure the total costs to be accounted for (step 2) equal the total costs accounted for (step 5).

ILLUSTRATION OF PROCESS COSTING WITHOUT BEGINNING INVENTORY

Before considering additional complexities of process costing, let's summarize the basic aspects of process costing by preparing a cost of production report for a simplified situation with no beginning work in process inventory and a single production department. The Southeastern Chemical Company, identified earlier in Figure 4-1 as the manufacturer of Aqua-bright, will be used for all illustrations that follow. Raw materials in chemical powder form are added at the start of the production process in the Blending Department (for now, we will only be concerned with the one department). Manufacturing overhead is applied to the work in process inventory on the basis of direct labor hours, which are incurred continuously throughout the production process. During January, 1987, the following data were accumulated as production took place:

Units in beginning work in process	–0–
Units started	50,000 gallons
Units finished	42,000 gallons

Units in ending work in process (40% complete as to the conversion process)	8,000 gallons
Raw materials requisitioned	$ 71,000
Direct labor cost	94,920
Manufacturing overhead cost	117,520

PREPARATION OF A COST OF PRODUCTION REPORT

Using the steps identified earlier, we can prepare the cost of production report for the January, 1987, production performance of the Blending Department shown in Figure 4-4 as follows (the steps are numbered in color where they are used in the figure):

SOUTHEASTERN CHEMICAL COMPANY
Blending Department
Cost of Production Report
Month Ended January 31, 1987

		Equivalent Units		
	Total Units	Raw Materials Cost	Direct Labor Cost	Manufacturing Overhead
Physical Flow Schedule				
Beginning work in process	–0–			
Units started	50,000			
Units to be accounted for	50,000 ①			
Units finished	42,000	42,000	42,000	42,000
Ending work in process	8,000	8,000	3,200*	3,200*
Units accounted for	50,000	50,000	45,200	45,200

Costs to Be Accounted For

Cost Element	Beginning Costs	Current Costs ②	Total Costs	Equivalent Units ③	Unit Cost ④
Raw materials	$–0–	$ 71,000	$ 71,000	50,000	$1.42
Direct labor	–0–	94,920	94,920	45,200	2.10
Manufacturing overhead	–0–	117,520	117,520	45,200	2.60
Costs to be accounted for	$–0–	$283,440	$283,440 ⑥		$6.12

Costs To Be Accounted For

Units transferred to			
Finishing Department	(42,000 gallons × $6.12) ⑤		$257,040
Ending work in process			
Raw materials	(8,000 gallons × 100% × $1.42)	$11,360	
Direct labor	(8,000 gallons × 40% × $2.10)	6,720	
Manufacturing overhead	(8,000 gallons × 40% × $2.60)	8,320	26,400
Costs accounted for			$283,440 ⑥

*8,000 gallons × 40%

Step 1. The firm had no work in process inventory at the beginning of the month, started 50,000 gallons during the month, finished 42,000 gallons, and had 8,000 gallons left in process on January 31. The ending work in process was 40% completed as far as the conversion process, but 100% completed as far as raw materials are concerned. Note that the firm must account for all units in the physical flow schedule. In this simple case, the 42,000 gallons completed plus the 8,000 left in process equal the 50,000 gallons to be accounted for.

Step 2. During the month, raw materials, direct labor, and manufacturing overhead costs of $71,000, $94,920, and $117,520, respectively, were accumulated with the firm's process costing system. Consequently, the total costs to be accounted for are $283,440.

Step 3. Since the raw materials are added at the beginning of the process, all 50,000 units started are equivalent units of production for raw materials computations. The ending work in process is at the 40% stage of conversion so additional raw materials are not required. However, the 8,000 gallons in work in process represent only 3,200 (8,000 gallons × 40%) equivalent units for the conversion costs so their total equivalent units are 45,200 (the 3,200 gallons in work in process plus the 42,000 gallons completed).

Step 4. The Blending Department's unit cost for each gallon produced is $6.12, comprised of $1.42 for raw materials, $2.10 for direct labor, and $2.60 for manufacturing overhead. The costs accumulated in step two are divided by the related equivalent units of production identified in step three to compute the individual unit costs.

Step 5. Since the $6.12 represents the unit cost required to produce a gallon of Aqua-bright in the Blending Department, it can be multiplied times the 42,000 gallons completed to determine the cost of the finished products, or $257,040. This total cost would be transferred from the Blending Department. But, recall from step 2 that the department must account for costs totaling $283,440. The difference between $283,440 and $257,040 must be left in the ending work in process inventory. This is shown by dividing the cost of the ending work in process inventory into its three cost components: raw materials, direct labor, and manufacturing overhead. A distinction between raw materials and the conversion costs is necessary because the related equivalent units of production are different. Since all raw materials have been added, their unit cost of $1.42 is multiplied times the 8,000 gallons in process for a dollar total of $11,360. For the conversion costs, the 8,000 gallons are reduced to 3,200 equivalent units that are multiplied times the labor and overhead rates of $2.10 and $2.60, respectively, to get additional costs of $6,720 and $8,320 for the ending work in process inventory. Consequently, the total costs assigned to the ending work in process are $26,400 ($11,360 + $6,720 + $8,320), and the total costs accounted for in the finished products and ending work in process inventory are $283,440 ($257,040 + $26,400).

Step 6. The total costs to be accounted for by the Blending Department ($283,440) are equal to the total costs accounted for ($283,440). The process costing results in this illustration are summarized in Figure 4-5.

Figure 4-5
Summary of
Process Costing
Results Without a
Beginning Inventory

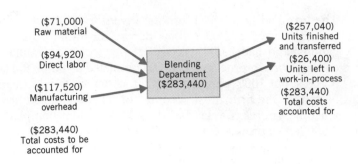

IMPACT OF BEGINNING WORK IN PROCESS INVENTORY

Objective 7:
Treatment of beginning work in process inventory

The preceding example showed that the total costs to be accounted for in a processing center at the end of a period must be distributed between (1) the units finished and transferred out of the center and (2) those left in the ending work in process inventory. The existence of a beginning work in process inventory in a processing center complicates a process costing application because the costs previously assigned to the beginning inventory also must be distributed to the center's output. If the products' unit costs remain the same from month to month, the process costing results will be the same regardless of how the beginning work in process inventory is treated. However, the unit costs often will change from one period to the next because of different prices or quantities of materials, labor, or overhead used in the production process.

This situation is similar to that of a merchandising business that pays different prices for inventory purchased on different dates. Recall from your financial accounting course that a merchandising firm must select a flow assumption to determine which unit costs are left in ending inventory and which are charged to cost of goods sold. Examples of popular flow assumptions are weighted-average, first in, first out (FIFO), and last in, first out (LIFO). The choice of the best flow assumption is required for a proper matching of revenue and cost of goods sold.

In a process costing system, managerial accountants must also use a flow assumption to account for costs in a beginning work in process inventory and those incurred during a current period. The basic question is *which of these costs should be transferred out of a processing center at the end of an accounting period and which should be left in the ending work in process inventory?*

The two flow assumptions most commonly used for process costing are the **weighted-average method** and the **FIFO method**. The major difference between the two methods is whether the costs of the beginning work in process inventory are kept separate from (FIFO method) or combined with (weighted-average method) the current period's production costs in determining unit costs. If unit costs fluctuate significantly from period to period, management will want to monitor the differences for control purposes with the FIFO method. Otherwise, the weighted-average method may be used because it is simpler and the results will be essentially the same. The choice between the two methods also will dictate how equivalent units are calculated.

Let's examine how the two flow assumptions are applied in process costing by continuing the Southeastern Chemical Company illustration to the month of February, 1987. The January 31 work in process inventory shown in Figure 4-4 becomes the beginning work in process inventory for February. Assume that the following data summarize the Blending Department's operating performance for February:

Beginning Work in Process Data

Units in beginning inventory (40% completed as to the conversion process)	8,000
Raw materials cost	$11,360
Direct labor cost	6,720
Manufacturing overhead cost	8,320

February Processing Data

Units started	42,000 gallons
Units finished	40,000 gallons
Units in ending work in process (30% completed as to the conversion process)	10,000 gallons
Raw materials requisitioned	$ 70,140
Direct labor cost	83,580
Manufacturing overhead	103,480

EQUIVALENT UNITS WITH THE WEIGHTED-AVERAGE METHOD

The computation of equivalent units of production with the weighted-average method is simpler than it is with the FIFO method; the reason is that we *combine* the beginning work in process inventory with the units started during the current period when the weighted-average method is used. As a result, the equivalent units of production with the weighted-average method will be equal to the completed units plus the equivalent units in the ending work in process inventory. To illustrate, the equivalent units of production for the Blending Department's February processing performance with the weighted-average method are calculated in Figure 4-6:

Objective 8: Computing equivalent units with a beginning work in process inventory

Figure 4-6

SOUTHEASTERN CHEMICAL COMPANY
Equivalent Units of Production—Weighted-Average Method
Month Ended February 28, 1987

	Equivalent Units		
	Raw Materials Cost	Direct Labor Cost	Manufacturing Overhead
40,000 gallons completed	40,000	40,000	40,000
Plus equivalent units in ending inventory of 10,000 gallons			
10,000 gallons × 100%	10,000		
10,000 gallons × 30%		3,000	3,000
Equals equivalent units with weighted-average method	50,000	43,000	43,000

Since the ending work in process inventory is at different stages of completion in terms of raw materials and conversion costs, two equivalent units of production figures are computed (50,000 and 43,000). Note that the equivalent units for direct labor and manufacturing overhead are the same (43,000) because the overhead is applied on the basis of direct labor hours. Thus, both cost elements are at the same stage of completion. Note also that we ignored the beginning inventory in the computation of equivalent units of production with the weighted-average method. This is always done when the weighted-average method is used because units in the beginning inventory are assumed to be started and finished during the current period. That is, we simply pool the units from the beginning inventory and those from the current period's production together without any concern for the source of the units. Thus, the weighted-average assumption greatly simplifies the calculation of equivalent units of production as we will see next.

EQUIVALENT UNITS WITH THE FIFO METHOD

When the FIFO method is used, a *distinction* is made between the units in the beginning inventory and those started during the current period. The stage of completion of both the beginning work in process inventory and the ending work in process inventory must be considered in a FIFO method application. The first in, first out assumption indicates that the units in the beginning work in process inventory are the first ones finished. Thus, the 8,000 gallons in the Blending Department's work in process inventory on February 1 are assumed to be completed before any of the 42,000 gallons started during the month. Remember that the 8,000 gallons were 40% finished as of February 1 so 60% additional work must be performed during February to complete them. The additional work requires conversion costs only since the 8,000 gallons are complete as far as raw materials are concerned (the raw materials are added at the beginning of the process).

The equivalent units of production with the FIFO method are computed by adding the units completed during the month to the equivalent units in the ending inventory (just like we did with the weighted-average method) and then subtracting the equivalent units in the beginning inventory. The equivalent units in the beginning inventory must be deducted to compute the equivalent units of production in the current period because they represent work that was performed in the previous period. When the FIFO method is used, the units and costs of the previous period are kept separate from those of the current period. As a result, separate unit costs can be computed for each period's production results.

The Blending Department would calculate the equivalent units of production for February with the FIFO method as shown in Figure 4-7. Note that the only difference in the equivalent units of production found in Figures 4-6 and 4-7 is the subtraction of the equivalent units in the beginning inventory. For example, the equivalent units for raw materials with the weighted-average method are 50,000 gallons compared with 42,000 gallons with the FIFO method. The 8,000-gallon difference represents the equivalent units in the beginning inventory. For the conversion costs, the equivalent units of production with the weighted-average method are 43,000 gallons compared with 39,800 gallons with the FIFO method. The 3,200-gallon difference is attributable to the equivalent units in the beginning inventory (8,000 gallons $\times$ 40% = 3,200 gallons). Thus, the difference in the equivalent units with the two methods results from the way we treat the beginning inventory.

When the weighted-average method is used, the beginning inventory is combined with the units started in February and no distinction is made between the unit costs of different months. The monthly unit costs are simply averages between the two months. In contrast, the beginning inventory is kept separate from the units started in February with the FIFO method, enabling the firm to compute separate unit costs for each month. The equivalent units with the FIFO method (42,000 and 39,800) relate to the February production results

Figure 4-7

SOUTHEASTERN CHEMICAL COMPANY
Equivalent Units of Production — FIFO Method
Month Ended February 28, 1987

	Equivalent Units		
	Raw Materials Cost	Direct Labor Cost	Manufacturing Overhead
40,000 gallons completed	40,000	40,000	40,000
Plus equivalent units in ending inventory of 10,000 gallons			
10,000 gallons × 100%	10,000		
10,000 gallons × 30%		3,000	3,000
Less equivalent units in beginning inventory of 8,000 gallons			
8,000 gallons × 100%	8,000		
8,000 gallons × 40%	_____	3,200	3,200
Equals equivalent units with FIFO method	42,000	39,800	39,800

only, whereas the equivalent units with the weighted-average method (50,000 gallons and 43,000 gallons) relate to units worked on in January and February. We will see how these differences in equivalent units of production affect the computation of unit costs next by considering cost of production reports with the two flow assumptions.

COST OF PRODUCTION REPORT — WEIGHTED-AVERAGE METHOD

A cost of production report prepared with the weighted-average method is shown in Figure 4-8. As the name suggests, the **weighted-average method** combines the costs assigned to the beginning work in process inventory with those incurred during the current period. At the same time, the units in the beginning work in process inventory are combined with those entered into production during the current period, as we saw in the previous section. In other words, there is no separate accounting for the costs and units in the beginning inventory versus those of the current period. Note that this treatment is essentially the same as what you observed when a merchandising firm used the weighted-average method in your financial accounting course. The following process costing steps are needed to prepare the cost of production report (the steps are numbered in color on the report):

Objective 9:
Use of cost of production reports with a beginning work in process inventory

Step 1. The Blending Department began the month of February with 8,000 gallons that were 40% converted. (Remember that all the raw materials were added in January.) 42,000 gallons were entered into production during the month, 40,000 gallons were completed, and 10,000 gallons were left in the ending work in process (30% converted). Note that 60% of the conversion process had not been performed on the beginning work in process inventory as of January 31 and must be accomplished during February to have products ready to be transferred out of the Blending Department.

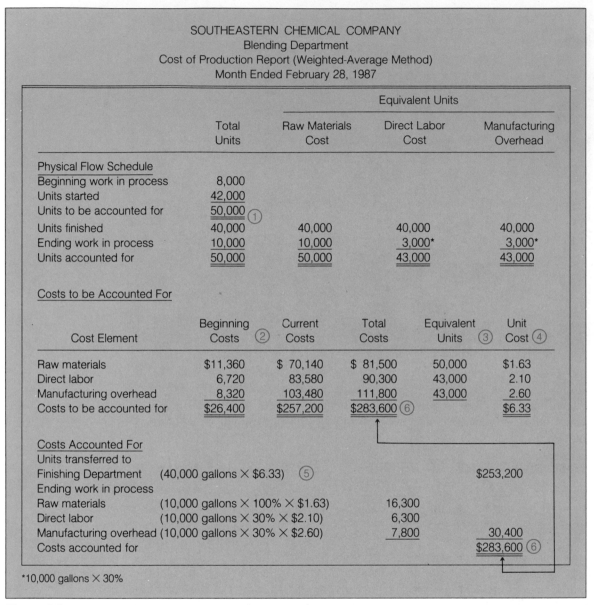

SOUTHEASTERN CHEMICAL COMPANY
Blending Department
Cost of Production Report (Weighted-Average Method)
Month Ended February 28, 1987

	Total Units	Equivalent Units		
		Raw Materials Cost	Direct Labor Cost	Manufacturing Overhead
Physical Flow Schedule				
Beginning work in process	8,000			
Units started	42,000			
Units to be accounted for	50,000 ①			
Units finished	40,000	40,000	40,000	40,000
Ending work in process	10,000	10,000	3,000*	3,000*
Units accounted for	50,000	50,000	43,000	43,000

Costs to be Accounted For

Cost Element	Beginning Costs ②	Current Costs	Total Costs	Equivalent Units ③	Unit Cost ④
Raw materials	$11,360	$ 70,140	$ 81,500	50,000	$1.63
Direct labor	6,720	83,580	90,300	43,000	2.10
Manufacturing overhead	8,320	103,480	111,800	43,000	2.60
Costs to be accounted for	$26,400	$257,200	$283,600 ⑥		$6.33

Costs Accounted For

Units transferred to			
Finishing Department	(40,000 gallons × $6.33) ⑤		$253,200
Ending work in process			
Raw materials	(10,000 gallons × 100% × $1.63)	16,300	
Direct labor	(10,000 gallons × 30% × $2.10)	6,300	
Manufacturing overhead	(10,000 gallons × 30% × $2.60)	7,800	30,400
Costs accounted for			$283,600 ⑥

*10,000 gallons × 30%

Figure 4-8

Step 2. The costs carried forward in the work in process inventory to February total $26,400, consisting of raw materials amounting to $11,360, direct labor of $6,720, and manufacturing overhead of $8,320. The costs assigned to each cost element must be kept separate because they will be added individually to the respective amounts incurred during February so unit costs can be computed for each cost element. The Blending Department recorded raw materials costs of $70,140, direct labor costs of $83,580, and manufacturing overhead of $103,480 with the process costing system in February. Consequently, the total costs to be accounted for in the Blending Department at the end of February are $283,600 (beginning inventory costs of $26,400 plus current costs of $257,200).

Step 3. Since the costs and units in the beginning work in process inventory are combined with those of the current period, the total equivalent units for each cost element are computed by adding the units completed in the processing center during February to the equivalent units in the ending work in process, as we saw in Figure 4-6. This means that the stage of completion of the beginning work in process is not important. It does not matter whether the completed units came from the group started during February or those carried forward from January. As a result, the equivalent units for raw materials, direct labor, and manufacturing overhead are 50,000 gallons, 43,000 gallons, and 43,000 gallons, respectively.

All 50,000 units are equivalent units in terms of raw materials because no more materials have to be added. However, only 3,000 equivalent units are in the ending work in process inventory in terms of direct labor and manufacturing overhead since the conversion process is only 30% finished on the average.

Step 4. Since the combined costs (beginning inventory plus current period) for each cost element and their equivalent units of production are now known, the unit costs can be calculated. By dividing the costs by the equivalent units, the results are unit costs of $1.63, $2.10, and $2.60 for raw materials, direct labor, and manufacturing overhead, respectively. Note that the unit cost for raw materials was higher in February than it was in January ($1.63 versus $1.42). Remember that the unit costs shown for February are averages, so the actual unit cost of raw materials incurred during that month must have been more than $1.63, as we will see when we consider the FIFO method.

Step 5. Once the unit costs are computed, the procedures used to allocate the total costs to be accounted for ($283,600) to the units finished and transferred from the Blending Department and to those left in the ending work in process inventory are the same as they were earlier without a beginning inventory. The $6.33 unit cost of each gallon is multiplied by the 40,000 gallons finished to obtain the total amount of $253,200 transferred from the department. The balance of the total costs accounted for of $30,400 is assigned to the ending work in process inventory, divided as $16,300 for raw materials, $6,300 for direct labor, and $7,800 for manufacturing overhead.

Step 6. The total costs to be accounted for by the Blending Department ($283,600) are equal to the total costs accounted for ($283,600). The process costing results with the weighted-average method are summarized in Figure 4-9.

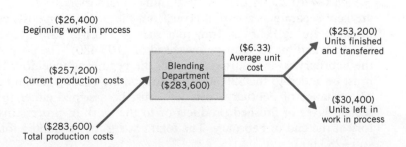

Figure 4-9
Summary of
Process Costing
Results with
Weighted-Average
Method

COST OF PRODUCTION REPORT—FIFO METHOD

As we noted earlier, the **FIFO method** keeps the accounting for the units in the beginning work in process separate from the units started during the month. This is accomplished by assigning the production costs to two layers of finished inventory and maintaining the identity of each layer until it is transferred to the next step in the process. The FIFO method is actually a modified FIFO application because only two cost categories are used, one for the beginning work in process inventory and one for the current production, regardless of how many different costs a firm may experience (e.g., various raw materials prices) during a period.

In addition, current production costs are combined with those of the beginning inventory to the extent necessary to complete the units in the beginning work in process inventory. For example, in the Blending Department of the Southeastern Chemical Company, February conversion costs are required to provide the 60% factor needed to complete the 8,000 units in the beginning work in process inventory. Figure 4-10 shows how the FIFO method is used in the preparation of a cost of production report (the following steps are numbered in color within the report).

Step 1. Tracing the physical flow with the FIFO method involves the same procedures followed with the weighted-average method, as shown in Figure 4-10. The Blending Department had 8,000 gallons in work in process on February 1, entered 42,000 gallons into production during February, completed 40,000 gallons, and was left with 10,000 gallons on February 28. However, we must now be concerned with the stage of completion for the beginning inventory since the units involved are accounted for as a separate layer.

Step 2. Two layers of finished inventory are accounted for with the FIFO method. The beginning work in process inventory is one layer to be finished, and the units started and completed during a period are a second layer. The units in the beginning work in process inventory are assumed to be completed and transferred first according to the FIFO flow. Keep in mind that the units assumed to be in the two layers may not actually be there because the FIFO method is a flow assumption used for costing purposes only. It does not necessarily reflect the actual movement of the units through the production process. Since the two layers are accounted for separately, equivalent units of production must be based on the *current period's production results.* Part of the current period's work will be directed toward completing the beginning unfinished units, and part will be for the units started during the period and either finished by the end of the period or left in the work in process inventory.

Figure 4-10 shows that the beginning inventory costs of $26,400 are kept separate as a partial layer from the production costs accumulated during February (raw materials of $70,140, direct labor of $83,580, and manufacturing overhead of $103,480). The portion of the February costs incurred to finish the beginning inventory layer must be added to the $26,400 to complete the costing of that layer. The balance of February costs left must be assigned either to the second layer of finished products or to the work in process inventory at the end of February. The total costs to be accounted for are still $283,600.

SOUTHEASTERN CHEMICAL COMPANY
Blending Department
Cost of Production Report (FIFO Method)
Month Ended February 28, 1987

	Total Units	Equivalent Units Raw Materials Cost	Equivalent Units Direct Labor Cost	Equivalent Units Manufacturing Overhead
Physical Flow Schedule				
Beginning work in process	8,000	(8,000)	(3,200)*	(3,200)*
Units started	42,000			
Units to be accounted for	50,000 ①			
Units finished	40,000	40,000	40,000	40,000
Ending work in process	10,000	10,000	3,000**	3,000**
Units accounted for	50,000	42,000	39,800	39,800

Costs To Be Accounted For

Cost Element	Amount of Cost	Equivalent Units	Unit Cost
Beginning work in process	$ 26,400		
Current cost elements	②	③	④
Raw materials	70,140	42,000	$1.67
Direct labor	83,580	39,800	2.10
Manufacturing overhead	103,480	39,800	2.60
Costs to be accounted for	$283,600 ⑥		$6.37

Costs Accounted For

Beginning inventory finished (8,000 gallons) ⑤			
Beginning work in process cost		$26,400	
Direct labor added	(8,000 gallons × 60% × $2.10)	10,080	
Manufacturing overhead added	(8,000 gallons × 60% × $2.60)	12,480	
Total cost of beginning inventory			48,960
Units started, finished, and transferred to Finishing Department	(32,000 gallons × $6.37)		203,840
Total cost of inventory finished			$252,800
Ending work in process inventory			
Raw materials	(10,000 gallons × 100% × $1.67)	16,700	
Direct labor	(10,000 gallons × 30% × $2.10)	6,300	
Manufacturing overhead	(10,000 gallons × 30% × $2.60)	7,800	30,800
Costs accounted for			$283,600 ⑥

*8,000 gallons × 40%
**10,000 gallons × 30%

Figure 4-10

Step 3. As mentioned earlier, the equivalent units with the FIFO method are those related to the current period's production results because the two layers of inventory must be kept separate. As we see in Figure 4-10 (and from the presentation of equivalent units with the FIFO method in Figure 4-7), the equivalent units for raw materials are 42,000 gallons and for the conversion costs 39,800 gallons. With the equivalent units for the month of February, the unit costs for the month can be computed and the portion of the costs incurred in February to complete the beginning inventory can be identified. The remainder of the February costs will be assigned to the second inventory layer or left in ending work in process. The computation of the equivalent units for February's production is based on the work performed on the beginning work in process inventory, the units started and finished, and the units started and left in ending work in process inventory.

Step 4. The equivalent units computed for February are divided into the costs for the month to determine the unit costs of $1.67 for raw materials, $2.10 for direct labor, and $2.60 for manufacturing overhead. The unit cost of producing one gallon of Aqua-bright in February is $6.37. The cost of the beginning work in process inventory was ignored in computing the unit costs in order to keep the two layers of inventory separate.

Step 5. In the allocation of the total costs to be accounted for ($283,600), the costs needed to complete layer one, the beginning work in process inventory, must be identified. The 8,000 gallons in the layer are completed in terms of raw materials but only 40% finished as to the conversion costs. Consequently, an additional 60% of the conversion process is needed to complete them. This means that equivalent units of 4,800 (8,000 gallons × 60%) are involved. The 4,800 equivalent units are multiplied by the unit costs computed in step 4 for direct labor ($2.10) and manufacturing overhead ($2.60) to find the conversion costs needed to complete the products in February. The result is additional costs of $10,080 for direct labor and $12,480 for manufacturing overhead. The total costs assigned to the first layer of finished inventory are $48,960 ($26,400 + $10,080 + $12,480).

Since 8,000 gallons of the 40,000 gallons finished have been accounted for, 32,000 gallons must have been started and finished during February as layer two. They are costed by multiplying 32,000 gallons by the unit cost of $6.37 for total costs of $203,840. The balance of the total costs to be accounted for ($283,600 − $48,960 − $203,840 = $30,800) is left in the ending work in process inventory.

Once again, the ending inventory is finished in terms of raw materials but will require additional conversion costs in March since it is only 30% through the process. The amount of raw materials in the ending inventory ($16,700) is calculated by multiplying 10,000 gallons times the unit cost of $1.67. The 3,000 equivalent units for the conversion costs (10,000 × 30%) are multiplied by the unit costs of $2.10 and $2.60 to determine the direct labor and manufacturing overhead in the ending inventory ($6,300 and $7,800, respectively).

Step 6. Once again, the total costs accounted for ($283,600) are equal to the total costs to be accounted for. The process costing application with FIFO is summarized schematically in Figure 4-11.

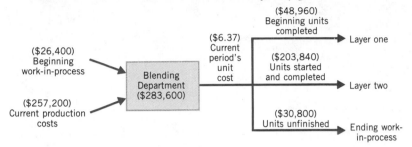

Figure 4-11
Summary of Process Costing Results with FIFO Method

COMPARISON OF THE RESULTS WITH THE WEIGHTED-AVERAGE AND FIFO METHODS

Figure 4-12 shows a comparison of several items computed earlier in Figures 4-8 and 4-10, which should help us understand the differences in process costing results with the weighted-average method and those with the FIFO method. Figure 4-12 shows that the cost of the units finished in the Blending Department is $253,200 with the weighted-average method and $252,800 with the FIFO method. The relatively small $400 difference between the two methods is the same amount (but in the opposite direction) for the ending work in process inventories because the amount with the weighted-average method is $30,400 compared to the $30,800 figure with the FIFO method. In both cases, the total costs accounted for are $283,600 so the difference in the two methods is the way the costs are assigned to finished units versus the ending work in process inventory.

For cost control purposes, the FIFO method is better than the weighted-average method because it enables management to evaluate changes in unit costs between periods. If the changes are significant, management will want to evaluate them for potential corrective action rather than having the differences obscured by the averaging process. If the changes are insignificant, the cost results with the weighted-average method will be essentially the same as those with the FIFO method. Although the FIFO method is more complex than the weighted-average method, computer applications are readily available to deal with the added calculations involved.

In Figure 4-12, we see that the total unit cost with the weighted-average method is $6.33, compared with $6.37 with the FIFO method. Note also that the unit costs for the direct labor cost and manufacturing overhead are the same with each method ($2.10 and $2.60). Since the average unit cost for each of the conversion costs is the same as the actual cost incurred in February, there must not have been any change in these unit costs from January to February. This can be confirmed by dividing the amount of direct labor cost included in the beginning inventory for February ($6,720) by the related equivalent units (8,000 gallons $\times$ 40% = 3,200 gallons), or a unit cost of $2.10. In addition, the amount of manufacturing overhead in the beginning inventory for February was $8,320, which also is divided by the 3,200 equivalent units for a unit cost of $2.60.

Figure 4-12

SOUTHEASTERN CHEMICAL COMPANY
Summary of Weighted-Average Method and FIFO Method Results

	Weighted-Average Method	FIFO Method
Unit cost – raw materials	$1.63	$1.67
Unit cost – direct labor	2.10	2.10
Unit cost – manufacturing overhead	2.60	2.60
Total unit cost	$6.33	$6.37
Total costs to be accounted for	$283,600	$283,600
Total costs accounted for	283,600	283,600
Cost of units finished and transferred	253,200	252,800
Cost of units left in ending inventory	30,400	30,800

Thus, the difference in the total unit cost for each gallon of Aqua-bright must have been caused by a change in the cost of raw materials from January to February. The unit cost of raw materials with the weighted-average method is $1.63, and the unit cost with the FIFO method is $1.67. Since the unit cost of raw materials in February is higher than the average between the raw materials costs in the beginning inventory and those incurred in February, the unit cost in February must be higher than that of January. This can be confirmed by comparing Figure 4-4 with Figure 4-10. In Figure 4-4, we see that the unit raw materials cost in January is $1.42, whereas Figure 4-10 indicates that the unit cost for raw materials in February is $1.67. Thus, the unit cost increased by $.25 from January to February. The same conclusion is drawn by comparing the unit cost for raw materials in February's beginning inventory with the $1.67 unit cost for the February production. The firm began the month with raw materials cost of $11,360 assigned to the 8,000 units in the beginning inventory, or a unit cost of $1.42 ($11,360/8,000).

The cost of production report prepared with the weighted-average method shown in Figure 4-8 does not disclose the monthly differences because they are averaged in the unit raw materials cost of $1.63. The average unit raw materials cost of $1.63 is the result of combining 8,000 gallons of beginning inventory with the 42,000 gallons started in February as follows:

8,000 gallons at a cost of $1.42 =	$11,360
42,000 gallons at a cost of $1.67 =	70,140
Total cost involved (a)	$81,500
Divided by the total units (b)	50,000
Weighted-average unit cost (a/b)	$ 1.63

When the FIFO method is used in Figure 4-10, the beginning inventory is costed at the $1.42 price and the units started and finished during the month are costed at the higher price of $1.67. In contrast, the total units finished (40,000) are costed at the $1.63 unit cost with the weighted-average method. As a result, the total cost of the 40,000 gallons finished is $400 higher with the weighted-average method than it is with the FIFO method, shown as follows:

Raw materials cost in finished units
   with the weighted-average method — 40,000 gallons × $1.63 = $65,200
Raw materials cost in finished units

with the FIFO method — 8,000 gallons × $1.42 = $11,360

plus

                   32,000 gallons × $1.67 = $53,440   64,800

Difference between the two methods $ 400

When unit costs are rising, we would expect higher finished inventory costs with the weighted-average method than with the FIFO method; more of the cost increases will be charged to the inventory finished and transferred with the weighted-average method than the FIFO method and less to the ending work in process inventory. Remember that the use of the FIFO method results in the latest (and in this case the highest) costs left in the ending inventory.

ACCOUNTING FOR MULTIPLE PROCESSING CENTERS

We noted earlier that the physical flow of production and related costs may become complicated when a firm operates multiple processing centers, organized on a sequential or parallel basis. This situation does not introduce any special accounting problems other than the need to recognize that the output of one processing center is the input of the next center, both in terms of the units transferred and the production costs associated with the units.

Objective 10: Treatment of costs from a preceding department

The costing process is *cumulative* since the costs transferred into a particular center are the production costs recorded in *all* preceding centers. When the last center in the production process finishes its work, the total costs accumulated in all processing centers are charged to finished goods inventory. A cost of production report is prepared for each processing center when multiple centers are used. A separate category is added to the costs to be accounted for section and costs accounted for section whenever costs are transferred in from other departments.

The category, called **"transferred in costs"** or **"previous department costs,"** consists of the raw materials, direct labor, and manufacturing overhead assigned in all preceding departments. In essence, think of it as being like a raw materials cost that is usually added at the beginning of the process for the computation of equivalent units and unit costs in the processing center receiving the transferred products.

To illustrate how transferred in costs are accounted for, let's continue to use the Southeastern Chemical Company case by considering the February production performance of the second processing center, the Finishing Department. Remember that the Finishing Department is *sequentially dependent* on the production output of the Blending Department. Thus, we must look at the units finished in the Blending Department and transferred to the Finishing Department to determine the units started in the second department.

Referring to either Figure 4-8 or Figure 4-10, we see that 40,000 gallons of Aqua-bright were transferred from the Blending Department to the Finishing Department during February. However, we must know which flow assumption was used by the Blending Department to determine the costs associated with the transfer of products. Figure 4-8, which contains a cost of production report prepared with the weighted-average method, indicates that a total cost of $253,200 was assigned to the units transferred. When the FIFO method was used in Figure 4-10, $252,800 was the amount of cost transferred to the Finishing Department. We assume in this illustration that the weighted-average method was used, so the relevant transferred in costs figure for the Finishing Department is $253,200.

To mainly concentrate on the accounting steps required for the transferred in costs in the Finishing Department illustration, we further assume that the department had no beginning inventory for February so we do not have to consider the flow assumption issue again. A cost of production report prepared for the Finishing Department's February performance should show the costs incurred by that department during the month as well as those transferred in from the Blending Department. The February production performance of the Finishing Department involved the following facts:

February Processing Data

Units started	40,000 gallons
Units finished	38,000 gallons
Units in ending inventory	
(50% finished as to the conversion process)	2,000 gallons
Raw materials cost	$ 30,400
Direct labor cost	46,800
Manufacturing overhead	56,160
Costs transferred in from the	
Blending Department	253,200
Total cost to be accounted for	$386,560

Raw materials are added in the Finishing Department at the end of the process.

The cost of production report presented in Figure 4-13 summarizes the Finishing Department's February performance. Note that the transferred in costs are the only addition to the report from others we have considered. These transferred in costs simply represent another cost category for which the Finishing Department must account. The cost of production report shown in Figure 4-13 is prepared with the following steps (the steps are numbered in color within the report):

Step 1. The Finishing Department began the month of February with no beginning work in process inventory, started the 40,000 gallons transferred in from the Blending Department, finished 38,000 gallons during the month, and had 2,000 gallons left in the ending work in process inventory—50% completed as to the conversion process. Thus, all 40,000 gallons to be accounted for have been accounted for.

Step 2. During February, the Finishing Department incurred raw materials cost amounting to $30,400, direct labor cost of $46,800, and manufacturing overhead of $56,160. In addition, the department must account for the transferred in costs of $253,200. Consequently, the total costs to be accounted for are $386,560 ($30,400 + $46,800 + $56,160 + $253,200).

Step 3. All 40,000 gallons transferred into the Finishing Department are equivalent units for the transferred in costs because they are complete in terms of the Blending Department's work. Since the raw materials are added at the end of the process in the Finishing Department, none are in the ending work in process inventory (it is not at that point yet since it is only 50% finished) and the equivalent units are equal to those physically finished, or 38,000. Because the ending inventory is 50% completed, the 2,000 gallons must be converted to 1,000 equivalent units for the conversion costs; the total equivalent units for direct labor and manufacturing overhead

SOUTHEASTERN CHEMICAL COMPANY
Finishing Department
Cost of Production Report
Month Ended February 28, 1987

	Total Units	Equivalent Units			
		Raw Materials Cost	Direct Labor Cost	Manufacturing Overhead	Transferred in
Physical Flow Schedule					
Beginning work in process	–0–				
Units started	40,000				
Units to be accounted for	40,000 ①				
Units finished	38,000	38,000	38,000	38,000	38,000
Ending work in process	2,000	–0–*	1,000**	1,000**	2,000***
Units accounted for	40,000	38,000	39,000	39,000	40,000

Costs to be Accounted For

Cost Element	Beginning Costs	Current Costs ②	Total Costs	Equivalent Units ③	Unit Cost ④
Transferred in costs	$ –0–	$253,200	$253,200	40,000	$6.33
Raw materials	–0–	30,400	30,400	38,000	.80
Direct labor	–0–	46,800	46,800	39,000	1.20
Manufacturing overhead	–0–	56,160	56,160	39,000	1.44
Costs to be accounted for	$ –0–	$386,560	$386,560 ⑥		$9.77

Costs Accounted For

Units transferred to finished goods (38,000 gallons × $9.77) ⑤			$371,260
Ending work in process			
Transferred in costs	(2,000 gallons × 100% × $6.33)	12,660	
Raw materials	(2,000 gallons × 0% × $.80)	–0–	
Direct labor	(2,000 gallons × 50% × $1.20)	1,200	
Manufacturing overhead	(2,000 gallons × 50% × $1.44)	1,440	15,300
Costs accounted for			$386,560 ⑥

*2,000 gallons × 0%
**2,000 gallons × 50%
***2,000 gallons × 100%

Figure 4-13

are 39,000 (38,000 gallons finished + 1,000 equivalent units in the ending inventory).

Step 4. The total unit cost required to complete one gallon of Aqua-bright in the Blending Department and the Finishing Department is $9.77, consisting of:

Blending Department costs transferred to Finishing Department	$6.33
Raw materials added in the Finishing Department	.80
Direct labor incurred by the Finishing Department	1.20
Manufacturing overhead applied in the Finishing Department	1.44
Total unit cost for one gallon of Aqua-bright	$9.77

Each of the unit costs is computed by dividing the costs accumulated in step 2 by the equivalent units determined in step 3. Since the Finishing Department is the final stage of the production process, the $9.77 unit cost is used to transfer the completed products to the finished goods inventory.

Step 5. The Finishing Department completed 38,000 gallons of Aquabright during February so costs of $371,260 (38,000 gallons × $9.77) are transferred out of the department and into finished goods inventory. The difference between the costs to be accounted for ($386,560) and the cost of the finished units ($371,260), or $15,300, is left in the work in process inventory at the end of February. The $15,300 consists of three cost elements: transferred in costs of $12,660 (2,000 gallons × $6.33), direct labor of $1,200 (2,000 gallons × 50% × $1.20), and manufacturing overhead of $1,440 (2,000 gallons × 50% × $1.44). No raw materials cost is included in the ending work in process inventory, which is only at the 50% point of completion. The total cost of the units transferred from the Finishing Department to finished goods inventory and those left in the ending work in process of the Finishing Department is $386,560 ($371,260 + $15,300).

Step 6. The total costs to be accounted for ($386,560) in the Finishing Department are equal to the total costs accounted for ($386,560).

JOURNAL ENTRIES FOR PROCESS COSTING

Objective 11: Preparing journal entries for process costing

Journal entries are required to record the production cost flows with process costing just like they were with job order costing. They are used to accumulate costs within each processing center and to transfer cumulative costs between centers. A separate Work in Process Inventory account is established for each center. This account is debited for all costs to be accounted for in the center as production takes place. When the center has completed its work, the products are transferred to the next step in the process and the costs accumulated to that point are debited to the next center's Work in Process Inventory account or to the Finished Goods Inventory account if the last center is involved. The same amount of costs is credited to the transferring center's Work in Process Inventory account.

The required journal entries can be summarized by considering those needed by the Southeastern Chemical Company in February to record the costs incurred in the two processing centers, to transfer the products from the Blending Department to the Finishing Department, to transfer the completed products to finished goods inventory, and to record the sales for the month. We assume that the weighted-average method was used in the Blending Department (Figure 4-8) for this illustration (as well as in the Finishing Department from Figure 4-13). In addition, assume that the Southeastern Chemical Company sold 36,000 gallons at a selling price of $13.50, for total sales of $486,000 during February.

The journal entries needed to record the February performances of the Blending Department and the Finishing Department are shown next.

Feb.	28	Work in Process – Blending Dept.	257,200		
		Raw Materials		70,140	
		Accrued Manufacturing Payroll		83,580	
		Manufacturing Overhead		103,480	
		(Record the production costs incurred in the Blending Dept. during February. See Figure 4-8.)			
		Work in Process – Finishing Dept.	253,200		
		Work in Process – Blending Dept.		253,200	
		(Record the total costs of the 40,000 gallons transferred to the Finishing Dept. See Figures 4-8 and 4-13.)			
		Work in Process – Finishing Dept.	133,360		
		Raw Materials		30,400	
		Accrued Manufacturing Payroll		46,800	
		Manufacturing Overhead		56,160	
		(Record the production costs incurred in the Finishing Dept. during February. See Figure 4-13.)			
		Finished Goods Inventory	371,260		
		Work in Process – Finishing Dept.		371,260	
		(Record the total costs of 38,000 gallons transferred to Finished Goods. See Figure 4-13.)			
		Accounts Receivable	486,000*		
		Sales		486,000	
		Cost of Goods Sold	351,720**		
		Finished Goods Inventory		351,720	
		(Record the sale of 36,000 gallons of Aquabright.)			
		* (36,000 gallons × $13.50)			
		** (36,000 gallons × $9.77)			

COMPARISON OF JOB ORDER COSTING AND PROCESS COSTING

In the discussion of product costing, we have described many characteristics of job order costing and process costing. In some ways, the two methods are similar while in many other ways they are different. Figure 4-14 shows a comparison of the most important characteristics of job order costing and process costing.

Objective 12: Comparing job order costing with process costing

Figure 4-14
Comparison of Job Order Costing and Process Costing

Characteristic	Job Order Costing	Process Costing
Basic purpose	Accumulate manufacturing costs	Same as job order costing
Cost flows	Raw materials to work in process to finished goods to cost of goods sold	Same as job order costing
Type of production	Heterogeneous	Homogeneous
Examples of firms using the method	Furniture, heavy equipment, printing, and construction	Chemical, oil, flour, plastics, and paint
Focal point	Job	Processing center
Control document	Job order cost sheet	Cost of production report
Reporting period	Life of a job	Time period such as a month
Unit cost computation	By job	By processing center
Flow of products	Separated by jobs	Continuous
Product requirements	Different for each job	Same for all products
Measurement of output	Number of jobs produced	Equivalent units of production
Direct versus indirect costs	Separation based on jobs as cost objectives	Direct as to the processing centers only
Manufacturing costs to be reported	All costs incurred for a job	All costs incurred for a processing center
Recordkeeping required	Very detailed because of job accounting	Less detailed than job order costing

SUMMARY

A process costing system is used by a manufacturing firm that has a continuous production flow and homogeneous products. Industries that produce chemicals, rubber, plastics, wine, petroleum, small electronics, and pharmaceuticals utilize process costing. Many nonmanufacturing firms also rely on process costing concepts and procedures to accumulate the costs incurred in performing activities, such as food preparation in a fast-food restaurant.

The focal point of process costing is the processing center(s) in which the work is performed during a specified period of time. The recordkeeping required is less detailed than it is in job order costing because the costs assigned to a processing center are not reassigned to individual products as jobs. Direct materials, direct labor, and manufacturing overhead are charged to a Work in Process Inventory account established for each processing center with procedures similar to those used in job order costing but without the detail of job accounting.

When multiple processing centers are used, the relationships between the centers must be clearly defined to accurately accumulate the production costs as they flow through the centers to finished goods inventory. The processing centers are organized on the basis of a sequential product flow or a parallel product flow. Production costs accumulated in each processing center are transferred along with the related products to the next center that will work on the products.

Unit costs are computed in each center by dividing the total costs of the center for a specified period by the center's production output for the same period. Computing these unit costs is complicated by beginning and ending work in process inventories, different timing of the various manufacturing cost elements, and the presence of multiple processing centers. Equivalent units of production are used to convert partially finished units into the number of completed units that would have been produced if all the work had been performed on completed units.

The control document used in a process costing system is called a cost of production report. It provides management with a complete description of the cost performance and production activity of a processing center during a particular time period, usually a month. A cost of production report shows:

1. An accounting of the production units for which a processing center is responsible.
2. The total costs assigned to the units.
3. The equivalent units of production.
4. The unit costs involved.
5. An allocation of the total costs to be accounted for to either products finished in that center or left in ending work in process.

When a beginning work in process inventory exists, a flow assumption is needed to determine which costs are to be assigned to the finished units of a period and which are to be left in the ending work in process inventory. The two most popular flow assumptions for process costing are the weighted-average method, which combines the beginning work in process inventory with the current production results, and the FIFO method, which keeps the two separate. Whenever multiple processing centers are involved, an added cost category is needed to account for the costs transferred into a particular center.

GLOSSARY

AVERAGE UNIT COST.   The unit cost determined in a process costing system by dividing the costs of a processing center for a specific time period by the center's production output for that period (p. 104).

COST OF PRODUCTION REPORT.   The control document used in a process costing system to account for the production activity and the related costs in a processing center during a specified time period (p. 108).

EQUIVALENT UNITS OF PRODUCTION.   A measure of how many whole units of production are represented by the units finished plus the units partially completed (p. 105).

FIFO METHOD.   The flow assumption used in process costing that accounts for the beginning work in process inventory separately from the products entered into production during the period (p. 112).

PARALLEL PRODUCT FLOW.   The arrangement of multiple processing centers in which certain phases of the work are performed concurrently and then are combined for further processing or completion (p. 103).

PROCESS COSTING SYSTEM.   A product costing system used when a firm produces homogeneous units with a continuous production flow (p. 100).

PROCESSING CENTER.   A segment of a manufacturing firm in which homogeneous units are produced and process costing is used to account for the manufacturing costs incurred (p. 101).

SEQUENTIAL PRODUCT FLOW.   A product flow in which production starts in the first processing center and flows through every processing center with each succeeding center being dependent on the preceding work perform-ance (p. 102).

TRANSFERRED IN COSTS (PREVIOUS DEPARTMENT COSTS). The total production costs transferred into a particular processing center that have been required in all preceding centers to produce the related products (p. 123).

WEIGHTED-AVERAGE METHOD. The flow assumption used in process costing that combines the costs and units in the beginning work in process inventory with those of the current period (p. 112).

DISCUSSION QUESTIONS

1. Why would a manufacturing firm operate a continuous production flow in producing its products?
2. How does a process costing system compare with a job order costing system?
3. What type of manufacturing firm is likely to use process costing? Give some examples.
4. What kind of nonmanufacturing firm will use a process costing approach in determining the cost of a particular activity? Give some examples.
5. What is the focal point in process costing?
6. Are the accounting procedures required with process costing usually more or less detailed than those used with job order costing?
7. Explain the basic differences in the orientation of the costing procedures required with process costing and those used in job order costing.
8. Compare and contrast the use of sequential and parallel product flows in the operation of a process costing system.
9. What is meant by the average unit cost in process costing? What are the major problems encountered in the calculation of an average unit cost?
10. What are equivalent units and why are they necessary with process costing?
11. Becker Company began the period with no beginning work in process inventory, started producing 112,500 units, and had 15,000 units in ending work in process inventory that were one-fourth finished in terms of conversion costs. How many equivalent units were involved for the conversion costs that are incurred uniformly throughout the process? Assume that raw materials are added at the beginning of the production process. How many equivalent units are involved for raw materials? Assume instead that the raw materials are added at the end of the process. How many equivalent units are involved?
12. What is the role of a cost of production report? What are the three major sections of such a report?
13. Distinguish between the costs to be accounted for and the costs accounted for in a process costing application.
14. What are the major steps followed in the preparation of a cost of production report?
15. How is the cost of the ending work in process inventory computed in a cost of production report?
16. Why should we distinguish between transferred in costs and those associated with raw materials added in a particular processing center?
17. Compare and contrast the use of the weighted-average method and the

FIFO method in dealing with beginning work in process inventories in a process costing application.

18. The Flow-through Company operates a process costing system. At the beginning of March, the firm had 2,000 units in the beginning work in process inventory that were 40% completed for conversion costs. During the month, 10,500 units were started, and 2,500 units were left in process at the end of the month, 50% completed for conversion costs. How many equivalent units were involved for the month if the weighted-average method is used? If the FIFO method is used?

EXERCISES

Exercise 4-1 Computing Equivalent Units of Production
A manufacturing firm producing rubber soled shoes uses a process costing system to accumulate costs during the production operation. In the Stamping Department, during February, 1987, 63,000 units were started. Of these 63,000 units, 60,000 were completed and transferred to the Finishing Department. Those units not completed were 100% finished in terms of raw materials (rubber) and 75% finished as to conversion costs. No units were included in inventory in the Stamping Department at the beginning of February.

Required:
Compute the number of equivalent units of production in the Stamping Department during February for:

1. Raw materials
2. Conversion costs

Exercise 4-2 Calculating Equivalent Units of Production
The CEW Company manufactures several products using three departments. Raw materials are added at the beginning of Department 1's process. Manufacturing overhead and direct labor are incurred evenly throughout the manufacturing process. During March, Department 1 incurred the following costs:

Raw materials	$ 75,000
Direct labor	194,000
Applied manufacturing overhead	436,500

100,000 units were started during the month (no beginning inventory) in Department 1. 90,000 were completed and transferred to Department 2. Unfinished units were 100% complete in terms of raw materials and 70% complete in terms of direct labor and manufacturing overhead.

Required:
A. Calculate equivalent units of production for:
  1. Raw materials
  2. Direct labor
  3. Manufacturing overhead
B. Calculate the unit cost for:
  1. Raw materials
  2. Direct labor
  3. Manufacturing overhead
C. What is the total unit cost for any unit completed during March in Department 1?

Exercise 4-3 Equivalent Units with a Beginning Inventory

The Adjustomatic Company produces a product that must go through two departments, X and Y. Data for Department X are shown below:

		% Complete	
	Units	**Direct Materials**	**Conversion Costs**
Work in process, 4/1/87	6,000	100%	70%
Started during April	134,000		
Work in process, 4/30/87	8,000	90%	60%

Required:

Using the weighted-average method, determine the equivalent units of production for:

1. Direct materials
2. Conversion costs

Exercise 4-4 Equivalent Units with a Beginning Inventory

The Frazier Company uses a process costing system. Selected data from Department 2 for the month of June are listed below:

Beginning inventory	7,000 units
Received from Department 1	50,000 units
Ending inventory	2,000 units

The beginning inventory contained 100% of the raw materials, as did the ending inventory. The beginning inventory was 75% completed as to the conversion costs. The units remaining at the end of the month were 30% completed as to the conversion costs.

Required:

A. What were the equivalent units of production for June in terms of raw materials and conversion costs with:
   1. Weighted-average method
   2. FIFO method
B. Why are the equivalent units different with the two methods?

Exercise 4-5 Computing Unit Costs with Process Costing

Refer to Exercise 4-4.

The following costs were incurred by the Frazier Company during June:

Raw materials cost	$170,000
Manufacturing overhead cost	151,050
Direct labor	75,525

Required:

Calculate the following using the FIFO method:

A. Unit costs for each manufacturing cost element.
B. Total unit cost assigned for each product during the month of June.

Exercise 4-6 Process Costing versus Job Order Costing

For each of the following types of business, indicate which would be more appropriate — job order costing or process costing:

1. Custom welding shop
2. Manufacturing of radial tires
3. Tractor manufacturer
4. Producer of soft drinks

5. Fast food restaurant
6. Mail-order seed company
7. Prefabricated homes
8. Weapons manufacturer
9. A tailor
10. A caterer

Exercise 4-7 Computing Equivalent Units

Below are process costing flow data for four independent situations:

	Situation			
	A	**B**	**C**	**D**
Beginning inventory	–0–	6,400	26,000	2,000
Percentage complete	—	25	50	70
Units transferred in	12,000	38,400	104,000	30,000
Ending inventory	4,000	–0–	20,800	5,000
Percentage complete	40	—	20	70

Required:
A. Compute the equivalent units of production for each of the above situations, assuming a FIFO basis.
B. Compute the equivalent units of production for each of the above situations, assuming a weighted-average basis.

Exercise 4-8 Computing Equivalent Units

The following data show the activity from a processing center of the Parrot Company for the month of June:

		% Completed	
	Units	**Materials**	**Conversion Costs**
Work in process inventory, 6/1	20,000	75	50
Work in process inventory, 6/30	30,000	50	10

This processing center entered 60,000 units into production during the month and transferred 50,000 completed units to finished goods.

Required:
A. Compute the equivalent units of production for June, assuming the FIFO method of accounting for units and costs.
B. Compute the equivalent units of production for June, assuming the weighted-average method of accounting for units and costs.

Exercise 4-9 Cost of Production Report—No Beginning Inventory

The Kleenmore Company manufactures paint thinner, which is sold by the gallon. Below are October cost data for the firm's first production process.

Beginning work in process inventory	–0–
Units started during October	104,000
Materials cost	$338,000
Direct labor cost	444,600
Manufacturing overhead cost	140,400
Ending work in process inventory	20,800 units (all materials, 50% conversion)

Required:
Prepare a cost of production report for October.

Exercise 4-10 Preparing a Basic Cost of Production Report

The Sellew Company manufactures carbonated mineral water that is sold in large drums. The following data pertain to the 1987 production performance of Department 1, in which minerals are added:

Work in process, 1/1/87	–0–
Drums started	25,000
Units completed & transferred	21,000
Raw materials cost	$25,000
Direct labor cost	49,600
Manufacturing overhead cost	74,400

Ending inventory is 95% complete in terms of labor and overhead; 100% complete in terms of raw materials.

Required:

Prepare a cost of production report for Department 1's 1987 performance.

Exercise 4-11 Preparing a Basic Cost of Production Report

Mugsy, Inc. produces vinyl covers for pocket calculators. The covers are produced in three departments. Below are data for Department A's operation:

Units started	37,000
Direct materials cost	$37,000
Direct labor cost	3,660
Applied manufacturing overhead	5,490
Beginning work in process	–0–

The ending work in process consists of 2,000 units with 80% conversion costs and 100% materials.

Required:

Prepare a cost of production report for Department A.

Exercise 4-12 Process Costing Flows

The Bronco Company produces a product that passes through two processing centers, Baking and Shaping. The following T-accounts show the flow of costs through the two processing centers for February:

Work in Process–Baking

Bal. 2/1	16,000	Transferred to Shaping	
Direct materials	57,600	Department	240,000
Direct labor	64,000		
Manufacturing overhead	128,000		

Work in Process–Shaping

Bal. 2/1	9,600	Transferred to finished	
Transferred in	240,000	goods	392,000
Direct labor	51,200		
Manufacturing overhead	102,400		

Required:

Prepare journal entries to record the flow of costs through the two processing centers during February.

PROBLEMS

Problem 4-1   Equivalent Unit Computations

The Ade Company produces one product in a continuous flow process that goes through two departments. All materials are added in Department One at the beginning of the process. The following data are available for July:

	Units
Work in process on July 1 (40% complete as to conversion costs)	800
Units started	3,200
Transferred to Department Two	3,360
Work in process on July 31 (25% complete as to conversion costs)	640

Required:
Compute the equivalent units of production for July, using the

1. FIFO method
2. Weighted-average method

Problem 4-2   Process Costing Flows and Journal Entries

The Johnson Company manufactures a small engine on an assembly line and uses a process costing system. Inventories at the beginning of the year were as follows:

Raw materials	$ 51,000
Work in process	100,500
Finished goods	187,500

Manufacturing overhead is applied at the rate of $12 per direct labor hour. The following transactions took place during the year:

1. Material purchases were $429,000.
2. Direct labor of $433,500 was incurred, based on 52,500 direct labor hours.
3. Additional costs incurred for production were:

Raw materials	$406,500
Utilities	69,000
Depreciation	108,000
Supervisory and other salaries	273,000
Other manufacturing overhead	203,250

4. Finished inventory transferred from work in process to finished goods amounted to $1,294,500.
5. Sales were $1,971,000 with a cost of goods sold of $1,227,000.

Required:
A. Prepare journal entries to record the above transactions.
B. Determine the ending balances in each inventory account, assuming a FIFO flow.

Problem 4-3   Process Costing Procedures

The Softskin Company manufactures body lotion and utilizes a process cost accounting system. The lotion is produced in the Blending Department and then is transferred to the Bottling Department. The company assigns overhead using the relationship between direct labor cost and manufacturing overhead cost. The firm's budget for 1987 showed that manufacturing overhead should be 1.6 times as much as direct labor cost. The inventory balances as of August 1, 1987 were:

Raw materials	$40,000
Work in process – Blending	64,000
Work in process – Bottling	48,000
Finished Goods	30,400

During August, the following transactions took place:

1. Raw materials requisitioned to Blending – $72,000
   Raw materials requisitioned to Bottling – $56,000
2. Direct labor costs incurred by Blending – $67,200
   Direct labor costs incurred by Bottling – $49,600
3. Other production expenses for August were:

Rent	$24,000
Supplies	19,200
Utilities	33,600
Depreciation	84,800
Repairs	22,400

4. Inventory with an assigned cost of $280,000 was transferred from Blending to Bottling.
5. Inventory with an assigned cost of $480,000 was transferred from Bottling to finished goods.
6. Finished goods with an assigned cost of $304,000 were sold for $364,800.
7. Raw materials purchased were $112,000.
8. Manufacturing overhead was applied in each department.

Required:
A. Prepare journal entries to record the August transactions. Use a single Manufacturing Overhead account and assume all expenses were paid when incurred (except depreciation).
B. Calculate the ending work in process inventory balances in each department.
C. Was overhead underapplied or overapplied in August?

Problem 4-4 Calculating Equivalent Units of Production
Calculate the equivalent units for each of the following independent departments using (1) the weighted-average method and (2) the FIFO method:

	Department			
	1	**2**	**3**	**4**
Beginning work in process	4,000	–0–	10,000	4,000
% complete – materials	100	100	100	30
% complete – conversion	20	50	30	70
Units completed	20,000	40,000	90,000	75,000
Ending work in process	5,000	12,000	3,000	4,000
% complete – materials	100	100	100	100
% complete – conversion	30	40	20	50

Problem 4-5 Determining Equivalent Units
A summary of the physical flow of products through three processing centers for a given month is shown below:

Center 1
Beginning Inventory: 2,000 units – all materials, 70% conversion costs
Units Started: 10,000
Ending Inventory: 1,000 units – all materials, 80% conversion costs

Center 2
Beginning Inventory: 6,500 units – all materials, 80% conversion costs
Units Started: 12,000
Ending Inventory: 2,500 units – 40% materials, 75% conversion costs
Center 3
Beginning Inventory: 3,000 units – 4/6 materials, 2/6 conversion costs
Units Started: 62,000
Ending Inventory: 7,000 units – 2/5 materials, 3/5 conversion costs

Required:
Calculate the number of equivalent units of production in each center for the month using:

1. Weighted-average method
2. FIFO method

Problem 4-6 Process Costing with No Beginning Inventory
The Knox Company manufactures window glass and uses a process costing system to accumulate product costs. The data below were recorded in the final department involved in the process, Department C.

1. Beginning work in process: none.
2. Units transferred in from Department B – 10,000 (cost = $22,000).
3. Materials used during the period – $27,000.
4. Direct labor cost for the month – $17,000.
5. Manufacturing overhead applied during the month – $44,200.
6. Ending work in process: 3,000 units all materials, 50% conversion costs.

Required:
Prepare a cost of production report for Department C.

Problem 4-7 Cost of Production Report with Weighted-Average Method
The DCM Company produces a special type of diesel fuel conditioner used in large trucks. This fuel conditioner is produced sequentially in three departments. The following production data pertain to the third and final department:

1. Beginning inventory: 12,000 gallons, 4/5 finished as to direct materials and 1/5 finished as to conversions costs.
2. Beginning inventory cost: preceding departments – $6,000; direct materials – $960; direct labor – $288; manufacturing overhead – $720.
3. Units received from Department 2: 20,000 gallons costing $10,000.
4. Direct materials used in Department 3 during current period – $2,240.
5. Direct labor recorded in Department 3 during current period – $3,492.
6. Manufacturing overhead applied in Department 3 during current period – $8,730.
7. Ending work in process: 2,000 gallons, all materials included and 75% of the conversion costs.

Required:
Prepare a cost of production report for Department 3. Use the weighted-average method.

Problem 4-8 Cost of Production Report with Beginning Inventory
The Timely Corporation manufactures a digital stopwatch, which is manufactured in a continuous process system. The firm's accounting records show the following work in process inventory as of December 31:

	Units	Costs
Work in process (50% complete as to labor and overhead)	600,000	$1,544,000

The cost of the ending inventory consists of raw materials ($520,000), direct labor ($640,000), and manufacturing overhead ($384,000).

Materials are added to production at the beginning of the manufacturing process and manufacturing overhead is applied to each product at the rate of 60% of direct labor costs. There was no finished goods inventory at the beginning of the year.

A review of the firm's inventory cost records disclosed the following information:

		Costs	
	Units	Materials	Labor
Work in process, January 1 (80% complete as to labor and overhead)	400,000	$280,000	$640,000

Units started in production during the year totaled 2 million and costs incurred were materials cost of $2,600,000 and direct labor cost of $3,560,000. Units completed during the year totaled 1,800,000.

Required:
A. Prepare a cost of production report for the year using the weighted-average method.
B. Repeat (A) above using the FIFO cost method.
C. Explain any difference in unit costs between the two methods.

Problem 4-9 Process Costing with Beginning Inventory
The Daly Company manufactures products with a continuous flow process. Below are June data for the Assembly Department, which is the third phase of a four-phase operation.

	Units	Conversion Costs
Work in process at June 1	40,000	$ 35,200
Units started and costs incurred during June	216,000	$228,800
Units completed and transferred to next department during June	160,000	

Conversion costs for the Assembly Department were 80% complete as to beginning work in process and 50% complete as to ending work in process. The company uses the FIFO cost method.

Required:
A. What were the conversion costs in the work in process inventory in the Assembly Department at June 30?
B. Calculate the conversion costs per equivalent unit of production for April and June.
C. Assuming the weighted-average method is used, what is the per-unit conversion cost for June?

Problem 4-10 Process Costing with Beginning Inventory
The Green Gravy Company manufactures gravy using three sequential processes: Blending, Cooking, and Packaging. Materials are added continuously in the Blending Department and at the beginning of the Packaging Department. All conversion costs are incurred continuously.

The beginning inventory costs for November are:

	Blending	Cooking	Packaging
Costs from previous department	—	$79,680	$146,880
Raw materials	$15,360	—	16,320
Conversion costs	11,200	9,600	4,352
Total costs	$26,560	$89,280	$167,552

The production costs for November are:

	Blending	Cooking	Packaging
Raw materials	$251,520	—	$65,280
Conversion costs	183,400	$130,900	99,328

Production data in gallons are:

	Beginning Inventory	% Complete	Ending Inventory	% Complete	Gallons Completed and Transferred
Blending	32,000	20	24,000	30	104,000
Cooking	19,200	40	14,400	25	?
Packaging	27,200	20	12,800	50	?

Required:
A. Calculate the unit cost of the gallons completed in each of the three processes using the weighted-average method.
B. Prepare a cost of production report for the November operating performance of the Blending Department (weighted-average method).

Problem 4-11 Calculating Unit Costs with Process Costing

The Morgan Company produces gold products in three sequential processes: Cutting, Molding, and Packaging. Materials are added at two points—at the beginning of the Cutting process and at the end of the Packaging process. At the end of the month, 9,600 units were transferred to finished goods.

Production data in units are as follows:

	Beginning Inventory	% Complete	Units Started	Ending Inventory	% Complete
Cutting	4,800	30	17,600	6,400	25
Molding	2,400	40	?	5,600	20
Packaging	?	30	?	3,520	30

Beginning inventory costs are:

	Cutting	Molding	Packaging
Previous department	—	$27,840	$4,272
Materials	$40,800	—	—
Conversion costs	4,464	1,680	192
Totals	$45,264	$29,520	$4,464

Production costs incurred during the month are:

	Cutting	Molding	Packaging
Materials	$149,600	—	$14,400
Conversion costs	50,096	22,680	21,120

Required:
Calculate the unit cost of production for each process, using the weighted-average method.

Problem 4-12 Process Costing with Two Departments
The Lawnkeep Company produces liquid chemicals and uses a process costing system to accumulate product costs. Two departments operate sequentially to produce the chemicals. The following data have been collected for the firm's July operating performance:

Department 1
Beginning inventory: 1,500 units – all materials, 40% completed as to conversion costs
Costs assigned to beginning inventory:
  Raw materials $2,825
  Conversion costs   3,060
During the month, 8,000 units were started
Ending inventory: 1,000 units – all materials, 80% completed as to conversion costs
Costs recorded during July:
  Raw materials $17,600
  Conversion costs   44,370

Department 2
Beginning inventory: 2,000 units – all materials, 70% completed as to conversion costs
Costs assigned to beginning inventory:
  Previous department costs $14,500
  Raw materials   4,800
  Conversion costs   1,520
Ending inventory: 600 units – all materials, 50% completed as to conversion costs
Costs recorded during July:
  Previous department costs   ?
  Raw materials $20,400
  Conversion costs   35,200

Required:
A. Prepare a cost of production report for Department 1 using the
   1. Weighted-average method
   2. FIFO method
B. Explain any unit cost differences between the two methods.
C. Prepare a cost of production report for Department 2 assuming the weighted-average method is used in both departments.

5

COST BEHAVIOR AND CONTRIBUTION MARGIN REPORTING

CHAPTER OVERVIEW AND OBJECTIVES

This chapter describes the essential features of cost behavior and its impact on a firm's income statement. After studying this chapter, you should be able to:

1. Recognize the limitations of a functional income statement for managerial use.
2. Develop an income statement with a contribution margin format.
3. Explain the meaning of a cost function.
4. Identify the cost functions involved with variable costs, fixed costs, and mixed costs.
5. Determine how certain costs that are not completely variable or fixed are treated in managerial accounting applications.
6. Understand how the concept of the relevant range is used with cost behavior.
7. Analyze cost behavior with three methods—visual fit of a scatter diagram, high-low, and linear regression.
8. Recognize how variable costing is used for internal reporting.
9. Reconcile the difference between variable costing net income and absorption costing net income.
10. Discuss the benefits and limitations of variable costing.

COST BEHAVIOR AND THE INCOME STATEMENT

Chapter 2 introduced the subject of cost behavior, which is the measure of how a cost responds to changes in the level of business activity. Up to this point, we have treated all manufacturing costs as product costs without any consideration of the cost behavior involved. Thus, the production performance results reported on the income statement make no distinction between the variable product costs and the fixed product costs. Both types of cost behavior are simply combined and reported as cost of goods sold or as ending inventory, depending upon whether the related products are sold during the period. In addition, cost behavior patterns of the operating expenses (selling and administrative expenses) have not been considered.

An income statement prepared using this costing approach is called a *functional income statement* or a *conventional income statement* because the costs involved are classified by business function (e.g., manufacturing, selling, and administrative). In financial accounting, you saw how functional income statements are used in service and merchandising firms. A manufacturing firm prepares such an income statement on the basis of an inventory valuation method called **absorption costing** or **full costing** because all production costs are inventoried as product costs, regardless of their cost behavior. Note that we used the absorption costing approach in our previous coverage of manufacturing operations because we were concerned with determining the full or total cost of producing products.

A functional income statement is required by generally accepted accounting principles for external reporting to present the results of operations for a given period. As such, a functional income statement is used by the business and investment communities to evaluate a firm's historical earnings performance. Business managers also use the functional income statement to measure how effectively their stewardship responsibilities are being performed. However, a functional income statement has serious limitations for managers who are more concerned about the future operating performance of the firm than that of the past.

An alternative form of income statement, called a contribution margin income statement, can be developed for use by managers to plan operations, control costs, and make decisions. The cost information required for a contribution margin income statement is more detailed than that contained in a functional income statement. Each significant cost item involved must be analyzed to identify its cost behavior pattern. Managers need to be able to predict the way costs change in relation to different levels of business activity and the consequent effect on future income statements. Thus, cost behavior considerations should be incorporated into an income statement used for internal reporting.

LIMITATIONS OF A FUNCTIONAL INCOME STATEMENT FOR PROJECTING A FUTURE EARNINGS PERFORMANCE

Objective 1:
Limitations of
functional income
statement for
management

One of the main concerns with any historical income statement is the extent it can be used to predict profit performance in the future. To project a future income statement, often called a **pro forma income statement**, management must be able to evaluate how profits will fluctuate with changes in sales volume. Although a functional income statement may be factual regarding the earnings performance of a specific period, it does not provide an accurate indication of the earnings performance with a different sales volume in the future.

Consider, for example, the functional income statement of the Deats Manufacturing Company shown in Figure 5-1. The firm earned net income of $240,000, which was 12% of sales, during 1987. Suppose management expects sales to increase by $400,000 to $2,400,000, or 20% in 1988 because more units will be sold and wants to predict the net income the company should earn. Can management simply multiply the projected sales revenue of

$2,400,000 by the profit margin of 12% to predict a 1988 net income of $288,000 (which also would be a 20% increase)? The answer is a resounding "no." Many of the costs involved are fixed and will not change with the increase in sales volume. In a functional income statement, fixed manufacturing overhead costs will be included in the cost of goods sold section of the income statement because they are assigned to the products during the production operation. Also, the selling and administrative expenses usually will contain both variable and fixed items. Even if the Deats Manufacturing Company were a merchandising business, its operating expenses most likely would be partially variable and partially fixed. Thus, the fixed costs would remain constant at the higher sales level projected, whereas the variable costs would increase.

Figure 5-1

DEATS MANUFACTURING COMPANY
Income Statement — Functional Format
Year Ended December 31, 1987

		Amount	Percentage
Sales		$2,000,000	100
Less cost of goods sold		1,040,000	52
Gross profit		960,000	48
Less operating expenses:			
Selling expenses	$400,000		20
Administrative expenses	320,000		16
Total		720,000	36
Net income		$ 240,000	12

DEVELOPING AN INCOME STATEMENT WITH A CONTRIBUTION MARGIN FORMAT

**Objective 2:
Use of a contribution margin income statement**

In Figure 5-2, the Deats Manufacturing Company's income statement for 1987 has been revised. To eliminate the deficiencies of a functional income statement, many businesses use cost behavior patterns to construct the income statement prepared for internal reporting purposes. Here, the emphasis is on the **contribution margin,** which is the sales revenue less *all* variable costs (those from manufacturing, selling, and administrative).

The **contribution margin rate** or percentage is found by dividing the contribution margin by sales revenue. The contribution margin represents the amount of sales revenue available first to cover the fixed costs and then to contribute toward profit. The contribution margin itself will vary directly as a fixed percentage of sales because only the variable costs have been deducted from revenue to compute the margin.

Before preparing an income statement that emphasizes the contribution margin, each cost item must be carefully analyzed to determine how it will change, if at all, over different levels of sales or production activity. For now, assume that the cost behavior classifications shown in Figure 5-2 have been developed for the 1987 income statement of Deats Manufacturing Company. We can see that the biggest change from the functional format is how each functional cost category has been recast in terms of the distinction between variable and fixed costs. The variable cost of goods sold and the variable operating expenses are subtracted from sales to determine the contribution margin in dollar amount and as a percentage of sales. All fixed costs are deducted from the contribution margin to compute the net income of the period.

Figure 5-2

DEATS MANUFACTURING COMPANY
Income Statement—Contribution Margin Format
Year Ended December 31, 1987

		Amount	Percentage
Sales		$2,000,000	100
Less variable costs:			
Variable cost of goods sold	$800,000		40
Variable operating expenses	400,000		20
Total		1,200,000	60
Contribution margin		800,000	40
Less fixed costs:			
Manufacturing	240,000		12
Selling & administrative	320,000		16
Total		560,000	28
Net income		$ 240,000	12

The information contained in the revised income statement shown in Figure 5-2 will enable management to evaluate the effect on net income of a change in sales volume. If sales of $2,400,000 are expected in 1988, the resulting net income can be computed as follows:

Projected contribution margin ($2,400,000 × 40%)	$960,000
Fixed costs	560,000
Net income	$400,000
Net income as a percentage of sales	16.7

The $400,000 net income projected for 1988 is a higher percentage of sales than that of 1987 because the fixed costs remain at $560,000. Only the total variable costs have increased at the rate of 60% of sales. Thus, the contribution margin increases in dollar amount from $800,000 to $960,000, but remains at a constant 40% of sales. Alternatively, the $160,000 increase in net income can be computed by multiplying the $400,000 sales increase projected by the contribution margin rate of 40%. To understand how a contribution margin income statement is developed, we must examine the subject of cost behavior more thoroughly.

COST BEHAVIOR: A CLOSER LOOK

In Figure 5-2, we have considered the two most basic cost behavior patterns, variable costs and fixed costs. Many other types of cost behavior, such as mixed costs, are encountered in the business world. Unfortunately, we cannot simply examine a particular firm's chart of accounts and automatically classify every cost item by its cost behavior. Some cost behavior classifications are obvious, but many are not because of differences in *management policies, operating circumstances, economic conditions, cost control procedures,* and *contractual agreements.* As a result, a particular cost item may not even be treated the same within a given firm from period to period. Also, a cost that behaves a certain way for one business may be different in another firm. These differences must be evaluated carefully.

Consider, for example, how depreciation on equipment is calculated. In most cases, depreciation expense is a fixed cost for financial reporting purposes because the straight-line method is used. However, the cost will be variable if management chooses a productivity method of depreciation such as the units of output produced. Here, the more the asset is used, the more it is depreciated.

The three most important cost behavior patterns for managerial accounting are variable, fixed, and mixed. We saw in Chapter 2 that a variable cost will vary in total amount proportionately with some measure of activity or volume such as sales dollars, units produced, or direct labor hours. In nonmanufacturing operations, cost variability can be measured in such terms as miles driven, hospital beds occupied, condominium units built, insurance policies processed, patients treated, and gallons consumed. The choice of activity or volume measure depends on the one that will provide the best linkage between a given cost and the activity measure. This means that the activity measure chosen will be the one that really causes the cost to vary. Examples of variable costs include direct materials, direct labor, sales commissions, and the cost of merchandise sold by a retailer.

The opposite of a variable cost is a fixed cost. Fixed costs do not change in total amount over a wide range of activity. That is, they remain the same during an accounting period whether the level of activity is high or low. Examples include executive salaries, depreciation (with the straight-line method), rent for office space, and real estate taxes. A third type of cost behavior is a **mixed cost** (sometimes called a semivariable cost), which contains both variable and fixed components. For example, maintenance costs often are classified as mixed costs.

IMPORTANCE OF LINEAR COST FUNCTIONS

The managerial accountant must be able to evaluate each cost item incurred by the firm to determine the cost function that best describes the item's cost behavior. This is true for manufacturing and nonmanufacturing costs alike. In its most basic form, a **cost function** is a relationship between a certain cost as a dependent variable and some measure of activity or volume as an independent variable. For example, total manufacturing cost depends on the number of units produced, so that cost would be the dependent variable and the number of units produced would be the independent variable. In more complicated cases (which are beyond the scope of this book), more than one independent variable may be considered.

Many businesses actually experience nonlinear cost functions, which means that they are not in the form of a straight line. In managerial accounting applications, however, these same cost functions usually are converted to **linear (straight line) relationships** because (1) the relevant range concept discussed later in this chapter justifies the conversion and (2) the linear function is a close approximation of the real cost function and is accurate enough for the estimates needed to project the future with all its uncertainties. For example, we will see in the next chapter that a fundamental assumption of cost-volume-profit analysis is that all cost functions considered are linear, which means they are in the form of straight lines. As such, the rate of change, or slope, for each cost function is constant over all levels of activity and thus is easy to predict. In

Objective 3:
Importance of
cost functions

contrast, a nonlinear cost function has a slope that changes with different levels of activity so it is much more difficult to evaluate.

A linear cost function is expressed in the form of a linear equation as follows:

$$y = a + bx$$

{ You should recall from your algebra course that this is called the slope-intercept form of the equation for any straight line.

where: y = the total cost as a dependent variable
a = the fixed cost portion of the total cost (also called the y intercept because it is the point where a linear cost function that is graphed touches the vertical axis as we will see later)
b = the variable cost rate that is the slope (rate of change) of the linear cost function
x = the measure of activity or volume as an independent variable sales dollars, units produced, and direct labor hours

Objective 4:
Identifying different cost functions

The three basic cost functions—variable, fixed, and mixed—can be graphed with this linear equation as shown in Figure 5-3.

Many firms experience costs that are not exactly variable and others that are not exactly fixed over the entire range of activity possible. That is, they do not have the same pattern of behavior at all levels of activity. Nevertheless, these atypical variable or fixed costs are classified as being either "true" variable costs or "true" fixed costs. We need to consider some of the characteristics of the atypical variable and fixed cost behavior patterns to understand why the costs involved can be treated as variable or fixed costs in managerial accounting applications.

VARIABLE COST BEHAVIOR

Objective 5:
Treatment of certain costs that are not completely variable or fixed

Few variable costs behave exactly as linear functions with constant slopes over all levels of activity. Two common nonlinear costs, a curvilinear function and a step-variable cost function, are incurred by many businesses. Figure 5-4 presents a graphic version of each of these cost functions.

CURVILINEAR COST FUNCTIONS AND THE RELEVANT RANGE

The **curvilinear variable cost** shown in graph (a) of Figure 5-4 is the result of what economists describe as economies and diseconomies of scale. At extremely low levels of activity, a firm does not have sufficient volume to take advantage of such factors as automation and the specialization of labor. Conse-

Figure 5-3
Linear Cost Functions

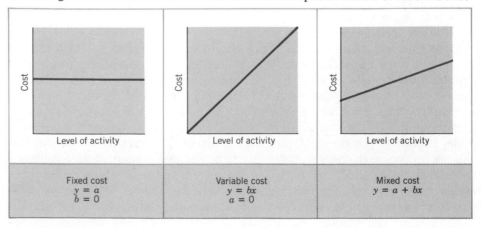

Fixed cost	Variable cost	Mixed cost
$y = a$	$y = bx$	$y = a + bx$
$b = 0$	$a = 0$	

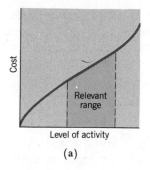

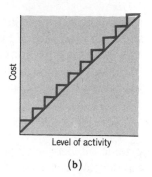

Figure 5-4
Curvilinear and
Step Cost Functions

quently, the variable cost function increases at a decreasing rate. For example, consider the manufacturing operation of a firm that produces a pocket size stereo cassette player that sells in a retail store for $29.95. If the firm only produced 10 units each month, it could not afford to invest in a highly automated assembly line so all the work would have to be done by hand. The result would be a large direct labor cost, perhaps more than the selling price of the product would justify. In contrast, if the firm produces thousands of units each month, the use of automation is economically sound and the amount of direct labor required for each unit produced will decrease significantly. That is, most of the work will be performed by the equipment involved.

When unusually high levels of activity are achieved, inefficiencies and bottlenecks occur so the variable cost again increases at an increasing rate. In the case of the stereo cassette player manufacturer, a monthly production volume that is more than the intended capacity of the highly automated assembly line will create problems and result in increased variable costs. For example, it may be necessary to pay overtime wages to the workers just to produce the required number of units. In addition, the equipment is likely to malfunction more than normal, resulting in a significant amount of maintenance costs and idle labor time.

Within the shaded area of graph (a) of Figure 5-4, however, the cost function is approximately linear because the rate of increase is relatively constant. The shaded area of the graph is called the relevant range. The **relevant range** is defined as the normal range of activity within which a firm expects to operate. For the stereo cassette player manufacturer, the relevant range would contain the level of production activity for which the automated assembly line was intended. Since a business does not expect to operate outside the relevant range, the curvilinear cost behavior at very low or very high levels of activity can be ignored. The relevant range concept is important in managerial accounting applications because it provides the justification for the linearity assumption without any significant loss of accuracy as long as the firm's activity stays within the relatively narrow limits.

Objective 6:
Importance of the
relevant range

STEP-VARIABLE COST FUNCTION

A **step-variable cost function,** such as the one shown in graph (b) of Figure 5-4, is representative of some variable cost items that cannot be purchased in divisible units. For example, labor services normally are acquired on the basis of 40 hours per week. The associated costs cannot be inventoried for future use since they must be utilized or lost (through idle time) as each workday passes. Consequently, each worker's wages represent a narrow step in the cost function in graph (b) of Figure 5-4. The cost function increases abruptly as an additional worker is hired to satisfy the needs of a higher level of activity. Again, the managerial accountant converts the step-variable cost function into a linear function, as shown in graph (b) of Figure 5-4, by connecting the points representing the highest level of activity for each step. The justification for the conversion is that the business will want to fully utilize the labor cost for any given step by attaining the highest level of activity possible.

FIXED COST BEHAVIOR

Note the trade-off between variable costs and fixed costs in the case of the stereo cassette player manufacturer discussed earlier. In order to achieve the direct labor cost savings required for a competitive selling price, the firm must invest in the equipment required for a highly automated assembly line operation. The result will be higher fixed costs relative to the variable costs because the equipment must be depreciated if it is purchased, or expensed when periodic payments are made if it is leased. Thus, a variable cost (direct labor) is replaced with a fixed cost (the cost of automation) in order to achieve the production efficiency required to compete in the electronics industry.

This switch from variable costs to fixed costs because of automation is happening throughout the business world today so it is important for managers to thoroughly understand fixed costs and their impact on a firm's earnings. A major disadvantage of a highly fixed cost structure is the loss of flexibility involved. Effective planning is crucial for a financially successful operation because management cannot as quickly reduce or increase fixed costs as it can the variable costs. *Unused capacity, excess costs,* and *reduced profitability* can occur when wrong decisions are made that commit a firm to a high fixed cost structure that cannot be utilized effectively.

IMPACT OF DISCRETIONARY AND COMMITTED FIXED COSTS

A **step-fixed cost function** such as those presented in Figure 5-5 often is incurred for either the total level of fixed costs or the behavior of certain cost items within the total amount. The relevant range concept also allows management to assume that the total fixed costs will remain constant over a range of activity. In reality, the total fixed costs may change over a complete range of activity in wide steps, as shown in graph (a) of Figure 5-5.

Many fixed costs are defined as **discretionary fixed costs** because they can be reduced or discontinued by management if adequate time is available. Thus, *time* is a key variable for this type of cost. At low levels of activity, management may decide to reduce or eliminate such discretionary fixed costs as advertising, research and development, and employee training programs. At an extremely low level of activity such as one caused by a prolonged labor strike, drastic measures may be necessary to eliminate all but the committed fixed costs through layoffs and curtailments.

The **committed fixed costs** are those required even if the operation has extremely low activity, including the possibility of being shut down temporarily. They consist of such items as depreciation, real estate taxes, insurance, and top management salaries. Once management makes the decision to incur a committed cost such as the real estate taxes associated with the purchase of a building, a relatively long time period usually is required to eliminate the cost because of the legal ramifications involved (the building must be sold).

At the other extreme, additional operating capacity is necessary at an excep-

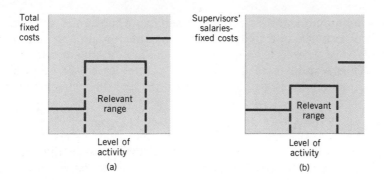

Figure 5-5
Fixed Cost Functions

tionally high level of activity to satisfy the market demand for the firm's products or services so many fixed costs, such as depreciation and managerial salaries, will increase. This in turn will cause the firm's fixed cost function to increase as an additional step.

Again, the *relevant range concept* permits management to ignore the low and the high levels by concentrating on the normal range of operation. Within the relevant range, the fixed costs will remain constant in total amount. Most firms plan each year's activities with a budgeting process (discussed in Chapter 8) that identifies all estimated costs, including the fixed costs for the year (discretionary and committed). For example, the advertising costs required to achieve the sales goals of the period are identified in the budget (in many cases, this results in contractual agreements with various media and related discretionary fixed costs for the entire ycar).

At the same time, the annual budget defines the relevant range within which the firm plans to operate and the total fixed costs for that range of activity. If an expansion of the firm's operating capacity is planned for the next year, the additional fixed costs required will be identified and the relevant range will be revised to the increased level of activity.

INDIVIDUAL FIXED COST ITEMS AS STEP FUNCTIONS

Some individual fixed cost items also behave as step functions as illustrated in graph (b) of Figure 5-5. These step-fixed cost functions are similar to the one shown in graph (b) of Figure 5-4 for a variable cost except here the steps are much wider. An example of a step-fixed cost would be the salaries paid to production supervisors, each of whom can manage the activities of 12 workers at most. As long as the firm employs 12 or fewer workers, the supervision cost remains constant. When the thirteenth worker is hired, a second supervisor must be added, and his or her salary increases the step function abruptly. The same change would take place every time the firm hires a new supervisor. The relevant range concept also is used to choose a particular level for a step-fixed cost that the firm expects to incur in a given period.

MIXED COST BEHAVIOR

As seen in Figure 5-3, a mixed cost contains both fixed and variable components. Consequently, a mixed cost increases or decreases linearly with changes in activity (because of its constant slope) but has a positive amount at zero activity (due to the fixed costs involved). The fixed portion of a mixed cost represents the minimum cost of obtaining a service, whereas the variable element results from a change in activity. For example, the rental of an automobile will be a mixed cost when a fixed amount per day and a certain rate per mile are charged. Other examples of mixed costs in many cases are utilities, maintenance costs, sales salaries, employees' insurance, and office machine rental.

METHODS FOR ANALYZING COST BEHAVIOR

Objective 7:
Analyzing cost
behavior

For mixed costs to be planned and controlled, they must be divided into their variable and fixed components. A number of techniques based on the equation $y = a + bx$ can be used for the separation of mixed costs. The three most popular techniques are the visual fit of a scatter diagram method, high-low method, and linear regression analysis. All three techniques are based on the collection of historical data that represent the mixed costs incurred at different levels of activity.

The objective of **cost behavior analysis** is to develop a cost function that best reflects the cost behavior pattern of the mixed costs. To illustrate the three techniques, assume that a manufacturing firm has experienced the following maintenance costs and machine hours during the past 12 months:

Month	Maintenance Costs	Machine Hours
January	$13,224	3,504
February	13,728	4,350
March	15,206	5,256
April	16,008	5,702
May	17,280	7,183
June	18,096	8,700
July	20,088	10,368
August	18,533	8,580
September	17,400	7,830
October	16,589	6,864
November	14,414	6,006
December	14,366	5,220

VISUAL FIT OF A SCATTER DIAGRAM METHOD

The **visual fit of a scatter diagram method** can be used to estimate the cost function of a mixed cost. This method is often used because it is quick, easy, and a reasonably accurate approximation of the cost function involved. The major advantage of this method is that all available relationships between cost and activity are considered. Its biggest limitation is that the method depends on the judgment of the person preparing the analysis because he or she must visually choose the best fit. Different people may draw different lines through the same scatter diagram so the method is subject to significant error. The following five steps are used to estimate the cost behavior of a particular mixed cost by visually fitting a scatter diagram:

1. Gather data related to the amount of cost incurred at different activity levels in the past. In the illustration above, the monthly maintenance costs recorded for the monthly machine hours have been identified. Machine hours are chosen as the independent variable because their incurrence causes the need for maintenance costs. This data would be taken from the accounting records for January through December.

2. Plot the data points representing combinations of cost and the level of activity on a graph with cost (the dependent variable) on the vertical axis (y)

and the level of activity (the independent variable) on the horizontal axis (*x*). The result is called a scatter diagram of data points. For example, the data point from January in our illustration is the combination of $13,224 for maintenance cost and 3,504 for machine hours.

3. Draw a straight line through the data points that comes as close to as many points as possible. This means that the differences between the data points and the straight line are the smallest compared with other lines that might be drawn through the same scatter diagram. Visual inspection of the data is the basis for identifying the best fit for the line through the data.

4. Determine the fixed component of the cost function by extending the line until it touches the vertical axis. The result of the line touching the *y* axis is the intersection that defines the total amount of fixed costs estimated to be necessary regardless of the level of activity. In the example above, the point at which the line touches the vertical axis is the monthly fixed maintenance costs expected to be incurred for all activity levels.

5. Compute the variable costs for any level of activity by subtracting the fixed costs determined in step 4 from the total costs observed from the line for that level of activity. The variable cost rate can be estimated by dividing the resulting variable costs by the related measure of activity. Continuing with the example above, this step would be used to find the variable maintenance costs that would change as a function of machine hours and the rate at which the change would take place.

The monthly maintenance costs can be plotted as a function of machine hours, as shown in Figure 5-6. The line touches the vertical axis at approximately $9,500, which is the estimate of the fixed portion of the maintenance costs. The variable costs can be found for any given number of machine hours by subtracting the fixed costs of $9,500 from the total costs related to that level of activity. For example, total maintenance costs of $17,660 are estimated for 8,000 machine hours, so the variable costs would be $8,160 ($17,660 less $9,500). In turn, the variable cost rate is approximately $1.02 per machine hour ($8,160/8,000). Consequently, the maintenance cost function is equal to *$9,500 + $1.02 per machine hour*. If 5,000 machine hours are expected during

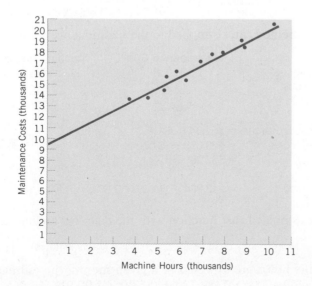

Figure 5-6
Scatter Diagram—
Maintenance Costs

a given month, the maintenance costs estimated with the visual fit of a scatter diagram method are $14,600 [$9,500 + ($1.02 × 5,000)].

HIGH-LOW METHOD

The **high-low method** is a quantitative technique that can be used to estimate a mixed cost function. As long as the costs at both the highest and lowest levels of activity are representative of the straight line that best describes a cost function, they provide useful information for cost estimation. The analyst must visually evaluate the two points to make sure that a line drawn through them would be essentially the same as one that best fits all the data points. This can be accomplished by completing steps one and two for the visual fit of a scatter diagram method identified earlier.

In many cases, the high and low points will not be representative of the true cost function. If a visual analysis indicates that this is the case, the high-low method can be modified. In the modified approach, the highest and lowest points are ignored and the analysis is performed with the second highest and second lowest points if they are observed to be representative of all the data points included.

To illustrate data points for which the high-low method would produce erroneous results, graph (a) in Figure 5-7 shows high and low points that are not representative of the entire data set. In contrast, graph (b) in the same figure contains valid high and low points. Many firms use the visual fit of a scatter diagram method and the high-low method together since they can be applied quickly and serve as checks on each other.

The high-low method is based on the same procedures used to determine the slope of any linear function because it compares the cost at the highest level of activity with the cost at the lowest level. The difference in total cost between the high and low points, caused by the change in the variable costs, is divided by the related difference in activity to find the variable cost rate. Once the variable costs for a given level of activity are known, they can be subtracted from the total costs to determine the fixed costs. Since the variable cost rate is the slope of a mixed cost function, we can find it as follows:

$$\text{Variable cost rate} = \frac{\text{Change in total cost}}{\text{Change in activity level}}$$

The high-low method can be applied to the maintenance cost data as follows:

	Maintenance Cost	Machine Hours
High point	$20,088	10,368
Low point	13,224	3,504
Difference	$ 6,864	6,864

Variable cost rate = $6,864/6,864 = $1.00 per hour
Fixed costs = $20,088 − ($1.00 × 10,368)
= $9,720

or:
Fixed costs = $13,224 − ($1.00 × 3,504)
= $9,720

As a result, the estimated cost function with the high-low method can be stated as:

Maintenance costs = $9,720 + ($1 × Machine hours)

If 5,000 machine hours are expected in a given month, the estimated maintenance costs would be $14,720 [$9,720 + ($1.00 × 5,000)].

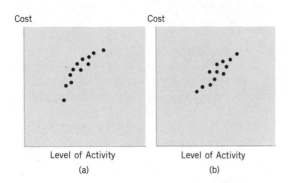

Cost   Cost

Level of Activity   Level of Activity
        (a)   (b)

Figure 5-7
Evaluation of Data
Points for High-
Low Method

LINEAR REGRESSION ANALYSIS

Each of the cost estimation methods discussed above has a potentially serious weakness. The visual fit of a scatter diagram method is subject to judgmental error even though it considers all the available data. The high-low method eliminates most of the judgment required but only considers a limited amount of the data available—the high and low points that are being analyzed. In addition, neither method tells us how good the answer we find really is.

Linear regression analysis is a more accurate cost estimation technique because it mathematically determines the straight line (called the **regression line**) that minimizes the sum of the squared differences between that line and the various data points. The **least squares method** provides the underlying mathematics for linear regression. When only two variables are considered (as is the case here with maintenance costs and machine hours), the analysis is referred to as simple linear regression analysis. When more than two variables are considered, multiple linear regression analysis is needed.

In essence, linear regression analysis is a mathematical version of the visual fit of a scatter diagram method. It uses all the available data and eliminates the analyst's personal judgment. In addition, linear regression analysis provides important statistical information that can be used in evaluating the quality of the independent variable (level of activity) as a predictor of the future performance of the dependent variable (a mixed cost).

The mathematics involved in linear regression analysis can be reduced to the solution of the following two equations that are derived from the basic equation for a straight line ($y = a + bx$):

$$b = \frac{n\Sigma xy - (\Sigma x)(\Sigma y)}{n\Sigma x^2 - (\Sigma x)^2}$$

$$a = \Sigma y/n - b(\Sigma x/n)$$

At first glance, the two equations may seem complicated, but actually they are easy to work with. Keep in mind that the objective of cost behavior analysis in all cases is to determine the variable cost rate (b) and the amount of fixed costs (a). The number of observations, n, will be defined by the number of data points (relationships between the dependent and independent variables) being considered. In the maintenance cost illustration, we have 12 data points so $n = 12$. The rest of the terms in the two equations deal with sums for the two variables, x and y, or certain squared terms required to satisfy the mathematical conditions of the method of least squares. As used in the maintenance cost illustration, the terms are defined as follows:

$\Sigma y =$ the total of the 12 values for the dependent variable (maintenance costs) observed in the data collected

$\Sigma x =$ the total of the 12 values for the independent variable (machine hours) observed in the data collected

$\Sigma xy =$ the total of the products of each pair of values observed for maintenance costs and machine hours

$\Sigma x^2 =$ the total of the squared values of the independent variable (machine hours)

$(\Sigma x)^2 =$ the total of the values for the independent variable (machine hours) squared

Computer software packages and small calculators are readily available for solving linear regression problems so the important thing is to understand the purpose of the technique and be able to define the various terms involved. The two equations can be used to determine the maintenance costs as a function of machine hours in our illustration as follows. (To facilitate the calculations involved, we have altered the original values for x and y by dividing each one by 1,000.)

	Maintenance costs (000)	Machine hours (000)		
	y	**x**	**xy**	**x²**
January	13.224	3.504	46.337	12.2780
February	13.728	4.350	59.717	18.9225
March	15.206	5.256	79.923	27.6255
April	16.008	5.702	91.278	32.5128
May	17.280	7.183	124.122	51.5955
June	18.096	8.700	157.435	75.6900
July	20.088	10.368	208.272	107.4954
August	18.533	8.580	159.013	73.6164
September	17.400	7.830	136.242	61.3089
October	16.589	6.864	113.867	47.1145
November	14.414	6.006	86.570	36.0720
December	14.366	5.220	74.991	27.2484
Totals	194.932	79.563	1,337.767	571.4799

$$b = \frac{12\,(1{,}337.767) - (79.563)\,(194.932)}{12\,(571.4799) - 6{,}330.2710}$$

$$= \frac{543.8293}{527.4878} = 1.031$$

$$a = 194.932/12 - 1.031\,(79.563/12)$$
$$= 9.4085$$

Since the values for the dependent and independent variables were expressed in thousands, the value calculated for a (the fixed costs) of 9.4085 must be multiplied by 1,000 to get back to the basis of the original data, or a total of 9,408.50. We do not have to restate b, or 1.031, because both the numerator and denominator for the calculation of b were expressed in thousands. Adding the necessary dollar signs, the maintenance cost function with linear regression analysis is:

Maintenance costs $= \$9{,}408.50 + (\$1.031 \times$ Machine hours$)$

If the firm expects to incur 5,000 machine hours in a given month, the estimated maintenance costs are $14,563.50 [$9,408.50 + ($1.031 × 5,000)].

SUMMARY OF COST ESTIMATION RESULTS

As shown in the following chart, the results of estimating the cost behavior of the maintenance costs in this illustration are about the same with all three methods—visual display of a scatter diagram, high-low, and linear regression analysis. This is not always the case, given the data involved, and the most accurate results can be expected from linear regression analysis.

	Variable Cost Rate	**Fixed Costs**
Scatter diagram method	$1.020	$9,500.00
High-low method	1.000	9,720.00
Linear regression method	1.031	9,408.50

EXTENSIONS WITH LINEAR REGRESSION ANALYSIS

As mentioned earlier, another advantage of linear regression analysis is that it makes available a great deal of statistical data for evaluating just how good the fit of the estimated line is. An example is the correlation coefficient which is a statistic used to measure the direction and degree of correlation for the relationship between two variables such as the maintenance costs and machine hours. When the correlation coefficient is close to one, a high positive correlation exists between the two variables being considered. This means that the two variables will increase or decrease together in the same direction. A correlation coefficient close to minus one indicates a high negative correlation. In such a situation, the two variables move together but in opposite directions. A correlation coefficient value close to zero indicates that the two variables are not related.

A small computer or a calculator with a linear regression capability also can be used to calculate the correlation coefficient. While the computations involved with this statistic are beyond the scope of this book, we should note that the correlation between maintenance costs and machine hours in the example above is approximately .97, indicating that the two variables are highly related with a positive correlation and that machine hours can be used reliably to estimate future maintenance costs. You should also be aware that a complete application of linear regression analysis is more complicated than the presentation in this chapter and many *potential pitfalls* must be avoided.

USE OF ABSORPTION COSTING VERSUS VARIABLE COSTING

As mentioned earlier in this chapter, absorption costing must be used for external reporting purposes because generally accepted accounting principles require both fixed and variable manufacturing overhead costs to be included as product costs. However, we have seen that management often needs income statement information that is useful in predicting the impact of changes in sales volume on the costs and profits of a firm. This information is difficult, if not impossible, to obtain with absorption costing since there is no clear-cut distinction between variable and fixed costs.

Variable costing (also called **direct costing**) is an alternative inventory valuation method that can be used for internal reporting purposes. With variable costing, only the variable manufacturing costs (direct materials, direct labor, and variable manufacturing overhead) are treated as product costs. This method eliminates the problems associated with unit costs that vary inversely with production volume because the fixed manufacturing costs are accounted for as *period costs*.

Objective 8:
Use of variable
costing

Three major steps are involved in the application of variable costing:

1. All costs—manufacturing, selling, and administrative—are analyzed carefully to determine which are variable and which are fixed. A mixed cost is separated into its variable and fixed components with one of the cost estimation methods discussed in the previous section.
2. Variable manufacturing costs—direct materials, direct labor, and variable manufacturing overhead—are assigned as product costs. Therefore, the work in process inventory, finished goods inventory, and cost of goods sold are costed on the basis of the manufacturing costs that vary proportionately with the level of production volume.
3. All fixed manufacturing overhead costs, as well as all selling and administrative expenses, are treated as period costs and charged to the income statement of the period in which they are incurred. However, the variable selling and administrative expenses are separated from the fixed selling and administrative expenses for presentation on the income statement. The variable selling and administrative expenses are deducted from sales revenue along with the variable cost of goods sold to determine the contribution margin of a period. In contrast, the fixed selling and administrative expenses are subtracted (along with the fixed manufacturing overhead costs) from the contribution margin to determine the net income of a period.

An income statement developed with variable costing has the same basic format as the one shown in Figure 5-2 (the contribution margin format). The only difference may be the presentation of a manufacturing margin, which is optional. This **manufacturing margin** is the difference between sales revenue and the variable cost of goods sold. The **manufacturing margin rate** is the manufacturing margin expressed as a percentage of sales. The distinction between the manufacturing margin and the contribution margin is often made so management can easily evaluate the performance of the manufacturing operation separately from the selling and administrative functions.

Proponents of variable costing support its format because it differentiates the *costs of doing business* (the variable costs deducted to determine the contribution margin) from the *costs of being in business* (the fixed costs subtracted from the contribution margin). The costs of doing business will rise and fall as the level of business activity increases and decreases. Examples include direct materials cost, direct labor cost, and sales commissions. In contrast, the costs of being in business represent capacity costs that will be required regardless of the volume of business achieved (subject to our earlier discussion about the relevant range). Examples include rent expense, depreciation expense, top management salaries, and insurance costs.

The cost flows associated with variable costing are summarized in Figure 5-8.

COMPARING VARIABLE COSTING AND ABSORPTION COSTING NET INCOMES

Objective 9: Difference between variable costing and absorption costing net incomes

The major difference between variable costing and absorption costing is the timing of the fixed manufacturing overhead costs as deductions on the income statement. The variable costing method charges the fixed manufacturing overhead costs to the income statement as these costs are incurred. Absorption costing applies the fixed manufacturing overhead costs to the products produced during a period; these costs are then deducted from the income state-

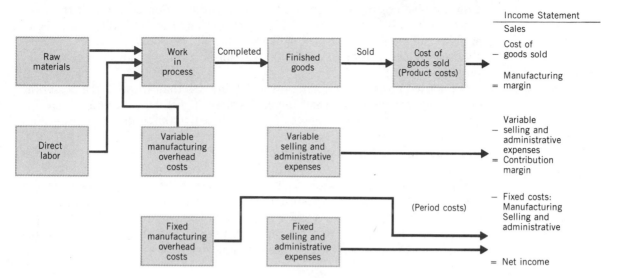

Figure 5-8
Variable Costing Cost Flows

ment when the related products are sold. The amount of fixed manufacturing overhead costs left on the balance sheet at the end of a given period with absorption costing is proportionate to the number of units left in ending inventory as compared with the total number of units produced.

When sales units and production units in a specific period are equal, inventories do not increase or decrease (e.g., if 100,000 units are produced and sold, the change in inventory is zero). In such cases, the same amount of fixed manufacturing overhead costs will be charged to the income statement of the period with both methods. Consequently, the net income with variable costing will be equal to the net income with absorption costing.

If the sales volume and the production volume are different, variable costing net income and absorption costing net income also will be different. When the production units exceed the sales units, part of the fixed manufacturing overhead costs inventoried with absorption costing will be deferred in inventory to a future period. As a result, absorption costing net income will be greater than variable costing net income (less cost will be on the income statement with absorption costing).

In contrast, variable costing net income will be higher than that of absorption costing when the sales units exceed the production units. As inventory is depleted to make up the difference between sales and production, the fixed manufacturing overhead costs of a previous period will be combined with those of the current period with absorption costing. Using variable costing, those same fixed manufacturing overhead costs carried forward would have been expensed on the income statement of the previous period (because all fixed costs are period costs with variable costing).

In general, the difference in net incomes of a given period with the two methods can be reconciled by comparing the fixed manufacturing overhead costs in the ending inventory with those in the beginning inventory when absorption costing is used. When the fixed costs in the ending inventory exceed those in the beginning inventory, absorption costing net income will be higher than variable costing net income by the difference. For example, if the fixed costs in the ending inventory are $165,000 compared to $125,000 in the beginning inventory, absorption costing net income will be $40,000 higher than variable costing net income (the $40,000 will appear on the balance sheet with absorption costing).

If the fixed costs in the ending inventory are less than those in the beginning inventory, variable costing net income will be higher by the same difference. For example, variable costing net income will be $40,000 more than absorption costing net income when the fixed costs in the ending inventory are $125,000 and those in the beginning inventory are $165,000 (the $40,000 will be included in the income statement with absorption costing).

The basic impact of inventory change on the net incomes with variable and absorption costing can be visualized in the following way. In a simplified case with a single type of product and a fixed manufacturing overhead cost rate per unit produced that remains the same from period to period, the difference between net income with variable costing and absorption costing can be computed as follows:

$$\begin{array}{c} \text{Difference in} \\ \text{net income} \end{array} = \begin{array}{c} \text{Change in} \\ \text{inventory} \\ \text{units} \end{array} \times \begin{array}{c} \text{Fixed manufacturing} \\ \text{overhead cost rate} \\ \text{per unit} \end{array}$$

The change in inventory during any period will be the difference between sales units and production units for that period. When no change in inventory occurs, there will be no difference in net income with variable costing and absorption costing. If the change in inventory is positive (production exceeds sales), the increase in inventory units multiplied by the fixed manufacturing overhead cost rate per unit will be the amount by which absorption costing net income is greater than variable costing net income. In contrast, if the change in inventory is negative (sales exceed production), the decrease in inventory units multiplied by the fixed manufacturing overhead cost rate per unit will equal the excess of net income with variable costing over that of absorption costing.

For example, assume that a firm's fixed manufacturing overhead cost rate per unit produced is $4. If the firm produces and sells 80,000 units during a period, the net income with either inventory valuation method will be the same because an equal amount of fixed manufacturing overhead costs will be charged to the income statement. If the same firm produces 80,000 units but only sells 60,000 units, absorption costing net income will exceed variable costing net income by $80,000 (20,000 units × $4) because 20,000 units are left in ending inventory along with the related fixed costs of $80,000 (also 20,000 units × $4). The 20,000 units will appear on the balance sheet instead of the income statement.

If the firm produces 70,000 units but sells 80,000 units, it obviously must have used up inventory that was produced in a previous period so the fixed manufacturing overhead costs in essence will overlap between periods with absorption costing. That is, fixed costs of a previous period will be charged to the current period's income statement along with those of the current period. Consequently, the decrease in inventory of 10,000 units multiplied by the fixed manufacturing overhead cost rate of $4 will equal the amount by which variable costing net income exceeds absorption costing net income for the period, or $40,000.

Figure 5-9 shows a summary of the essential features of variable costing compared with those of absorption costing.

Figure 5-9
Comparison of
Variable Costing
and Absorption
Costing

	Variable Costing	*Absorption Costing*
Basic purpose	Internal reporting	External reporting
Income statement format	Sales	Sales
	—Variable costs	—Cost of goods sold
	=Contribution margin	=Gross margin
	—Fixed costs	—Operating expenses
	=Net income	=Net income
Product costs	Variable manufacturing costs	All manufacturing costs
Period costs	Variable selling and administrative expenses	All selling and administrative expenses
	All fixed costs— manufacturing, selling, and administrative	
Net income comparison:		
Production equals sales	Net income same as absorption costing	Net income same as variable costing
Production more than sales	Net income less than absorption costing	Net income more than variable costing
Production less than sales	Net income more than absorption costing	Net income less than variable costing
Net income difference		Fixed costs in ending inventory compared with those in beginning inventory

UNIT COST COMPUTATIONS WITH VARIABLE COSTING AND ABSORPTION COSTING

To illustrate how unit costs differ with variable costing and absorption costing, assume the following facts for the Irvin Company, which manufactures a single product (a component used in microcomputers):

Variable costs per unit produced:	
Direct materials	$3
Direct labor	6
Manufacturing overhead	1
Selling and administrative	2
Fixed costs for a year:	
Manufacturing overhead	$600,000
Selling and administrative	100,000
Expected annual production	50,000 units

Remember that only manufacturing costs are charged to the products during the production process. Selling and administrative expenses are *never* inventoried, regardless of whether variable costing or absorption costing is used. Also, the fixed portion of the manufacturing overhead rate for absorption costing in this case is $12 per unit ($600,000/50,000 units). The unit cost for each component with the two inventory valuation methods is computed as:

Absorption Costing

Direct materials	$ 3
Direct labor	6
Variable manufacturing overhead	1
Fixed manufacturing overhead	12
Total unit cost	$22

Variable Costing

Direct materials	$ 3
Direct labor	6
Variable manufacturing overhead	1
Total unit cost	$10

Note that the unit cost with absorption costing is $12 more than it is with variable costing ($22 versus $10). This is because absorption costing treats the $12 per unit manufacturing overhead rate as a product cost while variable costing treats the fixed manufacturing overhead costs totaling $600,000 as period costs. When the Irvin Company sells one unit of product valued with absorption costing, the income statement will show $22 as cost of goods sold. If variable costing is used, only $10 will be charged to cost of goods sold. In addition, units that are not sold at the end of the accounting period will be valued at $22 on the balance sheet with absorption costing and $10 with variable costing.

ILLUSTRATION OF VARIABLE COSTING VERSUS ABSORPTION COSTING

The data presented for the Irvin Company will now be used to illustrate variable costing and absorption costing. Assume that the firm began business on January 1, 1986 with *no* beginning inventory. It sells its single product for $30 per unit. During the three-year period 1986–1988, the selling price and all costs remained the same each year, while actual production and sales in units were as follows:

Year	Production	Sales
1986	50,000	50,000
1987	50,000	40,000
1988	40,000	50,000

Income statements with absorption costing and variable costing for the three-year period 1986–1988 are presented in Figures 5-10 and 5-11, respectively. In 1986, production and sales are equal, so the net income is the same with both inventory valuation methods ($200,000).

During 1987, production exceeded sales by the 10,000 units transferred to ending inventory at a cost of $220,000 with absorption costing. The variable costs in the ending inventory are $100,000 (10,000 units × $10) as shown in Figure 5-11 (the income statement with variable costing). The rest of the ending inventory with absorption costing consists of fixed costs totaling $120,000 (⅕ of the annual fixed overhead costs of $600,000 since the ending inventory is ⅕ of the units produced, or 10,000/50,000). Net income with absorption costing is greater than if variable costing had been used by the same $120,000 since one-fifth of the fixed manufacturing overhead costs are deferred from the 1987 income statement. In contrast, the total fixed manufacturing overhead costs of $600,000 are charged to the 1987 income statement with variable costing.

The situation is reversed in the third year, 1988, when sales exceed production by 10,000 units. The fixed manufacturing overhead costs charged to the

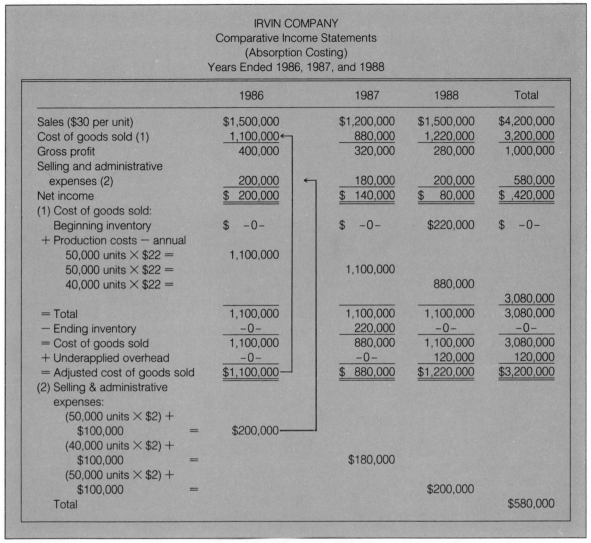

Figure 5-10

1988 income statement under absorption costing are the $600,000 incurred during 1988 plus the $120,000 balance carried into the year from 1987. Note that in Figure 5-10 an adjustment of $120,000 has been made to cost of goods sold for underapplied manufacturing overhead. Recall that the firm applies manufacturing overhead on the basis of a predetermined overhead rate. The fixed portion of the rate was $12 ($600,000/50,000 units). Since the firm only produced 40,000 units in 1988, the fixed costs applied amounted to $480,000 (40,000 units × $12) instead of $600,000.

Assuming that the firm adjusts any overapplied or underapplied overhead to cost of goods sold (as discussed in Chapter 3), $120,000 must be added to the cost of goods sold for 1988 to determine the adjusted cost of goods sold based on an absorption of the total fixed manufacturing overhead costs of $600,000. The underapplied overhead of $120,000 can also be calculated as 10,000 units (the units the company expected to produce but did not) multiplied by the $12 manufacturing overhead rate. Once again, the fixed manufacturing overhead

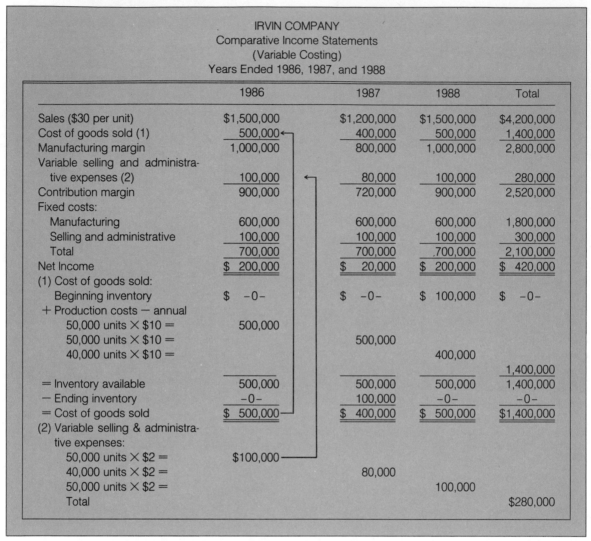

IRVIN COMPANY
Comparative Income Statements
(Variable Costing)
Years Ended 1986, 1987, and 1988

	1986	1987	1988	Total
Sales ($30 per unit)	$1,500,000	$1,200,000	$1,500,000	$4,200,000
Cost of goods sold (1)	500,000	400,000	500,000	1,400,000
Manufacturing margin	1,000,000	800,000	1,000,000	2,800,000
Variable selling and administrative expenses (2)	100,000	80,000	100,000	280,000
Contribution margin	900,000	720,000	900,000	2,520,000
Fixed costs:				
Manufacturing	600,000	600,000	600,000	1,800,000
Selling and administrative	100,000	100,000	100,000	300,000
Total	700,000	700,000	700,000	2,100,000
Net Income	$ 200,000	$ 20,000	$ 200,000	$ 420,000
(1) Cost of goods sold:				
Beginning inventory	$ –0–	$ –0–	$ 100,000	$ –0–
+ Production costs – annual				
50,000 units × $10 =	500,000			
50,000 units × $10 =		500,000		
40,000 units × $10 =			400,000	
				1,400,000
= Inventory available	500,000	500,000	500,000	1,400,000
– Ending inventory	–0–	100,000	–0–	–0–
= Cost of goods sold	$ 500,000	$ 400,000	$ 500,000	$1,400,000
(2) Variable selling & administrative expenses:				
50,000 units × $2 =	$100,000			
40,000 units × $2 =		80,000		
50,000 units × $2 =			100,000	
Total				$280,000

Figure 5-11

costs shown in the variable costing income statement are only $600,000, so the company's net income is $120,000 higher than the net income with absorption costing. During the three-year period, both sales and production equal 140,000 units, so the total net income is $420,000 with either method.

EVALUATION OF THE NET INCOME RESULTS

Figure 5-11 shows that the variable costing net income moves in the same direction as sales. The manufacturing margin (sales less the variable cost of goods sold) is a constant percentage of sales, or 66.7%. The contribution margin is also a constant percentage of sales (60%). Consequently, management can easily predict the impact of a change in sales volume on net income because of the linear relationships involved. When sales increased by $300,000 from 1987 to 1988, the increase in net income of $180,000 is logical because of the following computation:

$$\frac{\text{Increase in}}{\text{sales volume}} \times \frac{\text{Contribution}}{\text{margin rate}} = \frac{\text{Increase in}}{\text{net income}}$$

$$\$300,000 \quad \times \quad .6 \quad = \quad \$180,000$$

The same approach can be taken to determine the decrease in net income from 1986 to 1987 when sales decreased from $1,500,000 to $1,200,000.

$$\frac{\text{Decrease in}}{\text{sales volume}} \times \frac{\text{Contribution}}{\text{margin rate}} = \frac{\text{Decrease in}}{\text{net income}}$$

$$\$300,000 \quad \times \quad .6 \quad = \quad \$180,000$$

The absorption costing results, however, are much more difficult to interpret and explain. Despite the fact that sales increased by $300,000 from 1987 to 1988, the net income of 1988 was actually $60,000 lower than that of 1987. The reason these results are so inconsistent is that net income with absorption costing is affected by changes in inventory (sales not equal to production) because of the absorption of fixed manufacturing overhead costs as product costs. As such, absorption costing net income is a function of both sales and production, whereas variable costing net income is a function of sales only.

An Irvin Company manager will naturally expect a higher profit when the sales volume increases, selling prices remain constant, and all costs are the same. Unless the manager fully understands the impact of fixed manufacturing overhead costs on profits with absorption costing, he or she will have trouble interpreting these results. Another obvious inconsistency with absorption costing arises from the fact that net income in 1986 was $200,000 on sales of $1,500,000, whereas the same sales volume produced net income of only $80,000 in 1988 even though selling prices and all costs remained the same. These absorption costing deficiencies have made variable costing very popular for internal reporting purposes.

ABSORPTION COSTING NET INCOME VERSUS VARIABLE COSTING NET INCOME

The difference between the absorption costing net income and the variable costing net income in the Irvin Company case can be reconciled as follows (a positive result indicates a higher net income with absorption costing; a negative result indicates a higher net income with variable costing):

	1986	1987	1988
Change in inventory units	–0–	10,000	(10,000)
× Fixed manufacturing overhead cost rate	$12	$ 12	$ 12
= Difference in net incomes	0	$120,000	($120,000)

Many firms use variable costing for internal reporting purposes during an accounting period and convert to absorption costing at the end of the period by adding fixed manufacturing overhead costs to inventories and cost of goods sold. Let's now consider the primary benefits and limitations of variable costing. Both must be evaluated carefully to ensure that the inventory valuation method is used properly.

Objective 10:
Knowing the benefits and limitations of variable costing

BENEFITS OF VARIABLE COSTING

The major benefits of variable costing are:

1. Variable costing forces management to evaluate the cost behavior pattern of each cost item, thus making the managers aware of how sensitive costs are to changes in the level of activity.
2. The variable costing income statement format closely follows management's thinking about profit performance because net income is a function of sales, not some combination of both production and sales.
3. The information needed for cost-volume-profit analysis (discussed in Chapter 6) can be obtained directly from the income statement instead of from special analysis that is independent of the income statement.
4. The effect of fixed costs on profits is emphasized because the total fixed costs are treated as period costs and are reported in one place on the income statement rather than being scattered throughout the statement.
5. Variable costing provides the basis for the preparation of a flexible budget (discussed in Chapter 11) in which variable and fixed costs are separated.
6. Since variable and fixed costs are divided, variable costing assists management in such decision-making activities as profit planning, cost control, pricing, and resource allocations.

LIMITATIONS OF VARIABLE COSTING

Like most managerial accounting techniques, variable costing does have certain limitations, including:

1. The separation of many cost behavior patterns into variable and fixed components often is very difficult, and the results are only approximations at best.
2. Variable costing is not acceptable for external reporting or income tax reporting.
3. Variable costing may give the misleading impression that only the variable costs must be considered in pricing decisions. In the long run, both variable and fixed costs must be recovered before net income can be earned. As will be seen in Chapter 7, short-run pricing may be based on variable costing in special situations.
4. Balance sheet inventories valued with variable costing will be understated in terms of the total costs required to produce them, and various liquidity measures such as working capital and the current ratio will be adversely affected.

SUMMARY

A functional (or conventional) income statement does not identify cost behavior patterns. This is a drawback for internal reporting and managerial applications. Managers are mainly concerned about any historical income statement to the extent that it can be used to predict the future earnings performance. To project a future income statement, management must be able to evaluate how costs and profits will fluctuate with changes in sales volume.

Cost behavior is the measure of how a cost responds to changes in the level of business activity. Many types of cost behavior are found in the business world, but the three most common patterns are variable costs, fixed costs, and mixed costs. A variable cost will vary in total amount proportionately with some measure of business activity such as sales dollars. In contrast, a fixed cost will remain constant in total amount over a wide range of activity. A mixed cost (sometimes called a semivariable cost) contains both variable and fixed components.

A cost function must be developed to describe the cost behavior of each of the costs incurred in a given business. A linearity assumption is made in managerial accounting because of the relevant range concept and future orientation of the data. The relevant range concept enables management to eliminate many nonlinear cost behaviors because with it management can ignore extreme levels of business activity and concentrate on the normal range of operation.

Cost behavior analysis is required to separate the mixed costs. The three most important techniques used for cost behavior analysis are the visual fit of a scatter diagram method, high-low method, and linear regression analysis method. The basic objective with all three techniques is to obtain data concerning relationships between a cost and some measure of activity, and to find an estimated line that best fits the data points.

Variable costing is an inventory valuation method used for internal reporting by a manufacturing firm. It is an alternative to absorption costing, which is required by generally accepted accounting principles. A separation of variable and fixed costs is built into the income statement with variable costing, and the focus is on the contribution margin—sales less all variable costs. The major difference between variable costing net income and absorption costing net income is the timing of the fixed manufacturing overhead costs as deductions on the income statement. Variable costing charges all fixed manufacturing overhead costs to the income statement as they are incurred instead of when the related products are sold.

GLOSSARY

ABSORPTION (FULL) COSTING.   The inventory valuation method required for a manufacturing firm by generally accepted accounting principles in which all manufacturing costs are inventoried, regardless of their cost behavior (p.142).

COMMITTED FIXED COST.   Fixed cost that is required even if the operation has extremely low activity (p. 148).

CONTRIBUTION MARGIN.   Sales revenue less all variable costs (manufacturing, selling, and administrative) (p.143).

CONTRIBUTION MARGIN RATE.   The contribution margin divided by the related sales revenue (p.143).

CORRELATION COEFFICIENT.   A statistic available with linear regression analysis that measures the direction and degree of correlation of the relationship between two variables such as cost and production volume (p. 155).

COST BEHAVIOR ANALYSIS.   The evaluation of how a cost responds to changes in the level of activity (p. 150).

COST FUNCTION.   The relationship between a cost as a dependent variable and some measure of the level of activity as an independent variable (p.145).

CURVILINEAR VARIABLE COST.   Cost function with a slope that is not constant over all levels of activity (p.146).

DISCRETIONARY FIXED COST.   Fixed cost that can be reduced or discontinued by management if adequate time is available (p. 148).

HIGH-LOW METHOD. A cost behavior analysis technique based on the changes in costs and levels of activity between the highest and lowest points (p.152).

LEAST SQUARES METHOD. The mathematical technique underlying linear regression analysis (p.153).

LINEARITY ASSUMPTION. The assumption used in managerial accounting to reduce nonlinear cost functions to straight-line cost functions (p.145).

LINEAR REGRESSION ANALYSIS. A statistical technique used to mathematically determine the line that best fits a scatter of data points (p.153).

MANUFACTURING MARGIN. Sales revenue less the variable cost of goods sold (p.156).

MANUFACTURING MARGIN RATE. The manufacturing margin divided by the related sales revenue (p.156).

MIXED COST. A cost that has both a variable component and a fixed component (sometimes called a semivariable cost) (p. 145).

PRO FORMA INCOME STATEMENT. An income statement projected for a future period (p.142).

REGRESSION LINE. The line fit to the scatter of data points (representing relationships between a dependent variable and an independent variable), such that the sum of the squared deviations between the data points and the line is minimized (p.153).

RELEVANT RANGE. The range of activity within which a business expects to operate and incur variable costs with constant slopes as well as fixed costs that are constant in total amount (p. 147).

STEP-FIXED COST FUNCTION. Cost function that changes abruptly after remaining constant over a wide range of activity (p.148).

STEP-VARIABLE COST FUNCTION. Cost function that changes abruptly after remaining constant over a narrow range of activity (p.147).

VARIABLE (DIRECT) COSTING. The inventory valuation method used by a manufacturing firm for internal reporting in which only the variable manufacturing costs are treated as product costs (p.155).

VISUAL FIT OF A SCATTER DIAGRAM METHOD. A cost behavior estimation technique with which the analyst draws a straight line through the data points so that the line comes as close to as many points as possible (p.150).

DISCUSSION QUESTIONS

1. Why does cost behavior have such an important influence on the income statement?
2. What are the limitations of a functional income statement in predicting the future profit performance of a firm?
3. What is the contribution margin? Why is it an important managerial accounting measure?
4. How does an income statement with a contribution margin format enable managers to forecast future profitability?
5. The Vander Company earned $130,000 on sales of $1,300,000 in 1986. While forecasting the 1987 income performance for the firm, the sales

manager expects sales revenue to increase by 40% to $1,820,000 even though selling prices will remain the same as they were in 1986. As a result, the sales manager believes that the firm's net income also will increase by 40% to $182,000. Do you agree? Explain.

6. What is meant by cost behavior classifications and why are managers concerned with them?

7. Why do cost behavior classifications differ between firms?

8. Identify typical measures of activity for determining variability of costs in a manufacturing firm. In a nonmanufacturing firm.

9. What is a cost function? What are its major components?

10. Why is the linearity assumption of significance in the development of a cost function?

11. If we have a cost function in the form of $y = a + bx$, what do each of these letters refer to in terms of the cost performance? In terms of an x/y display on a graph?

12. Explain the three basic cost functions—variable, fixed, and mixed.

13. Why are many variable cost functions actually curvilinear to some extent? What do managerial accountants do to eliminate the curvilinear behavior?

14. What is the significance of the relevant range in developing a variable cost function?

15. Why is a step cost function frequently incurred for a variable cost?

16. Explain why fixed costs often do not remain constant over an entire range of activity. What is the significance of the relevant range for fixed costs?

17. Distinguish between a discretionary fixed cost and a committed fixed cost. Give an example of each.

18. What are the three most popular techniques to choose from in separating mixed costs? Which of the three is the most accurate?

19. The Hi-Lo Company wants to estimate the cost behavior of its manufacturing supplies. Selected data are as follows:

Manufacturing Supplies	Production Level
$34,920	6,480 hours
31,320	4,680 hours

Using these data, estimate the cost behavior of manufacturing supplies.

20. What is a scatter diagram and how is it used by managers?

21. Explain why linear regression is an accurate cost estimation technique.

22. What are the major characteristics of variable costing? How does it differ from absorption costing?

23. How can variable costing net income and absorption costing net income be reconciled for a given accounting period?

24. What are the benefits and limitations of variable costing?

25. The McCabe Company uses variable costing for internal reporting and absorption costing for external reporting. During the previous year, the firm produced 90,000 units and sold 112,500 units. The variable costs required to manufacture one unit were $3.30 and the fixed costs were $9 per unit. Which of the two methods, variable costing or absorption costing, would report the highest net income? By how much, based on the facts given?

EXERCISES

Exercise 5-1 Comparing Income Statements with Functional and Contribution Margin Formats

Barlow Corporation reported sales for the year ended December 31, 1987 of $11,240. Cost of goods sold for the period was $5,800. Of that amount, $1,000 was attributed to fixed manufacturing costs. Selling expenses for the year were $1,500, of which half were variable and half were fixed. Administrative expenses were fixed at $1,200 for the year.

Required:
A. Prepare an income statement for this firm using the functional format.
B. Prepare an income statement for this firm using a contribution margin format.

Exercise 5-2 Evaluating the Effect of Sales Increase on Profit

Given the income statement below, what would projected net income for 1988 be if sales are expected to double?

PRICE BUSINESS PRODUCTS
Income Statement
For the Year Ended December 31, 1987

Sales		$1,680,500
Less variable costs:		
Variable cost of goods sold	$660,000	
Variable operating expenses	213,860	
Total		873,860
Contribution margin		806,640
Less fixed costs:		
Manufacturing	130,000	
Selling and administrative	210,000	
Total		340,000
Net income		$ 466,640

Exercise 5-3 Basic Contribution Margin Income Statement

The following information relates to a new product being produced by the Wompler Corporation:

Selling price per unit	$ 30
Manufacturing costs:	
Variable cost per unit produced	16
Total fixed	50,000
Selling & administrative costs:	
Variable cost per unit sold	6
Total fixed	30,000

There was no beginning inventory. During the year, 25,000 units were produced and 20,000 units were sold.

Required:
Prepare an income statement for the year using a contribution margin format.

Exercise 5-4 Basic Contribution Margin Income Statement

Below are data for the Dellinger Company pertaining to the year ending December 31, 1987:

Units manufactured	120,000
Units sold	90,000
Fixed manufacturing overhead	$210,000
Fixed selling & administrative expenses	120,000
Selling price per unit	18
Direct materials per unit	4.50
Direct labor cost per unit	3.00
Variable manufacturing overhead per unit	3.00
Variable selling and administrative expenses per unit	1.50

Required:

Prepare a contribution margin income statement for 1987 assuming there was no beginning inventory.

Exercise 5-5 Basic Cost Behavioral Patterns

The graphs below relate to the behavior of certain costs at a local day care school.

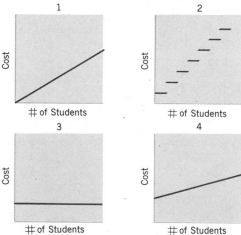

Required:

A. Identify each graph by its cost behavior (fixed, variable, etc.).
B. For the costs listed below, select the graph which is best matched with the cost.

   1. Teachers' salaries. A teacher is required for every 25 children.
   2. Cost of food for daily meals.
   3. Repairs and maintenance. The maintenance person is on salary. Other repairs and labor depend on the funds provided as the number of students increases.
   4. Rent on school building.

Exercise 5-6 Identifying Cost Behavior Classifications

Following is a list of costs that you are to classify into their most likely category:

	Fixed	Variable	Mixed
1. Rent on factory building–$2,000 per month			
2. Cost of tires installed on products			

3. Depreciation on machinery—
   straight line
4. Cost of paint used on products
5. Fire insurance on plant
6. Direct labor
7. Plant superintendent's salary
8. Computer lease cost—$500 per
   month plus $40 per hour of
   computer time.
9. Property taxes on plant
10. Controller's salary
11. Electricity costs for plant
12. Indirect labor

Exercise 5-7 Determining a Cost Equation and Graphing the Cost Function

The Rogers Furniture Company is reviewing its advertising program. An analysis of cost and volume data for the past four years shows that marketing expenses were $40,000 a year plus $.05 for each dollar of sales.

Required:

A. Develop the cost equation that describes the company's total annual advertising cost. What is the slope of this equation? Why?
B. Based on your equation in part A, estimate advertising costs for annual sales of $3,000,000 and $4,000,000.
C. Graph the advertising total cost line.

Exercise 5-8 Evaluating Cost Behavior Patterns

During the first eight months of the year, the Williamson Company recorded the following production activity and manufacturing overhead costs:

Month	Direct Labor Hours	Manufacturing Overhead Costs
January	43,000	$317,000
February	47,000	331,000
March	58,500	324,000
April	67,600	354,000
May	48,000	338,000
June	52,000	318,000
July	65,000	378,000
August	72,000	380,000

Required:

A. Plot the above data on a scatter diagram and draw the estimated cost function involved.
B. Calculate the estimated fixed and variable components of the manufacturing overhead costs from the graph in part A.
C. Using the data above, compute the fixed and variable cost components for manufacturing overhead costs using the high-low method.

Exercise 5-9 Evaluating Cost Behavior Patterns

The management of the Mauller Company is reviewing the cost of operating its maintenance department during the past five years. The following data have been collected:

Year	Units Produced	Maintenance Costs
1983	11,000	$160,000
1984	14,000	185,000

1985	22,000	230,000
1986	26,000	250,000
1987	20,000	220,000

Required:
A. Determine the variable and fixed costs using the high-low method.
B. Calculate the estimated maintenance cost for 1988 if 28,000 units are to be produced.
C. Use linear regression analysis to determine the variable and fixed costs for the firm.

Exercise 5-10   Evaluating Cost Behavior

The Bloomtown Hospital has collected the following data concerning laundry costs for the past six months:

Month	Laundry Costs	Direct Labor Hours
1	$8,360	3,020
2	9,000	3,500
3	7,600	2,900
4	8,000	3,000
5	9,600	3,600
6	9,200	3,700

Required:
A. Graph the data for laundry costs as a function of direct labor hours and visually draw the best fit for the cost function involved.
B. Compute the fixed and variable components of the laundry costs using the high-low method.
C. Compute the fixed and variable components of the laundry costs using regression analysis.
D. Discuss the strengths and weaknesses of each of the cost estimation techniques above.

Exercise 5-11   Graphing a Mixed Cost

Redbird Enterprises has chosen to be billed by the telephone company based on its usage of the system plus a fixed monthly charge. The agreement states that Redbird will be charged $20 per month plus $.10 for each outgoing call.

Required:
Graph the cost function for Redbird Enterprises' telephone bill. Assume a relevant range of at most 300 calls per month.

Exercise 5-12   Using the High-Low Method

Henderson Corporation has experienced the following maintenance costs for the first six months of 1987:

Month	Maintenance Costs	Machine Hours
January	$54,850	2,125
February	55,500	2,300
March	62,000	2,400
April	57,925	1,800
May	44,000	1,500
June	51,750	1,750

Required:
Using the high-low method, determine Henderson Corporation's maintenance cost function.

Exercise 5-13 Preparing a Scatter Diagram
Pauley Printing publishes the local weekly newspaper. The company has gathered information for the last two years concerning its overhead cost in relation to the number of newspapers printed. This information is summarized as follows:

Quarter	Number of Newspapers	Overhead Cost
1st – 1985	10,000	$1,500
2nd – 1985	12,000	1,400
3rd – 1985	15,000	1,700
4th – 1985	17,000	2,000
1st – 1986	16,000	1,700
2nd – 1986	18,000	1,800
3rd – 1986	22,000	2,000
4th – 1986	21,000	2,200

Required:
Plot a scatter diagram to estimate the fixed portion of the overhead cost for Pauley Printing.

Exercise 5-14 Basic Linear Regression
Pete Johnson produces custom designed wooden storm doors in his basement. Because he lives in an area where electricity is quite expensive, he has carefully monitored the costs of operating his power machines. For the past seven months, the number of doors completed and the cost of electricity involved have been:

Month	1	2	3	4	5	6	7
Doors completed	7	8	5	9	8	3	9
Electricity used	$110	$120	$90	$150	$130	$80	$160

Required:
Perform regression analysis to determine the fixed and variable portions of Johnson's electricity cost.

Exercise 5-15 Use of Linear Regression
The following data have been accumulated during the past seven months for the direct labor hours worked and the related maintenance costs incurred by the Jenkins Company:

Month	Direct Labor Hours	Maintenance Costs
January	4,000	$10,000
February	8,000	12,000
March	8,000	14,000
April	9,000	16,000
May	10,000	16,000
June	12,000	20,000
July	6,000	12,000

Required:
A. Use regression analysis to separate the maintenance costs into their fixed and variable components.

B. Discuss the reasoning for using direct labor hours in explaining maintenance costs. Would you suggest any better way?

Exercise 5-16 Evaluating Committed and Discretionary Fixed Costs

For the following fixed costs, answer "C" if the item is most likely to be a committed cost or "D" for a discretionary cost.

1. Liability insurance
2. Long-term leases
3. Marketing costs
4. Pension benefits
5. New systems development costs
6. Rental of office space
7. Real estate taxes on warehouse
8. Clerical staff salaries

Exercise 5-17 Basic Comparison of Absorption and Variable Costing

The cost structure of the Smith Manufacturing Company is summarized as:

Variable manufacturing costs per unit	$ 35
Variable selling and administrative costs per unit	4
Total annual fixed manufacturing overhead costs	96,000
Total annual fixed selling and administrative costs	40,000

32,000 units were produced during the year, and 24,000 units were sold at a price of $50 per unit. There were no beginning inventories.

Required:

A. Compute the ending inventory costs for absorption costing and variable costing.

B. Compute net income under both methods and reconcile the difference between the two methods.

Exercise 5-18 Net Income with Absorption and Variable Costing

The Bike-ease Company produces a special part for bicycles. Each part sells for $20 and the company's normal level of sales and production is 250,000 parts a year. Cost data for last year are presented below:

Direct materials	$3/unit
Direct labor	$2.50/unit
Manufacturing overhead	$1/unit plus $1,750,000 fixed costs per year
Selling and administrative expenses	$2/unit plus $750,000 fixed costs per year

Required:

A. If the company produces 250,000 parts and sells 225,000 of them, calculate net income using variable and absorption costing.

B. Explain why there is a difference between the net incomes in part A.

Exercise 5-19 Absorption and Variable Costing Income Statements

Otter Manufacturing Company provides the following information concerning its 1987 operations:

Number of units produced		45,000
Budgeted production – units		45,000
Selling price per unit	$	36
Variable costs:		
Direct labor		6

Direct materials	7
Manufacturing overhead	3
Selling and administrative	2
Fixed costs:	
Manufacturing overhead	180,000
Selling and administrative	85,000
Units sold	33,000

There was no beginning inventory for the firm.

Required:

A. Prepare an absorption costing income statement for the Otter Manufacturing Company.

B. Prepare a variable costing income statement for Otter Manufacturing.

Exercise 5-20 Absorption and Variable Costing Comparison

Hartford, Inc. uses absorption costing for its external financial statements and variable costing for managerial planning and control purposes. By the end of 1987, the following data had been gathered:

	Units	Variable Costing Unit Cost	Absorption Costing Unit Cost
Beginning inventory	12,000	$ 8	$11
Ending inventory	10,000	10	12

42,000 units were sold during 1987.

Required:

A. How many units were produced in 1987?

B. By how much will the net income be different when comparing the absorption and variable costing results?

C. Which method will give the larger net income?

PROBLEMS

Problem 5-1 Income Statements with Functional and Contribution Margin Formats

Archer Auto Parts is a manufacturing company with sales of $798,400 for the fiscal year ended October 31, 1987. Gross profit for the period was 42% of sales. Only 25% of the cost of goods sold is a fixed manufacturing cost.

Sales salaries are the only selling expenses. The sales force has total base salaries of $80,000. Commissions for the year were an additional $33,000.

Administrative expenses for the year totaled $86,000. This included $57,000 of committed fixed costs and $29,000 of discretionary fixed costs.

Required:

A. Prepare an income statement with a functional format for Archer Auto Parts.

B. Prepare an income statement with a contribution margin format for Archer Auto Parts.

Problem 5-2 **Evaluating Income Statement Performance**

For the year ended December 31, 1987, Orbit Sales Company reported net sales of $2,185,680. Cost of goods sold totaled $980,000. Operating expenses during the period were·$795,000. Net sales for the year ending December 31, 1988 are projected to increase by 20%.

Required:

Compute the projected net income for 1988 under each of these situations:

1. 75% of cost of goods sold is a variable cost. 75% of operating expenses are variable costs.
2. 75% of cost of goods sold is a fixed cost. 75% of operating expenses are fixed costs.
3. Cost of goods sold and operating expenses are each 50% variable and 50% fixed.

Problem 5-3 **Evaluating Changes with a Contribution Margin Income Statement**

Below is the 1987 income statement for the Cleaver Company. In 1988, management is expecting direct materials cost to increase by 10%, direct labor cost to increase by 12%, and variable manufacturing overhead to increase by 10%.

CLEAVER COMPANY
Income Statement
For the Year Ended December 31, 1987

Sales		$500,000
Cost of goods sold:		
Direct materials	$ 80,000	
Direct labor	100,000	
Variable manufacturing overhead	50,000	
Fixed manufacturing overhead	100,000	330,000
Gross margin		170,000
Variable selling & admin. expenses		95,000
Fixed selling & admin. expenses		68,000
Net income		$ 7,000

Required:

A. Prepare a contribution margin income statement for 1987.
B. Prepare a contribution margin income statement for 1988 with the anticipated cost increases.
C. Management is considering an advertising program in 1988 that should increase sales by $150,000 and add $24,000 to fixed costs. Prepare a contribution margin income statement to show if the advertising program should be implemented or not (the other cost increases also will occur).

Problem 5-4 **Effects on Income Due to Cost and Revenue Changes**

Presented next are data for a company that is considering changes in an effort to increase net income:

Selling price per unit	$ 80
Variable costs per unit:	
Variable manufacturing expenses	24
Variable selling expenses	2
Fixed costs per year:	
Rent	16,000
Advertising	14,000
Other	5,000
Current annual sales level in units	1,000

In order to increase profitability, management is considering the following changes:

1. Increase sales commissions which will raise variable selling expenses to $5 per unit. The increase in commissions would provide additional incentive to sales representatives and is expected to increase unit sales by 5%.
2. Increase advertising expense by $4,000 a year, which is expected to increase unit sales by 15%.
3. Implement both of the above cost increases, thereby increasing sales by 20%.

Required:
A. Calculate current net income using a contribution margin format.
B. Calculate net income if only proposal 1 is implemented.
C. Calculate net income if only proposal 2 is implemented.
D. Calculate net income if both proposals are implemented.

Problem 5-5 Evaluating Cost Behavior
The Production manager of the RJS Company is analyzing the cost of water used to cool the plant machinery. She has accumulated the following data for the first 10 months of the year:

Month	Machine Hours	Water Costs
1	6,000	$ 2,500
2	6,500	2,700
3	5,500	2,100
4	4,500	1,900
5	4,000	1,800
6	5,000	2,000
7	4,500	1,900
8	5,500	2,000
9	4,000	1,800
10	4,500	2,100
Total	50,000	$20,800

Required:
A. Determine the fixed and variable components of the cost function associated with water costs using the:
   1. Linear regression analysis method
   2. High-low method
B. If 7,000 machine hours are used next month, what would be the expected water costs for each of the methods used in part A above?

Problem 5-6 Identifying Specific Cost Patterns (CPA)
Presented here are a number of cost behavior patterns that might be found in a

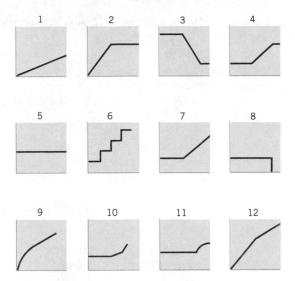

company's cost structure. The vertical axis on each graph represents cost, and the horizontal axis represents the level of activity.

Required:
A. For each of the following situations, identify the graph that best illustrates the cost pattern involved. A graph may be used more than once.
1. The cost of raw materials, when the cost decreases $.05 per unit for each of the first 100 units purchased, after which it remains constant at $3.50 per unit.
2. Water bill—a flat fixed charge, plus a variable cost after a certain number of gallons are used.
3. Depreciation of equipment, where the amount is computed by the straight-line method.
4. Rent on a building made available by the city, where the agreement calls for a fixed fee payment unless 100,000 labor hours are worked, in which case no rent needs to be paid.
5. Salaries of repairmen, where one repairman is needed for every 500 hours of machine-hours or less (i.e., 0 to 500 hours requires one repairman, 501 to 1,000 hours requires two repairmen, etc.).
6. Use of a machine under a lease, where a minimum charge of $2,000 is paid up to 400 hours of machine time. After 400 hours of machine time, an additional charge of $2 per hour is paid up to a maximum charge of $2,000 per period.
B. How would knowledge of cost behavior patterns such as those above be of use to a manager in analyzing the cost structure of the firm?

Problem 5-7   Use of Contribution Margin Analysis
The Westlake Company manufactures and sells only one product. The selling price of the product is $720 per unit, variable expenses are $540 per unit, and annual fixed expenses are $810,000. Annual production and sales are 20,000 units.

Required:
A. Calculate net income using the contribution margin format for the current situation.

B. Calculate net income under each of the following independent situations:
1. Sales volume in units decreases by 25%.
2. Sales price increases by 20%.
3. Fixed costs increase by 25%.
4. Variable expenses decrease by 20%.
5. Sales price increases by 20%, sales volume in units decreases by 25%, and fixed costs decrease by 25%.

Problem 5-8 Using the High-Low Method

Ervine Products has always purchased its employees' insurance from the All-good Insurance Agency. In 1987, Ervine expects to expand, increasing its number of employees to 900.

The following information represents the firm's insurance costs and number of employees for the past 10 years:

Year	No. of Employees	Insurance Cost
1977	206	$12,090
1978	223	13,504
1979	260	16,256
1980	400	19,851
1981	416	20,107
1982	493	24,003
1983	610	30,500
1984	621	31,251
1985	735	40,106
1986	758	41,208

Required:
Using the high-low method, estimate Ervine's insurance cost for 1987.

Problem 5-9 Applying the High-Low Method

The maintenance department of Realgood Appliances Company needs an estimate of repair costs for 1987. Management has found repair costs to be related to the number of units produced. The company estimates that output for 1987 will be 28,000 units and provides the following information for the previous 10 years:

Year	Units of Output	Repair Costs
1977	10,000	$150,000
1978	12,000	155,000
1979	11,000	160,000
1980	14,000	180,000
1981	15,000	200,000
1982	18,000	230,000
1983	22,000	235,000
1984	25,000	230,000
1985	30,000	260,000
1986	26,000	250,000

Required:
After analyzing the data involved, correctly use the high-low method to estimate the firm's repair costs for 1987.

Problem 5-10 Use of the High-Low Method

In the Archer Company's operation, maintenance costs fluctuate with the level of production. Production for the fourth quarter of 1987 is estimated at 28,000 units. Data concerning the maintenance costs and production levels for the previous seven quarters are as follows:

	Quarter	Units Produced	Maintenance Cost
1986	1st	10,000	$ 6,000
	2nd	13,000	7,500
	3rd	16,000	8,000
	4th	20,000	9,500
1987	1st	26,000	10,500
	2nd	30,000	11,000
	3rd	24,000	10,000

Required:
Using the high-low method, estimate maintenance costs for the fourth quarter of 1987.

Problem 5-11 High-Low Cost Estimation
Hadley Company estimates that each machine hour should cost $2.25. The following is a schedule of units produced and the number of machine hours used for each month of 1986.

	Units	Machine Hours
January	8,000	95
February	10,000	105
March	13,000	110
April	13,500	115
May	12,000	110
June	14,000	120
July	18,000	140
August	16,000	125
September	15,000	125
October	12,000	105
November	9,000	95
December	7,000	85

Required:
The average monthly production in 1987 is projected to be 15,500 units. What is the estimated annual cost of production for 1987?

Problem 5-12 Linear Regression Analysis
Quality Furniture creates handmade dining tables. Information on units produced and overhead costs for the previous six months appears below:

Units produced	17	23	19	26	18	21
Overhead costs (in $100s)	$55	$71	$61	$78	$52	$60

Required:
A. Use regression analysis to determine the overhead cost function.
B. What is the expected overhead cost for next month if production is projected to be 24 units?

Problem 5-13 Regression Analysis Compared to the High-Low Method
Jaquard, Inc. needs an estimate of its 1987 manufacturing overhead costs. Direct labor hours for 1987 are expected to be 60,000. The following additional information is available:

Year	Direct Labor Hours	Manufacturing Overhead Cost
1982	38,000	$250,000
1983	36,000	244,000
1984	39,000	265,000
1985	46,000	291,000
1986	55,000	320,000

Required:
A. Use the high-low method to estimate manufacturing overhead cost for 1987.
B. Use regression analysis to estimate manufacturing overhead cost for 1987.
C. Which result should be more accurate? Why?

Problem 5-14 Interpreting Absorption and Variable Costing Information

The following are selected items of information about Hapley Company's 1986 operations:

	Units	Direct Labor	Direct Materials	Applied Overhead Fixed	Applied Overhead Variable
Beginning inventory	14,000	$10/unit	$ 8/unit	$8/unit	$4/unit
Ending inventory	9,000	$11/unit	$10/unit	$7/unit	$5/unit

Underapplied overhead = $22,000
Sales = 21,000 units @ $42 each
Variable selling expenses = $54,000
Fixed selling and administrative expenses = $78,000

Required:
From the data provided, determine:

1. The number of units produced.
2. Cost of ending inventory using absorption costing.
3. Cost of ending inventory using variable costing.
4. Total contribution margin.
5. Difference in net income between absorption and variable costing.

Problem 5-15 Comparing Absorption and Variable Costing

The Boller Company sells a product for $60 per unit. Variable manufacturing costs per unit are $32, variable selling costs per unit are $12, total fixed manufacturing costs are $100,000 per year, and total fixed selling and administrative expenses are $60,000 per year. There was no beginning inventory, and during the year 12,500 units were produced and 10,000 units were sold.

Required:
A. Determine the cost of the ending inventory assuming:
  1. Variable costing
  2. Absorption costing
B. Determine the total fixed costs charged to the period assuming:
  1. Variable costing
  2. Absorption costing
C. Prepare an income statement for the year assuming:
  1. Variable costing
  2. Absorption costing

Problem 5-16   Comparing Variable and Absorption Costing

The Hillside Manufacturing Company produces a single product and the following data is available:

Product Costs	
Direct materials	$ 2.40 per unit
Direct labor	1.60 per unit
Manufacturing overhead:	
Fixed	240,000 per year
Variable	.80 per unit
Selling and administrative expenses:	
Fixed	128,000 per year
Variable	.80 per unit
Additional Data	
Expected production:	100,000 units per year
Beginning inventory:	–0–
Units produced during the year	100,000
Units sold during the year	80,000
Selling price	$11.10 per unit

Over-or underapplied overhead is closed directly to cost of goods sold at year-end.

Required:

A. Calculate the cost of inventory at year-end using:
   1. Absorption costing
   2. Variable costing
B. Calculate net income for the year using:
   1. Absorption costing
   2. Variable costing
C. Explain why there is a difference in net income between absorption and variable costing.

Problem 5-17   Comparison of Absorption and Variable Costing

The Controller of the Thompson Company has prepared the firm's income statement for January, 1987. The statement has been prepared on the variable costing basis and is reproduced below. The firm has just adopted the variable costing method for internal reporting purposes.

THOMPSON COMPANY Income Statement (000 omitted) Month Ended January 31, 1987		
Sales		$6,240
Less: Variable cost of goods sold		3,120
Contribution margin		3,120
Fixed costs:		
Manufacturing	$1,560	
Selling and administrative	1,040	
Net income		2,600
		$ 520

The controller attached the following notes to the statements: The unit sales price for January averaged $62.40. The unit manufacturing costs for the month were:

Variable costs	$31.20
Fixed costs	10.40
Total costs	$41.60

The unit price for fixed manufacturing costs is a predetermined rate based upon a normal monthly production of 150,000 units. Production for January was 45,000 units in excess of sales. The inventory at January 31 consisted of 80,000 units.

Required:
A. The controller is not satisfied with the variable costing basis and wonders what the net income would have been under the prior absorption costing basis.
   1. Present the January income statement on an absorption cost basis.
   2. Reconcile and explain the difference between the variable costing and the absorption costing net income figures.
B. Explain the features associated with variable costing income measurement that should appeal to the firm's sales manager.

Problem 5-18 Comparison of Absorption and Variable Costing
Below is a budget related to the production and sales of a talking doll made by the Whamco Company:

Sales	$800,000
Manufacturing costs:	
Fixed	100,000
Variable	300,000
Selling & admin. expenses:	
Fixed	80,000
Variable	200,000
Net income	$120,000

100,000 units represent the budgeted operating level used for the budgeted information above and to apply fixed manufacturing overhead costs to production. All fixed costs are incurred uniformly throughout the year. Over- and underapplied fixed manufacturing costs are not closed to cost of goods sold until year-end.

At the end of the first six months, the following information is available:

Sales	30,000 units
Actual production	60,000 units

Required:
A. Calculate the amount of fixed manufacturing overhead cost assigned to the product during the first six months under absorption costing.
B. Calculate the reported net income (loss) for the first six months under variable costing and absorption costing.
C. Reconcile the difference between absorption and variable costing income.

Problem 5-19 Evaluating an Income Performance with Variable Costing
The Gallion Company produces and sells medium-priced wines. The firm has

not been able to achieve profit results that are acceptable to its president. Demand for the products in recent years has been increasing and production last year was very near the limit of the firm's capacity of 1 million bottles per year. The firm's most recent income statement, prepared with absorption costing, shows the following operating results:

Sales (980,000 bottles @ $6.40)		$6,272,000
Cost of goods sold:		
Beginning inventory (10,000 bottles @ $5.76)	$ 57,600	
Production cost (985,000 bottles @ $5.76)	5,673,600	
Total	5,731,200	
Ending inventory (15,000 bottles @ $5.76)	86,400	
Cost of goods sold		5,644,800
Gross profit		627,200
Selling and administrative expenses		544,000
Net income before tax		$ 83,200

The president has hired you to find ways to improve the firm's profitability. Your first step is to evaluate the cost behavior patterns involved as follows:

Production costs:
  Variable—$3.20 per bottle
  Fixed—$2,521,600 for 985,000 bottles, or $2.56 per bottle
Selling and administrative expenses:
  Variable—$.16 per bottle sold
  Fixed—$387,200

Required:
A. Prepare an income statement for the firm using variable costing.
B. Why is the net income in requirement A different from that shown earlier with absorption costing?
C. The company's marketing manager believes that a $32,000 increase in advertising expenses will result in sales of 1 million bottles. Should this decision be made?
D. In addition to the $32,000 in advertising expenses, the firm can increase its capacity to 1.2 million bottles per year by increasing the fixed manufacturing costs by $576,000. There will not be any change in the variable manufacturing costs or selling and administrative expenses. Assuming all 1.2 million bottles can be sold, what would be the effect on the firm's net income?

Problem 5-20 Absorption and Variable Costing Income Statements (CPA)
Maximum productive capacity for Childers Manufacturing is 200,000 units per year. Normal capacity is regarded as 180,000 units per year. Budgeted variable manufacturing costs are $10 per unit. Fixed factory overhead is $315,000 per year. Variable selling expenses are $4 per unit and fixed selling expenses are $260,000 per year. The selling price is $22 per unit.

Operating results for 1987 are: sales, 160,000 units; production, 170,000 units; and beginning inventory, 15,000 units.

Required:
A. Prepare in good form a 1987 income statement using absorption costing.
B. Prepare in good form a 1987 income statement using variable costing.

PART 3

USE OF MANAGERIAL ACCOUNTING FOR DECISION MAKING WITH A PLANNING FOCUS

6

COST-VOLUME-PROFIT RELATIONSHIPS

CHAPTER OVERVIEW AND OBJECTIVES

This chapter covers cost-volume-profit relationships as an extension of the cost behavior topics presented in Chapter 5. After studying this chapter, you should be able to:

1. Describe the importance of cost-volume-profit (CVP) analysis as a managerial accounting technique.
2. Explain how an income statement with a contribution margin format provides the information needed in CVP analysis.
3. Recognize the limiting assumptions of CVP analysis.
4. Calculate and evaluate a break-even point.
5. Prepare a CVP chart using different formats.
6. Realize how managers use the margin of safety as a measure of risk.
7. Use CVP analysis to plan profits.
8. Evaluate the impact of changes in selling prices, sales volume, sales mix, and costs using "what-if" analysis.
9. Perform CVP analysis for a multiproduct firm.
10. Describe the concept of operating leverage as it is used to evaluate the sensitivity of profits to changes in sales volume.

IMPORTANCE OF COST-VOLUME-PROFIT ANALYSIS

Objective 1: Use of cost-volume-profit analysis

In the previous chapter, we examined the relationship between cost behavior and the type of income statement needed by managers for planning, control, and decision making. Cost behavior information is a prerequisite for **cost-volume-profit (CVP) analysis,** a managerial accounting technique used to evaluate how costs and profits are affected by changes in the level of business activity. Managers are constantly faced with decisions about selling prices, sales volume, sales mix, and costs (variable and fixed) in order to find the right combination of these four factors that will produce acceptable profits. The amounts incurred for the four factors and the interrelationships between them change constantly as a firm's own operating conditions or its economic environment change. An essential part of successful management is anticipating and evaluating the effect of these changes so a firm's resources are acquired and used profitably. CVP analysis can assist managers in answering such questions as:

1. What is the firm's break-even point—the sales level at which the business will neither earn a profit nor incur a loss?
2. What effect will increased advertising expenditures have on sales volume and profit?
3. What level of sales must be achieved to earn the desired amount of net income?
4. How will sales volume be affected if selling prices are increased or decreased?
5. What will be the impact on profits of a variable cost (such as direct labor) being replaced by a fixed cost (such as depreciation on a robotics system)?
6. How much additional sales volume is required to offset a pending increase in direct materials cost by a supplier?
7. If additional plant capacity is acquired, increasing fixed manufacturing overhead costs, how will net income change?
8. What is the most profitable sales mix?
9. What market share must a firm achieve to attain its required return on investment?
10. What level of risk is associated with management's projection of sales for the upcoming year—that is, by how much do the estimated sales exceed the firm's break-even point?

Based on this line of questioning, another popular name for CVP analysis is **"what-if" analysis.** Considerations such as "What if selling prices are reduced 10%?," "What if sales volume declines 4%?," "What if the sales mix changes so more units of a product with a lower contribution margin are sold?," and "What if fixed costs increase because of a proposed rate increase by a local utility?" are examples of "what-if" analysis. This type of analysis enables management to change key variables in the cost-volume-profit relationships and quickly see the effects of the changes on the firm's profit performance.

When it is combined with the budgeting process discussed in Chapter 8, CVP analysis provides the means of planning and revising the firm's profit goals. Through the use of CVP analysis, managers can develop an understanding of the various interrelationships between the key profit variables and their implications for satisfactory profit results.

USE OF A CONTRIBUTION MARGIN INCOME STATEMENT

The income statement with a contribution margin format introduced in the previous chapter provides the information needed for CVP analysis. Recall that such an income statement features cost behavior by distinguishing between the variable costs and the fixed costs. All variable costs are subtracted from sales revenue as costs of doing business to determine the contribution margin. None of the fixed costs are inventoried since they are considered costs of being in business and thus are treated as period costs. Consequently, they are subtracted from the contribution margin in the period in which they are incurred. The distinction between the variable and fixed costs provides the foundation for the development of linear equations that can be used to estimate costs and profits at different sales volumes. These equations, covered in this chapter, are an essential part of CVP analysis.

Objective 2:
Contribution margin income statement and CVP analysis

ASSUMPTIONS UNDERLYING CVP ANALYSIS

The uncertainties of the future, the possibility of nonlinear cost behavior patterns, and the ever-changing nature of the business world require certain limiting assumptions in the use of conventional CVP analysis. (More sophisticated versions of the technique are available for nonlinear relationships and conditions of uncertainty but are beyond the scope of this book.) The limitations of CVP analysis must be evaluated carefully to make sure that the assumptions are realistic for a given set of "real world" operating conditions. In general, the limiting assumptions of CVP analysis are necessary because this managerial accounting technique is not sophisticated enough to precisely consider all the complex conditions possible in the business world.

CVP analysis represents a static model of business conditions even though those same conditions in the "real world" are dynamic (ever changing). As such, management must revise the facts included in a particular CVP analysis whenever the business conditions being considered change. Despite these limitations, CVP analysis usually is a close approximation of the results obtained when a more sophisticated analysis is performed for a specific set of operating conditions so it is a valuable managerial accounting tool. The assumptions underlying CVP analysis that limit its accuracy are:

1. The unit sales prices remain constant throughout the period being considered.
2. All costs can be identified as being either variable or fixed with a reasonable amount of accuracy.
3. Variable costs will change in total amount proportionately with volume.
4. Total fixed costs will remain constant over the entire range of activity being considered.
5. Efficiency remains constant—that is, no productivity gains or losses will occur during the period.
6. Whenever more than one product is sold, total sales will be in some predictable proportion or sales mix.
7. Variable costing is used if a manufacturing operation is involved or, if absorption costing is used, the number of units sold will equal the number of units produced. (The reason for this assumption is the deferral of fixed manufacturing overhead costs from one period to another with absorption costing.)

PROFIT PLANNING WITH CVP ANALYSIS

Let's consider how management can use CVP analysis to evaluate the interrelationships of selling prices, sales volume, sales mix, and costs so that acceptable profits can be planned. As we will see in Chapter 8, profit goals are established during the budgeting process and are reevaluated continuously throughout the budget period. In order to plan profits effectively, management must estimate as accurately as possible the selling price of each product, the variable costs required to produce and sell it, and the fixed costs expected for a given period. This information is then combined with estimates concerning the projected sales volume and sales mix to project the expected earnings performance.

In the illustration in this chapter, CVP analysis will be performed for the Water Sports Company, which began manufacturing a single model of water skis on January 2, 1986, in a Florida plant. The variable costing income statement for the firm's first year of operation shows:

WATER SPORTS COMPANY Income Statement — Variable Costing Year Ended December 31, 1986		
	Amount	% of Sales
Sales (12,000 units @ $50)	$600,000	100.0
Variable cost of goods sold	360,000	60.0
Manufacturing margin	240,000	40.0
Variable selling & admin. expenses	60,000	10.0
Contribution margin	180,000	30.0
Fixed costs:		
Manufacturing	$150,000	25.0
Selling & administrative	75,000	12.5
Total	225,000	37.5
Net income (loss)	$ (45,000)	(7.5)

BREAK-EVEN ANALYSIS: A STARTING POINT

Break-even analysis is the typical starting point of CVP analysis. Each unit of product sold is expected to provide revenue in excess of its variable costs and contribute to fixed costs as well as to profit. Remember that the total variable costs rise and fall proportionately with total sales revenue. The contribution margin is the amount of revenue left to (1) recover the fixed costs and (2) then earn a profit for the period. Since the total fixed costs remain constant during a given period, enough units must be sold to provide a total contribution margin in dollars (units sold multiplied by the contribution margin per unit) that is equal to the fixed costs of the period before a profit can be earned.

Objective 4:
Use of the
break-even point

The **break-even point** is the sales volume at which revenue and total costs are equal, with no net income or loss. Net income is earned above the break-even point, whereas a net loss is incurred below it. Both the variable and fixed costs are covered by sales revenue at the break-even point. Although a break-even point is not normally a desired performance target because of the absence of profit, it does indicate the level of sales necessary to avoid a loss. As such, the break-even point represents a target of the minimum sales volume a business must achieve. In addition, break-even analysis provides valuable information concerning the impact of cost behavior patterns at different sales levels. We will see later in this chapter that the basic procedures of break-even analysis can be expanded to plan for a desired amount of profit and to evaluate the margin of safety associated with the expected sales volume.

USE OF THE BREAK-EVEN EQUATION

The break-even point can be determined mathematically or graphically and can be expressed in either sales units or sales dollars. The mathematical approach, using a **break-even equation,** is based on a basic income statement with a contribution margin format stated as:

Sales − Variable costs − Fixed costs = Net income

or

Sales = Variable costs + Fixed costs + Net income

which can be expanded to

$$\begin{array}{c} \text{No. of units sold} \\ \times \\ \text{Selling price} \end{array} = \begin{array}{c} \text{No. of units sold} \\ \times \\ \text{Variable cost rate} \end{array} + \text{Fixed costs} + \text{Net income}$$

At the break-even point, the net income obviously is zero. Note that the left side of the last equation consists of: (1) the number of units that must be sold; (2) the selling price required; and (3) the total sales dollars found by multiplying (1) times (2). Thus, we can apply break-even analysis by determining the required amount of one or more of these three items, depending on our objective. If we know the selling price, we can find the number of units that must be sold. If we know the number of units expected to be sold, we can use the equation to determine the selling price needed to break even. Finally, we can let the total sales dollars required to break even be the unknown, without dividing the left side of the equation into the number of units and the selling price.

To illustrate the use of the break-even equation, consider the variable costing income statement presented earlier for the Water Sports Company. The firm operated below its break-even point in 1986 because it incurred a net loss of $45,000. Note that the total fixed costs were $225,000 and variable costs were 70% of sales [($360,000 + $60,000)/$600,000], or $35 per unit ($420,000/ 12,000 units). The number of units required for break-even sales can be established as an unknown (S) and determined as (the equations that follow are numbered for later reference):

(1)
$$\$50S = \$35S + \$225,000$$
$$\$15S = \$225,000$$
$$S = 15,000 \text{ units}$$

The break-even sales in units can be converted to sales dollars of $750,000 by multiplying the 15,000 units by the selling price of $50. If we had expected to sell 15,000 units and wanted to determine the selling price needed to break even (without knowing the $50 price given), we could do so by letting the selling price be the unknown (S) as follows:

(2)
$$15,000S = 15,000 \, (\$35) + \$225,000$$
$$15,000S = \$525,000 + \$225,000$$
$$15,000S = \$750,000$$
$$S = \$50$$

Finally, we can use the cost-volume-profit relationships to find the total sales dollars required to break even as the unknown (S):

(3)
$$S = .7S + \$225,000$$
$$.3S = \$225,000$$
$$S = \$750,000$$

The break-even sales dollars can be converted to sales units of 15,000 by dividing $750,000 by $50, the selling price. The break-even analysis indicates that the Water Sports Company must increase its sales level by 25% (from $600,000 or 12,000 units to $750,000 or 15,000 units) in order to break even financially. We can prove that sales revenue of $750,000 will produce break-even results by preparing the following income statement:

WATER SPORTS COMPANY
Pro forma Income Statement
Year Ending December 31, 1987

Sales (15,000 units × $50)	$750,000
Variable costs (15,000 units × $35)	525,000
Contribution margin	225,000
Fixed costs	225,000
Net income	$ –0–

CONTRIBUTION MARGIN APPROACH TO BREAK-EVEN ANALYSIS

Remember that the contribution margin is found by subtracting all variable costs from sales. The contribution margin rate or percentage is determined by dividing the contribution margin by sales revenue. The contribution margin is identified in the process of solving for (S) on the left side of equations (1) and (3) in the previous section. In the first equation, $15S$ represents the contribution margin as a dollar amount since each unit sold will have a contribution margin of $15. The total contribution margin earned will be $15 multiplied by the number of units determined for (S), the unknown. The third equation includes the contribution margin $(.3S)$ as a percentage (30%) of sales. By multiplying total sales dollars as (S) by .3, we can determine the total contribution margin.

These two equations illustrate two important rules to remember in break-even analysis:

1. When the contribution margin is expressed as a dollar per unit figure, the break-even point is calculated in sales units; and
2. When the contribution margin is stated as a percentage of sales, the break-even point is computed in sales dollars.

An alternative way to calculate a break-even point is by directly using the **contribution margin** as follows:

$$\text{Break-even sales} = \frac{\text{Fixed costs}}{\text{Unit contribution margin}} = \frac{\$225,000}{\$15} = 15,000 \text{ units}$$

or

$$\text{Break-even sales} = \frac{\text{Fixed costs}}{\text{Contribution margin \%}} = \frac{\$225,000}{30\%} = \$750,000$$

GRAPHIC APPROACH TO CVP ANALYSIS

A graph often is developed so managers can visualize the break-even point and the profitability of various combinations of revenues and costs over a range of volume. The graphic approach is especially helpful to managers in evaluating the effects of changes from past volume levels or those projected for the future. By using a graph, managers can eliminate the mathematical calculations otherwise required each time a different volume level is considered.

Objective 5: Preparing CVP charts

Such a graph often is called a "break-even chart," but this term is too limited because the break-even point is only a small part of the total information presented. The graph is more appropriately referred to as a **cost-volume-profit (CVP) chart,** an example of which is shown in Figure 6-1. The vertical axis of the CVP chart in Figure 6-1 represents dollars of revenue and costs in thousands, while the volume of units in thousands is measured along the horizontal axis. The steps used to prepare this cost-volume-profit chart are:

1. Plot the revenue line, which begins at the origin (zero $ and zero units) and increases at the rate of $50 (the selling price) per unit. As such, the revenue is $0 at zero volume and increases to $1,200,000 at 24,000 units.
2. Plot the fixed costs line as a horizontal line at the level of $225,000 for all volume levels.
3. Draw a line that starts at the level of fixed costs on the vertical axis (the intersection of $225,000) and increases at the variable cost rate of $35 per unit. Do this by selecting a sales volume above zero and calculating the total costs for that point. For example, at a sales volume of 10,000 units, we would project total costs of $575,000 [(10,000 × $35) + $225,000]. Then draw a line from the $225,000 point on the vertical axis to the $575,000 point at sales of 10,000 units. Note that the line drawn represents the total cost function, and the difference between it and the fixed cost line is the amount of variable costs at any level of sales volume.

Figure 6-1 indicates that the Water Sports Company's break-even point is $750,000 in sales revenue or 15,000 units—the same results obtained earlier with the mathematical approaches. The profit or loss anticipated for any sales volume between zero units and 24,000 units can be found on the chart. If the company does not achieve sales of $750,000, it will incur an operating loss, as

Figure 6-1
Cost-Volume-Profit
Chart

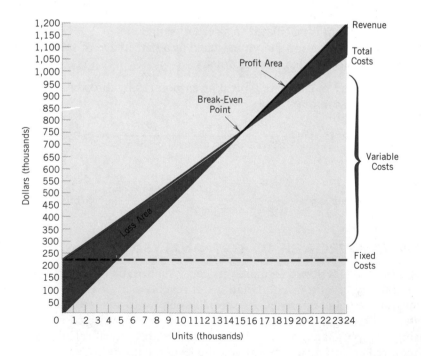

indicated by the colored area. A profit will be earned when sales exceed $750,000 (the black area). The chart provides management with valuable information to use in evaluating the profit results associated with different volume levels.

Alternative forms of CVP charts are presented in Figures 6-2 and 6-3. Some managers prefer these alternate forms because they emphasize contribution margin and net income. Note that Figure 6-1 does not allow us to read the amount of contribution margin directly from the graph because we started with the fixed costs and then added the variable costs. Thus, we can compare sales revenue to the total costs or to the fixed costs but not to the variable costs as needed for the contribution margin. The CVP chart in Figure 6-2 is used frequently because the contribution margin can be read directly from the graph. In this alternative format, the CVP chart is prepared by plotting the variable cost line, which begins at the origin and increases at the rate of $35 per unit, and then plotting the total cost line from the $225,000 level at the vertical axis so that it runs parallel to the variable cost function. By comparing the variable costs with revenue, we can directly determine the contribution margin in dollars at any sales volume from the CVP chart. For example, the contribution margin at the break-even point is the $225,000 needed to cover the fixed costs.

A third approach to a CVP chart, called a **profit-volume chart,** is shown in Figure 6-3. Some managers prefer a profit-volume chart because it emphasizes how profit changes in relation to volume. The major limitation is that it does not present a complete picture of how costs vary with changes in the volume level. Profit is shown on the vertical scale, while sales volume in units is presented on the horizontal axis. Alternatively, sales volume in dollars can be shown on the horizontal axis.

A profit-volume chart is prepared by connecting the point at which a firm

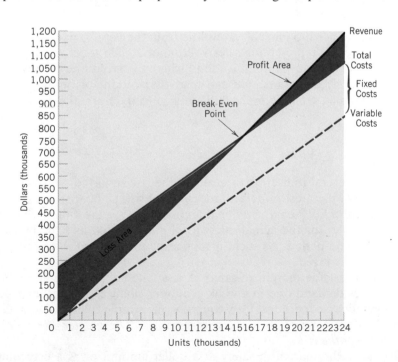

Figure 6-2
Cost-Volume-Profit
Chart

Figure 6-3
Profit-Volume
Chart

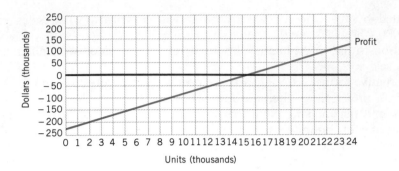

incurs the maximum loss with another point representing the expected profit or loss at a particular volume level. The maximum loss, consisting of the fixed costs not covered by any revenue, occurs at zero volume (as long as a firm has a positive contribution margin). In the case of the Water Sports Company, the fixed costs amount to $225,000, which is the first connecting point on the vertical axis. As volume increases and revenue is earned, a proportionate amount of contribution margin is available. A loss is incurred until the break-even point is reached—that is, when the total contribution margin is equal to the fixed costs. On the graph, that happens at the point where the profit line touches the horizontal axis. Any volume level above zero can be selected as the second point needed to plot the profit function. For example, let's consider the profit results if 20,000 units are sold. The expected profit at this level is:

Sales (20,000 units @ $50)	$1,000,000
Variable costs (20,000 units @ $35)	700,000
Contribution margin (20,000 units @ $15)	300,000
Fixed costs	225,000
Net income	$ 75,000

Therefore, we need to plot the profit line from the vertical axis at $(225,000) to the second point representing sales volume of 20,000 units and net income of $75,000. The break-even point is found where the profit line crosses the horizontal axis, or 15,000 units. We can read the amount of profit anticipated from sales ranging from 0 to 24,000 units directly from the profit-volume chart.

MARGIN OF SAFETY CONCEPT

Objective 6:
Measuring risk
with the margin
of safety

Managers use several indicators to evaluate the risk involved with operating a business. One of the most important measures of risk is the **margin of safety**—an integral part of CVP analysis. The margin of safety is the difference between the budgeted sales (or the actual sales) for a given period and the break-even sales for the same period. As such, it represents the amount sales can decline before a loss is incurred.

A firm with a large margin of safety is less vulnerable to the effects of decreases in sales demand due to a weak economy, changes in consumer behavior, or competitive conditions. Consequently, the simple rule used to apply the margin of safety concept in a given business is: *The greater the margin of safety, the lower the risk.*

We can state the margin of safety as a dollar amount or as a percentage of sales. For example, assume that the Water Sports Company expects sales of $937,500 in 1987 without any change in its break-even point of $750,000. The margin of safety is $187,500 ($937,500 − $750,000) or 20% ($187,500/ $937,500). As a result, the firm can incur a decline in sales of $187,500, or 20%, and still be operating at its break-even point.

PROJECTING PROFIT TARGETS

The basic procedures of break-even analysis can also be used to determine the sales volume needed to earn a **target** or **desired net income**. A profit goal can be expressed as a fixed amount of net income, as a percentage of sales, or as a return on investment. Return on investment analysis is covered later in Chapter 13. The contribution margin income statement provides the information used to find the sales volume required for the target profit. Assume that the Water Sports Company wants to earn a net income before tax of $90,000 in 1987 and expects the same selling price and costs as those experienced in 1986 (the before-tax net income will be taxed at the firm's total tax rate for any federal, state, and local income taxes applicable). We can compute the necessary sales target as:

S = Sales dollar target
S = Variable costs + Fixed costs + Target net income before tax
S = $.7S$ + $225,000 + $90,000
$.3S$ = $225,000 + $90,000
S = $1,050,000 [or 21,000 units ($1,050,000/$50)]

With the sales of $1,050,000, the following income statement shows that the net income before tax will be $90,000:

Sales (21,000 units @ $50)	$1,050,000
Variable costs (21,000 units @ $35)	735,000
Contribution margin	315,000
Fixed costs	225,000
Net income before tax	$ 90,000

Alternatively, assume that management's goal is to achieve before-tax profits that are 10% of sales. The equation required to determine the sales target is:

S = Sales dollar target
S = $.7S$ + $225,000 + $.1S$
$.2S$ = $225,000
S = $1,125,000 [or 22,500 units ($1,125,000/$50)]

Note that the target net income is expressed as a variable amount because the firm wants to earn a profit that is dependent on sales (10% or $.1S$). Again, an income statement can be prepared to prove that a sales level of $1,125,000 will produce a before-tax profit equaling 10% of sales:

Sales (22,500 units @ $50)	$1,125,000	
Variable costs (22,500 units @ $35)	787,500	
Contribution margin	337,500	10%
Fixed costs	225,000	
Net income before tax	$ 112,500	

CONSIDERATION OF AFTER-TAX PROFIT

Many firms choose to define their target profit as net income after tax (all income taxes are considered as costs), in which case an additional computation is required to determine the net income before tax. To do so, the net income after tax can be divided by the factor (1 − tax rate) to convert it to the related amount of before-tax profit. The tax rate involved is the total rate for all income taxes combined (federal, state, and local). For example, assume that the Water Sports Company's profit goal for 1987 is to earn net income after tax of $63,000 with an expected tax rate of 30%. We can calculate the required sales dollar volume as follows:

$$S = \text{Variable costs} + \text{Fixed costs} + \text{Target net income before tax}$$
$$S = .7S + \$225,000 + [\$63,000/(1 - .3)]$$
$$S = \$1,050,000 \text{ [or 21,000 units } (\$1,050,000/\$50)]$$

Alternatively, we can calculate the income before tax as follows:

$$X = \text{Net income before tax}$$
$$.3X = \text{Tax}$$
$$X - .3X = \text{Net income after tax}$$
$$X - .3X = \$63,000$$
$$.7X = \$63,000$$
$$X = \$90,000$$

The $90,000 can then be inserted into the equation used earlier to solve for S, the sales volume required to earn an after-tax profit of $63,000. Note that the sales level necessary to achieve the net income after tax of $63,000 is the same as the one we found earlier for net income before tax of $90,000 since $63,000/.7 = $90,000.

EVALUATING THE IMPACT OF CHANGE WITH "WHAT-IF" ANALYSIS

Objective 8:
Use of "what-if"
analysis

Once the cost-volume-profit relationships of a firm are known, management can use that information to find the combination of revenues and costs that will produce satisfactory profits. CVP analysis is particularly important to management during the budgeting process (described in Chapter 8) when various alternative strategies regarding the future financial performance must be evaluated. Acceptable target profits rarely are found when management first estimates amounts for the factors involved with CVP analysis. Instead, additional steps must be taken to evaluate alternative combinations of the factors. Effective profit planning must be concerned with the impact on profits of:

1. Changes in selling price
2. Changes in sales volume
3. Changes in sales mix
4. Changes in variable costs
5. Changes in fixed costs

To illustrate the CVP analysis used to evaluate potential changes with "what-if" questioning, we will continue to use the 1986 financial data of the Water Sports Company. Management undoubtedly would be dissatisfied with its first year financial results since a net loss of $45,000 occurred. Assume that the initial version of the profit planning process for 1987 has been completed with the 1986 selling prices and costs, but that sales volume is expected to increase by 3,000 units (from 12,000 units to 15,000 units). As a result, the initial pro forma income statement for 1987 (that will be used to evaluate the effects of certain changes next) has been prepared as follows:

WATER SPORTS COMPANY
Pro forma Income Statement
Year Ending December 31, 1987

Sales (15,000 units @ $50)	$750,000
Variable costs (15,000 units @ $35)	525,000
Contribution margin	225,000
Fixed costs	225,000
Net income	$ –0–

Although the projected performance for 1987 is better than the results of 1986, we assume that it is not acceptable to management because the firm will only operate at break-even sales. Consequently, management is considering a number of changes and will apply CVP analysis to evaluate their impact on profits. We will consider each change independently for illustrative purposes, although these changes usually would be evaluated concurrently in a real life situation.

CHANGE IN SELLING PRICE

The sales manager of the Water Sports Company estimates that a price reduction of 10% (from $50 to $45) will increase the number of units sold by 30%, from 15,000 units to 19,500 units. If this happens, the impact on break-even sales and net income is:

$$S = \text{Break-even sales}$$
$$\$45S = \$35S + \$225,000$$
$$\$10S = \$225,000$$
$$S = 22,500 \text{ units [or } \$1,012,500 \ (22,500 \times \$45)]$$

	Initial Pro forma Income Statement	Revised Pro forma Income Statement	Difference from Selling Price Change
Sales:			
(15,000 units × $50)	$750,000		
(19,500 units × $45)		$877,500	$127,500
Variable costs:			
(15,000 units × $35)	525,000		
(19,500 units × $35)		682,500	157,500
Contribution margin:			
(15,000 units × $15)	225,000		
(19,500 units × $10)		195,000	(30,000)
Fixed costs	225,000	225,000	–0–
Net income (loss)	$ –0–	$(30,000)	$(30,000)

Despite the increase in sales revenue of $127,500 (from $750,000 to $877,500) with this potential change of selling price, the firm would incur a net loss of $30,000 instead of operating at its break-even point. The reason is the $5 loss of contribution margin per unit (from $15 to $10), which is not offset by selling 4,500 additional units (19,500 units versus 15,000 units). Even though the sales revenue would increase by $127,500 with the proposed change, the variable costs would rise even more (from $525,000 to $682,500, or $157,500); so the loss of contribution margin is $30,000, the same amount as the net loss involved. The break-even point also increases from the $750,000 to $1,012,500, so this change would not produce favorable results for the firm.

CHANGE IN VARIABLE COSTS

In many situations, businesses cannot increase prices to improve their profit performance because of competitive forces and consumer resistance in their markets. Instead, managers must find a way to reduce costs by such measures as purchasing less expensive materials, more efficiently utilizing labor, or decreasing certain discretionary fixed costs such as employee training.

Here, let's assume that the production manager for the Water Sports Company believes that certain modifications to the manufacturing process will utilize labor more efficiently and reduce the variable costs by $3 per unit. The impact on the firm's break-even sales and its net income would be:

$$S = \text{Break-even sales}$$
$$\$50S = \$32S + \$225,000$$
$$\$18S = \$225,000$$
$$S = 12,500 \text{ units [or } \$625,000 \ (12,500 \times \$50)]$$

	Initial Pro forma Income Statement	Revised Pro forma Income Statement	Difference from Variable Cost Change
Sales (15,000 units × $50)	$750,000	$750,000	$ –0–
Variable costs:			
(15,000 units × $35)	525,000		
(15,000 units × $32)	_____	480,000	(45,000)
Contribution margin:			
(15,000 units × $15)	225,000		
(15,000 units × $18)		270,000	45,000
Fixed costs	225,000	225,000	–0–
Net income	$ –0–	$ 45,000	$45,000

The improved efficiency will increase the firm's profit by $45,000 because the contribution margin per unit will be $18 instead of $15. The additional contribution margin per unit of $3 multiplied by the 15,000 unit sales projection equals the increased net income of $45,000. In addition, the break-even point is reduced from 15,000 units to 12,500 units because of the improvement in productivity with this proposed change.

CHANGE IN FIXED AND VARIABLE COSTS

We have noted before that many management decisions regarding cost behavior involve a trade-off between variable and fixed costs. Thus, an important change to be evaluated with CVP analysis is the impact on profits of such a trade-off. The management of the Water Sports Company wants to evaluate the effect of changing the method used to compensate its sales manager, whose

1986 compensation consisted of an annual salary of $25,000 plus 5% of all sales revenue. In 1986, the sales manager was paid $55,000 [$25,000 + (.05 × $600,000)]. As an alternative, management wants to consider paying the sales manager a straight salary of $56,200 in 1987, an increase of $1,200 over the total compensation paid in 1986. Doing this would decrease the variable costs from 70% to 65% of sales; fixed costs would increase by $31,200 (the new salary of $56,200 less the old salary of $25,000). Consequently, the total fixed costs for 1987 would be $256,200 ($225,000 + $31,200), and the new contribution margin would be 35% of sales. The revised contribution margin per unit would be $17.50, which is the initial contribution margin of $15 per unit plus the variable cost savings with the sales commission of $2.50 per unit ($50 × 5%). The effect on the firm's break-even point and net income would be:

$$S = \text{Break-even sales}$$
$$S = .65S + \$256,200$$
$$.35S = \$256,200$$
$$S = \$732,000 \text{ [or 14,640 units (\$732,000/\$50)]}$$

	Initial Pro forma Income Statement	Revised Pro forma Income Statement	Difference from Salary Change
Sales (15,000 units × $50)	$750,000	$750,000	$ –0–
Variable costs:			
(15,000 units × $35)	525,000		
(15,000 units × $32.50)		487,500	(37,500)
Contribution margin:			
(15,000 units × $15)	225,000		
(15,000 units × $17.50)		262,500	37,500
Fixed costs	225,000	256,200	31,200
Net income	–0–	$ 6,300	$ 6,300

Note that net income increased by $6,300 with this proposed change because the total contribution margin increases by $37,500 (15,000 units × $2.50 per unit) while the fixed costs increase by only $31,200. In addition, the break-even point declines from $750,000 to $732,000 so from strictly a financial perspective, this proposed change is attractive.

CHANGE IN FIXED COSTS AND SALES VOLUME

Another proposal being considered by the management of the Water Sports Company is an advertising campaign that would cost the firm $45,000 each year. The sales manager estimates that the additional advertising will cause a 25% increase in sales units (from 15,000 units to 18,750 units). The new break-even point and net income would be:

$$S = \text{Break-even sales}$$
$$\$50S = \$35S + \$225,000 + \$45,000$$
$$\$15S = \$270,000$$
$$S = 18,000 \text{ units or } \$900,000 \text{ (18,000} \times \$50)$$

	Initial Pro forma Income Statement	Revised Pro forma Income Statement	Difference from Advertising Costs
Sales:			
(15,000 units × $50)	$750,000		
(18,750 units × $50)		$937,500	$187,500
Variable costs:			
(15,000 units × $35)	525,000		
(18,750 units × $35)		656,250	131,250
Contribution margin:			
(15,000 units × $15)	225,000		
(18,750 units × $15)		281,250	56,250
Fixed costs	225,000	270,000	45,000
Net income	$ –0–	$ 11,250	$ 11,250

The break-even point would increase by 3,000 units because an additional contribution margin of $45,000 (3,000 units × $15) is necessary to cover the proposed advertising expenditures. Note that the expected sales are 750 units above the break-even point with the increase of 3,750 units above the initial estimate for 1987. Consequently, the projected net income will be $11,250 — the result of earning a contribution margin of $15 for each of the 750 units above the break-even point.

SPECIAL PRICING SITUATIONS

CVP analysis also can assist managers in establishing selling prices. We saw earlier that the foundation for CVP analysis is an income statement with a contribution margin format that can be expressed as:

$$\text{Sales} = \text{Variable costs} + \text{Fixed costs} + \text{Net income}$$

Remember that sales also can be divided into the number of units sold multiplied by the selling price.

In the previous illustrations, we knew the selling price (e.g., $50 for a pair of water skis) but wanted to determine the sales volume for each given situation. If management knows the sales volume that will occur or can estimate it with reasonable accuracy, the same basic procedures can be used to find the selling price as an unknown in CVP analysis.

Let's assume again that the management of the Water Sports Company is faced with the break-even point established in the initial pro forma income statement for 1987 ($750,000 or 15,000 units). Suppose too, that the sales manager of the firm has decided to consider a request for 5,000 pairs of water skis from a wholesale sporting goods company on the West Coast. The Water Sports Company has not previously sold its products in that market area, so management does not believe there will be any adverse effect on its regular customers if a selling price below the normal price of $50 is quoted for the 5,000 units. The wholesaler has told the company that it wants a private label on the skis, has asked other manufacturers for competitive bids, and does not expect to pay nearly as much as $50 per pair of skis. The variable costs per pair of skis are expected to remain at $35, and a fixed cost of $15,000 will be required for the special label requested by the wholesaler. In addition, the sales manager has decided that the firm should earn a profit of $25,000 on the 5,000 pairs of skis. The selling price necessary to achieve this profit objective is $43 for each pair of skis, computed as follows:

$$X = \text{Selling price}$$
$$\text{Sales} = \text{Variable costs} + \text{Fixed costs} + \text{Net income}$$
$$5,000X = (5,000 \times \$35) + \$15,000 + \$25,000$$
$$5,000X = \$215,000$$
$$X = \$43$$

Note that only the fixed costs directly associated with the special order have been considered in the analysis to determine the $43 selling price. The $225,000 fixed costs forecast for 1987 in the earlier illustrations have been ignored. The company had already projected 15,000 units as its regular business for 1987, and these units represented the break-even sales so the fixed costs of $225,000 would be covered by the related contribution margin. Given the nature of the special order, only the additional fixed costs of $15,000 have to be considered in the analysis, along with the related variable costs and desired profit. We will discuss the use of managerial accounting data for different types of pricing strategies in more detail in Chapter 7. That discussion will cover the legal and other nonquantitative factors that must be considered in pricing decisions.

EXTENSION OF CVP ANALYSIS TO MULTIPLE PRODUCTS

For illustrative purposes, we have assumed until now that the Water Sports Company sells only one product. In reality, few businesses are so limited, although the analysis previously presented can be used for all products considered collectively. We now extend our discussion of CVP analysis to evaluate its application with multiple products.

Objective 9: Applying CVP analysis to multiple products

Different selling prices and different variable costs cause products to have different contribution margins. Products having higher contribution margins contribute more to fixed costs and profits than products with lower contribution margins. Thus, when products with high contribution margins make up a relatively large proportion of total sales, profits are greater than they are when the same sales level consists of products with low contribution margins. Consequently, the sales mix itself is a variable that managers must carefully plan and control as they seek satisfactory profits.

Earlier, we stated as a basic assumption of CVP analysis that total sales must be in some predictable proportion or sales mix whenever more than one product is sold. The term **"sales mix"** refers to the relative quantities of each product sold. CVP analysis can be performed for a multiproduct firm by using a **weighted average contribution margin** for a given sales mix. This analysis can be accomplished on the basis of a sales mix in units or a sales mix in dollars. In the illustration that follows, we will only consider a sales mix in units.

Assume that the Water Sports Company produces and sells two types of water skis, a Standard Model and a Deluxe Model, with the following data:

	Standard Model	Deluxe Model
Selling price	$50	$80
Variable costs	35	45
Contribution margin	$15	$35
Contribution margin %	30.00	43.75

Note that the Deluxe Model is most profitable with a contribution margin of $35 per pair of skis (or 43.75% of the selling price). The Standard Model has the same contribution margin used in the earlier illustration ($15 per unit or 30% of the selling price). The firm's fixed costs are $300,000, and the product mix consists of three Standard Models for each Deluxe Model. That is, the Water Sports Company sells three times as many Standard Models as it does Deluxe Models, so 75% of the products sold are Standard Models and 25% are Deluxe Models. The weighted average contribution margin per unit is $20, computed as follows:

$$\text{Weighted average contribution margin per unit} = (.75 \times \$15) + (.25 \times \$35)$$
$$= \$11.25 + \$8.75$$
$$= \$20$$

We can use the weighted average contribution margin per unit to compute the firm's break-even point with the same procedures described earlier for the single product situation. Break-even sales with the two products would be:

$$S = \text{Break-even sales}$$

$$S = \frac{\text{Fixed costs}}{\text{Weighted average contribution margin per unit}}$$

$$S = \frac{\$300,000}{\$20}$$

$$S = 15,000 \text{ units}$$

Since the break-even point consists of total units that must be sold, we use the sales mix again to determine how many units of each product are involved. The sales mix is 75% Standard Models and 25% Deluxe Models, so the 15,000 units are divided into 11,250 Standard Models and 3,750 Deluxe Models (.75 × 15,000 = 11,250 Standard Models and .25 × 15,000 = 3,750 Deluxe Models). The .75 and .25 are the results of the 3:1 ratio, the summation of which is 4 and the individual components are 3/4 and 1/4. The break-even income statement will be:

	Standard Model	Deluxe Model	Total
Sales – units	11,250	3,750	15,000
Sales – dollars	$562,500	$300,000	$862,500
Variable costs	393,750	168,750	562,500
Contribution margin	$168,750	$131,250	300,000
Fixed costs			300,000
Net income			$ –0–

PROFIT PLANNING WITH MULTIPLE PRODUCTS

We can use the same approach presented above to plan profits with multiple products. Assume that the Water Sports Company wants to earn a before-tax profit of $100,000 during 1987. To do so, total sales of 20,000 units are needed (15,000 Standard Models and 5,000 Deluxe Models) as shown in the following analysis:

$$S = \text{Sales target}$$

$$S = \frac{\text{Fixed costs} + \text{Target profit}}{\text{Weighted average contribution margin}}$$

$$S = \frac{\$300,000 + \$100,000}{\$20}$$

$$S = 20,000 \text{ units}$$

	Standard Model	Deluxe Model	Total
Sales – units	15,000	5,000	20,000
Sales – dollars	$750,000	$400,000	$1,150,000
Variable costs	525,000	225,000	750,000
Contribution margin	225,000	175,000	400,000
Fixed costs			300,000
Net income			$ 100,000

EFFECT OF CHANGE IN SALES MIX

Since the different products produced and sold in a multiproduct firm usually have different contribution margins, a change in the sales mix affects the break-even point and the profitability of the business. For example, one of the most serious problems encountered by the automobile industry during the late 1970s was the shift of consumer preference from large to small cars because of increased fuel costs. The profit margins on small cars were lower than those of large cars, so most auto dealerships earned less net income with the revised sales mixes even if they sold as many units as they did before the change. Management of every business must be able to evaluate the effects of changes in sales mix to make sure the business is selling enough products with adequate profit margins.

Let's see how a change in the sales mix will affect the Water Sports Company. Assume that the sales manager believes that a more aggressive sales effort will result in a shift in the sales mix to an equal number of Standard Models and Deluxe Models. Thus, the sales mix will be 50% Standard Models and 50% Deluxe Models. The impact on the break-even point and the sales needed to earn a before-tax profit of $100,000 with the revised weighted average contribution margin per unit is as follows:

$$\text{Weighted average contribution margin per unit} = (.5 \times \$15) + (.5 \times \$35)$$
$$= \$7.50 + \$17.50$$
$$= \$25$$

$$S = \text{Break-even sales}$$

$$S = \frac{\text{Fixed costs}}{\text{Weighted average contribution margin per unit}}$$

$$S = \frac{\$300,000}{\$25}$$

$$S = 12,000 \text{ units}$$
$$(6,000 \text{ Standard Models and } 6,000 \text{ Deluxe Models})$$

and

$$X = \text{Target sales for before-tax profit of } \$100,000$$

$$X = \frac{\text{Fixed costs} + \text{Target profit}}{\text{Weighted average contribution margin per unit}}$$

$$X = \frac{\$300,000 + \$100,000}{\$25}$$

$X = 16,000$ units
(8,000 Standard Models and 8,000 Deluxe Models)

Consequently, the shift of the sales mix to one Standard Model for every Deluxe Model has raised the weighted average contribution margin from $20 to $25 per unit. As a result, the break-even point has been lowered from 15,000 units to 12,000 units, and the number of units needed to earn net income before tax of $100,000 has decreased from 20,000 units to 16,000 units. This change in the sales mix will have a positive effect on the profitability of sales at all volume levels.

PROFIT SENSITIVITY TO VOLUME CHANGES

Objective 10:
Use of operating leverage

Cost structures differ from firm to firm and industry to industry because of the relationship between variable and fixed costs. At one extreme, a business may have high variable costs (small contribution margin) and low fixed costs. At the other extreme, a firm may have low variable costs (large contribution margin) and high fixed costs. Many firms have cost structures that are in between these two extremes. A given company's cost structure will have a significant effect on how sensitive its profit performance is to changes in sales volume. A business with a large contribution margin will benefit greatly from an increase in volume because a significant portion of each additional sales dollar is available to contribute to the fixed costs and profit. In contrast, a firm with a small contribution margin will experience little benefit from each additional sales dollar because the related variable costs rise so rapidly.

EVALUATION OF FIXED COSTS UTILIZATION WITH OPERATING LEVERAGE

As indicated earlier in this book, the typical firm's cost structure has become more fixed in recent years because of the increasing popularity of automation, including the use of robotics and computers. An important management objective is assuring that the fixed costs are used effectively because they will be incurred regardless of the level of business activity actually achieved. A managerial accounting calculation called **operating leverage,** which is a measure of how profits respond to changes in sales volume, can be used to evaluate the extent to which fixed costs are being utilized.

Let's illustrate the concept of operating leverage by evaluating the cost structures of three firms and their profits' sensitivity to changes in sales volume, as follows:

	Company A		Company B		Company C	
	Amount	**%**	**Amount**	**%**	**Amount**	**%**
Sales	$100,000	100	$100,000	100	$100,000	100
Variable costs	20,000	20	60,000	60	80,000	80
Contribution margin	80,000	80	40,000	40	20,000	20
Fixed costs	70,000	70	30,000	30	10,000	10
Net income	$ 10,000	10	$ 10,000	10	$ 10,000	10

Although each of the three companies shows a net income of $10,000, they have considerably different cost structures and amounts of operating leverage. Company A has the combination of the largest contribution margin (80% of sales) and highest fixed costs ($70,000), so it will have the most operating leverage. This means that a given sales dollar increase will yield more additional profit for Company A than for either of the other two companies. Company B has the next highest contribution margin and fixed costs of the three companies with 40% and $30,000, respectively. Company C has the least amount of operating leverage with a relatively small contribution margin (20% of sales) and low fixed costs ($10,000).

To evaluate the three firms' sensitivity to volume changes, assume that additional sales volume of $20,000 or 20% ($20,000/$100,000) with the same selling price are predicted for each company. We can see in the above income statements that all three companies are operating above their break-even points since net income of $10,000 has been earned by each firm. This means that the contribution margin more than covers the fixed costs in every case. We can evaluate the sensitivity of profits to the increase in sales volume of $20,000 as follows:

	Increase in Sales	×	Contribution Margin %	=	Increase in Profits
Company A	$20,000	×	.80	=	$16,000 (160%)
Company B	$20,000	×	.40	=	$ 8,000 (80%)
Company C	$20,000	×	.20	=	$ 4,000 (40%)

As a result, a 20% sales volume increase for Company A ($20,000/$100,000) will result in a 160% increase in net income ($16,000/$10,000). This shows the significant impact on profit results from sales increases for a company with high operating leverage. Companies B and C have less operating leverage since the same $20,000 sales volume increase produces additional profits of only 80% and 40%, respectively. However, a firm with high operating leverage will be exposed to more risk with sales declines and will have higher break-even points than businesses with low operating leverage. For example, if sales are expected to decrease by $20,000 from $100,000 to $80,000, the net incomes of the three companies would fall by the same amounts they increased in the calculations above. In addition, a firm with high operating leverage also will have a relatively high break-even point as we can see in the following analysis with Companies A, B, and C.

Break-even sales = Fixed costs/Contribution margin %
Company A = $70,000/.8 = $87,500
Company B = $30,000/.4 = $75,000
Company C = $10,000/.2 = $50,000

ANALYSIS WITH AN OPERATING LEVERAGE FACTOR

To help you understand why profits increase or decrease at a higher rate for a company with greater operating leverage, we need to consider the **operating leverage factor,** which is calculated as follows:

$$\text{Operating leverage factor} = \frac{\text{Contribution margin in dollars}}{\text{Net income}}$$

The operating leverage factor is a measure of how much a percentage change in sales volume from a *given sales level* will affect profits. For Companies A, B, and C, the operating leverage factors at the $100,000 sales level are:

$$\text{Company A} - \frac{\$80,000}{\$10,000} = 8$$

$$\text{Company B} - \frac{\$40,000}{\$10,000} = 4$$

$$\text{Company C} - \frac{\$20,000}{\$10,000} = 2$$

Remember that operating leverage factors are only valid for a given level of sales, or $100,000 in this case. These operating leverage factor results indicate that a given percentage change in sales volume will produce a change eight times as great in the net income of Company A, a change four times as great in the net income of Company B, and a change twice as great in the net income of Company C. Thus, if sales are expected to increase 20% from the $100,000 level (as they were earlier), we would predict that the three firm's net income will increase by:

	% Increase in Sales Volume	Operating × Leverage = Factor	% Increase in Net Income
Company A	20	8	160
Company B	20	4	80
Company C	20	2	40

Note that these are the same percentages of increased net income found earlier, but the use of the operating leverage factors helps explain why a 20% sales increase causes the higher percentage increases in the three firms' net incomes. It is also important to know that the operating leverage factor is greatest at sales levels near a firm's break-even point and decreases as net income rises. To illustrate, the operating leverage factors for Company A at three sales levels above its break-even point of $87,500 decrease as the sales volume increases as follows:

Sales	$90,000	$120,000	$150,000
Less variable costs (@ 20%)	18,000	24,000	30,000
Contribution margin (a)	72,000	96,000	120,000
Less fixed costs	70,000	70,000	70,000
Net income (b)	$ 2,000	$ 26,000	$ 50,000
Operating leverage factor (a)/(b)	36	3.69	2.4

Remember that earlier we determined that a 20% increase in sales from the $100,000 sales level for Company A resulted in a 160% increase in net income. However, the same 20% increase above a sales level of $150,000 will only raise net income by 48% (20% × 2.4). The use of the operating leverage factor enables management to quickly evaluate the impact of percentage changes in sales volume on profit results without preparing complete income statements for different sales levels.

SUMMARY

Management is constantly faced with decisions regarding selling prices, sales volume, sales mix, and costs as it looks for a combination of these factors that will produce satisfactory profits. Cost-volume-profit analysis is an important managerial accounting technique used to evaluate the interrelationships of these factors and to plan a firm's profit performance. An income statement with a contribution margin format provides the information needed to perform CVP analysis. Certain limiting assumptions of traditional CVP analysis must be evaluated carefully to make sure its application is realistic for the business conditions involved.

The beginning point of CVP analysis usually is break-even analysis, which is concerned with finding the sales level where all costs are covered by revenues but a profit is not earned nor is a loss incurred. The break-even point can be calculated mathematically or can be plotted graphically. CVP charts can provide management a visual display of the relationships between costs and revenues at various volume levels. Break-even analysis is also utilized by management to evaluate a firm's margin of safety as an indication of the risk associated with a given level of sales. The basic procedures of break-even analysis can be extended to determine the sales level needed to earn a target net income established as a profit goal. We can identify the target net income as either a constant amount or a variable amount that changes in relation to sales volume.

Managers can use "what-if" analysis to examine the effect of changes in selling price, sales volume, sales mix, and costs in the search for acceptable profits. When a business sells more than one product, different selling prices and variable costs usually are encountered; CVP analysis can be performed using a weighted average contribution margin approach. Whenever the sales mix changes, the weighted average contribution margin also changes, and this has an impact on the firm's break-even point and its profitability. Consequently, shifts in the sales mix must be carefully evaluated to assure that they result in more profitable products whenever possible.

The sensitivity of profits to changes in sales volume is another important aspect of CVP analysis. Operating leverage is a measure of how volatile profits are to changes in sales volume. Businesses with high contribution margins and high fixed costs will have the largest operating leverage and can earn significantly higher profits with relatively small increases in sales volume. Thus, operating leverage assists management in evaluating how important sales volume increases are for a firm.

GLOSSARY

BREAK-EVEN EQUATION. Mathematical expression used to compute a break-even point (p. 189).

BREAK-EVEN POINT. The sales volume at which revenues and total costs are equal, with no net income or loss (p. 189).

CONTRIBUTION MARGIN APPROACH TO BREAK-EVEN ANALYSIS. An alternative method used to calculate break-even sales by dividing fixed costs by the contribution margin per unit or percentage (p. 191).

COST-VOLUME-PROFIT (CVP) ANALYSIS. A managerial accounting technique used to evaluate how costs and profits are affected by changes in the level of business activity (p. 186).

COST-VOLUME-PROFIT CHART. A graphic display of the break-even point and the net income or loss for a range of activity (p. 192).

MARGIN OF SAFETY. The amount by which sales can decrease before a loss results (p. 194).

OPERATING LEVERAGE. A measure of how much profits respond to changes in sales volume (p.204).

OPERATING LEVERAGE FACTOR. A measure of how much a percentage change in sales volume from a given sales level affects net income (p. 205).

PROFIT-VOLUME CHART. A graphic display showing how profit changes in relation to volume (p. 193).

SALES MIX. The relative quantities of each product sold by a multiproduct firm (p. 201).

TARGET (DESIRED) NET INCOME. A profit goal expressed as a fixed or variable amount that is included in CVP analysis to determine the sales level necessary to earn that amount of net income. (p. 195).

WEIGHTED AVERAGE CONTRIBUTION MARGIN. The overall contribution margin based on the contribution margins per unit of the individual products weighted by their relative quantities (p. 201).

"WHAT-IF" ANALYSIS. Use of CVP analysis to evaluate the effect of changes in selling price, sales volume, sales mix, or costs (p. 187).

DISCUSSION QUESTIONS

1. Why is cost-volume-profit (CVP) analysis such an important managerial accounting subject?
2. Identify some examples of how CVP analysis can be used.
3. How are a contribution margin income statement and CVP analysis integrated for important managerial accounting applications?
4. What are the basic assumptions underlying CVP analysis?
5. Why is this chapter titled cost-volume-profit relationships instead of break-even analysis?
6. Define the following terms:
   a. Break-even point
   b. Break-even analysis
   c. Cost-volume-profit chart
   d. Profit-volume chart
   e. Margin of safety
7. What is the difference between the use of a break-even equation and the contribution margin approach to break-even analysis?
8. How can break-even analysis be extended to determine the sales volume required to earn a desired net income?
9. What information other than the break-even point can be obtained by managers from a CVP chart?
10. The Hare Company sells a product for $30. Variable costs are $18 per unit and fixed costs are $36,000 per month.
    a. What is the firm's break-even point?
    b. If the firm wants to earn a before-tax profit of $9,000 per month, how many units must be sold?
    c. If the firm wants to earn a before-tax profit of 16% of sales, what sales volume is necessary?

11. Why is the margin of safety an important part of CVP analysis for managers?
12. How is after-tax net income dealt with in CVP analysis?
13. What is meant by "what-if" analysis in the evaluation of CVP relationships?
14. Identify the major factors that can be evaluated with "what-if" analysis.
15. In recent years, the airlines have received a great deal of publicity with their "no frills" airfares. Since these fares are discounted significantly, how can they be justified on the basis of CVP relationships?
16. What are the major changes that must be evaluated to find the combination of revenue and costs that will produce acceptable profits?
17. What is meant by the weighted average contribution margin when CVP analysis is applied to multiple products? How is a weighted average contribution margin computed?
18. How does a change in the sales mix affect the weighted average contribution margin?
19. What is meant by operating leverage? Why is this concept important to managers?
20. Would we expect the typical business firm to experience a cost structure with large amounts of variable or fixed costs in today's business world? Justify your answer and explain the significance of this situation to management.
21. Explain what is meant by an operating leverage factor.

EXERCISES

Exercise 6-1 Contribution Margin and Break-even Analysis
Financial performance data for three companies are shown below:

Company	Sales	Variable Costs % of Sales	Fixed Costs
A	$204,000	40	$90,000
B	100,000	60	25,000
C	70,000	30	42,000

Required:
A. Prepare an income statement with a contribution margin format for each of the three companies.
B. Compute the break-even point for each company.

Exercise 6-2 Basic Break-even Equation
The income statement for the JT Company is as follows:

Sales (50,000 units)	$500,000
Variable costs	300,000
Contribution margin	200,000
Fixed costs	150,000
Net income	$ 50,000

Required:
A. Calculate the break-even point using the break-even equation.

B. Calculate the margin of safety in dollar amount and as a percentage of sales.

C. Graph the break-even point.

Exercise 6-3 Contribution Margin and CVP Analysis

Financial performance data for three companies are shown below:

Company	Number of Units Sold	Selling Price per Unit	Variable Cost per Unit	Fixed Costs
A	14,000	$ 5	$4	$ 10,000
B	20,000	10	6	75,000
C	40,000	12	8	140,000

Required:

A. Compute the break-even point for each company in units. In dollars.

B. Prepare an income statement with a contribution margin format for each company.

C. How many units must be sold by each company to earn a before-tax profit of 10% of sales?

Exercise 6-4 Developing a Simple CVP Graph and Evaluating the Results

Below are cost behavior data for the Brooks Company:

Sales price	$5.00/unit
Variable costs	3.50/unit
Fixed costs	6,000

Required:

A. Develop a cost-volume-profit graph, identifying the total revenue line, the total cost line, the fixed cost line, and the break-even point.

B. From the above graph, determine net income at a sales level of 6,000 units.

Exercise 6-5 Break-even Analysis and Margin of Safety

The following is the annual income statement for the Partee Company:

Sales (120,000 units)		$1,080,000
Cost of goods sold:		
Direct materials	$240,000	
Direct labor	180,000	
Variable manufacturing overhead	60,000	
Fixed manufacturing overhead	160,000	640,000
Gross profit		440,000
Variable selling expenses		100,000
Fixed selling expenses		74,000
Variable administrative expenses		140,000
Fixed administrative expenses		66,000
Net income		$ 60,000

Required:

A. Calculate the contribution margin per unit.

B. Calculate the break-even point in units and sales dollars.

C. Calculate the margin of safety.

Exercise 6-6 Basic CVP Chart

A CVP chart, as shown below, is a useful technique for visualizing relationships between costs, volume, and profits.

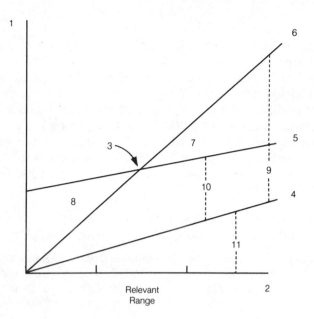

Relevant
Range

Required:
A. Identify the numbered parts of this CVP chart.
B. Discuss the significance of the "relevant range" to break-even analysis.

Exercise 6-7 Evaluating a Break-even Point

The CTH Company sells its only product for $60 per unit. It is produced and sold at a variable cost of $45 per unit. The president has learned about a new piece of equipment which can reduce variable costs by 20% if it is installed. Currently, fixed costs are $78,000, and if the new equipment is installed the fixed costs will increase to $115,200.

Required:
A. Calculate the present break-even point and the new break-even point if the equipment is installed.
B. Graph the present break-even point and the new break-even point.

Exercise 6-8 Evaluating CVP Relationships

The Gnaw Bone Company manufactures and sells a single product. The product sells for $20, fixed expenses are $60,000, and the contribution margin rate is 30%.

Required:
A. Calculate the variable cost per unit.
B. Using the equation technique,
   1. What is the break-even point in units and in dollar sales?
   2. What sales levels in units and in dollar sales are required to earn a profit of $30,000?
   3. If the contribution margin rate is raised to 40%, what is the new break-even point in units and dollar sales?
C. Repeat requirement B above, using the contribution margin approach.

Exercise 6-9 Evaluating Changes with CVP Analysis

The Thompson Knife Company sells a knife for $30 that has a contribution margin rate of 40%, and fixed costs of $240,000 per year. Annual sales were 50,000 units during the previous year.

Required:

A. Calculate the increase in net income for the next year if sales increase by 15,000 units.
B. Calculate the increase in net income if sales increase by $120,000 next year due to additional units.
C. The vice-president of sales proposes that a $60,000 increase in advertising would increase sales by $100,000. Should his proposal be accepted?
D. The sales manager proposes reducing the selling price by 20% and increasing the advertising budget by $50,000. He predicts that if both of these changes are implemented, unit sales will increase by 50%. Should his proposal be accepted?

Exercise 6-10 CVP Analysis with Multiple Products

The sales and cost data for the Roberts Company are as follows:

Product	Selling Price	Variable Cost	Sales Volume
A	$10	$ 6	5,000 units
B	20	10	3,000 units
C	40	16	2,000 units

Total fixed costs are $78,400.

Required:

A. Compute the net income for the year.
B. Compute the break-even point in total units and units of each product.
C. What is the firm's margin of safety?

Exercise 6-11 CVP Analysis with Multiple Products

The Top Notch Shoe Company produces three types of shoes, which have contribution margins as follows:

	Product A	Product B	Product C
Sales price per pair	$30	$20	$16
Variable cost per pair	20	12	10
Contribution margin per pair	$10	$ 8	$ 6
Total fixed costs are $205,000.			

Required:

A. Assume that the mix of sales units for the different types of shoes is 30%, 50%, and 20% for A, B, and C, respectively. Calculate the break-even point in pairs and dollars for each product.
B. Assume the sales mix changes to 50%, 30%, and 20%. Calculate the new break-even point in pairs and dollars for each product.
C. Explain why the break-even points calculated in B are different than those in A.

Exercise 6-12 CVP Analysis with Multiple Products

The Bedford Boot Bowery produces two types of boots. Expected data for the coming year are:

	High Top	Low Top
Expected sales (units)	30,000	20,000
Selling price per pair	$60	$50
Variable costs per pair	40	38
Total fixed costs for the year are expected to be $806,400.		

Required:
A. If sales volume, prices, and costs are as expected, what is the break-even point for each type of boot and what is the expected net income?
B. Assume that costs and prices are as expected, but the sales mix actually is 20,000 pairs of high tops and 30,000 pairs of low tops. What effect will this change have on expected net income?

Exercise 6-13 Evaluating Operating Leverage
Refer to Exercise 6-3.

Required:
A. Which company has the most operating leverage? Compute their operating leverage factors.
B. If each company can increase the number of units sold by 20%, what will be the effect on their profits?

PROBLEMS

Problem 6-1 Evaluating the Impact of Change with CVP Analysis
The RJS Company has prepared its projected 1988 income statement, which is presented below. The company is evaluating four independent situations and has asked for your assistance.

Sales (10,000 units)	$128,000
Variable expenses	73,600
Contribution margin	54,400
Less fixed expenses	44,800
Net income	$ 9,600

Required:
A. If a new marketing method would increase variable expenses (by an unknown amount that you are to determine), increase sales units 10%, decrease fixed costs 5%, and increase net income by 25%, what would be the company's break-even point in terms of dollar sales if it adopts this new method? Assume that the sales price per unit would not be changed.
B. If sales units increase 30% in the next year and net income increases 150%, did the manager perform better or worse than expected in terms of net income? Assume that there was adequate capacity to meet the increased volume without increasing fixed costs.
C. Assume variable costs would decrease 10% per unit due to a change in the quality of direct materials and sales would decrease 5% in spite of increasing advertising costs of $5,000. Should the company make the change in the materials used in production?
D. If the company hires an additional salesperson at a salary of $10,200, how much must sales increase in terms of dollars to maintain the company's current net income?

Problem 6-2 Evaluating Change with CVP Analysis

The Easy-Doze Company manufactures a popular sleeping pill that is sold throughout the Midwest. The company sells an average of 300,000 bottles per month. The following are the cost data related to the sleeping pills:

Selling price per bottle		$ 1.00
Variable costs per bottle		.30
Fixed monthly costs:		
Salaries		25,000
Rent on building		16,000
Advertising		50,000
Depreciation on equipment		16,000
Other		33,000

Required:

A. What is the monthly break-even point in bottles of sleeping pills and the firm's margin of safety?

B. How many bottles would have to be sold for the company to earn a monthly profit of $28,000?

C. If the company loses its current building lease and must move to a building which costs $30,000 per month, what will be the new break-even point in bottles?

D. The marketing vice-president believes that an additional advertising expense of $10,000 per month would generate a 10% increase in the number of bottles sold. Would you recommend the increased advertising? (Ignore part C.)

E. Refer to the original data. The company is considering a change in the production process which would decrease the variable cost per bottle by $.05 and would increase monthly fixed costs by $20,000. At a sales level of 300,000 bottles, would you recommend this change?

F. If the changes in D and E above are both implemented, what is the:
1. New break-even point
2. New margin of safety
3. Net income at sales of 300,000 bottles

Problem 6-3 Evaluating Profit Sensitivity with CVP Analysis

Mr. High and Mr. Lowe are the presidents of their respective companies. The two firms manufacture and sell the same product, and due to the competitive nature of the market, they charge the same selling price.

High and Lowe differ regarding their production and management philosophies. The High Company is almost completely automated, and the labor force is paid on a fixed salary basis. The Lowe Company uses a high degree of manual labor paid on an hourly basis. The sales force at the High Company is paid fixed annual salaries with very small commissions, whereas the sales force at Lowe Company is paid strictly on a commission basis. Mr. Lowe constantly makes fun of Mr. High's operations, saying the High Company is inflexible and unable to adjust costs as sales volume fluctuates.

During 1986, both firms reported net income of $12,000 on sales of $120,000. However, Mr. Lowe was shocked when examining the results for 1987, which showed that High Company's profits were far ahead of Lowe

Company's, even though Lowe Company had higher sales. The results for the two years are as follows:

	High Company		Lowe Company	
	1986	*1987*	*1986*	*1987*
Sales revenue	$120,000	$150,000	$120,000	$180,000
Total costs	108,000	114,000	108,000	156,000
Net income	$ 12,000	$ 36,000	$ 12,000	$ 24,000
Net income as a percentage of sales	10%	24%	10%	13⅓%
Fixed costs for each year	$ 84,000		$ 12,000	

Mr. Lowe is trying to figure out why the profit increase of his company was less than that of High Company. His company's accountants carefully examined the costs for each year and found no operating inefficiencies or costs that were out of line. He has hired you as a consultant to help solve the dilemma.

Required:
A. Present the income statements for 1986 and 1987 for both companies in contribution margin format.
B. Compute the break-even point in dollar sales and the margin of safety for each company.
C. Prepare an explanation for Mr. Lowe showing why Lowe Company's profits for 1987 were lower than those reported by High Company despite the fact that Lowe Company's sales were higher. Use the concept of operating leverage for your analysis.
D. What volume of sales would Lowe Company have to achieve to make the same profit as High Company in 1987?
E. Comment on the relative position of the two companies if sales in the future begin to decline.

Problem 6-4   Break-even Analysis with a Change in Contribution Margin
The TJ Company is the exclusive wholesale distributor of a brand of gourmet cookies. The company's president is developing his firm's financial strategy for the coming year. He has accumulated the following data regarding next year's operations:

Expected annual sales volume	624,000 boxes
Selling price per box	$ 6.40
Fixed costs	704,000
Variable costs:	
Cost of cookies	3.20/box
Selling and administrative	.64/box

After accumulating the above data, the president was informed that the manufacturers of the cookies will increase the cost of the cookies by 15% next year due to an increase in the cost of sugar.

Required:
A. What is the current contribution margin per box?
B. What is the current break-even point in dollars and boxes before the cost increase?

C. What is the expected net income before the cost increase?
D. If the 15% increase in the cost of the cookies occurs, what would the new selling price have to be if the company wants to maintain the current contribution margin rate?
E. If the cookies increase in cost by 15% and the selling price stays at $6.40/box, what will be the new break-even point in dollars and boxes?

Problem 6-5   CVP Analysis and the Evaluation of Changes

The Wharton Company produces a product which had the following sales and cost data for the current year:

Sales	$2,080,000
Variable costs:	
Manufacturing	936,000
Selling and administrative	312,000
Fixed costs:	
Manufacturing	390,000
Selling and administrative	312,000
Management expects the following	
cost increases in the coming year:	
Variable manufacturing	10%
Variable selling and administrative	6%
Fixed manufacturing	$ 23,400
Fixed selling and administrative	70,400

Required:
A. Calculate the break-even point in dollars for the current year.
B. Calculate the break-even point in dollars for the coming year if the expected cost increases actually occur.
C. Calculate the level of sales for the current year that would provide the company with a target net income of $390,000.
D. Repeat C above for the coming year assuming the expected cost increases occur.

Problem 6-6   Determining a Selling Price with CVP Analysis

The Clampett Company produces small wooden wine casks which are sold for $10 each. The costs associated with the casks are as follows:

Fixed costs	$120,000 per year
Variable manufacturing costs	6 per cask
Variable selling costs	10% of sales price (commission paid to salespersons)

A wine producer in California has proposed a one-time special order from Clampett to buy 10,000 casks at a yet to be determined price. Clampett Company has excess capacity for the order and operates at a profitable level. Since the deal is arranged directly by the president of the Clampett Company, no sales commission would be paid.

Required:
Determine the price that the Clampett Company must charge per cask in order to earn additional profit of $35,000 on this special order.

Problem 6-7   Break-even Analysis with Multiple Products

The Bonkers Company manufactures three toys that sell for $4 each and have the following sales and cost data:

	Toy R	Toy S	Toy T
Sales	$240,000	$40,000	$120,000
Variable costs	180,000	20,000	96,000

Total fixed costs are $74,880.

Required:
A. Calculate the break-even point in total units and sales dollars.
B. Calculate the break-even point in units and sales dollars for each individual toy.
C. Assume that the sales level remains the same as above, but the sales mix changes to 30%, 40%, 30%, for Toy R, Toy S, and Toy T, respectively. In addition, fixed costs increase to $80,400. Calculate the new break-even point in total sales dollars and in units for each individual toy.

Problem 6-8 Evaluating Multiple Products' Changes with CVP Analysis

The president of the North Bay Sales Company is examining projected sales and cost data for the coming year. The company sells three products, each of which has the same selling price. The projected activity for the year is as follows:

	Product 1	Product 2	Product 3	Total
Sales ($1/unit)	$50,000	$30,000	$20,000	$100,000
Variable costs:				
Cost of goods sold	30,000	21,000	16,000	67,000
Other operating costs	7,500	4,500	3,000	15,000
Total	37,500	25,500	19,000	82,000
Contribution margin	$12,500	$ 4,500	$ 1,000	$ 18,000
Fixed costs				13,140
Net income				$ 4,860

Required:
A. The company is considering a special advertising campaign, but does not want to dilute the effectiveness of the campaign by trying to promote more than one product. Which product should the company choose to promote in the advertising campaign?
B. The company is examining possible ways to increase profitability. The purchasing department has found an alternate supplier for each of its products. Each supplier will sell to the company at a price 10% lower than is currently being paid. However, the quality of the products would not be as high; therefore a reduction in sales of 15% is anticipated. The company can change suppliers for only one product at a time. For which product, if any, should the company change suppliers? Support your answer.
C. Assume that the company did not initiate the advertising campaign, nor did it change suppliers for any product. At the end of the year, the company showed a net income of $360 on sales of $110,000. Analysis of the sales mix for the year showed the following:

	Sales
Product 1	$ 30,000
Product 2	20,000
Product 3	60,000
Total	$110,000

The president is baffled as to why net income was so low when sales had exceeded the forecasted amount. Explain the reasons why net income was lower than projected.

Problem 6-9 Use of CVP Analysis

William Grey plans to open a day care center for young children at the beginning of next year. He recently has arranged to rent a building and has estimated that the following annual costs will be required to operate the center:

Salaries for three teachers	$46,000
Salaries for two assistants	16,000
Rent	16,000
Utilities	3,600
Miscellaneous	2,400
Supplies	$40 per child
Meals and snacks	$380 per child

Based on the space in the building and the three teachers available, Grey believes that the maximum number of children that can be cared for is 120.

Required:

A. Assume the day care center can attract 120 children when it opens. Determine the annual fee per child that must be charged in order for the center to break even financially.

B. If Grey finds out he can charge $1,620 per child annually, how many children must be attracted for the center to break even?

C. If Grey decides that he wants to earn an annual before-tax profit of $30,000 from the center and can charge $1,620 per child, how many children must be attracted?

Problem 6-10 Use of CVP Analysis in a Hospital

The controller of the Bloomingdale Hospital is evaluating ways to increase revenues. The financial objective of the hospital is to operate above its break-even point. The hospital currently refers approximately 2,500 patients each year to a nearby laboratory for a popular blood test. The lab charges $30 for each test. The equipment needed to perform the test can be leased for $34,250 per year and a technician would have to be hired at $14,000 annually. Other fixed annual costs for the tests are expected to be $8,000. The controller estimates variable costs (e.g., supplies) will be $5 for each test.

Required:

A. If the hospital charges $30 per test, how many tests must be performed each year to break even on the service?

B. If the hospital can perform 2,500 tests per year, how much should be charged for each test to break even?

C. Assume that the hospital wants to offset operating losses of $12,500 from another department with profit from the blood tests. If $30 per test is charged, how many patients must be treated annually?

Problem 6-11 Use of CVP Analysis

The McCabe Company just finished its first year of operations. The annual income statement showed the following results:

McCABE COMPANY
Income Statement
Year Ended December 31, 1987

Sales (40,000 units at $10)		$400,000
Direct materials	$ 52,000	
Direct labor	88,000	
Manufacturing overhead	132,000	272,000
Gross profit		128,000
Operating expenses:		
Selling	48,000	
Administrative	110,000	158,000
Net loss		$ (30,000)

The president of the company is quite disturbed by these operating results and wants to improve the profit performance for 1988. The firm's controller has provided the following additional information:

Variable manufacturing overhead is $.30 per unit.

Variable selling expenses are $.20 per unit.

The firm has the capacity to produce 60,000 units annually.

Required:

A. Prepare a variable costing income statement for 1987.
B. What is the firm's break-even point?
C. The firm's sales manager wants to reduce the selling price by 10%. She believes this will enable the company to produce and sell 60,000 units each year. Should this change be made? What will be the impact on the firm's break-even point?
D. What is the firm's margin of safety if the change in part C is made?
E. Instead of reducing the selling price, the firm is considering an advertising campaign that will cost an additional $20,000 annually and should increase the number of units sold by 25%. What effect would this change have on net income?

Problem 6-12 Use of CVP Analysis

Bill Lawyer started a pizza restaurant in a college town five years ago. The business has grown significantly and annual net income has more than doubled during the five-year period. The firm's accountant has prepared a projected income statement for the next year, 1987, as follows:

LAWYER COMPANY
Projected Income Statement
Year Ending December 31, 1987

Sales		$270,000
Cost of food sold	$81,000	
Wages and fringe benefits	65,000	

Rent	6,000	
Professional services	3,600	
Depreciation	10,400	
Utilities	5,000	
Supplies	1,980	172,980
Net income before tax		97,020
Income tax at 30%		29,106
Net income		$ 67,914

The restaurant's average pizza sells for $3.

Required:

A. What is the break-even point in number of pizzas that must be sold?

B. Mr. Lawyer would like an after-tax net income of $84,000. How many pizzas must be sold to reach that objective?

C. Mr. Lawyer is considering adding a campus delivery service with three trucks that have the oven capacity required to prepare pizzas away from the restaurant. Each truck costs $12,000 and will be depreciated on a straight-line basis over a three-year period. Additional annual fixed costs of $24,000 will be required to operate the trucks. In addition, a 10% commission will be paid to the delivery persons for each pizza sold. The average price of a delivered pizza is expected to be $4 with food preparation amounting to 30% of the selling price. What is the break-even point for the delivery business?

D. Evaluate the firm's operating leverage in selling 10% more pizzas from the income statement shown above using the operating leverage factor concept. (Ignore part C.)

Problem 6-13 Evaluating Changes with CVP Analysis

The Hennesy Company produces and sells a single product. It sold 30,000 units last year with the following results:

HENNESY COMPANY
Income Statement
Year Ended December 31, 1986

Sales		$750,000
Variable costs	$450,000	
Fixed costs	180,000	630,000
Net income before tax		120,000
Income tax (45%)		54,000
Net income		$ 66,000

The firm is evaluating ways to improve its product. One suggestion is to replace a component part used for the finished product that costs $2.50 each with a better one that costs $4.50 each. A new machine costing $36,000 also is being considered. The machine has a useful life of six years and no residual value. Straight-line depreciation is used on all plant assets.

Required:

A. What was the firm's break-even point in units last year?

B. How many units would the firm have had to sell last year to earn $77,000 in net income after tax?

C. If the company charges the same price in 1987 as it did in 1986 and makes the suggested changes, how many units must be sold to break even?

D. If the company has the same selling price in 1987 as it did in 1986 and makes the suggested changes, how many units must be sold to earn the same net income after tax as that of 1986?

E. If the company wants to maintain the 1986 contribution margin rate, what selling price per unit must be charged to cover the increased materials cost?

F. Use operating leverage analysis to evaluate the impact of a 20% increase in sales units from the 1986 level without any other changes.

Problem 6-14 CVP Analysis for a Hospital (CPA)

The Home Hospital operates a general hospital that rents space and beds to separate departments that provide such services as pediatrics, maternity, and surgery. Home Hospital charges each department for common services to departmental patients such as meals, laundry, billing, and collections. Space and bed rentals are fixed for the year.

For the year ended June 30, 1987, the Pediatrics Department charged each patient an average of $65 per day, had a capacity of 60 beds, operated 24 hours each day for 365 days, and had revenues of $1,138,800. Expenses charged to the Pediatrics Department for the year were:

	Basis for Allocation	
	Patient Days	**Bed Capacity**
Dietary	$ 42,952	
Janitorial		$ 12,800
Laundry	28,000	
Laboratory	47,800	
Pharmacy	33,800	
Maintenance	5,200	7,140
General administrative services		131,760
Rent		275,320
Billings/collections	40,000	
Bad debt expense	47,000	
Other	18,048	25,980
Totals	$262,800	$453,000

The only personnel directly employed by the Pediatrics Department are supervising nurses, nurses, and aides. The hospital has minimum personnel requirements based on total annual patient days. Hospital requirements, beginning at the minimum expected level of operation are:

Annual Patient Days	Aides	Nurses	Supervising Nurses
10,000–14,000	21	11	4
14,001–17,000	22	12	4
17,001–23,725	22	13	4
23,726–25,550	25	14	5
25,551–27,375	26	14	5
27,376–29,200	29	16	6

The staffing levels shown above are full-time equivalents, and it should be assumed that the Pediatrics Department always employs only the minimum number of required full-time equivalent personnel. Annual salaries for each class of employee are:

Supervising nurses	$18,000
Nurses	13,000
Aides	5,000

Salary expense for the year ended June 30, 1987 was:

Supervising nurses	$ 72,000
Nurses	169,000
Aides	110,000

The Pediatrics Department operated at 100% capacity during 111 days during the past year. It is estimated that during 90 of these full capacity days, the patient demand averaged 17 patients above capacity. The hospital has an additional 20 beds available for rent during the year ending June 30, 1988.

Required:
A. How many patient days were experienced by the Pediatrics Department during the past year? Each day a patient is in the hospital is a patient day.
B. What was the variable cost per patient day for the past year?
C. What were the total fixed costs for the department during the past year (allocated and direct)?
D. What was the break-even point for the Pediatrics Department during the past year?
E. Assuming that patient demand, revenue per patient day, cost per patient day, cost per bed, and employee salaries remain the same for the year ending June 30, 1988 as they were in the previous year, should the Pediatrics Department rent the additional beds from the hospital? The beds must be rented every day even though they may not be used during a given day. Show the annual gain or loss from the additional 20 beds.

7

DECISION MAKING BASED ON RELEVANT INFORMATION

CHAPTER OVERVIEW AND OBJECTIVES

This chapter describes the role of managerial accounting in decision making. After studying this chapter, you should be able to:

1. Describe how the managerial decision-making process works and identify the relevant managerial accounting information required for good decisions.
2. Explain what is meant by differential analysis.
3. Describe how relevant costs (revenues), differential costs (revenues), unavoidable costs, sunk costs, and opportunity costs are used in decision making.
4. Evaluate a special order pricing situation.
5. Evaluate the addition or deletion of products.
6. Evaluate a make or buy decision.
7. Distinguish between the treatment of joint product costs for inventory valuation and for decision-making purposes.
8. Evaluate the replacement of equipment.
9. Recognize how product mix decisions should be made when a firm's scarce resources and other constraints are considered.
10. Explain and compare market demand-oriented pricing and cost-oriented pricing.
11. Understand three cost-oriented pricing methods: markup pricing, cost plus target income pricing, and target return on investment pricing.
12. Describe the basic legal implications of pricing decisions.

MANAGERIAL ACCOUNTING AND DECISION MAKING

We noted in Chapter 1 that managers at different levels of an organization must make a variety of decisions ranging from *strategic decisions at the top management level* to *operating decisions at lower levels*. In this chapter, we are

Objective 1:
Importance of
decision making

primarily concerned with (1) operating decisions directed toward the short run (usually one year or less) and (2) the managerial accounting information required to make these decisions. Managers must make good operating decisions if their firm is to utilize the existing capacity of the business in a profitable way. Many of the subjects discussed here are also useful to top management for strategic decision making (long-term decision making is covered in Chapter 9).

We saw previously that managers make decisions continuously as they plan activities, organize resources, direct operations, and control performance. The managerial accounting topics covered in previous chapters assist management in making decisions, either directly or indirectly. Many concepts and procedures discussed in this chapter are extensions of managerial accounting topics presented earlier—including product costing, cost behavior analysis, and a contribution margin oriented income statement.

Decision making involves a choice between alternative courses of action, and that choice is usually made on the basis of some measure of profitability or cost savings. What products to produce, how to produce them, how to sell them, what price to charge, where to buy raw materials, when to replace equipment, how to allocate scarce resources, and whether to expand production capacity are examples of management decisions. Of special importance to most firms is the choice among alternative selling prices of products or services. The prices must be competitive to attract customers, yet high enough to produce the sales revenue needed to attain profit goals.

In general, the quality of decision making depends on the quality of the information available to the decision maker. Good information typically leads to correct decisions, while bad information usually leads to incorrect decisions. A basic understanding of the general decision-making process must precede our coverage of the role of managerial accounting information in decision making.

BASICS OF MANAGERIAL DECISION MAKING

Managerial decisions range from the routine and repetitive to the complex and nonrecurring. Except for the simplest cases, managerial decision making is both an art and a science because a combination of *qualitative (subjective)* and *quantitative (objective) factors* are involved. Although managerial accounting is primarily concerned with the quantitative aspects of decisions, the qualitative factors involved cannot be ignored in most cases. Such qualitative factors as public image, management intuition, social responsibility, consumer reaction, competitive responses, and employee attitudes often have an important bearing on a decision.

At the same time, managers attempt to structure a decision-making situation in quantitative terms as much as possible so a choice between alternatives can be made on a systematic basis. This means that the decision maker (1) follows a well-defined, logical process in selecting between alternatives, (2) can justify each of the steps taken, and (3) can evaluate the results achieved. Managerial accounting provides most of the quantitative information (e.g., revenues, costs, invested capital, and operating statistics) required to evaluate alternative courses of action.

GENERAL DECISION-MAKING PROCESS

There is no universal way managers make decisions. Methods vary according to the type of decision, management style, personal opinion, nature of the business, and environmental influences. However, most managers find it beneficial to follow a general **decision-making process** that consists of these four steps:

1. Define the problem with an emphasis on the objective to be accomplished.
2. Identify alternative courses of action.
3. Obtain relevant information while discarding that which is irrelevant.
4. Make the decision.

In order to define the limits of the decision, the manager should develop a *complete understanding* of both the problem itself and the objective to be accomplished. The problem should be precisely identified, and all pertinent facts associated with it should be interpreted carefully. This first step is essential because the other phases of the decision-making process depend on it. If the problem is incorrectly defined, the company's time and resources will be wasted on ineffective decision making.

The second step is selecting the possible alternative courses of action. In some cases, only two alternatives are considered. For example, a firm may decide whether to produce or purchase a certain part needed in the production process. Complex decisions often involve more than two alternatives. In such cases, it is important to limit the analysis to a manageable number of alternatives. For example, assume that the management of a medical clinic is trying to decide what kind of computer to install for data processing. Instead of considering every company selling computers, the clinic should only look at those firms known for their expertise in the health care field.

The third step in the decision-making process involves collecting information so that the various alternatives can be evaluated effectively. Only relevant information should be considered — that is, *information that will have a bearing on the decision being made.* All irrelevant information should be discarded, but both qualitative and quantitative information should be included. Some of the information will be internal to the business, some external. Any information that is the result of past experience should be recast as a projection of what is expected or desired in the future.

The last step, making a decision, occurs after the pertinent facts have been thoroughly analyzed. The final choice between alternative courses of action is the one the decision maker believes will lead to the desired objective identified in step one. In many cases, a **decision model,** which is a formalized method for evaluating alternatives, is used as an aid in the selection process. The cost-volume-profit analysis methods discussed in Chapter 6 are examples of decision models that can be used to evaluate the profitability of various alternatives. Other decision models based on mathematical or statistical procedures also are available for decision making in well-structured situations, as discussed in Chapter 15. Next, we will consider differential analysis — an important decision model used in managerial accounting.

USE OF DIFFERENTIAL ANALYSIS

Differential analysis or **incremental analysis** is a decision model that can be used to evaluate the differences in revenues and costs associated with alternative courses of action. The costs considered in differential analysis are not necessarily those costs used in conventional financial reporting. As we saw in Chapter 2, there are different costs for different purposes. For decision-making

**Objective 2:
Application of
differential
analysis**

purposes, relevant costs, differential costs, unavoidable costs, sunk costs, and opportunity costs are important classifications.

COSTS RELEVANT TO DECISION MAKING

Objective 3: Identifying the components of differential analysis

Relevant costs are the expected future costs that will differ between the alternatives being considered in a decision. The difference between the relevant costs of two or more alternatives is called a **differential cost.** For example, if a production manager is deciding which of two robotic systems to buy, the wages that will be paid to the operator of the equipment may or may not be relevant. If the same skilled labor with an hourly rate of $15 is required to operate either system and an equal number of hours are needed, the labor cost is not relevant. However, if one system requires less skill with a $12 per hour operator, the labor cost is relevant and the differential cost is $3 per hour.

All costs other than unavoidable costs are relevant in decision making. **Unavoidable costs** are either future costs that will not differ between alternatives —such as the $15 labor cost needed with both robotic systems in the above example—or sunk costs. **Sunk costs** are not relevant in decision making because they already have been incurred and cannot be changed. An example of a sunk cost is the book value of an item of equipment that a business is trying to decide whether to replace. Assume that the equipment does not have any residual value. If the item is replaced, the book value will be written off in the period of the disposal. If it is kept, the same amount will be depreciated over the remaining life of the asset. In either event, the book value will be expensed, so it is a sunk cost that is irrelevant. It should be noted, however, that the timing involved with the book value treatment may be important for two reasons: (1) the manager responsible for making the decision may prefer to have the item expensed in the future in order to show higher profits in the current year and (2) the time value of money will affect the true economic impact of the decision, as we will see in Chapter 9.

USE OF OPPORTUNITY COSTS IN DECISION MAKING

An **opportunity cost** is the benefit forfeited by rejecting one alternative while accepting another. Opportunity costs are not found in the general ledger, but they are considered either formally or informally when most decisions are made. For example, if a student decides to attend summer school instead of accepting a job that will pay $2,400, the true cost of attending school is more than just books, tuition, and housing. The opportunity cost of $2,400 must be added to the other costs to determine the true costs of making the decision to attend summer school. An opportunity cost also would be involved in a situation where the owner of a pizza parlor located near a university is considering redecorating the restaurant. Assume that the restaurant must be closed for two weeks for the remodeling. The opportunity cost of the remodeling project is the profit lost while the business is closed. In this instance, the opportunity cost can be minimized by timing the construction to coincide with a period when school is not in session.

APPLYING DIFFERENTIAL ANALYSIS TO REVENUES

The concepts of relevance and differential also can be applied to revenues. **Relevant revenues** are those that differ between alternatives; **differential revenue** is the difference between the relevant revenues of two or more alternatives. Whenever there are no relevant revenues (meaning that the differential revenue is zero) for a given decision, the selection between alternatives is made on the basis of the lowest cost. For an example of relevant revenue, assume that a given firm is considering the addition of a new product to utilize available production capacity. Two choices are being considered: cross-country skis or downhill skis. The projected revenue with cross-country skis is $343,200 while that of downhill skis is $391,200, or a differential revenue of $48,000. The related costs also would be considered if they are relevant.

DECISION MAKING WITH DIFFERENTIAL ANALYSIS

Differential analysis can assist management in making several types of business decisions, such as:

* Should a special sales order be accepted when the selling price is lower than normal?
* Should a product or department be discontinued?
* Is it better to produce or purchase a part needed in manufacturing?
* Does a product need further processing or should it be sold now?
* Should a fixed asset be replaced with a newer model?

Let's see how differential analysis can be applied to these decisions.

EVALUATION OF A SPECIAL SALES ORDER

Business firms often must decide whether to accept a special sales order, usually at a price lower than the normal selling price. If a business is to be profitable, its long-term pricing policy must be based on a consideration of all costs incurred. When idle capacity exists, however, a special sales order may be attractive even though a lower than normal selling price is involved. Differential analysis can be applied to evaluate the differential revenues and costs associated with a special order. Remember that a pricing decision based on differential analysis is valid for a one-time order but normally not for a firm's regular line of business.

Objective 4:
Example of a
special order
pricing situation

To illustrate a decision concerning a special sales order, let's refer to the Eastern Hardball Company, a manufacturer of baseballs sold with an Eastern label to sporting goods stores located throughout the United States. The firm has the capacity to produce 120,000 baseballs per month, although the sales forecast for January is only 90,000 because of seasonal demand for the product. An exporter located in New Orleans has offered to purchase 20,000 baseballs at a price of $1.80 each for distribution in a South American country. The normal selling price per baseball is $2.50.

The variable costs required to produce a baseball are $.90, and the monthly fixed manufacturing costs are $111,000. All selling and administrative expenses are fixed and total $15,000 each month. No additional selling and administrative expenses will be required with the order, but $10,000 must be spent on a machine needed to imprint a special label on each baseball. The machine can only be used for the special order. Should the offer be accepted? If the decision is made on the basis of the average production cost per baseball with the order, the offer will be rejected because the $1.80 selling price is less than the average cost of $2 ($.90 + $121,000/$110,000). However, the average cost of production is irrelevant, as shown by differential analysis:

	With Order	Without Order	Differential Analysis	
Sales				
(90,000 units × $2.50)	$225,000	$225,000		
(20,000 units × $1.80)	36,000		$36,000	(Differential revenue)
Variable costs:				
(90,000 units × $.90)	81,000	81,000		
(20,000 units × $.90)	18,000		18,000	(Differential costs)
Contribution margin	162,000	144,000	18,000	
Fixed costs:				
Manufacturing—regular	110,000	110,000		
—additional	10,000		10,000	(Differential costs)
Selling & administrative	15,000	15,000		
Net income	$ 27,000	$ 19,000	$ 8,000	

The firm's net income will be $8,000 higher with the special sales order even though the price is lower than normal. This happens because the sales order has a total contribution margin of $18,000 (20,000 units × $.90) but only results in incremental fixed costs of $10,000. Note that the special order has a contribution margin per baseball of $.90 ($1.80 − $.90). The regular fixed manufacturing costs of $110,000 and the fixed selling and administrative expenses of $15,000 are unavoidable since they will be incurred with or without the special order. Thus, they are irrelevant costs for this decision. As long as the company does not have a better alternative use of the production capacity and is certain that the special order will not have an adverse effect on its regular business, the offer should be accepted.

Note that the concept of an opportunity cost can be applied to this situation if the firm has alternative uses for the production capacity. The profit forfeited from any alternative use of the capacity must be considered in evaluating any special sales order. For example, assume that the unused capacity could also be used to produce racquetballs. The profit from the sales of racquetballs is estimated to be $12,000, so this opportunity cost exceeds the net income with the special sales order for baseballs by $4,000. Thus, the opportunity cost of the decision regarding baseballs is greater than the profit from the special sales order so racquetballs should be produced based on economic considerations only.

ADDITION OR DELETION OF DEPARTMENTS OR PRODUCTS

Objective 5: Example of adding or deleting products

Managers are constantly faced with decisions involving the selection of a combination of products (the sales mix) that will produce acceptable profits. As new products become available, their revenues and costs must be evaluated carefully to ensure that the related profit returns are large enough to justify selling them. In contrast, old products often become unpopular and unprofitable as consumer preferences change so these products must be eliminated from the sales mix. The decision-making process used for the addition or deletion of individual products also may be extended to product lines, departments, or other business segments such as a store or a plant. An important consideration in the decision to add or delete products is whether it will improve the future net income of the firm. Differential analysis can be used to evaluate the impact on future profits of adding or deleting products.

To illustrate how differential analysis can be applied to a situation in which a product or products are added or deleted, consider the following income statement for the Star Hardware Store, which currently operates three departments —Tools, Hardware, and Paint:

	Tools Department	Hardware Department	Paint Department	Total
Sales	$300,000	$450,000	$250,000	$1,000,000
Variable costs	231,000	288,000	150,000	669,000
Contribution margin	69,000	162,000	100,000	331,000
Fixed costs:				
Sales salaries	40,000	52,000	32,000	124,000
Advertising	24,000	36,000	20,000	80,000
Insurance	900	1,350	750	3,000
Property taxes	1,500	2,250	1,250	5,000
Depreciation	21,000	31,500	17,500	70,000
Miscellaneous	600	900	500	2,000
Total	88,000	124,000	72,000	284,000
Net income	$(19,000)	$ 38,000	$ 28,000	$ 47,000

An analysis of these operating results shown above may lead to the conclusion that the Tools Department is so unprofitable that management should consider eliminating it. The net loss of $19,000 may suggest that profits would have been $66,000 instead of $47,000 without the Tools Department. But is this an accurate conclusion? Although the Tools Department does not have a sufficient amount of contribution margin to cover all fixed costs assigned to it, the department is nevertheless making a contribution to the firm's profit results. We know that the firm will lose the department's contribution margin amounting to $69,000 if it is eliminated, but we need further analysis to determine which of the fixed costs can be avoided by closing the department.

Remember that unavoidable costs will be incurred regardless of the alternative selected. Consequently, before the department is eliminated, each cost assigned to the Tools Department must be evaluated to determine which costs are avoidable and which are unavoidable. Only then can the true impact on the firm's profitability from eliminating the department be accurately assessed.

The variable costs shown in the income statement represent cost of goods sold, so they can be avoided by discontinuing the Tools Department. (Remember, this is a retail business and cost of goods sold consists of merchandise inventory cost only.) Assume that the sales salaries for the Tools Department are paid to salespersons who work exclusively in that department so the people involved can be eliminated by discontinuing the department. Also assume that the rest of the fixed costs are common to the entire store and are allocated to specific departments. Recall from Chapter 3 that an allocated cost cannot be traced directly to a department but instead must be assigned to it in some reasonable proportion to the benefits received from the common cost. Since the common fixed costs are incurred for all departments, they cannot be avoided by eliminating any department. Examples are advertising, insurance, property taxes, and depreciation.

Applying differential analysis, we can see that the Star Hardware Store actually would earn less net income if the Tools Department is eliminated, as can be seen in the following illustration:

	With Tools Department	Without Tools Department	Differential Analysis
Sales	$1,000,000	$700,000	$300,000
Variable costs	669,000	438,000	231,000
Contribution margin	331,000	262,000	69,000
Fixed costs:			
Avoidable (sales salaries)	124,000	84,000	40,000
Unavoidable ($284,000 − $124,000)	160,000	160,000	−0−
Total	284,000	244,000	40,000
Net income	$ 47,000	$ 18,000	$ 29,000

The store's net income declines from $47,000 with the Tools Department to $18,000 without it—a decrease of $29,000. This decrease in profit occurs because the two remaining departments have a combined contribution margin of $262,000 ($162,000 + $100,000), which has to cover the two departments' own avoidable fixed costs of $84,000 ($52,000 + $32,000) plus the unavoidable fixed costs amounting to $160,000 ($284,000 − $124,000). The result is a net income of $18,000, so the elimination of the Tools Department would not be a wise choice.

A more complete analysis of the decision involving the possible elimination of the Tools Department would take into consideration alternative uses of the space currently occupied by it (the opportunity cost concept) and any adverse effect on the sales of the Hardware and Paint Departments from its closing. Customers may want to shop at a store with all three product lines, so the elimination of tools may cause them to go elsewhere to buy hardware and paint. If management does not consider this to be a problem, any alternative use of the space currently occupied by the Tools Department that will add more than $29,000 in profit with differential analysis should be considered. For example, plumbing supplies would be a potential alternative, given the nature of the business.

EVALUATING A MAKE OR BUY DECISION

Objective 6: Example of a make or buy decision

Most manufacturing firms use many component parts in the assembly of their finished products. These parts can either be produced by the manufacturer or purchased from an outside source. For example, an automobile manufacturer may produce its own engine but purchase tires. In turn, certain parts of the engine (such as nuts and bolts) may be acquired from other manufacturers.

Whenever a firm has both the production capacity and the expertise to produce a given part, the decision to make it or buy it should be based on the relevant costs of each alternative. Differential analysis can be used to evaluate the relevant costs of making or buying a part. For example, assume that the Maxwell Company has been operating at 75% of capacity and has been paying $12 each to purchase a small gear used in its production process. A forecast of the future sales indicates that regular production will remain at approximately 75% of capacity. As a means of utilizing some of the unused capacity, the firm is considering the possibility of producing 20,000 gears instead of purchasing them. Based on the firm's product costing approach with absorption costing, the following costs are estimated for the production of 20,000 gears:

Direct materials cost	$ 63,000
Direct labor cost	109,500
Variable manufacturing overhead	30,000
Fixed manufacturing overhead	82,500
Total manufacturing costs (a)	$285,000
Total gears produced (b)	20,000
Cost of each gear (a)/(b)	$ 14.25

At first glance, it may appear that the cost of producing a gear exceeds the purchase price by $2.25 ($14.25 less $12). However, differential analysis requires a review of the manufacturing costs to determine which ones actually are avoidable if the gears are purchased. Assume that such a review at the Maxwell Company shows that direct materials cost, direct labor cost, variable manufacturing overhead, and fixed manufacturing overhead of $7,500 can be eliminated by purchasing the gears. The remaining fixed manufacturing overhead of $75,000 is not a relevant cost because it will be incurred whether the gears are produced or purchased. Differential analysis shows:

	Make the Gears	Buy the Gears	Differential Analysis
Direct materials cost	$ 63,000		$ 63,000
Direct labor cost	109,500		109,500
Variable manufacturing overhead	30,000		30,000
Fixed manufacturing overhead	82,500	75,000	7,500
Purchase costs (20,000 units × $12)		240,000	(240,000)
Total costs	$285,000	$315,000	$ (30,000)

The relevant costs of producing the gears are $210,000 ($63,000 + $109,500 + $30,000 + $7,500), or $10.50 per unit. Therefore, a cost savings of $1.50 per unit ($12 less $10.50) will result if the firm produces the gears—for a total cost savings of $30,000.

The firm also should consider any alternative uses of the unused capacity—such as producing another salable product with a contribution margin in excess of $30,000—since they could generate even higher profits than the production of gears. Also, the desire to control the quality of the gears internally may be an important factor in the analysis. Other considerations are any adverse effect on the business relationship with the outside supplier of the gear, who may provide other components used in the production process, and the future prices the supplier is likely to charge for the gears.

JOINT PRODUCT COST TREATMENT— INVENTORY VALUATION VERSUS DECISION MAKING

Manufacturing firms in many industries produce several products from common raw materials or from the same production process. These multiple products are called **joint products.** An oil refinery, for example, will use crude oil to produce gasoline, fuel oil, kerosene, lubricating oils, naphtha, diesel fuel, and paraffin. The chemical, lumber, mining, plastics, and meatpacking industries are others in which it normally is not possible to produce a single product without producing other products.

Objective 7: Identifying the proper treatment of joint product costs

The common costs required to produce joint products—that is, before they are identifiable as separate units of output—are termed **joint product costs.** The point in the production process at which the joint products become separable products is called the **split-off point.** Some of the products may be in salable form at the split-off point while others may require further processing before they can be sold. Graphically, the production flow of a manufacturing firm with two products (A and B) that are salable at the split-off point and one product (C) that must be processed further is:

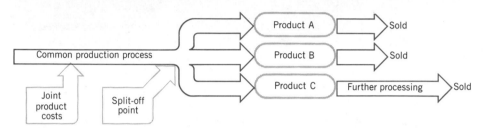

In the treatment of joint product costs, there are two separate and distinct considerations: (1) *the valuation of the inventories for income reporting purposes* and (2) *determining at what point joint products should be sold.*

Inventory Valuation with Joint Product Costs

Joint product costs are common costs that must be allocated to the individual products involved in order to value the related inventories for financial reporting purposes. The most common practice is to allocate joint product costs on the basis of the products' relative sales values. For example, assume that a chemical company incurs joint product costs of $162,000 while producing 18,000 gallons of Anoline and 9,000 gallons of Banoline. Anoline sells for $8 per gallon and Banoline sells for $9 per gallon. Therefore, the sales of Anoline are $144,000 and the sales of Banoline are $81,000, for total sales of $225,000. Using the products' relative sales values, the joint product costs of $162,000 would be assigned to the two products as follows:

$$\text{Anoline} \quad \frac{\$144,000}{\$225,000} \times \$162,000 = \$103,680$$

$$\text{Banoline} \quad \frac{\$ 81,000}{\$225,000} \times \$162,000 = \underline{\quad 58,320}$$

$$\text{Total joint costs allocated} \qquad \underline{\underline{\$162,000}}$$

The allocation of joint product costs must be performed so that the production costs can be divided between the inventories left on the balance sheet at the end of a period and the cost of goods sold for the period. Like any cost allocation procedure, the results must be interpreted carefully since they are only approximations of the true costs required to produce the individual products.

Determining the Point of Sale for Joint Products

Managers often must decide whether to sell a joint product at the split-off point or to process it further. Joint product costs (such as the $162,000 in the above example) are irrelevant in such decisions since they are sunk costs and therefore should not be allocated to the joint products involved for decision-making purposes. Instead, differential analysis should be used to evaluate the relevant costs and revenues. For example, assume that the two products, Anoline and Banoline, can either be sold at the split-off point for $8 and $9 per gallon, respectively, or can be processed further and subsequently sold. The following data are relevant:

Product	Selling Price per Gallon at Split-off Point	Further Processing Costs per Gallon	Selling Price per Gallon after Further Processing
Anoline	$8	$4	$14
Banoline	$9	$3.50	$12

PROFIT ANALYSIS—THE WRONG APPROACH

We can illustrate how the inclusion of joint product costs in the determination of the best point of sale for joint products can lead to erroneous results with the following income statement analysis:

	Anoline	Banoline	Total
Quantity (gallons)	18,000	9,000	27,000
Without Further Processing			
Revenue:			
18,000 gallons × $8	$144,000		
9,000 gallons × $9		$ 81,000	$225,000
Joint product costs (allocated by revenue):			
$162,000 × $144,000/$225,000	103,680		
$162,000 × $81,000/$225,000		58,320	162,000
Profit	$ 40,320	$ 22,680	$ 63,000
With Further Processing			
Revenue			
18,000 gallons × $14	$252,000		
9,000 gallons × $12		$108,000	$360,000
Separate costs			
18,000 gallons × $4	72,000		
9,000 gallons × $3.50		31,500	103,500
Joint product costs (allocated by revenue):			
$162,000 × $252,000/$360,000	113,400		
$162,000 × $108,000/$360,000		48,600	162,000
Profit	$ 66,600	$ 27,900	$ 94,500

The results of this analysis appear to indicate that both products should be processed further because the profit from each product will increase, giving the firm a total profit of $94,500. However, look closely at the change that takes place with further processing of Banoline. The income statement analysis indicates that profit increases by $5,220 (from $22,680 to $27,900). Note that the amount of joint product costs allocated on the basis of revenue decreased by $9,720 (from $58,320 to $48,600) even though the total joint product costs remained at $162,000. The added revenue from further processing ($108,000 − $81,000 = $27,000) was actually less than the added costs involved ($31,500) by $4,500. Thus, the reported profit increase of $5,220 is not the result of earning revenue from further processing that exceeds the required additional costs.

The profit increase is the result of allocating less of the common costs ($58,320 − $48,600 = $9,720), reduced by the amount the additional costs exceeded the additional revenue ($4,500), or $5,220. Since a disproportionate amount of the joint product costs have been allocated to Anoline, its incremental profit must be understated. Thus, the true incremental results of the decision concerning further processing of the two products have been misstated by the inclusion of the joint product costs amounting to $162,000, which remain constant regardless of the decision made. This erroneous information can lead to bad managerial decisions so it is important to *differentiate* between the treatment of joint product costs for *inventory valuation* and *decision making*. To avoid these erroneous conclusions, differential analysis should be applied.

PROFIT ANALYSIS — THE RIGHT APPROACH

The joint product costs of $162,000 are ignored in differential analysis because they are sunk costs; that is, they have already been incurred and will remain the same regardless of which alternative is selected. Anoline should be processed further and sold for $14 per gallon, whereas Banoline should be sold at the split-off point for $9 because of the following differential analysis:

Product	Differential Revenue with Further Processing	Differential Cost of Further Processing	Profit (Loss) of Further Processing
Anoline	$6 ($14 − $8)	$4	$6 − $4 = $2
Banoline	$3 ($12 − $9)	$3.50	$3 − $3.50 = $(.50)

The third column indicates that the firm will earn $2 more for each gallon of Anoline that is processed further, but it will lose $.50 for each gallon of Banoline sold beyond the split-off point. The profit earned by selling Anoline after further processing and Banoline at the split-off point would be $99,000 [(18,000 × $14) + (9,000 × $9) − (18,000 × $4) − $162,000]. This is $36,000 higher than the $63,000 profit ($225,000 − $162,000) that would have been earned by selling both products at the split-off point. The additional income of $36,000 (18,000 × $2) earned by the further processing of Anoline gives this result. In contrast, profits would be $4,500 less if Banoline is processed further because each of the 9,000 units would earn $.50 less.

Note the significant difference between these results and those obtained earlier with the joint product costs included in the analysis. There, both products were processed further with a total profit of $94,500. Using incremental analysis, we see that the best decision is to sell Banoline at the split-off point and process further only Anoline, thus producing the total profit of $99,000.

EVALUATING THE REPLACEMENT OF EQUIPMENT

Objective 8: Example of equipment replacement

Periodically, managers must evaluate the equipment being used in their businesses to ensure that they have adequate and modern operating capacity. One of the most confusing aspects of this analysis is the role of the book value of the equipment being considered for replacement. Recall from financial accounting that the book value of a fixed asset is its cost less accumulated depreciation. We mentioned earlier in this chapter that book value is a sunk cost that is irrelevant for decision making because the cost already has been incurred and nothing can be done about it. However, managers sometimes look at book value and erroneously conclude that its existence automatically will result in an unacceptable loss if the related equipment is discarded. Consequently, many managers feel more comfortable waiting for equipment to be fully depreciated before they replace it. This may not be economically sound thinking, as can be shown with differential analysis.

To illustrate, assume the following facts concerning a certain business that is considering the replacement of an old machine (original expected life of 10 years) with a newer and more efficient machine:

Old Machine		**New Machine**	
Cost	$50,000	Cost	$60,000
Book value	25,000	Estimated life	5 years
Remaining life	5 years	Disposal value in 5 years	–0–
Current disposal		Annual variable	
value	$10,000	operating expenses	$20,000
Annual variable		Annual revenue	
operating expenses	35,000	from sales	75,000
Annual revenue			
from sales	75,000		

If the old machine is disposed of, an accounting loss must be immediately recognized as follows:

Disposal value	$ 10,000
− Book value	25,000
Loss on disposal	$(15,000)

At first glance, management may hesitate to dispose of the machine because the loss will be shown on the income statement in the year of the disposal. The tendency is to think that this loss can be avoided by keeping the machine for its entire useful life, thereby maximizing the profits generated with the machine. This in turn will allow the business to fully recover its investment in the machine, and then management can consider replacing it with a new machine.

However, evaluating the incremental effect of the book value for both keeping or replacing the old machine shows us that this line of reasoning is erroneous. The book value of $25,000 is a sunk cost, so it is irrelevant for the decision-making process. We can see this by applying differential analysis to the projected operating performance of the firm for the next five years.

	Five-Year Performance		
	Keep Old Machine	**Buy New Machine**	**Differential Analysis**
Revenue	$375,000	$375,000	$ –0–
Variable operating expenses	(175,000)	(100,000)	75,000
Depreciation of old machine or its write			
off at disposal	(25,000)	(25,000)	–0–
Disposal value of old machine		10,000	10,000
Depreciation of new machine		(60,000)	(60,000)
Net income—five years	$175,000	$200,000	$ 25,000

For financial reporting purposes, the $25,000 book value of the old machine and the $10,000 received for it at disposal would be netted off to show the $15,000 loss identified earlier.

Replacing the old machine will increase the firm's net income by $25,000 over the five-year period. The savings in the variable operating costs make the purchase of the new machine economically attractive even though the disposal loss ($15,000) must be recognized in the first year. Note that the book value of the old machine is charged to the income statements of the five-year period whether the machine is kept or replaced.

If the old machine is retained, the $25,000 is depreciated, whereas the same amount is written off in the first year if the machine is replaced. Consequently, the book value is irrelevant for this decision. The relevant factors in the analysis are the *variable operating expenses,* the *disposal value of the old machine,* and the *cost of the new machine.* The savings in variable operating costs over the five-year period are $75,000; the disposal value of the old machine is $10,000. The sum of the two ($85,000) exceeds the $60,000 cost of the new machine by $25,000, which is the increase in net income for the five-year period.

We should point out that both the time value of money and the income tax consequences have been ignored in the illustration to emphasize the concept of relevancy. In Chapter 9, we will consider these two issues as they relate to similar investment decisions.

MAKING PRODUCT MIX DECISIONS WITH CONSTRAINTS

Objective 9: Evaluating product mix decisions

Businesses that sell more than one product must constantly evaluate the profitability of the various products to determine the most profitable product mix. In most cases, this cannot be done by simply selecting the products with the highest individual contribution margins. Every business faces scarce resources that must be used in the most optimal way to earn maximum profits. These scarce resources are limitations (also called constraints) for managerial decision-making purposes because they restrict how the firm can operate. For example, a manufacturing firm will have a limited amount of production capacity as measured by direct labor hours or machine hours. In a department store, a primary limitation is the amount of floor space available so management has to restrict the inventory items sold.

The most profitable product mix is determined in a multiple-product situation by relating the *contribution margins of the products* to the *constraints of the firm.* In this way, management can maximize the total contribution margin in relation to the firm's constraints, thus ensuring that the scarce resources are used in the best way. For example, assume that a particular company produces and sells two types of furniture (tables and chairs) with these per-unit selling prices and variable costs:

	Table	Chair
Selling price	$60	$48
Variable costs	30	36
Contribution margin per unit	$30	$12
Contribution margin – % of selling price	50	25

At first glance, management may decide that tables are the more profitable products and thus try to produce as many tables as the firm can sell. Assume, however, that the same machines are used to produce both tables and chairs. Only 60,000 machine hours are available each month. Six machine hours are required to produce a table, and two machine hours are needed for each chair. The maximum number of tables or chairs that can be produced is calculated as follows:

	Tables	Chairs
Maximum number of machine hours available (a)	60,000	60,000
Machine hours required for one unit (b)	6	2
Maximum number of units that can be produced (a)/(b)	10,000	30,000

If 10,000 tables or 30,000 chairs can be sold, only chairs should be produced because they are more profitable on the basis of contribution margin per machine hour:

	Tables	Chairs
Contribution margin per unit (a)	$30	$12
Machine hours needed for one unit (b)	6	2
Contribution margin per machine hour (a)/(b)	$ 5	$ 6
Total contribution margin with each product:		
Machine hours available	60,000	60,000
× Contribution margin per machine hour	$5	$6
= Total contribution margin	$300,000	$360,000

By producing a maximum of 30,000 chairs (60,000 machine hours/2 machine hours per chair), the total contribution margin earned will be $360,000 (30,000 chairs × $12 per chair). This is the same total contribution margin found above (60,000 machine hours × $6 = $360,000). In contrast, the total contribution margin with tables is only $300,000. Thus, this illustration shows that the product with the highest contribution margin per unit may not be the one that produces the highest total contribution margin when the related constraints are considered.

It is unlikely, however, that an unlimited number of chairs can be sold since the market usually imposes constraints that must be recognized in product mix decisions. For example, a minimum number of tables may have to be produced just to satisfy the needs of customers who want to buy both tables and chairs. In addition, the maximum number of chairs that can be sold may be fewer than 30,000. Other constraints such as limited raw materials and direct labor hours may also have to be considered.

In most cases, more than two products with several constraints must be evaluated, so the determination of the most profitable product mix is a complex decision and the approach taken above is not effective. Linear programming is a quantitative technique that can be used to overcome the complexities of multiple products and multiple constraints. We will discuss the subject of linear programming in Chapter 15.

RELEVANT COSTS AND PRICING DECISIONS

We noted in Chapter 6 that selling price is one of the four profit variables management must plan and control. Business managers often must make pricing decisions to be sure that their products or services are competitively and profitably priced. In some firms, these pricing decisions are relatively simple because the products or services are either regulated by a governmental agency (such as an electric utility) or sold in a market in which competitive forces completely establish prices (such as agricultural products). In regulated industries, the major pricing decisions involve the justification of requests for price increases or decreases. Such price changes are usually made on the basis of changes in a firm's cost structure. Managers selling a highly competitive product such as a farm commodity face prevailing market conditions that determine prices on any given day. Such firms cannot charge a higher price because it will not be accepted, and they have no incentive to charge a lower price because all their products can be sold at the market price. The major managerial decisions in such cases involve cost control and the amount to produce.

Objective 10:
Use of pricing
strategies

Most firms, however, do have some degree of control over the prices they charge. These firms face complex decisions involving such diverse considerations as:

- The firm's cost structure
- Profit goals
- Type of business
- Market share objectives
- Competitive reaction
- Public image
- Economic conditions
- Need for a complete product line
- Governmental influence
- Legal implications

These complex pricing decisions should be made on the basis of as much information as management can gather from both external and internal sources. It is advantageous for managers of all businesses to understand the general conditions underlying pricing decisions and the specific factors they must consider when the decisions are made. Two approaches are generally used for pricing decisions—a market demand-oriented approach and a cost-oriented approach.

MARKET DEMAND-ORIENTED PRICING

A **market demand-oriented pricing** approach is an important part of microeconomics that provides a theoretical structure for a general understanding of how prices are established, given certain limiting assumptions. Although this approach may not be directly useful for a specific business because the detailed information needed to implement it is absent *or* the assumptions involved are unreasonable, it does describe the general movement of prices with various combinations of *supply and demand.* For example, a market demand-oriented approach will not explain why a gallon of a certain brand of gasoline is priced at one price in a given Florida city and at another price elsewhere in the same state. However, it does explain why worldwide oil prices decline when the major oil producing countries' production output has increased substantially.

The market demand-oriented approach to pricing decisions is based on the premise of an *equilibrium price,* which is found where the related quantity of a certain product supplied is equal to the quantity demanded by buyers. In addition, the subject of microeconomics theorizes that the optimum selling price is found where a firm's marginal revenue (the added revenue resulting from the sale of one additional unit) is equal to its marginal cost (the added cost incurred in the sale of one additional unit). Since the concept of a market demand-oriented approach to pricing is mainly valuable as a theoretical tool with which the general price structure can be evaluated, we will defer a complete discussion of it to microeconomics or marketing courses. Next, we will consider the cost-oriented approach to pricing, which is most pertinent to managerial accounting and its application in specific businesses.

**Objective 11:
Applying cost-oriented methods**

COST-ORIENTED PRICING

The most widely used means of setting selling prices in the business world is with a **cost-oriented pricing** approach. That is, a business starts with the actual or estimated costs identified with a product or service and then adds an amount of profit that management desires. This does not mean that the demand for the related product can be ignored; the interaction of cost and demand always must be considered. A price that is too high or too low typically will not result in profits that are compatible with management's goals. If the price is too high, customers won't buy enough of the related product to justify selling it. If the price is too low, even high unit sales may not prevent the firm from operating at a loss because the profit margin per unit is inadequate. Competitive conditions usually prevent a firm from passing more than a reasonable amount of cost and profit on to its customers. Thus, *cost control* and *realistic profit goals* are extremely important when a cost-oriented pricing approach is used.

Many different cost-oriented pricing techniques are utilized in the business world. Most firms establish different pricing strategies for the short run and the long run. Earlier in this chapter, we discussed special order pricing in which the selling price may be lower than normal. We justified such a policy for short-term decisions only because of the incremental profits that may be involved.

In the long run, however, total cost provides the floor below which prices cannot fall for a firm to be profitable. As such, all costs are relevant for long-term pricing decisions. A total-cost pricing approach includes both product and period costs. This means that all manufacturing, selling, and administrative costs must be considered (or whatever functional costs are incurred by a particular business). It also means that both variable and fixed costs must be covered by selling prices. Managerial accounting data obtained from a firm's accounting system provide the basis for applying a cost-oriented pricing technique. Let's examine some of the most important cost-oriented pricing techniques available to managers.

Markup Pricing

Many firms establish their selling prices through the use of **markup pricing** percentages. This approach is particularly popular with merchandising businesses, but it also is used by many manufacturing firms. A markup can be expressed as a percentage of either a cost base or the selling price. It should be large enough to cover all the costs involved plus the amount of profit management desires.

In a merchandising firm, the determination of the costs to be considered is relatively straightforward because the products are purchased, not produced. Consequently, we can refer to the purchase invoice to identify the cost base that provides the starting point for establishing the selling price. When markup pricing is used by a manufacturing firm, we must know whether absorption costing or variable costing is being used before we can select the appropriate cost base. In either case, fixed costs must be considered in establishing selling prices. Since only variable manufacturing costs are inventoried with variable costing, the markup must be *larger* than it is with absorption costing to cover the fixed costs.

Let's illustrate the basics of markup pricing in a merchandising operation and then extend the application of the technique to a manufacturer. Assume that the Computer Store sells several types of microcomputers and a wide range of supporting software. The store owner's policy is to mark up the purchase cost of all hardware products by 25% and all software products by 100%. If a particular type of computer costs the store $2,100 and the related software costs $900, the total price quoted to the customer is computed as follows:

$$\text{Selling price of the computer} = \$2,100 + (25\% \times \$2,100) = \$2,625$$
$$\text{Selling price of the software} = \$900 + (100\% \times \$900) = \$1,800$$
$$\text{Total selling price} = \$2,625 + \$1,800 = \$4,425$$

If management wants to express the markup as a percentage of the selling price but at the same time consider the desired markup on cost, it can easily convert the cost markup to a selling price markup as follows:

$$\frac{\text{Markup as a}}{\text{percentage of selling price}} = \frac{\text{Markup as a percentage of cost}}{100\% + \text{Markup as a percentage of cost}}$$

Consequently, the markups as percentages of selling prices for hardware and software at the Computer Store would be found as follows:

$$\text{Hardware markup as a percentage of selling price} = \frac{25\%}{100\% + 25\%} = 20\%$$

$$\text{Software markup as a percentage of selling price} = \frac{100\%}{100\% + 100\%} = 50\%$$

Alternatively, we can convert a markup on selling price to a markup on cost with this formula:

$$\text{Markup as a percentage of cost} = \frac{\text{Markup as a percentage of selling price}}{100\% - \text{Markup as a percentage of selling price}}$$

$$\text{Hardware} = \frac{20\%}{100\% - 20\%} = 25\%$$

$$\text{Software} = \frac{50\%}{100\% - 50\%} = 100\%$$

Extension of Markup Pricing to a Manufacturing Firm. The same markup-pricing approach can be taken with a manufacturing firm, except that the total product costs that are to be marked up as a cost base must be *carefully defined.* In Chapter 5, we saw that products can be costed with either *absorption costing or variable costing.* The markup percentage selected to reflect a specific profit goal depends on which of these product costing methods is being used.

Markup Pricing with Absorption Costing. Under absorption costing, the cost base to be marked up is the total cost required to produce one unit of product. The markup must be large enough to cover both a share of the selling and administrative expenses and the desired amount of profit. Since fixed manufacturing costs are treated as product costs with the absorption costing approach, the number of units that will be produced during a period must be estimated (just as we did when we computed the predetermined overhead rate). This production estimate is divided into the fixed manufacturing costs of the same period to determine the fixed manufacturing costs per unit.

To illustrate markup pricing with absorption costing, assume that the TRL Company produces microcomputers and is about to market a new portable computer. The firm's managerial accountant has compiled the following costs that are expected in the production and sale of 5,000 portable computers:

Direct materials	$2,350,000
Direct labor	2,450,000
Variable manufacturing overhead	450,000
Fixed manufacturing overhead	2,250,000
Total manufacturing costs	$7,500,000
Variable selling and administrative expenses	750,000
Fixed selling and administrative expenses	1,250,000
Total operating expenses	$2,000,000

The total cost of producing one portable computer under absorption costing is $1,500 ($7,500,000/5,000 units). Assume that management wants a markup on cost of 40%. The selling price of each portable computer would be $2,100, or the unit base cost of $1,500 plus 40% of $1,500.

Note that we cannot ignore the demand for the product while using this approach because management must estimate how many units will be sold in order to compute the fixed manufacturing cost per unit. Once the selling price is initially determined ($2,100 in our example) management must evaluate carefully whether the sales volume target is realistic at that price. If it is not, the process must be repeated until an acceptable combination of selling price and sales volume is found.

Consequently, the results of this form of markup pricing must be loosely interpreted and usually are used as a starting point for establishing a selling price rather than the final answer. By evaluating the reasonableness of several combinations of price and demand, management often can minimize the potential difficulties associated with the *circular reasoning* that price is dependent on full cost which is dependent on volume which is dependent on price.

Markup Pricing with Variable Costing. When variable costing data are used for markup pricing, the selling prices are based on the same contribution margin approach we first introduced in Chapter 5. Using the contribution margin approach, selling prices are established on the basis of cost behavior instead of on costs classified by function. Thus, managers can see the relationship between prices and the costs that fluctuate directly with sales.

As a result, the cost base to be marked up consists of the total variable costs related to the product rather than the total costs incurred to produce it. We must consider all variable costs, whether they are manufacturing, selling, or administrative. Since fixed costs are not included in the cost base to be marked up, the markup percentage must be large enough to cover the *total fixed costs plus the desired profit*. If we again use the TRL Company as an example, the total variable costs for each portable computer are $1,200, computed as follows:

Direct materials cost ($2,350,000/5,000 units)	$470
Direct labor cost ($2,450,000/5,000 units)	490
Variable manufacturing overhead ($450,000/5,000 units)	90
Variable selling and administrative expenses ($750,000/5,000 units)	150
Total variable costs per unit	$1,200

If management of the TRL Company decides to price the portable computer with a 75% markup on the total variable costs as a cost base, the selling price will be the same as it was with absorption costing, or $2,100 [$1,200 + (75% × $1,200)]. Although the selling prices in this illustration are the same with either absorption or variable costing, different markups are used because the cost bases are different. Whichever of the two methods is used, the results usually are only first approximations of the ultimate selling price. The impact of other factors such as competition's prices, customer reactions, promotional efforts, and less expensive products must be considered carefully in light of the total complexities associated with pricing decisions.

Cost Plus Target Income Pricing

In Chapter 6, we demonstrated that cost-volume-profit (CVP) analysis can be used to establish prices. This is another type of cost-based pricing approach in which the objective is to cover all related costs and produce the amount of profit management desires. The **cost plus target income pricing** approach often is used by *service businesses* that can reasonably estimate the service activity expected during a given period. Target profits are established either on the basis of a fixed amount or a variable amount as a percentage of revenue. The total costs involved and the target profit desired by management are used in a CVP analysis formula to determine how much should be charged for the service.

To illustrate, consider the case of Lucille Sutton, a Certified Public Accountant (CPA), who has just resigned from an international public accounting firm in order to open her own office. After renting office space, hiring two clerical employees, purchasing equipment, and making arrangements for the other costs necessary to operate an accounting practice (such as utilities, insurance, and automobile expenses), she is ready to decide how much to charge per hour for her services. She estimates that the total fixed costs required to operate the office will be $40,000 per year and that she will have 1,500 billable hours annually (billable hours are those charged to clients for services rendered). In addition, she wants to earn a profit of $20,000 during the first year of practice. To find the hourly billing rate needed, she would make the following calculation:

$$\text{Hourly billing rate} = \frac{\$40,000 + \$20,000}{1,500 \text{ hours}} = \$40 \text{ per hour}$$

The CPA must evaluate the $40 hourly rate to determine if it is realistic in terms of what competing firms are charging for the same services. If the rate is not realistic, she will have to adjust accordingly by working *more hours, reducing costs,* or *accepting a lower profit.* Consequently, as we emphasized earlier, a cost base usually provides the first step in the pricing process, and the results must be evaluated to see if they are realistic for the market conditions involved.

Pricing Based on a Target Return on Investment

Many companies use a pricing policy based on a **return on investment (ROI)** as the target profit goal. With this approach, management must determine both the profit desired and the investment in assets required to earn the profit. In Chapter 13, we will consider the subject of **return on investment** in more detail, but for now we will define it as being net income divided by the investment in assets required to earn the income. Once the desired ROI is determined, the total costs involved with a product or service are added to it to find the price that will cover the costs and earn enough profit to justify the investment in the related assets.

To illustrate, assume that the Rider Company, which produces and sells a wide range of chemical products, is evaluating the feasibility of introducing a new product that would be sold in gallon containers and used for swimming pool maintenance. The firm's sales manager estimates that 100,000 gallons will be sold each year. The investment in assets needed to produce and sell the new chemical amounts to $800,000, and management has decided that it wants to earn 15% on its investment. Total costs associated with the new product are estimated to be $650,000. The selling price required is calculated as follows:

$$\begin{aligned}\text{Selling price} &= [\$650,000 + (15\% \times \$800,000)]/100,000 \text{ gallons} \\ &= (\$650,000 + \$120,000)/100,000 \text{ gallons} \\ &= \$7.70 \text{ per gallon}\end{aligned}$$

Again, we should note that each of the cost-oriented pricing methods previously considered has the limitation of being highly dependent on the accuracy of the projected sales volume. Unit fixed costs, unit target profit, and unit selling price will vary according to the forecast sales volume. If an overly optimistic sales forecast is used, the selling price may be set so low that the firm cannot achieve its profit goal. Conversely, an unrealistically low sales forecast may produce a high selling price that is not competitive in the marketplace.

Despite this weakness, most managers consider cost-oriented pricing to be the best approach available. To counteract the demand problem, many managers use "what-if" analysis (also called sensitivity analysis) to evaluate combinations of price and demand to find the one that appears to be the most realistic for the future. This analysis consists of evaluating the impact of changes in the demand for a given product or service on selling prices and the likely competitiveness of the results.

PRICE DISCRIMINATION UNDER THE ROBINSON-PATMAN ACT

Businesses must be certain that their pricing decisions are in compliance with various laws that deal with price setting and price discrimination. Our discussion of pricing concludes with a brief discussion of one of the most important of these laws, the Robinson-Patman Act. The act was passed by the U.S. Congress in 1936 to prevent price discrimination by businesses engaged in interstate commerce. The law, enforced by the Federal Trade Commission (FTC), prohibits offering different prices for commodities of like grade and quality to different customers who compete with each other.

Objective 12: Consideration of the legal implications of pricing decisions

For our purposes, the most important aspect of the act is that it is directed toward price discrimination, not all price differentials. This means that a business can establish different prices on a limited basis as long as it can justify the differences in a way permitted by the Robinson-Patman Act. Although such defenses are complicated and have resulted in numerous court cases, the justifications for price differentials are:

1. Interstate commerce is not involved, or
2. The prices are needed to meet competition, or
3. The products involved are not alike, or
4. Competition is not affected, or
5. The price differentials are based on differences in the cost of producing and distributing the same product to different customers.

Whenever a company relies on the fifth justification, the government insists on detailed cost information to support the price differences. Both the FTC and the courts have consistently ruled that the cost base used to support price differences must involve full costing (absorption costing), not just the incremental or variable costs. The complexities associated with the technical aspects of the five defenses must be evaluated carefully whenever a business considers offering different prices to different customers who compete with each other. A coverage of these complexities is beyond the scope of this textbook.

SUMMARY

Managers need relevant information to make good business decisions at all levels of an organization. In general, decision making consists of four steps: (1) defining the problem; (2) selecting alternative courses of action; (3) obtaining relevant information; and (4) making a decision. Good information typically leads to correct decisions, whereas bad information usually leads to incorrect decisions. In most cases, decision making is both an art and a science because both qualitative and quantitative factors must be considered. To provide a structured approach to decision making, managers often use a decision model, which is a formalized method for evaluating alternatives. Differential analysis (incremental analysis) is a decision model used to evaluate the differences in revenues and costs for alternative courses of action.

Relevant costs, differential costs, unavoidable costs, sunk costs, and opportunity costs are important ways of classifying costs for differential analysis. Relevant costs are expected future costs, which will differ among the alternatives being considered. The difference between the relevant costs of two or more alternatives is a differential cost. Unavoidable costs will be the same regardless of the alternative selected. Sunk costs have already been incurred and cannot be changed. They are, therefore, irrelevant. Opportunity costs are important in decision making because they represent the benefits foregone by rejecting one alternative while accepting another. Differential analysis assists managers in making decisions such as evaluating a special sales order, considering whether or not a product or department should be discontinued, determining whether to purchase or produce a part used in the production process, and analyzing the replacement of a fixed asset.

Pricing decisions are among the most important ones made in most businesses. A selling price is generally determined by using a market demand-oriented approach or a cost-oriented approach. The market demand-oriented approach is most useful in explaining general price movements; a cost-oriented approach is most frequently utilized by businesses to set actual products' or services' selling prices. Examples of cost-oriented pricing methods are markup pricing, cost plus target income pricing, and target return on investment pricing. The basic objective of each cost-oriented pricing method is to determine the selling price that will cover the firm's total costs and yield a profit that is acceptable to management. Even when management utilizes a cost-oriented pricing method, the demand for a product or service must be considered carefully.

The legal ramifications of the Robinson-Patman Act must be evaluated to ensure that a firm is not guilty of price discrimination. This law is complex, but price differentials are permitted in certain situations such as when a firm is reacting to a competitor's price, the products involved are not alike, or there are differences in the cost of serving different customers.

GLOSSARY

COST-ORIENTED PRICING. An approach used to price products and services in which we begin with the actual or estimated costs involved and add the amount of profit management desires (p. 238).

COST PLUS TARGET INCOME PRICING. The use of cost-volume-profit (CVP) analysis to establish a selling price based on the costs involved and the profit goals of the firm (p. 242).

DECISION MAKING. Making a choice between alternative courses of action (p. 224).

DECISION-MAKING PROCESS. Defining the problem, selecting alternative courses of action, obtaining relevant information, and arriving at a decision (p. 225).

DECISION MODEL.   A formalized method for evaluating alternative courses of action (p. 225).

DIFFERENTIAL ANALYSIS (INCREMENTAL ANALYSIS).   A decision model used to evaluate the differences in relevant revenues and costs between alternative courses of action (p. 225).

DIFFERENTIAL COSTS.   The difference between the relevant costs of two alternatives (p. 226).

DIFFERENTIAL REVENUE.   The difference between the relevant revenues of two alternatives (p. 226).

JOINT PRODUCT COSTS.   Common costs required to produce joint products before they are identifiable as separate units (p. 232).

JOINT PRODUCTS.   The name given to multiple products produced from common raw materials or by the same production process (p. 231).

MARKET DEMAND-ORIENTED PRICING.   A theoretical approach to pricing in which the primary focus is on the relationship of supply and demand in the marketplace (p. 238).

MARKUP PRICING.   Determining selling prices by using a markup percentage that is large enough to cover the cost base involved and yield the amount of profit management desires (p. 239).

OPPORTUNITY COST.   The potential benefit forfeited by rejecting one alternative while accepting another (p. 226).

RELEVANT COSTS.   Expected future costs that will differ between alternatives (p. 226).

RELEVANT REVENUES.   Expected future revenues that will differ between alternatives (p. 226).

RETURN ON INVESTMENT (ROI).   The comparison of profit results with the investment in assets required to earn them (p. 242).

SPLIT-OFF POINT.   The point in the production process at which joint products become separable products (p. 232).

SUNK COSTS.   Costs that are not relevant in decision making because they already have been incurred and cannot be changed (p. 226).

TARGET RETURN ON INVESTMENT PRICING.   A pricing method with which a desired return on investment is added to the cost base involved to establish a selling price (p. 242).

UNAVOIDABLE COSTS.   Either future costs that will not differ between alternatives or sunk costs (p. 226).

DISCUSSION QUESTIONS

1. What is decision making? What are the basic steps followed in the decision-making process?
2. Distinguish between operating decisions and strategic decisions.
3. You recently heard a business manager make the following comment: "Quantitative analysis may be all right for some businesses, but I'd rather make decisions based on my intuition and years of experience." Do you agree? Explain.
4. What qualitative factors must be considered in a typical business decision? How are they different from quantitative factors for managerial accounting purposes?

5. What is differential analysis and how does it contribute to managerial decision making?

6. Define each of the following terms:
   a. Relevant costs
   b. Differential costs
   c. Unavoidable costs
   d. Sunk costs
   e. Opportunity costs

7. "All future costs are relevant costs." Do you agree?

8. The All-Sports Company produces golf balls that are sold for $9 per dozen. Under what circumstances might the firm consider an order at a price lower than $9?

9. What is the most potentially misleading feature of the analysis required to consider the elimination of a product or a product line?

10. The Back Camper Company uses a number of parts to produce several models of campers. The company has been purchasing a certain part from another firm at a price of $159 even though it has the expertise to produce the part internally. The controller has estimated that the following costs would be incurred in the production of each of the parts:

Direct costs	$135
Variable manufacturing overhead	15
Fixed manufacturing overhead	30
Total	$180

Do you agree that the firm should buy the part based on this analysis? Explain.

11. Define the following terms:
   a. Joint products
   b. Joint product costs
   c. Split-off point for joint products

12. What is the basic difference between the treatment of joint costs for inventory valuation and decision making concerning the choice of selling them at the split-off point or processing them further?

13. Is book value ever a relevant cost in a decision involving the replacement of old equipment? Explain. How about any disposal value for the old equipment?

14. Why can't a firm simply select the products with the highest contribution margin per unit to find the most profitable product mix?

15. What is meant by the contribution margin per machine hour or per direct labor hour? How do marketing constraints affect the choice of the most profitable product mix?

16. Identify some of the major factors management must consider in selecting the firm's selling prices.

17. Why is the market demand-oriented pricing approach advocated by economists impractical for most businesses?

18. Identify and explain the basic cost-oriented pricing techniques available to management.

19. Why are cost-based pricing methods so popular in the real world of business?

20. What is the biggest problem associated with markup pricing?

21. Explain cost plus target income pricing. Why is target return on investment pricing an effective means of selecting selling prices?

22. You recently heard a company president say, "My firm does not bother with fixed costs in setting selling prices because we base everything on a contribution margin approach." Do you agree with this approach? Explain.
23. What is the main purpose of the Robinson-Patman Act?
24. Identify the major defenses for price differentials that are permitted by the Robinson-Patman Act.

EXERCISES

Exercise 7-1 **Evaluating a Special Order**

The Pigskin Company manufactures footballs and has enough idle capacity to accept a special order for 20,000 footballs to be sold for $12 each. The footballs normally sell for $20 each. The variable manufacturing costs are $9 per ball, and fixed manufacturing overhead is $3 per ball. There will be no additional selling or administrative costs related to the special order, and the special order will not affect normal sales.

Required:
Calculate the effect on net income if the special order is accepted.

Exercise 7-2 **Evaluating a Special Order**

The Clean-out Company produces cleaning kits for shotguns. The production capacity available will enable the firm to produce 500,000 kits annually. A projected income statement for next year shows:

Sales (460,000 kits)	$4,600,000
Cost of goods sold	2,960,000
Gross profit	1,640,000
Selling and administrative expenses	1,250,000
Net income	$ 390,000

Fixed manufacturing overhead costs included in the cost of goods sold are $1,120,000. A 10% sales commission is paid to sales representatives for each kit sold. The purchasing department of a large discount chain has offered to purchase 30,000 kits at $6 each. The Clean-out Company sales manager's initial response is to refuse the offer because he concludes that the $6 price is below the firm's average cost ($2,960,000/460,000). The sales commission would not be paid on the special order.

Required:
A. Should the special offer be accepted? What would be the impact on net income?
B. Assume that the offer was for 50,000 kits. Should it still be accepted? Show your calculations.
C. Ignore part B. What is the lowest price the firm could accept if it wants to earn annual net income of $480,000?

Exercise 7-3 **Elimination of a Department**

The Discount Apparel Store operates three departments: Children's Clothing, Men's Clothing, and Women's Clothing. The store manager is considering the elimination of the Men's Clothing Department because income statements prepared by the store's accountant consistently show a net operating loss for the department. For example, the departmental operating performances during the past year (1987) were as follows:

DISCOUNT APPAREL STORE
Income Statement
Year Ended December 31, 1987

	Children's Clothing	Men's Clothing	Women's Clothing
Sales	$288,000	$192,000	$480,000
Cost of goods sold	187,200	144,000	288,000
Gross profit	100,800	48,000	192,000
Direct expenses	28,800	24,000	48,000
Indirect expenses–allocated to departments	50,400	33,600	84,000
Net income	$ 21,600	$ (9,600)	$ 60,000

In analyzing these operating results, the store's accountant determines that advertising expenses amounting to $4,800 are the only indirect expenses that can be avoided if the Men's Clothing Department is terminated. All direct expenses are avoidable.

Required:
What would be the effect on the store's profits of eliminating the Men's Clothing Department?

Exercise 7-4 Evaluating a Make-Buy Situation
The Yoomahoo Company manufactures motorcycles and purchases a major component from another firm. The company has a significant amount of idle capacity. Yoomahoo has been purchasing the component for $265. The controller has said that the component could be produced internally at the following costs:

Direct materials	$150
Direct labor	75
Variable manufacturing overhead	25
Fixed manufacturing overhead	50
Total	$300

Required:
A. Identify the following for the company:
1. Unavoidable costs
2. Relevant and differential costs
B. Based on your analysis, should Yoomahoo continue to purchase the component?

Exercise 7-5 Evaluating a Make-Buy Situation
A manufacturer of television sets is considering ways to increase the firm's plant capacity utilization because it has recently been operating at 70% of capacity. One proposal is to make a component which is currently being pur-

chased for $74 per unit. Based on a study by the firm's controller, the cost to produce the component is as follows:

Direct materials	$24.00
Direct labor (3 hours @ $11.20/hr)	33.60
Manufacturing overhead (applied based on direct labor hours)	24.00
Total	$81.60

The anticipated work activity for the year is 250,000 direct labor hours. Fixed manufacturing overhead for the year is budgeted at $1,500,000.

Required:
You have been asked by the controller to determine if the component should be built internally or purchased. Calculate the per unit cost differential between making and buying the component.

Exercise 7-6 Consideration of Joint Products
The CY Company manufactures two lotions, CY regular and CY super. The lotions are made from a joint process. The sales value at split-off was $75,000 for 6,000 bottles of regular, and $37,500 for 2,000 bottles of super. Joint product cost allocated to the super lotion was $45,000 using the relative sales value method at the split-off point.

Required:
Determine the amount of total joint product costs incurred by the company.

Exercise 7-7 Evaluating an Equipment Replacement Decision
The Bain Company is evaluating the purchase of a new machine to replace an existing machine used in the production operation. The new machine will provide a significant increase in the firm's productivity. Selected information about the two machines is as follows:

	Existing Machine	New Machine
Original cost	$80,000	$120,000
Accumulated depreciation	20,000	–0–
Residual value	18,000	–0–
Estimated annual cost savings from new machine		28,000
Years of useful life	5	5

Required:
Determine whether the new machine should be acquired. Ignore income taxes.

Exercise 7-8 Evaluating the Replacement of Equipment
The Orvis Car Rental Company installed a new car washing machine two weeks ago at a cost of $25,600. The machine has an annual operating cost (excluding depreciation) of $19,200. It is expected to have a useful life of four years with no residual value.

Today, a car washing machine sales representative provides Orvis with information about a new, improved machine that costs $32,000 and has an annual operating cost (excluding depreciation) of $12,800. The new machine also has a four-year life with no residual value. The machine currently in use can be sold for $14,400.

Required:

A. Identify the relevant costs in this decision.

B. Should Orvis buy the new machine or keep the current machine? Calculate the annual cost differential between the machines.

Exercise 7-9 Determining the Best Product Mix with Constraints

The Maxwell Company produces three types of stereo headphones, X-11, X-12, and X-13. The production of all three types requires the use of a special machine, which can only be operated 200 hours each month. The following data are provided by the controller:

	X-11	X-12	X-13
Selling price per unit	$84	$112	$147
Variable cost per unit	49	56	70
Machine time required in minutes	6	10	15

The demand for all three types has been very strong, and the firm can sell as many headphones as it can produce.

Required:

A. Given the capacity constraint imposed by the special machine, which type should be made?

B. If all types required the same amount of machine time, which style should be produced?

Exercise 7-10 Choice of Products with Constraints

The Holder Company produces three products in a highly automated manufacturing process. During a month, only 400 machine hours are available for production of the three products. Relevant financial and production data for the three products are:

	Product A	Product B	Product C
Selling price	$12	$16	$22
Variable costs	7	8	10
Contribution margin	$ 5	$ 8	$12
Machine time required – in minutes	12	20	30

The firm can sell as much of any product as it can manufacture.

Required:

A. Which product should be manufactured? How much total contribution margin will be earned?

B. How much would the selling price of the second most profitable product have to increase to be as profitable as the answer to A?

Exercise 7-11 Basic Considerations of Pricing Decisions

The management of the Miller Company is attempting to establish the selling price for its newest product. The product has the following cost data:

	Per Unit	Total
Direct materials	$52.00	
Direct labor	78.00	
Variable manufacturing overhead	19.50	
Fixed manufacturing overhead	45.50	$2,275,000
Fixed selling and administrative expenses	26.00	1,300,000

The expected production capacity and sales for the year are 50,000 units. Management is considering using cost plus pricing with a markup of 50% on the manufacturing costs to determine selling price.

Required:
Compute the selling price for the new product assuming the company uses:

1. Variable costing
2. Full (absorption) costing

Exercise 7-12 Basics of Target Return on Investment Pricing

The Stone Company has developed a new product, and the controller is attempting to determine what price to charge. The company requires a 10% return on investment from all products, and the product has required an $800,000 investment. The estimated costs related to the new product are as follows:

	Per Unit	Annual Total
Direct materials	$12.50	
Direct labor	10.50	
Variable manufacturing overhead	7.40	
Variable selling and administrative expenses	1.60	
Fixed manufacturing overhead	—	$400,000
Fixed selling and administrative expenses	—	240,000

For all of its products, the company uses cost plus pricing based on the variable costs involved.

Required:
A. If the company expects to sell 30,000 units each year, what percentage mark-up would be required to achieve the target ROI? With this markup, what is the selling price per unit?
B. Repeat question A, assuming expected sales are 50,000 units each year.

Exercise 7-13 Multiple-choice Questions—Relevant Information and Decision Making

1. In a make or buy decision involving relevant costs:
   a. Only variable costs are relevant
   b. Fixed costs that can be avoided in the future are relevant
   c. Only prime costs are relevant
   d. Future costs that will continue regardless of the decision are relevant
   e. None of the above
2. In a make or buy decision, which of the following qualitative factors is usually important?
   a. Quality control of the production process
   b. Labor skills available
   c. Technology requirements
   d. Special material requirements
   e. All of the above
3. The Metzger Company uses 20,000 units of a certain part in its production process. The following information concerning production costs is available:

Direct materials	$ 4
Direct labor	16
Variable manufacturing overhead	8
Fixed manufacturing overhead applied	10
Total	$38

The company has an offer from an outside supplier to purchase the part for $35 per unit. If this is done, the released manufacturing facilities could not otherwise be used productively and 60% of the fixed overhead applied will continue. The total relevant costs of making the part are:

   a. $560,000
   b. $640,000
   c. $700,000
   d. $750,000
   e. None of the above

4. In question 3 above, which alternative is more profitable for the firm and by what amount?

   a. Buy, $80,000
   b. Make, $80,000
   c. Buy, $60,000
   d. Make, $60,000
   e. None of the above

5. In considering a special order that will enable a company to utilize currently idle production capacity, which of the following costs are irrelevant?

   a. Direct materials
   b. Equipment depreciation
   c. Direct labor
   d. Variable overhead
   e. None of the above

6. Production of a special order will increase gross profit when the incremental revenue from the special order is more than:

   a. The fixed costs incurred in producing the order
   b. The incremental costs incurred in producing the order
   c. The direct materials incurred in producing the order
   d. The depreciation charge associated with the order
   e. None of the above

7. The Kemper Company sells a product at a price of $21 per unit. Kemper's cost per unit based on a full capacity utilization of 200,000 units is:

Direct materials	$ 4
Direct labor	5
Manufacturing overhead (2/3 of which is fixed)	6
Total	$15

A special order for 20,000 units has been offered by a foreign importer if Kemper can price the product more competitively than $21 per unit. The only selling costs that would be incurred with the special order are $3 per unit for shipping. Kemper has enough existing capacity to produce the 20,000 units. The minimum selling price it should set is:

   a. $12
   b. $15
   c. $16
   d. $18
   e. None of the above

8. Refer to question 7. To increase its profits by $40,000, Kemper should establish a selling price of:

   a. $12

    b. $14
    c. $16
    d. $21
    e. None of the above

9. Relay Company produces batons. Relay can manufacture 300,000 batons a year at a variable cost of $750,000 and a fixed cost of $450,000. Relay forecasts that 240,000 batons will be sold at the normal selling price of $5 each. In addition, a special order was recently offered to Relay for 60,000 batons to be sold at a 40% discount off the normal price. If the offer is accepted, Relay's profits will change by:
    a. $60,000 decrease
    b. $30,000 increase
    c. $36,000 increase
    d. $180,000 increase
    e. None of the above

10. Which of the following methods would be used to determine the lowest price that would be quoted for a special order that would utilize what otherwise would be idle capacity?
    a. Process cost
    b. Job order cost
    c. Variable cost
    d. Absorption cost
    e. None of the above

Exercise 7-14 Multiple-choice Questions—Relevant Information and Decision Making

1. The Wayout Company has a limited number of machine hours available for the production of Products A and B. Both products have a $10 selling price, but Product A has a contribution margin of 60% and Product B one of 70%. Four units of Product A can be produced in the same time required by three units of B. Assume that there is no limit on how many units of each product the firm can sell. How should the firm's capacity be used?
    a. 100% for A
    b. 100% for B
    c. 50% for each product
    d. None of the above

2. The Richards Company has a used machine with a book value of $90,000 and a residual value of $12,000. The remaining life of the machine is 12 years. A new machine, costing $228,000, is available with a life of 12 years. It will do the same thing as the old machine at a cost savings of $20,000 per year. Based on this information, which is the best answer?
    a. The new machine will have a total advantage of $24,000 over the 12-year period
    b. The new machine will have a total advantage of $36,000 over the 12-year period
    c. The old machine will have a total advantage of $28,000 over the 12-year period
    d. The old machine will have a total advantage of $36,000 over the 12-year period
    e. None of the above

3. The Johnson Company has some obsolete inventory that cost $60,000 and

can be sold today for $20,000. If it is further processed, the inventory can be sold for $70,000, but additional costs of $46,000 are required for the work. The incremental effect of further processing for Johnson is:

a. An advantage of $4,000
b. A disadvantage of $4,000
c. An advantage of $16,000
d. A disadvantage of $16,000
e. None of the above

4. The Carrier Company has 6,000 machine hours available for manufacturing two products with the following facts:

	Product A	Product B
Selling price	$50	$40
Variable costs	40	28
Time required to produce one unit (in minutes)	7.5	12

The contribution margins per machine hour for A and B are:

a. $10 for A and $12 for B
b. $75 for A and $144 for B
c. $80 for A and $60 for B
d. $50 for A and $40 for B
e. None of the above

5. In question 4 above, the firm can maximize profits by producing:

a. 48,000 units of B
b. 48,000 units of A
c. 30,000 units of A
d. 30,000 units of B
e. None of the above

6. The maximum profitability for the Carrier Company using the facts in questions 4 and 5 above is:

a. $480,000
b. $360,000
c. $200,000
d. $210,000
e. None of the above

PROBLEMS

Problem 7-1   Evaluating a Special Order

The Stay-Fresh Company produces flower vases. The operating results of the preceding year were:

Sales (77,000 units @ $8)	$616,000	
Cost of goods sold:		
Direct materials	115,500	
Direct labor	154,000	
Manufacturing overhead	92,400	
Total	361,900	
Gross profit	254,100	
Selling expenses	38,500	
Administrative expenses	23,100	
Total operating expenses	61,600	
Net income	$192,500	

The company has received a special order to buy 10,000 vases at a unit cost of $6.90. Material costs per unit would not change, but the labor costs for the special order would be 25% greater than normal since some overtime wages would be incurred. Fixed manufacturing overhead is 50% of the variable manufacturing overhead at the present level of production. Fixed manufacturing overhead would not change and there would be no additional variable or fixed selling expenses. The administrative expenses, which are all fixed, would increase $2,000 if the special order is accepted. Current variable selling expenses are $.20 per unit. The company has a maximum capacity of 85,000 vases so the company would have to reduce its regular sales by 2,000 units if it accepts the special order.

Required:
A. Should the company accept the special order? Why?
B. What would be the effect on the firm's profits?

Problem 7-2 Evaluating a Special Order

The Cook-Out Company manufactures gas grills and is considering expanding production. A distributor has asked the company to produce a special order of 8,000 grills to be sold overseas. The grills would be sold under a different brand name and would not influence Cook-Out Company's current sales. The plant is currently producing 95,000 units per year. The company's maximum capacity is 100,000 units per year so the company would have to reduce the production of units sold under its own brand name by 3,000 units if the special order is accepted. The company's income statement for the previous year is presented below:

Sales (95,000 units)		$7,125,000
Cost of goods sold:		
Direct materials	$2,375,000	
Direct labor	1,900,000	
Manufacturing overhead	1,425,000	5,700,000
Gross profit		1,425,000
Selling expenses	575,000	
Administrative expenses	237,500	812,500
Net income		$ 612,500

The company's variable manufacturing overhead is $10 per unit and the variable selling expense is $5 per unit. The administrative expense is completely fixed and would increase by $5,000 if the special order is accepted. There would be no variable selling expense associated with the special order and variable manufacturing overhead per unit would remain constant.

The company's direct labor cost per unit for the special order would increase 5% while direct materials cost per unit for the special order would increase 10%. Fixed manufacturing overhead and fixed selling expense would not change.

Required:
If the distributor has offered to pay $67 per unit for the special order, should the company accept the offer? Justify your answer.

Problem 7-3 Evaluating a Special Order

Tom Mandel is the owner of a small company that produces electric motors. He has two production lines, one for a standard motor that is also made by several other firms and one for specialty motors produced specifically for customers' specifications. Results of the firm's operations for the previous year are as follows:

	Special Motors	Standard Motors	Total
Sales	$125,000	$62,500	$187,500
Direct materials	25,000	20,000	45,000
Direct labor	50,000	22,500	72,500
Rent	15,000	2,500	17,500
Depreciation	15,750	9,000	24,750
Utilities	1,500	250	1,750
Other fixed overhead	4,500	750	5,250
Net income	$ 13,250	$ 7,500	$ 20,750

The building has been leased for 15 years at $17,500 per year. The rent, utilities, and other overhead are allocated based on the amount of floor space occupied by each production line. Depreciation is specifically allocated to the machines used by each product line.

Mr. Mandel has received an order from his best customer to manufacture 12,500 specialized motors. Mandel is currently working at capacity and is required by contract to produce all special orders already received. He could reduce his production of standard motors by one-half for the next year in order to produce the new special order. The customer will pay $17.50 per motor with the new order. The direct costs will be $14 per unit, and Mandel will have to buy a new tool costing $5,000 for the special motor. The tool will be worthless when the job is finished.

Required:
Should Mandel accept the order? In your answer, be sure to identify the following:

1. Differential revenue and costs
2. Unavoidable costs
3. Opportunity costs

Problem 7-4 Considering the Deletion of a Department

Joe Gossup, president of the National Publishing Company, is analyzing the firm's financial statements for the past year. The firm publishes magazines weekly, monthly, and quarterly. Data for the past year are as follows:

	Quarterly Magazine	Monthly Magazine	Weekly Magazine	Total
Sales	$125,000	$175,000	$200,000	$500,000
Variable expenses	62,500	70,000	80,000	212,500
Fixed expenses:				
Depreciation of special				
equipment	7,500	8,750	11,250	27,500
Salary of editor	20,000	20,000	22,500	62,500
Common costs				
allocated*	43,750	61,250	70,000	175,000
Net income (loss)	$ (8,750)	$ 15,000	$ 16,250	$ 22,500

* Allocated based on sales dollars

The equipment used is very specialized and has no resale value if its use is discontinued. Mr. Gossup is considering discontinuing the quarterly magazine, because he claims it is decreasing the company's profitability.

Required:

As Mr. Gossup's advisor, assist him in determining whether to continue the quarterly magazine. Use a contribution margin income statement to support your advice.

Problem 7-5 Considering the Deletion of a Product

The controller of the Bartlett Company is reviewing the financial summary of the company's three products. He is attempting to find a way to increase the firm's profitability. The financial data for the past twelve months are as follows:

	Product A	Product B	Product C	Total
Sales	$ 31,500	$25,000	$45,000	$101,500
Cost of goods sold	34,920	11,875	17,640	64,435
Gross profit	(3,420)	13,125	27,360	37,065
Selling & admin. expenses	7,065	4,975	7,440	19,480
Net income	$(10,485)	$ 8,150	$19,920	$17,585
Sales price per unit	$3.50	$5.00	$7.50	
Variable cost of goods sold per unit	3.25	1.25	1.50	
Variable selling & admin. expenses per unit	.50	.59	.63	
Units sold	9,000	5,000	6,000	

Required:

A. The controller analyzes the above data and decides that Product A should be discontinued because it is showing a net loss. What will be the effect on net income if it is discontinued?

B. If Product A is discontinued causing an additional loss of 100 units of Product C, what will be the total impact on net income?

Problem 7-6 Elimination of a Department

The Discount Furniture Showcase Company operates three departments at its Grand Rapids location—a Commercial Furniture Department, a Residential Furniture Department, and an Assemble-Yourself Furniture Department for budget conscious customers. The store's accountant has prepared an income statement by department for the most recent year, and for the third year in a row the Assemble-Yourself Furniture Department has shown a loss. If the company decides to eliminate the unprofitable department, 60% of the space occupied by the Assemble-Yourself Furniture Department will be used by the Residential Furniture Department and the remaining 40% will be used by the Commercial Furniture Department. The firm does not believe that eliminating the third department, while at the same time enlarging the remaining two departments, will change the sales or gross profits of the Residential and Commercial Departments. The accountant has also provided the following information:

1. The president's salary of $75,000 per year has been allocated equally between the departments.

2. At present, there are three salespersons and a manager in the Assemble-Yourself Furniture Department. If the department is eliminated, the manager would be transferred to the Commercial Furniture Department and the three salespersons would be terminated. The manager's salary is $35,000 per year.

3. The utilities, rent, and insurance are allocated on the basis of square foot-

age. The insurance would decrease $2,000 a year if the department is eliminated; the rent and utilities would not change.

4. Indirect advertising in the amount of $80,000 was allocated to the departments on the basis of sales. The direct advertising expenditures incurred by the Assemble-Yourself Furniture Department would be eliminated.

5. The equipment in the Assemble-Yourself Furniture Department would be transferred to the other departments—70% to the Commercial Furniture Department and 30% to the Residential Furniture Department.

DISCOUNT FURNITURE SHOWCASE COMPANY
Income Statement
Year Ended December 31, 1987

	Commercial Furniture	Residential Furniture	Assemble-Yourself Furniture	Total
Sales	$850,000	$510,000	$340,000	$1,700,000
Cost of goods sold	340,000	229,500	119,000	688,500
Gross profit	510,000	280,500	221,000	1,011,500
Operating expenses:				
Salaries	160,750	82,500	89,750	333,000
Utilities	15,400	18,100	14,500	48,000
Advertising	140,000	87,000	96,000	323,000
Rent on building	28,000	37,000	25,000	90,000
Depreciation on equipment	35,000	26,000	22,000	83,000
Insurance	8,100	12,150	6,750	27,000
Total operating expenses	387,250	262,750	254,000	904,000
Net income (loss)	$122,750	$ 17,750	$ (33,000)	$ 107,500

Required:
A. Should the Assemble-Yourself Furniture Department be eliminated?
B. Prepare a departmental income statement reflecting the results if the department is dropped.

Problem 7-7 Elimination of a Department
The Klondike Company operates a hardware store with three departments—Hardware, Plumbing, and Paint. For the past three years, the Paint Department has shown a net loss and the owner of the store has asked you to determine whether the Paint Department should be eliminated. If the owner decides to eliminate the Paint Department, 75% of the space occupied by the department will be used by the Hardware Department and the remaining 25% will be used by the Plumbing Department. Neither sales nor gross profits of the Hardware or Plumbing Departments will change if the Paint Department is eliminated. The following additional information describes the expenses currently related to the Paint Department:

1. The owner's salary of $30,000 has been allocated equally among the three departments.

2. At present, there is one salesperson and a manager in the Paint Department. If the Paint Department is eliminated, the manager would be trans-

ferred to the Hardware Department and the salesperson would be terminated. The salesperson's salary is $12,000.

3. The office expense, telephone expense, and supplies expense are allocated on the basis of sales. The supplies expense would decrease by $1,000 if the Paint Department is eliminated, but the office expense and telephone expense would not change.

4. The rent expense is allocated on the basis of square footage and would not change if the Paint Department is eliminated.

KLONDIKE COMPANY
Income Statement
Year Ended July 31, 1987

	Hardware	Plumbing	Paint	Total
Sales	$171,600	$92,400	$ 45,500	$309,500
Cost of goods sold	79,850	43,150	13,650	136,650
Gross profit	91,750	49,250	31,850	172,850
Operating expenses:				
Salaries	51,000	29,000	35,000	115,000
Office expenses	6,000	4,320	1,680	12,000
Telephone	2,750	1,980	760	5,490
Supplies	11,000	7,920	3,080	22,000
Rent	8,000	4,500	3,500	16,000
Total operating expenses	78,750	47,720	44,020	170,490
Net income (loss)	$ 13,000	$ 1,530	$(12,170)	$ 2,360

Required:

A. Should the Paint Department be eliminated?

B. Prepare a departmental income statement showing the results if the department is dropped.

Problem 7-8 Evaluating a Make-Buy Decision

The Blow-Out Company produces air compressors. The motors for the compressors are purchased directly from an outside supplier at a cost of $46 each. The company has some factory space that it currently rents to a firm as warehouse space. The annual rental income is $50,000. If the company decides to manufacture the motors, it would have to purchase a new machine at a cost of $75,000. The new equipment would enable the firm to produce its annual requirement of 5,000 motors and would have no residual value at the end of a five-year useful life. In addition, the company has compiled the following costs per unit, which do not reflect the cost of the new machine:

Direct labor	$12
Direct materials	15
Variable manufacturing overhead	8
Fixed manufacturing overhead – direct	2
Fixed manufacturing overhead – allocated	5
Total	$42

Required:

Should the firm make or buy the motors for the air compressors?

Problem 7-9 Evaluating a Make-Buy Decision

The Lake Company has realized a significant increase in demand for its products and is presently producing at a full capacity level of 100,000 units. The company is considering expanding output to 125,000 units by the adoption of one of the following alternatives:

1. The additional 25,000 units could be purchased from an outside source at a price of $6 per unit.
2. The company could expand its production capacity, which would result in added direct fixed expenses of $50,000 per year.

The company's sales and cost data at the 100,000-unit level of output are:

Sales	$750,000
Direct materials	100,000
Direct labor	150,000
Variable overhead	50,000
Direct fixed overhead	250,000
Allocated fixed overhead	75,000
Net income	$125,000

Common fixed costs allocated to production would increase from $75,000 to $93,750 since the common fixed overhead is allocated on the basis of sales volume, although the firm's total common fixed costs would not increase under either alternative.

Required:
Which of the two alternatives should the company adopt?

Problem 7-10 Evaluating a Make-Buy Decision

The Hoosier Generator Company manufactures small electric motors for which a small part is needed. The following cost data have been accumulated for the 16,000 parts the company manufactured during the previous year:

Direct materials	$ 32,000
Direct labor	88,000
Variable manufacturing overhead	72,000
Fixed manufacturing overhead	112,000

The company can buy the part from another firm for $18.80 per unit. If the firm buys the item, it will be able to reduce fixed manufacturing overhead costs by $64,000 per year. It will also be able to rent some of the facilities currently used to make the part to another firm for $34,000.

Required:
Should Hoosier Generator continue to make the part, or should it be purchased from the other firm?

Problem 7-11 Differential Analysis and Joint Products

The Candle Chemical Company produces two products, A and B, at a joint product cost of $24,000. The company can sell 8,000 units of Product A for $2 per unit or the units can be processed further at a cost of $10,000 to produce 3,000 units of Product X, 4,000 units of Product Y, and 1,000 units of Product Z. The unit selling prices for Products X, Y, and Z are $3, $2, and $4, respectively. The company can sell 5,000 units of Product B or they can be processed further to produce 2,000 units of Product C and 3,000 units of Product D. The additional processing to produce Products C and D will cost $3,000. The per unit selling prices are $3 (Product B); $5 (Product C); and $3 (Product D).

Required:
Which of the products should be sold at the split-off point and which should be processed further?

Problem 7-12 Differential Analysis and Joint Products
The Borl Company produces two joint products, X and Y. The annual production is 10,000 units of X and 6,000 units of Y at a joint cost of $104,000. Product X can be sold for $10 per unit at the split-off point and Product Y can be sold for $16 per unit. Product Y can be further processed at a cost of $2,000 into Products A and B. The additional processing will produce 4,000 units of A and 2,000 units of B. The selling price of Product A is $12 per unit and Product B sells for $20 per unit. Product X can be processed further at an annual cost of $20,000 and sold for $20 per unit.

Required:
Which products should be sold at the split-off point and which should be processed further?

Problem 7-13 Joint Product Decision Making
The Columbia Corporation produces four chemicals from a joint production process. The chemicals can be processed beyond the split-off point with the following sales and cost data:

Product	Processing Costs after Split-off	Sales Value after Split-off
Chem-1	$176,000	$288,000
Chem-2	96,000	211,200
Chem-3	64,000	83,200
Chem-4	24,000	19,200

Joint product costs are $128,000. The firm could sell the chemicals at split-off for the following amounts:

Product	Sales Value at Split-off
Chem-1	$128,000
Chem-2	57,600
Chem-3	16,000
Chem-4	-0-

Required:
Determine which products should be sold at the split-off point and which ones should be processed further.

Problem 7-14 Evaluating Cost-Based Pricing
The General Appliance Company has developed a new air-conditioning system that will be sold during the next year. Cost data for the system are as follows:

	Per Unit Cost	Total Cost
Direct materials	$480	
Direct labor	240	
Variable manufacturing overhead	160	
Fixed manufacturing overhead	—	$576,000
Variable selling & admin. expenses	112	
Fixed selling & admin. expenses	—	355,000

The expected production capacity and sales level are 2,000 systems per year. The company normally uses a pricing formula of full production cost plus 50%. A recently hired accountant says that in college he learned that full costs should not be used as a pricing base. He suggests that the price be set at 225% of total variable costs.

Required:
A. Compute the difference in selling price between the full cost approach and the variable cost approach.
B. For all other products that the company sells, it earns a 20% profit on sales. What selling price is necessary for the air-conditioning system to achieve the same profit-sales relationship?

Problem 7-15 Computing Markup Percentages for Pricing
The Removal Company has developed a new cleaning solvent sold in drums. The new solvent will require a permanent investment of $640,000 for equipment and working capital. The following costs are estimated for the production of the solvent:

	Per Drum	Total Annual Costs
Direct materials and labor	$34.56	—
Variable manufacturing overhead	3.84	—
Variable selling and admin. expenses	1.60	—
Fixed manufacturing overhead*	—	$192,000
Fixed selling and administrative expenses	—	232,000

*Based on annual production of 20,000 drums

The company uses cost-plus pricing for all its products and has a 15% target return on investment.

Required:
A. Compute the markup percentage needed for the company to achieve its target ROI, assuming the company uses absorption (full) costing.
B. Using the markup percentage calculated in A above, compute the selling price for a drum of solvent.
C. Compute the markup percentage needed for the company to achieve its target ROI, assuming the company uses the variable costing method.
D. Using the markup percentage calculated in C above, compute the selling price for a drum of solvent.

Problem 7-16 Using Cost Information for Pricing
Johnson Engineering Company produces electronic air filters for commercial and residential use. The firm normally prices the filters by adding a markup of 75% to its variable costs, a policy that has enabled the company to operate

above 90% of capacity. Recently, the company has been asked to bid on a state government order for 2,000 air filters. The controller has prepared the following cost estimates for the 2,000 filters:

Direct materials	$160,000
Direct labor	100,000
Variable manufacturing overhead	20,000
Allocated fixed manufacturing overhead	110,000
Allocated administrative costs	10,000
Total	$400,000
Divided by	2,000
Cost per electronic air filter	$ 200

If Johnson Engineering Company receives the government bid, it will have to eliminate regular sales of $315,000. The fixed costs allocated to the bid above represent what will otherwise be unused capacity to the firm.

Required:
A. If the firm's normal pricing policy is used, what price should be charged for the 2,000 filters?
B. How much contribution margin will be lost from regular sales if the government order is accepted?
C. What is the lowest price the company can bid on the government order without decreasing current profits?

Problem 7-17 Pricing in a Service Business
Sheri Keller recently started a personal financial consulting firm. She wants to establish hourly billing rates to charge her clients. Her annual costs needed to perform the related services are estimated to be:

Office rent	$12,000
Professional liability insurance	3,000
Salaries	40,000
Utilities	4,000
Automobile	5,500
Depreciation	12,000
Other	3,500
Total	$80,000

In addition, Ms. Keller wants to earn a profit of $30,000 during the first year of operation. She estimates that she will be able to charge clients for 2,000 hours per year.

Required:
A. Based on the projected financial data, how much should Ms. Keller charge per hour for her services?
B. What other factors should she consider in establishing the hourly billing rate?

Problem 7-18 Variable Cost Pricing
Cabalt, Inc. produces custom-made powerboats in a price range of $15,000 to $30,000. The pricing policy of the firm is to set prices based on the estimated costs of direct materials, direct labor, and the firm's overhead (manufacturing, selling, and administrative). A markup of 20% typically is added to the total

estimated costs in order to set the selling price per boat. As an example, a recent price was established for a particular boat as follows:

Direct materials	$ 5,000
Direct labor	8,000
Overhead	2,000
Total	15,000
Plus 20%	3,000
Selling price	$18,000

If a customer rejects a price, the firm often decreases the markup to as little as 5% over the estimated costs involved. The annual average markup typically is 15% because of this policy.

The company's controller has suggested that pricing based on variable costs only would be better than the current approach. He has determined that the firm's total overhead is expected to be $180,000, of which $108,000 is fixed. The remainder is variable in proportion to direct labor cost of $720,000.

Required:

A. Assume that during a month when the firm has slack capacity, a customer rejects both the $18,000 price shown for the boat above and a $15,750 offer (the selling price with a 5% markup). The customer says he will pay $14,600 for the boat. Should the firm accept the offer?

B. What is the minimum selling price the firm can charge for the boat in part A without reducing or increasing net income?

C. What advantages does the policy of basing prices on variable costs have over the policy used historically?

D. What are the disadvantages of a pricing policy based on variable costs?

8

BUDGETING: A MANAGEMENT TOOL FOR FINANCIAL PLANNING AND CONTROL

CHAPTER OVERVIEW AND OBJECTIVES

This chapter presents the basic concepts and procedures used to develop budgets that assist management in planning and controlling a firm's financial performance. After studying this chapter, you should be able to:

1. Explain how a master budget is used as a management tool.
2. Define the need for goal congruence in an organization.
3. List the benefits and limitations of budgeting.
4. Identify the key steps involved in preparing a master budget.
5. Recognize the significance of an accurate sales forecast for the budgeting process and the methods used to predict sales.
6. Distinguish between an operating budget and a financial budget.
7. Prepare and use each of the individual budgets included in the master budget.
8. Discuss the importance of inventory level decisions made during the budgeting process.
9. See how budget performance reports are used for control purposes.
10. Describe the major considerations involved with budgeting in nonmanufacturing operations.

THE PURPOSE OF BUDGETING

A **budget** is a detailed plan that shows how resources are expected to be acquired and used during a specified time period. Virtually every person and every organization use some form of budget with the objective of achieving an efficient and effective utilization of scarce resources. A master budget prepared

Objective 1:
Importance of budgeting as a management tool

by a business, however, is typically more detailed and formalized than a budget for an individual. The budgeting process used to prepare a master budget is vital to efficient, effective business management. Budget information is utilized throughout the management process, although its primary application is in the planning and controlling functions.

As a management tool, a budget can be compared to the architectural drawings used by a contractor to build a house. To build the house efficiently (with an economical amount of labor, materials, and overhead) and effectively (so the results are compatible with the predetermined specifications), the contractor must follow the blueprint drawings carefully. A budget serves the managers of a business in the same manner by providing a formal plan for the firm's future courses of action according to well-defined organizational goals.

Initially, budgeting identifies certain financial and operating targets that become management's goals for the future. These targets, which provide the direction for the firm's activities and transactions, are expected to lead to satisfactory profit results. As the actual performance occurs, it is monitored and checked against the related targets for control purposes. If significant variances between the actual and planned performance are found, they are investigated and corrected whenever possible using the concept of management by exception (discussed in Chapter 1). When budgeting is combined with responsibility accounting (see Chapter 13), the result is an effective organizational framework for planning and controlling a firm's financial performance.

IMPORTANCE OF GOAL CONGRUENCE IN AN ORGANIZATION

Objective 2: Achieving goal congruence in an organization

Every organization must be certain that all of its segments work toward common goals. Since the performances of the various segments are interrelated in many ways, segment managers must each know (1) their own roles and (2) how their individual roles interact with the rest of the organization. For example, the accounting, finance, marketing, personnel, production, and purchasing functions of a manufacturing firm must be closely coordinated. The same is true for the agencies of a government, the services of a bank, or the departments of a hospital. Disorder and confusion are inevitable if the various segments of an organization operate without knowing or caring about the impact of their actions on other segments. As a result, inefficiency and ineffectiveness in the allocation and utilization of scarce resources are likely.

Coordination does not occur automatically since individuals within an organization and the organization as a whole usually have different goals. Consider, for example, the potential conflict that could develop within a manufacturing firm from differing inventory policies of the managers responsible for production and marketing. The production manager is primarily concerned with (1) using the manufacturing facilities efficiently and (2) maintaining stable inventory levels by producing at a steady rate.

In contrast, the marketing manager's goal is having enough inventory available at all times to meet customers' demands — even if large variations in sales volume occur between periods. Stable inventory levels and sufficient amounts of inventory at all times usually are not compatible goals, and a compromise between production and marketing is necessary.

Without a formal coordination system, individual managers would tend to operate in different directions and in many cases against the best interests of the organization. This problem becomes increasingly difficult as an organization grows and management responsibility is delegated to more people. Goal congruence occurs when the managers of a firm accept the organizational goals as their own. The various activities of a business must be planned and controlled with the full participation and support of the managers responsible for them.

BENEFITS OF BUDGETING

Achieving satisfactory profits in today's competitive and uncertain business world is no easy matter. For example, the average profit margin (net income after tax divided by net sales) for large U.S. corporations is only about 5%. This means that the typical company can use approximately five cents out of every sales dollar to pay dividends, retire debt, and reinvest in the business. Figure 8-1, which shows the biannual profit margins of 8 large corporations from 1978 to 1984, illustrates just how small corporate profits really are.

Objective 3: Identifying the benefits and limitations of budgeting

Tight profit margins leave little room for error, and management must do everything possible to protect and improve them. A firm's financial performance must be planned and controlled through sound budgeting procedures in order to achieve and maintain acceptable profit results. To ensure that budgets are effectively used, both their benefits and limitations must be carefully considered. The benefits of budgeting are:

1. **Planning.** Budgeting forces management to plan ahead and systematically anticipate the future. Most managers are very busy with their day-to-day activities and may avoid formalized planning unless budgeting is part of their job. Nevertheless, every successful manager knows what he or she wants to accomplish and when it should be done. The regularity of the budgeting process forces managers to formalize their thinking about the future and participate in the firm's goal setting activities.
2. **Organizing.** Budgeting assists in (1) placing economic and human resources in the most financially rewarding areas and (2) making the managers aware of the scarcity of resources.

Figure 8-1
Profitability Performance for Eight Large Corporations

| | Profit Margin Percent | | | |
Company	1978	1980	1982	1984
American Airlines	4.5	def.*	def.	4.8
Ford Motor Company	4.1	def.	def.	4.2
General Foods	3.5	3.7	3.4	3.7
Holiday Inns	5.6	7.6	5.2	7.8
IBM Corporation	14.7	13.2	11.8	13.7
Pabst Brewing	1.6	1.3	0.1	0.5
Sears, Roebuck and Co.	4.7	2.2	2.4	3.6
Texas Instruments	5.6	5.3	3.2	def.

*def. indicates a net loss for the period.
Source: "Annual Report on American Industry," Forbes (January 1979, 1981, 1983, 1985).

3. **Controlling.** Budgeting provides managers with realistic performance targets against which actual results can be compared. Management by exception is performed by identifying significant variances (differences between actual and budgeted amounts) that require corrective action if the firm is to achieve its goals.

4. **Coordination.** Budgeting coordinates the various segments of the organization and makes each manager aware of how the different activities fit together. Goal congruence can be achieved by the unifying effect budgeting has on an organization — particularly when it is combined with responsibility accounting as we will see in Chapter 13.

5. **Communication.** Budgeting serves as a communication device that the various managers use to (a) exchange information concerning goals, ideas, and achievements and (b) interact and develop an awareness of how each of their activities contributes to the firm's overall operation.

6. **Motivation.** Budgeting provides managerial motivation in the form of goals. Few people work for the sheer joy of it; most of us need some form of stimulus to work hard and maintain an enthusiastic attitude toward our jobs. Budget goals and periodic reports comparing actual performance with the goals are a major source of managerial stimulus whenever budgeting is properly used. Unfortunately, an improperly applied budget may have an adverse effect on the motivation of managers — who may then criticize the process as being unfair.

Two key aspects of a good budgeting application are (1) the budgeted level of performance should be attainable with a reasonably efficient amount of effort and (2) the managers evaluated with a budget should actively participate in its development. Managers will be more highly motivated with self-imposed budgets than with those established by someone at a higher level in the organization.

LIMITATIONS OF BUDGETING

Like other managerial accounting tools, budgeting is not a panacea because it does have some limitations that can adversely affect its usefulness. In fact, many people have the wrong impression about budgeting, identifying it with unrealistic goals, unreasonable restrictions, authoritative decision making, excessive pressure, lack of participation, and too much guesswork. These views can impede the use of budgeting in financial planning and control. To avoid such negative perceptions, the following limitations of budgeting should be understood so they can be avoided whenever possible or at least minimized:

1. In many cases, a budget tends to *oversimplify the facts of a real-world situation* and does not truly represent the complexities faced by management. This can be particularly true of environmental factors such as the economy, the labor market, social changes, and the impact of competition.

2. A budget *may emphasize results* (e.g., actual net income compared with the amount budgeted) *but not reasons* (e.g., explanations for why marketing costs were higher than expected) when both are important.

3. The participative theme of budgeting *demands complete management support and involvement.* If managers are not convinced of budgeting's benefits, they are not likely to spend the time required for successful budgeting.

4. The budget may *undermine management's initiative* by discouraging new developments and actions not covered in the budget.

5. If *excess pressure* is applied to individual managers for the achievement of budget goals, the managers may react with decisions that adversely affect organizational goals. For example, a department manager who is having trouble keeping spending within the budget may decide to defer preventive maintenance expenditures on machinery to the future, thereby meeting the budget targets in the short run but causing costly breakdowns and repairs later.
6. The budgeting process is *not an exact science* and good judgment plays an essential role. Thus, budgeting is somewhat subjective and is based on the best information available. Constant revision is needed as new facts become known.

PROFIT PLANNING WITH BUDGETING

The primary objective of the profit planning phase of budgeting is identifying how managers intend to achieve organizational goals by acquiring and using the firm's resources during a budget period. A master budget—that is, a budget consisting of several interrelated budgets—provides the basis for profit planning. These are the major steps in developing a master budget:

1. Identify the organizational goals for the budget period—including those that are financially oriented such as *desired net income, profit margins, return on investment, liquidity, share of the market,* and *financial position.*
2. Have the managers of the various business segments *participate* in developing the parts of the master budget for which they are responsible.
3. Forecast sales for the budget period.
4. Have responsible managers estimate (1) the product costs and (2) the period costs to be included on the budgeted income statement.
5. Assign priorities for capital expenditures (investments in facilities and equipment) of the budget period.
6. Convert accrual accounting to cash basis accounting in order to determine the cash receipts and cash disbursements of the budget period. Consider any nonoperating sources or uses of cash (such as the sale of stock, issue of debt, payment of dividends, or retirement of debt).
7. Prepare a set of pro forma financial statements based on the initial version of the financial performance projections.
8. Compare the budgeted financial performance results with the organizational goals. Revise as necessary to make the final version of the budget compatible with the overall organizational goals.

Objective 4:
Key steps in preparing a master budget

IMPORTANCE OF THE SALES FORECAST

Sales information provides the basis for preparing a sales budget, predicting cash receipts, and constructing a variety of expense budgets. Thus, an accurate **sales forecast** is the cornerstone of successful budgeting. Virtually everything else is dependent on it. The basic objectives of sales forecasting are (1) evaluating the total market potential for the firm's products or services and (2) estimating the business' anticipated market share, given its resource limitations.

The sales forecast usually is the most difficult part of the budgeting process because of the typical uncertainty regarding future sales. Unless a business firm has numerous unfilled orders that guarantee future sales or a highly consistent demand for its products or services, sales forecasts are merely management's

Objective 5:
Significance of an accurate sales forecast

best estimates of what will happen in the future. The following are examples of factors that will influence the reliability of a sales forecast:

1. The general economy
2. Industry conditions
3. The effect of proposed advertising expenditures
4. Actions of competitors
5. Consumer buying habits
6. Population changes
7. Technological developments
8. The firm's pricing policies

A combination of several methods is usually used to forecast sales. The most popular methods are *predictions by members of the sales staff, group estimates prepared by top management, test marketing,* and the *use of statistical or mathematical techniques.* The sales force should participate actively in the preparation of the sales forecast because of its awareness of current market conditions. Field surveys can be conducted to predict revenues by products or services, geographical areas, customers, and sales representatives. In large companies, a market research staff may be available to conduct the field studies of consumer demand and develop sales revenue estimates.

Many businesses predict the sales of a new product based on *test (also called target) market results.* A test market that is considered representative of all the markets in which the firm operates is selected. The product is then offered for sale in that market to test consumer response to the product. The sales results are later extended to the firm's overall market to estimate the total sales expected from the product.

The members of the management team—including production, finance, purchasing, and general administrative officers—should develop their own estimates of expected revenues based on their personal knowledge of both the total business and the environment in which the firm operates. In addition, statistical and mathematical techniques, such as trend analysis (an evaluation of changes in sales over time) based on regression analysis, are available for sales forecasting. The alternative forecasting methods discussed above are used because they provide checks on each other and produce a compromise representing management's best estimate of sales revenue.

STRUCTURE OF THE MASTER BUDGET

The **master budget** is a set of separate but closely interrelated budgets representing a comprehensive plan of action for a specified time period. A budget committee normally is appointed by top management and given the responsibility of coordinating the development of the master budget. This budget is typically prepared for the 12-month period representing a firm's fiscal year. It is then subdivided into shorter periods (such as months or quarters) to facilitate timely comparisons of actual and budgeted results. Alternatively, the master budget may be developed for a continuous period of 12 months or more by adding a month or a quarter in the future as the month or quarter just ended is eliminated.

Even in an annual budgeting application, the budgeted targets must be revised frequently as new information concerning the business and its environment becomes available. Many businesses also prepare long-term budgets for periods of three to five years that typically are less detailed than an annual budget. This approach is becoming more popular because of management's increasing concern for long-term planning and the availability of sophisticated computerized budgeting packages.

The master budget consists of two major components: (1) the operating budget and (2) the financial budget. The **operating budget** is a detailed description of the revenues and costs required to achieve satisfactory profit results. The **financial budget** shows the funding and financial position needed for the planned operations. Each of these two components has several separate but interrelated budgets, such as those shown schematically in Figure 8-2 for the Campus Specialty Company. The page numbers shown refer to the presentation of the related budgets in an illustration involving the company later in the chapter. Essentially the same budgeting cycle as the one illustrated in Figure 8-2 is applicable in a nonmanufacturing business, although some of the individual budgets may differ (for example, a merchandising firm would not need a production budget).

The master budget for a manufacturing firm would contain the following budgets:

Objective 6:
Comparing an operating budget with a financial budget

Master Budget

Operating Budget	Financial Budget
Sales budget	Capital expenditures budget
Production budget	Cash budget
Direct materials budget	Budgeted balance sheet
Direct labor budget	Budgeted statement of cash
Manufacturing overhead budget	flows
Cost of goods sold budget	
Selling expenses budget	
Administrative expenses budget	
Budgeted income statement	

MASTER BUDGET PREPARATION ILLUSTRATION

The preparation of a master budget involves a sequence of steps, many of which are dependent on the previous step. Let's illustrate the preparation of a master budget by referring to the Campus Specialty Company, which produces two types of medallions that are sold to campus bookstores in the Midwest. The medallions are decorative items on which a university's name and emblem are imprinted. A Deluxe Medallion is larger and requires more direct labor than a Standard Medallion. Campus Specialty Company purchases metal alloy by the ounce and uses skilled labor to produce the medallions. The following data represent the direct (prime) costs estimated for the production of each medallion:

Objective 7:
Preparing and using individual budgets

	Deluxe	**Standard**
Direct materials	5 ounces @ $2 per ounce	4 ounces @ $2 per ounce
Direct labor	2 hours @ $10 per hour	1 hour @ $10 per hour

The master budget is prepared for a calendar year and is subdivided into quarters. In the following illustration, we are concerned with a summary of the steps taken by the Campus Specialty Company to prepare the 1987 master budget. We assume that work in process inventories are negligible so they are ignored here in order to concentrate on the basic principles of budgeting. Our objective is to examine the most essential steps in the budgeting process and consider the most important concepts, procedures, and interrelationships involved.

Figure 8-2
Master Budget
Interrelationships

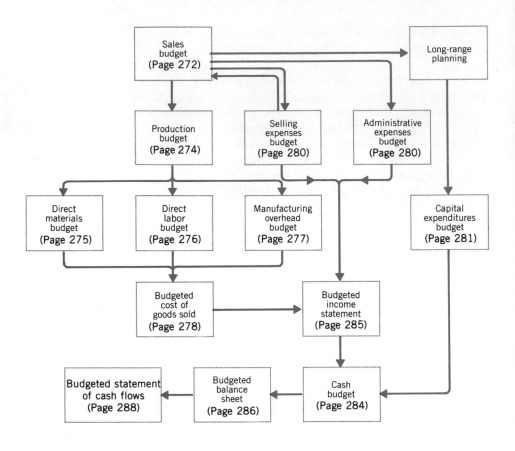

Figure 8-3

CAMPUS SPECIALTY COMPANY					
Sales Budget					
Year Ending December 31, 1987					
	Quarter				
	1	2	3	4	Total
Deluxe Medallion					
Budgeted sales units	4,800	7,200	7,800	6,000	25,800
× Budgeted price per unit	$72	$72	$72	$72	$72
= Budgeted sales dollars	$345,600	$518,400	$561,600	$432,000	$1,857,600
Standard Medallion					
Budgeted sales units	7,200	9,600	10,200	8,400	35,400
× Budgeted price per unit	$42	$42	$42	$42	$42
= Budgeted sales dollars	$302,400	$403,200	$428,400	$352,800	$1,486,800
Total					
Budgeted sales dollars	$648,000	$921,600	$990,000	$784,800	$3,344,400

SALES BUDGET

As noted earlier, almost every phase of the master budget depends on the sales forecast. The sales budget is prepared from the sales forecast. Detailed information concerning sales volume, selling prices, and sales mix is presented in the sales budget as an expansion of the original sales forecast. Assume that we have used the forecasting methods discussed earlier in this chapter to prepare the 1987 sales forecast leading to the sales budget shown in Figure 8-3.

Most of the information used to develop the sales forecast originated in a market survey performed by the firm's sales representatives. These representatives called on each midwestern school served by the Campus Specialty Company and discussed the expected medallion sales with bookstore managers. This information was then evaluated by all of the company's managers in relation to such factors as past sales, general economic conditions, projected school enrollments, and the expectations of the managers concerning future sales.

Trend analysis from past sales was also used to project the 1987 sales. These trend results were combined with the market survey data to determine the most likely sales forecast. In addition, the firm's sales manager considered the influence of selling expenses such as advertising on the projected demand for the two products. That is, the level of advertising spending was correlated with the expected sales revenue shown in Figure 8-3.

PRODUCTION BUDGET

Once the sales budget is prepared, we can consider the production requirements for the period, which are determined as:

$$\begin{matrix} \text{Production} \\ \text{units} \\ \text{required} \end{matrix} = \begin{matrix} \text{Forecast} \\ \text{sales} \\ \text{units} \end{matrix} + \begin{matrix} \text{Desired ending} \\ \text{finished} \\ \text{goods} \end{matrix} - \begin{matrix} \text{Beginning} \\ \text{finished} \\ \text{goods} \end{matrix}$$

Note that an inventory level decision must be made before the production requirements can be established. Campus Specialty Company plans its inventory for each product to have an adequate number of units available to satisfy the expected sales demand for a current quarter and have enough ending inventory for future sales. The right amount of inventory is an important factor for the firm's profitability. An excessive inventory will result in unnecessary costs, such as insurance, handling, and the opportunity costs for funds invested. In contrast, inventory shortages will cause lost sales, dissatisfied customers, and production scheduling problems.

Objective 8: Importance of inventory level decisions

We assume that the company has decided that the desired ending finished inventory for a particular quarter should be set equal to the expected sales for the first month of the succeeding quarter. This policy has enabled the company to maintain the right amount of ending inventory in the past. For example, the desired ending inventory for Deluxe Medallions at the end of the first quarter is set equal to the sales expected for April. Since the production budget is developed before the budget year 1987 starts, we will have to estimate the beginning inventory. The production budget for 1987 is shown in Figure 8-4.

DIRECT MATERIALS BUDGET

After we have determined the production requirements for the period, the direct materials budget, direct labor budget, and manufacturing overhead budget

CAMPUS SPECIALTY COMPANY
Production Budget
Year Ending December 31, 1987

	\multicolumn{5}{c}{Quarter}				
	1	2	3	4	Total
Deluxe Medallion					
Forecast sales units (Figure 8-3)	4,800	7,200	7,800	6,000	25,800
+ Desired ending finished goods	3,600	2,580	1,980	2,340	2,340
= Total units needed	8,400	9,780	9,780	8,340	28,140
− Beginning finished goods	1,620	3,600	2,580	1,980	1,620
= Production required − units	6,780	6,180	7,200	6,360	26,520
Standard Medallion					
Forecast sales units (Figure 8-3)	7,200	9,600	10,200	8,400	35,400
+ Desired ending finished goods	3,000	3,600	3,000	2,880	2,880
= Total units needed	10,200	13,200	13,200	11,280	38,280
− Beginning finished goods	2,400	3,000	3,600	3,000	2,400
= Production required − units	7,800	10,200	9,600	8,280	35,880

Figure 8-4

can be developed since each of these budgets contains the costs required for the production process. To prepare the **direct materials budget,** we again must make inventory level decisions. Essentially the same approach used for the production budget is taken with budgeted direct materials purchases calculated as:

$$\begin{matrix} \text{Budgeted} \\ \text{purchases} \\ \text{in units} \end{matrix} = \begin{matrix} \text{Budgeted} \\ \text{direct} \\ \text{materials} \\ \text{usage} \end{matrix} + \begin{matrix} \text{Desired} \\ \text{ending} \\ \text{direct} \\ \text{materials} \end{matrix} - \begin{matrix} \text{Beginning} \\ \text{direct} \\ \text{materials} \end{matrix}$$

The direct materials required are initially determined in ounces and then converted to dollars by multiplying the ounces needed by the cost of an ounce of metal alloy. We need five ounces of direct materials to produce one Deluxe Medallion and four ounces for a Standard Medallion. Each ounce costs $2. In Chapter 10, we will discuss how the prices and quantities of the resources needed for production can be predetermined as standard costs, which are used by many manufacturing firms. We have also decided to utilize a one-month supply for the estimate of desired ending direct materials inventory. The total purchases of direct materials projected are $549,240, as shown in Figure 8-5.

DIRECT LABOR BUDGET

The **direct labor budget,** which provides important information concerning the size of the labor force that is necessary each quarter, is also developed from the production budget. The primary objective of this budget is to maintain a labor force large enough to satisfy the production requirements but not so large that it results in costly idle time. At the same time, it must be big enough to avoid an excessive amount of overtime charges, which also would be costly.

CAMPUS SPECIALTY COMPANY
Direct Materials Budget
Year Ending December 31, 1987

	Quarter				
	1	2	3	4	Total
Deluxe Medallion					
Production units (Figure 8-4)	6,780	6,180	7,200	6,360	26,520
× Ounces of materials per unit	5	5	5	5	5
= Ounces of materials required	33,900	30,900	36,000	31,800	132,600
+ Desired ending materials	10,200	12,000	10,700	11,200	11,200
= Ounces needed	44,100	42,900	46,700	43,000	143,800
− Beginning materials	10,500	10,200	12,000	10,700	10,500
= Purchases required – ounces	33,600	32,700	34,700	32,300	133,300
× Cost per ounce	$2	$2	$2	$2	$2
= Cost of purchases	$ 67,200	$ 65,400	$ 69,400	$ 64,600	$266,600
Standard Medallion					
Production units (Figure 8-4)	7,800	10,200	9,600	8,280	35,880
× Ounces of materials per unit	4	4	4	4	4
= Ounces of materials required	31,200	40,800	38,400	33,120	143,520
+ Desired ending materials	13,500	12,800	11,000	11,700	11,700
= Ounces needed	44,700	53,600	49,400	44,820	155,220
− Beginning materials	13,900	13,500	12,800	11,000	13,900
= Purchases required – ounces	30,800	40,100	36,600	33,820	141,320
× Cost per ounce	$2	$2	$2	$2	$2
= Cost of purchases	$ 61,600	$ 80,200	$ 73,200	$ 67,640	$282,640
Total purchases	$128,800	$145,600	$142,600	$132,240	$549,240

Figure 8-5

The first step in the development of the direct labor budget is to estimate the time needed to produce each type of medallion. Two hours are required for one Deluxe Medallion and one hour is needed for a Standard Medallion. The next step is computing the total labor required for each type of medallion by multiplying these hourly measures by the number of medallions to be produced. For the year, 53,040 direct labor hours are projected for Deluxe Medallions and 35,880 hours for Standard Medallions, for a total of 88,920 direct labor hours. The final step is finding the total annual direct labor costs. This is done by multiplying the total direct labor hours (88,920) by the hourly labor rate of $10 to find the total direct labor costs of $889,200 for the year, as shown in Figure 8-6.

MANUFACTURING OVERHEAD BUDGET

The **manufacturing overhead budget** provides a schedule of all production costs except direct materials and direct labor. We assume that cost behavior analysis has been used to separate variable and fixed costs, with the results shown in Figure 8-7. Remember that every manufacturing firm must decide between absorption and variable costing to value its inventories. Absorption costing is used for external reporting; it charges both variable and fixed production costs to inventory.

CAMPUS SPECIALTY COMPANY
Direct Labor Budget
Year Ending December 31, 1987

	Quarter				
	1	2	3	4	Total
Deluxe Medallion					
Production units (Figure 8-4)	6,780	6,180	7,200	6,360	26,520
× Direct labor hours per unit	2	2	2	2	2
= Total hours required	13,560	12,360	14,400	12,720	53,040
× Labor rate per hour	$10	$10	$10	$10	$10
= Direct labor cost	$135,600	$123,600	$144,000	$127,200	$530,400
Standard Medallion					
Production units (Figure 8-4)	7,800	10,200	9,600	8,280	35,880
× Direct labor hours per unit	1	1	1	1	1
= Total hours required	7,800	10,200	9,600	8,280	35,880
× Labor rate per hour	$10	$10	$10	$10	$10
= Direct labor cost	$ 78,000	$102,000	$ 96,000	$ 82,800	$358,800
Total direct labor cost	$213,600	$225,600	$240,000	$210,000	$889,200
Total direct labor hours	21,360	22,560	24,000	21,000	88,920

Figure 8-6

In contrast, variable costing provides better information for internal purposes because only the variable manufacturing costs are charged to inventory with this approach. Since the master budget being prepared for Campus Specialty Company is an internal report, variable costing will be utilized for applying manufacturing overhead to the products during the budgeting process. The fixed manufacturing overhead costs are treated as period costs that are charged to the quarter in which they are projected to be incurred. As a result, the predetermined overhead rate used for budgeting consists only of the variable manufacturing overhead costs.

Note in Figure 8-7 that we have considered variability on the basis of direct labor hours (manufacturing overhead is the dependent variable and direct labor hours the independent variable), which also are used for the predetermined variable overhead cost rate computed as follows:

Overhead Item	Estimated Variable Rate per Direct Labor Hour
Indirect labor	$ .60
Indirect materials	.30
Employee benefits	1.60
Utilities	.50
Total	$3.00

The total variable manufacturing overhead costs will fluctuate with the production level on the basis of $3 per direct labor hour. For example, the total variable manufacturing overhead costs in the first quarter are $64,080 (21,360 hours × $3), and they increase to $67,680 in the second quarter because the estimated direct labor hours rise from 21,360 to 22,560.

CAMPUS SPECIALTY COMPANY
Manufacturing Overhead Budget
Year Ending December 31, 1987

	Rate per Hour	Quarter				Total
		1	2	3	4	
Variable Costs						
Indirect labor	$ .60	$ 12,816	$ 13,536	$ 14,400	$ 12,600	$ 53,352
Indirect materials	.30	6,408	6,768	7,200	6,300	26,676
Employee benefits	1.60	34,176	36,096	38,400	33,600	142,272
Utilities	.50	10,680	11,280	12,000	10,500	44,460
Total variable costs	$3.00	$ 64,080	$ 67,680	$ 72,000	$ 63,000	$266,760
Direct labor hours		21,360	22,560	24,000	21,000	88,920
Predetermined overhead rate		$3	$3	$3	$3	$3
Fixed Costs						
Supervision		$ 50,600	$ 50,600	$ 50,600	$ 50,600	202,400
Property taxes		6,500	6,500	6,500	6,500	26,000
Insurance		7,200	7,200	7,200	7,200	28,800
Maintenance		11,500	11,500	11,500	11,500	46,000
Utilities		10,600	6,600	9,600	6,600	33,400
Depreciation		24,000	24,000	24,000	24,000	96,000
Other		3,000	3,000	3,000	3,000	12,000
Total fixed costs		$113,400	$109,400	$112,400	$109,400	$444,600
Total manufacturing overhead		$177,480	$177,080	$184,400	$172,400	$711,360

Figure 8-7

By definition, the fixed manufacturing costs do not fluctuate in relation to the direct labor hours. Note, however, in Figure 8-7 that the total fixed manufacturing overhead costs are not the same each quarter. These differences are the result of seasonal fluctuations rather than volume changes. The only fixed manufacturing overhead cost item that changes from quarter to quarter is utilities cost. The budgeted utilities reflect high winter heating costs and high summer air-conditioning costs ($10,600 for the first quarter and $9,600 for the third quarter). In contrast, the utilities budgeted as fixed costs in the second and fourth quarters amount to $6,600. These fixed utilities costs will be the same each quarter regardless of the number of direct labor hours budgeted.

Note, too, that Figure 8-7 shows another variation of cost behavior analysis because it separates the total utilities cost (a mixed cost) into its variable and fixed components. The cost of the electricity needed to operate the firm's machinery is variable because this cost rises and falls with the use of the machinery at the rate of $.50 per direct labor hour. Other utility costs such as those related to heating, air-conditioning, and lighting are fixed costs because the same amounts are required regardless of how many medallions are produced or direct labor hours are worked. Thus, the total utilities cost is a mixed cost with a constant variable cost rate of $.50 per direct labor hour and a fixed cost component that changes from quarter to quarter (e.g., $10,600 for the first quarter).

COST OF GOODS SOLD BUDGET

The next step in the budgeting process is the preparation of a cost of goods sold budget based on the data accumulated in Figures 8-3 to 8-7. Keep in mind that we are using variable costing so only the variable manufacturing costs are included in the cost of goods sold calculation. The cost of goods sold budget is shown in Figure 8-8. The cost of goods sold estimated for the Deluxe Medallions is $928,800 and the amount for the Standard Medallions is $743,400. The total cost of goods sold is $1,672,200.

Remember that we are ignoring work in process inventories in this illustration. The unit variable production costs are $36 and $21 for Deluxe Medallions and Standard Medallions, respectively. We can compute the cost of goods sold for each product by multiplying the unit cost times the number of units in the sales forecast. The budgeted sales of Deluxe Medallions are 25,800 units (Figure 8-3), for a cost of goods sold of $928,800 (25,800 × $36), while 35,400 Standard Medallions are planned at a cost of $743,400 (35,400 × $21). Thus, the total budgeted cost of goods sold is $1,672,200. Campus Specialty Company must be sure that the selling prices of the two types of product are high enough to cover the cost of goods sold, all period costs, and the company's desired profit.

As shown in Figure 8-8, the complete computation of cost of goods sold in-

Figure 8-8

CAMPUS SPECIALTY COMPANY
Cost of Goods Sold Budget
Year Ending December 31, 1987

	Deluxe Medallion		Standard Medallion		Total	
Beginning finished goods		$ 58,320		$ 50,400		$ 108,720
+ Direct materials used:						
Beginning direct materials	$ 21,000		$ 27,800		$ 48,800	
+ Budgeted purchases (Fig. 8-5)	266,600		282,640		549,240	
− Ending direct materials	22,400		23,400		45,800	
= Direct materials used		265,200		287,040		552,240
+ Direct labor (Fig. 8-6)		530,400		358,800		889,200
+ Variable manufacturing overhead (direct labor hours × $3)		159,120		107,640		266,760
= Total manufacturing costs		954,720		753,480		1,708,200
− Ending finished goods		84,240		60,480		144,720
= Cost of goods sold		$928,800		$743,400		$1,672,200
Unit costs per product:						
Direct materials	5 oz @ $2 = $10			4 oz @ $2 = $8		
Direct labor	2 hr @ $10 = $20			1 hr @ $10 = $10		
Variable manufacturing overhead	2 hr @ $3 = $6			1 hr @ $3 = $3		
Unit cost	$36			$21		

volves the same basic cost of goods sold schedule we introduced in Chapter 2 (that is, adding the beginning finished goods inventory to the total manufacturing costs of the period and subtracting the ending finished goods inventory). In turn, the total manufacturing costs of the period are found by adding the direct materials budgeted, the direct labor budgeted, and the variable manufacturing overhead budgeted for the period. The direct materials expected to be used are calculated by adding the beginning materials to the budgeted purchases and subtracting the estimated ending materials. The finished goods inventories consist of the number of medallions shown in the production budget (Figure 8-4) multiplied by the unit costs (either $36 or $21). For example, Campus Specialty Company expects to begin 1987 with 1,620 Deluxe Medallions and 2,400 Standard Medallions. Thus, the total beginning finished goods inventory is $108,720 [(1,620 × $36) + (2,400 × $21)]. The same approach is taken with the beginning and ending direct materials inventories using unit cost of $2 each. For example, the firm estimates a beginning direct materials inventory of $21,000 for Deluxe Medallions (10,500 units × $2) and $27,800 for Standard Medallions (13,900 units × $2).

SELLING EXPENSES BUDGET

Since the firm's marketing efforts (e.g., the amount of advertising) will influence the level of sales volume, the effect of selling expenses on the sales forecast must be carefully evaluated. The sales manager of the Campus Specialty Company does this by preparing the initial version of the selling expenses budget concurrently with the sales forecast. The final version of the firm's selling expenses budget is presented in Figure 8-9. Cost behavior analysis is again performed to distinguish between the variable and fixed costs. Since we are dealing with selling expenses, variability is related to sales dollars, not some measure of production performance.

As shown in Figure 8-9, Campus Specialty Company has two variable selling expenses, advertising and sales commissions. Advertising is budgeted at 2% of sales dollars, so the total sales of $3,344,400 (from Figure 8-3) multiplied times 2% equals the advertising expenses budgeted for 1987, or $66,888. The quarterly sales dollars multiplied by 2% equals the quarterly advertising expenses. In addition, the company pays its sales representatives a commission of 8% of sales dollars, which amounts to $267,552 ($3,344,400 × 8%) in the 1987 budget. The rest of the selling expenses are fixed. They total $49,000 each quarter, and $196,000 for the year.

ADMINISTRATIVE EXPENSES BUDGET

The administrative expenses budget shown in Figure 8-10 contains the estimated expenses of general administration for 1987. This category includes the costs related to the president's office, the accounting department, and the personnel function. We have determined that all these costs are fixed; their total is $295,992, divided evenly among the quarters of 1987.

Administrative expenses are typically fixed because their total amount does not change with different sales levels; that is, they are committed or discretionary costs. An exception would be a bonus paid to certain managers based on a percentage of sales dollars.

CAMPUS SPECIALTY COMPANY
Selling Expenses Budget
Year Ending December 31, 1987

	Quarter				
	1	2	3	4	Total
Variable Expenses					
Advertising	$ 12,960	$ 18,432	$ 19,800	$ 15,696	$ 66,888
Sales commissions	51,840	73,728	79,200	62,784	267,552
Total variable expenses	64,800	92,160	99,000	78,480	334,440
Fixed Expenses					
Sales salaries	38,000	38,000	38,000	38,000	152,000
Travel	3,600	3,600	3,600	3,600	14,400
Entertainment	2,400	2,400	2,400	2,400	9,600
Insurance	600	600	600	600	2,400
Property taxes	400	400	400	400	1,600
Utilities	300	300	300	300	1,200
Depreciation	3,000	3,000	3,000	3,000	12,000
Other	700	700	700	700	2,800
Total fixed expenses	49,000	49,000	49,000	49,000	196,000
Total selling expenses	$113,800	$141,160	$148,000	$127,480	$530,440

Figure 8-9

Figure 8-10

CAMPUS SPECIALTY COMPANY
Administrative Expenses Budget
Year Ending December 31, 1987

	Quarter				
	1	2	3	4	Total
Administrative Expense					
Management salaries	$40,848	$40,848	$40,848	$40,848	$163,392
Clerical salaries	17,000	17,000	17,000	17,000	68,000
Insurance	2,150	2,150	2,150	2,150	8,600
Property taxes	1,200	1,200	1,200	1,200	4,800
Utilities	600	600	600	600	2,400
Supplies	1,400	1,400	1,400	1,400	5,600
Depreciation	10,000	10,000	10,000	10,000	40,000
Other	800	800	800	800	3,200
Total	$73,998	$73,998	$73,998	$73,998	$295,992

CAPITAL EXPENDITURES BUDGET

Before the budgeted income statement can be prepared, we must determine if the Campus Specialty Company will incur interest expense from borrowing money. Later, we will see from the company's balance sheet that the firm does not have any long-term debt or any other interest-bearing liabilities at the beginning of 1987. However, short-term borrowing may be necessary to finance the cash flow requirements of the firm's operating performance. In addition, some form of debt may be required for capital expenditures planned during 1987. Any type of debt will involve interest charges that must be expensed on the income statement. A cash budget will indicate whether the Campus Specialty Company expects to borrow money during 1987 based on its planned operating performance and capital expenditures.

We must consider the capital expenditures budget for the year before the cash budget can be developed. In turn, the cash budget is prerequisite to the completion of the budgeted income statement so any interest expense required is properly recognized. Note that the capital expenditures budget and the cash budget are both financial budgets.

The capital expenditures budget included in the master budget shows the acquisition of facilities and equipment of significant amounts planned for 1987. Capital expenditures are investments that are expected to yield benefits over a relatively long-term period. Most firms, including the Campus Specialty Company, prepare long-term capital expenditures budgets for periods of five or more years. Thus, the amounts shown in Figure 8-11 would represent the current portion of the long-term budget planned for 1987. Capital budgeting, the subject dealing with the planning and financing of capital expenditures, is discussed in Chapter 9.

As shown in Figure 8-11, the Campus Specialty Company expects to spend $150,000 for capital expenditures during the last quarter of 1987. The company's policy is to finance capital expenditures of this size out of operating income and, if required, from short-term borrowing.

CASH BUDGET

We assume that all of Campus Specialty Company's sales are made on credit. In addition, we should note that in a real-life situation, the firm probably

Figure 8-11

CAMPUS SPECIALTY COMPANY
Capital Expenditures Budget
Year Ending December 31, 1987

| | Quarter | | | | |
	1	2	3	4	Total
Computer equipment				$ 80,000	$ 80,000
Vehicles				70,000	70,000
Total				$150,000	$150,000

would have to prepare cash budgets more often than quarterly to guard against cash shortages within the quarter. The revenues and costs of the operating budgets must be translated into cash receipts and cash disbursements for financial planning purposes. The main purpose of the cash budget is to evaluate a business' ability to pay its bills as they come due. The cash budget (Figure 8-13) is used to plan an adequate but not excessive cash balance throughout the period. Excess cash can be used more productively by investing it in earning assets (e.g., short-term investments such as a certificate of deposit or a money market fund).

A profitable income statement does not guarantee sufficient liquidity (ability of a firm to satisfy its short-term obligations) because of the time lags between accrual and cash accounting. Consequently, we must carefully estimate the time lag between revenues recognized on the income statement and cash receipts as well as the time lag between expenses deducted and cash disbursements. In addition, we must eliminate any noncash expenses (such as depreciation) in the preparation of the cash budget since they will not require a cash outflow.

We have analyzed the company's previous experience with cash receipts from sales and determined that 60% of sales are collected in the quarter of the sales, 30% are collected in the quarter after the sales, and 10% are collected two quarters after the sales. Bad debts are negligible, so they are ignored for budgeting purposes. We also estimate that 80% of the company's raw materials purchases will be paid for in the quarter in which they are acquired and 20% will be paid for in the following quarter. The next step is the preparation of a schedule showing the cash receipts from sales and the cash disbursements for purchases, as shown in Figure 8-12.

The cash receipts and cash disbursements schedule in Figure 8-12 provides essential information needed to prepare the cash budget shown in Figure 8-13. We assume that Campus Specialty Company pays for direct labor, manufacturing overhead, selling expenses, and administrative expenses in the quarter in which they occur. Depreciation expense (amounting to $148,000) has been ignored in the preparation of the cash budget ($96,000 from manufacturing overhead in Figure 8-7, $12,000 from selling expenses in Figure 8-9, and $40,000 from administrative expenses in Figure 8-10) because it is a noncash expense.

Based on past experience, we have decided that the company requires a minimum cash balance of $30,000 at all times. A line of credit has been arranged with the firm's bank at a current interest rate of 12%, so money can be borrowed short term whenever the cash balance drops below $30,000. If a cash deficiency is forecast for a particular quarter, as it is for the first quarter of 1987, enough money will be borrowed at the beginning of that quarter to bring the projected cash balance up to the $30,000 minimum. The company will then pay the money back as soon as it has enough cash at the end of a succeeding quarter.

Figure 8-13 shows that $37,118 must be borrowed at the beginning of the first quarter because a cash deficit of $7,118 is projected. The estimated cash position at the end of the second quarter is $70,282, so the company can repay the $37,118 loan plus the interest accrued for six months of $2,227 ($37,118 $\times$ .12 $\times$ ½). No additional borrowings are expected to be necessary during 1987 since we are projecting cash receipts from sales sufficient to make all payments.

CAMPUS SPECIALTY COMPANY
Schedule of Cash Receipts and Disbursements
Year Ending December 31, 1987

	Quarter				
	1	2	3	4	Total
Cash Receipts					
From beginning accounts receivable balance of $377,000 (Fig. 8-15)	$301,000*	$ 76,000**			$ 377,000
From 1st quarter sales of $648,000 (Fig. 8-3)	(.6) 388,800	(.3) 194,400	(.1) $ 64,800		648,000
From 2nd quarter sales of $921,600 (Fig. 8-3)		(.6) 552,960	(.3) 276,480	(.1) $ 92,160	921,600
From 3rd quarter sales of $990,000 (Fig. 8-3)			(.6) 594,000	(.3) 297,000	891,000
From 4th quarter sales of $784,800 (Fig. 8-3)				(.6) 470,880	470,880
Total cash receipts	$689,800	$823,360	$935,280	$860,040	$3,308,480
Cash Disbursements					
For beginning accounts payable balance of $28,000 (Fig. 8-15)	28,000				28,000
For 1st quarter purchases of $128,800 (Fig. 8-5)	(.8) 103,040	(.2) 25,760			128,800
For 2nd quarter purchases of $145,600 (Fig. 8-5)		(.8) 116,480	(.2) 29,120		145,600
For 3rd quarter purchases of $142,600 (Fig. 8-5)			(.8) 114,080	(.2) 28,520	142,600
For 4th quarter purchases of $132,240 (Fig. 8-5)				(.8) 105,792	105,792
Total cash disbursements	$131,040	$142,240	$143,200	$134,312	$550,792

* .30 (4th quarter sales of $760,000) + .10 (3rd quarter sales of $730,000)
** .10 (4th quarter sales of $760,000)

Figure 8-12

Note that in addition to the cash disbursements for the various expenses, the company will pay a quarterly dividend of $20,000 plus an extra dividend of $20,000 at the end of the year, for total dividends of $100,000. Also, quarterly estimated tax payments of $40,000 will be made, and the capital expenditures budgeted in Figure 8-11 will be paid for in the fourth quarter. The remaining balance of the estimated tax liability shown on the budgeted income statement in Figure 8-14 ($2,000), or whatever amount is actually due, will be paid when the tax returns are filed.

The cash budget in Figure 8-13 shows that the Campus Specialty Company expects to begin the year with $36,000 in cash and end it with $102,469. Adequate liquidity will be maintained throughout 1987 according to this budget. In addition, the company should consider ways to invest excess cash (any amount above $30,000) during the third and fourth quarters.

CAMPUS SPECIALTY COMPANY
Cash Budget
Year Ending December 31, 1987

	Quarter				
	1	2	3	4	Total
Beginning cash balance	$ 36,000	$ 30,000	$ 30,937	$ 153,619	$ 36,000
Cash Receipts					
Cash collections from sales (Fig. 8-12)	689,800	823,360	935,280	860,040	3,308,480
Total cash available for disbursements	725,800	853,360	966,217	1,013,659	3,344,480
Cash Disbursements					
Payments for materials purchases (Fig. 8-12)	131,040	142,240	143,200	134,312	550,792
Direct labor (Fig. 8-6)	213,600	225,600	240,000	210,000	889,200
Manufacturing overhead (Fig. 8-7)	153,480	153,080	160,400	148,400	615,360
Selling expenses (Fig. 8-9)	110,800	138,160	145,000	124,480	518,440
Administrative expenses (Fig. 8-10)	63,998	63,998	63,998	63,998	255,992
Capital expenditures (Fig. 8-11)	–0–	–0–	–0–	150,000	150,000
Cash dividends	20,000	20,000	20,000	40,000	100,000
Estimated tax payments	40,000	40,000	40,000	40,000	160,000
Total cash disbursements	732,918	783,078	812,598	911,190	3,239,784
Change in cash without borrowing or payment on debt	(7,118)	70,282	153,619	102,469	104,696
Borrowing required for $30,000 minimum balance	37,118				37,118
Repayment—principal		(37,118)			(37,118)
—interest		(2,227)			(2,227)
Ending cash balance	$ 30,000	$ 30,937	$153,619	$ 102,469	$ 102,469

Figure 8-13

BUDGETED INCOME STATEMENT

The budgeted income statement shown in Figure 8-14 is developed from the information concerning revenues and expenses contained in the individual budgets discussed previously. Note that a contribution margin format is presented because we are using variable costing for internal reporting.

At first glance, the statement may appear to be the result of simply combining the end products of the other budgets once they are available. However, remember that the basic premise of budgeting is a planned financial performance that is acceptable to management. If we were considering the entire budgeting process in an actual situation, we probably would see that the managers involved must evaluate several combinations of selling prices, sales volume, sales mix, and costs before they arrive at an income statement with an acceptable profit projection.

Top management starts the budgeting process by establishing certain guidelines within which the entire business plans its financial performance. Through participative management, each manager then evaluates how his or her area of responsibility will contribute to the overall goals. These guidelines may pertain to such goals as *profit margins, return on investment, share of the market, growth rate, cash flow, research and development, cost control, financial position,* and *productivity.*

For example, the Chairman of the Board of 3M Company stated in the firm's 1982 annual report that the growth and profitability goals of the business included average sales growth, adjusted for inflation, of 10% a year, before-tax profit margins of 20% or better, and return on stockholders' equity approaching 25%.

Since we are concentrating on the basic steps of the budgeting process, we will assume that the guidelines of the Campus Specialty Company's top management are founded on two major profitability goals: (1) to achieve a before-tax profit margin of approximately 12% and (2) to achieve a before-tax return on average stockholders' equity in the range of 20% to 22%. The stockholders' equity is calculated from the balance sheets presented in Figure 8-15 by adding the 1987 beginning balance of stockholders' equity ($1,803,452) to the ending balance ($1,940,393) and dividing the total of $3,743,845 by two. The result is an average stockholders' equity of approximately $1,871,923. The before-tax net income is budgeted at $398,941 (Figure 8-14), which is about 12% of sales ($398,941/$3,344,400) and approximately a 21.3% before-tax return on average stockholders' equity ($398,941/$1,871,923).

Note that the link between the cash budget (Figure 8-13) and the budgeted income statement (Figure 8-14) is the interest expense of $2,227 from the

Figure 8-14

CAMPUS SPECIALTY COMPANY Budgeted Income Statement Year Ending December 31, 1987			
	Deluxe Medallion	Standard Medallion	Total
Sales–units (Fig. 8-3)	25,800	35,400	61,200
Sales–dollars (Fig. 8-3)	$1,857,600	$1,486,800	$3,344,400
Cost of goods sold (Fig. 8-8)	928,800	743,400	1,672,200
Manufacturing margin	928,800	743,400	1,672,200
Variable selling expenses (Fig. 8-9)	185,760	148,680	334,440
Contribution margin	743,040	594,720	1,337,760
Fixed costs:			
Manufacturing (Fig. 8-7)			444,600
Selling (Fig. 8-9)			196,000
Administrative (Fig. 8-10)			295,992
Total fixed costs			936,592
Net operating income			401,168
Interest expense (Fig. 8-13)			2,227
Net income before tax			398,941
Estimated income tax*			162,000
Net income after tax			$ 236,941

* Based on estimated net income with absorption costing required for income tax reporting.

short-term borrowing required in the first quarter. The budgeted income statement is an important part of the budgeting process because it summarizes how management's profit goals are to be achieved. The control feature of the budgeted statement is exercised when management takes the necessary action to correct deficiencies found by comparing the actual earnings with those planned, as we will see later in this chapter.

BUDGETED BALANCE SHEET

Since the 1987 budget is prepared by the Campus Specialty Company before the end of 1986, we must estimate the balance sheet as of December 31, 1986. It is shown in Figure 8-15 and provides the beginning balances for the 1987 budgeting process.

Once the actual financial results are known, the estimated 1986 balance sheet shown in Figure 8-15 will have to be revised if significant differences occur. The budgeted balance sheet for December 31, 1987, also presented in Figure 8-15, is the result of converting the beginning balances of the balance sheet items through the 1987 budgeting process into ending balances. For example, cash increases from $36,000 to $102,469 as a result of the cash receipts and disbursements shown in the cash budget (Figure 8-13). The total cash receipts are $3,308,480 and the total cash disbursements including the payment for interest are $3,242,011 ($3,239,784 + $2,227), for an increase in cash of $66,469 ($36,000 to $102,469). Accounts receivable increase by $35,920 (from $377,000 to $412,920) because of the projected sales that are not expected to be collected during 1987 (estimated sales are $3,344,400 in Figure 8-3, while the expected collections are $3,308,480 in Figure 8-12). The other ending balances can be reconciled by referring to their respective budgets.

We must evaluate the budgeted balance sheet carefully to make sure that it reflects a sufficiently strong financial position. If the projected balance sheet is not acceptable, potential budgetary revisions that will improve it must be considered.

BUDGETED STATEMENT OF CASH FLOWS

A budgeted statement of cash flows is presented in Figure 8-16 as an extension of the cash budget discussed earlier (see Figure 8-13). The advantage of the format used in Figure 8-16 is that cash flows are classified on an annual basis by operating activities, investing activities, and financing activities. These three activities involve different kinds of business decisions and transactions (e.g., the sale of inventory versus the sale of productive assets). In turn, the three activities will have different prospects concerning similar future cash flows from or for them that management must be able to assess. As a result, management should be able to classify cash flows by operating activities, investing activities, and financing activities so all three types can be planned and controlled effectively. A complete description of the statement of cash flows, as proposed by the Financial Accounting Standards Board, is presented in Chapter 17.

The Campus Specialty Company expects to generate net cash flows from operating activities of $316,469. This amount is determined (with what is explained as the indirect method in Chapter 17) by adjusting the budgeted net income of $236,941 (from Figure 8-14) to the net cash flow from operations.

CAMPUS SPECIALTY COMPANY
Budgeted Balance Sheet
December 31, 1987
(With Comparative Estimates as of December 31, 1986)

	1986		1987	
Assets				
Cash		$ 36,000		$ 102,469
Accounts receivable		377,000		412,920
Finished goods inventory*		108,720		144,720
Raw materials inventory		48,800		45,800
Total current assets		570,520		705,909
Land		550,000		550,000
Building and equipment	$1,330,932		$1,480,932	
Accumulated depreciation	(620,000)	710,932	(768,000)	712,932
Total assets		$1,831,452		$1,968,841
Liabilities				
Accounts payable		$ 28,000		$ 26,448
Accrued taxes		0		2,000
Total current liabilities		28,000		28,448
Stockholders' Equity				
Common stock (500 shares outstanding, no par)		500,000		500,000
Retained earnings*		1,303,452		1,440,393
Total stockholders' equity		1,803,452		1,940,393
Total liabilities and stockholders' equity		$1,831,452		$1,968,841

* Based on variable costing. Retained earnings and the finished goods inventories would be adjusted to reflect absorption costing for external reporting.

Figure 8-15

Changes in the various accounts that have contributed to accrual based net income but do not influence the firm's expected cash flows from operating activities are used to make the required adjustment. In addition, the firm expects to invest $150,000 in plant assets and to have a net cash outflow of $100,000 for financing activities (the proposed dividends are a return on the stockholders' investment. As a result, an increase in the firm's cash balance of $66,469 is projected during 1987 when all operating activities, investing activities, and financing activities are evaluated.

CONTROL ASPECTS OF BUDGETING

The control phase of budgeting consists of three major steps:

Objective 9:
Using budget performance reports for control purposes

1. Comparing the actual financial performance results with the budget estimates.
2. Identifying any significant variances (differences between the actual performance and the budget estimates).
3. Deciding whether management should take corrective or adaptive action.

The emphasis of budgetary control is on both efficiency and effectiveness measures. **Budget performance reports** that show significant variances between the actual and planned performance provide the feedback necessary to evaluate the financial and operating results on the basis of *management by exception.*

Unfavorable variances are investigated to determine whether corrective action can be taken to improve the future performance. Even significantly large favorable variances should be evaluated to be sure the related estimates were correct. If they were too easy to attain, the future estimates should be changed.

We noted in Chapter 1 that management must settle for an adaptive response at times in any control process because corrective action is not possible. This happens when a variance is investigated and the targeted performance involved is deemed unrealistic when evaluated with current information. The original budget target is then revised to reflect the present conditions. For example, a new union contract may make the labor rates originally used in the budget obsolete, so the budget has to be revised accordingly.

Only *controllable revenues and costs* should be included in the performance

---

CAMPUS SPECIALTY COMPANY
Budgeted Statement of Cash Flows
Year Ending December 31, 1987

Net income after tax (Fig. 8-14)		$236,941
Adjustments to convert net income to net cash flows from operations:		
Increase in accounts receivable (Fig. 8-15)	$(35,920)	
Increase in finished goods inventory (Fig. 8-15)	(36,000)	
Decrease in raw materials inventory (Fig. 8-15)	3,000	
Decrease in accounts payable (Fig. 8-15)	(1,552)	
Increase in accrued taxes (Fig. 8-15)	2,000	
Depreciation expense ($96,000 from Fig. 8-7, $12,000 from Fig. 8-9, and $40,000 from Fig. 8-10)	148,000	79,528
Net cash flow from operating activities		316,469
Cash flow from investing activities:		
Purchase of plant assets (Fig. 8-11)		(150,000)
Cash flow from financing activities:		
Proceeds from loan (Fig. 8-13)	37,118	
Repayment of loan (Fig. 8-13)	(37,118)	
Cash dividends (Fig. 8-13)	(100,000)	(100,000)
Net increase in cash		$ 66,469

Figure 8-16

reports; it would be unfair to hold managers accountable for uncontrollable items. We will discuss the concept of controllability in more detail in Chapter 13 when we consider responsibility accounting. Remember, however, that we defined a controllable cost in Chapter 2 as one that can be influenced by the manager held responsible during the time period involved.

Figure 8-17 illustrates the basic format of a budget performance report. This report, which was prepared for the sales manager of the Campus Specialty Company, includes the controllable costs of the sales department during the first quarter of 1987 (originally budgeted in Figure 8-9). We assume that actual sales for the quarter were the same as projected ($648,000). In Chapter 11, we will see why this assumption is necessary because of the changes in budgeted variable costs that must be considered over different volume levels (called a flexible budget).

The "actual" column of the performance report shows the actual costs incurred by the department. The "budget" column contains the budget estimates for each item. The U indicates an unfavorable variance, while the F refers to a favorable variance. The sales department incurred expenses that exceeded its budget by $6,680. These results will have an adverse effect on the firm's profits and will require corrective action if the Campus Specialty Company is to achieve its financial goals of future quarters.

BASIC BUDGETING CONSIDERATIONS FOR NONMANUFACTURING ORGANIZATIONS

Many of the concepts and procedures involved with the master budget discussed in this chapter are applicable in all types of organizations. For example, the use of budgeting for goal congruence is important for merchandising businesses, service firms, not-for-profit organizations, and manufacturing operations. However, a wide range of variations from the master budget are required in nonmanufacturing organizations because of their nature and objectives.

Objective 10: Use of budgeting in nonmanufacturing organizations

Although a complete coverage of budgeting in every type of organization is beyond the scope of this book, some of the basic issues involved will be introduced so you can develop a fundamental awareness of how organizational differences affect the budgeting process. We will consider three general types of nonmanufacturing organizations: merchandising, service, and not-for-profit.

MERCHANDISING FIRMS

The budgeting process for a merchandising firm is much simpler than it is for a manufacturing business because of the absence of the production function. Consequently, such budgets as the production budget, direct materials budget,

Figure 8-17

```
                    CAMPUS SPECIALTY COMPANY
                         Sales Department
                     Budget Performance Report
                   Quarter Ending March 31, 1987
```

Controllable Expenses	Budget	Actual	Variance
Advertising	$ 12,960	$ 15,560	$2,600 U
Sales commissions	51,840	51,840	–0–
Sales salaries	38,000	41,200	3,200 U
Travel	3,600	4,100	500 U
Entertainment	2,400	2,800	400 U
Utilities	300	280	20 F
Total	$109,100	$115,780	$6,680 U

F indicates a favorable variance
U indicates an unfavorable variance

direct labor budget, and manufacturing overhead budget are not required. The budgeting process is directed toward desired profit results for both the merchandising business as a whole and for each of its individual departments.

A master budget, similar to the one presented earlier for a manufacturing firm, is used by a merchandising firm. The master budget includes the sales, purchases, cost of goods sold, operating expenses, capital expenditures, cash flow, and financial statements projected for the budget period. The emphasis of the budgeting process is on efficient and effective merchandise management.

Purchases and sales must be carefully planned and controlled to ensure that satisfactory profit margins and inventory turnover are achieved with adequate but not excessive inventory levels. Inventory planning and control can be complicated because the typical merchandising business purchases and sells an extremely large number of products, often in the thousands. Constant attention must be directed toward developing and revising the inventory aspects of the master budget to coincide with current business conditions, style changes, new products, competitive considerations, and customers' buying habits. Inventory turnover measurement is emphasized throughout the budgeting process to minimize the problems of inventory obsolescence and low profit margins. In general, financial planning and control for a merchandising firm consists of three major steps:

1. Developing a realistic plan of operations, formalized as a master budget, based on management's profit goals for a specific time period.
2. Directing the various activities of the business toward the attainment of the targeted performance.
3. Preparing and issuing budget performance reports that show a comparison of the actual results with those planned.

SERVICE FIRMS

The absence of inventory in a service firm does not eliminate the need for budgeting but it does alter the focus of its application. Service firms such as a public accounting firm, a law practice, a medical clinic, an architectural firm, or an advertising agency are typically labor intensive because their most important resources are the *people* who perform the revenue-producing services. These people often engage in numerous nonrepetitive activities because no two jobs are exactly alike. This lack of predictability of the services to be performed complicates the projection of the revenues and costs associated with the services.

The primary financial consideration is ensuring that the professional staff is kept busy, thereby generating enough revenue to support the operation. Consequently, the budgeting emphasis is on the labor budget to provide an adequate but not excessive amount of labor to satisfy the demand for the services being performed. In most cases, billing rates or fees for the services are established from the firm's budget, so budgetary accuracy is important if the organization is to charge enough to achieve its financial goals.

The budget of a service firm is usually developed on the basis of a "bottom-up approach," unlike manufacturing firms which use "top-down procedures." In the earlier illustration of budgeting for the Campus Specialty Company, we saw that the forecast of sales demand is the first step in the development of a master budget, which in turn determines the resources needed to produce and sell the products involved. Thus, the budgeting process flows from revenues to costs and is referred to as a top-down approach. In contrast, the size and composition of the professional staff of a service firm is relatively fixed for a particular budget period. The basic concern is an efficient and effective utilization of the professional staff in the performance of the services offered. The total labor cost is the starting point for determining how much revenue must be earned from the labor capacity available to absorb all costs and return an acceptable amount of profit to the owners of the firm. Thus, we have a bottom-up approach as the budgeting process flows from costs to revenues. An example of a bottom-up approach was the pricing strategy used by the Certified Public Accountant in Chapter 7.

NOT-FOR-PROFIT FIRMS

The primary objective of not-for-profit organizations is to use available resources to provide the best possible services or programs. Examples are educational institutions, governmental agencies, hospitals, and charitable organizations. Since profit measurement is not involved, the success of these organizations is evaluated on the basis of how much service they provide and the quality level of their results. Budgeting must be performed in a not-for-profit organization to determine the expenditures necessary to provide the services during the budget period. The level of expenditures, in turn, will determine how much revenue the organization must generate from the services.

The revenue sources tend to be fixed in amount as a result of the budgeting process. This means they cannot be changed to coincide with a different level of services or programs than the one originally planned (e.g., revenues provided by real estate taxes). Consequently, the budget imposes a permanent cap on the money that can be spent for the various functions, and the amount cannot be increased even if more or better services could be offered. These budgetary limitations usually are imposed by either legal requirements or the governing board charged with the stewardship of the economic resources involved. Several approaches to this more legalistic version of budgeting are used. Two examples worth noting because of their business orientation are program budgeting and zero-base budgeting.

Program budgeting provides an analytical framework for evaluating the benefits of the services or programs offered by a not-for-profit organization and for allocating the resources needed to accomplish the objectives involved in a cost-effective way. The emphasis of program budgeting is on the output or final results of the performance instead of the inputs or money expended. An example is the planning, programming, budgeting system (PPBS) developed some time ago by the Department of Defense. Program budgeting focuses on a *cost/benefit evaluation* of every service or program and is particularly popular within the federal government.

The concept of **zero-base budgeting** is used by many governmental and business organizations. Otherwise, governmental budgeting can result in the use of the last year's budget plus a certain increment for a new period (e.g., a past budget of $2,000,000 plus 8% for the next year). As the name suggests, a complete version of zero-base budgeting requires each manager to justify every dollar spent as if the services or programs involved were being requested for the first time. All of the costs incurred in the past are considered irrelevant, so the managers must start from scratch (the zero point) with no ongoing expenditures automatically authorized. In contrast with most traditional budgeting processes which start with the historical performance and build from it in anticipation of the future, zero-base budgeting completely ignores the past.

As a practical matter, most applications of this budgeting method are based on what can best be termed a zero-base review. That is, each service or program is studied completely every few years rather than each year. This eliminates the excessive time and cost that would be required to implement the procedures involved each year in an organization with numerous services and programs, yet still provides the benefits of the justification process.

Even though the approach taken may not be specifically identified as zero-base budgeting, most successful businesses use many of its concepts because the managers responsible for the various activities have to periodically justify their budget requests on the basis of future profitability. The major advantage of zero-base budgeting in such cases is to provide a set of formal procedures for the evaluation process.

SUMMARY

Budgeting is an essential phase of managing the activities of any type of organization. A budget is a detailed plan that shows how resources should be acquired and used during a specific period. The budgeting process provides the targets for managing a business in an efficient and effective manner. Although budget information is used throughout the management process, its primary application is in the planning and controlling functions. Goal congruence is a major consideration for every organization to ensure that all segments of the organization work toward common goals.

The most important benefits of budgeting are that it (1) forces managers to plan, (2) provides desired performance targets, (3) shows how resources should be allocated, (4) coordinates the various segments of an organization toward common objectives, (5) serves as an effective communication device, and (6) motivates managers to work to achieve the organizational goals.

The sales forecast serves as the cornerstone of budgeting because almost everything else in the budget depends on it. A combination of predictions by the sales staff, estimates prepared by management, test marketing, and statistical or mathematical techniques usually is used to deal with the complexities of sales forecasting.

The master budget is a set of interrelated budgets, which in turn, are classified as either operating or financial budgets. The operating budget is a detailed description of the revenues and costs required for the profit goals of the firm. The financial budget shows the funding and financial position required to achieve these goals.

Managerial control with budgeting consists of (1) comparing actual results with the budget estimates, (2) identifying significant variances, and (3) deciding what managerial action should be taken. A budget performance report is used to make each responsible manager aware of deviations between his or her segment's actual performance and the one planned during the budgeting process.

Budgeting is an important part of management in nonmanufacturing organizations as well as manufacturing firms. A merchandising business concentrates on the master budget to ensure that the inventory is purchased and sold with profitable results. A service firm is most concerned with planning and controlling the costs associated with its most important resource, the labor needed to produce service revenue. Not-for-profit organizations use a budgeting process that is different from one found in a business firm because revenue is founded on the estimated expenditures and usually cannot be changed once the budget is finalized, regardless of any alterations in the services or programs involved. Program budgeting and zero-base budgeting are two popular budgeting methods used by not-for-profit organizations.

GLOSSARY

ADMINISTRATIVE EXPENSES BUDGET. A schedule of the estimated administrative expenses for the budget period (p. 279).

BUDGET. A quantitative plan showing how resources are expected to be acquired and used during a specified time period (p. 265).

BUDGET PERFORMANCE REPORT. A management report comparing the actual and budgeted performance with an emphasis on any significantly large variances (p. 287).

CAPITAL EXPENDITURES BUDGET. The budget showing the acquisition of long-term assets planned during a particular period (p. 281).

CASH BUDGET. A projection of the cash receipts and disbursements expected during the budget period (p. 282).

COST OF GOODS SOLD BUDGET. The cost of goods sold estimated for the budgeted income statement of a future period (p. 278).

DIRECT LABOR BUDGET. An estimate of the direct labor needs of a budget period based on the expected production level (p. 274).

DIRECT MATERIALS BUDGET. A projection of the direct materials that must be purchased to satisfy the production requirements of a budget period (p. 274).

FINANCIAL BUDGET. The component of the master budget that shows the funding and financial position needed for the planned operations (p. 271).

GOAL CONGRUENCE. The reconciliation of the goals of individual managers with those of the organization (p. 267).

MANUFACTURING OVERHEAD BUDGET. A projection of the manufacturing overhead cost items required to support the expected production level (p. 275).

MASTER BUDGET. A set of interrelated budgets representing a comprehensive plan of action for a specified time period (p. 270).

OPERATING BUDGET. The component of the master budget that shows a detailed description of the revenues and costs required to achieve a firm's profit goals (p. 271).

PRODUCTION BUDGET. A projection of the number of units that will be manufactured during the budget period to satisfy the requirements of the sales forecast (p. 273).

PROGRAM BUDGETING. A budgeting approach used by not-for-profit organizations emphasizing the benefits of the services or programs involved rather than their costs (p. 291).

SALES BUDGET. A translation of the sales forecast for a budget period into detailed information concerning the products or services expected to be sold (p. 273).

SALES FORECAST. The projection of the potential sales for an entire industry as well as those expected for the firm preparing the forecast (p. 269).

SELLING EXPENSES BUDGET. A schedule showing the estimated selling expenses needed to generate the expected sales volume for the budget period (p. 279).

ZERO-BASE BUDGET. A budget prepared without allowing any consideration of past costs because each cost must be justified currently by the managers involved (p. 291).

DISCUSSION QUESTIONS

1. What is the basic reason that every person and every organization must resort to budgeting of some sort?
2. How is a budget used for:
   a. Planning?
   b. Control?
3. Why is goal congruence such an important managerial accounting concept? Give an example of a potential goal congruence conflict in a business.
4. Identify the major benefits of budgeting. What are its most essential limitations?
5. Describe the basic steps involved with the development of the master budget.
6. Why is an accurate sales forecast essential for effective budgeting? Why is it difficult to forecast sales accurately?
7. What are the most popular methods used to forecast sales?
8. Why can it be said that the budgeting process actually consists of multiple budgets?
9. What are the two major components of a master budget?
10. Distinguish between a sales forecast and a sales budget.
11. What is the difference between a sales budget and a production budget?
12. Why are inventory level decisions essential in the budgeting process?
13. The Wright Company expects to sell 90,000 units during the upcoming year. It wants to have 18,000 units on hand at the end of the year and has 13,500 available at the beginning of the year. How many units should the firm produce during the year?
14. Why is a reliable cash budget required even with an accurate prediction of a business's income statement?
15. You recently overheard a local businesswoman say, "My business involves too many uncertainties for budgeting to be practical." Do you agree? Explain.
16. Why is it important to distinguish between fixed and variable costs in preparing a manufacturing overhead budget?
17. How does budgeting assist management in developing its employment policies?
18. Is the budgeted income statement simply the product of combining a number of revenue and expense budgets?
19. Why do we develop the cash budget before we prepare the budgeted income statement in the budgeting process?
20. What are the major steps in the control phase of budgeting?
21. How should management decide what costs to include in budget performance reports?
22. What is the emphasis of a budgeting process used in a merchandising

firm? Why are the procedures used less complicated than those required in a manufacturing operation?

23. What is the most important aspect of a budget prepared for a service firm?

24. What is the primary objective of a budget used in a not-for-profit organization?

25. How is the concept of program budgeting applied in a not-for-profit organization? What is zero-base budgeting and what kind of organization would be most likely to use this form of budgeting?

EXERCISES

Exercise 8-1   Preparing a Sales Budget

The Tootsie Toy Company produces three dolls that are sold to retail stores throughout the Midwest. The sales manager expects the following levels of sales for the coming year:

Doll	Selling Price	Annual Sales in Units
Arlene	$ 8.00	60,000
Rick	10.00	40,000
Butch	12.00	80,000

The budgeted annual sales are distributed by month in the following percentages:

Month	Percent of Annual Sales
January	6
February	8
March	4
April	4
May	2
June	10
July	8
August	12
September	14
October	6
November	8
December	18

Required:

Prepare a monthly sales budget in units and dollars for the three dolls.

Exercise 8-2   Basic Production Budget Preparation

The Addrite Company produces two models of calculators, Basic and Memory. The projected operating performance data for the month of July include the following:

	Basic	Memory
Estimated beginning inventory (units)	2,500	2,100
Estimated July sales (units)	6,600	6,150
Desired ending inventory (units)	2,750	1,950

Required:

Prepare a production budget for July.

Exercise 8-3   Developing Production/Purchases Budgets

The sales, purchasing, and production managers of the Dalton Company are meeting to determine the firm's operating needs for the final six months of the year. The sales budget for this period is as follows:

Month	Budgeted Sales in Units
July	19,200
August	22,400
September	17,600
October	25,600
November	30,400
December	20,800

The production manager attempts to maintain a raw materials inventory at the end of a month equal to the budgeted production needs for the next two months. Each unit produced requires five pounds of raw materials that cost $4 per pound. The sales manager likes to maintain a finished goods inventory at 150% of the following month's budgeted sales. As of June 30, the firm had 272,000 pounds of raw materials in inventory and 27,200 units of finished goods.

Required:
A. Prepare a production budget (in units) for as many months as possible.
B. Prepare a raw materials purchases budget (in pounds) for as many months as possible.

Exercise 8-4 Developing a Direct Labor Budget

The Brown County Woodshop produces two types of wooden clocks. The expected production in units for the first four months of the year are as follows:

	Budgeted Production	
	Oak Clock	Walnut Clock
January	600	700
February	800	800
March	900	400
April	500	600

Each oak clock requires three hours of labor and a walnut clock requires four hours of labor. The labor rate is $10 per hour.

Required:
Prepare a direct labor budget by month, assuming no beginning or ending inventories.

Exercise 8-5 Preparing a Direct Labor Budget

Joe Brown is a wood craftsman who makes high quality wood sculptures. Each sculpture requires the following labor:

Carving	15 hours
Finishing	5 hours

Mr. Brown charges $15 per hour of labor time when computing the cost of his sculptures. He attempts to maintain an inventory of sculptures equal to 20% of the following month's expected sales. On December 31, he has four finished sculptures in inventory. Anticipated sales for the first four months of the year are as follows:

January	20 sculptures
February	25 sculptures
March	30 sculptures
April	40 sculptures

Required:

Prepare a direct labor budget for January, February, and March.

Exercise 8-6 Preparing a Budgeted Income Statement and a Purchases Budget

The Top Notch Clothing Store is preparing its budget for the coming year. Budgeted sales for the first part of the year are as follows:

January	$208,000
February	260,000
March	312,000
April	390,000

Inventory on December 31 is budgeted at $166,400. This is based on the company's policy that inventory is maintained at 200% of the following month's budgeted cost of goods sold. The cost of goods sold percentage is 40% of sales, and all other variable costs are 20% of sales. Fixed costs are $52,000 per month.

Required:

A. Prepare a budgeted income statement for each month of the first quarter.
B. Prepare a purchases budget for each month of the first quarter.

Exercise 8-7 Evaluating Cash Receipts and Disbursements

The Bartlett Company has the following budgeted activity for January 1987:

Sales	$875,000
Gross profit as a percentage of sales	30%
Increase in inventory during January	$ 12,500
Increase in accounts receivable during January	25,000
Increase in accounts payable during January	–0–

Total selling and administrative expenses are $88,750 per month plus 10% of total sales. Included in the total for selling and administrative expenses is $50,000 per month of depreciation expense. Variable selling and administrative expenses include a charge for uncollectible accounts of 1% of sales. The accounts receivable shown above are presented net of the allowance for doubtful accounts.

Required:

Compute the estimated cash receipts and cash disbursements for January.

Exercise 8-8 Calculating Budgeted Cash Receipts

The Kaline Department Store's budgeted monthly gross sales for January through July are presented below. The company's experience is that 80% of the monthly sales are on credit. All payments received during the month of sale are subject to a 2% cash discount. This policy applies to both cash and credit sales. Approximately 50% of the credit sales are collected in the month of sale, 35% in the month following the sale, 14% in the second month following the sale, and 1% is never collected. The budgeted gross sales by month are as follows:

January	$104,000
February	156,000
March	130,000
April	143,000
May	117,000
June	169,000

Required:
Calculate the budgeted cash receipts for April, May, and June.

Exercise 8-9 Determining Budgeted Purchases and Cash Disbursements

The Bean Blossom Department Store has prepared a sales budget for the fiscal year ending June 30, 1987 and has provided the following data:

Purchases for May 1986	$252,000
Purchases for June 1986	268,800
Ending inventory–June 30, 1986	320,040
Budgeted sales: July 1986	420,000
August 1986	378,000
September 1986	448,000
October 1986	406,000

The cost of goods sold is 60% of sales, and it is company policy to maintain a month-end inventory balance sufficient to meet the projected sales requirement for the following month and 30% of the sales requirements for the second following month. The company pays for 50% of its purchases in the month of purchase, 40% in the following month, and 10% in the second month following sale.

Required:
A. Calculate the amount of purchases for July and August 1986.
B. Calculate the cash disbursements in July and August for merchandise purchased.

Exercise 8-10 Evaluating Future Cash Flows

The Hofman Company is preparing a cash budget for June 1987 and has provided the following information:

1. Of each month's sales, 60% are on account, with 70% of the accounts being collected in the month of sale. The remaining accounts are collected the following month.
2. The cost of goods sold equals 70% of sales. Of all purchases, 70% are paid in the month of sale and 30% are paid the following month.
3. The company's policy is to maintain an inventory level equal to 40% of the next month's sales requirement. The requirement was met on June 1, 1987.
4. Selling and administrative expenses are budgeted at $10,000 for June. They include $3,000 of depreciation. All selling and administrative expenses, except depreciation, are paid in the month incurred.
5. Cash balance, June 1 $ 25,200
   May sales   84,000
   June sales   124,800
   July sales   108,000
   May purchases   67,860

Required:
A. Prepare a budgeted income statement for June.
B. Prepare a cash budget for June.

Exercise 8-11 Evaluating Future Cash Flows

The Sanders Company has prepared a budgeted income statement for the month of July. The company pays for 70% of its merchandise purchased in the month of purchase and 30% in the month following the purchase. Of all sales, 60% are collected in the month of sale and 40% in the following month. The annual insurance premium was prepaid in January and the annual property taxes are due in October. All other cash expenses are paid currently. The company maintains a minimum cash balance of $500, and the cash balance as of July 1 was $750. A new piece of equipment costing $400 will be paid for in July. Additional information:

June sales	$2,240
June purchases	1,260
July purchases	1,680

SANDERS COMPANY
Budgeted Income Statement
For the Month of July

Sales		$2,800
Cost of goods sold		1,260
Gross profit		1,540
Operating expenses:		
Insurance	$105	
Property taxes	126	
Rent	210	
Wages	770	
Depreciation	70	
Total		1,281
Net income		$ 259

Required:
A. Prepare a cash budget for the month of July.
B. How much cash can the owners of the Sanders Company withdraw during July and maintain the minimum cash balance required?

Exercise 8-12 Evaluating Budgeted Cash Flows
The Williamson Company prepared the following financial data for the first five months of the year:

Month	Sales	Purchases
January (actual)	$187,200	$109,200
February (actual)	171,600	124,800
March (actual)	156,000	93,600
April (actual)	202,800	140,400
May (budgeted)	171,600	156,000

The company's collections normally are 60% in the month of the sale, 30% in the month following the sale, 9% in the second month following the sale, and 1% is uncollectible. The company's policy for purchases is to always take advantage of the 3% discount allowed on purchases which are due on the 10th of the following month. The cash balance on May 1 was $57,200, and cash disbursements for operating expenses in May are expected to be $37,440.

Required:
A. Calculate the expected cash disbursements for May.
B. Calculate the expected cash collections for May.
C. Calculate the expected cash balance on May 31.

Exercise 8-13 Preparing a Budget Performance Report

The controller for the Southern Indiana University has prepared the following annual budget for the Psychology Department's controllable costs:

	Fixed	Variable Cost per Student Enrolled
Personnel salaries	$52,000	$ .50
Utilities	17,000	.15
Maintenance	18,000	1.20
Supplies	14,000	.80
Duplicating	22,000	6.00
Travel	24,000	–0–

Actual enrollment for the Psychology Department for the year was 4,000 students. The actual expenses incurred for the year were as follows:

Personnel salaries	$61,000
Utilities	18,200
Maintenance	21,700
Supplies	17,100
Duplicating	28,200
Travel	25,500

Required:

Prepare a budget performance report for the year.

Exercise 8-14 Analysis of the Budgeting Process

Choose the best answer to each of the following questions:

1. The normal starting point for the preparation of a master budget is:
   a. Direct labor budget
   b. Budgeted income statement
   c. Production budget
   d. Sales forecast
2. Which of the following would not normally be part of a firm's operating budget?
   a. Sales budget
   b. Production budget
   c. Direct labor budget
   d. Budgeted balance sheet
3. Which of the following would not normally be part of a firm's financial budget?
   a. Capital budget
   b. Selling expense budget
   c. Cash budget
   d. Budgeted balance sheet
4. The concept of management by exception refers to management:
   a. Considering only unusual items
   b. Developing a sample of all items
   c. Considering only unfavorable items
   d. Considering only those items that deviate significantly from plan
5. Another term for budgeted financial statements is:
   a. Sample budgets
   b. Historical budgets
   c. Pro forma statements

    d. Price level adjusted statements
6. Budgets in not-for-profit organizations serve as:
    a. Planning documents
    b. Tools to motivate managers
    c. Controlling and organizing means
    d. Performance evaluation
    e. All of the above
7. Which of the following is not a benefit of budgeting?
    a. Performance evaluation
    b. Increased communication
    c. Effective communication
    d. Required planning
    e. None of the above
8. The proper role of a budget committee should be to:
    a. Have line authority over those involved with the budget
    b. Have no coordinating responsibility for the budget process
    c. Meet quarterly to discuss the budget
    d. Advise management on budgetary issues
9. The term zero-base budgeting refers to:
    a. A failure to project expenditures
    b. The review of each cost item from a cost/benefit perspective
    c. No budgeting at all
    d. A review of changes made to historical data
10. Whenever a business prepares a sales forecast:
    a. It does not represent a firm commitment
    b. It should be based only on sound quantitative analysis
    c. It should always be an extension of a past performance
    d. It should be more detailed than the sales budget that is later developed

PROBLEMS

Problem 8-1 Preparing a Sales Forecast

The Dalton Company manufactures a line of water heaters designed for apartment use. The company markets this line in two cities—Cheraw and Kingstree. Approximately 50% of all new apartment complexes in the two cities will have an individual water heater installed in each apartment. The firm has also projected that 10% of the existing apartments will install new individual water heaters to improve existing systems or replace old individual heaters that cannot be repaired. Based on past experience, the Dalton Company anticipates it can obtain 25% of the new apartment construction market and 10% of the replacement market.

    The Company sells two models of water heaters—the standard model and the deluxe model, a more energy-efficient unit. Builders will use the standard model in 60% of the apartments they construct and the deluxe model in 40%. When an existing complex installs new water heaters, it typically will use the standard model in 30% of the apartment units and the deluxe model in 70%. The other information available is:

	Cheraw	Kingstree
Number of units to be constructed	56,000	65,000
Number of existing units	400,000	300,000
Selling price – standard	$300	$300
Selling price – deluxe	400	390

Required:
Prepare a sales forecast for the Dalton Company by market area.

Problem 8-2 Developing Production and Direct Materials Budgets

The Steen Company manufactures an industrial cutting tool. The production of the tool requires two different direct materials, X and Y. One tool requires two pounds of Material X and one pound of Material Y.

The company's inventory policy is that at the end of each month, the finished inventory (tools) should be 20% of the following month's estimated sales. Also, month-end inventories of direct materials should be sufficient for the following month's production of the tool. The following inventories are on hand on December 31:

Cutting tools	19,200 units
Material X	192,000 pounds
Material Y	96,000 pounds

Estimated sales of the cutting tool (in units) for the first four months of the year are as follows:

January	96,000
February	128,000
March	112,000
April	128,000

Required:
A. Prepare a production budget for the first three months of the year.
B. Prepare a direct materials budget for the first three months of the year.

Problem 8-3 Evaluating Budgeted Materials Requirements

The RJS Company produces two products, regular and super. The following data pertain to the planned production, direct materials requirements, and inventory levels for the coming month:

	Regular	Super
Budgeted production	7,800 units	5,200 units
Materials requirements:	Each regular unit requires 2 units of Material C7 and 9 units of Material C8. Each super unit requires 4.5 units of C7 and 8 units of C8.	

Raw materials inventory:

	Beginning	Ending	Price per Unit
C7	3,200	7,800	$5
C8	15,000	18,000	$3

Required:
A. Calculate the amount of raw materials (in units) necessary to produce the two products and the total cost of materials used in production.

B. Calculate the amount of raw materials (in units) to be purchased during the month and the total cost of direct materials purchases.

Problem 8-4 Preparing a Production Budget and Related Budgets

The Parteen Company manufactures patio and lawn furniture. The manager in charge of the production of picnic tables has been asked to prepare a production budget, a direct materials budget, and a direct labor budget for part of 1987 based on management's sales forecast.

The materials and labor requirements per table are:

	Quantity	**Cost**
Lumber	18 feet	$.70 per foot
Stain	1 quart	4 per quart
Cutting labor	4 hours	10 per hour
Finishing labor	7 hours	14 per hour

The company requires a finished goods ending inventory for each quarter that equals 50% of expected sales for the next quarter. Also, the ending inventory balance of direct materials should equal 40% of the next quarter's production requirements. The inventory balances on January 1, 1987 are forecasted as:

Lumber	36,000 feet
Stain	2,000 quarts
Picnic tables	2,500 units

The forecasted quarterly sales in units are:

First quarter, 1987	5,000
Second quarter, 1987	7,000
Third quarter, 1987	6,000
Fourth quarter, 1987	4,000

Required:
A. Prepare a quarterly production budget for the first three quarters of 1987.
B. Prepare a quarterly direct materials budget for the first two quarters of 1987.
C. Prepare a quarterly direct labor budget for the first two quarters of 1987.

Problem 8-5 Preparing a Manufacturing Overhead Budget

The Magnabox Company produces two types of microwave ovens, the Magna-Reg and the Magna-Deluxe. The manufacturing overhead costs related to the production operation for the year are as follows:

Variable costs:	
Indirect materials	$.16/direct labor hour
Indirect labor	.24/direct labor hour
Utilities	.48/direct labor hour
Other	.08/direct labor hour
Fixed costs:	
Production supervisors' salaries	$56,000
Depreciation	48,000
Insurance	16,000
Miscellaneous	8,000

Sales for the year are expected to be 3,200 units of Magna-Reg and 8,000 units of Magna-Deluxe. Each Magna-Reg oven requires 15 hours of direct labor, and each Magna-Deluxe requires 10 hours.

Required:
A. Prepare a manufacturing overhead budget at the expected activity level.
B. Calculate the manufacturing overhead rate based on direct labor hours.

Problem 8-6 Preparing a Cash Budget and Budgeted Income Statement
The balance sheet for the Hunter Company on 12/31 is as follows:

Cash	$ 12,800
Accounts receivable (net of allowance for uncollectible accounts of $3,200)	60,800
Inventory	25,600
Fixed assets (net of accumulated depreciation of $96,000)	64,000
Total assets	$163,200
Accounts payable (for inventory purchases)	$132,000
Common stock	20,000
Retained earnings	11,200
Total liabilities and stockholders' equity	$163,200

Projected sales for January and February are $176,000 and $192,000, respectively. The gross profit is 25% of sales.

Cash collections for accounts receivable are estimated to be 50% in the month of sale, 48% in the following month, and 2% are uncollectible.

Purchases of inventory each month are 75% of the next month's projected sales. Purchases are paid in full the following month. Depreciation is $8,000 per month. Other expenses, amounting to $26,400 per month, are paid in cash in the month incurred.

Required:
Prepare a projected cash budget and income statement for the month of January.

Problem 8-7 Preparing Budgeted Financial Statements
The Thompson Company is preparing its quarterly budget for the three months ending March 31, 1987. The information available for the budget is as follows:

1. Cash sales represent 40% of all monthly sales. Of all credit sales, 70% are collected in the month of sale and the remainder in the month following the sale.
2. Merchandise purchases that are made on account equal 60% of the forecasted sales for the month. Of the purchases, 60% are paid in the month of purchase, and 40% are paid the following month.
3. Ending inventory on March 31, 1987 is projected to be $36,800.
4. Equipment purchases for the first quarter are budgeted at $3,200.
5. Other quarterly expenses are budgeted as follows: utilities, $7,360; rent, $20,800; salaries, $40,000. These expenses are paid when incurred.
6. Depreciation for the first quarter will be $6,400.
7. The balance sheet as of December 31, 1986 contained the following accounts:

Cash	$11,360	Accumulated depreciation	$38,400
Accounts receivable	7,840	Accounts payable	3,840

| Inventory | 16,000 | Common stock | 32,800 |
| Equipment | 89,600 | Retained earnings | 49,760 |

8. Budgeted sales are: January, $83,200; February, $80,000; March, $76,800.
9. Ignore income taxes.

Required:
Prepare a budgeted income statement and a budgeted balance sheet for the quarter ending March 31, 1987.

Problem 8-8 Developing Manufacturing Budgets and a Budgeted Income Statement

The Poorina Dog Chow Company produces one type of dog food that is sold in 40-pound boxes. The firm's controller is preparing budgets for the first quarter of 1987 and has the following data available:

- First quarter budgeted sales are 72,000 boxes @ $25/box.
- Production of one box of dog food requires 10 pounds of meat residue and 30 pounds of vegetable residue.
- Budgeted inventory levels are:

	January 1	March 1	Cost
Completed boxes of dog food	19,200	14,400	—
Pounds of meat residue	104,000	84,000	$ .95/lb
Pounds of vegetable residue	184,000	152,000	.16/lb
Boxes (empty)	48,000	32,000	1.18 each

- Direct labor required to produce and fill one box of dog food requires eight minutes and the direct labor rate is $12/hr.
- Fixed costs:
  Manufacturing overhead cost – $32,000/month
  Selling and administrative expenses – $18,000/month
- Variable costs:
  Manufacturing overhead costs – $.72/box
  Selling and administrative – 5% of sales dollars

Required:
A. Prepare a production budget for the first quarter of 1987.
B. Prepare a raw materials purchases budget for the meat residue, vegetable residue, and empty boxes, in both dollars and pounds/boxes.
C. Calculate the budgeted unit cost per box of dog food using variable costing.
D. Prepare a budgeted variable costing income statement for the first quarter.

Problem 8-9 Preparing a Cash Budget

The Bennet Company is in the process of preparing a cash budget for 1987. The company collects 60% of its sales in the quarter the sale is made, 30% in the quarter following the sale, and the remainder in the subsequent quarter. Of all purchases, 70% are paid for in the quarter in which they are purchased, with the remaining 30% paid for in the following quarter.

Selling expenses are $18,000 each quarter plus 10% of sales dollars. Administrative expenses are $90,000 per quarter, including $30,000 of depreciation expense. The company is planning to buy equipment during the second quarter at a cost of $16,000 and to pay a $9,000 dividend in the first quarter. The cash balance of January 1, 1987 is $19,000.

The following sales and purchases data have been compiled for the preparation of the budget:

	Sales	Purchases
Third quarter, 1986	$180,000	$72,000
Fourth quarter, 1986	162,000	64,800
First quarter, 1987	189,000	75,600
Second quarter, 1987	198,000	66,600

Required:

Prepare a cash budget by quarter and in total for the first two quarters of 1987.

Problem 8-10 Comprehensive Budgeting Problem—Merchandising Firm

The Acme Fashion Store has the following sales data available on July 1:

May	$299,000 (actual)
June	286,000 (actual)
July	312,000 (estimated)
August	286,000 (estimated)
September	299,000 (estimated)
October	312,000 (estimated)
November	338,000 (estimated)

The store sells all merchandise on account, with the following collection performance:

60% in month of sale

30% in the following month

9% in the second month following the sale

1% uncollectible

Inventory levels in units at the end of each month should be equal to the next 1½ months' sales. The average gross margin is 35%, and all purchases are paid in the month following the month of purchase. Other expenses are as follows:

Fixed–$65,000 per month, which includes $15,600 of depreciation

Variable–10% of gross sales dollars

All expenses are paid for in the month incurred

The balance sheet as of June 30 is as follows:

Cash	$104,000
Accounts receivable (net of allowance for uncollectible accounts)	138,450
Inventory	295,750
Fixed assets (net of accumulated depreciation)	390,000
Total assets	$928,200
Accounts payable (inventory purchases)	$194,350
Common stock	260,000
Retained earnings	473,850
Total liabilities and stockholders' equity	$928,200

Required:

A. Prepare a schedule of cash collections for the third quarter of the year (July, August, and September).

B. Prepare a schedule of inventory purchases in dollars for the third quarter.

C. Prepare a cash budget for the third quarter.

D. Prepare a budgeted income statement for the third quarter.

E. Prepare a budgeted balance sheet as of September 30.

Problem 8-11 Comprehensive Budgeting Problem—Manufacturing Firm

The Thompson Corporation manufactures and sells two products, PW1 and PW2. Projected data for 1987 are as follows:

Sales Forecast for 1987

Product	Price	Units
PW1	$40	30,000
PW2	60	20,000

Inventory Forecast for 1987

Product	Expected Inventory 1/1/87	Expected Inventory 12/31/87
PW1	10,000 units	12,500 units
PW2	4,000 units	4,500 units

The raw materials requirements for the products are as follows:

Materials—PW1	
A	2 pounds
B	1 pound

Materials—PW2	
A	2.5 pounds
B	1.5 pounds
C	1 item

Anticipated data for 1987 related to raw materials are as follows:

Material	Purchase Price	Anticipated Inventory 1/1/87	Anticipated Inventory 12/31/87
A	$4.00/lb	16,000 lbs	18,000 lbs
B	2.50/lb	14,500 lbs	16,000 lbs
C	1.50 each	3,000 each	7,000 each

PW1 requires two direct labor hours per unit at $8/hr. PW2 requires three direct labor hours per unit at $9/hr. Manufacturing overhead is applied at the rate of $2 per direct labor hour.

Required:

A. Calculate projected sales (in dollars) in 1987 for each product.
B. Calculate the budgeted production in units for each product for 1987.
C. Calculate the raw materials purchases requirements for materials A, B, and C, for 1987 in quantity and in dollars.
D. Calculate the direct labor requirements for 1987 in hours and in dollars.
E. Calculate the dollar value of the finished goods inventory on 12/31/87 for PW1 and PW2 based on absorption costing.

Problem 8-12 Budgeting for a Service Firm

Kevin Smith is an attorney in a large northern city who specializes in automobile accident settlements. He has a staff consisting of four attorneys and three clerical workers. The staff attorneys are paid $3,600 per month, and the clerical workers are paid $1,200 per month. Other operating expenses are fixed at $9,640 per month.

Mr. Smith charges his clients based on the number of hours worked. The fee structure is as follows:

	Charge per Hour
Mr. Smith	$70
Staff attorneys	45
Clerical workers	16

Mr. Smith's practice has been highly seasonal in the past. Due to snow and ice during the winter, a dramatic increase in automobile accidents occurs from November through February. Below is an analysis of the average hours charged to clients per month:

	November–February	March–October
Mr. Smith	160	100
Staff attorneys	170 each	110 each
Clerical workers	150 each	80 each

Required:
Prepare an annual budget of revenue and expenses for the law firm. Separate the budget into quarterly periods, and summarize the results as an annual budget.

Problem 8-13   Budgeting for a Retail Store (CMA)

Kelly Company is a retail sporting goods store that uses accrual accounting for its records. Facts regarding Kelly's operations are as follows:

Sales are budgeted at $220,000 for December, 1987 and $200,000 for January, 1988.

Collections are expected to be 60% in the month of sale and 38% in the month following the sale. Uncollectible sales are expected to be 2%.

Gross margin is 25% of sales.

A total of 80% of the merchandise for resale is purchased in the month prior to the month of sale and 20% is purchased in the month of sale. Payment for merchandise is made in the month following the purchase.

Other expected monthly expenses to be paid in cash are $22,600.

Annual depreciation is $216,000.

Kelly Company's Statement of Financial Position at the close of business on November 30, 1987 is shown next:

KELLY COMPANY
Statement of Financial Position
November 30, 1987

Assets	
Cash	$ 22,000
Accounts receivable (net of $4,000 allowance for uncollectible accounts)	76,000
Inventory	132,000
Property, plant, and equipment (net of $680,000 accumulated depreciation)	870,000
Total assets	$1,100,000

Liabilities and Stockholders' Equity	
Accounts payable	$ 162,000
Common stock	800,000
Retained earnings	138,000
Total liabilities and stockholders' equity	$1,100,000

Required:
Select the best answer:

1. The budgeted cash collections for December, 1987 are:
   a. $208,000
   b. $132,000
   c. $203,600
   d. $212,000
   e. Some amount other than those given above.
2. The pro forma income (loss) before income taxes for December, 1987 is:
   a. $32,400
   b. $28,000
   c. $14,400
   d. $10,000
   e. Some amount other than those given above.
3. The projected balance in accounts payable on December 31, 1987 is:
   a. $162,000
   b. $204,000
   c. $153,000
   d. $160,000
   e. Some amount other than those given above.
4. The projected balance in inventory on December 31, 1987 is:
   a. $160,000
   b. $120,000
   c. $153,000
   d. $150,000
   e. Some amount other than those given above.

Problem 8-14 Preparing a Pro forma Balance Sheet (CMA)
Einhard Enterprises has a comprehensive budgeting program. Pro forma statements of earnings and financial position are prepared as the final step in the budget program. Einhard's projected financial position as of June 30, 1987 is presented below. Various 1987–1988 master budget schedules based upon the plans for the fiscal year ending June 30, 1988, appear on the next page.

All sales are made on account. Raw materials, direct labor, manufacturing overhead, and selling and administrative expenses are credited to vouchers payable. Federal income tax expense is charged to income taxes payable. The federal income tax rate is 40%.

EINHARD ENTERPRISES
Pro forma Statement of Financial Position as of June 30, 1987
($000 omitted)

Assets

Cash	$ 800
Accounts receivable	750
Direct materials inventory	506
Finished goods inventory	648
Total current assets	$ 2,704
Land	$ 1,500
Property, plant & equipment	11,400
Less accumulated depreciation	(2,250)
Total long-term assets	$10,650
Total assets	$13,354

Liabilities and Equity

Vouchers payable	$ 1,230
Income taxes payable	135
Notes payable (due 12/30/87)	1,000
Total current liabilities	$ 2,365
Common stock	$10,200
Retained earnings	789
Total equity	$10,989
Total liabilities and equity	$13,354

Sales Schedule in Units and Dollars

Unit Sales	Selling Price per Unit	Total Sales Revenue
2,100,000	$16	$33,600,000

Production Schedule in Units and Dollars

Production in Units	Cost per Unit	Total Manufacturing Cost
2,110,000	$12.00	$25,320,000

Raw Materials Purchases Schedule in Units and Dollars

Purchases in Pounds	Cost per Pound	Total Purchase Cost
4,320,000	$2.75	$11,880,000

Two pounds of raw materials are needed to make one unit of finished product.

Direct Labor Schedule in Units and Dollars

Production in Units	Direct Labor Cost per Hour	Total Direct Labor Cost
2,110,000	$8	$8,440,000

Each unit requires one-half hour of direct labor time.

Manufacturing Overhead Schedule in Dollars
(Expected activity level—
1,055,000 direct labor hours)

Variable expenses	$2,954,000*
Depreciation	600,000
Other fixed expenses	1,721,000*
Total manufacturing overhead	$5,275,000

* All require cash expenditures. The manufacturing overhead rate is $5.00 per direct labor hour ($5,275,000 ÷ 1,055,000)

Selling and Administrative Expenses Schedule in Dollars

Selling expenses	$2,525,000
Administrative expenses	2,615,000
Total	$5,140,000

All selling and administrative expenses require the expenditure of cash.

Beginning Inventory Schedule in Units and Dollars

	Quantity	Cost per Unit	Total Cost
Direct materials	184,000 pounds	$ 2.75 per lb.	$506,000
Finished goods	54,000 units	$12.00 per unit	$648,000

Cash Receipts and Disbursements Schedule
($000 omitted)

Cash balance 7/1/87 (estimated)	$ 800	
Cash receipts		
Collection of accounts receivable	33,450	
Total cash available		$34,250
Cash disbursements		
Payment of vouchers payable		
Direct materials	$11,900	
Direct labor	8,400	
Manufacturing overhead	4,650	
Selling and administrative expenses	5,200	
Total vouchers payable	$30,150	
Income taxes	1,100	
Purchase of equipment	400	
Cash dividends	820	
Total cash disbursements		$32,470
Excess cash		$ 1,780
Financing		
Repayment of note payable 12/30/87	$ 1,000	
Interest expense	50	
Total financing cost		$ 1,050
Projected cash balance 6/30/88		$ 730

Required:

Construct a pro forma statement of financial position for Einhard Enterprises as of June 30, 1988.

Problem 8-15 Projecting Cash Flows for a Service Business (CMA)

Prime Time Court Club (PTCC) has been in business for five years. The club has experienced cash flow problems each year, especially in the summer when court use is quite low and new membership sales are insignificant. Temporary loans have been obtained from the local bank to cover the summer shortages. Additional permanent capital has also been invested by the owners.

The owners and the bank have decided some action needs to be taken at this time to improve PTCC's net cash flow position. They would like to review a quarterly cash budget based upon a revised fee structure that hopefully would increase club revenues. The purpose of the cash budget would be to better anticipate both the timing and amounts of the probable cash flow of the club and to determine if the club can survive.

John Harper, Club Manager, recommended that the membership dues be increased and that the hourly court time fees be replaced with a monthly charge for unlimited court use. He believes that this plan will increase membership and that the cash flow and timing problem should be reduced. The proposed fee schedule, which is consistent with rates at other clubs, is presented below. In his opinion, the proportions of the different membership categories should not change, but the total number of members will increase by 10%. Court use will also increase an estimated 20% as a result of this new program. The pattern of use throughout the year is not expected to change.

The present fee structure, the distribution among membership categories, and the projected 1988 operating data including membership status, court usage, and estimated operating costs are presented below. The projected operating data presented in the table were based on the present fee structure before Harper's proposed fee schedule was recommended.

Proposed Fee Schedule

Membership Category	Annual Membership Fees	Monthly Court Charges
Individual	$ 75	$10
Youth	45	8
Family	150	18

Present Fee Structure

Annual membership dues	
Individual	$ 45
Youth	30
Family	100
Court time fees	
Prime	$10 per hour
Regular	6 per hour

Membership Distribution

Individual	50%
Youth	20
Family	30
	100%

Projected Operating Data

Quarter	Membership Renewal or New Memberships	Court Time in Hours		Costs	
		Prime	Regular	Fixed Costs*	Variable Costs
1	600	5,500	6,000	$ 56,500	$ 57,500
2	200	2,000	4,000	56,500	30,000
3	200	1,000	2,000	56,500	15,000
4	600	5,500	6,000	56,500	57,500
	1,600			$226,000	$160,000

* Includes a quarterly depreciation charge of $12,500.

Required:

A. Construct a quarterly cash budget for one year for PTCC assuming the new fee structure is adopted and John Harper's estimates of increases in membership and court use occur. Assume the transition from the old to the new fee structure is immediate and complete when preparing the budget.

B. Will John Harper's proposal solve the summer cash shortfall problem? Explain your answer.

C. Will John Harper's proposal support a conclusion that the club can become profitable and survive in the long run? Explain your answer.

9

CAPITAL BUDGETING

CHAPTER OVERVIEW AND OBJECTIVES

This chapter describes how capital budgeting is used by management for long-term decision making that establishes a firm's operating capacity. After studying this chapter, you should be able to:

1. Recognize why capital budgeting decisions are so important to management.
2. Identify the major characteristics of capital budgeting decisions.
3. Determine the role of cash flows in capital budgeting decisions.
4. List the typical cash inflows and cash outflows involved in capital budgeting decisions.
5. Explain how the time value of money is used in capital budgeting decisions.
6. Evaluate an investment with the net present value method and rank investments with the profitability index.
7. Define the essential features of a firm's cost of capital.
8. Evaluate an investment with the internal rate of return method.
9. Discuss the concept of depreciation as a tax shield and explain how different depreciation methods affect cash flows.
10. Compute an investment's payback period and recognize how this method is used in capital budgeting decisions.
11. Calculate an investment's average rate of return and explain how this method is used in capital budgeting.

IMPORTANCE OF CAPITAL BUDGETING

Objective 1: Importance of capital budgeting to management

We mentioned in Chapter 8 that the capital expenditures budget prepared during the annual budgeting process is usually only part of a long-term capital expenditures budget (e.g., five years or longer). The master budget emphasizes the most profitable short-term utilization of the existing operating capacity rather than determining how much capacity is needed. The short-term decision-making focus of Chapter 7 also was on utilizing operating capacity in the most profitable way. We now turn to capital budgeting, which is an important long-term decision-making tool used by management to establish a firm's operating capacity. The expenditures made to establish operating capacity are referred to as *capital expenditures* because they involve investments with long lives.

Capital budgeting is the process used to evaluate capital expenditures such as the construction of a building, replacement of equipment, introduction of a new product line, substitution of automation for labor, and expansion of production facilities. The primary objective in a capital budgeting decision is to add to the value of a business by selecting investments that meet the goals of the organization and provide the highest rates of return. A capital budgeting decision is concerned with a current investment that will pay for itself and yield an acceptable rate of return over its life. As such, capital budgeting decisions are critical for the long-term profitability of a business. Once these decisions are implemented, the related operating capacity will be available and management must make sure it is utilized efficiently and effectively. Unused or misused operating capacity will have an adverse effect on a firm's profitability when measured by the return on the assets involved.

To give you a better appreciation of the magnitude and nature of typical capital budgeting decisions, let's consider the following excerpts from the 1982 annual reports of two large companies:

The Proctor and Gamble Company. *Capital expenditures totaled $625 million, up $60 million over the previous year. New disposable diaper plants came on-stream at Crailsheim, Germany and Akashi, Japan. In the United States, we began production of health and personal care products at a new plant in Greensboro, North Carolina. Over the past three years, we have completed 10 new plants at locations throughout the world, making this the largest construction program in our history to meet the capacity needs of the business.*

Cost savings projects designed to improve productivity and efficiency were up significantly over the previous year and accounted for nearly one-fourth of total capital spending. We anticipate that this greater emphasis on cost savings projects will continue over the next few years. These projects, both here and abroad, are helping us to offset the impact of inflation on our costs and to keep our selling prices as competitive as possible.

Ford Motor Company. *This product improvement program, which required an investment of almost $3 billion in North America, began last fall with the new Ford LTD and Mercury Marquis, the Mustang convertible, and the Capri three-door "bubble back." They were followed in mid-February by the Ford Thunderbird and Mercury Cougar with their combination of aerodynamic design and efficiency, and in March by the multipurpose four-wheel-drive Bronco II. In late spring, Ford Tempo and Mercury Topaz, a new family of midsize front-wheel-drive cars, will be introduced. All these products contain substantial technological advances in the form of new gasoline and diesel engines, multicapacity electronic engine controls, and new transmissions and functional design features. We believe they respond directly to the needs of customers for fuel-efficiency, satisfying and reliable overall vehicle performance, value, and style.*

CHARACTERISTICS OF CAPITAL BUDGETING DECISIONS

**Objective 2:
Evaluating the
major character-
istics of capital
budgeting
decisions**

The experiences of these two companies show us the significant impact capital budgeting decisions have on the long-term operating performance of a business. Such decisions must be considered carefully because:

1. They involve large sums of money, and the success or failure of a firm may be dependent on a single decision.
2. The resources invested are committed for a long time period.
3. They cannot be reversed easily because the investment becomes a sunk cost that can be recovered only through the productive use of the related assets or their ultimate sale, if possible, for their residual value.
4. Since they are oriented toward the long term, substantial risk is involved because of uncertainties such as economic conditions, technological developments, consumer preferences, and social responsibilities. For example, consider the $3 billion investment described earlier by Ford Motor Company. That money will have been spent unwisely if consumers do not buy enough of the new automobiles to justify the investment.

EVALUATING CAPITAL EXPENDITURES

A number of methods are available for evaluating capital expenditures, including the *net present value method, internal rate of return method, payback period method,* and *average rate of return method.* These capital budgeting methods, in the form of decision models (as defined in Chapter 7), all involve the consideration of two factors: (1) the amount of the required investment, and (2) some measure of the return or yield expected from the investment in the future. These are the same two factors you would consider if you were evaluating investing money in stocks, bonds, real estate, or a money market fund. You would not want to invest a certain amount of money currently with the expectation of only receiving that same amount back at a later date. Instead, you want a return on your investment in the form of dividends, interest, rent, or stock price appreciation in addition to receiving the original investment back at a later date. The same is true for all types of investments, including capital expenditures made by a business. All companies have to deal with the issue of scarce resources (e.g., lack of cash or the inability to obtain capital), so effective capital budgeting is an essential part of management.

Regardless of the specific capital budgeting method selected as a decision model, a business should follow these general steps in making capital expenditure decisions:

1. Identify the capital expenditures requested by the firm's managers to provide the operating capacity needed to achieve the organization's long-term goals.
2. Obtain relevant information related to the cost of the investments requested and the return expected from them.
3. Select the capital budgeting method or methods to be used to evaluate each of the investment opportunities.
4. Evaluate each of the investments requested with the capital budgeting method or methods chosen.
5. Rank the investment opportunities in terms of their potential returns and risks.
6. Select the best investments, given the opportunities and resources available.
7. Reevaluate each of the unfunded capital expenditures contained in the

long-term budget as new information regarding business conditions and alternative investments becomes available.

The next issue to be considered is how to measure the return on an investment in order to evaluate whether it has a sufficiently high rate of return to justify spending the money.

USE OF CASH FLOWS IN CAPITAL BUDGETING

Most capital budgeting methods require the use of cash flows to evaluate the return from an investment. The analysis often involves a cash outlay made currently or in the future to obtain future net cash flows (cash receipts in excess of cash disbursements or, instead, the cash savings involved) from the investment. An exception to the use of cash flows is the average rate of return method, which we will discuss later in this chapter. The basic reason for using cash flows instead of accounting net income to measure the return from an investment is the time value of money, a concept presented in detail in Appendix A at the end of the book. Cash received from an investment today is worth more than the same amount of cash received next month or next year.

Since net income is based on accrual accounting, it typically does not reflect the flow of cash in and out of a business. The cash flows associated with an accrual income statement may precede or follow the net income reported. Sales usually do not produce immediate cash receipts because of the time needed to collect receivables. In addition, expenses may require cash payments before they appear on the income statement (e.g., the depreciation on equipment and the inventory included in the cost of goods sold) or after the income statement period (e.g., accrued salaries and taxes). Consequently, accrual accounting must be converted to cash accounting before the time value of money can be accurately evaluated in the capital budgeting process. A more complete discussion of the conversion of accrual accounting to cash accounting is presented in Chapter 17.

Objective 3: Role of cash flows

TYPICAL CASH FLOWS IN A CAPITAL BUDGETING DECISION

The most common cash outflows considered in a capital budgeting decision are:
1. The initial cost of the investment.
2. Incremental operating costs needed for the investment.
3. Maintenance and repairs associated with the investment.
4. Any increase in working capital (current assets minus current liabilities) required to support the investment.

Objective 4: Identifying cash flows

Typical cash inflows associated with capital budgeting decisions are:
1. Incremental revenues from an investment.
2. Cost reductions from an investment that improves the firm's efficiency.
3. Any residual value at the end of the useful life of the investment.
4. Any decrease in working capital that may occur at the end of the investment's life.

We should emphasize that the revenues and operating costs considered in the analysis are incremental revenues and incremental operating costs. That is, they represent the additional revenues earned because the investment is made and the additional annual cash outlays required once the investment becomes operational. Examples of operating costs are wages, insurance, taxes, and utilities.

Note that we include increases and decreases of working capital in the capital budgeting analysis. The reason is easiest to see for increases in working capital as cash outflows. As you learned in financial accounting, every business must maintain a certain amount of working capital for liquidity purposes. If an incremental amount of working capital (e.g., more accounts receivable and inventory) is required to support a new investment, the increment should be treated for capital budgeting purposes as being part of the initial investment. In contrast, if the working capital can be reduced at the end of the investment's life because the higher amount no longer is required, the decrease should be treated as a cash inflow. The same dollar amount of increase and decrease in working capital will not simply cancel out in the analysis because of the time value of money.

We also should emphasize that depreciation *does not* require a cash outlay when it is recorded each year, so it *should not* be included as an annual cash outflow for capital budgeting purposes. The related cash outflow is recognized in capital budgeting when the initial investment is made.

TIME VALUE OF MONEY: AN OVERVIEW

Objective 5:
Use of the time
value of money

We mentioned earlier that a complete discussion of the time value of money is presented in Appendix A at the end of the book. If you need a complete review of the subject or have not considered it before, you should read Appendix A now. The basic issue with the **time value of money** is that a dollar held today is worth more than a dollar held anytime in the future. The time value of money can be evaluated in terms of either its future value or its present value.

The money we have today can be invested to earn interest. Thus, it will grow in amount as future periods pass. For example, $1,000 invested today at 12% compounded annually (the interest is calculated once a year) will become $1,120 one year later [$1,000 + (.12) $1,000]. In other words, we can say that next year's $1,120 is only worth $1,000 today. The $1,120 is the future value of the $1,000 because of the interest earned for one year. Conversely, $1,000 is the **present value** of the $1,120 if we discount the future value back to today. The process of converting a future value into what has to be a smaller present value is called **discounting.** We use the term **"discount rate"** to indicate that a present value is being calculated rather than a future value involving an interest rate. However, the interest rate and discount rate are both the same amount in a given future value/present value relationship (i.e., 12% in the above example).

The same basic concepts of the time value of money can be applied to an **annuity,** which is a series of equal payments over a specific number of time periods. For example, monthly mortgage payments made over a 20-year period to pay back a building loan are an example of an annuity. The future value of an annuity is the sum of all payments made plus the interest accumulated on each payment. For example, quarterly deposits in a money market fund yielding 10% that are made for 10 years will accumulate as the future value of an annuity at the end of the 10-year period.

In contrast, the present value of an annuity is the amount that would have to be invested today at a certain interest rate (e.g., 10%) to receive a series of future payments over a specific time period. This means that the future payments are discounted to their present value by removing the amount of interest involved. If we consider a capital expenditure as an investment made today to receive a series of equal annual payments over the life of the investment that will recover the original amount invested and yield a desired rate of return, we have an example of the present value of an annuity.

The tables presented in Appendix A are used to evaluate the time value of money to avoid the tedious mathematics that otherwise would be involved. Since capital budgeting decisions consist of present value applications, we will use Tables A-3 and A-4 in the illustrations of discounted cash flows. Table A-3 provides factors for various combinations of interest rates and number of periods related to the present value of a single amount, whereas Table A-4 contains the factors for the present value of an annuity.

APPLYING TIME VALUE OF MONEY TO CAPITAL BUDGETING DECISIONS

The net present value method and the internal rate of return method are two important capital budgeting techniques that are based on the time value of money. To illustrate these two methods, assume that the Naples Company is evaluating the possibility of producing a new product, which will require the acquisition of a new robotics system. The system, which will cost $229,201 (including installation and transportation charges), has a useful life of five years with no residual value. The company estimates that the new product will increase its annual net cash flows by $70,000, computed as:[1]

Estimated cash inflows from sales of the new product	$250,000
Estimated operating costs requiring cash payments (including income taxes)	180,000
Net cash flows each year	$ 70,000

Let's consider the net present value method first.

NET PRESENT VALUE (NPV) METHOD

FEATURES OF THE NPV METHOD

Discounted cash flows can be used to compare the present value of an investment with the present value of the net cash flows expected from it in the future. For example, the Naples Company is considering an investment of $229,201 in current dollars, which will yield expected net cash flows of $70,000 for each of five years (a total of $350,000). In making any investment decision, the expected net cash flows must be compared with the amount of investment required to obtain them. As we demonstrated earlier, however, a dollar expected in the future is not equivalent to a dollar held today because of the time value of money.

The net present value method is a discounted cash flow technique, which is used to compare the discounted cash inflows from an investment with its discounted cash outflows. Another way to describe the NPV is that it is the present value of all the expected future benefits from an investment less the present value of its current and expected future costs. The discount rate chosen for the discounting process is the firm's required rate of return from its investments, often called the cost of capital. Other terms used for this discount rate are the hurdle rate or minimal rate of return.

Objective 6:
Evaluating an investment with the net present value method

[1] For illustrative purposes, we assume here that the net cash flow is the same each year. Later, we will consider the impact of uneven net cash flows.

ROLE OF COST OF CAPITAL

Objective 7:
Defining the cost
of capital

The **cost of capital** or **hurdle rate** is the firm's cost of obtaining funds in the form of debt and owners' equity. As such, the cost of capital is not the same as the interest rate at which money can be borrowed because the cost of all means of financing used by a firm must be considered. For example, a given firm may use three types of financing—debt, preferred stock, and common equity (common stock and retained earnings). The concepts and calculations involved with a complete coverage of the cost of capital are complex and beyond the scope of this book, so they are deferred to a finance textbook. However, the basic principles involved can be illustrated with a simple example. Assume that the after-tax cost of the Naples Company's debt, preferred stock, and common equity are 8%, 12%, and 14%, respectively. Further, the capital structure of the firm consists of the following:

Type of Financing	Percent of Total Capital
Debt	30
Preferred stock	10
Common equity	60

The cost of capital is a weighted average, computed as the sum of the products of each financing source's cost multiplied by its percentage of the total capital, or in this case:

$$\text{Cost of capital} = (.08).3 + (.12).1 + (.14).6$$
$$= .024 + .012 + .084$$
$$= .12 \text{ or } 12\%$$

As long as an investment offers a rate of return higher than the cost of capital (12% in this case), it is potentially attractive because the return will exceed the cost of the funds used to finance it. This will occur when the NPV is positive (the discounted cash inflows exceed the discounted cash outflows). A negative NPV indicates that an investment should be rejected since the discounted cash outflows will exceed the discounted cash inflows, resulting in an inadequate return. If the NPV of an investment is zero, management will be indifferent about accepting or rejecting it because the true cost of the investment will be the same as the return earned from it. Thus, no value will be added to the business.

BASIC ILLUSTRATION OF NPV METHOD

To illustrate the NPV method, the management of the Naples Company requires a return in excess of its cost of capital (12%). As long as the present value of the net cash flows discounted at 12% is greater than the current cost of the equipment, the investment is potentially attractive. The expected net cash flows of $70,000 can be discounted by one of two approaches:

1. They can be discounted year by year, using the present value of $1 table as shown in Figure 9-1 (the factors in the third column are taken from Table A-3 in Appendix A, the present value of $1 table).
2. They can be discounted using Table A-4, the present value of an annuity of $1 table (12% and five periods), since the amount received is the same each

Figure 9-1

NAPLES COMPANY
Analysis with Net Present Value Method

Year	(a) Expected Net Cash Flow	(b) Present Value of $1 at 12%	(a) $\times$ (b) Present Value of Net Cash Flow
1	$70,000	.8929	$ 62,503
2	70,000	.7972	55,804
3	70,000	.7118	49,826
4	70,000	.6355	44,485
5	70,000	.5674	39,718
Total present value of net cash flows			$252,336
Cost of investment			229,201
Net present value (NPV)			$ 23,135

year. With this approach, the annual net cash flows of $70,000 are considered as annuity payments that must provide a return on investment of at least 12%.

Note that the annual net cash flows of $70,000 in Figure 9-1 have present values that decrease with the passage of time. That is, the longer the company has to wait for the money, the less it is worth in the beginning because of the 12% discount rate and an increasing number of years. We see in Figure 9-1 that the NPV for the equipment investment is $23,135, which means that the actual rate of return is attractive because it is significantly higher than 12%.

We can obtain the same NPV with the annuity treatment by using a 3.6048 factor (12% and five years from Table A-4) multiplied by the annual net cash flows and comparing the results to the cost of the investment as follows:

Present value of expected net cash flows (3.6048 $\times$ $70,000)	$252,336
Cost of investment	229,201
Net present value (NPV)	$ 23,135

Whenever the net cash flows involved in a capital budgeting decision are not constant each year, they must be discounted on a year-by-year basis with the present value of $1 table as we have done in Figure 9-1 because an annuity is a series of equal payments. The total present value of $252,336 represents the maximum amount the Naples Company could pay for the equipment and still earn the required 12%. However, the investment can be made for only $229,201. As a result, the actual rate of return is significantly higher than the minimum of 12% required. We will see later in this chapter that the second discounted cash flow technique, the internal rate of return method, will enable us to determine what the actual rate of return is for the equipment investment.

We should also note that the total present value of the net cash flows would have been lower than $252,336 if a discount rate higher than 12% had been used. In contrast, a discount rate lower than 12% would have produced a total present value of the net cash flows in excess of $252,336. Thus, an inverse relationship exists between the discount rate chosen and the present value of future net cash flows. This means that a business will be willing to pay more for an investment when it requires a lower return on the investment.

RANKING INVESTMENTS WITH A PROFITABILITY INDEX

When the NPV method is used to evaluate capital expenditures, all projects with positive net present values are acceptable and all projects with negative net present values are unacceptable. Managers, however, usually face two conditions that complicate the evaluation of NPV results: (1) the various investments being considered have different costs; and (2) the firm does not have sufficient funds to invest in all the projects available.

An extension of the NPV method, called a profitability index, can be used to ensure that a firm uses its limited resources for investments with the largest returns. The NPV of one investment cannot be compared directly with the net present value of another investment unless both of them are of equal size. For example, a NPV of $5,000 from an investment of $25,000 is more attractive than a NPV of $5,000 from an investment of $250,000.

A **profitability index** is computed by dividing the present value of the net cash flows by the amount of the investment required. This index provides the relative measurement needed to compare two or more investments of different sizes. In the case of the Naples Company, the profitability index is determined as:

$$\text{Profitability index} = \frac{\text{Present value of net cash flows}}{\text{Cost of investment}}$$

$$= \frac{\$252,336}{\$229,201}$$

$$= 1.101$$

When a firm cannot obtain sufficient funds to finance all the investments being considered, the profitability index is used to distinguish between those chosen and those postponed or rejected, based strictly on the returns involved. The simple decision rule used with the profitability index is that *the investment with the largest index is preferred over others with lower indexes.* For example, the Naples Company will choose the investment illustrated above with its profitability index of 1.101 rather than another project with an index of 1.050 even though both may have the same NPV. Using the index, investments are ranked in their descending order of profitability. Investments with the highest profitability indexes are accepted until the firm's resources have been consumed. A profitability index of less than one reveals a negative NPV.

EVALUATING INVESTMENTS WITH DIFFERENT LIVES

Another important consideration when a firm is comparing alternative investments is the possibility that they may have different lives. Basically the same procedures discussed earlier for the NPV method are still applicable, but we must refine the analysis somewhat. In such cases, the useful lives of the investments must be *equalized.* For example, assume that we are comparing the returns from an asset with a useful life of five years and one having a useful life of 10 years. We can equate the lives involved by assuming that the first asset is replaced after five years at its estimated replacement cost then. As such, the two assets will be evaluated over a 10-year period. In more complicated cases, we may have to pick a point in the future that does not represent the ends of the useful lives of the assets being evaluated in order to have a common denominator for the analysis.

To illustrate the treatment of investments with unequal lives, assume that Naples Company has an alternative to the five-year asset discussed above. Another robotics system with a useful life of 10 years is available for the production of the new product being considered. The relevant facts are as follows:

Initial cost of alternate system	$621,522
Estimated annual net cash flows for 10 years with alternate system	110,000

Since the alternatives involve investments for different periods of time, we will equalize their lives over a 10-year period by assuming that the five-year asset can be replaced at the end of its life for an estimated cost of $250,000. The $20,799 increase in five years from its current cost of $229,201 is based on management's best estimate of the future replacement cost. We futher assume that the annual net cash flows of $70,000 from the five-year asset are expected to occur over the entire 10-year period. The firm's cost of capital is still 12%. The two assets are evaluated as follows:

Five-Year Asset

Net cash flows of $70,000 discounted to their present value at 12% for 10 years (Table A-4 factor) ($70,000 × 5.6502)	$395,514
Initial cost of $229,201 at its present value	(229,201)
Replacement cost of $250,000 discounted to its present value at 12% for 5 years (Table A-3 factor) ($250,000 × .5674)	(141,850)
Net present value (NPV)	$ 24,463

Ten-Year Asset

Net cash flows of $110,000 discounted to their present value at 12% for 10 years (Table A-4 factor) ($110,000 × 5.6502)	$621,522
Initial cost of $621,522 at its present value	(621,522)
Net present value (NPV)	$ –0–

As we see above, the $250,000 expected cost of the five-year asset's replacement at the end of its useful life is discounted to $141,850, which is the present value of the future expenditure. Based on the comparison above, the firm should choose the five-year asset because of its higher NPV. However, we should point out that the company must carefully evaluate other factors such as:
1. The reliability of the replacement cost estimate for the five-year asset.
2. Technological changes that may occur in the future and affect the time it wants to be committed to a particular robotics system.

IMPACT OF UNEVEN CASH FLOWS — INCLUDING RESIDUAL VALUE

Cash flows from an investment can differ from year to year for several reasons. For example, the annual net cash flows from operations may be different, a major expenditure for an overhaul may be required at a future date, or the asset may have an estimated residual value at the end of its useful life. To illustrate, let's change the facts with the Naples Company case and assume that the $229,201 investment is expected to produce the following net cash flows over its five-year life:

Year	Amount
1	$ 50,000
2	60,000
3	70,000
4	80,000
5	90,000
Total	$350,000

Note that the total net cash flows over the five-year period are $350,000, the same as they were in the original case. The timing of the net cash flows, however, is different. Assume further that the firm will have to spend $15,000 on an overhaul of the equipment at the end of the third year to keep it operational, and that the equipment is expected to have a residual value, less income taxes, of $25,000 at the end of its five-year life. The residual value must be reduced by any income taxes expected with the disposition because we are concerned with cash flows. In general, the excess of the selling price of such an asset over its book value at the time of the sale is taxed. Thus, to estimate the cash flow from the ultimate disposition of the equipment, we must consider the income taxes involved. The discounted cash flows in this case, using the firm's 12% cost of capital are shown in Figure 9-2.

The NPV in this case is $18,516, indicating that the actual rate of return is higher than 12%. Thus, the investment is attractive to the firm. The original investment cost is not discounted because it already is in current dollars. The unequal annual net cash flows from operations ranging from $50,000 to $90,000 are discounted at 12% on a year-to-year basis using factors from Table A-3. Since the major overhaul is required at the end of the third year, its estimated cost (a cash outflow) of $15,000 is converted to current dollars with a factor of .7118.

INTERNAL RATE OF RETURN (IRR) METHOD

Objective 8:
Use of the
internal rate of
return method

The **internal rate of return** (also called the time adjusted rate of return or true rate of return) is defined as the discount rate that can be used to make the discounted cash inflows from an investment equal to its discounted cash outflows (that is, the NPV is equal to zero). What would happen, for example, if we discounted the net cash flows of $70,000 in the Naples Company illustration at 20% and compared the results with the cost of the investment? Using the

Figure 9-2

NAPLES COMPANY Analysis with NPV Method				
Year	Item	(a) Cash Flow	(b) Present Value of $1 @ 12%	(a) × (b) Present Value of Cash Flows
Current	Original investment	$(229,201)	1.0000	$(229,201)
1	Annual net cash flow	50,000	.8929	44,645
2	Annual net cash flow	60,000	.7972	47,832
3	Annual net cash flow	70,000	.7118	49,826
3	Major overhaul	(15,000)	.7118	(10,677)
4	Annual net cash flow	80,000	.6355	50,840
5	Annual net cash flow	90,000	.5674	51,066
5	Residual value (after income taxes)	25,000	.5674	14,185
Net present value (NPV)				$ 18,516

2.9906 factor for 20% and five years from Table A-4, we find a negative NPV of $19,859, as follows:

Present value of expected net cash flows (2.9906 × $70,000)	$209,342
Cost of the investment	229,201
Net present value (NPV)	$ (19,859)

Keep in mind that the NPV was $23,135 at 12%, and we have just seen that it is a negative $19,859 at 20%. Since we have a positive NPV at 12% and a negative NPV at 20%, the actual rate of return is somewhere between 12% and 20%. The NPV can be either positive or negative depending on the discount rate used, so there must be a discount rate that will make the NPV exactly zero. This will occur when the discounted cash inflows equal the discounted cash outflows.

In turn, the discount rate that produces a NPV of zero is the IRR. Since (1) the net cash flows are the same each year and (2) the investment is paid for initially in the Naples Company case, the calculation of the IRR is relatively easy. We simply treat the net cash flows as an annuity and find the factor from Table A-4 that makes the discounted net cash flows equal to the cost of the investment. The required annuity factor for the IRR can be determined as follows:

$$\text{Internal rate of return factor} = \frac{\text{Cost of the investment}}{\text{Annual net cash flows}}$$

$$= \frac{\$229,201}{\$70,000}$$

$$= 3.2743$$

Remember that a specific factor from a time value of money table, such as Table A-4, represents a particular combination of discount (interest) rate and number of time periods. Since we know that five years are involved, we look for the 3.2743 factor in the five-period row and find it in the 16% column. Consequently, the IRR for the investment of the Naples Company is 16% because that discount rate makes the discounted net cash flows equal to the cost of the investment (that is, 3.2743 × $70,000 = $229,201).

APPROXIMATING THE IRR OR USING INTERPOLATION

In many cases, the fraction used above to compute the IRR factor produces a number that does not appear in Table A-4. The table is based on whole percentages (e.g., 12% and 16%) and does not refer to every percentage, so all factors are not represented. (We should note, however, that more complete tables based on fractional interest rates are available.) The question then is "How accurate does the IRR have to be?"

At times, we don't care about finding the exact figure because an approximation is adequate for comparison with the firm's cost of capital. If the approximate rate is significantly higher than the cost of capital, the investment is acceptable; if it is clearly lower, the investment is not acceptable. To approximate the IRR in such cases, we simply find a factor in the table that is closest to the factor we want on the high side and a second factor that is closest on the low side. These two factors establish a narrow range for the correct rate. For example, assume that the investment being considered by the Naples Company will cost $241,500 instead of $229,201 with same expected annual net cash flows of $70,000. Using the method introduced earlier to compute the IRR factor, we find:

$$\text{Internal rate of return factor} = \frac{\$241,500}{\$70,000} = 3.4500$$

Referring again to the five-year row in Table A-4, we can see that the factor 3.4500 is between the factors in the 13% to 14% columns (3.5172 and 3.4331). Thus, the IRR is in the 13% to 14% range and is closer to 14%. Since this result is larger than the firm's cost of capital of 12%, the investment is still potentially attractive.

If we want to compute the exact internal rate of return in such cases, interpolation must be used. **Interpolation** is a mathematical technique with which fractional rates of return that do not appear in a table can be computed. To illustrate its use, we know that the IRR for the Naples Company is between 13% and 14% when the cost of the investment is $241,500. The factor from Table A-4 for an interest rate of 13% is 3.5172, and for 14% it is 3.4331. In addition, the IRR factor is 3.4500. Using these values to interpolate to the correct IRR, we find:

	Five-Year Factors from Table A-4	
Factor for 13%	3.5172	3.5172
IRR factor	3.4500	
Factor for 14%		3.4331
Difference	.0672	.0841

$$\text{IRR} = 13\% + [.0672/.0841\ (1\%)] = 13.799\%$$

The 1% in the equation above is the difference between the two rates used (14%–13%). The IRR in this case is actually 13.799%. Since this rate is higher than the firm's cost of capital of 12%, the investment is potentially attractive. Computer software packages and small computers are available to determine IRRs with even more precise results.

COMPUTING THE IRR WITH UNEVEN CASH FLOWS

We illustrated earlier with the NPV method that the cash flows from an investment may not be the same from year to year because of such factors as unequal annual net cash flows, maintenance costs, and residual value. In such cases, the annuity approach to computing the IRR will not work because the denominator of the fraction used will not be constant. Instead, we must use a trial-and-error process to determine the IRR. This consists of choosing an arbitrary discount rate and calculating the NPV of the cash flows. If the NPV is found to be positive, we know the discount rate being tried is lower than the IRR, and the calculation must be repeated with a higher rate. This process continues until we find a net present value that is negative. Once the IRR is bracketed between two interest rates (one with a positive NPV and one with a negative NPV), we proceed by testing other rates within that range until we find the rate with a net present value of zero. The result is the IRR. This trial-and-error process can be quite time-consuming in complex cases, but fortunately computer programs and calculators that eliminate the need for tedious manual computations are readily available.

LIMITING ASSUMPTIONS OF DISCOUNTED CASH FLOW METHODS

When cash flows are discounted to recognize the time value of money in capital budgeting decisions as illustrated earlier with the NPV method and the IRR method, *two limiting assumptions are made.* The first assumption is that all cash flows from an investment occur at the end of the time periods. In reality, this assumption is somewhat unrealistic because the cash flows normally occur throughout a given period. The treatment as an ordinary annuity (one in which the payments occur at the end of a period), however, simplifies the computations involved without any significant loss of accuracy in most cases.

The second assumption is that the business is immediately able to reinvest the cash flows from a given investment in another project. In addition, the rate of return from the reinvestment must be at least as large as the discount rate used for the cash flows from the original investment. The discount rate involved is either the firm's cost of capital (with the net present value method) or the original investment's internal rate of return (with the internal rate of return method). Unless the reinvestment rate of return is at least as large as the discount rate used, the true rate of return from the original investment will be overstated and its evaluation will be incorrect. For example, if we are using a 12% discount rate to evaluate a given capital expenditure, we assume that the cash flows from it can be invested in a second project that has a rate of return of at least 12%. If the second investment will only yield 10% per year, the true return on the first investment will be less than 12%.

CONFLICTING RESULTS WITH NPV METHOD AND IRR METHOD

Whenever alternative investments require different amounts of money, have different lives, or produce different patterns of annual cash flows, the two discounted cash flow techniques, NPV method and IRR method, often produce *conflicting results.* That is, the most attractive investment as measured with one of the two methods is not the same as the best investment according to the other method. The reason for this difference is the second assumption underlying the use of the discounted cash flow techniques discussed earlier. The reinvestment rate for the net cash flows generated from an investment is different for the two methods, NPV and IRR. The NPV method assumes that the reinvestment takes place at the firm's cost of capital, which is lower than the IRR for all acceptable investments. In contrast, the IRR method assumes that the net cash flows are reinvested at the IRR throughout the life of the investment. Thus, the two reinvestment rates are different, which in turn can cause a ranking difference between the NPV method and IRR method. Consequently, the choice between the NPV method and the IRR method is often made on the basis of the reinvestment rate that is most realistic. Since the cost of capital stays the same from investment to investment but the internal rate of return can change with each investment, the NPV method usually is preferred over the IRR method.

To illustrate how a ranking difference can occur between the NPV method and the IRR method, consider the case of the Stanley Company, which has a cost of capital of 10%. Two alternative investments, Project A and Project B with different patterns of annual net cash flows, are being considered. The two projects are alternatives because only one of them will be chosen. The following data have been prepared by the firm's management:

	Project A	**Project B**
Initial cost	$10,000	$10,000
Expected life	3 years	3 years
Net cash flows:		
Year 1	$ 4,747.21	–0–
Year 2	4,747.21	–0–
Year 3	4,747.21	$16,430.00
Net present value	1,805.84[a]	2,343.86[b]
Internal rate of return	20%[c]	18%[d]

[a] $4,747.21 discounted at 10% for 3 years using factor from Table A-4:

2.4869 × $4,747.21 = $11,805.84 − $10,000.00 = $1,805.84

[b] $16,430.00 discounted at 10% for 3 years using factor from Table A-3:

.7513 × $16,430 = $12,343.86 − $10,000.00 = $2,343.86

[c] $10,000/$4,747.21 = 2.1065 or 20% from 3-year row of Table A-4

[d] $10,000/$16,430 = .6086 or 18% from 3-year row of Table A-3

Note that the pattern of the annual net cash flows is significantly different for the two projects. Project A will generate annual net cash flows of $4,747.21 for three years, or a total of $14,241.63. Project B will produce zero net cash flows for the first two years of its life and $16,430 during the third and final year. In this case, the differences in the annual cash flows cause conflicting rankings of the two investments with the NPV method and the IRR method. Project A has the highest IRR of 20% (compared with 18% for Project B), whereas Project B has the largest NPV of $2,343.86 (compared with $1,805.84 for Project A). Even though Project A produces less total net cash flows, it returns the net cash flows faster and the assumption with the IRR method is that these funds are available for reinvestment at the 20% rate (when the time value of money is relatively high). The choice between the two methods with these conflicting results depends on the rate at which the firm can reinvest the net cash flows. If Project A's IRR of 20% or better is not realistic for all reinvestments, Project B should be selected because of its higher NPV.

EFFECT OF DEPRECIATION ON CASH FLOWS

Objective 9: Impact of depreciation as a tax shield

We emphasized earlier that depreciation should not be included as an annual cash outflow in capital budgeting because it does not require a cash payment. Instead, the cost of the asset is a cash outflow when it is paid for. However, depreciation does affect the amount of income taxes paid because (1) it is deductible for tax purposes, and (2) income taxes require cash outflows. Consequently, the choice of depreciation method will have an impact on the cash flows evaluated in a capital budgeting decision. We are concerned with the depreciation method used for income tax reporting, not the one used for financial reporting purposes, in capital budgeting. The specific methods allowable for federal income tax purposes in a given year depend on the tax law, which changes over time.

Until 1981, the same methods used for financial reporting were allowable for tax reporting (straight line, declining balance, sum-of-the-years' digits, and units of production). The Economic Recovery Act (ERTA) of 1981 significantly changed the way depreciation was computed for tax purposes by introducing the concept of an **accelerated cost recovery system (ACRS)**. The purpose of ACRS was to permit more rapid depreciation than was allowed under previous tax laws. According to ACRS, all depreciable assets placed in service after 1980 were included in one of five property classes, regardless of their useful life. For example, business equipment and machinery that did not specifically qualify for one of the other classes were depreciated over a five-year period according to the following schedule:

Year	% of the Asset's Cost Recovered
1	15
2	22
3	21
4	21
5	21

The Tax Reform Act of 1986 modified ACRS for property placed in service on or after January 1, 1987. Eight classes of property were established for the fastest cost recovery possible with different lives and depreciation methods for the various classes. For example, the cost of depreciable nonresidential real property is recovered with the straight line method over a period of 31.5 years, regardless of the actual useful life involved. In addition, numerous types of personal property used in business are depreciated with the 200% (double) declining balance method over a period of five years. Residual value is ignored with the different classes of property under the Tax Reform Act of 1986. In addition, the straight line method can be elected over ACRS for those assets otherwise qualifying for a 200% – or 150% declining balance class.

In order to establish the cost recovery (depreciation) schedule for a particular asset with the modified ACRS, a business must match that asset with one of the eight classifications. The **Class Life Asset Depreciation Range (usually referred to as ADR) System** that is identified in the tax law is the starting point for identifying the appropriate class for a particular type of asset that is included in the ADR system. The ADR system is a listing of different types of depreciable assets with a range of lives for each type based on the lowest life allowed, the mid-point life, and the highest life allowed. A business matches an asset acquired with the related category in the ADR system and identifies the mid-point life involved, as established by the tax law. That mid-point life, in turn, is matched with the appropriate class of property set forth in the Tax Reform Act of 1986 to determine the depreciable life of the asset.

To illustrate, assume that a business purchases an asset for $10,000 at the beginning of 1987. The asset has an estimated useful life of ten years but is classified for tax purposes as one with an ADR mid-point life of eight years. All assets with an ADR mid-point life of more than four years but less than ten years are depreciated as five-year assets under the modified ACRS using the 200% declining balance method. In general, the recovery period begins in the middle of the year in which the property is placed in service (half year convention). Thus, a half year of depreciation is allowed in the first year as well as the sixth year (a total of five years depreciation). In addition, the business can switch to the straight line method at the point when it provides a larger deduction than the 200% declining balance method. The useful life of ten years would be ignored for tax purposes as would any residual value involved, and the cost of the asset would be recovered with the 200% declining balance method according to the following schedule:

Year	Book Value at Beginning of Year	Rate	Annual Depreciation	Book Value at End of Year
1987	$10,000	20%*	$2,000	$8,000
1988	8,000	40%	3,200	4,800
1989	4,800	40%	1,920	2,880
1990	2,880	40%	1,152	1,728
1991	1,728	**	1,152	576
1992	576	**	576	-0-

* 200% of straight line rate = 20% × 2 = 40%. First year's depreciation expense with half year convention = 40%/2 = 20%.
** Switch to straight line depreciation because it is more than double declining balance depreciation and the asset must be fully depreciated. As of January 1, 1991, the remaining life is 1.5 years. Therefore, the depreciation expense in 1991 is $1,152 ($1,728/1.5). In 1992, one-half year of depreciation expense is recognized ($1,152/2 = $576).

DEPRECIATION AS A TAX SHIELD

Since depreciation is deductible for tax purposes, it shields income from tax. Thus, depreciation is called a **tax shield**. The amount of tax savings from a tax shield depends on the tax rate involved. If a company has a 40% tax rate, the savings from a $10,000 depreciation deduction is $4,000, based on the following general formula:

Tax saving from depreciation tax shield = Depreciation deduction × Tax rate

The net cash flows will be $4,000 more with the depreciation than they would have been without it. We can see the tax shield effect in the following comparison of the tax liability of Company X, which has such a deduction, with Company Y, which does not have the $10,000 depreciation deduction. To illustrate the impact of the depreciation only on net cash flows, we assume that the sales for each company are equal to cash receipts and that all operating expenses other than depreciation are paid in cash.

	Company X	Company Y	Difference
Sales (equal to cash receipts)	$100,000	$100,000	$ -0-
Less expenses:			
Cash operating expenses	60,000	60,000	-0-
Depreciation (1)	10,000	-0-	10,000
Net income before taxes	30,000	40,000	(10,000)
Income taxes @ 40%	12,000	16,000	(4,000)
Net income after taxes (2)	18,000	24,000	(6,000)
Net cash flows (1) + (2)	$ 28,000	$ 24,000	$ 4,000

Note that Company X has $4,000 less income taxes and higher net cash flows of the same amount because it has the $10,000 depreciation tax shield. The net cash flows for the two companies are determined by adding depreciation, which does not require a cash outflow, back to the net income after taxes. Alternatively, the net cash flows can be computed by subtracting all cash outflows from the sales (for Company X, this would be $100,000 − $60,000 − $12,000 = $28,000; and for Company Y, it would be $100,000 − $60,000 − $16,000 = $24,000). Even though Company Y has $6,000 more net income than Company X, the depreciation tax shield has resulted in the larger net cash flows of $4,000 for Company X.

COMPREHENSIVE ILLUSTRATION OF DISCOUNTED CASH FLOWS

As a final illustration of capital budgeting with discounted cash flows, let's apply the net present value method to a situation in which uneven net cash flows are involved because of income tax ramifications and a variety of other cash flows. The Pestle Company is evaluating the possibility of producing a new product, which will require the acquisition of a new machine at the beginning of the current year. The machine will cost $80,000 and will qualify as a five-year asset for tax purposes, although the firm estimates that its useful life will be eight years.

The 200% declining balance method will be used to depreciate the machine, and residual value will be ignored for cost recovery purposes. At the end of the eight-year period, the firm expects to sell the machine for its residual value of $10,000. The company's regular tax rate is 40%, and the $10,000 sale of the machine will be fully taxed at the 40% rate because the book value of the asset will be zero (initial cost of $80,000 less accumulated depreciation of $80,000). Working capital of $30,000 will be required to support the investment because of increased accounts receivable and inventory that are offset only partially by additional accounts payable. Management expects to be able to reduce the working capital needed at the end of the project's eight-year life by the same $30,000 as the accounts receivable and inventory are turned into cash and accounts payable from inventory purchases are reduced to zero.

The cash from the sales forecast for the new product and the conversion of the operating results to net cash flows from the new product for the eight-year period are shown in Figure 9-3. Annual sales from the new product are estimated at $212,000, while the cash operating expenses are expected to be $180,000 each year, thereby producing operating income before depreciation and income tax of $32,000. Annual depreciation is $16,000 in year one (half year convention) and $25,600 in year two. The annual depreciation expense then decreases each year (except in year 5) until the asset is fully depreciated in year six. Note the significant impact on the net cash flows from depreciation as a tax shield. This impact is easy to see in Figure 9-3 because the annual sales, cash operating expenses, and tax rate are the same each year. Using year one as an example, the effect of the tax shield on the net cash flows can be observed directly as follows:

$$
\begin{aligned}
\text{After-tax cash from operations} &= \$32,000 \times 60\% = \$19,200 \\
+ \text{Depreciation tax shield} &= \$16,000 \times 40\% = \underline{6,400} \\
= \text{Net cash flow} - \text{year 1} & = \underline{\underline{\$25,600}}
\end{aligned}
$$

The highest net cash flow occurs in the second year because of the large amount of depreciation ($25,600). The net cash flow decreases after the second year due to the reduced tax savings from the depreciation tax shield. In years five and six, the straight line method is used to depreciate the asset over its remaining life of 1.5 years.

The importance of depreciation as a tax shield is emphasized in years seven and eight because the machine is fully depreciated at the end of the sixth year; therefore, no depreciation can be recorded for tax purposes during the last two years of the project. As a result, the net cash flows decline to $19,200 for each

PESTLE COMPANY
Analysis of Operating Cash Flows from New Product

	Year			
	1	2	3	4
Cash from sales	$212,000	$212,000	$212,000	$212,000
Cash operating expenses	180,000	180,000	180,000	180,000
Operating income before depreciation and tax (1)	32,000	32,000	32,000	32,000
Depreciation (2) (a below)	16,000	25,600	15,360	9,216
Taxable income	16,000	6,400	16,640	22,784
Income taxes (@ 40%) (3)	6,400	2,560	6,656	9,114
Net income (4)	9,600	3,840	9,984	13,670
Net cash flow (1) − (3) or (2) + (4)	$ 25,600	$ 29,440	$ 25,344	$ 22,886
(a) Depreciation schedule				
$80,000 × .20	$16,000			
$64,000 × .40		$25,600		
$38,400 × .40			$15,360	
$23,040 × .40				$9,216

	Year			
	5	6	7	8
Cash from sales	$212,000	$212,000	$212,000	$212,000
Cash operating expenses	180,000	180,000	180,000	180,000
Operating income before depreciation and tax (1)	32,000	32,000	32,000	32,000
Depreciation (2) (a below)	9,216	4,608	−0−	−0−
Taxable income	22,784	27,392	32,000	32,000
Income tax (@ 40%) (3)	9,114	10,957	12,800	12,800
Net income (4)	13,670	16,435	19,200	19,200
Net cash flow (1) − (3) or (2) + (4)	$ 22,886	$ 21,043	$ 19,200	$ 19,200
(a) Depreciation schedule				
$13,824/1.5 years	$ 9,216			
($13,824/1.5 years) ½		$ 4,608		
			−0−	
				−0−

Figure 9-3

of the last two years since the absence of the tax shield increases income taxes significantly. The annual operating net cash flows are combined with other related cash flows in Figure 9-4, so we can evaluate the net present value of the investment in the machine required to produce the new product and the working capital needed to support it.

Management has decided to use a discount rate of 16%, which is the firm's cost of capital, to discount the cash flows involved with the new product. The NPV in this case is $5,989, which means that the investment is attractive because the actual return from it over the eight-year period is larger than 16%. If

Figure 9-4

PESTLE COMPANY
Net Present Value Analysis of Cash Flows

Item	Year	Expected Cash Flows	Present Value of $1 @ 16%	Present Value of Cash Flows
Investment in machine	Current	$(80,000)	1.0000	$(80,000)
Additional working capital	Current	(30,000)	1.0000	(30,000)
Operating net cash flows	1	25,600	.8621	22,070
	2	29,440	.7432	21,880
	3	25,344	.6407	16,238
	4	22,886	.5523	12,640
	5	22,886	.4761	10,896
	6	21,043	.4104	8,636
	7	19,200	.3538	6,793
	8	19,200	.3050	5,856
Sale of machine less tax ($10,000 × .6)	8	6,000	.3050	1,830
Recovery of working capital	8	30,000	.3050	9,150
Net present value (NPV)				$ 5,989

we wanted to compute the IRR for the project, we could use the trial and error method discussed earlier.

Note that in Figure 9-4 the investments in the machine and working capital are in current dollars. Thus, they already represent present values. The other cash flows occur after the investment is made, so they must be discounted using the 16% rate from the year of their occurrence to make them comparable to the cost of the investments. The annual net cash flows from operations found in Figure 9-4 are discounted with the appropriate factors representing the present value of $1 at 16% (Table A-3).

The estimated selling price of the machine at the end of the eighth year will produce a net cash inflow of $6,000 after the tax of $4,000 ($10,000 × .40) is paid. The $6,000 is discounted to current dollars by multiplying it times the present value factor of .3050. Finally, the recovery of the working capital must be recognized, but it will not be worth the full $30,000 in current dollars since the firm must wait 8 years before the funds can be used for another project. Thus, the $30,000 is discounted with the eight-year present value factor of .3050 to arrive at the current value of $9,150. The discounted cash outflows are $110,000 (all in current dollars) and the discounted cash inflows total $115,989, thereby resulting in the NPV of $5,989.

OTHER CAPITAL BUDGETING METHODS— DEPARTURES FROM TIME VALUE OF MONEY

The two discounted cash flow techniques discussed earlier (net present value and internal rate of return) are the most accurate capital budgeting methods because they are based on the time value of money. However, the business world uses several other less theoretically sound capital budgeting methods. Some managers prefer these other methods because: (1) they are simpler and

(2) they may be sufficiently accurate since any method is subject to uncertainties of the future that may adversely affect the estimates being used. We will now examine two of the most popular alternative methods: payback period and average rate of return.

PAYBACK PERIOD METHOD

Objective 10: Computing the payback period

The **payback period** is the length of time required to recover the cost of an investment from the net cash flows it generates; that is, the period of time needed for an investment to pay for itself. The payback period is simple to compute and easy to understand. Generally, it is desirable to use the shortest possible payback period because:

1. The sooner the cash is recovered, the sooner it can be reinvested in other productive assets, which is particularly important in times of high inflation.
2. A quick payback period may reduce the risk of the investment since uncertainty usually increases with the passage of time.

The primary disadvantages of this method are that it ignores the total life of the investment and the time value of money. An investment selected because of its short payback period may, therefore, be less profitable over its entire life than an alternative investment with a longer payback period and longer total life. Managers may use this method to maximize short-term profits and make themselves look good, even though the long-term results are detrimental to the business. In addition, cash flows in later years are assumed to be equivalent to those in early years—a serious violation of the time value of money concept. Nevertheless, many firms use the method to make a final choice among alternatives when other methods of evaluation indicate they are equally attractive.

Whenever the annual cash flows from an investment are equal each year, the following formula can be used to compute the payback period:

$$\text{Payback period} = \frac{\text{Initial cost of investment}}{\text{Annual net cash flows}}$$

To see how this formula is applied, let's assume that the Ditto Computer Services Company is evaluating which of two computer systems to buy to provide certain data processing services for its clients. A minicomputer can be purchased for $40,000, and the firm estimates that its annual net cash flows (cash collected from services performed less the cash operating expenses incurred to perform the services) will be $8,000. Alternatively, a microcomputer that has a more limited use can be acquired at a cost of $9,000 and should produce annual net cash flows of $3,000 from client services. The payback periods for the two computers are:

$$\text{Minicomputer:} \quad \frac{\$40,000}{\$8,000} = 5 \text{ years}$$

$$\text{Microcomputer:} \quad \frac{\$9,000}{\$3,000} = 3 \text{ years}$$

Note that the payback formula is the same as the one we used earlier to determine the annuity factor for the internal rate of return. The payback concept is an easy way to remember this important step in computing the IRR.

Impact of Uneven Net Cash Flows

When the annual net cash flows are not the same each year, the payback period calculation must be modified. For example, assume that the Ditto Computer Services Company is considering another small specialized computer system that is expected to generate increasing net cash flows from year to year. The cost of the equipment is $12,000, and the net cash flows forecast for the future are as follows:

Year	Annual Net Cash Flows	Cumulative Net Cash Flows
1	$ 800	$ 800
2	1,200	2,000
3	3,600	5,600
4	6,400	12,000
5	7,600	19,600
6	7,800	27,400
7	8,000	35,400
8	8,200	43,600

To find the payback period, we must determine when the cumulative net cash flows equal the equipment's initial cost of $12,000. This will happen after the fourth year, so the payback period is four years. We can take the same approach when uneven annual net cash flows result from the use of accelerated depreciation, a situation discussed earlier with discounted cash flows. However, it should be emphasized again that a weakness of the payback period method is that it ignores the time value of money by assuming that $1 of net cash flows from the first year is worth the same amount as $1 of net cash flows from a later year.

Use of Payback Reciprocal Method

A useful extension of the payback period method in some capital budgeting decisions is the **payback reciprocal method**. Whenever the life of an investment is significantly longer than the related payback period and annual net cash flows are relatively even, it can be shown mathematically that the payback reciprocal (1/payback period) will be a reasonably close approximation of the investment's internal rate of return (IRR). For example, the payback reciprocals for the minicomputer and the microcomputer in the Ditto Computer Services Company case discussed earlier are:

$$\text{Minicomputer: Payback reciprocal} = \frac{1}{\text{Payback period}} = \frac{1}{5} = 20\%$$

$$\text{Microcomputer: Payback reciprocal} = \frac{1}{\text{Payback period}} = \frac{1}{3} = 33.3\%$$

We would then compare the expected life of each asset with the payback period to determine how valid the payback reciprocal is as an estimate of the related internal rate of return. If the expected life is more than twice as long as the payback period, the approximation should be reasonably accurate.

In all cases, the payback reciprocal is higher than the internal rate of return, but the difference between the two decreases as the difference between the payback period and the useful life of the investment increases.

To illustrate the relationship of the payback reciprocal to the internal rate of return, assume that the minicomputer in the Ditto Computer Services Company case has an expected useful life of 15 years. The internal rate of return can be determined from Table A-4 in Appendix A using a factor of 5.0000 ($40,000/$8,000) and the 15-year row. We can see from Table A-4 that the internal rate of return is between 18% and 19% (5.0916 versus 4.8759). With interpolation (as defined earlier), we can find the internal rate of return of 18.42%, which is close to the payback reciprocal of 20%. As a general rule, many businesses choose investments with relatively short payback periods (e.g., three to five years) of no more than one half of their expected useful lives, thereby obtaining high rates of return.

AVERAGE RATE OF RETURN METHOD

**Objective 11:
Use of the
average rate of
return method**

The **average rate of return method** (also called the simple rate of return method or accounting rate of return method) is a rough approximation of an investment's profitability over its life as measured with accrual accounting rather than cash flows. It is calculated as:

$$\frac{\text{Average annual net income after tax from an investment}}{\text{Average amount of the investment}}$$

Alternatively, the average rate of return sometimes is based on the initial investment involved. The alternative approach will result in a rate of return that is significantly lower than it is with the average investment because the initial investment, or denominator of the fraction above, is always higher than the average investment. When straight-line depreciation is used, the book value of an asset decreases uniformly over its life. As a result, the average investment is computed as:

$$\text{Average investment} = \frac{\text{Initial investment} + \text{Residual value}}{2}$$

When the residual value is zero, the average investment is simply the amount of the initial investment divided by two. To illustrate the average rate of return method, assume that a firm is evaluating whether to purchase a machine with which a new product can be produced. The machine costs $162,000 and is expected to have a residual value of $18,000 at the end of its expected life of 10 years. The company estimates that the new product will increase its annual net income by $21,600 after all expenses, including straight-line depreciation, are deducted from the sales revenue that is forecast.

The depreciation considered with the average rate of return method is the amount included on the income statement, not the tax return, since we are basing the analysis on accrual net income rather than cash flows. The average investment is $90,000 [($162,000 + $18,000)/2], and the average rate of return from the investment is:

$$\text{Average rate of return} = \frac{\text{Average net income}}{\text{Average investment}} = \frac{\$21,600}{\$90,000} = 24\%$$

The 24% return would be compared with the returns of alternative investments and with the minimum return required by management to determine whether it should be accepted.

The proponents of the average rate of return method support it on the premise that it follows the income statement in measuring the return on an investment. Opponents of the method, however, criticize it for the income statement orientation. They base this argument on the fact that accountants tend to expense items on the income statement very quickly but some of these items, such as research and development costs and sales promotional expenses, should actually be part of the investment base involved. Thus, the investment base can be seriously understated.

Unlike the payback period method, the average rate of return method does consider the profitability of an investment over its useful life. However, its most serious weakness is that it does not consider the time value of money. That is, the use of average net income ignores the timing of cash receipts and cash disbursements. Consequently, the net cash flow from an investment's last year of life is valued the same as that of its first year.

SUMMARY

Capital budgeting decisions involve the planning and selection of capital expenditures such as the construction of a building, replacement of equipment, introduction of a new product line, and expansion of production facilities. As such, capital budgeting decisions establish the long-term operating capacity of a business. These decisions are important because (1) they involve large sums of money and often determine the success or failure of a firm, (2) they commit resources for a long period of time, (3) they cannot be reversed easily, and (4) they may have significant risk.

Managers use a number of capital budgeting methods to consider the amount of investment required and the rate of return expected from the investment. Examples are the net present value (NPV) method, internal rate of return (IRR) method, payback period method, and average rate of return method. They can choose between these capital budgeting methods to evaluate and rank the various alternative investments available so the resources of the business are allocated profitably.

Cash flows are used to evaluate the return from an investment in most capital budgeting methods because of the time value of money. The analysis involves a cash outlay made currently or in the future to obtain net cash flows from the investment in future years. A conversion of an accrual based income statement is necessary to determine the related cash flows. For example, depreciation is not included in the cash flow analysis because it does not require a cash outlay when it is recorded. However, the impact of depreciation on after-tax cash flows must be considered.

The NPV method and the IRR method are two important capital budgeting techniques based on the application of the time value of money. When the NPV method is used, the cost of an investment is compared with the discounted future net cash flows, which are discounted with the firm's required rate of return. If the NPV is positive, the actual rate of return from the investment is greater than the discount rate being applied and the investment is attractive because its benefits exceed the related cost. A profitability index can be computed for the ranking of investments by dividing the present value of the net cash flows by the amount of investment required.

The second discounted cash flow method is called the internal rate of return, which is defined as the discount rate that will make the discounted cash inflows from an investment equal to its discounted cash outflows. This method is used to find the actual rate of return that will be earned over the life of an investment. Since the discounted cash inflows are equal to the discounted cash outflows with the internal rate of return, the NPV is zero.

Although depreciation is not included as a cash outflow in a capital budgeting decision, it must be considered because of its impact on income taxes. The depreciation method considered is the one used for tax purposes because we are using cash flows, not financial reporting net income. Since depreciation is a tax shield, it will affect the amount of taxes paid and consequently the cash outflows.

When an increase in working capital is needed to support a capital budgeting project, that amount must be considered as a current cash outflow needed for the investment. If the working capital is expected to be released at the end of the project, the present value of the amount recovered should be factored into the analysis of discounted cash flows.

Two other capital budgeting methods, which are of limited value because they are not based on the time value of money, are the payback period method and the average rate of return method. The payback period is the length of time required to recover the cost of an investment from the net cash flows it generates. The average rate of return method is a rough measure of an investment's profitability over its life as measured by accrual accounting instead of cash flows. The method is easy to apply and understand because it follows the income statement over the total expected life of the investment.

GLOSSARY

ACCELERATED COST RECOVERY SYSTEM (ACRS). A form of accelerated depreciation used to depreciate assets purchased after 1980 for federal income tax purposes (p.329).

ANNUITY. A series of equal payments over a specified number of time periods, with a particular interest rate included in the payments (p.318).

AVERAGE RATE OF RETURN METHOD. A capital budgeting method that provides a rough approximation of an investment's profitability as measured with net income from the income statement (p.336).

CAPITAL BUDGETING. The process used to evaluate capital expenditures (p.315).

CLASS LIFE ASSET DEPRECIATION RANGE (ADR) SYSTEM. A listing in the tax law of different types of assets with a range of lives for each type. (p.329).

COST OF CAPITAL (HURDLE RATE). A firm's cost of obtaining funds in the form of debt and owners' equity, which represents the firm's minimal rate of return from an investment that is acceptable to management (p.320).

DISCOUNTED CASH FLOWS. Use of present values to convert the cash inflows and cash outflows from an investment to equivalent or current dollars (p.319).

DISCOUNTING. Applying a discount rate to convert future values to present values (p.318).

DISCOUNT RATE. The rate used to convert future values to present values (p.318).

HURDLE RATE. Another term used for the cost of capital or the minimal rate of return required from an investment (p.320).

INTERNAL RATE OF RETURN (IRR) METHOD. The use of a discount rate that will exactly equate the discounted cash outflows from an investment with its discounted cash inflows, thus making the net present value zero (p.324).

INTERPOLATION. A mathematical technique used to compute an interest or discount rate bracketed by two known rates (p. 326).

NET PRESENT VALUE (NPV) METHOD. A capital budgeting method used to evaluate the discounted cash flows associated with an investment (p.319).

PAYBACK PERIOD METHOD. A capital budgeting method used to determine the length of time required to recover the cost of an investment from the net cash flows it generates (p.334).

PAYBACK RECIPROCAL METHOD. A capital budgeting method based on the inverse of the payback period that provides a reasonably close approximation of the internal rate of return when the life of an investment is significantly longer than its payback period and the net cash flows from the investment are relatively equal each year (p.335).

PRESENT VALUE. The current value of some future sum of money or series of payments, discounted with a specific discount rate (p.318).

PROFITABILITY INDEX. The present value of the net cash flows from an investment divided by its cost (p.322).

TAX SHIELD. A tax deductible item, such as depreciation, which shields income that otherwise would be taxed (p.330).

TIME VALUE OF MONEY. Money held at an early date such as today is more valuable than the same amount of money available at a later date because of the interest that can be earned on the money over time (p.318).

DISCUSSION QUESTIONS

1. Define capital budgeting. How does it relate to a master budget?
2. Why is capital budgeting such an important management responsibility?
3. What are the major characteristics of capital budgeting decisions?
4. Explain why a capital budgeting method is a type of decision model.
5. Differentiate between the use of a cash-flow approach and a noncash-flow approach to capital budgeting.
6. What are the most common cash inflows considered in a capital budgeting decision? The most common cash outflows?
7. How is working capital accounted for in a capital budgeting application? Since cash, accounts receivable, and inventory are classified as current assets, how can they be considered as "long-term assets" in capital budgeting decisions?
8. What is the basic objective of any capital budgeting method?
9. What is meant by the "time value of money?" Why is this concept important for capital budgeting?
10. Distinguish between the future value of money and the present value of money. Which of the two are most important in capital budgeting? Why?
11. Is the amount of cash flow or the timing of cash flow most important in determining net present value? Explain.
12. You recently overheard a prominent manager say, "The only important thing for our firm in making a capital budgeting decision is how long it takes to get the money back." Do you agree with this policy? Explain.
13. What is meant by the term "discounting" and why is it important in capital budgeting?

14. Define the net present value method. Is the net present value always positive in a capital budgeting decision?
15. What is the basic purpose of the net present value method?
16. How do we handle even net cash flows while applying the net present value method? What changes are required when the net cash flows are uneven from year to year?
17. How is a firm's cost of capital computed and used in capital budgeting?
18. If a firm has to pay 12% to borrow money at the bank, its cost of capital must be 12%. Do you agree? Explain.
19. What is a profitability index? How is it used in capital budgeting?
20. Explain how assets with different lives are considered in the application of the net present value method.
21. Define the internal rate of return. How is it different from the net present value?
22. What is the basic problem involved with calculating the internal rate of return with uneven net cash flows?
23. What are the two limiting assumptions with the two discounted cash flow methods?
24. Why are the results with the net present value method often in conflict with those from the internal rate of return method?
25. If the net present value of an investment is zero, does this mean that no profit will be earned from the investment?
26. It has been said that "the problem with discounted cash flow methods of capital budgeting is that they ignore depreciation expense." Do you agree? Explain.
27. Is an accelerated depreciation method or a nonaccelerated depreciation method preferred in capital budgeting?
28. What is meant by a tax shield? How does it affect a capital budgeting decision?
29. "Discounting future cash flows at 16% provides a higher net present value than discounting them at 14%." Do you agree? Why?
30. What is the payback period method of capital budgeting? Identify its major weaknesses.
31. What is the payback reciprocal and how can it be used in capital budgeting?
32. Explain the basic purpose of the average rate of return method and relate it to a typical income statement. What are the method's major limitations?

EXERCISES

Exercise 9-1 Basics of Present Value Analysis

The Monroe Company wants to evaluate a possible investment in a machine used for manufacturing. The asset has a useful life of four years. The company's cost of capital is 10%. The data below are representative of the asset being considered.

Year	Expected Net Cash Flows	Present Value of $1 at 10%
1	$50,000	.9091
2	50,000	.8264
3	50,000	.7513
4	50,000	?

Required:
A.   Calculate the present value of the asset's expected net cash flows.
B.   What is the maximum amount the company would pay for the machine?

Exercise 9-2   Basic Present Value Calculations

The Spencer Company is considering the acquisition of a new asset. The asset is expected to generate $60,000 per year over its five-year useful life. The asset is expected to require an investment of $200,288. Spencer estimates that its cost of capital is 12%.

Year	Expected Net Cash Flows	Present Value of $1 at 12%
1	$60,000	.8929
2	60,000	.7972
3	60,000	?
4	60,000	?
5	60,000	?

Required:
Using the information above, calculate the present value of the net cash flows from the asset.

Exercise 9-3   Calculating the Net Present Value

The Cougar Manufacturing Company is presently trying to decide if a proposed investment of $200,000 is financially attractive. The company's cost of capital is 12%. Assume that the company expects the investment to generate net cash flows of $70,000 for each year of its five-year useful life.

Required:
Calculate the net present value of the investment.

Exercise 9-4   Computing the Net Present Value for an Investment

The Greg Wilson Company is trying to decide whether or not to invest in a new operating division. This new division is expected to generate $125,000 in net cash flows during each of the next six years. At that time, the division would be discontinued with no residual value.

Required:
The new division is priced at $527,000, and the company wants to earn a minimum return on investment of 12%. Should the company invest in it? Why or why not?

Exercise 9-5   Using the Net Present Value Method

The following data pertain to an investment opportunity of a corporation located in the Midwest:

1.   Initial cost of investment: $140,165
2.   Expected net cash flows:

Year	Amount
1	$30,000
2	40,000
3	50,000
4	50,000
5	50,000
6	60,000

3.   Firm's cost of capital: 14%

Required:
Using the net present value method, determine whether the corporation should accept the investment.

Exercise 9-6 Use of a Profitability Index
Compute the profitability indices for Exercises 9-2 through 9-5 above. If one and only one of the four investments can be funded, which one would you choose? Explain.

Exercise 9-7 Computing the Cost of Capital
The Deal Company wants to determine its cost of capital to use in capital budgeting decisions. The firm's capital structure is as follows:

Source of Capital	Amount
Debt financing	$ 40,000
Preferred stock	20,000
Common equity	140,000

The firm's president has determined that the after-tax costs of the three financing sources are 8%, 12%, and 18%, respectively.

Required:
Compute the firm's cost of capital.

Exercise 9-8 Basics of the Internal Rate of Return Method
If an investment should generate annual net cash flows of $120,000 for four years, and will cost $364,476, what is the internal rate of return factor for this investment? To what internal rate of return does this factor correspond?

Exercise 9-9 Interpolation and IRR
A particular investment being considered by the Baldwin Company is priced at $159,000. It is expected to produce $52,000 in annual net cash flows over its four-year life. What is the internal rate of return of the investment?

Exercise 9-10 Comparing NPV with IRR

	Project A	Project B
Initial cost	$20,000	$20,000
Expected life	3 years	3 years
Net cash flows:		
Year 1	$9,494.42	–0–
Year 2	9,494.42	–0–
Year 3	9,494.42	$33,704.08

The firm's cost of capital is 17%.

Required:
Compute the net present value and internal rate of return for each project. Which project should be accepted first? Explain.

Exercise 9-11 Comparing NPV with IRR
A company must decide between two projects, A and B. The following data pertain to each project. You are to decide which project should be accepted. The company's cost of capital is 12%.

Project A: Initial cost	$100,000	
Expected life	4 years	
Net cash flows:		
Year 1	$36,453.78	
Year 2	36,453.78	
Year 3	36,453.78	
Year 4	36,453.78	
Project B: Initial cost	$100,000	
Expected life	4 years	
Net cash flows:		
Year 1	-0-	
Year 2	-0-	
Year 3	-0-	
Year 4	$174,886.32	

Required:

A. Evaluate each project with the NPV method.

B. Evaluate each project with the IRR method.

Exercise 9-12 Evaluating Relationships Between NPV and IRR

Given below are four independent cases in which the life of each investment is 10 years, with no residual value.

Case	Initial Investment Cost	Annual Net Cash Flows	Cost of Capital	Internal Rate of Return	Net Present Value
1	—	$ 70,000	12%	16%	—
2	$193,328	—	—	16%	$32,680
3	282,510	—	10%	—	24,720
4	—	100,000	—	16%	(64,070)

Required:

Fill in the blanks based on the relationships between the initial cost of the investment, the annual net cash flows, the cost of capital, the internal rate of return, and the net present value.

Exercise 9-13 Evaluating Depreciation as a Tax Shield

The controller of the Jill Company, a new company just beginning operations, is trying to evaluate the after-tax effect of depreciation on the firm's cash flows. The company has recently purchased depreciable assets costing $200,000, with no residual value at the end of a 10-year life. Assume that the firm has two options for the annual rates of depreciation, shown as follows:

Year	Option 1	Option 2
1	.15	.10
2	.22	.10
3	.21	.10
4	.21	.10
5	.21	.10
6	—	.10
7	—	.10
8	—	.10
9	—	.10
10	—	.10

The firm expects to have to pay income taxes each year with either option at a tax rate of 35%. It has a cost of capital of 12%.

Required:
Compute the discounted tax savings with each option.

Exercise 9-14   Use of Capital Budgeting Methods
The Lunar Company is evaluating the purchase of a new machine that will cost $33,540 and have no residual value. Annual net cash flows (including tax payments) for each of the next 10 years are expected to be $8,000. The related annual net income is expected to be $4,696, and depreciation is computed for financial reporting purposes on a straight-line basis. The company has a cost of capital of 12%.

Required:
A.   Compute the payback period.
B.   Compute the net present value.
C.   Compute the internal rate of return.
D.   Compute the return on average investment.

Exercise 9-15   Use of Discounted Cash Flows and Payback Period
The Kopel Company is considering the purchase of a new machine, which will cost $70,000 and which will be paid for in cash. The machine has a useful life of seven years with no residual value. Annual before-tax cash savings from better productivity are expected to be $18,000. The company has a cost of capital of 12% and an income tax rate of 35%. For tax purposes, the machine will be depreciated over five years with the 200% declining balance method (modified ACRS).

Required:
A.   Determine the annual after-tax cash savings from the machine.
B.   What is the payback period for the investment?
C.   What is the net present value of the investment?

Exercise 9-16   Computing the Payback Period
Compute the payback period for the following investments:

	Investment			
	1	**2**	**3**	**4**
Initial cost	$10,000	$50,000	$ 75,000	$60,000
Expected life (in years)	3	4	5	8
Total net cash flows over the life of the investment	$12,000	$80,000	$125,000	$96,000

The firm's cost of capital is 12%.

Exercise 9-17   Use of the Payback Period Method
Compute the payback period for the following investment with an initial cost of $56,000:

Year	Annual Net Cash Flows
1	$ –0–
2	15,000
3	25,750
4	15,250

5	23,940
6	57,060

Exercise 9-18 Use of the Payback Reciprocal Method

Using the payback reciprocal method, calculate the estimated internal rate of return for the investments shown below:

	Investment		
	1	**2**	**3**
Initial cost	$27,000	$512,000	$642,000
Expected life	12 years	20 years	18 years
Annual net cash flows	$ 9,000	$ 51,200	$ 80,250

Exercise 9-19 Use of the Average Rate of Return Method

Calculate the average rate of return from the following investment opportunities. If the firm desires a 15% minimum return, which investment should be chosen?

	1	**2**
Initial investment	$114,000	$137,000
Residual value	12,000	8,000
Average annual after-tax net income	11,340	8,700

Exercise 9-20 Capital Budgeting Evaluations

The Davis Company is evaluating three investment alternatives and has compiled the following information:

	Investment		
	A	**B**	**C**
Initial investment	$91,276	$151,632	$83,946
Net cash inflows:			
Year 1	20,000	40,000	30,000
2	20,000	40,000	30,000
3	20,000	40,000	30,000
4	20,000	40,000	30,000
5	20,000	40,000	—
6	20,000	—	—
7	20,000	—	—

The company requires a 12% minimum return on new investment.

Required:
A. Calculate the payback period for each investment.
B. Calculate the net present value for each investment.
C. Determine the profitability index for each investment.
D. Calculate the internal rate of return for each investment.

PROBLEMS

Problem 9-1 Basics of Cost of Capital

The Holmes Company is attempting to decide whether to invest in a new asset. The Holmes Company's after-tax cost of debt, preferred stock, and common equity are 10%, 12%, and 16%, respectively. The firm's capital structure consists of the following:

Debt	$ 60,000
Preferred stock	10,000
Common equity	130,000
Total capital	$200,000

Required:
Determine the Holmes Company's cost of capital.

Problem 9-2 Computing Net Present Value

Assume the following about the asset being considered in Problem 9-1:

Initial cost	$172,200
Annual net cash flows:	
Year 1	$ -0-
2	75,000
3	77,450
4	40,300
5	35,500
6	29,500

Required:
A. Calculate the net present value of the asset.
B. Should the company invest in the asset? Why or why not?

Problem 9-3 Use of NPV Method

The Shatter Company must decide on one investment from the two alternatives being considered. Using the data below and the net present value method, which investment would you recommend? Explain.

	Investment	
	A	**B**
Initial cost	$210,000	$229,854
Annual net cash flows:		
Year 1	110,000	110,000
2	90,000	100,000
3	80,000	90,000
4	70,000	80,000
Cost of capital	15%	15%

Problem 9-4 Use of NPV Method with Unequal Lives

The Eva Marie Company has two investments to choose from. The first investment has an initial cost of $300,000 and is expected to generate $80,000 in annual net cash flows over its entire five-year life. At the end of its useful life, another machine costing $900,000 with a 10-year expected life, generating the same yearly cash flows would have to be purchased. The alternative investment has an initial cost of $200,000, net annual cash flows of $60,000, and is expected to last 15 years. Assume a 17% cost of capital.

Required:
A. Using the net present value method, which investment is most attractive?
B. What assumptions must be made about your choice?

Problem 9-5 Use of NPV Method

The Shell Company has purchased a new asset that cost $280,000 with a five-year life. The residual value, net of tax, is estimated to be $10,000. The machine purchased will have to be overhauled after the fourth year at a cost of $40,000. Annual net cash flows are:

Year	
1	$ 70,000
2	80,000
3	90,000
4	100,000
5	110,000

Assume a 13% cost of capital for the company.

Required:
Calculate the NPV of this investment.

Problem 9-6 Computing the IRR

Compute the internal rate of return for each of the following independent situations and state which should be accepted:

Situation	Initial Cost	Annual Net Cash Flows	Cost of Capital	Useful Life
1	$1,899,094	$ 580,000	13%	5 years
2	3,571,346	820,000	12%	6 years
3	6,428,000	1,347,137	16%	9 years
4	1,147,055	182,000	16%	14 years

Problem 9-7 Interpolating to Find the IRR

The Florence Agnes Company is considering a new investment. Management has determined that every investment must yield at least 14.5% to be acceptable. If the investment being evaluated generates annual net cash flows of $60,000 and has an initial cost of $205,800, should Florence Agnes purchase the investment, which has a five-year useful life? Use the internal rate of return method.

Problem 9-8 Evaluating Depreciation as a Tax Shield

The Junction Company owns an asset that cost $425,000, has an expected residual value of $20,000, and has an estimated life of 10 years. The asset qualifies as a five-year asset for tax purposes. The Junction Company's cost of capital is 12%. What are the tax savings of the depreciation expense (in present dollars)? Use a 40% tax rate.

Problem 9-9 Capital Budgeting Evaluations

The Payton Company is considering a project that would require the purchase of a new machine at a cost of $59,812. The new machine would have a five-year life and no residual value at the end of its life. The new project would produce a net cash flow of $20,000 each year. The company has a cost of capital of 12%.

Required:
A. What is the payback period for the machine?
B. Calculate the net present value of the machine.
C. Determine the internal rate of return for the machine.

Problem 9-10 Using Alternative Capital Budgeting Methods

The president of the Bennett Company is evaluating three investment projects. The net cash flows for each project are estimated as follows:

	Investment Project		
Year	1	2	3
1	$ 90,000	$ 60,000	$ 50,000
2	90,000	60,000	50,000
3	90,000	60,000	50,000
4	—	60,000	50,000
5	—	60,000	50,000
6	—	—	50,000
7	—	—	50,000
8	—	—	50,000
Initial cost	216,162	227,448	217,180

The firm's cost of capital is 12%.

Required:
A. Compute the payback period for each investment.
B. What is the net present value for each investment?
C. What is the profitability index for each investment?
D. Calculate the internal rate of return for each investment.

Problem 9-11 Use of Capital Budgeting Methods

The Rush Company is considering three investments for the upcoming year. The firm has a cost of capital of 16%. Summary information concerning the net cash flows of the investments and their initial costs is shown here.

	Investment		
Year	A	B	C
1	$ 70,000	$ 50,000	$ 30,000
2	70,000	50,000	30,000
3	70,000	50,000	30,000
4	70,000	50,000	30,000
5	—	50,000	30,000
6	—	50,000	30,000
7	—	—	30,000
8	—	—	30,000
9	—	—	30,000
10	—	—	30,000
11	—	—	30,000
12	—	—	30,000
Initial cost	181,209	205,570	155,913

Required:
A. Calculate the payback period for each investment.
B. What is the net present value for each investment?
C. What is the profitability index for each investment?
D. Compute the internal rate of return for each investment.

Problem 9-12 Estimating and Calculating the IRR (Uneven Net Cash Flows)

Rex Windel, a CPA, has purchased personal computer software that is to be used primarily in his consulting business. The software is expected to be useful for seven years, after which it will be obsolete with no residual value. Mr. Windel paid $8,225 for the software and related operating manual. He has prepared the following estimates:

Year	Annual Net Cash Flows
1	$1,265
2	2,025
3	2,175
4	2,760
5	3,600
6	3,000
7	1,200

Required:
A. Using the payback period reciprocal method, estimate the internal rate of return for the software.
B. Compute the exact internal rate of return (to two decimal places).
C. Is your estimate in part A reasonable?
D. Was the software purchase a profitable choice?

Problem 9-13 Evaluating a Capital Budgeting Decision

The Compute-it Company operates a computer service bureau that provides data-processing services to the business community. The firm is currently considering the purchase of a new specialized computer that will cost $110,000 and have no residual value at the end of its five-year life. The straight line depreciation method is used for tax purposes and for financial reporting. The firm's accountant expects the revenues and expenses associated with operating the computer to be about equal to cash receipts and cash disbursements, except for depreciation. The projected operating performance is summarized as:

Year	Revenue	Expenses (Excluding Depreciation)
1	$ 86,450	$58,000
2	96,000	61,500
3	102,250	61,500
4	108,500	61,500
5	114,750	61,500

The company's expected tax rate is 20%, and its cost of capital is 12%. Income taxes are not included in the expenses shown.

Required:
A. Compute the average rate of return for the computer.
B. Determine the annual net cash flows (after tax) expected from the operation of the computer.
C. Calculate the net present value for the investment.
D. Determine the profitability index for the investment.

Problem 9-14 Evaluating Capital Budgeting Decisions

The I.M. Trucking Company must replace some obsolete equipment. Three alternative investments are available. The net cash flows for each alternative are given below. No residual values are expected for any of the replacements. The firm's estimated cost of capital is 17%.

Year	Alternative A	Alternative B	Alternative C
1	$100,000	$150,000	$140,000
2	100,000	150,000	140,000
3	100,000	150,000	140,000
4	100,000	150,000	140,000
5	100,000	150,000	140,000
6	—	150,000	140,000
7	—	—	140,000
8	—	—	140,000
Initial investment	300,000	600,000	700,000
Annual net income	40,000	50,000	53,000

Required:
Rank the three investments using:

1. Net present value method
2. Internal rate of return method (use approximate amounts)
3. Payback period method
4. Payback reciprocal method
5. Average rate of return method (assume straight-line depreciation)

Problem 9-15 Evaluating Capital Budgeting Decisions

The POWR Company is in the process of evaluating three different investment possibilities. The firm's cost of capital is 15%. Each alternative requires an initial cash outlay of $70,000 and has a useful life of seven years. The net cash flows involved are as follows:

Year	Alternative X	Alternative Y	Alternative Z
1	$27,250	$10,000	$25,000
2	33,750	20,000	25,000
3	9,000	30,000	20,000
4	8,000	10,000	15,000
5	7,000	(5,000)	10,000
6	6,000	20,000	5,000
7	5,000	30,000	2,500

Required:
A. Rank the alternatives using:
   1. Net present value
   2. Payback period
   3. Payback reciprocal
B. True or False: Investment Y is the best because it provides the greatest amount of net cash flow.

Problem 9-16 Evaluating a Capital Budgeting Decision

Deere Electronics is an engineering consulting firm specializing in the installation of highly sophisticated electronic communications systems. The company is considering the purchase of testing equipment that would be used on jobs. The equipment would cost $132,000 and would have no residual value at the end of its five-year life. Straight-line depreciation would be used for financial reporting and for tax purposes if the equipment is purchased. The firm's accountant projects revenues and expenses with the operation of the equipment that are equal to the cash receipts and cash disbursements associated with it, except for depreciation. A summary of the cash flows expected from the equipment (without considering taxes) is as follows:

Year	Revenue	Expenses (Excluding Depreciation)
1	$103,740	$69,600
2	115,200	73,800
3	122,700	73,800
4	130,200	73,800
5	137,700	73,800

The firm's expected tax rate is 20%, and its cost of capital is 12%.

Required
A. Compute the average rate of return for the equipment.
B. Determine the annual net cash flows (after tax) expected from the operation of the equipment.
C. Calculate the net present value for the investment.
D. Determine the profitability index for the investment.

Problem 9-17 Capital Budgeting Analysis (CMA)

Yipann Corporation is reviewing an investment proposal. The initial cost as well as the estimate of the book value of the investment at the end of each year, the net after-tax cash flows for each year, and the net income for each year are presented in the schedule below. All cash flows are assumed to take place at the end of the year. The residual value of the investment at the end of each year is equal to its book value. There would be no residual value at the end of the investment's life.

Investment Proposal

Year	Initial Cost and Book Value	Annual Net After-Tax Cash Flows	Annual Net Income
0	$105,000		
1	70,000	$50,000	$15,000
2	42,000	45,000	17,000
3	21,000	40,000	19,000
4	7,000	35,000	21,000
5	0	30,000	23,000

Yipann uses a 24% after-tax target rate of return for new investment proposals. The discount figures for a 24% rate of return are as follows:

Year	Present Value of $1 Received at the End of Period	Present Value of an Annuity of $1 Received at the End of Each Period
1	.81	.81
2	.65	1.46
3	.52	1.98
4	.42	2.40
5	.34	2.74
6	.28	3.02
7	.22	3.24

Required:
Select the best answer to the following:

1. The payback period for the investment proposal is:
   a. .875 years
   b. 1.993 years
   c. 2.250 years
   d. Over five years
   e. Some period other than those given above

2. The accounting rate of return for the investment proposal over its life using the initial value of the investment is:
   a. 36.2%
   b. 18.1%
   c. 28.1%
   d. 38.1%
   e. Some percentage other than those given above

3. The net present value for the investment proposal is:
   a. $4,600
   b. $10,450
   c. $(55,280)
   d. $115,450
   e. Some amount other than those given above

4. The payback reciprocal is often used as an approximation of an investment proposal's internal rate of return. Which one of the following is the correct reason for not being able to use the payback reciprocal to approximate the internal rate of return for this investment proposal?
   a. The life of an investment proposal must be at least twice the payback period
   b. The life of an investment proposal must be at least 10 years
   c. The net after-tax cash flows must be constant over the life of the investment
   d. Only straight-line depreciation can be employed when determining the net after-tax cash flows
   e. The profitability index must be greater than one

5. When there are two mutually exclusive investments, management should select the project:
   a. That generates cash flows for the longer period of time
   b. Whose net after-tax flows exceed the initial investment
   c. That has the greater accounting rate of return
   d. Whose cash flows vary less
   e. That has the greater profitability index

Problem 9-18 Use of the NPV Method (CMA)

Wyle Co. is considering a proposal to acquire new manufacturing equipment. The new equipment has the same capacity as the current equipment but will provide operating efficiencies in direct and indirect labor, direct materials usage, indirect supplies, and power. Consequently, the savings in operating costs are estimated at $150,000 annually for six years.

The new equipment will cost $300,000 and will be purchased at the beginning of the year when the project is started. The equipment dealer is certain that the equipment will be operational during the second quarter of the year it is installed. Therefore, 60% of the estimated annual savings can be obtained in the first year. Wyle will incur a one-time expense of $30,000 to transfer the production activities from the old equipment to the new equipment. No loss of sales will occur, however, because the plant is large enough to install the new equipment without interfering with the operations of the current equipment. The equipment dealer states that most companies use a five-year life when depreciating this equipment for tax purposes.

The current equipment has been fully depreciated and is carried in the accounts at zero book value. Management has reviewed the condition of the current equipment and has concluded that it can be used an additional five years. Wyle Co. would receive $5,000 net of removal costs if it elected to buy the new equipment and dispose of its current equipment at this time.

The company uses the 200% declining balance depreciation method (modified ACRS). A half year's depreciation is taken in the first year the asset is put into use.

The company is subject to a 40% income tax rate and requires an after-tax return of at least 12% on any investment.

Required:
A. Calculate the annual incremental after-tax cash flows for Wyle Co.'s proposal to acquire the new manufacturing equipment.
B. Calculate the net present value of Wyle Co.'s proposal to acquire the new manufacturing equipment using the cash flows calculated in requirement A and indicate what action Wyle Co.'s management should take. For ease in calculation, assume all recurring cash flows take place at the end of the year. Use the following present value tables:

Discount Factors

Period	Present Value of $1 Received at the End of the Period		Present Value of an Annuity of $1 Received at the End of each Period	
	12%	20%	12%	20%
1	.89	.83	.89	.83
2	.80	.69	1.69	1.52
3	.71	.58	2.40	2.10
4	.64	.48	3.04	2.58
5	.57	.40	3.61	2.98
6	.51	.33	4.11	3.33

Problem 9-19 Use of Capital Budgeting Methods (CMA)

Hazman Company plans to replace an old piece of equipment which is obsolete and is expected to be unreliable under the stress of daily operations. The equipment is fully depreciated, and no residual value can be realized upon its disposal.

One piece of equipment being considered would provide annual cash savings of $7,000 before income taxes. The equipment would cost $18,000 and have an estimated useful life of five years. No residual value would be used for depreciation purposes because the equipment is expected to have no value at the end of five years.

Assume that Hazman uses the straight-line depreciation method on all equipment for both book and tax purposes. The company is subject to a 40% tax rate. Hazman has an after-tax cost of capital of 14%.

Required:
A. Calculate for Hazman Company's proposed investment in new equipment the after-tax:

1. Payback period
2. Average rate of return
3. Net present value
4. Profitability index
5. Internal rate of return

Assume all operating revenues and expenses occur at the end of the year. Appropriate discount tables are presented below.

B. Identify and discuss the issues Hazman Company should consider when deciding which of the five decision models identified in requirement A it should employ to compare and evaluate alternative capital investment projects.

Present Value of $1 Received at the End of Period

Period	8%	10%	12%	14%	16%	18%	20%	22%	24%
1	.93	.91	.89	.88	.86	.85	.83	.82	.81
2	.86	.83	.80	.77	.74	.72	.69	.67	.65
3	.79	.75	.71	.67	.64	.61	.58	.55	.52
4	.73	.68	.64	.59	.55	.52	.48	.45	.42
5	.68	.62	.57	.52	.48	.44	.40	.37	.34

Present Value of an Annuity of $1 Received at the End of Each Period

Period	8%	10%	12%	14%	16%	18%	20%	22%	24%
1	.93	.91	.89	.88	.86	.85	.83	.82	.81
2	1.79	1.74	1.69	1.65	1.60	1.57	1.52	1.49	1.46
3	2.58	2.49	2.40	2.32	2.24	2.18	2.10	2.04	1.98
4	3.31	3.17	3.04	2.91	2.79	2.70	2.58	2.49	2.40
5	3.99	3.79	3.61	3.43	3.27	3.14	2.98	2.86	2.74

Problem 9-20 **Extensions of NPV Method (CMA)**

The WRL Company makes cookies for its chain of snack food stores. On January 2, 1984, WRL Company purchased a special cookie cutting machine; this machine has been utilized for three years. WRL Company is considering the purchase of a newer, more efficient machine. If purchased, the new machine would be acquired on January 2, 1987. WRL Company expects to sell 300,000 dozen cookies in each of the next four years. The selling price of the cookies is expected to average $.50 per dozen.

WRL Company has two options: (1) continue to operate the old machine; or (2) sell the old machine and purchase the new machine. No trade-in was offered by the seller of the new machine. The following information has been assembled to help decide which option is more desirable:

	Old Machine	New Machine
Original cost of machine at acquisition	$80,000	$120,000
Residual value at the end of useful life for depreciation purposes	10,000	20,000
Useful life from date of acquisition	7 years	4 years
Expected annual cash operating expenses:		
Variable cost per dozen	$.20	$.14
Total fixed costs	15,000	14,000
Assumed depreciation method	Straight-line	Straight-line
Estimated cash value of machines:		
January 2, 1987	$40,000	$120,000
December 31, 1990	7,000	20,000

WRL Company is subject to an overall income tax rate of 40%. Assume that all operating revenues and expenses occur at the end of the year. Assume that any gain or loss on the sale of machinery is treated as an ordinary tax item and will affect the taxes paid by WRL Company at the end of the year in which it occurred.

Required:

A. Use the net present value method to determine whether WRL Company should retain the old machine or acquire the new machine. WRL requires an after-tax return of 16%.

Discount Factors for 16% (Rounded)

Period	Present Value of $1	Present Value of an Annuity of $1 Per Period — Received at the End of the Period
1	.86	.86
2	.74	1.60
3	.64	2.24
4	.55	2.79

B. Identify and discuss the advantages and disadvantages of using discounted cash flow techniques (e.g., the net present value method) for capital investment decisions.

USE OF MANAGERIAL ACCOUNTING FOR DECISION MAKING WITH A CONTROL FOCUS

10

STANDARD COSTS: DIRECT MATERIALS AND DIRECT LABOR

CHAPTER OVERVIEW AND OBJECTIVES

This chapter discusses standard costs for direct materials and direct labor. After studying this chapter, you should be able to:

1. Recognize why standard costs are used by a manufacturing firm.
2. List the benefits and limitations of standard costs.
3. Describe the different ways standard costs are developed.
4. Distinguish between ideal standards and attainable standards.
5. Explain how price and quantity standards are developed for direct materials.
6. Explain how rate and efficiency standards are developed for direct labor.
7. Identify the basic steps taken in cost variance analysis.
8. Develop a general model for direct cost variance analysis.
9. Compute cost variances for direct materials and direct labor.
10. Identify potential causes of direct manufacturing cost variances and the managers responsible for them.
11. Determine what is a significant cost variance.
12. Analyze cost performance with a control chart.
13. Prepare journal entries to record a standard cost performance.

INTRODUCTION TO STANDARD COSTS

Standard costs are carefully predetermined costs that are used as performance targets for an efficient manufacturing operation. They are analogous to performance targets used as a basis for measuring the level of achievement in other aspects of our lives. Examples are a B+ academic performance for scholastic recognition, a .300 batting average for a major league baseball player, a recipe used by a restaurant to prepare a pizza, and the engineering specifications followed in the production of a microcomputer.

In order to plan and control a manufacturing cost performance with acceptable profit results, managers need to know not only what costs have been but also what they should be before products are produced. Standard costs for direct materials, direct labor, and manufacturing overhead provide the most effective way to define what costs should be. These standard costs define both the prices that should be paid for each of the resource inputs (manufacturing cost elements) and the quantities of the inputs that should be used. To achieve profit goals, managers are expected to pay the lowest possible prices, consistent with the quality level of the products involved, for the resource inputs. In addition, managers are responsible for an efficient utilization of the resource inputs in producing products according to well-defined engineering specifications. Standard costs provide the information needed by the managers to accomplish these two important functions.

The application of standard costs to direct materials and direct labor is described in this chapter, followed by the use of standard costs with manufacturing overhead in Chapter 11. Although our primary concern in this chapter is with standard costs in manufacturing firms, we should also be aware that these costs are used in a wide range of other businesses such as hospitals, restaurants, accounting firms, banks, and automobile service centers. In practice, standard costing is potentially applicable whenever the activities of a business are repetitive.

LIMITATIONS OF HISTORICAL COSTS AND NEED FOR STANDARD COSTS

Chapters 3 and 4 demonstrated how a cost accumulation system can be used to determine the actual costs of producing a product. This information furnishes management with a detailed record of the manufacturing costs that are incurred in the performance of a job or the operation of a processing center. The cost data are also used in the inventory valuation and income determination aspects of financial reporting. However, these results have serious limitations concerning the measurement of the efficiency of the manufacturing operation. Management planning must be founded on reliable projections of an efficient utilization of resources. Management control begins with a comparison of actual results with those planned and ends with corrective or adaptive action, as we saw in the discussion of budgeting.

Objective 1: Need for standard costs

Historical or actual cost data are of limited value because they represent what happened, which is not necessarily what should have happened. Consequently, it is difficult to determine a reliable performance base with historical cost data. Are costs too high? If so, who is responsible? How can these costs be reduced? Are the costs representative of the future? These typical questions are difficult to answer with historical cost data.

Efficiency evaluations with actual costs only are limited to historical comparisons such as unit costs from month to month and to management's judgment about what costs should be. The problem with the monthly comparisons is that there is no guarantee that the operation was efficient to begin with. Thus, it may be meaningless to compare the costs of one period with those of another period. In addition, difficulties will be encountered in assessing the impact of changes in such factors as the volume of production, wage rates, product quality levels, productivity, raw materials prices, and the cost of manufacturing overhead items. Management judgment about what costs should be is hindered by the same limitations.

The basic objective with standard costing is to establish a standard cost for each unit of product (output) by predetermining the cost per unit of the direct materials, direct labor, and manufacturing overhead (inputs) required to produce it. Thus, standard costing is often referred to as input/output analysis. Both the dollar amounts to be paid for the manufacturing cost elements and the quantity of each that should be used are identified. As such, a standard cost has two components: (1) a **price standard** component based on such measures as dollars per pound or wage rate per hour and (2) a **quantity standard** component expressed in terms of input measures such as pounds or hours per unit of output.

BENEFITS OF STANDARD COSTS

Objective 2: Benefits and limitations of standard costs

As we study standard costs, we must keep in mind that they do not replace actual costs. Instead, actual and standard costs complement each other because the combination of the two provides comparative information with which managers can determine when and why an actual cost performance is significantly different from the one planned. The following are the most important benefits of standard costs:

1. **Planning in budgeting.** Standard costs provide reliable estimates for the planning phase of budgeting. We noted in Chapter 8 that accurate projections for direct materials, direct labor, and manufacturing overhead are necessary to perform effective budgeting. Since standard costs are carefully predetermined, they provide the best basis for estimating future cost performance. Consequently, standard costs contribute significantly to the planning function of management.

2. **Performance evaluation.** Standard costs serve as targets in the application of management by exception to evaluate performance and to control manufacturing costs. The standard costs represent measures of what costs should be, so any variances between them and the actual costs incurred can be investigated for potential corrective action. Cost control does not necessarily mean minimizing costs, but it does mean keeping them within acceptable limits. Responsible managers receive periodic reports that reveal any significant variances through management by exception. Thus, both the cause of the variance and the type of managerial response needed can be determined.

3. **Recordkeeping cost savings.** Standard costs can be used for inventory valuation with cost savings in the recordkeeping function. Inventories are maintained on the basis of standard costs without the detailed accounting of the actual costs needed in an actual costing system. Since standard costs are predetermined costs, they are used to record the materials, labor, and manufacturing overhead as production takes place. For example, materials requisition forms and labor time tickets can be standardized and completed in advance of production rather than being prepared as production takes place. A reconciliation of the actual costs is made at the end of an

accounting period with variance analysis, thus eliminating much of the detailed accounting work and clerical cost incurred during the period.

4. **Managerial decision making.** Standard cost information is available on a timely basis for managerial decision making. In Chapter 7, we observed that a significant amount of relevant cost information must be available for managers to make correct decisions about the future. Managers must make decisions regularly concerning such activities as product pricing, make/buy situations, product profitability analysis, departmental performance evaluation, and the utilization of resources. In many cases, standard costs can be used without waiting for the results of the actual performance.

5. **Cost awareness.** Standard costs make employees more aware of costs and their impact on the operation. Most employees are not trained accountants and are more concerned with operating results than with the costs associated with them. Since the standard costs represent what costs should be, they make the employees more cost- and time-conscious, thus promoting an efficient use of resources. An incentive wage system, tied in with standard costs, can be implemented to further increase the benefits from cost awareness. For example, a bonus may be offered to employees who perform their work within the standard amount of time allowed.

LIMITATIONS OF STANDARD COSTS

The limitations of standard costs also should be understood so they can be minimized and kept in proper perspective. Otherwise, these limitations may negate many of the benefits of standard costs and create behavioral problems in an organization. The most significant limitations encountered in the use of standard costs are the following:

1. Many standards are founded on judgment rather than fact and, as a result, are subject to human error. If the plan is faulty to begin with, future comparisons of actual and standard performance are meaningless.

2. Standards that are either too tight or too loose can lead to unsatisfactory behavior on the part of the employees involved. If the standards are too tight, the employees will either (1) be frustrated and look for ways to "beat the system" or (2) simply ignore the standards as unattainable performance targets. In contrast, standards that are too loose will encourage underachievement on the part of the workers and will not provide any incentive for improvement.

3. Standard costs must be reviewed constantly to determine if revision is warranted. This requires valuable management time to obtain and evaluate information concerning external or internal changes that may have occurred and affected the current standard costs. For example, price changes in an inflationary economy frequently make materials price standards and labor wage standards obsolete, thus requiring constant managerial attention.

4. The use of management by exception can create frustrations on the part of responsible managers. They may feel that an excessive amount of concern is directed toward the problems of the business without adequate recognition of the positive aspects of the performance. In turn, the morale of the workers involved may be adversely affected by the perception that they are informed of bad performance but are not praised for satisfactory results.

ESTABLISHING STANDARD COSTS

Objective 3:
Establishing
standard costs

As we noted earlier, standard costs are made up of a standard unit price and a standard input quantity. The standard direct materials cost consists of a standard price per unit of material multiplied by the standard number of units to be used. The standard direct labor cost is composed of a standard labor rate per hour multiplied by the standard number of hours required. (Remember that we will consider standard costing for manufacturing overhead in the next chapter.) For example, the production of one finished product may require three gallons of direct materials at a price of $6 per gallon. The standard direct materials cost would be $18 per finished unit. The same product may call for two hours of direct labor at $8 per hour, for a standard labor cost of $16. Consequently, the standard direct manufacturing costs (direct materials and direct labor) for the product would be $34 ($18 + $16).

Product specifications must be considered carefully when standard costs are established to ensure that desired quality levels are maintained for the finished products. The product specifications usually are established by engineers at the same time they design the products. Once established, the product specifications dictate certain quality requirements for the resource inputs needed, which in turn are translated into unit prices and quantities for the standard costs used.

METHODS FOR ESTABLISHING STANDARDS

Management usually establishes standard costs in conjunction with the product specifications through the use of one or a combination of the following three methods:

1. **Engineering approach.** Time studies, work sampling, learning curves, and synthesizing procedures are examples of engineering techniques that can be used to develop standards. Their major purpose is to determine economical quantities of materials and labor on a scientific basis. For example, a time study may be performed to determine the best combination of labor steps needed for a particular job.
2. **Analysis of historical performance data.** Even though historical cost data may have the deficiencies discussed earlier, they should not be ignored. The most recent past, in particular, can provide valuable insights into what to expect in the future. For example, the direct labor hours required to produce last year's products should be evaluated carefully in establishing this year's standards.
3. **Management judgment concerning the future.** The managers responsible for the various personnel, production, and purchasing activities are the persons closest to the day-to-day operations, so their opinions and knowledge must be considered in identifying the costs that should be incurred. This is particularly important whenever external influences (such as union negotiations for wage rates and market conditions for materials prices) are involved. In many businesses, a cost standards committee is formed to coordinate the development and revision of standard costs.

CHOICE OF EXPECTED PERFORMANCE LEVEL FOR STANDARDS

Objective 4:
Ideal versus at-
tainable stan-
dards

Management must also decide what type of standards the firm will use. The choice between ideal standards and attainable standards depends on how demanding management wants the planned performance level to be. **Ideal stan-**

dards require the highest possible amount of effort if they are to be achieved. Consequently, they represent maximum efficiency and do not include allowances for factors such as waste, spoilage, fatigue, purchases based on urgency or supplier loyalty, work interruptions, and human error. Few businesses use ideal standards, even if they are based on sound engineering results, because they (1) will produce significant variances from all but the very best performances and (2) may discourage average or above average workers from even trying to achieve such high standards.

Attainable standards are preferred because they represent targets that can be achieved with a reasonably efficient effort. As such, they are difficult but possible to attain and include allowances for departures from maximum efficiency. Once the standards are established, they should be reviewed regularly and revised whenever necessary to coincide with internal changes (such as new production methods) and external changes (such as direct materials market conditions). A change in the number of direct labor hours required to produce a product often is necessary because a business and its union agree to restrictions on the pace of the work performance.

DEVELOPING STANDARDS FOR DIRECT MANUFACTURING COSTS

To illustrate how standards are developed for the direct manufacturing costs, let's consider the use of standard costing in the Carolina Boat Building Company. The firm produces a fiberglass sailboat hull that is sold to marinas throughout the Southeast. The sail, mast, and all hardware are purchased by the marinas from other suppliers and assembled after the hulls have been delivered. The end product is a small fiberglass sailboat that can be transported on the top of an automobile. The Carolina Boat Building Company operates a single production department for the mixing and molding processes needed to manufacture a sailboat hull.

Production of the hulls requires a great deal of skill and accuracy so that the fiberglass ingredients are mixed and molded correctly. If one or more steps in the production process are incorrect, the hull being worked on must be scrapped and will have no salvage value.

The company has been experiencing cost problems in the hull manufacturing process, which have caused significant operating losses for the company during the last two years. The firm's controller decided to install a standard cost system, so the cost problems can be identified and corrected. The firm will only use *attainable standards* in the new system. The monthly production target for the firm's production department is 1,000 hulls. In Chapter 11, we will continue this illustration by considering standard costs for manufacturing overhead in the same company.

DIRECT MATERIALS STANDARDS

A direct materials price standard should represent the delivered cost of the materials required, net of any discounts involved. Carolina Boat Building Company must purchase the highest quality fiberglass ingredients because of the structural specifications of its sailboat hulls. Two types of materials — fiberglass fabric and fiberglass mix — are required. After evaluating bids submitted from several suppliers, it has been determined that the following price standards

Objective 5:
Developing standard costs for direct materials

should be established for the two raw materials:

Fiberglass fabric
Purchase price per square foot	$.75
Transportation cost	.02
Receiving and handling cost	.22
Purchase discount	(.09)
Standard price per square foot	$.90

Fiberglass mix
Purchase price per pound	$1.00
Transportation cost	.05
Receiving and handling cost	.30
Purchase discount	(.15)
Standard price per pound	$1.20

After considering all costs and discounts associated with the purchases of the two raw materials, the firm plans to spend $.90 per square foot for the fiberglass fabric and $1.20 per pound for the fiberglass mix.

The next step is determining the quantities of each of the raw materials required to produce a sailboat hull. Since the company is using attainable standards, an allowance must be made for waste and rejects based on what is normal for a reasonably efficient operation, as shown below:

Fiberglass fabric
Square feet needed for each hull per engineering specifications	130
Plus allowance for normal waste and defective units (square feet)	10
Standard quantity for each hull (square feet)	140

Fiberglass mix
Pounds for each hull per engineering specifications	45
Plus allowance for normal waste and defective units (pounds)	5
Standard quantity for each hull (pounds)	50

Thus, the firm is planning to use 140 square feet of fiberglass fabric and 50 pounds of fiberglass mix to produce each sailboat hull. By combining the price and quantity standards determined above, standard direct materials cost of $186 for each hull is computed as follows:

Fiberglass fabric — 140 square feet @ $.90 per foot =	$126
Fiberglass mix — 50 pounds @ $1.20 per pound =	60
Standard direct materials cost per hull	$186

DIRECT LABOR STANDARDS

Objective 6: Developing standard costs for direct labor

The standard direct labor wage rate usually consists of the direct compensation paid in the form of wages plus an allowance for payroll taxes and fringe benefits (such as vacation time, insurance, and retirement plan contributions). This approach is taken in the Carolina Boat Building Company case to develop the standard direct labor rates shown next for the production department:

Wage rate per hour	$ 8.00
Plus allowance for payroll taxes and fringe benefits	2.00
Standard labor rate per hour	$10.00

Note that a single labor rate is used for the department even though different workers may earn different wages because of seniority and skill levels. Alternatively, a standard labor rate could be established for each separate wage classification, but the additional recordkeeping required usually is not justified. Management of the company is most concerned with the average use of the labor rates. Thus, the comparison of the average standard rate as shown above with the average actual rate enables management to evaluate how efficiently the labor is being scheduled. (See also the later discussion of the labor rate variance.)

The quantity component of the labor standard is an efficiency measure concerning the number of labor hours required to produce one fiberglass hull. Industrial engineering procedures may be used to separate the various manual activities needed during the production process. The total time required to produce a unit could be broken down into more than one measure of the standard time allowed. For illustrative purposes, we will assume that a single measure of the time required to produce a hull has been determined and has been adjusted for a normal amount of idle time as follows:

Direct labor hours needed per hull	4.6
Plus allowance for idle time (in hours)	.4
Standard direct labor hours per hull	5.0

Consequently, the firm expects to use 5 standard direct labor hours to produce one hull, and the standard direct labor cost per hull is $50 (5 hours × $10). If everything happens according to plan, the direct manufacturing costs incurred to produce a hull should be $236 ($186 for direct materials and $50 for labor). Remember that these standards should be revised anytime a significant change affecting them occurs.

STANDARD COST VARIANCES: DIRECT MATERIALS AND DIRECT LABOR

BASIC CONCERN FOR VARIANCES

Standard cost variances arise when actual costs are different from standard costs. These cost variances enable managers to evaluate the efficiency of the manufacturing operation and to improve the cost performance whenever possible. Standard cost variance analysis is used (1) to calculate the amount of any difference between actual and standard costs and (2) to determine the cause of the deviation.

To accomplish both of these steps, however, we need more detailed information than a comparison of the actual total costs and the standard total costs. For example, it would not be very meaningful to only know that the actual total manufacturing costs for a month were $550,000 when the total standard costs should have been $495,000. We need more complete information than

Objective 7: Basics of cost variance analysis

total results to assist us in deciding how to reduce the total variance in the future. Standard cost variance analysis provides this valuable information by considering five basic questions:

1. **When did the variance occur?** A good standard cost system should identify a variance as soon as it arises.
2. **Where did the variance occur?** A good standard cost system should identify the segment of the organization in which the variance occurred.
3. **Why did the variance occur?** A good standard cost system should identify the specific cause of the variance so management can decide what to do about it.
4. **Who is responsible for the variance?** Some variances will be predetermined as the responsibility of a specific manager, whereas others must be evaluated after being identified to determine who is accountable.
5. **What can be done about the variance?** Once we have answers to the first four questions, we can decide what should be done. Whenever possible, corrective action should be taken to improve the future performance. If we discover that the standard itself was wrong, adaptive action should be taken to change the plan for the future.

IDENTIFYING STANDARD COST VARIANCES

Standard costs can be used for analytical purposes only or can be incorporated into the formal accounting system. When they are used only for analytical purposes, standard cost variances are shown on management performance reports used to control manufacturing costs. As such, they are not recorded in the general ledger, and the recordkeeping savings benefits of standard costs are not available.

The more complete treatment in identifying standard cost variances is to establish cost variance accounts that are used to accumulate any differences between the actual and standard cost performance in the general ledger. When the cost variances are recognized in the general ledger, the costs charged to inventories (and ultimately to cost of goods sold) are standard costs rather than the actual costs incurred. An unfavorable cost variance will have a debit balance since it is, in essence, an *added cost*. In contrast, a favorable variance will have a credit balance because it represents a *reduced cost*. Standard cost variances will be recorded in general ledger accounts in our discussion of variance analysis since this is the most complete approach to the subject of standard costing.

GENERAL MODEL FOR DIRECT MANUFACTURING COST VARIANCE ANALYSIS

Objective 8:
Use of a general model for direct cost variance analysis

In Chapter 1, we described efficiency as an economical relationship between a firm's resource inputs and its outputs of products. Standard cost variance analysis is a form of input/output analysis because it shows how efficiently inputs are converted into outputs. The three production inputs required to produce outputs in the form of finished products are direct materials, direct labor, and manufacturing overhead.

In the Carolina Boat Building Company illustration introduced earlier, the production inputs needed to produce one sailboat hull as a unit of output are fiberglass fabric (140 square feet @ $.90 each), fiberglass mix (50 pounds @ $1.20 each), and direct labor (5 hours @ $10 each). Remember that two standards are established for each of the direct manufacturing costs: (1) The first standard is the *price* that should be paid for a production input and (2) the second standard is the *quantity* of a production input that should be used to produce one unit of output.

If the actual price paid for a production input differs from the standard price, the difference is called a **materials price variance** for direct materials and a **labor rate variance** for direct labor. When the actual quantity of input used for a given amount of output is different from the **standard quantity allowed** for that output, the result is called a **materials quantity variance** or **usage variance** for direct materials and a **labor efficiency variance** or **usage variance** for direct labor. Thus, the two types of variances possible for each of the direct manufacturing costs relate back to the two types of standards established originally for them.

The algebraic sum of the materials price variance and the materials quantity variance equals the total materials variance, that is, the difference between the actual materials cost and the standard materials cost. Likewise, the algebraic sum of the labor rate variance and the labor efficiency variance equals the total labor variance, that is, the difference between the actual labor cost and the standard labor cost. Breaking the total variance for each of the direct manufacturing costs into these two components is necessary if we want to use variance analysis for *cost control* and *performance evaluation* by answering the five questions discussed earlier.

Another important reason for the division is that the direct materials usually are purchased and used at *different points in time* and, as we saw earlier, an important objective of variance analysis is to identify a variance as soon as it arises. For control purposes, a materials price variance should be recognized when the related materials are purchased and the actual price is known. A materials quantity variance, on the other hand, will ideally be identified when the materials are used for production, possibly weeks or months after the purchase. In many process costing situations, it even may be necessary to wait until the end of the accounting period in which the work is performed to compute the materials quantity variance because the output for the period is not known until then.

We will see in the next section that standard cost variances for the two direct manufacturing costs can be calculated with the general variance analysis model shown as Figure 10-1 in a columnar format. Developing the general model requires a comparison of three calculations: (1) actual quantity of input times actual price; (2) actual quantity of input times standard price; and (3) standard quantity of input allowed for the output produced times standard price. We should develop a basic understanding of the general model shown in Figure 10-1 before we refine it for application to direct materials or direct labor.

In Figure 10-1, column (1) consists of the actual cost incurred for either direct materials or direct labor since we insert the actual quantity of input multiplied by the actual price paid for each of the units of input. Column (3) represents the standard costs that should have been incurred for the units of output produced. Here, the standard quantity of input allowed for the output achieved is multiplied times the standard price of each unit of input. The difference between columns (1) and (3) is the total standard cost variance, that is, the devia-

Figure 10-1
General Model for
Direct Manufacturing Cost Variance
Analysis

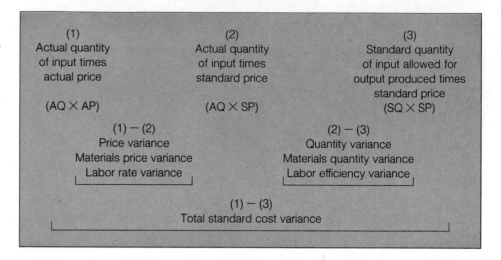

tion between the actual costs incurred and the standard costs that should have been necessary for the output produced.

This total variance is divided into its price and quantity components by inserting column (2), the product of the actual quantity of input multiplied by the standard price that should have been paid for each input. Basically, variance analysis considers each source of variance independently, while holding any other source constant. We know that the total variance consists of a price component and a quantity component. By comparing columns (1) and (2) in the general model, we are using actual quantity in both calculations and allowing only price to vary between actual and standard. Thus, the difference between the two columns is a price variance for the actual quantity involved.

In contrast, the standard price is used in both columns (2) and (3). However, the quantity shown in column (2) is the actual amount, whereas the quantity included in column (3) is the **standard quantity allowed** for the output achieved. As a result, the quantity is varied between actual and standard so the difference between columns (2) and (3) is a quantity variance costed at the standard price that should have been incurred. The algebraic sum of the price variance and the quantity variance is the total standard cost variance.

We will illustrate the use of this general model as we consider the four types of variances possible for the direct manufacturing costs—materials price variance, materials quantity variance, labor rate variance, and labor efficiency variance—in relation to the Carolina Boat Building Company. Assume that during March the firm produced 950 sailboat hulls and incurred the following actual costs:

Purchased and used 138,000 square feet of fiberglass fabric @ $.96 per square foot	$132,480
Purchased and used 49,000 pounds of fiberglass mix @ $1.10 per pound	53,900
Recorded 4,950 actual direct labor hours @ an average cost of $10.20 an hour (including payroll taxes and fringe benefits)	50,490
Total actual direct manufacturing costs	$236,870

Next, the sources of the difference between the total actual direct manufacturing costs of $236,870 and the standard direct manufacturing costs that should have been incurred must be identified. Earlier, we established standard direct manufacturing costs of $236 for one sailboat hull, so the total standard direct manufacturing costs for the 950 hulls produced should have been $224,200 (950 hulls × $236). Consequently, the firm incurred an unfavorable total variance of $12,670 ($236,870 less $224,200) for the direct manufacturing costs during March. We can evaluate each of the four variances possible to determine the sources of the unfavorable total cost variance of $12,670.

DIRECT MATERIALS VARIANCE ANALYSIS

MATERIALS PRICE VARIANCE

Any differences between the actual direct materials cost and the standard direct materials cost can be explained by a combination of a materials price variance and a materials quantity variance. A **materials price variance** is the result of purchasing an actual quantity of materials at an actual price that is different from the standard price. This variance is used to:

Objective 9: Computing cost variances

1. Control the cost of direct materials,
2. Evaluate the performance of the purchasing function, and
3. Measure the effect of price increases or decreases on the firm's profit results.

If the two are different, the materials price variance should be computed for the actual quantity purchased instead of the actual quantity used because: (1) the point of purchase will precede usage, and the time delay that can result from waiting until usage to recognize a price variance may eliminate the possibility of corrective action and (2) identifying a price variance at the time of purchase enables a firm to record increases and decreases to the raw materials inventory account at standard prices. The result is significant savings in the recordkeeping function. We should note, however, that some firms wait until the direct materials are utilized to recognize the materials price variance because prices do not change much from period to period. The only difference in the calculation of the materials price variance in such cases is that the actual quantity of direct materials requisitioned to production is used instead of the actual quantity purchased.

The general model presented in Figure 10-1 must be adjusted when the materials price variance is recognized at the point of purchase and the quantity purchased is not equal to the quantity issued to production during the period. The adjustment would be accomplished by using different actual quantities of input for the materials price variance and the materials quantity variance. The actual quantity purchased is used for the price variance, whereas the actual quantity requisitioned is used for the quantity variance, shown as follows:

General Model Column	Computation	Variance
Column 1—Actual quantity of input purchased × Actual price Column 2—Actual quantity of input purchased × Standard price		Materials Price Variance
Column 2—Actual quantity of input used × Standard price Column 3—Standard quantity of input allowed × Standard price		Materials Quantity Variance

Thus, the only adjustment to the general model is the distinction between the amount of materials purchased and those used in the production operation (column 2).

The person who is usually responsible for the materials price variance is the manager responsible for the purchasing function, often called the purchasing agent. Typical causes of a materials price variance include:

Objective 10: Potential causes of cost variances

1. A wrong selection of quantity size that affects the planned purchases discount
2. An incorrect choice of quality
3. A rush order purchase requiring higher than normal transportation charges
4. The use of the wrong supplier
5. Price changes in the marketplace
6. An outdated standard price

The calculation of the materials price variances for the Carolina Boat Building Company are shown in Figure 10-2. Note that the production inputs of the

Figure 10-2

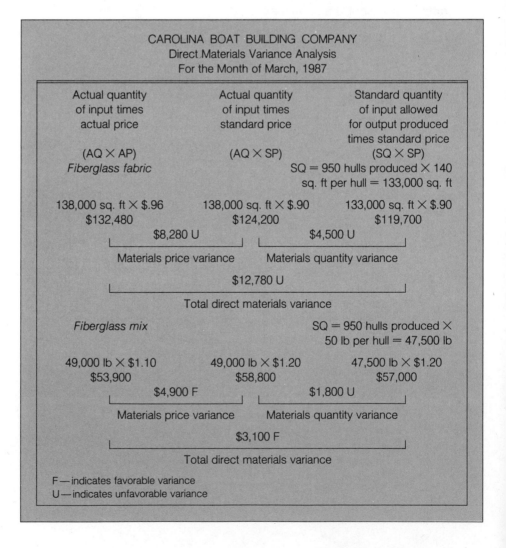

CAROLINA BOAT BUILDING COMPANY
Direct Materials Variance Analysis
For the Month of March, 1987

general variance analysis model are expressed as square feet and pounds for fiberglass fabric and fiberglass mix, respectively. We can reduce the calculations involved with the materials price variance from those of the general model to a more simplified form as follows:

General model: $(AQ \times AP) - (AQ \times SP) =$ Materials price variance
Simplified calculation: $AQ (AP - SP) =$ Materials price variance

Using the simplified calculation for the materials price variances incurred by the Carolina Boat Building Company, we get the same answers as those shown in Figure 10-2, or:

Fiberglass fabric
Materials price variance
$= AQ (AP - SP)$
$= 138,000$ sq. ft $(\$.96 - \$.90)$
$= 138,000$ sq. ft $(\$.06)$
$= \$8,280$ Unfavorable

Fiberglass mix
Materials price variance
$= 49,000$ lb $(\$1.10 - \$1.20)$
$= 49,000$ lb $(\$.10)$
$= \$4,900$ Favorable

The simplified calculation is used to prepare the performance report shown in Figure 10-3. The report is prepared periodically for the manager of the Carolina Boat Building Company's purchasing department to evaluate and explain any materials price variances. In this case, we assume that, upon investigation, management discovered that the variances were caused by an *urgent order* and by the purchase of *lower quality* materials than those planned (as a result, at a lower cost).

An unfavorable materials price variance was incurred for fiberglass fabric because $.96 per pound was paid instead of the standard price of $.90. The $.06 difference multiplied by the 138,000 square feet purchased equals the unfavor-

Figure 10-3

CAROLINA BOAT BUILDING COMPANY						
Purchasing Department Performance Report						
For the Month of March, 1987						
	(1)	(2)	(3)	(4) (2) − (3)	(5) (1) × (4)	
Type of materials	Amount purchased	Actual price	Standard price	Difference in price	Price variance	Explanation
Fiberglass fabric	138,000 sq. ft	$ .96	$ .90	$.06	$8,280 U	Urgent purchase-stock out
Fiberglass mix	49,000 lb	$1.10	$1.20	($.10)	$4,900 F	Tried lower quality materials
F—indicates favorable variance						
U—indicates unfavorable variance						

able variance of $8,280. In contrast, a favorable materials price variance of $4,900 resulted from purchasing fiberglass mix. The difference between the actual price and the standard price was $.10 ($1.10 versus $1.20). The $.10 difference multiplied times the 49,000 pounds purchased equals the favorable price variance of $4,900.

Materials Price Variance — Quantity Purchased Different from Quantity Used in Production

To illustrate the calculation of the materials price variance when the quantity of materials purchased and the amount requisitioned to production are not equal, consider the following change in the facts above. Assume that the Carolina Boat Building Company purchased 148,000 square feet of fiberglass fabric at $.96 per square foot during March but only used 138,000 square feet. The computation of the materials price variance for fiberglass fabric would be as follows:

$$\text{Materials price variance} = AQ\,(AP - SP)$$
$$= 148{,}000 \text{ sq. ft } (\$.96 - \$.90)$$
$$= 148{,}000 \text{ sq. ft } (\$.06)$$
$$= \$8{,}880 \text{ Unfavorable}$$

In this revised case, the unfavorable materials price variance for the fiberglass fabric is $8,880, which is $600 higher than the same variance when only 138,000 square feet were purchased. The 10,000 square feet of fiberglass fabric that were purchased but not used (148,000 − 138,000) can be multiplied by the $.06 difference between the actual price and the standard price ($.96 − $.90 = $.06) to determine the additional unfavorable materials price variance. The 10,000 square feet of fiberglass fabric that were purchased but not used will be left in raw materials inventory at the end of March. The difference between the quantity purchased and the quantity used will not affect the calculation of the materials quantity variance, which is always based on the amount of materials requisitioned to production.

MATERIALS QUANTITY VARIANCE

The materials quantity variances for fiberglass fabric and fiberglass mix also are shown in Figure 10-2. A **materials quantity variance** results from using an actual amount of direct materials that is different than the standard quantity allowed for the products produced.

The starting point for the calculation of the materials quantity variance is the conversion of the actual units of output produced to the standard quantity of materials allowed for that level of production. *We do this by multiplying the actual units produced by the standard amount of direct materials that should be used to produce one unit.* The difference between the actual materials used and the standard amount allowed costed at the standard price is the materials quantity variance. Again, we can reduce the calculations for the materials quantity variance from those of the general model as follows:

General model: $(AQ \times SP) - (SQ \times SP) = $ Materials quantity variance

Simplified calculation: $SP\,(AQ - SQ) = $ Materials quantity variance

For the Carolina Boat Building Company, the application of the simplified version of the materials quantity variance is as follows:

Fiberglass fabric
Materials quantity variance = SP (AQ − SQ)
$$= \$.90 \ (138,000 \text{ sq. ft} - 133,000 \text{ sq. ft})$$
$$= \$.90 \ (5,000 \text{ sq. ft})$$
$$= \$4,500 \text{ Unfavorable}$$

Fiberglass mix
Materials quantity variance = $1.20 (49,000 lb − 47,500 lb)
$$= \$1.20 \ (1,500 \text{ lb})$$
$$= \$1,800 \text{ Unfavorable}$$

When the simplified calculation is used, the standard price is multiplied by the difference between actual quantity and standard quantity, thus holding the price constant and considering only the effect of a quantity change. As we see, the simplified calculation produces the same unfavorable materials quantity variances of $4,500 and $1,800 for fiberglass fabric and fiberglass mix, respectively, as those shown in Figure 10-2.

The materials quantity variance provides a measure of a production department's *efficiency in utilizing direct materials.* Normally, it is the responsibility of the manager in charge of the related manufacturing activity. Common causes of materials quantity variances include:

1. Materials with an inferior quality
2. Inexperienced labor
3. Inadequate supervision
4. Faulty equipment
5. An exceptionally good work performance
6. Undetected defective materials
7. Mistakes made during the production process
8. Outdated standards

Note that there can be an important interrelationship between a materials price variance and a materials quantity variance. For example, a firm may purchase materials with a lower quality than called for in the standard, thus incurring a favorable price variance. If an excessive amount of waste results from the inferior materials, an unfavorable materials quantity variance occurs even if the production workers are efficient in their handling of the materials. Consequently, the cause of the materials quantity variance is *uncontrollable* for the production operation in such cases and must be traced back to the purchasing function for corrective action.

Carolina Boat Building Company produced 950 hulls during March with standard quantities of 140 square feet per hull and 50 pounds per hull for fiberglass fabric and fiberglass mix, respectively. As a result, the standard quantity allowed for fiberglass fabric is 133,000 square feet (950 hulls × 140 square feet) and the standard quantity allowed for fiberglass mix is 47,500 pounds (950 hulls × 50 pounds). The actual usage of fiberglass fabric was 138,000 square feet, so an unfavorable materials quantity variance of $4,500 resulted [(138,000 − 133,000) × $.90], as shown in Figure 10-2.

Remember that we apply the standard price to compute a quantity variance because we want to hold constant any price effect. An unfavorable materials quantity variance also is calculated for fiberglass mix because 49,000 pounds actually were used compared with the standard quantity of 47,500 pounds. The difference of 1,500 pounds multiplied by the standard price of $1.20 equals the unfavorable variance of $1,800. A performance report such as the one shown in Figure 10-4 is prepared monthly to inform the manager of the company's production department about the materials quantity variances.

DIRECT LABOR VARIANCE ANALYSIS

LABOR RATE VARIANCE

A difference between the actual direct labor cost and the standard direct labor cost can be divided into a labor rate variance and a labor efficiency variance. A **labor rate variance** occurs for the actual labor hours worked when the actual labor rate is different than the standard rate expected. In many cases, standard labor rates are determined through a collective bargaining agreement with a union according to employees' experience, skills, and seniority. In other situations, the rates are established by the personnel department in conjunction with information provided by top management. Consequently, the responsibility for a labor rate variance must be assigned carefully since it may not be controllable by the manager who supervises the work activities.

The manager in charge of the production performance is accountable for scheduling workers with the correct wage rates to specific jobs. If an employee earning a wage rate different from the standard rate specified is assigned to a job, a labor rate variance that is controllable by the related manager will arise. For example, a highly skilled worker may be assigned to a task requiring less skill and a lower labor rate. The result will be an unfavorable labor rate variance, which may be offset somewhat by a favorable labor efficiency variance if the work is performed faster than the standard labor hours allowed. This trade-off is particularly beneficial when an excessive amount of highly skilled labor is available and would otherwise be idle if it is not assigned to the lower skilled work.

Figure 10-4

CAROLINA BOAT BUILDING COMPANY Production Department Performance Report — Direct Materials For the Month of March, 1987						
Type of materials	(1) Standard price	(2) Actual quantity used	(3) Standard quantity allowed	(4) (2) − (3) Difference in quantity	(5) (1) × (4) Quantity variance	Explanation
Fiberglass fabric	$ .90	138,000 sq. ft	133,000 sq. ft	5,000 sq. ft	$4,500 U	Bad handling of materials
Fiberglass mix	$1.20	49,000 lb	47,500 lb	1,500 lb	$1,800 U	Inferior quality
U—indicates unfavorable variance						

The computations for the labor rate variance incurred by the Carolina Boat Building Company during March are illustrated in Figure 10-5. The labor rate variance calculations used in the general model presented in Figure 10-5 can be reduced to a more simple form as follows:

General model: $(AQ \times AP) - (AQ \times SP) =$ Labor rate variance
Simplified calculation: $AQ (AP - SP) =$ Labor rate variance

Applying the simplified calculation to the Carolina Boat Building Company illustration, we get the same result as that shown in Figure 10-5:

$$\begin{aligned} \text{Labor rate variance} &= AQ (AP - SP) \\ &= 4{,}950 \text{ hr } (\$10.20 - \$10.00) \\ &= 4{,}950 \text{ hr } (\$.20) \\ &= \$990 \text{ Unfavorable} \end{aligned}$$

When the simplified calculation is used, the actual direct labor hours are multiplied by the difference between the actual hourly rate and the standard hourly rate, thus holding the quantity constant and considering only the rate deviation. An unfavorable labor rate variance of $990 occurred in March because the actual rate was $10.20 compared with a standard rate of $10 and 4,950 actual labor hours were recorded. The $.20 difference between the two rates is multiplied by the 4,950 actual labor hours to compute the $990 unfavorable labor rate variance. A performance report such as the one presented in Figure 10-6 is prepared for the manager of the production department to identify the amount of the labor rate variance and provide the basis for corrective action in the future.

Figure 10-5

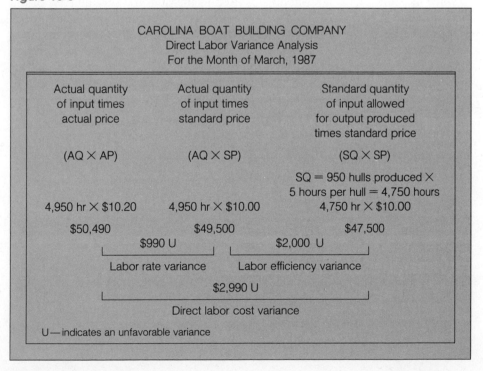

CAROLINA BOAT BUILDING COMPANY
Direct Labor Variance Analysis
For the Month of March, 1987

Actual quantity of input times actual price	Actual quantity of input times standard price	Standard quantity of input allowed for output produced times standard price
(AQ × AP)	(AQ × SP)	(SQ × SP)
		SQ = 950 hulls produced × 5 hours per hull = 4,750 hours
4,950 hr × $10.20	4,950 hr × $10.00	4,750 hr × $10.00
$50,490	$49,500	$47,500

$990 U — Labor rate variance

$2,000 U — Labor efficiency variance

$2,990 U — Direct labor cost variance

U—indicates an unfavorable variance

LABOR EFFICIENCY VARIANCE

As the name suggests, a **labor efficiency variance** is the result of using more or less direct labor hours as production input than the standard quantity (in hours) allowed for the units of output produced. The labor efficiency variance measures the productivity of a firm's labor force, so it is an important factor in achieving satisfactory profit results. **Labor productivity** is defined as the output of products actually produced divided by the number of labor hours required to achieve that output. If a firm's labor productivity is rising, the business is producing more units of output with a given number of labor hours—which in turn has a positive effect on unit product costs and profits. In contrast, when productivity is declining unit costs of the output will rise and the firm will have trouble competing with more efficient companies.

The standard hours allowed are determined by multiplying the units of output produced by the standard direct labor hours per unit. The actual direct labor hours used are then compared with the standard hours allowed to determine how efficiently the labor has been used. The standard hours allowed are the result of converting output to input—that is, the number of units produced multiplied by the standard hours per unit. Typical causes of a labor efficiency variance include:

1. Faulty equipment
2. Inexperienced workers
3. Poor quality materials
4. Inadequate supervision
5. A superior work performance
6. Changes in production methods
7. An outdated standard

Since the labor efficiency variance is used to measure the productivity of the labor force in achieving production results, it is the responsibility of the manager in charge of the manufacturing operation. The computations involved with a labor efficiency variance using the general model are illustrated in Figure 10-5. This general model can be reduced to the more simplified form shown next. The results can then be used to prepare a performance report for the manager of the production department (see Figure 10-6).

General model: $(AQ \times SP) - (SQ \times SP) =$ Labor efficiency variance
Simplified calculation: $SP (AQ - SQ) =$ Labor efficiency variance

The simplified calculation can be applied to the Carolina Boat Building Company case as follows:

$$\begin{aligned} \text{Labor efficiency variance} &= SP (AQ - SQ) \\ &= \$10 (4{,}950 \text{ hr} - 4{,}750 \text{ hr}) \\ &= \$10 (200 \text{ hr}) \\ &= \$2{,}000 \text{ Unfavorable} \end{aligned}$$

The Carolina Boat Building Company incurred an unfavorable labor efficiency variance of $2,000 during March. The standard direct labor hours allowed for the production output were 4,750 (950 hulls times five standard hours per hull), whereas 4,950 actual direct labor hours were recorded. The difference of 200 hours multiplied by the standard labor rate of $10 equals the $2,000 unfavorable labor efficiency variance. By combining the unfavorable labor rate variance of $990 and the unfavorable labor efficiency variance of $2,000, we find the total unfavorable direct labor variance of $2,990. The manager of the production department has to look at both labor variances to determine what corrective action is required. The performance report shown in Figure 10-6 provides the analysis needed to investigate the labor variances further.

RECAP OF VARIANCES

By combining the variances computed for the direct manufacturing costs, we can account for the unfavorable $12,670 difference between the total actual direct manufacturing costs and the total standard direct manufacturing costs as follows:

Materials price variance — fiberglass fabric	$ 8,280 U
Materials price variance — fiberglass mix	4,900 F
Materials quantity variance — fiberglass fabric	4,500 U
Materials quantity variance — fiberglass mix	1,800 U
Labor rate variance	990 U
Labor efficiency variance	2,000 U
Total direct manufacturing cost variance	$12,670 U

F indicates a favorable variance
U indicates an unfavorable variance

We should note that the reason the sum of the individual variances is equal to the total direct manufacturing cost variance of $12,670 is the fact that the *quantity of materials purchased is equal to the quantity used* in this case. When-

Figure 10-6

CAROLINA BOAT BUILDING COMPANY
Production Department Performance Report — Direct Labor
For the Month of March, 1987

Labor rate variance	(1) Actual hours worked	(2) Actual labor rate	(3) Standard labor rate	(4) (2) − (3) Difference in labor rate	(5) (1) × (4) Labor rate variance	Explanation
	4,950	$10.20	$10	$.20	$990 U	Error made scheduling workers

Labor efficiency variance	(1) Standard labor rate	(2) Actual hours worked	(3) Standard hours allowed	(4) (2) − (3) Difference in labor hours	(5) (1) × (4) Labor efficiency variance	Explanation
	$10	4,950	4,750	200	$2,000 U	Equipment breakdown

ever the two quantities are different, the materials price variance will be based on the quantity purchased instead of the quantity used for the production output achieved. In such cases, this variance cannot be added to the other variances (materials quantity variance, labor rate variance, and labor efficiency variance) as we have done above to reconcile the total variance of $12,670, which is based on the 950 units produced. That is, the different variances are not related to the same measures of the quantities involved. For example, reconsider what happened earlier in the Carolina Boat Building Company case when we changed the quantity purchased to 148,000 square feet but continued with the actual usage of 138,000 square feet. The result was an unfavorable materials price variance of $8,880, which was $600 higher than the $8,280 variance shown above. Recall also that the 10,000 square feet of materials purchased but not used were left in inventory at the end of March. As a result, the $600 additional variance recognized in March would relate to inventory to be used in the future rather than to the production output of March.

DECIDING WHICH VARIANCES ARE SIGNIFICANT

Objective 11: Defining a significant variance

Once cost variances have been computed and reported, management must decide whether the deviations from plan are important enough to justify further investigation. Since the standards are based on estimates about uncertain future events, some amount of deviation is inevitable. If every variance were investigated, the management time required and related costs incurred would be prohibitive. For control purposes, managers should only be concerned with *significant variances* between actual costs and standard costs. This approach enables managers to "troubleshoot"—that is, spend their time attempting to improve operations by investigating the problem areas of the business where the cost performance is not happening according to plan.

The definition of a significant variance is often a difficult task because there are so many sources and causes of cost variances. In addition, the cost variances associated with some cost items are more important than others. Many cost variances will be repetitive while others will be nonrecurring. Thus, different types of operations will be concerned with different variances. For example, a labor-intensive operation will be mainly concerned with direct labor variances that are large and recurring. Extremely large variances should be investigated in all situations because their size justifies the costs of the investigation process.

Keep in mind that unfavorable and favorable variances alike should be investigated if they are significant. While we have been concerned mainly with unfavorable variances as potential sources of corrective action, a significant favorable variance may signal that the related standard was too easy to attain and should be revised. In addition, a favorable variance may point out an efficient activity that can be duplicated in another phase of the operation.

RANDOM AND NONRANDOM CAUSES OF VARIANCES

How can managers decide when a cost variance is large enough to require investigation? They usually do so by separating variances caused by random or chance fluctuations from those resulting from nonrandom sources. **Random fluctuations** are characteristic of all repetitive processes. Such processes simply do not operate perfectly all the time even if management exercises complete control over them. Nor can the imperfections be traced to a single cause controllable by management. For example, a worker may have a temporary slump in productivity because of illness or worry about a sick child, but then is fine the next day.

Random fluctuations tend to balance out over time and produce a stable pattern of variability as a range around the standard cost involved. As long as the actual cost results are so small that they are within this range of random fluctuations, the cost performance involved is considered to be in a state of acceptable control and further investigation is not worthwhile. In contrast, an actual cost that is outside the acceptable range is a signal that the cost performance is out of control because a **nonrandom variation** caused by a controllable factor has occurred. Examples of nonrandom fluctuations include:

1. Defective direct materials
2. Equipment breakdowns
3. Changes in product design
4. Production scheduling problems
5. Inexperienced workers
6. Inadequate supervision

Nonrandom fluctuations in the production process usually cause larger cost variances than random variations. This type of fluctuation *should be investigated* because it is potentially controllable by management. The two most popular ways to distinguish between random and nonrandom fluctuations are with management judgment guidelines and control chart analysis.

IDENTIFYING NONRANDOM FLUCTUATIONS WITH MANAGEMENT JUDGMENT GUIDELINES

Based on past experience and their expectations of the future, managers often will develop general guidelines to separate random and nonrandom fluctuations. These guidelines typically are based on an absolute dollar amount of a variance, a variance as a percentage of the standard amount, or a combination of the two. For example, a business may decide that any variance that differs from the related standard by $500 or more should be investigated. Smaller variances are assumed to be the result of uncontrollable random fluctuations.

The problem with using an absolute amount such as $500 is that it is difficult to develop a perspective concerning the relative importance of the single amount involved. If the standard cost is $1,000, a $500 variance is much more important than it is if the standard cost is $100,000.

The advantage of a percentage approach is that relative importance is considered. An example of the percentage approach would be to decide that any variance of 10% or more from the related standard should be investigated. The rationale for the 10% limit is that a variance of at least that size is highly likely to reveal a situation that is out of control and requires corrective action.

There is a serious problem with the percentage approach, however. The problem arises because the absolute dollars involved may not be large enough to warrant further investigation. For example, a variance of 10% would be significant if the related standard is $100,000, but insignificant for a standard of $100. The costs and potential benefits involved would favor investigation of a $10,000 variance but not a $10 variance unless it is incurred repeatedly.

Most firms using management judgment guidelines combine the absolute dollar approach and the percentage approach to minimize their individual weaknesses. The combined rule for determining whether a variance should be investigated is that it must deviate from standard *by a certain minimum dollar amount and by a certain minimum percentage.* For example, a variance would be considered significant if it differed from the related standard by at least $50 and 10%. Different absolute amounts and percentages may be established for different cost items (e.g., direct materials, direct labor, and manufacturing overhead) to recognize their relative importance.

USE OF CONTROL CHART ANALYSIS

Objective 12: Analyzing cost performance with a control chart

Control chart analysis can be used to graphically portray the management judgment guidelines discussed above. In addition, such an analysis can be extended to establish statistical rules for distinguishing between random and nonrandom fluctuations. The statistical techniques used to develop acceptable control limits for control charts are discussed in Chapter 15, and we will consider only the general use of control charts here.

A control chart, such as the one shown in Figure 10-7, defines **upper and lower control limits** within which variances from standard due to chance or random fluctuations are expected to occur. The actual cost performance is sampled periodically, and the sample results are plotted on the control chart to see if they fall within the acceptable range. If they do, the cost performance is considered in control. Further investigation is not warranted in such cases because the causes of the variances are assumed to be uncontrollable by management. In contrast, a sample result that falls outside the control limits is likely to be caused by nonrandom fluctuations that signal the need for investigation by the manager who is responsible for the related cost performance.

The standard cost being monitored with the control charts in Figure 10-7 is the labor efficiency standard of the Carolina Boat Building Company. Remember that we established a standard of 5 direct labor hours at a rate of $10 each for the production of each sailboat hull, or a standard cost of $50. Assume that a sample of the actual hours recorded for the production of sailboat hulls has been taken and costed using the standard rate of $10 to consider the labor efficiency variance only. The results are then plotted on the control chart (as x's) to see if they fall within the acceptable control limits.

We have set the control limits of the control chart in Figure 10-7 in terms of absolute dollars. The range of assumed random fluctuations is from $45 to $55 compared with the standard cost of $50. Note that 9 of the 10 sample results

Figure 10-7
Control Chart with
Dollar Control
Limits-Labor
Efficiency Variance

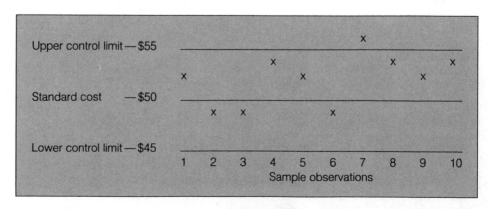

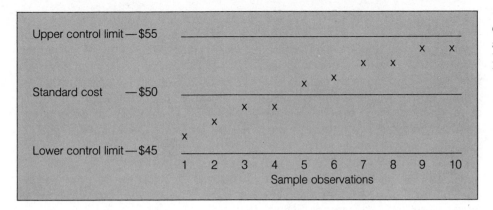

Figure 10-8
Control Chart with
a Trend Pattern—
Labor Efficiency
Variance

fall within the acceptable range and, therefore, would not require further investigation. The seventh observation is outside the upper limit of $55, so it should be investigated to determine what has caused the potentially significant variance from the $50 standard.

Another advantage of a control chart is that it permits us to visualize the pattern of sample results plotted on the chart. Even if the observations fall within the acceptable range, a pattern of fluctuations that signals a potential problem now or in the near future may develop. For example, we may spot a trend in the fluctuations, such as the one found in Figure 10-8, which suggests that the cost performance may be out of control soon. Alternatively, we may observe a situation such as the one illustrated in Figure 10-9 where the results are regularly around the upper control limit. These results should be investigated to make sure they do not move to an out-of-control state in the future.

JOURNAL ENTRIES FOR STANDARD COSTS

When standard costs are used in the formal accounting system, they are recorded through journal entries to value the work in process inventory at standard cost, rather than at actual cost. Variance accounts are established for the materials price variance, materials quantity variance, labor rate variance, labor efficiency variance, and manufacturing overhead variances. We mentioned earlier that an unfavorable variance has a debit balance because it is an added cost for the standard amount being recorded. Conversely, a favorable cost variance has a credit balance since it is a reduced cost resulting from an actual cost that is less than the standard amount that was expected.

**Objective 13:
Preparing journal
entries for
standard costs**

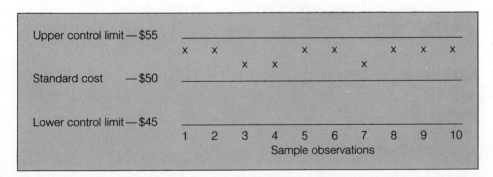

Figure 10-9
Control Chart with
Consistently High
Values—Labor
Efficiency Variance

As the journal entries are recorded in a standard cost system, a major objective is isolating the variances as soon as possible so management has current information to use in evaluating the cost performance. The materials price variance and labor rate variance are usually recognized when the related costs are incurred. The materials quantity variance and labor efficiency variance are recorded as soon as the actual production output can be identified (e.g., typically as production occurs in job order costing and at the end of an accounting period with process costing). Let's illustrate the journal entries required for the standard direct manufacturing costs by considering the entries prepared by the Carolina Boat Building Company to record the cost performance discussed earlier. These entries are also shown in Figure 10-10 in T account form as a summary of the cost flows involved. The journal entries are numbered for cross-referencing to the T accounts in Figure 10-10.

Materials Purchases

(1)

Raw Materials Inventory (138,000 sq. ft @ $.90)	124,200	
Materials Price Variance	8,280	
Accounts Payable (138,000 sq. ft @ $.96)		132,480
To record the purchases of fiberglass fabric.		

(2)

Raw Materials Inventory (49,000 lb @ $1.20)	58,800	
Accounts Payable (49,000 lb @ $1.10)		53,900
Materials Price Variance		4,900
To record the purchases of fiberglass mix.		

Direct Materials Usage

(3)

Work in Process Inventory (133,000 sq. ft @ $.90)	119,700	
Materials Quantity Variance	4,500	
Raw Materials Inventory (138,000 sq. ft @ $.90)		124,200
To record the usage of fiberglass fabric for 950 hulls.		

(4)

Work in Process Inventory (47,500 lb @ $1.20)	57,000	
Materials Quantity Variance	1,800	
Raw Materials Inventory (49,000 lb @ $1.20)		58,800
To record the usage of fiberglass mix for 950 hulls.		

Direct Labor Cost Recorded

(5)

Direct Labor Payroll (4,950 hr @ $10)	49,500	
Labor Rate Variance	990	
Accrued Payroll (4,950 hr @ $10.20)		50,490
To record the actual direct labor payroll.		

Direct Labor Hours Used

(6)

Work in Process Inventory (4,750 hr @ $10)	47,500	
Labor Efficiency Variance	2,000	
Direct Labor Payroll (4,950 hr @ $10)		49,500
To record the direct labor hours used for 950 hulls.		

CAROLINA BOAT BUILDING COMPANY
Summary of Standard Cost Flow—Direct Manufacturing Costs

Figure 10-10

Raw Materials Inventory				Work in Process Inventory			Accounts Payable		
(1)	124,200	(3)	124,200	(3)	119,700		(1)	132,480
(2)	58,800	(4)	58,800	(4)	57,000		(2)	53,900
				(6)	47,500			

Direct Labor Payroll				Accrued Payroll			Materials Price Variance		
(5)	49,500	(6)	49,500			(5) 50,490	(1)	8,280	(2) 4,900

Materials Quantity Variance			Labor Rate Variance			Labor Efficiency Variance		
(3)	4,500		(5)	990		(6)	2,000	
(4)	1,800							

Notice the similarities between the general model used earlier in Figure 10-1 for variance analysis and the computations involved in the journal entries above:

- When the direct manufacturing costs are incurred, the actual quantity of input times the standard price is charged to either Raw Materials Inventory or the Direct Labor Payroll account. The corresponding credit to Accounts Payable or Accrued Payroll is the actual quantity of input times the actual price, which is the actual amount owed for that cost item. The difference between the debit and credit is the price (rate) variance.
- The Work in Process Inventory account is debited for standard costs only, that is, the standard quantity of input allowed for the output produced times the standard price. The corresponding credit is also recorded at the actual quantity of input times the standard price, so the difference between the debit and credit is the quantity (efficiency) variance.

When the journal entries for the direct manufacturing costs are completed, both standard prices (rates) and standard quantities are included in work in process inventory so we have an inventory valued with *standard costs only.* We should also note that the Direct Labor Payroll account is an example of a clearing account used to facilitate the identification of the labor variances. The term "clearing" simply means that the amount debited to the account during an accounting period will always equal the amount credited to it. For example, in this case we debited and credited the account for $49,500, identifying the labor rate variance with the debit entry and the labor efficiency variance with the credit entry.

SUMMARY

Standard costs are carefully predetermined measures of what costs should be based on the quality specifications of the products produced. The actual costs recorded in the accounting system are compared with the standard costs to determine whether a business is operating according to its plan. Standard costs are especially important for manufacturing firms but are also used effectively by other businesses with repetitive activities. The major benefits of standard costs are that they: (1) provide reliable estimates for budgeting; (2) represent control targets for management by exception; (3) are used for inventory valuation with recordkeeping savings; (4) contribute to managerial decision making; and (5) make employees more cost conscious.

A standard unit price and a standard input quantity make up the standard cost of each direct manufacturing cost. These two standards must be consistent with the quality level of the products being produced. The three methods most commonly used to establish standard costs are: (1) an engineering approach; (2) an analysis of historical data; and (3) management judgment concerning the future cost performance.

Management must also decide how difficult the standards should be to achieve. Ideal standards are the most demanding because they require the highest possible level of effort if they are to be achieved. As a result, they do not represent realistic targets for most firms because significant variances regularly arise from all but the very best performance. Attainable standards are the ones used by most manufacturing businesses since they represent targets that are achievable with a reasonably efficient effort. Such standards are difficult but possible to attain and include allowances for departures from maximum efficiency.

Standard cost variances occur when actual costs are different from standard costs. They are computed, evaluated, reported, and investigated if they are significant using the principle of management by exception. Standard cost variance analysis is performed by considering *when* a variance occurred, *where* it took place, *why* it happened, *who* is responsible for it, and *what* can be done about it.

The total direct materials variance is divided into price and quantity components. The total direct labor variance is divided into rate and efficiency components. The price and rate variances result when a firm pays a different price or rate for the actual materials and labor recorded than it planned. In contrast, the quantity and efficiency variances arise because more or less units of materials and labor inputs are used during an accounting period than the standard quantity allowed for the production output achieved.

These variances are reported to the responsible managers who must determine if the deviations from the planned performance are significant and, if they are, what should be done about them. Common causes of cost variances are inadequate supervision, inexperienced workers, poor quality materials, faulty equipment, price changes in the marketplace, and outdated standards. Management judgment guidelines and control chart analysis are often used to determine whether cost variances are significant enough to warrant further investigation.

GLOSSARY

ATTAINABLE STANDARDS. Cost performance targets that can be achieved with a reasonably efficient effort (p.363).

CONTROL CHART ANALYSIS.   The use of a graphic display to evaluate whether cost results are within acceptable control limits (p. 380).

IDEAL STANDARDS.   Cost performance targets that can be achieved only with an optimal effort (p.362).

LABOR EFFICIENCY (USAGE) VARIANCE.   The difference between the actual labor hours used and the standard hours allowed multiplied times the standard labor rate. It is used to measure the productivity of the labor force (p. 367).

LABOR PRODUCTIVITY.   The output of products actually produced divided by the number of labor hours required to achieve that output (p.376).

LABOR RATE VARIANCE.   The difference between the actual labor rate and the standard labor rate multiplied by the actual hours worked. It is used to measure how well a firm stayed within its labor rate limits (p.367).

MATERIALS PRICE VARIANCE.   The difference between the actual price paid for raw materials and the standard price that should have been paid multiplied by the actual quantity of materials purchased or used. It is utilized to measure the performance of the purchasing department and evaluate the effect of price changes on profits (p.367).

MATERIALS QUANTITY (USAGE) VARIANCE.   The difference between the actual direct materials used for production and the standard quantity expected multiplied by the standard price of the materials. It is used to measure the efficiency of direct materials utilization (p. 367).

NONRANDOM FLUCTUATIONS.   Causes of variances that should be investigated because they are identifiable and controllable (p. 379).

PRICE STANDARD.   The amount that should be paid for a unit of direct materials or an hour of direct labor (p. 360).

QUANTITY STANDARD.   The units of input in the form of direct materials or direct labor that should be used for a specified output of products (p. 360).

RANDOM FLUCTUATIONS.   Causes of variances resulting from chance that are not controllable by management because they are inevitable in every repetitive process (p. 378).

STANDARD COSTS.   Carefully predetermined costs that should be incurred to produce a product or perform an operation (p. 358).

STANDARD COST VARIANCE CONTROL LIMITS.   The upper and lower boundaries of a control chart defining a range of cost performance that is assumed to be the result of random fluctuations uncontrollable by management (p. 380).

STANDARD COST VARIANCES.   The differences between actual costs and standard costs, which can be used to control a cost performance with management by exception (p. 385).

STANDARD QUANTITY ALLOWED.   The number of units of direct materials or direct labor hours that should have been used for the production of a specified amount of product output (p. 367).

DISCUSSION QUESTIONS

1. What are standard costs? Why are they better measures of performance than simply comparing current results with those of the past?

2. What is wrong with comparing actual performance with past performance to evaluate a firm's efficiency?
3. Are standard costs useful in manufacturing firms only?
4. What does the standard direct materials cost consist of? The standard direct labor cost?
5. What are the benefits of standard costs? The limitations?
6. How are standard costs established?
7. Distinguish between ideal and attainable standard costs.
8. Why are items other than the expected purchase price included in the standard price of materials?
9. How is a materials quantity standard established?
10. What is included in a labor rate standard? A labor efficiency standard?
11. What is meant by standard cost variance analysis?
12. Identify the five basic questions that should be considered in standard cost variance analysis. Why are they important to managers?
13. Describe the general model that is used for direct cost variance analysis.
14. Who is usually responsible for a materials price variance? A materials quantity variance?
15. What are typical causes of a materials price variance? A materials quantity variance?
16. Who is usually responsible for a labor rate variance? A labor efficiency variance?
17. Identify some typical causes of a labor rate variance. A labor efficiency variance.
18. What is the basic difference between calculating a variance and determining its cause?
19. The Johnson Company has a standard labor rate of $9.46 per hour. Each of its finished products requires 4.4 hours of labor. During June, 5,720 units are produced with 25,080 labor hours and a labor cost of $243,276. What is the total labor cost variance? How much of it is attributable to labor rate? Labor efficiency?
20. Why is it important for managers to be able to evaluate the significance of standard cost variances? How is this typically done?
21. Differentiate between variances caused by random fluctuations and those resulting from nonrandom sources. Why is this distinction important?
22. How is management judgment used to separate random and nonrandom fluctuations?
23. What is control chart analysis as it is used to evaluate a cost performance?

EXERCISES

Exercise 10-1 Computing Materials Variances

The Dudley Company produces a laundry detergent known as Clean-Up. The firm uses a standard cost system to control costs. The standard direct materials required for one box of Clean-Up are as follows:

Chemical compound—4 pounds at $1.10 per pound
Container—1 box at $.05 per box

During August, the company purchased and used 80,000 pounds of chemical compound at $1.25 each and 22,000 containers at $.04 each. The actual production of Clean-Up amounted to 21,200 boxes.

Required:
A. Compute the materials price variances.
B. Compute the materials quantity variances.
C. Who would be responsible for these variances?

Exercise 10-2 Computing Labor Variances

The Dudley Company introduced in Exercise 10-1 has the following direct labor performance associated with the production of Clean-Up during August:

	Standard Hours	**Standard Rate**
One box	.3 hour	$8.50
Actual hours worked – 6,690		
Actual direct labor cost – $58,203		

Required:
A. Compute the labor rate variance.
B. Compute the labor efficiency variance.
C. Who would be responsible for these variances?

Exercise 10-3 Materials Price Variance — Amount Purchased and Used Unequal

Assume that the Dudley Company introduced in Exercise 10-1 purchased 86,000 pounds of chemical compound at $1.25 each and 23,000 containers at $.04 each. The actual usage of the materials was the same as that indicated earlier.

Required:
A. Compute the materials price variances with these changes.
B. Who would be responsible for this variance?

Exercise 10-4 Computing Materials Variances

The Monroe Company uses a standard cost system that specifies that 30 board-feet of lumber at $3.50 per board-foot should be used to manufacture one office desk. The company used 9,900 board-feet of lumber to produce 300 desks. The total purchase price of the materials used in production was $33,660.

Required:
Calculate the materials price and quantity variances.

Exercise 10-5 Computing Labor Variances

The Darlington Company has decided that the labor standards for each unit produced are three hours of assembly labor at $8.75 per hour and two and one half hours of finishing labor at $9.50 per hour. During May, the company produced 700 units using 1,890 hours of assembly labor and 2,100 hours of finishing labor. The company's direct labor payroll was $16,821 for assembly labor and $20,160 for finishing labor.

Required:
Calculate the labor rate and efficiency variances for the assembly labor and the finishing labor.

Exercise 10-6 Calculating Materials Variances

The Almar Company produces office furniture. In one of the firm's departments, formica tops are installed on desks produced in another department. The formica is purchased in large sheets, trimmed to size, and glued to the desks. Each desk requires 24 square feet of formica at a cost of $.90 per square foot. During June, 1,800 desks were finished. 48,000 square feet of formica were purchased at a cost of $.93 per square foot. The formica used in production amounted to 45,000 square feet.

Required:
A. Compute the materials price variance.
B. Compute the materials quantity variance.
C. Identify some likely causes of these variances.

Exercise 10-7 Calculating Labor Variances

The Scott Company produces electronic equipment and uses a standard cost system. A particular model of automobile stereo system requires the following standard direct labor performance: 14.5 hours at $12.10 per hour.

During 1987, 3,800 stereo systems were produced at a total direct labor cost of $741,000. Actual direct labor hours of 57,000 were recorded during the period.

Required:
A. How much direct labor cost should have been incurred during 1987? What is the total labor cost variance?
B. Divide the total labor cost variance into its rate and efficiency components.
C. Identify some likely causes of these variances.

Exercise 10-8 Computing Direct Cost Variances

The Cleanit Company produces an industrial cleaning solvent. Each gallon of solvent requires 1.2 gallons of a liquid chemical and 1.7 pounds of a chemical compound. In addition, .2 direct labor hour is needed for each gallon of solvent at a standard rate of $8.90. The liquid chemical is purchased in drums at a cost of $3 per gallon subject to a 2% discount if paid for within 10 days. The Cleanit Company's policy is to take advantage of all discounts. The chemical compound has a standard cost of $50 per 100 pounds.

During 1987, the firm experienced the following:

Actual production of solvent was 109,100 gallons

Actual purchases of raw materials:
    Liquid chemical 163,650 gallons at $492,586.50
    Chemical compound 218,200 pounds at $98,190.00

Actual usage of raw materials:
    Liquid chemical   141,830 gallons
    Chemical compound   180,015 pounds

Actual direct labor – 24,000 hours at $216,018.

Required
A. Calculate the materials price variance assuming they are based on the amounts purchased.
B. Calculate the materials quantity variance.

C. Calculate the labor rate variance.
D. Calculate the labor efficiency variance.

Exercise 10-9   Consideration of Standard Costing Features

Select the best answer to the following questions:

1. When standard costs are used, the materials price variance is computed by multiplying the:
   a. Actual price by the difference between the actual quantity purchased and the standard quantity used.
   b. Standard price by the difference between the standard quantity purchased and standard quantity used.
   c. Standard quantity purchased by the difference between the actual price and the standard price.
   d. Actual quantity purchased by the difference between the actual price and the standard price.

2. What materials variances for price and quantity will arise if the actual number of pounds used exceeds standard pounds allowed but actual cost was less than standard cost?

	Price	Quantity
a.	Favorable	Unfavorable
b.	Favorable	Favorable
c.	Unfavorable	Favorable
d.	Unfavorable	Unfavorable

3. Which of the following conditions would be least likely to cause an unfavorable materials quantity variance?
   a. Machinery that has not been maintained adequately.
   b. Workers with skills that are compatible with those required by the standard.
   c. Scheduling of a significant amount of overtime.
   d. Direct materials of lower quality than called for in the specifications.

4. Information on the Ryder Company's direct materials costs is as follows:

Standard price per unit	$7.20
Actual quantity purchased	1,600
Standard quantity allowed for actual production	1,450
Materials price variance for units purchased – favorable	$ 480

   The actual purchase price per unit is:
   a. $6.12
   b. $6.90
   c. $6.22
   d. $7.50

5. Assume that AH = Actual hours, SH = Standard hours allowed for actual production, AR = Actual rate, and SR = Standard rate. Which formula should be used to calculate the labor efficiency variance?
   a. $AR (AH - SH)$
   b. $SH (AR - SR)$
   c. $SR (AH - SH)$
   d. $AH (AR - SR)$

6. An unfavorable labor efficiency variance indicates that:
   a. The actual labor rate was higher than the standard labor rate

    b. The total labor variance must be unfavorable
    c. Overtime labor was utilized during the period
    d. Actual direct labor hours exceeded standard direct labor hours for the production level actually achieved
7. A debit balance in the labor efficiency variance account indicates that:
    a. Actual hours exceeded standard hours
    b. Standard hours exceeded actual hours
    c. Standard rate and standard hours exceed actual rate and actual hours
    d. Actual rate and actual hours exceed standard rate and standard hours
8. Information on the Spiller Company's direct labor costs for the month of June is as follows:

Actual direct labor rate	$ 7.50
Standard direct labor hours allowed	11,000
Actual direct labor hours	10,000
Direct labor rate variance – favorable	$5,500

    What was the standard direct labor rate used during June?
    a. $6.95
    b. $7.00
    c. $8.00
    d. $8.05

Exercise 10-10 Evaluating Direct Labor Cost Variances
Select the best answer to each of the following questions:

1. The Davis Company uses a standard cost system. Direct labor information for the month of September is as follows:

Standard labor rate	$6.00 per hour
Actual labor rate paid	6.10 per hour
Standard hours allowed for actual production	1,500
Labor efficiency variance – unfavorable	$600

    What were the actual hours worked?
    a. 1,400
    b. 1,402
    c. 1,598
    d. 1,600
2. The difference between the actual labor rate multiplied by the actual hours worked and the standard labor rate multiplied by the standard labor hours is the
    a. Total labor variance
    b. Labor rate variance
    c. Labor efficiency variance
    d. No variance
3. Listed below are four terms for different kinds of standards when a standard cost system is used. Which one describes the labor costs that should be incurred with reasonably efficient operations?
    a. Maximum efficiency
    b. Maximum effectiveness
    c. Ideal
    d. Attainable

4. Excess direct labor costs resulting from overtime premiums will be disclosed in which type of variance?
 a. Labor rate
 b. Labor efficiency
 c. Labor usage
 d. No labor variance

5. The Johnson Manufacturing Company's direct labor costs for April are as follows:

Standard direct labor hours	42,000
Actual direct labor hours	40,000
Standard direct labor rate per hour	6.30
Direct labor rate variance – favorable	8,400

What was Johnson's total direct labor cost for April?
 a. $243,600
 b. $244,000
 c. $260,000
 d. $260,400

Exercise 10-11 Evaluating Cost Variances with Incomplete Data

The Pointe Company uses a standard costing system. During January, the firm recorded the following performance for the only product produced:

Purchased 8,500 pounds of materials

Used 8,000 pounds of materials

Worked 825 direct labor hours

Produced 1,500 finished units

Standard cost specifications for the product are:

	Standard Quantity	Standard Price
Direct materials	5 pounds	$ 4
Direct labor	.5 hour	$10

The unfavorable total materials cost variance during January was $4,850. The unfavorable total labor cost variance was $915.

Required:
A. What was the actual price paid for materials?
B. What was the actual labor rate?

Exercise 10-12 Evaluating the Significance of Variances

The production manager of the Nichols Company exercises management by exception by reviewing materials usage and labor efficiency variances incurred during any given week. His decision rule is that any variance that is greater than $5,000 or more than 10% of the standard cost involved should be investigated to determine the underlying cause. During last week, the company's operating performance included the following:

Units produced — 5,000

Direct materials used (21,500 lb @ $18.20)

Direct labor hours worked (8,240 hr @ $12.30)

Standard cost specifications for each unit produced are:

Direct materials—4 lb at $18 each
Direct labor—1.6 hr @ $12.30 each

Required:
A. Calculate all cost variances for direct materials and direct labor.
B. Should the production department manager investigate either of the variances for which he is responsible?
C. Identify three possible causes of each of the variances for which the manager is responsible.

Exercise 10-13 Use of Control Chart Analysis

The Muth Company uses control chart analysis to monitor the direct labor cost performance of its Mixing Department. An average direct labor cost of $500 per batch has been established as the target, with control limits of $450 and $550. A batch is a certain number of gallons mixed. During the first two weeks of April, the following data were collected:

Day	Batches Processed	Total Direct Labor Cost	Day	Batches Processed	Total Direct Labor Cost
1	20	$10,200	6	18	$ 9,684
2	22	11,330	7	22	11,880
3	18	9,450	8	21	11,340
4	24	12,720	9	23	12,512
5	16	8,480	10	22	12,012

Required:
A. Prepare a control chart for the two-week period.
B. Evaluate the results shown in part A.

PROBLEMS

Problem 10-1 Computing Materials Variances

The Moon Chemical Company produces a chemical called Moonglow that is used in various petroleum products. The standard materials cost of producing a batch of Moonglow is $540. The standard materials and related standard cost of each chemical used in each batch are:

Materials	Standard Input Quantity in Gallons	Standard Cost per Gallon	Total Cost
XJ3	400	$.40	$160
XJ4	200	.85	170
XJ5	500	.30	150
XJ6	100	.60	60

Below is a summary of the actual materials usage during the current production period. A total of 140 batches of Moonglow were manufactured during the current period.

Materials	Gallons Purchased	Total Purchase Price	Gallons Used
XJ3	57,000	$23,940	57,000
XJ4	28,000	22,400	28,000
XJ5	72,000	18,000	72,000
XJ6	15,000	15,000	15,000

Required:
Compute the following for each material used in the production of Moonglow:

A.   The materials price variance.
B.   The materials quantity variance.

Problem 10-2 Computing Labor Variances

The Starr Manufacturing Company used the following standards for production in 1987:

Labor Class	Standard Hourly Rate	Standard Hours Allowed for Output per Month
Experienced	$12.80	800
Mid-level	11.20	800
Apprentice	8.00	800

The standard rates were originally established in November of 1985, and were held constant during 1986. The actual wage rates for each labor class increased on January 1, 1987 due to negotiations with the local union. The standard wage rates shown above were not revised to reflect the new contract.

The actual labor used in production for the month of July was as follows:

Labor Class	Actual Hourly Labor Rate	Actual Labor Hours Used
Experienced	$13.60	880
Mid-level	12.00	1,040
Apprentice	8.64	600

Required:
A.   For each labor class, compute:
   1.   The labor rate variance for July
   2.   The labor efficiency variance for July
B.   What is the total labor variance for July?

Problem 10-3 Standard Cost Variances for Direct Costs

The Tahoe Tent Company produces a tent which requires two types of nylon —Nylon F4 and Nylon Q7. The raw material standards are as follows:

Material	Standard Quantity per Unit	Standard Cost
Nylon F4	10 yards	$12 per yard
Nylon Q7	6 yards	$24 per yard

The direct labor standards are eight hours per tent at $9 per hour. There were no beginning or ending work in process inventories. Actual production results for the year are as follows:

	Nylon F4	Nylon Q7
Direct materials:		
Purchases	122,000 yards	74,000 yards
Purchase price	$11.80 per yard	$24.60 per yard
Beginning inventory	8,000 yards	3,000 yards
Ending inventory	6,000 yards	5,000 yards

Direct labor – 95,200 hours @ $9.20 per hour
12,000 tents were produced during the year

Required:

A. Calculate the materials price and quantity variances.

B. Calculate the labor rate and efficiency variances.

Problem 10-4 Computing and Recording Direct Cost Variances

Aul Tuxedo Company produces a single line of formal wear. The standard costs for one suit are:

Direct materials:	
5 yards of black cloth at $1.75 per yard	$ 8.75
2.5 yards of white cloth at $1.50 per yard	3.75
Direct labor:	
2 hours at 9.25 per hour	18.50
Total standard cost per unit	$31.00

During February, 450 suits were produced. The costs incurred during the month were:

Materials purchased:
    2,500 yards of black cloth at $1.85 per yard
    1,200 yards of white cloth at $1.40 per yard

Materials used in production:
    2,200 yards of black cloth
    1,200 yards of white cloth

Direct labor:
    960 hours at $9 per hour

Required:

A. Compute the materials price and quantity variances and prepare all journal entries associated with direct materials for the month of February.

B. Compute the labor rate and efficiency variances and prepare the journal entries to record the incurrence of direct labor costs.

Problem 10-5 Evaluating Direct Manufacturing Cost Performance

Ice Products, Inc. is a large producer and distributor of packaged ice. The company uses standard costs for all of its different sized packages. The standard costs and actual costs for the month of August are given below for one of the company's product lines (per unit of product):

	Standard Cost	Actual Cost
Direct materials:		
Standard: 25 gal at $.45 per gal	$11.25	
Actual: 28 gal at $.40 per gal		$11.20
Direct Labor:		
Standard: .3 hour at $9.50 per hour	2.85	
Actual: .25 hour at $10.80 per hour		2.70
Total cost per unit	$14.10	$13.90

During the month of August, the company produced 18,400 units of product. A comparison of standard and actual costs for the period on a total cost basis is given below:

Actual costs:	18,400 units at $13.90	$255,760
Standard costs:	18,400 units at $14.10	259,440
Favorable cost variance		$ 3,680

There was no inventory of materials on hand at the beginning of August. During the month, 515,200 gallons of materials were purchased, all of which were used in production.

Required
A. For direct materials:
 1. Compute the price and quantity variances for August.
 2. Prepare journal entries to record all activity relating to direct materials for August.
B. For direct labor:
 1. Compute the rate and efficiency variances.
 2. Prepare a journal entry to record the incurrence of direct labor cost for August.
C. After seeing the favorable total cost variance of $3,680, the company's president stated, "Because we have experienced a favorable total cost variance, it is obvious that our performance is above standard and not in need of investigation." Is this statement correct? Explain.

Problem 10-6 Evaluating Direct Labor Performance with Cost Variances
JMF Helmet Company manufactures a single type of batting helmet sold to major league baseball teams. Cost information for the last month's direct labor usage is given below:

1. Standard hours allowed for output at the standard rate equaled $87,220.
2. Actual hours worked during the month – 10,000 hr
3. Total labor variance – $280 Unf.
4. Labor rate variance – $1,500 Fav.

Required:
A. Compute the direct labor efficiency variance.
B. Compute the actual labor rate and the standard labor rate for the month.
C. Compute the standard hours allowed for the month's production.

Problem 10-7 Evaluating Direct Manufacturing Costs
The standard materials and labor costs for one unit of product RJS-3 are as follows:

Direct materials: 6 pounds @ $4 per pound
Direct labor: 5 hours @ $12 per hour

The following data show the actual production results for 1,200 units of product RJS-3 during August:

Raw materials purchased and used	7,000 pounds
Materials price variance	$700 debit
Materials quantity variance	1,200 credit
Total labor variance	1,500 debit

Required:
For the month of August, compute:

1. The actual price per pound paid for direct materials.
2. The actual pounds of direct materials used.
3. The actual cost of direct labor used.

Problem 10-8 Calculating and Recording Cost Variances

The Folz Furniture Company manufactures a complete line of dining room furniture. The company recently developed standards for its new 10-person deluxe dinner table. The standard costs for this model are shown below:

36 board-feet of oak at $1.25 per board-foot	$45
3 direct labor hours at $7.00 per hour	21
Total direct materials and direct labor	$66

During the month of April, Folz purchased 45,000 board-feet of oak for $63,000 and used 40,800 board-feet in the production of 1,200 tables. The direct labor used during the month amounted to 3,840 hours and cost $28,800. The price variance for direct materials is recognized at the time of purchase.

Required:
A. Calculate the direct materials price and quantity variances.
B. Calculate the variances for direct labor for the month of April.
C. Prepare journal entries to record the standard costs and variances.

Problem 10-9 Computing Direct Manufacturing Cost Variances

The Hammer-n-Nail Company has recently acquired a subsidiary which produces custom doghouses. The company believes it can do well in the production of doghouses because it can supply some of the needed materials and labor. Hammer-n-Nail has established standards for its new company's product as shown below:

Materials – 46 sq. ft of plywood at $.50 per sq. ft.	$23
Direct labor – 2 hours at $7 per hour	14
Total direct materials and direct labor	$37

During the first month, the firm produced 600 doghouses and management is anxious to see an analysis of its operating results. The following costs were incurred:

Materials (purchased and used) – 27,000 sq. ft.	$16,200
Direct labor – 900 hours	5,400
Total direct materials and direct labor	$21,600

Required:
A. Compute the materials price and quantity variances.
B. Compute the labor rate and efficiency variances.

Problem 10-10 Evaluating Cost Variances for Further Investigation

Noret Flood, production manager of the Water Works Supply Company, is responsible for controlling the performance of operations. After examining a performance report, he investigates all variances greater than $1,000 to determine the possible causes and corrective actions. During July, the following occurred for the production of 6,200 units:

	Standard Cost	Actual Cost
Materials:		
Standard: 6 pounds at $.50 per pound	$3.00	
Actual: 5.5 pounds at $.60 per pound		$3.30
Labor:		
Standard: .25 hour at $10.00 per hour	2.50	
Actual: .30 hour at $9.00 per hour		2.70
Total cost per unit	$5.50	$6.00

Required:
A. Calculate the materials price and quantity variances.
B. Calculate the labor rate and efficiency variances.
C. Determine which variances should be investigated using the given criteria.

Problem 10-11 **Evaluating Standard Cost Performance with Incomplete Information**

Hayes Manufacturing Company produces a single product. The company has set standards as follows for direct materials and labor:

	Direct Materials	Direct Labor
Standard price or rate	?	$ 5
Standard quantity or hours per unit	5.8	?
Standard cost per unit	?	$19

During the last period, the company purchased 6,000 pounds of direct materials at a cost of $51,000. All of the materials were used to produce 1,000 units of product. The actual direct labor cost for the period totaled $19,248. Also, the following variances for the period are known:

Labor efficiency variance	$1,050 Unf.
Total materials variance	$ 620 Fav.

Required:
A. For direct labor:
  1. Compute the standard hours allowed per unit.
  2. Compute the actual direct labor rate per hour for the period.
  3. Compute the labor rate variance.
B. For direct materials:
  1. Compute the standard price per pound of materials.
  2. Compute the materials quantity variance.

Problem 10-12 **Evaluating Performance with Standards**

Pamela's Bakery specializes in the production of home-style bread. This company uses standards established by the National Bakery Association based on performances by the trade association members from various parts of the country. The first year's production results are available, and Pamela is anxious to see if her bakery is performing better than the national standards.

NBA Standards for 20 Loaves of Bread	
Direct labor: .2 hour at $12.50 per hour	$ 2.50
Direct materials: 35 pounds of dough at $.20 per pound	7.00
Total cost for 20 loaves	$ 9.50

Actual Operating Results for Pamela's Bakery

Number of loaves produced	90,000
Direct labor hours worked	850
Wage rate for direct labor	$12.00 per hour
Materials purchased	160,000 pounds
Materials used in production	150,000 pounds
Price paid for materials	$.19 per pound

Required:
A. Compute all labor and material variances.
B. Is Pamela's Bakery performing better than the national standards?

Problem 10-13 Use of Cost Variance Reports

The Mazda Company produces and sells wooden workstations used with microcomputers. In recent months, the firm's actual profit results have deviated unfavorably from those budgeted because of production cost problems. For example, the company's most recent income statement showed the following:

MAZDA COMPANY
Income Statement
Month Ended March 31, 1987

	Budgeted	Actual	Variance
Sales	$600,000	$600,000	$ –0–
Variable cost of goods sold	240,000	280,000	40,000 Unf.
Variable selling expenses	60,000	60,000	–0–
Contribution margin	300,000	260,000	40,000 Unf.
Fixed costs:			
Manufacturing	160,000	160,000	–0–
Selling and administrative	80,000	80,000	–0–
Net income	$ 60,000	$ 20,000	$40,000 Unf.

The firm's controller is disturbed by the profit results and wants to initiate the use of cost variance reports prepared on a monthly basis. The company has operated a standard cost system for several years. However, the standard costs have been used primarily for budgeting purposes and variances have been reviewed only in the controller's office. To achieve better cost control, the controller wants monthly cost variance reports prepared for the managers responsible for the related cost performance.

The standards established earlier for the direct costs required for each workstation are:

Walnut wood:	4 feet at $8 per foot	$32
Direct labor:	1.6 hours at $10 per hour	16
Total		$48

During March, 5,000 workstations were produced and sold. Raw materials are purchased on a "just in time basis" so the amount purchased is equal to that used. The following actual costs were recorded during March:

Raw materials—22,000 feet at $8.20 per foot

Direct labor—9,960 hours at $10.00 per hour

All manufacturing overhead is a fixed cost.

Required:
A. Prepare cost variance reports for:
   1. The purchasing department manager
   2. The production department manager

Identify all cost variances incurred during March in your reports.

B. List probable causes of the variances identified in part A.

Problem 10-14 Establishing Standard Labor Hours

The Cardwell Company produces several models of robots that are used to manufacture automobiles. The firm has been in existence for only five years and has experienced significantly higher production costs during the past three years. A job order cost system using actual cost data has been used to accumulate product costs. The president of the firm, Bill Cardwell, has an engineering background. He has analyzed the cost data from the performance of the past three years and is alarmed because labor costs have increased 50% during that period. In turn, the company's profits declined by 80%.

Mr. Cardwell hired an engineering consulting firm to evaluate the labor cost performance and establish labor standards for the future. In analyzing the report prepared by the engineering consulting firm, the president notes the following times required by several workers to perform a certain operation in the production of a particular robot:

Worker	Time Required (Hours)
J. Jones	5.5
H. Herff	5.5
J. Alkins	5.5
R. Merden	5.8
D. Madden	6.2
B. Kulsrod	6.2
V. Bingley	6.2
D. Douglas	6.6
B. Jordan	7.2
S. Burns	7.3
Average	6.2

In addition, the president is further confused because the engineering consulting firm has informed him that the operation in question should be performed in five hours if ideal operating conditions and labor efficiency existed. The firm's cost accountant advises the president that the standard labor quantity should be 5.5 hours for the operation. However, the production manager involved says that the average amount of labor (6.2 hours) should be used as the standard. The president believes that the choice of an appropriate labor standard for this operation is an important decision because the same thinking will be used for all production operations in order to control future labor costs.

Required:

A. What is the difference between an ideal standard cost and an attainable standard cost?

B. What should be established as the standard quantity of labor in this case? Why?

Problem 10-15 Use of Different Labor Rates

The Apple Company is a franchised moving company located in a midwestern college community. The business is very seasonal with a slack period from December through March. Standard labor rates are used to bid for moving jobs and to account for the various jobs. Interstate drivers are the highest paid employees at $12 per hour as established by a union contract.

During the winter months, these drivers are often used to pack household and office items involved with local moves. The regular packers are laid off during the slack period. They typically earn $8 per hour. The Packing Department manager is very disturbed with this policy because her department is charged for the $12 per hour even though the standard is only $8. Consequently, her department consistently shows a large labor rate variance even though the department is otherwise profitable.

Required:

Evaluate the firm's policy for the treatment of drivers' wages. Do you suggest any modifications?

11

FLEXIBLE BUDGETS AND STANDARD MANUFACTURING OVERHEAD COSTING

CHAPTER OVERVIEW AND OBJECTIVES

In this chapter, we continue the discussion of standard costing by applying it to manufacturing overhead. After studying this chapter, you should be able to:

1. Explain why a fixed budget is of limited value to management for control purposes.
2. Prepare a flexible budget and discuss how it is used.
3. Describe how a flexible budget performance report is used to control costs.
4. Discuss how standard manufacturing overhead is applied to the products produced.
5. Determine how a manufacturing overhead flexible budget is developed based on some measure of standard production activity.
6. Evaluate how the choice of production activity level affects the predetermined overhead rate.
7. Distinguish between the four definitions of production capacity.
8. Account for over- or underapplied manufacturing overhead.
9. Compute and evaluate standard manufacturing overhead cost variances with the two-variance method.
10. Compute and evaluate standard manufacturing overhead cost variances with the three-variance method.
11. Prepare journal entries to record manufacturing overhead cost variances in general ledger accounts.
12. Recognize how standard cost variances are presented in an income statement used for internal reporting.

TREATMENT OF MANUFACTURING OVERHEAD AS A STANDARD COST

In Chapter 10, we described how standard costs are established for the direct manufacturing costs and used for managerial planning, control, and decision making. Since the materials and labor are directly traceable to the products produced, the product specifications dictate both the standard quantity and standard price for each of the direct manufacturing costs. The standard cost treatment of manufacturing overhead is more complicated than it is for the direct manufacturing costs for four reasons:

1. As discussed in Chapter 3, manufacturing overhead cannot be traced directly to the products produced so it must be applied to them on the basis of a predetermined overhead rate. The use of a standard cost system does not change the indirect nature of manufacturing overhead; thus, standard inputs of manufacturing overhead *cannot* be directly related to the production output in the same manner as direct materials and direct labor.
2. Manufacturing overhead consists of several dissimilar types of costs (e.g., supplies, maintenance, insurance, idle time, and depreciation), many of which are relatively small in dollar amount. It would be *impractical* to try to develop a standard cost for each item separately.
3. The three major types of cost behavior—variable, fixed, and mixed—typically are experienced with manufacturing overhead. In contrast, the direct manufacturing costs are only variable costs.
4. The amount of manufacturing overhead applied to the products will depend on whether absorption costing or variable costing is used. For a complete coverage of product costing, the emphasis in this chapter is on *standard absorption costing.*

A **flexible budget** is the basic managerial accounting tool used to overcome these complications in the standard cost treatment of manufacturing overhead. This type of budget shows the expected future costs for a range of business activity instead of only a single level. A flexible budget format can be used for all types of costs as well as all types of budgets, including a manufacturing overhead budget prepared during the master budgeting process.

A manufacturing overhead flexible budget is based on some *measure of standard production activity* such as standard direct labor hours or standard machine hours. A predetermined overhead rate selected from the flexible budget is used to apply manufacturing overhead in standard amounts as production takes place. Standard cost variance analysis is later used to identify the sources of a difference between the actual manufacturing overhead incurred and the standard amount applied with the predetermined overhead rate. Before we discuss a flexible budget for manufacturing overhead, let's evaluate how a flexible budget generally is developed and used, beginning with the consideration of a fixed budget's basic limitation.

LIMITATION OF PERFORMANCE EVALUATION WITH A FIXED BUDGET

Objective 1: Evaluating the limitations of a fixed budget

The various budgets discussed in Chapter 8 are **fixed budgets** (or **static budgets**), because they consider only one level of sales or production activity. The starting point in the development of a master budget is the sales forecast for the budget period. The planning phase of the management cycle is served effectively by this approach since all the firm's activities are directed toward a common level of achievement. The production level and all budgets for manufacturing, selling, and administrative activities are based on the single estimate of sales.

A potential problem with using a fixed budget for control purposes is that it does not take into consideration the possibility that the firm may not achieve the sales or production goals. If the actual level of activity for sales or production *differs* significantly from what is planned, performance evaluation is difficult with a fixed budget. For example, consider the comparison of the budgeted performance and the actual cost results achieved by the production department of the Leil Manufacturing Company shown in Figure 11-1.

Can we really say that the production department's actual cost performance was $77,460 less than its budget? This might be the conclusion based on a fixed budget approach, although it would be erroneous. We also must note that the department only produced 20,000 of the 25,000 units budgeted, so the variable costs should automatically be lower than those budgeted.

The fixed budget estimates in Figure 11-1 simply do not reflect what costs should be for the actual units produced. We cannot compare the manufacturing costs of one production level with those of another production level and expect the results to be of any value for control purposes. Instead, a flexible budget should be used to provide a comparable basis for evaluating a cost per-

Figure 11-1

LEIL MANUFACTURING COMPANY			
Fixed Budget Performance Report			
Year Ended December 31, 1987			
	Budget	Actual	Variance
Production units	25,000	20,000	5,000 U
Variable costs:			
Direct materials	$150,000	$132,000	$18,000 F
Direct labor	360,000	312,000	48,000 F
Indirect materials	15,000	13,680	1,320 F
Indirect labor	22,500	19,440	3,060 F
Utilities	37,500	29,520	7,980 F
Total variable costs	585,000	506,640	78,360 F
Fixed costs:			
Supervision	72,600	73,680	1,080 U
Property taxes	10,440	10,440	–0–
Insurance	6,240	6,360	120 U
Maintenance	5,640	5,340	300 F
Depreciation	18,360	18,360	–0–
Total fixed costs	113,280	114,180	900 U
Total manufacturing costs	$698,280	$620,820	$77,460 F

F indicates a favorable variance
U indicates an unfavorable variance

formance when the actual level of activity is different from the one budgeted (see Figure 11-2 for a sample flexible budget).

PREPARATION OF A FLEXIBLE BUDGET

Objective 2: Developing and using a flexible budget

The basic steps used to prepare a flexible budget are:

1. Select the measure of activity to be used to prepare the budget (e.g., direct labor hours or units of production).
2. Define the relevant range of activity for the budgeted performance based on the measure of activity selected in step 1.
3. Identify the cost items to be included in the budget.
4. Determine the cost behavior of each cost item over the relevant range.
5. Separate the cost items into variable and fixed cost categories (a mixed cost is split between the two).
6. Select the specific levels of activity to be budgeted.
7. Use the cost behavior patterns identified in step 4 to estimate the budgeted amounts for each cost item at the different activity levels selected in step 6.

In Figure 11-2, we see that the Leil Manufacturing Company has used production units as the measure of activity or volume. Production units have been selected as the best overall choice in this case because of the inclusion of direct materials and direct labor in the flexible budget. Other measures of activity used for flexible budgets include direct labor hours and machine hours. The

Figure 11-2

LEIL MANUFACTURING COMPANY Flexible Budget Year Ended December 31, 1987				
	Per Unit	Levels of Activity		
Production units		20,000	25,000	30,000
Variable costs:				
Direct materials	$ 6.00	$120,000	$150,000	$180,000
Direct labor	14.40	288,000	360,000	432,000
Indirect materials	.60	12,000	15,000	18,000
Indirect labor	.90	18,000	22,500	27,000
Utilities	1.50	30,000	37,500	45,000
Total variable costs	$23.40	468,000	585,000	702,000
Fixed costs:				
Supervision		72,600	72,600	72,600
Property taxes		10,440	10,440	10,440
Insurance		6,240	6,240	6,240
Maintenance		5,640	5,640	5,640
Depreciation		18,360	18,360	18,360
Total fixed costs		113,280	113,280	113,280
Total manufacturing costs		$581,280	$698,280	$815,280

best choice among measures of activity will depend on the nature of the costs included in the flexible budget. The two key factors that should be considered in the choice of activity measure are:

1. The measure chosen should be the one whose activity is most closely related to the largest portion of the variable costs involved. That is, the measure of activity *should be the best predictor of the variable costs* at various activity levels because a causal relationship exists between these costs and the activity measure.
2. The measure of activity selected should only be affected by volume changes. Thus, dollar measures should be avoided because they are subject to price-level changes that will distort the measurement over time.

A flexible budget is developed for a multi-level range of activity, not just a single level. The range of activity considered is the relevant range, or the range of activity within which the firm expects to operate. In the case of the Leil Manufacturing Company, the relevant range is from 20,000 units of production to 30,000 units. The restriction to the relevant range only is important because cost behavior patterns for variable and fixed costs are valid within that area of operation. In contrast, different cost behavior may be experienced outside the relevant range. Since a flexible budget covers a range of activity, it is "dynamic" in nature rather than static. That is, managers can revise the budget to the activity level achieved once the actual performance is known. The revised budget will be representative of what costs should have been for the activity level achieved. The "dynamic" aspect of a flexible budget increases in importance as the difference between the actual and planned activity levels widens.

The flexible budget shown in Figure 11-2 contains both direct and indirect manufacturing costs. Later, we will restrict the use of a flexible budget to manufacturing overhead only. An essential step in the preparation of a flexible budget is distinguishing between the fixed and variable costs. The cost behavior of each cost item must be studied to see if it changes as the activity level changes. As we learned earlier, a variable cost will vary in total amount proportionately with changes in volume. The variable cost rate will be constant on a per unit basis. A fixed cost will remain constant in total amount over the entire relevant range but will vary inversely on a per unit basis. A mixed or semivariable cost contains both variable and fixed components that can be separated with the cost behavior analysis techniques discussed in Chapter 5.

In the case of the Leil Manufacturing Company, three manufacturing overhead items—indirect materials, indirect labor, and utilities—have been classified as variable costs along with the direct materials and direct labor. The firm has established the following variable cost rates for the manufacturing cost performance:

Cost Item	Variable Cost Rate per Unit
Direct materials	$ 6.00
Direct labor	14.40
Indirect materials	.60
Indirect labor	.90
Utilities	1.50
Total	$23.40

Within the relevant range of 20,000 units to 30,000 units, the total variable cost rate of $23.40 will remain unchanged. In addition, total fixed manufacturing overhead of $113,280 is budgeted for any activity level within the relevant range. Consequently, the flexible budget formula for the relevant range of production activity is as follows:

Total manufacturing costs = $113,280 + $23.40 (Number of units produced)

Note that this flexible budget formula is in the form of a linear equation ($y = a + bx$, as introduced in Chapter 5) and can be used to identify the total manufacturing costs expected for any production activity level within the relevant range. The variable cost portion of the flexible budget changes for different levels of production, as we see in the Leil Manufacturing Company's flexible budget presented in Figure 11-2. Three activity levels have been chosen for the flexible budget—20,000 units (the low end of the relevant range), 30,000 units (the high end of the relevant range), and 25,000 units (a level within the relevant range). More than one level between the ends of the relevant range may be necessary for better visual display of the budgeted amounts when the area involved is extremely wide.

Once the cost behavior patterns for the various cost items considered in the flexible budget are determined, the budgeted amounts for any activity level within the relevant range can be easily computed. For example, the total variable costs will be $468,000 for 20,000 units ($23.40 × 20,000), $585,000 for 25,000 units ($23.40 × 25,000), and $702,000 for 30,000 units ($23.40 × 30,000). The variable cost rates are multiplied by a specific number of units produced to determine the budgeted costs for the individual variable cost items at that level of production. In contrast, the five fixed cost items (totaling $113,280) remain constant over the entire range of activity. Consequently, the variable costs are the costs that "flex" over different levels of activity because they are the only items that should change as we move from one level to another.

PERFORMANCE EVALUATION WITH A FLEXIBLE BUDGET

Objective 3: Using a flexible budget performance report

The use of a flexible budget for cost performance reporting makes the budget estimates and actual results *comparable* since both are based on the same level of activity (20,000 units). Figure 11-3 presents a **flexible budget performance report** for the production department of the Leil Manufacturing Company. Instead of achieving the favorable financial results that were reported with the fixed budget in Figure 11-1, the department actually incurred an unfavorable total variance of $39,540. The flexible budget performance report represents a more realistic evaluation of the departmental cost performance than the fixed budget performance report.

The variances shown in Figure 11-3 have meaning since they relate to the cost performance alone. Production differences have been eliminated by revising the flexible budget to the level of 20,000 units. The performance report provides management with a realistic indication of the areas that should be investigated further in order to control the production costs. For example, direct materials cost and direct labor cost exceeded the budget estimates by $12,000 (10%) and $24,000 (8.3%), respectively. The Leil Manufacturing Company will have to determine the cause of these unfavorable variances and make corrections if future profitability goals are to be achieved.

Figure 11-3

LEIL MANUFACTURING COMPANY
Flexible Budget Performance Report
Year Ended December 31, 1987

	Budget	Actual	Variance
Production units	20,000	20,000	–0–
Variable costs:			
Direct materials	$120,000	$132,000	$12,000 U
Direct labor	288,000	312,000	24,000 U
Indirect materials	12,000	13,680	1,680 U
Indirect labor	18,000	19,440	1,440 U
Utilities	30,000	29,520	480 F
Total variable costs	468,000	506,640	38,640 U
Fixed costs:			
Supervision	72,600	73,680	1,080 U
Property taxes	10,440	10,440	0
Insurance	6,240	6,360	120 U
Maintenance	5,640	5,340	300 F
Depreciation	18,360	18,360	0
Total fixed costs	113,280	114,180	900 U
Total manufacturing costs	$581,280	$620,820	$39,540 U

F indicates a favorable variance
U indicates an unfavorable variance

The dynamic nature of a flexible budget permits management to revise the budget to any activity level within the relevant range. In the Leil Manufacturing Company case, the actual level of activity was the same as one of the levels in the original flexible budget (20,000 units). Even if we cannot find the activity level attained in the flexible budget, we can easily revise the budget to that level by using the company's flexible budget formula. For example, if the company had produced 22,400 units, we would compute the flexible budget amount for that level as follows:

$$\text{Total manufacturing cost} = \$113,280 + \$23.40 \ (22,400 \ \text{units})$$
$$= \$637,440$$

The budgeted costs totaling $637,440 would then be compared with the actual costs incurred to produce the 22,400 units in the same report format as Figure 11-3.

OVERVIEW OF STANDARD MANUFACTURING OVERHEAD

In effect, the predetermined overhead rate discussed in Chapter 3 is a standard cost because it is computed by dividing the estimated manufacturing overhead costs for a given time period by some measure of the estimated production activity for the same period. Both the numerator (manufacturing overhead costs) and the denominator (production activity) of the fraction are based on esti-

**Objective 4:
Applying standard manufacturing overhead**

mates rather than actual results. When we apply the predetermined overhead rate to some measure of actual production activity, such as the actual direct labor hours worked, the charge to work in process inventory is a *partial standard cost*. That is, a combination of a standard rate (the predetermined overhead rate) and the actual number of labor hours recorded is involved.

Recall from Chapter 10, however, that we want the work in process inventory to be costed with standard costs only in a standard cost system. The standard amounts of direct materials and labor were determined by multiplying the standard price (rate) times the standard quantity of inputs needed to produce a specified amount of output. Likewise, the **standard amount of manufacturing overhead** in a standard cost system is determined by multiplying the predetermined overhead rate times some measure of standard production activity such as standard direct labor hours or standard machine hours.

For example, assume that a firm has a predetermined overhead rate of $8 per standard direct labor hour and a particular product should require two standard direct labor hours. Even if three actual hours of labor are needed to produce one unit of the product, the standard amount of manufacturing overhead charged to the product would be $16 ($8 × 2 hours), not $24 ($8 × 3 hours). In a standard cost system, the actual hours worked are not considered in the application of manufacturing overhead since the applied overhead should not vary from the standard amount just because the actual and standard direct labor hours are different.

The difference between the application of manufacturing overhead in an actual cost system and in a standard cost system can be summarized in T account form as follows:

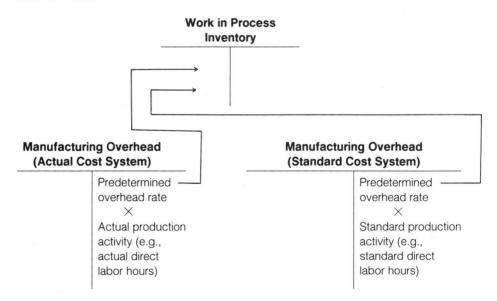

FLEXIBLE BUDGET FOR MANUFACTURING OVERHEAD

Objective 5:
Using a manufacturing overhead flexible budget

When the concept of a predetermined overhead rate was introduced in Chapter 3, we assumed for illustrative purposes that only one level of production activity had to be considered for the denominator in the rate calculation. As a result, we used a fixed budgeting approach, which is of limited value for control purposes because actual cost results can be compared only with budgeted costs for the single level of estimated activity. A flexible budget for manufacturing overhead should be utilized to avoid the limitations of a fixed budget. To do so, a flexible budget that separates the variable and fixed manufacturing overhead costs over the relevant range of production activity is prepared. Such a budget enables us to evaluate the impact of attaining an activity level that is different from the one planned.

The production levels established in a manufacturing overhead flexible budget are based on the *same* measure of standard production activity used to apply the overhead. As mentioned earlier, the measure of production activity, actual or standard, that is selected for a flexible budget should provide a close causal relationship between it and the variable manufacturing overhead costs. This means that the variable manufacturing overhead costs (the dependent variable) should vary as a result of changes in the measure of standard production activity (the independent variable). In addition, dollar measures should be avoided because of the potential distortion associated with price-level changes.

Two valid measures of standard production activity are standard direct labor hours and standard machine hours. The choice between the two depends on which method is the best predictor of the variable manufacturing overhead costs, given the type of production operation involved. A labor-intensive operation usually chooses standard direct labor hours, whereas a highly automated firm typically selects standard machine hours.

Whenever the standard production activity needed for the units of output produced is different from that planned, the original budget can be easily revised to compensate for the change. The budgeted fixed manufacturing overhead costs for the revised activity level remain the same as those in the original budget, but the variable overhead costs will change.

We will illustrate how to utilize a manufacturing overhead flexible budget by continuing the Carolina Boat Building Company case introduced in Chapter 10. Remember that the company established a standard of five direct labor hours for each sailboat hull produced. The firm applies manufacturing overhead on the basis of standard direct labor hours using the absorption costing method and has prepared the manufacturing overhead flexible budget shown in Figure 11-4. The budget represents the March portion of the 1987 annual flexible budget used by the firm to calculate a predetermined overhead rate and to provide a comparative basis for cost performance evaluation with variance analysis.

Standard direct labor hours are used to measure the level of production activity and range from 4,375 to 6,250 (the relevant range) for the month of March. Four production levels are budgeted as percentages of maximum production capacity for 70%, 80%, 90%, and 100%, respectively. Maximum production capacity is the measure of the highest production activity level a firm can achieve with its existing physical facilities and organizational structure. Because of the different definitions of production capacity discussed later and their effect on the predetermined overhead rate, it is useful to relate a firm's production activity level to its production capacity utilization. The Carolina Boat Building Company's maximum monthly production capacity is 6,250 standard direct hours or 1,250 sailboat hulls (6,250 hours/5 hours).

Remember from Chapter 10 that the company has a monthly production target of 1,000 sailboat hulls, so it plans to operate at 80% capacity or 5,000 standard hours (1,000 hulls divided by 1,250 hulls or 5,000 hours divided by

CAROLINA BOAT BUILDING COMPANY
Manufacturing Overhead Flexible Budget
Month of March, 1987

% of production capacity		70	80	90	100
Units of production		875	1,000	1,125	1,250
Standard direct labor hours		4,375	5,000	5,625	6,250
Budgeted manufacturing overhead:					
Variable costs:	Per hour				
Indirect materials	$ .20	$ 875	$ 1,000	$ 1,125	$ 1,250
Maintenance	1.20	5,250	6,000	6,750	7,500
Utilities	.60	2,625	3,000	3,375	3,750
Total variable costs	$2.00	8,750	10,000	11,250	12,500
Fixed costs:					
Supervision		11,400	11,400	11,400	11,400
Insurance		3,600	3,600	3,600	3,600
Property taxes		11,160	11,160	11,160	11,160
Supplies		2,640	2,640	2,640	2,640
Rent		7,200	7,200	7,200	7,200
Depreciation		18,000	18,000	18,000	18,000
Total fixed costs		54,000	54,000	54,000	54,000
Total manufacturing overhead		$62,750	$64,000	$65,250	$66,500
Predetermined overhead rate at 5,000 standard hours			$12.80		

Figure 11-4

6,250 hours). The variable manufacturing overhead costs change at a rate of $2 per standard direct labor hour within the relevant range of production activity. The fixed costs remain constant at $54,000 regardless of monthly production volume. As a result, the total manufacturing overhead at any level of activity within the flexible budget's relevant range can be calculated with the following formula:

$$\text{Manufacturing overhead costs} = \$54{,}000 + \$2 \text{ (Number of standard direct labor hours)}$$

IMPORTANCE OF PRODUCTION ACTIVITY LEVEL FOR PREDETERMINED OVERHEAD RATE

Objective 6: Choice of production activity level for a predetermined overhead rate

Keep in mind that we are using absorption costing in this analysis because fixed manufacturing overhead costs are related to production activity and later will be applied to the products produced. Since a range of production activity is considered in the flexible budget, a single level must be selected to calculate the predetermined overhead rate. Different predetermined overhead rates are computed for different levels of production activity. These differences occur because the fixed manufacturing overhead costs per standard hour decrease as the number of hours increase. The following schedule illustrates the effect of cost behavior on the calculation of a predetermined overhead rate from the flexible budget of the Carolina Boat Building Company.

% of Production Capacity	70	80	90	100
Standard direct labor hours (a)	4,375	5,000	5,625	6,250
Variable overhead costs (b)	$ 8,750	$10,000	$11,250	$12,500
Fixed overhead costs (c)	54,000	54,000	54,000	54,000
Total overhead costs (d)	62,750	64,000	65,250	66,500
Variable overhead rate per hour (b/a)	2.00	2.00	2.00	2.00
Fixed overhead rate per hour (c/a)	12.34	10.80	9.60	8.64
Total overhead rate per hour (d/a)	$14.34	$12.80	$11.60	$10.64

We can see in the schedule above that the total overhead rate decreases from $14.34 per hour to $10.64 per hour as the production activity level increases from 4,375 standard direct labor hours to 6,250 hours (or production capacity utilization increases from 70% to 100%). You should note that this is one of the biggest problems with absorption costing; that is, the unit costs are always changing depending on the level of production activity because of the fixed costs involved. If the correct production activity level is not selected at the beginning of the period, an incorrect amount of manufacturing overhead will be applied to the work in process inventory even if the actual cost performance is equal to its related budget estimates.

For example, if the Carolina Boat Building Company selects its predetermined overhead rate from the maximum production capacity level (6,250 standard hours), the fixed cost portion of the rate will be $8.64. If the firm works only 4,750 standard hours, the fixed manufacturing overhead costs applied will be $41,040 (4,750 hours × $8.64), despite the fact that the budgeted fixed costs were $54,000. Consequently, the fixed costs will be underapplied by $12,960 ($54,000 less $41,040) if the actual fixed manufacturing overhead costs also are $54,000. Variable manufacturing overhead costs do not cause the same problem since they automatically adjust to the level of 4,750 hours (the "flex" part of the budget) with the applied amount and budgeted amount being equal at $9,500 (4,750 hours × $2).

Since the fixed portion of most firms' manufacturing overhead has increased significantly in recent years because of the movement to automation, a correct choice of production activity level is an important management decision. If the right level is not selected prior to the beginning of a given period, the fixed manufacturing overhead costs will not be applied accurately and the unit product costs that result from the costing process will not be reliable.

DIFFERENT DEFINITIONS OF PRODUCTION CAPACITY

Up to now, we have discussed the importance of the production activity level choice without defining how the level selected compares with the total production capacity available. That is, should the production activity level chosen for the predetermined overhead rate be the maximum capacity of the production operation or something less? Initially determining the size or maximum capacity of a plant or factory is a capital budgeting decision as described in Chapter 9. Utilizing the available capacity, however, is a management decision that has an important bearing on the application of manufacturing overhead (with absorption costing) and the firm's profitability.

Objective 7: Identifying four definitions of production capacity

The choice of production activity level for the predetermined overhead rate should be made on the basis of a careful evaluation of a firm's existing production facilities and organizational structure as well as the sales demand anticipated for a given period. As such, the choice usually is made on the basis of the extent to which management plans to utilize the firm's production capacity (often called operating capacity) during a particular time period. The following four definitions of **production capacity** (production activity level) are used for different purposes in the business world:

1. **Maximum capacity.** The highest level of production activity possible if optimal operating conditions exist with no delays, material shortages, or maintenance problems. This measure assumes that the firm will operate continuously at peak efficiency, so it is the best possible performance.
2. **Practical capacity.** The maximum production activity level reduced by reasonable allowances for departures from an optimal performance. This measure recognizes that an operation cannot be perfect all the time and that a certain amount of inefficiency is unavoidable.
3. **Expected capacity.** The level of production activity anticipated during a specific year, given the firm's operating conditions and market demand for its products. This measure is based on the production requirements identified in the annual master budget as being necessary to meet the sales demand forecast for the period. Any anticipated cyclical fluctuations in sales demand between years are ignored with expected capacity because of its one-year focus.
4. **Normal capacity.** The average annual production activity that will satisfy the market demand over a relatively long time period, such as a three-to-five-year period. This measure is based on the consideration of cyclical fluctuations of market demand that are characteristic of many industries such as steel and automotive. In other words, wide swings of sales between years will cause a cyclical firm to produce at a high level one year and a lower level in the near future. The normal capacity concept normalizes the high and low production performances by considering the average annual production activity anticipated over a three-to-five-year period. Other firms use normal capacity to average out a trend in production activity over a period of several years.

Since sales demand is ignored with maximum and practical capacities, these measures are seldom used for predetermining a manufacturing overhead rate. If either of them are used, large variances between the overhead applied and the amount actually incurred will often occur and will be meaningless for managerial attention. They simply are caused by a fluctuating sales demand that *was not even considered* when the capacity level originally was selected. If the production volume does not change significantly from year to year, expected capacity and normal capacity will be approximately equal.

Most managers believe that the normal capacity produces the most accurate manufacturing overhead rates when significant fluctuations in production volume occur between years. The longer period normalizes the fluctuations between years and provides more consistent overhead application rates. For example, consider the differences in the annual predetermined overhead rates that would result in the following situation when expected and normal capacity are compared for a firm with a cyclical sales record over a three-year period. All of the firm's manufacturing overhead is fixed and is budgeted at $600,000 per year. The annual production level required for the sales demand ranges from a low of 10,000 units in the first year to a high of 50,000 units in the third year. The average annual production units budgeted for the three-year period are equal to the number of units budgeted in the second year or 30,000.

Year	1	2	3	Total
Budgeted fixed manufacturing overhead (a)	$600,000	$600,000	$600,000	$1,800,000
Budgeted production in units (b)	10,000	30,000	50,000	90,000
Predetermined overhead rate per unit produced (a)/(b)	$60	$20	$12	$20

If expected capacity is used, the predetermined overhead rate will change drastically from year to year even though the budgeted fixed manufacturing overhead is $600,000 each year. To avoid the significant inconsistency of the predetermined overhead rates and the resulting adverse impact on the unit costs of the products produced, the firm can use a normal capacity approach by selecting a $20 predetermined overhead rate for each of the three years. This approach normalizes the extreme production activity differences between years and results in more consistent unit product costs. As such, it is actually an extension of the basis upon which the predetermined overhead rate itself is justified.

Remember from Chapter 3 that a major reason for using a predetermined overhead rate, rather than actual overhead, in product costing is to avoid inconsistent unit cost results when the production volume changes significantly from month to month. The normal capacity concept extends this need to allocate the overhead costs to a time period longer than one year by considering the cyclical and trend fluctuations between years as well as any seasonal differences between months.

Remember too that the use of a predetermined overhead rate causes an over- or underapplied condition between months. We will find the same results between years when the normal capacity concept is used because overapplications of overhead in some years will be offset by underapplications in other years. For example, in the previous illustration, the use of a $20 predetermined overhead rate each year will cause an underapplication of overhead in the first year because the $20 normalized rate is lower than the $60 rate based on expected capacity. This underapplied condition will be offset in the third year when the normalized rate of $20 is greater than the $12 rate based on expected capacity, and overhead is overapplied as a result. We will see how to treat over- or underapplied overhead in a standard cost system later in this chapter.

CHOICE OF DENOMINATOR
FOR PREDETERMINED OVERHEAD RATE

Once a specific production capacity level has been chosen as the operating goal from the manufacturing overhead flexible budget, the denominator of the predetermined overhead rate (budgeted production activity level) is defined. Some firms call this measure the **denominator activity** used to apply manufacturing overhead. Remember from our discussion in Chapter 3 that once the denominator activity is selected, it remains unchanged throughout the accounting period involved because its main purpose is to provide a consistent predetermined overhead rate during the entire period rather than the changing rates that otherwise would prevail. The denominator activity—which is the best estimate of production activity for overhead application purposes—is divided into the total budgeted manufacturing overhead costs for the period. The resulting predetermined overhead rate consists of variable and fixed components. The variable part of the rate is the same as it would have been for any production activity level, but the fixed portion is valid only for that particular level.

As production takes place, manufacturing overhead costs are assigned to work in process inventory by applying the predetermined overhead rate to each standard measure of production activity recorded in the standard cost system. In the case of the Carolina Boat Building Company, the standard measure of production activity is standard direct labor hours as shown in Figure 11-4. We assume that the firm has used a normal capacity approach in defining its monthly production target of 5,000 standard direct labor hours. Normal capacity is utilized because the company experiences both seasonal and cyclical fluctuations in sales demand. A predetermined overhead rate for March of $12.80 per standard direct labor hour is computed in Figure 11-4. The company will apply the $12.80 rate to each standard direct labor hour allowed as the sailboat hulls are produced.

Note that the rate consists of a $2 variable cost component and a $10.80 fixed cost element. Instead of using the total rate of $12.80 to apply the overhead, the company could apply the variable and fixed costs separately with a $2 per hour rate for the variable costs and a $10.80 rate for the fixed costs. When this alternative treatment is chosen, overhead application is based on cost behavior as the two rates are charged separately to the standard direct labor hours allowed for production.

By adding the standard direct manufacturing costs needed to produce a sailboat hull to the amount of manufacturing overhead determined from the flexible budget (Figure 11-4), the total standard cost for each hull can be calculated as follows:

Direct materials:		
Fiberglass fabric (140 sq. ft. @ $.90)		$126
Fiberglass mix (50 lbs. @ $1.20)		60
Direct labor (5 hrs. @ $10)		50
Manufacturing overhead:		
Variable costs (5 hrs. @ $2)	$10	
Fixed costs (5 hrs. @ $10.80)	54	
Total manufacturing overhead		64
Standard cost per sailboat hull		$300

Consequently, the firm's goal is to produce each sailboat hull for $300 when all standard costs are considered.

USING THE PREDETERMINED OVERHEAD RATE

Remember from Chapter 10 that 4,750 standard direct labor hours were allowed for the Carolina Boat Building Company's March production performance (950 sailboat hulls produced × 5 standard direct labor hours per hull). The manufacturing overhead costs are applied to work in process inventory by charging the $12.80 predetermined overhead rate to each of the 4,750 standard hours allowed. Thus, total manufacturing overhead of $60,800 was charged to the sailboat hulls that were worked on during March (4,750 hours × $12.80).

The variable overhead costs applied amounted to $9,500 (4,750 × $2), and the fixed manufacturing overhead costs were $51,300 (4,750 × $10.80). Keep in mind that these are the *applied* manufacturing overhead costs, *not* the costs *actually* incurred. Once we know the actual manufacturing overhead costs, we will have to reconcile and account for the difference between the applied and actual overhead costs.

Note that the 4,950 direct labor hours actually worked during the Carolina Boat Building Company's March performance have been ignored in the overhead costing. As we mentioned earlier, the standard direct labor hours allowed, not the actual hours worked, are used to apply manufacturing overhead costs in a standard cost system. This approach enables the firm to charge each unit of product with the same amount of manufacturing overhead cost, the standard amount, or $64 per sailboat hull (5 standard hours allowed × $12.80). If actual direct labor hours were used, different amounts of manufacturing overhead would be applied to various products because of differences in the labor time spent on the products, not differences in the overhead itself. At the end of March, the Work in Process Inventory account and the Manufacturing Overhead account would show the following:

Work in Process Inventory		Manufacturing Overhead	
60,800		60,800	
		(4,750 hr × $12.80)	

OVERAPPLIED AND UNDERAPPLIED MANUFACTURING OVERHEAD

Remember from Chapter 3 that differences between the actual manufacturing overhead incurred and the overhead applied are inevitable because the applied amount is based on estimates. When the applied overhead is less than the actual amount, the difference is an *underapplied* manufacturing overhead variance. It is unfavorable because the work in process inventory has been undercosted when the higher actual overhead is considered. In contrast, an *overapplied* manufacturing overhead variance exists whenever the amount of manufacturing overhead applied exceeds the actual overhead incurred during a given period. An overapplied overhead variance is favorable because the work in process inventory has been charged with more overhead than the amount actually incurred. Thus, the product costs are higher than they need to be once the actual manufacturing overhead is known.

When you first consider an overhead variance, identifying an underapplied amount as unfavorable and an overapplied amount as favorable may seem contradictory because of the usual meaning of the terms "under" and "over." The two terms are not used, however, to explain whether actual manufacturing overhead costs are "under" or "over" those budgeted. They simply describe how accurate the estimates used for the predetermined overhead rate are once the actual manufacturing overhead for the period is known. An underapplied variance indicates that an inadequate amount of overhead has been applied to

Objective 8: Accounting for over- or underapplied manufacturing overhead

work in process inventory, whereas an overapplied variance means that the inventory would have been valued lower with actual costs.

In Chapter 3, we considered the accounting treatment of an over- or underapplied overhead variance needed to prepare financial statements for a manufacturing firm. We now turn our attention to how we can determine the sources of an over- or underapplied overhead variance in a standard cost system by using variance analysis. This analysis provides management with valuable information for corrective action and future profit improvement.

To illustrate manufacturing overhead variance analysis, assume that the following actual overhead costs were incurred by the Carolina Boat Building Company during March:

Actual variable manufacturing overhead costs	$10,600
Actual fixed manufacturing overhead costs	54,800
Actual total manufacturing overhead costs	$65,400

Remember that the applied manufacturing overhead for the company's March production performance was computed by multiplying the $12.80 predetermined overhead rate by the 4,750 standard direct labor hours allowed for a total of $60,800. As a result, an underapplied (unfavorable) overhead variance of $4,600 (actual overhead costs of $65,400 less the applied costs of $60,800) was incurred for the month of March. The next step is to determine the sources of the total overhead variance of $4,600. The T accounts shown earlier can be revised to reflect the actual versus applied manufacturing overhead as follows:

Work in Process Inventory		Manufacturing Overhead	
→ 60,800		65,400 (Actual)	60,800 (Applied)
			4,600 (Underapplied)

MANUFACTURING OVERHEAD VARIANCE ANALYSIS

The basic objective of manufacturing overhead variance analysis is dividing over- or underapplied overhead as a total variance into more detailed variances that help managers determine the reasons why the applied overhead and the actual overhead are not equal. The $4,600 unfavorable overhead variance incurred by the Carolina Boat Building Company only indicates that the actual overhead exceeded the applied overhead. In order to control manufacturing overhead, the firm's management must identify the sources of the unfavorable difference between the applied and actual overhead—just as it did with direct materials and direct labor. Thus, the breakdown of the total manufacturing overhead variance into more detailed variances is similar to the calculation of price (rate) and quantity (efficiency) variances for the direct manufacturing costs. In addition, the same five questions discussed in Chapter 10 are applicable to manufacturing overhead variance analysis:

1. When did the variance occur?
2. Where did the variance occur?

3. Why did the variance occur?

4. Who is responsible for the variance?

5. What can be done about the variance?

Two of the most widely used methods for manufacturing overhead variance analysis are the **two-variance method** and the **three-variance method.** The basic difference between the two methods is that the three-variance method provides more detail than the two-variance method. To illustrate the two methods, we will apply them to the Carolina Boat Building Company case. Before doing so, let's identify three important definitions of direct labor that should help you understand the calculations used in manufacturing overhead variance analysis. Remember that the Carolina Boat Building Company uses standard direct labor hours for the development of the manufacturing overhead flexible budget and the application of overhead to products produced. Direct labor hours are defined in three different ways in the operation of a standard cost system:

1. *Budgeted hours* (denominator activity) are the number of standard hours estimated at the beginning of a period for the predetermined overhead rate. In the Carolina Boat Building Company illustration, the budgeted hours are 5,000.

2. *Standard hours allowed* are the number of direct labor hours that should have been worked for the production results achieved during the period. That is, standard hours allowed represent the standard inputs needed for the actual outputs achieved and are an important part of overhead variance analysis when a firm such as Carolina Boat Building Company applies overhead on the basis of standard direct labor hours. During March, the company's standard hours allowed are 4,750 (950 hulls produced $\times$ 5 hours per hull). We will base the description of overhead variance analysis that follows on the use of standard direct labor hours although the same procedures are valid for other measures of standard production activity such as standard machine hours.

3. *Actual hours* are the number of direct labor hours that actually were worked during the period to achieve the production results. During March, 4,950 actual hours were worked by the production department of the Carolina Boat Building Company.

TWO-VARIANCE OVERHEAD ANALYSIS

Over- and underapplied manufacturing overhead as a total variance can be divided into two components: a budget variance and a capacity variance. A **budget** or **controllable variance** is the difference between the actual manufacturing overhead costs and the flexible budget based on the standard hours allowed for the actual production outputs achieved. Whenever the actual overhead costs are greater than the costs from the flexible budget, the budget variance is unfavorable. In contrast, a favorable budget variance arises if the actual overhead costs are less than the costs from the flexible budget.

A **capacity** or **denominator variance** is the difference between the flexible budget for the standard hours allowed and the total overhead applied to the products based on the standard hours allowed. If the overhead costs from the flexible budget exceed those applied, the capacity variance is unfavorable. Conversely, overhead costs from the flexible budget that are less than the costs applied result in a favorable capacity variance.

Objective 9:
Using the
two-variance
method of
overhead analysis

The following general analytical framework provides a useful, systematic way to compute and understand the budget variance and the capacity variance:

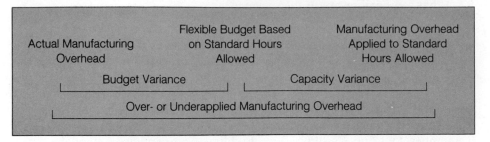

Note that this analytical framework is similar to the input/output models presented for the direct manufacturing cost variances in Chapter 10. Applying the analytical framework to the March manufacturing overhead performance of the Carolina Boat Building Company, we show the computation of the budget variance and the capacity variance in Figure 11-5.

To compute the two variances in Figure 11-5 we need three totals for the manufacturing overhead cost performance as shown in columns (2), (3), and (4):

Column (2)—Presents the actual manufacturing overhead incurred during the period. As indicated earlier, the firm recorded overhead costs totaling $65,400 during March.

Column (3)—Presents the flexible budget based on the standard hours allowed. This amount is determined from the flexible budget used to compute the predetermined overhead rate at the beginning of the period (Fig-

Figure 11-5

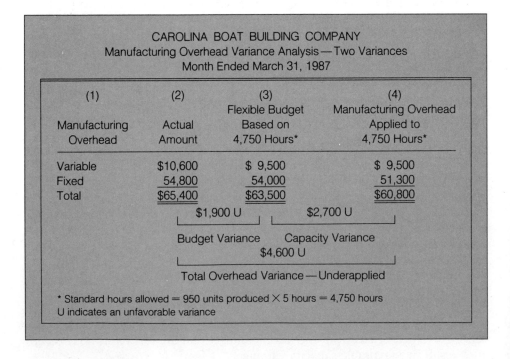

ure 11-4). To do so, we simply find the budgeted amount for the standard hours allowed in achieving the production output of the period. The company produced 950 units during March, and each unit required five standard hours. Thus, the standard hours allowed amounted to 4,750 (950 units × 5 hours). You should note that this is the same figure computed in Chapter 10 for the labor efficiency variance. Using the formula presented earlier, the flexible budget for 4,750 hours is:

$$
\begin{aligned}
\text{Budgeted manufacturing overhead} &= \$54,000 + \$2 \, (4,750 \text{ hours}) \\
&= \$54,000 + \$9,500 \\
&= \$63,500
\end{aligned}
$$

Column (4)—Presents the manufacturing overhead applied to the products produced on the basis of the standard hours allowed. The standard hours allowed in our illustration are 4,750 as computed above. The predetermined overhead rate computed at the beginning of the period is $12.80. Thus, the total manufacturing overhead applied during March is $60,800. (Note that this is the same amount identified earlier when we computed the underapplied overhead.)

Once we have determined the three amounts—actual manufacturing overhead ($65,400), budgeted overhead for the standard hours allowed ($63,500), and applied overhead ($60,800)—we can compute the two overhead variances. The budget variance is the difference between columns (2) and (3). The capacity variance is the difference between columns (3) and (4). The total overhead variance is the amount underapplied, computed by subtracting column (4) from column (2) ($65,400 − $60,800 = $4,600).

Budget Variance

The budget variance for the Carolina Boat Building Company's March performance is an unfavorable $1,900. Actual manufacturing overhead ($65,400) exceeded the flexible budget for the standard direct labor hours allowed ($63,500) by the $1,900. The budget variance is a measure of management's efficiency in utilizing the manufacturing overhead cost of the firm. This variance will be the responsibility of the manager in charge of the related manufacturing operation. Common causes of budget variances include:

1. Changes in the price or rate paid for items such as utilities or rent
2. An excessive use of overhead costs such as indirect materials or indirect labor
3. Urgent production orders requiring excessive amounts of overhead
4. Equipment breakdowns
5. An efficient operation
6. Unrealistic budgeted costs

Capacity Variance

An unfavorable capacity variance of $2,700 was also incurred by the Carolina Boat Building Company during March. The overhead applied was only $60,800 while the amount budgeted for the standard direct labor hours allowed amounted to $63,500. If the company had achieved its production target of

1,000 sailboat hulls or 5,000 standard direct labor hours, the amount originally budgeted (variable costs of $10,000 and fixed costs of $54,000) would have been applied because the applied overhead is determined by multiplying the $12.80 predetermined overhead rate times the standard hours allowed (5,000 hours $\times$ $12.80 = $64,000). But the firm did not achieve its production target since only 950 hulls were produced while 4,750 standard direct labor hours were used.

What effect did the difference in the planned production activity and the one attained have on the $4,600 unfavorable total overhead variance? We know from cost behavior analysis that the total variable costs decrease in proportion to declines in production. Consequently, as the production activity is reduced from 5,000 hours to 4,750 hours, the budgeted variable overhead costs also decrease at the rate of $2 per hour ($10,000 to $9,500).

This automatic adjustment with the variable overhead costs that takes place means that they cannot contribute to a capacity variance because the amount applied will always equal the amount budgeted for the standard direct labor hours allowed. That is, the flexible budget variable overhead costs in column (3) are computed by multiplying the $2 variable cost rate by the 4,750 standard direct labor hours. This is the same calculation used for the applied variable overhead costs in column (4).

However, we have the same problem with the fixed manufacturing overhead costs discussed earlier in this chapter because they remain constant in total amount over a range of production activity but vary inversely with a change in the level of production. We illustrated earlier that the $10.80 fixed portion of the predetermined overhead rate is valid only for a production level of 5,000 standard direct labor hours. Whenever the Carolina Boat Building Company works more or less standard direct labor hours, the use of the $10.80 fixed cost rate will cause the $54,000 fixed overhead costs to be misapplied. This is what happened in March when the firm recorded 4,750 standard direct labor hours instead of 5,000; thus, a capacity variance of $2,700 resulted. The $54,000 budgeted fixed overhead costs shown in column (3) are $2,700 more than the $51,300 applied fixed overhead costs in column (4), and the variance is the result of working at a capacity that was different from the one planned for the month.

As a result of this analysis, we can conclude that *only the fixed manufacturing overhead costs will be the source of any capacity variance.* Alternatively, we can compute the capacity variance for the Carolina Boat Building Company as follows:

Capacity variance = (Budgeted hours − Standard hours allowed) $\times$ Fixed cost rate
= (5,000 − 4,750) $\times$ $10.80
= 250 $\times$ $10.80
= $2,700 Unfavorable

An unfavorable capacity variance is an important measure of the cost of planned capacity available to the firm *but not utilized.* For example, in the Carolina Boat Building Company case, management's goal was to operate at a normal capacity of 5,000 standard direct labor hours, but only 4,750 standard direct labor hours were worked. As a result, the planned capacity of the firm was *underutilized* by 5% (250 hours/5,000 hours), and the $54,000 fixed costs could have been used for more production. This difference explains the unfavorable capacity variance of $2,700 (5% of $54,000 = $2,700). The $10.80 fixed cost portion of the predetermined overhead rate simply was not adequate to absorb all the budgeted fixed manufacturing overhead costs ($54,000).

The reasons for the idle capacity may range from manufacturing problems to a lack of sales orders. As a result, either the production department manager or the marketing manager may be responsible for a capacity variance, depending on the circumstances. An error in the choice of capacity level used for the predetermined overhead rate will also cause a capacity variance.

Use of a Budget Variance Report

The budget variance computed earlier is the result of spending performance only because the work performance is held constant by comparing the actual spending for the standard direct labor hours allowed with the related budgeted amounts. For a more detailed evaluation of the spending performance, each individual manufacturing cost could be itemized to show the actual and budgeted amounts rather than just showing the totals as we did in Figure 11-5. Since the more detailed information is only pertinent for assessing the budget variance, most firms list the itemized overhead costs in a budget variance report, such as the one presented in Figure 11-6. This report provides management with important information concerning the specific cost items involved in the total budget variance of $1,900. It extends the budget variance analysis

Figure 11-6

CAROLINA BOAT BUILDING COMPANY
Budget Variance Report — Production Department
Month Ended March 31, 1987

	Budget*	Actual	Variance
Variable manufacturing overhead costs:			
Indirect materials	$ 950	$ 1,140	$ 190 U
Maintenance	5,700	6,130	430 U
Utilities	2,850	3,330	480 U
Total variable costs	9,500	10,600	1,100 U
Fixed manufacturing overhead costs:			
Supervision	11,400	11,800	400 U
Insurance	3,600	3,600	–0–
Property taxes	11,160	11,160	–0–
Supplies	2,640	3,040	400 U
Rent	7,200	7,200	–0–
Depreciation	18,000	18,000	–0–
Total fixed costs	54,000	54,800	800 U
Total manufacturing overhead	$63,500	$65,400	$1,900 U

* Budgeted costs for the 4,750 standard hours allowed
U indicates an unfavorable variance

of Figure 11-5 and assists the manager responsible for the work performance in controlling manufacturing overhead spending.

THREE-VARIANCE OVERHEAD ANALYSIS

**Objective 10:
Using the
three-variance
method of
overhead analysis**

Many managers prefer the three-variance method for analyzing a manufacturing overhead performance because it adds a third dimension that can be important for control purposes. The term "three-variance method" refers to the division of the over- or underapplied overhead variance into three separate components: a *spending variance,* an *efficiency variance,* and a *capacity variance.* In the explanation of the two-variance method, we showed that the budget variance is the difference between the actual manufacturing overhead recorded and the flexible budget based on the standard hours allowed. We explained that this variance is the result of a firm's spending more or less than the amount allowed in the budget.

However, there is a dimension of this spending performance that we have not recognized because of the way the budget variance is computed. The consideration ignored is the impact of labor efficiency on the manufacturing overhead spending performance. At first, it may seem strange that labor efficiency could affect manufacturing overhead, but consider what happens to the variable overhead costs when more or less direct labor hours are required than those allowed in the standard cost system. By definition, the variable overhead costs will rise or fall with an increase or decrease in direct labor hours as the measure of production activity. For example, the Carolina Boat Building Company worked 4,950 actual direct labor hours compared with the 4,750 standard direct labor hours allowed. This 200-hour difference required incremental overhead support from the variable overhead costs that change as a function of production activity. In contrast, the fixed overhead costs should be $54,000 for either 4,950 direct labor hours or 4,750 direct labor hours.

The three-variance method further divides the budget variance with the two-variance method into spending and efficiency components to separate the true impact of spending from that of labor efficiency. The **spending variance** is the difference between the actual manufacturing overhead and the flexible budget based on the actual hours incurred during a period. The **overhead efficiency variance** is the difference between the flexible budget based on the actual hours and the flexible budget for the standard hours allowed. This approach provides management with additional control information because it shows the amount of variable overhead that could be saved if better labor efficiency is achieved. In the case of the Carolina Boat Building Company, the additional 200 hours of labor cost the firm $400 for the variable overhead costs (200 hours times the variable overhead cost rate of $2), so a better utilization of labor will also result in manufacturing overhead cost savings. Such information will be useful in deciding how to improve future profits but is not available with the two-variance approach in which the impact of efficiency is combined with that of spending.

The capacity variance with the three-variance method is defined and computed the same way it is with the two-variance method. Three-variance analysis can be performed with the general analytical framework presented next. To consider the overhead efficiency variance, we simply add another column for the flexible budget based on the actual direct labor hours worked during the period to the analytical framework used earlier for the two-variance method (Figure 11-5).

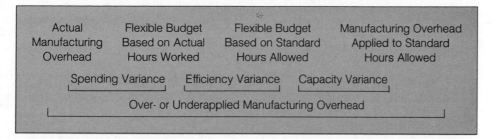

Part of the analytical framework is presented in Figure 11-7 to illustrate the computation of the spending and efficiency variances. The capacity variance calculation is *omitted* because it is the same with the three-variance method as it is in Figure 11-5.

By comparing columns (3) and (4) of Figure 11-7, we can see that only the budgeted variable overhead costs change as we move from one level of the flexible budget (4,950 hours) to another level (4,750 hours). Since we want to separate the true impact of spending from that of efficiency, we must first compare the actual manufacturing overhead incurred for the actual work performance in column (2) with the amount that should have been spent for the actual work performance in column (3). This comparison measures the impact of spending only because it eliminates any labor efficiency influence. As we see, the unfavorable spending variance is $1,500 for the Carolina Boat Building Company's March performance.

If we compare the manufacturing overhead budgeted for the actual hours worked in column (3) with the column (4) amount that should have been spent if the planned labor efficiency (the standard hours allowed) had been achieved, the difference is an unfavorable overhead efficiency variance of $400. Again, this efficiency variance is the result of the variable overhead costs only since the

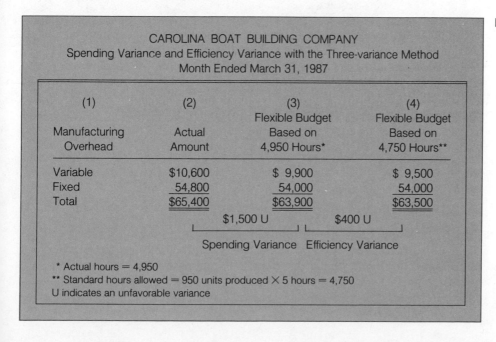

Figure 11-7

CAROLINA BOAT BUILDING COMPANY
Spending Variance and Efficiency Variance with the Three-variance Method
Month Ended March 31, 1987

(1) Manufacturing Overhead	(2) Actual Amount	(3) Flexible Budget Based on 4,950 Hours*	(4) Flexible Budget Based on 4,750 Hours**
Variable	$10,600	$ 9,900	$ 9,500
Fixed	54,800	54,000	54,000
Total	$65,400	$63,900	$63,500

$1,500 U — Spending Variance $400 U — Efficiency Variance

* Actual hours = 4,950
** Standard hours allowed = 950 units produced × 5 hours = 4,750
U indicates an unfavorable variance

fixed costs are $54,000 at both budget levels. By adding the unfavorable spending variance of $1,500 to the unfavorable efficiency variance of $400, we have the same amount identified earlier as an unfavorable budget variance with the two-variance method ($1,900).

COMPARISON OF STANDARD COST VARIANCES FOR DIFFERENT TYPES OF VARIABLE MANUFACTURING COSTS

Remember from Chapter 10 that standard cost variances for the direct manufacturing costs can be computed with a general price/quantity model. You may find it helpful to use the same general model to identify the variable manufacturing overhead costs considered when the three-variance method is applied. The general model can be used for the variable manufacturing overhead costs to determine the spending and efficiency variances because they are analogous to the price and quantity variances for the direct manufacturing costs (remember that a capacity variance is the result of fixed overhead costs only). The general model is used to compute the spending and efficiency variances for the variable manufacturing overhead cost performance of the Carolina Boat Building Company as follows:

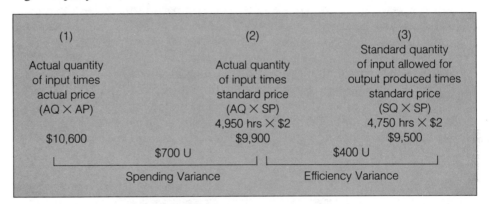

Column (1) consists of the actual variable overhead costs incurred during March and column (2) shows the actual direct labor hours (4,950) multiplied by the $2 variable overhead cost rate. The difference between columns (1) and (2) is the spending variance of $700 for the variable manufacturing overhead costs. Column (3) shows the standard direct labor hours allowed (4,750) multiplied times the $2 variable cost rate, so the difference between columns (2) and (3) is the $400 efficiency variance. These results are the same as those determined earlier for the variable overhead costs in Figure 11-7.

GRAPHIC ANALYSIS OF MANUFACTURING OVERHEAD VARIANCES

Figures 11-8 and 11-9 show graphic displays of the budget variance and the capacity variance, respectively, associated with the manufacturing overhead performance of the Carolina Boat Building Company during March. These two graphs should help you visualize what we previously determined mathematically for the budget and capacity variance components of the underapplied overhead variance.

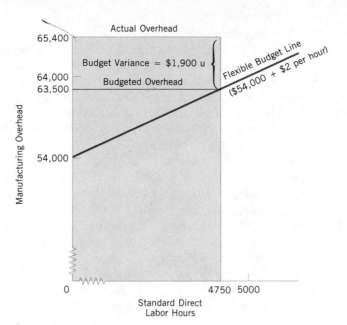

Figure 11-8
Budget Variance

Figure 11-8 shows the flexible budget line beginning at $54,000 (the fixed overhead cost) on the vertical axis and increasing at the rate of $2 per hour (the variable overhead cost rate). Whenever the actual manufacturing overhead costs incurred exceed the flexible budget line for the standard direct labor hours allowed, an unfavorable budget variance results. In contrast, actual manufacturing overhead incurred that is below the flexible budget line for the standard direct labor hours allowed produces a favorable budget variance. Since the Carolina Boat Building Company's actual overhead costs amounted to $65,400 compared with budgeted costs of $63,500 for 4,750 standard direct labor hours [$54,000 plus $2 (4,750 hours)], the $1,900 budget variance was unfavorable.

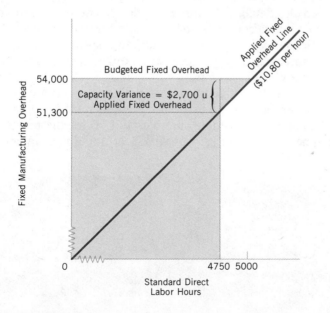

Figure 11-9
Capacity Variance

The firm's $2,700 unfavorable capacity variance is graphed in Figure 11-9. Remember that a capacity variance is the result of the fixed manufacturing overhead costs only, so the budgeted overhead costs considered in Figure 11-9 are $54,000. The applied fixed cost line begins at the origin (at zero activity, no fixed manufacturing overhead costs are applied) and increases at the rate of $10.80 (the fixed cost portion of the predetermined overhead rate).

A normal capacity level of 5,000 standard direct labor hours was chosen as the denominator activity for the allocation of the fixed overhead costs. As the graph indicates, the firm has to work the 5,000 standard direct labor hours to apply the $54,000 fixed overhead costs budgeted. If the standard direct labor hours allowed exceed 5,000, we will have a favorable capacity variance because the fixed overhead costs applied will exceed $54,000. In contrast, standard direct labor hours below 5,000 will result in an unfavorable capacity variance because all of the $54,000 fixed overhead costs will not be applied. This is what happened in the Carolina Boat Building Company case, as we see in Figure 11-9, since the 4,750 standard direct labor hours allowed multiplied by the $10.80 fixed cost rate only resulted in applied fixed costs of $51,300, which is below the $54,000 budget line for a capacity variance of $2,700.

JOURNAL ENTRIES FOR STANDARD MANUFACTURING OVERHEAD

Objective 11: Preparing journal entries for standard manufacturing overhead

In Chapter 3, we illustrated the journal entries needed to record manufacturing overhead with an actual costing system. Recall that the left side of the Manufacturing Overhead account was used to record the actual overhead incurred and the right side the overhead applied to the work in process inventory. The balance of the Manufacturing Overhead account at the end of an accounting period is the over- or underapplied overhead. We know now that the over- or underapplied overhead variance can be divided into more detailed variances using the two-variance or three-variance method. These variances are recorded in general ledger accounts with a standard cost system.

We can record the detailed variances by closing the over- or underapplied overhead variance into accounts established for a budget variance and a capacity variance with the two-variance approach or a spending variance, an efficiency variance, and a capacity variance with a three-variance approach. Again, a debit balance in a variance account is unfavorable because it is an added cost and a credit balance is favorable since it represents a reduced cost. Let's illustrate how journal entries are prepared for manufacturing overhead with the three-variance method by recording summary entries for the March manufacturing overhead performance of the Carolina Boat Building Company.

Mar.	31	Manufacturing Overhead		65,400	
		Accounts Payable			23,300
		Raw Materials Inventory			1,140
		Accrued Payroll			11,800
		Accrued Property Taxes			11,160
		Accumulated Depreciation			18,000
		(To record the manufacturing overhead actually incurred during March.)			

Work in Process Inventory	60,800	
Manufacturing Overhead		60,800
(To record the manufacturing overhead applied		
to the work in process inventory during March,		
or 4,750 standard direct labor hours times		
$12.80.)		
Overhead Spending Variance	1,500	
Overhead Efficiency Variance	400	
Overhead Capacity Variance	2,700	
Manufacturing Overhead		4,600
(To close the underapplied manufacturing		
overhead for March into the spending		
variance, efficiency variance, and capacity		
variance.)		

RECAP OF ACTUAL AND STANDARD COST PERFORMANCES

Now that we have completed the coverage of standard costs for the Carolina Boat Building Company, we can reconcile the difference between the actual manufacturing costs incurred during March with the standard costs that should have been incurred. Recall from Chapter 10 that the firm planned to produce each sailboat hull at a standard direct manufacturing cost of $236. In this chapter, we saw that the standard amount of manufacturing overhead per hull was $64 (five standard direct labor hours times the predetermined overhead rate of $12.80). Thus, the standard total cost expected for each hull was $300. Since 950 hulls were produced during March, the total standard costs should have been $285,000 (950 hulls × $300) during the month. Instead, the company incurred the following actual costs:

Fiberglass fabric (138,000 sq. ft @ $.96 per sq. ft)	$132,480
Fiberglass mix (49,000 lb @ $1.10 per lb)	53,900
Direct labor (4,950 hr @ $10.20 per hour)	50,490
Variable manufacturing overhead	10,600
Fixed manufacturing overhead	54,800
Total actual manufacturing costs	$302,270

As a result, we can see that the firm deviated as follows from its planned cost performance for the 950 sailboat hulls produced:

Total actual manufacturing overhead costs	$302,270
Total standard manufacturing costs (950 hulls × $300)	285,000
Total standard cost variance—unfavorable	$ 17,270

Assuming we are using the three-variance method for manufacturing overhead, the total standard cost variance of $17,270 can be explained with the cost variances computed previously.

Materials price variance–fiberglass fabric	$ 8,280 U
Materials price variance–fiberglass mix	4,900 F
Materials quantity variance–fiberglass fabric	4,500 U
Materials quantity variance–fiberglass mix	1,800 U
Labor rate variance	990 U
Labor efficiency variance	2,000 U

Overhead spending variance	1,500 U
Overhead efficiency variance	400 U
Overhead capacity variance	2,700 U
Total cost variance	$17,270 U

U indicates an unfavorable variance; F represents a favorable variance. This detailed cost variance information shows management why its planned cost performance was not achieved and where its attention should be directed for the improved cost control needed in the future.

TREATMENT OF STANDARD COST VARIANCES ON FINANCIAL STATEMENTS

Objective 12: Treatment of standard cost variances for income reporting purposes

We observed in Chapter 3 that an over- or underapplied overhead variance can be treated in one of three ways: (1) carried forward to the next period on the balance sheet for interim reporting; (2) closed to cost of goods sold; or (3) prorated between inventories and cost of goods sold. These same three alternative treatments are used for standard cost variances, and the choice between them depends on the size of the variances and how the financial statements involved are being utilized. The seven cost variances incurred by the Carolina Boat Building Company (or the six cost variances with the two-variance method for overhead) must be disposed of in the preparation of financial statements because they have been recorded in the general ledger.

The treatment of the standard cost variances typically is different in internal reporting than it is in external reporting for three reasons:

1. Internal reporting is not affected by generally accepted accounting principles (GAAP), which require the proration method for significant variances at the end of the year. GAAP also permit the balance sheet treatment for interim reporting and the adjustment to cost of goods sold at the end of the year for relatively small variances.
2. Since the standard costs represent management goals for a specific period, internal reporting should disclose any variances from the planned performance as they occur.
3. The detailed breakdown of the variances would be meaningless to external parties such as stockholders who do not participate in the day-to-day activities of the firm. Such outsiders are mainly concerned with the final profit results instead of the numerous steps leading to them.

The most widely-used treatment of standard cost variances for internal reporting is to present them in the income statement of the period in which they arise. As such, the variances are added to or subtracted from the period's standard cost of goods sold so management can evaluate their effect on profits. Unfavorable variances are added to the standard cost of goods sold since the related actual costs exceed the standard amounts. In contrast, favorable variances are subtracted from the standard cost of goods sold to reflect the "cost savings" involved.

To illustrate how the standard cost of goods sold is adjusted for the standard cost variances, assume that the Carolina Boat Building Company sold all the

950 sailboat hulls it produced in March. The cost of goods sold section of a monthly income statement prepared for management would show the following:

Standard cost of goods sold (950 hulls @ $300)		$285,000
Plus unfavorable cost variances:		
Materials price variance – fiberglass fabric	$8,280	
Materials quantity variance – fiberglass fabric	4,500	
Materials quantity variance – fiberglass mix	1,800	
Labor rate variance	990	
Labor efficiency variance	2,000	
Overhead spending variance	1,500	
Overhead efficiency variance	400	
Overhead capacity variance	2,700	22,170
Less favorable cost variances:		
Materials price variance – fiberglass mix		(4,900)
Adjusted cost of goods sold		$302,270

With this cost of goods sold information, management can see the total impact of deviations from the planned cost performance and can evaluate how to improve future profitability in the manufacturing operation.

SUMMARY

A fixed budget has a serious deficiency in many situations because it is based on a single level of estimated sales or production. Whenever the actual sales or production activity differs significantly from what was planned, meaningful performance evaluation is difficult with a fixed budget. A flexible budget can be used instead of a fixed budget to avoid the problem of a difference between the actual level of business activity and the one planned. A flexible budget is a series of budgets for different levels of activity. Since a range of activity is considered, managers can determine the specific volume level actually achieved and revise the budget to that level.

The most essential feature of a flexible budget is a well-defined distinction between the variable and fixed costs included because the variable costs are the only costs that change as a function of activity. The fixed costs remain the same as long as we stay within the relevant range of operation. The use of a flexible budget for cost performance reporting makes the budget estimates and actual results comparable since they both are based on the same level of activity.

Standard manufacturing overhead is applied to the work in process inventory by charging the predetermined overhead rate to some measure of standard production activity such as standard direct labor hours. The predetermined overhead rate is developed from a flexible budget prepared for manufacturing overhead. Since multiple levels of production activity are possible, management must decide on a specific activity level for the budget period. Four different measures of production capacity are used: (1) maximum capacity; (2) practical capacity; (3) expected capacity; and (4) normal capacity. Expected capacity and normal capacity are the two most popular measures used for the application of manufacturing overhead. The production activity level chosen from the flexible budget defines the denominator used to compute the predetermined overhead rate.

Over- or underapplied manufacturing overhead is the difference between the actual overhead incurred and the standard overhead applied to the work in process inventory. This total overhead variance can be further divided for analytical purposes into more detailed variances using the two-variance or three-variance method. The choice between the two methods depends on how much detail management wants for a given situation. The two-variance method consists of a budget variance and a capacity variance, whereas the three-variance method divides the budget variance into spending and efficiency components. These variances assist management in controlling manufacturing overhead costs for future profit improvements.

Journal entries are prepared to record the manufacturing overhead cost variances incurred during an accounting period. All standard cost variances must be disposed of in the preparation of financial statements. For internal reporting, the cost variances usually are adjusted to the cost of goods sold for the period in which they are incurred. The adjustment to cost of goods sold for the cost variances produces a different cost of goods sold than the amount based on standard costs. When this adjustment is made on an income statement prepared for management, the report shows the managers responsible for the cost standards what the impact of deviations from the planned production performance is on profits. GAAP require that significant standard cost variances must be prorated between ending inventories and cost of goods sold for year-end external reporting.

GLOSSARY

BUDGET (CONTROLLABLE) VARIANCE (OVERHEAD). The difference between the actual manufacturing overhead incurred and the flexible budget based on the standard hours allowed (or whatever measure of standard production activity being used) (p. 417).

CAPACITY (DENOMINATOR) VARIANCE (OVERHEAD). The difference between the flexible budget based on the standard hours allowed and the standard amount of manufacturing overhead applied to the work in process inventory (p. 417).

DENOMINATOR ACTIVITY. The production activity level chosen for the denominator of the predetermined overhead rate used to apply manufacturing overhead (p. 413).

EFFICIENCY VARIANCE (OVERHEAD). The difference between the flexible budget based on the actual hours and the flexible budget for the standard hours allowed (p. 422).

EXPECTED CAPACITY. The level of production activity expected for a specific year, given the firm's operating conditions and market demand for its products (p. 412).

FIXED (STATIC) BUDGET. A budget prepared for only one level of sales or production activity (p. 402).

FLEXIBLE BUDGET. A series of budgets for a range of business activity (p. 402).

FLEXIBLE BUDGET PERFORMANCE REPORT. A management report showing the variances between budgeted costs and actual costs when the budgeted amounts are revised to the level of business activity attained if it is different from the one originally planned (p. 406).

MAXIMUM CAPACITY. The highest level of production activity possible if optimal operating conditions exist (p. 412).

NORMAL CAPACITY. The average annual production activity that will satisfy the market demand over a relatively long time period, such as three to five years (p. 412).

PRACTICAL CAPACITY. The maximum production capacity of a firm less reasonable allowances for departures from an optimal performance (p. 412).

PRODUCTION CAPACITY. Some measure of the production activity a firm can achieve with its existing physical facilities and organizational structure. The four measures of production capacity are maximum, practical, expected, and normal (p. 412).

SPENDING VARIANCE (OVERHEAD). The difference between the actual manufacturing overhead incurred and the flexible budget based on the actual production activity (e.g., actual direct labor hours) (p. 422).

STANDARD AMOUNT OF MANUFACTURING OVERHEAD. The predetermined overhead rate multiplied by some measure of standard production activity, such as standard direct labor hours (p. 408).

THREE-VARIANCE METHOD. The division of an over- or underapplied manufacturing overhead variance into three components: a spending variance, an efficiency variance, and a capacity variance (p. 417).

TWO-VARIANCE METHOD. The division of an over- or underapplied manufacturing overhead variance into two components: a budget variance and a capacity variance (p. 417).

DISCUSSION QUESTIONS

1. How is standard costing applied to manufacturing overhead?
2. Differentiate between a fixed budget and a flexible budget.
3. What is the deficiency of a fixed budget for performance evaluation purposes?
4. What are the major steps involved in the preparation of a flexible budget?
5. "The flexible aspect of a flexible budget consists of the variable costs." Do you agree? Explain.
6. What do we mean by "adjusting a flexible budget to reflect actual performance"? Why is this step important for performance evaluation?
7. How is production activity measured in the use of a flexible budget and application of standard manufacturing overhead?
8. Why does the standard manufacturing overhead rate decrease as the production activity forecast increases?
9. Why is the determination of a specific capacity level important in the application of manufacturing overhead with a flexible budget?
10. Explain the following terms:
    a. Maximum capacity
    b. Practical capacity
    c. Expected capacity
    d. Normal capacity

11. How is the demand for a firm's products considered in each of the definitions of capacity shown in question 10 (if at all)?
12. What is overapplied manufacturing overhead? Underapplied manufacturing overhead?
13. Differentiate between two-variance overhead analysis and three-variance overhead analysis.
14. Why is cost behavior important for manufacturing overhead variance analysis?
15. Distinguish between a budget variance and a capacity variance in a two-variance overhead analysis.
16. Who is responsible for an overhead budget variance? What are typical causes of this variance?
17. Who is responsible for an overhead capacity variance? What are typical causes of this variance?
18. What is meant by a revised budget for standard hours allowed in overhead analysis? Why is this measure required?
19. Explain what is meant by a spending variance, an efficiency variance, and a capacity variance in three-variance overhead analysis.
20. Who is usually responsible for an overhead spending variance? What are typical causes of this variance?
21. Who is usually responsible for an overhead efficiency variance? What are typical causes of this variance?
22. Who is usually responsible for an overhead capacity variance? What are typical causes of this variance?
23. The Windwood Company uses normal capacity measured in standard direct labor hours to apply manufacturing overhead. During 1987, normal capacity was 10,000 standard direct labor hours while the standard direct labor hours allowed for the production level achieved amounted to 9,600. Actual hours worked were 10,200. The predetermined overhead rate was $6, of which $2 was variable. How much manufacturing overhead was applied to work in process? What was the capacity variance?
24. Explain the basic difference in disposing of standard cost variances in internal reports as compared with the treatment of them for external reporting.
25. What is meant by prorating cost variances in the preparation of financial statements? Why is this proration often required for external reporting?

EXERCISES

Exercise 11-1 Evaluating Flexible Budgets and Variances
The Schurman Company produces a single product. Direct materials are $6 per unit and direct labor is $4. Manufacturing overhead is $40,000 per month plus $5 per unit produced. The planned production each month is 25,000 units. During January, 21,500 units were produced with actual direct materials of $135,000, direct labor of $92,500, fixed manufacturing overhead of $40,500, and variable manufacturing overhead of $111,500.

Required:
A. Prepare a flexible budget formula.
B. What were the variances between budgeted and actual costs?

Exercise 11-2 Basic Concepts of a Flexible Budget

The Kelsey Company wants to prepare flexible budget cost estimates for the following items within a range of 10,000 to 12,000 direct labor hours:

	Fixed Cost	Variable Cost per Direct Labor Hour
Maintenance	$3,600	$.25
Depreciation	6,000	—
Supplies	840	.45
Utilities	1,800	.15
Rent	2,400	—
Insurance	3,600	—
Indirect labor	7,200	.75

Required:
A. Prepare a flexible overhead budget for 10,000, 11,000 and 12,000 direct labor hours.
B. Calculate the fixed, variable, and total predetermined overhead rates if 10,000 direct labor hours are chosen as the normal capacity.
C. Calculate the fixed, variable, and total predetermined overhead rates if 12,000 direct labor hours are chosen as the normal capacity.

Exercise 11-3 Developing a Flexible Budget and a Performance Report

The Robinson Company uses an annual flexible budget based on standard direct labor hours for the following manufacturing overhead items:

	Variable Cost per Standard Direct Labor Hour	Fixed Cost
Indirect labor	$.50	$3,600
Supplies	.15	4,500
Utilities	.25	8,100

During the year, the firm recorded 8,700 standard direct labor hours while working 9,100 actual direct labor hours and incurring the following actual costs:

Indirect labor	—	$ 8,000
Supplies	—	5,790
Utilities	—	10,315

Required:
A. Prepare a flexible budget for the three cost items using 8,000, 9,000, and 10,000 standard direct labor hours.
B. Prepare a flexible budget performance report for the three cost items, based on the firm's operating results for the year.

Exercise 11-4 Preparing a Flexible Budget

The Ferris Company has prepared the following incomplete flexible budget:

		Standard Direct Labor Hours			
Manufacturing Overhead	**Rate per Hour**	**20,000**	**24,000**	**28,000**	**32,000**
Variable costs:					
Indirect labor		$ 44,800			
Maintenance		64,400			
Utilities		30,800			
Total		140,000			
Fixed costs:					
Supervisory salaries		62,000			
Rent		22,000			
Insurance		14,500			
Depreciation		48,500			
Total		147,000			
Total manufacturing overhead		$287,000			

Required:
Complete the flexible budget for the Ferris Company.

Exercise 11-5 Cost Behavior and a Flexible Budget

A summarized version of a flexible budget used by the Greene County prosecutor's office for 1987 is as follows:

	Number of Cases Prosecuted		
Cost Item	**1,400**	**1,600**	**1,800**
Salaries and wages	$68,200	$70,800	$73,400
Supplies	3,220	3,680	4,140
Office expenses	23,200	24,800	26,400

During 1987, the prosecutor's office incurred the following actual costs while prosecuting 1,670 cases:

Salaries and wages	$73,350
Supplies	3,901
Office expenses	26,500

Required:
Prepare a budget performance report for 1987.

Exercise 11-6 Preparing a Basic Flexible Budget

The following cost functions for the Mears Company's manufacturing overhead items are being used to prepare the firm's flexible budget for 1987:

Cost Item	**Cost Function**
Maintenance	$30,000 + $2 per direct labor hour
Supervisory salaries	$75,000 + $4 per direct labor hour
Utilities	$.45 per direct labor hour
Depreciation	$42,000
Supplies	$.25 per direct labor hour
Indirect materials	$12,000 + $.80 per direct labor hour

The cost functions are valid for a relevant range of 10,000 to 14,000 direct labor hours.

Required:
Prepare a flexible budget for 10,000, 12,000, and 14,000 direct labor hours.

Exercise 11-7 Evaluating Performance with Variances

Refer to Exercise 11-6. Assume that the Mears Company actually worked 13,100 direct labor hours during 1987 with the following costs:

Cost Item	Amount
Maintenance	$ 58,200
Supervisory salaries	129,100
Utilities	5,695
Depreciation	42,000
Supplies	3,350
Indirect materials	21,380

Required:
Prepare a budget performance report for 1987.

Exercise 11-8 Computing Budget and Capacity Variances for Manufacturing Overhead

The Jenkins Company produces dishwashers and applies manufacturing overhead using standard direct labor hours. The company estimated that it would take 36,000 standard direct labor hours to produce 7,200 dishwashers during 1987. At the 7,200 unit level, the budgeted manufacturing overhead is:

Variable portion	$ 54,000
Fixed portion	162,000
Total	$216,000

Actual production during 1987 was 7,100 dishwashers and 37,000 direct labor hours with the following actual costs:

Variable manufacturing overhead	$ 59,100
Fixed manufacturing overhead	163,000
Total	$222,100

Required:
Compute the budget and capacity variances for 1987.

Exercise 11-9 Using the Three-Variance Method
Refer to Exercise 11-8.

Required:
Compute the spending, efficiency, and capacity variances for manufacturing overhead during 1987.

Exercise 11-10 Evaluating Overhead Efficiency and Capacity Variances
The following six companies apply manufacturing overhead on the basis of standard direct labor hours. For each company, the budgeted standard direct labor hours used to calculate the predetermined overhead rate, the actual direct labor hours worked, and the standard direct labor hours allowed for the actual production are presented.

Company	Budgeted Direct Labor Hours	Actual Direct Labor Hours	Standard Direct Labor Hours Allowed
A	14,400	12,600	13,200
B	19,200	20,360	19,200
C	15,600	16,800	17,400
D	12,000	13,200	12,240
E	13,200	12,000	12,000
F	18,000	18,600	18,600

Required:
Determine whether each company incurred an overhead efficiency variance

and an overhead capacity variance. Also specify whether each variance is favorable or unfavorable.

Exercise 11-11 Fixed Manufacturing Overhead and a Capacity Variance

The controller of the Kindig Company is evaluating the fixed manufacturing overhead costs associated with the production performance of the firm for the year 1987, which just ended. The following information has been collected:

Production activity:	
Number of units produced	12,000
Standard direct labor hours per unit	2
Standard direct labor hours used to compute the predetermined overhead rate	25,000

Manufacturing overhead is applied to work in process inventory on the basis of standard direct labor hours. The actual cost performance for 1987 included the following:

Fixed manufacturing overhead incurred	$179,000
Unfavorable budget variance	$ 4,000

Required:
A. How many standard direct labor hours were allowed for 1987?
B. What was the fixed portion of the predetermined overhead rate for 1987?
C. What was the capacity variance for 1987?

Exercise 11-12 Combining Labor and Overhead Variances

The Page Company uses a standard cost system. During October, the firm planned to produce 800 units of finished product. Each unit requires two standard direct labor hours. Budgeted manufacturing overhead for the month was:

Variable portion — $3 per standard direct labor hour
Fixed portion   — $9 per standard direct labor hour

These rates were based on the number of standard direct labor hours required for the planned production. Actual manufacturing overhead for October was:

Variable manufacturing overhead	$ 4,650
Fixed manufacturing overhead	14,900
Total	$19,550

The firm's October labor performance included the following:

Standard direct labor rate	$7.20 per hour
Actual direct labor rate	$7.40 per hour
Actual direct labor hours	1,650 hours
Unfavorable labor efficiency variance	$1,080

Required:
A. How many units must have been produced during October?
B. Calculate the labor rate variance for the month.
C. Using the two-variance method, compute the budget and capacity variances for overhead.
D. Using the three-variance method, compute the spending, efficiency, and capacity variances for overhead.

PROBLEMS

Problem 11-1   Cost Behavior and Manufacturing Overhead
Eversman Manufacturing wants to develop a flexible budget for manufacturing overhead costs. Below is the monthly cost and activity data for the last six-month period:

Month	Manufacturing Overhead Cost	Standard Direct Labor Hours
February	$42,000	1,700
March	48,000	2,000
April	56,000	2,400
May	46,000	1,900
June	52,000	2,200
July	49,000	2,100

Required:
Use the high-low method to determine the fixed and variable components of the manufacturing overhead cost.

Problem 11-2   Preparing a Flexible Budget
The Dot Tool Company uses a flexible budget to evaluate the production performance. The firm's controller has estimated the manufacturing overhead costs for the coming year as:

	Fixed Costs	Variable Cost Per Standard Machine Hour
Indirect labor	$24,000	$6.00
Supplies	6,000	.50
Maintenance	11,000	.20
Utilities	5,000	1.30
Depreciation	40,000	—

Required:
Prepare a flexible budget using 10,000, 15,000, and 20,000 standard machine hours.

Problem 11-3   Use of a Flexible Budget Performance Report
The Twisted Tom Food Company produces jumbo whole-grain pretzels. The company uses a flexible budget system for planning and controlling costs. Below are budgeted and actual production data for the last year:

	Budgeted	Budgeted	Actual
Number of pretzels	70,000	90,000	82,500
Supervision	$60,000	$76,000	$74,000
Materials	28,000	36,000	33,000
Maintenance	9,000	11,000	11,000
Depreciation	18,000	18,000	18,000
Utilities	7,000	9,000	8,500

Required:
A.   Determine the cost behavior pattern for each mixed cost.
B.   Prepare a flexible budget performance report for last year.

Problem 11-4 Use of a Flexible Budget Performance Report

The Frey Company has prepared a fixed budget performance report for the year ending December 31, 1987, as follows.

	Budget	Actual	Variance
Units of production	42,000	44,400	2,400 F
Manufacturing costs:			
Direct materials	$273,000	$296,148	$23,148 U
Direct labor	346,500	364,524	18,024 U
Manufacturing overhead:			
Variable costs			
Indirect labor:	68,040	75,036	6,996 U
Supplies	23,940	22,200	1,740 F
Repairs	13,860	15,984	2,124 U
Total variable overhead	105,840	113,220	7,380 U
Fixed costs:			
Insurance	4,800	5,040	240 U
Rent	14,400	14,400	-0-
Depreciation	12,000	12,000	-0-
Supervisory salaries	25,200	25,800	600 U
Total fixed overhead	56,400	57,240	840 U
Total manufacturing overhead	162,240	170,460	8,220 U
Total manufacturing costs	$781,740	$831,132	$49,392 U

Required:

Convert the fixed budget performance report to a flexible budget performance report.

Problem 11-5 Comparing Fixed and Flexible Budgets

Julken Manufacturing Company's 1987 budget contained the following costs, based on their cost behavior.

Cost Item	Fixed Costs	Variable Cost Rate per Unit
Utilities	$ 6,000	—
Supervision	38,000	—
Property taxes	10,000	—
Insurance	4,000	—
Maintenance	12,000	—
Depreciation	6,000	—
Rent	22,000	—
Direct materials	—	$2.20
Direct labor	—	7.40
Indirect materials	—	.50
Indirect labor	—	1.60

Actual operating results for 1987 were:

Utilities	$ 7,500
Supervision	36,500
Property taxes	12,750
Insurance	4,780
Maintenance	13,200
Depreciation	6,300
Rent	22,900
Direct materials	56,400
Direct labor	183,800

Indirect materials	13,600
Indirect labor	46,500
Units produced	25,000

Required:

A. Prepare a fixed budget performance report based on an estimated production level of 30,000 units compared with the actual cost performance.

B. Prepare a flexible budget performance report.

C. Milton Nag, the manager responsible for production costs, believes that a fixed budget performance report is the most appropriate cost measure to use this month while the owner, Bob Smarter, favors the flexible budget report. Which one do you believe is the best measure of performance and why does each person favor their respective reports?

Problem 11-6 Evaluating Manufacturing Overhead Variances

The Ester Company has provided the following information about the company's only product.

Standard direct labor rate	$8.20 per hour
Standard direct labor hours per unit	3 hours
Variable manufacturing overhead	$3 per standard direct labor hour
Fixed manufacturing overhead	7.50 per standard direct labor hour
Normal capacity for the month	7,200 units

During the preceding month, the actual production was 7,560 units. The average rate paid for the 22,800 hours of direct labor was $8.40 per hour. The actual variable manufacturing overhead was $67,080, and the actual fixed manufacturing overhead was $163,000.

Required:

A. Use the two-variance method to calculate the budget and capacity variances for overhead.

B. Use the three-variance method to compute the spending, efficiency, and capacity variances for overhead.

C. Identify likely causes for the variances calculated in parts A and B.

Problem 11-7 Computing Manufacturing Overhead Variances

The Arnold Company uses a standard cost system and has prepared the following flexible budget:

	75%	90%
Capacity		
Production in units	3,600	4,320
Manufacturing overhead:		
Variable costs:		
Indirect labor	$11,700	$14,040
Supplies	2,700	3,240
Repairs	720	864
Utilities	1,260	1,512
Total variable costs	16,380	19,656
Fixed costs:		
Rent	10,800	10,800
Insurance	6,000	6,000
Property taxes	3,600	3,600
Depreciation	2,064	2,064
Total fixed costs	22,464	22,464
Total manufacturing overhead	$38,844	$42,120

The standard cost data for the company's single product are:

Direct labor   — 5 hours at $8 per hour
Direct materials — 20 pounds at $2 per pound

Manufacturing overhead is five standard direct labor hours at an unknown cost per hour. The company uses normal capacity of 90% for the calculation of the predetermined overhead rate applied to standard direct labor hours. The company actually operated at 75% of capacity and produced 3,600 units. The actual costs were:

Direct labor: 18,640 hours at $7.80 per hour	$145,392
Direct materials: 71,640 pounds at $2.10 per pound	150,444
Rent	10,800
Insurance	6,000
Property taxes	3,600
Depreciation	2,064
Indirect labor	11,772
Supplies	2,556
Repairs	648
Utilities	1,440

Required:
A. Calculate the predetermined overhead rate.
B. Use the two-variance method to calculate the budget and capacity variances for overhead.
C. Use the three-variance method to calculate the spending, efficiency, and capacity variances for overhead.

Problem 11-8 Calculating Manufacturing Overhead Variances

The Arias Company has prepared the following summarized manufacturing overhead budget used in a standard cost system:

	90%	95%
Capacity		
Production in units	21,600	22,800
Manufacturing overhead:		
Variable costs	$ 64,800	$ 68,400
Fixed costs	171,000	171,000
Total	$235,800	$239,400

The standard cost data for the company's only product are:

Direct materials	18 pounds at $4 per pound
Direct labor	6 hours at $12 per hour
Manufacturing overhead	6 hours at $1.75 per hour

The company uses normal capacity of 95% for the calculation of the predetermined overhead rate, which is based on standard direct labor hours. The company actually operated at 90% of capacity, producing 21,600 units and incurring the following costs:

Direct materials — 391,500 pounds at $3.90 per pound	$1,526,850
Direct labor — 131,400 hours at $12.10 per hour	1,589,940
Variable manufacturing overhead	67,392
Fixed manufacturing overhead	172,300

Required:

A. Using the two-variance method, calculate the budget and capacity variances for overhead.

B. Using the three-variance method, compute the spending, efficiency, and capacity variances for overhead.

Problem 11-9 Evaluating Standard Overhead with Incomplete Information

Evaluate each of the following companies' performance independently. Each firm uses a flexible budget to compute the predetermined overhead rate and a standard cost system.

	Company A	Company B	Company C
Actual variable overhead	$ 42,000	—	$ 35,500
Actual fixed overhead	161,000	202,000	72,000
Denominator activity in hours	20,000	10,000	—
Standard hours allowed	18,000	—	—
Predetermined overhead rate:			
Variable portion	—	—	$3
Fixed portion	—	—	$6
Budgeted fixed overhead	$160,000	$200,000	$72,000
Total budgeted overhead	$200,000	$250,000	—
Standard variable overhead applied	—	—	$33,000
Standard fixed overhead applied	—	$180,000	—
Overhead spending variance	—	$-0-	—
Overhead efficiency variance	—	$1,000 U	—
Overhead capacity variance	—	—	—
Actual hours worked	19,000	—	10,500

Required:
Fill in the blanks with correct answers.

Problem 11-10 Computing Manufacturing Overhead Variances

Holly, Inc., bases its overhead rate on standard direct labor hours. For the next year's budget, standard direct labor hours allowed are estimated at 25,000. Fixed overhead is expected to be $150,000, and the variable overhead cost is budgeted at $100,000. Four direct labor hours are required to produce one unit of product. During the year, 6,000 units were produced using 24,500 actual direct labor hours. At the end of the year, the manufacturing overhead control account has a debit balance of $242,000.

Required:

A. Compute manufacturing overhead variances using the two-variance method.

B. Compute the spending and efficiency variances using the three-variance method.

Problem 11-11 Evaluating Overhead Variance Relationships

During the past year Kent Company incurred $362,000 of actual manufacturing overhead costs. Actual direct labor hours and standard direct labor hours were 29,000 and 30,000, respectively. Manufacturing overhead variances for the period are:

Spending	$10,000 Fav.
Efficiency	4,000 Fav.
Capacity	16,000 Unf.

Required:

A. Compute applied manufacturing overhead.
B. Compute the variable manufacturing overhead rate.
C. Compute the budgeted fixed manufacturing costs.
D. Compute the total manufacturing overhead rate.
E. Compute the fixed manufacturing overhead rate.
F. Compute the budgeted standard direct labor hours used to compute the predetermined overhead rate.

Problem 11-12 Evaluating Manufacturing Overhead Variances

After receiving a report from the controller's office, Rodney Franklin, President of Buddah Manufacturing, was delighted to learn that during the past fiscal year there was no overapplied or underapplied manufacturing overhead. Actual manufacturing overhead incurred to produce 11,200 units of finished product consisted of $56,000 variable costs and $145,600 fixed costs. Budgeted fixed costs were $145,600 and budgeted production output was 10,400 units. Manufacturing overhead was applied based on standard machine hours. Standard machine hours allowed for the period were 28,000. The actual machine hours worked exceeded the standard number allowed by 1,400.

Required:

A. Does the fact that actual manufacturing overhead was equal to applied manufacturing overhead justify not computing any other overhead variances?
B. Compute the predetermined overhead rate used by the firm.
C. Compute the fixed and variable components of the overhead rate.
D. Compute the actual number of machine hours worked.
E. Compute the number of standard machine hours allowed per unit of output.
F. Compute the spending, efficiency, and capacity variances, if any, and determine if any of them should be investigated.

Problem 11-13 Computing and Recording Overhead Variances

Rest-Easy Sofa Company is a highly automated manufacturer of living room furniture. The production process is capital-intensive so the company applies overhead based on standard machine hours. Estimated activity for the period is 15,000 standard machine hours and the predetermined overhead rate is $8.50 per standard machine hour, of which $1.80 is variable. Actual manufacturing overhead costs and production data are as follows:

Manufacturing overhead:		
Building occupancy	$48,500	
Maintenance	17,800	
Depreciation	31,600	
Indirect materials	14,900	
Indirect labor	9,200	
Total overhead		$122,000
Sofas produced		3,500
Actual machine hours		13,400
Machine hours allowed per sofa		4

Required:

A. Prepare the journal entry to record the manufacturing overhead actually incurred during the period (building occupancy and maintenance expenses should be credited to accounts payable).
B. Prepare the entry to record the manufacturing overhead applied to the work in process inventory during the period.
C. Compute all variances using the three-variance method.
D. Prepare the entry to close the overapplied (underapplied) manufacturing overhead for the period into the spending variance, efficiency variance, and capacity variance.

Problem 11-14 Standard Overhead Application and Variance Analysis

The operating results for Cassidy Company are now available and management wants an analysis of manufacturing overhead costs. A flexible budget prepared at the beginning of the year is given below:

		Standard Direct Labor Hours		
Manufacturing Overhead	**Cost Rate**	**5,000**	**7,000**	**9,000**
Variable costs:				
Maintenance	$0.25	$ 1,250	$ 1,750	$ 2,250
Indirect materials	0.35	1,750	2,450	3,150
Total variable costs	$0.60	3,000	4,200	5,400
Fixed costs:				
Insurance		3,800	3,800	3,800
Rent		6,000	6,000	6,000
Total fixed costs		9,800	9,800	9,800
Total overhead costs		$12,800	$14,000	$15,200

Seven hours of standard labor time are required per unit of product. The company had set its production activity level for the period at 7,000 hours (or 1,000 units). Actual results for the period:

Number of units produced	1,100
Actual direct labor hours	7,900
Actual variable overhead cost	$ 4,800
Actual fixed overhead cost	10,200

Required:
Calculate the following:

1. The predetermined overhead rate.
2. Use the two-variance method to calculate the budget and capacity variances for overhead.
3. Use the three-variance method to compute the spending, efficiency, and capacity variances for overhead.
4. Who would be responsible for the variances in part 3?

Problem 11-15 Overhead Application and Variance Analysis (CMA)

Wann Products developed its predetermined overhead rate from the current annual budget. The budget is based on an expected production output of 750,000 units that should require 3,750,000 standard direct labor hours (DLH). The company is able to schedule production uniformly throughout the year.

A total of 64,000 units requiring 340,000 DLH were produced during May. Actual manufacturing overhead costs for May amounted to $472,325. The actual manufacturing overhead costs as well as the annual budget and one-twelfth of the annual budget are shown below.

| | Annual Budget | | | | |
	Total Amount	Per Unit	Per DLH	Monthly Budget	Actual Costs for May
Variable costs:					
Indirect labor	$ 937,500	$1.25	$ .25	$ 78,125	$ 81,000
Supplies	1,500,000	2.00	.40	125,000	125,000
Fixed costs:					
Supervision	1,200,000	1.60	.32	100,000	102,500
Utilities	1,050,000	1.40	.28	87,500	85,700
Depreciation	937,500	1.25	.25	78,125	78,125
Total	$5,625,000	$7.50	$1.50	$468,750	$472,325

Required:
Calculate the following amounts for Wann Products' May performance:

1. Applied manufacturing overhead costs.
2. Overhead spending variance.
3. Overhead efficiency variance.
4. Overhead capacity variance.
5. Identify likely causes for each of the three variances.
6. Prepare a variance report that shows the spending variance for each manufacturing cost item.

Problem 11-16 Computing Manufacturing Overhead Variances (CMA)
Elizabeth Company has the following estimated standard manufacturing overhead costs per unit based on a capacity of 160,000 standard direct labor hours:

Variable portion	2 hours at $4 per hour =	$ 8
Fixed portion	2 hours at $6 per hour =	12
Total		$20

During July, 80,000 units were scheduled for production. However, 90,000 units were actually produced. The following additional data relate to July:

Actual direct labor cost incurred was $740,000 for 170,000 actual hours of work.

Actual manufacturing overhead incurred totaled $1,600,000 — $890,000 fixed and $710,000 variable.

All inventories are recorded at standard cost.

Required:
A. Use the two-variance method to calculate the budget and capacity variances for overhead.
B. Use the three-variance method to compute the spending, efficiency, and capacity variances for overhead.
C. List potential causes of the variances identified in part B.

Problem 11-17 Comprehensive Standard Costing Situation (CMA)
Moll Company has an automated production process so standard machine hours are used to apply manufacturing overhead to the products produced. An absorption costing system is operated by the company.

The annual profit plan for the next fiscal year is finalized in July of each year. The profit plan for the fiscal year ending August 31, 1987, called for 8,000 units requiring 40,000 machine hours to be produced. The predetermined overhead rate for the 1986–1987 fiscal year was determined using 8,000 units of planned production.

Moll Company developed a flexible budget for different levels of activity to use in evaluating performance. A total of 8,200 units were actually produced during the 1986–1987 fiscal year requiring 42,000 machine hours. The schedule presented below compares the company's actual costs for the 1986–1987 fiscal year with the profit plan and the budgeted costs for two different activity levels. The dollar figures shown are in thousands.

| | | Flexible Budgets for | | |
Item	Profit Plan (8,000 Units)	41,000 Standard Machine Hours	42,000 Standard Machine Hours	Actual Costs
Direct Materials:				
G27 aluminum	$ 104.0	$ 106.6	$ 109.2	$ 112.0
M14 steel alloy	336.0	344.4	352.8	350.0
Direct Labor:				
Assembler	312.0	319.8	327.6	326.0
Grinder	364.0	373.1	382.2	383.0
Manufacturing overhead:				
Maintenance	32.0	32.8	33.6	33.0
Supplies	172.0	176.3	180.6	182.0
Supervision	100.0	102.0	104.0	102.0
Inspection	174.0	177.0	180.0	181.0
Insurance	60.0	60.0	60.0	60.0
Depreciation	220.0	220.0	220.0	220.0
Total costs	$1,874.0	$1,912.0	$1,950.0	$1,949.0

Required:
A. The budgeted number of machine hours needed to produce one unit of product.
B. The actual cost of materials used for one unit of product.
C. The cost of materials that should be processed per machine hour.
D. The budgeted labor cost for each unit produced.
E. The manufacturing overhead formula based on a linear equation $(y = a + bx)$.
F. The manufacturing overhead spending variance for the 1986–1987 fiscal year.
G. The manufacturing overhead capacity variance for the year.
H. The total budgeted manufacturing overhead costs for the production of 8,050 units using the formula from part E.

12

PROFIT VARIANCE ANALYSIS

CHAPTER OVERVIEW AND OBJECTIVES

This chapter describes how differences between actual and planned profits can be evaluated with variance analysis as a continuation of the procedures presented in Chapters 10 and 11. After studying this chapter, you should be able to:

1. Discuss the nature and importance of profit variance analysis.
2. Identify the major sources of a profit variance.
3. Realize why variable costs and fixed costs should be separated in profit variance analysis.
4. Describe how contribution margin variance analysis is performed with a single product.
5. Distinguish between a sales volume variance, a selling price variance, and a variable cost variance.
6. Explain how fixed cost variance analysis is performed.
7. Consider a sales mix variance while performing contribution margin variance analysis with more than one product.
8. Report profit variances to managers and advise them of potential causes of the variances.
9. Combine contribution margin variances with standard cost variances to inform managers about the different sources of deviations from a planned profit performance.

IDENTIFYING THE SOURCES OF A PROFIT VARIANCE

Objective 1:
Using profit variance analysis

In Chapters 10 and 11, we concentrated on deviations from the planned cost phase of a firm's earnings performance in the discussion of standard cost systems. We now turn our attention to a complete coverage of deviations between actual and planned profits. A **profit variance** is the difference between the actual net income earned and the net income planned for the same period. Throughout the discussion of managerial accounting, we have stressed the importance of a planned profit performance for every type of business. The profit goals established during the budgeting process are the result of a concentrated effort by management to define an earnings performance that is a measure of a successful operation. In turn, these profit goals become the *responsibility* of the managers who are in charge of the various activities of the firm, and they should do everything possible to ensure that they contribute positively to the firm's overall profitability. We will consider this responsibility more closely in the next chapter when we discuss responsibility accounting.

But, meanwhile, what can be done about a planned profit performance that is not achieved? We know that the ultimate response to this question is *corrective action* to make the changes necessary for improved future financial results. To be able to take effective corrective action, however, managers must have (1) a complete and accurate description of the sources of profit performance deviations and (2) a list of the changes that should be considered. The cost variances considered thus far only provide a partial explanation of a profit performance deviation. Here, we will examine other reasons why actual profit results may be different from those planned and learn how to compute these variances.

Since we are concerned with an income statement used by managers in profit variance analysis, certain items such as extraordinary gains and losses that may appear on a statement reported to external parties will be ignored. Management's primary interest is with the operating section of the income statement, which is a report of the revenues and costs of the firm's principal operations. In addition, we will be mainly concerned with an income statement based on a contribution margin format because of the internal focus of profit variance analysis. The many variables that influence a firm's net income (e.g., market share, productivity, competition, and effectiveness) can be reduced for analytical purposes to the following five major accounting factors:

Objective 2: Identifying the sources of a profit variance

1. The sales volume representing the number of units sold
2. The selling price per unit sold
3. The sales mix or combination of units sold
4. The variable costs of producing and selling each unit
5. The fixed costs incurred for the manufacturing, selling, and administrative functions during an accounting period

If the expected amounts for each factor included in a profit plan are not actually achieved, the actual net income will deviate from the planned net income. The same five factors can be used to analyze a difference *between the net incomes of two periods,* such as the current year versus the previous year. In General Motors Corporation's 1981 annual report, top management summarized the major reasons why the firm's 1981 net income improved over the 1980 results in the following excerpt:

> *Reflecting the decline in retail sales, worldwide factory sales (sales of General Motors cars and trucks to its dealers) in 1981 also dropped to a level of 6.8 million* units, *5% below 1980.*
>
> *Worldwide sales dollars, however, increased 9% over 1980 and totaled $62.7 billion. Dollar sales in both years included* price *adjustments of $5.0 billion which were offset by decreased year-to-year* unit volume *in each year.*
>
> *The $3.72 per share earnings improvement in 1981 is primarily attributable to an improved* mix of products *sold and efficiencies obtained due to intensive* cost *reductions.*

The five factors involved with a firm's profitability often are interrelated, so a change in one of them affects another factor. For example, an increase in selling price may result in a decrease in the number of units sold. An increase in costs often prompts management to raise the selling price unless the higher costs can be offset by more units sold. To identify the effect of *each* of the five factors when unplanned profit results are being evaluated, *the impact of the other four factors must be held constant.* After the dollar amount of every type of deviation from the planned performance has been computed, we can algebraically add the individual deviations to find the total variance between the actual net income earned and the amount planned.

Next, we will develop an analytical framework to use in computing the individual variances associated with the five factors. This information is used to: (1) assign responsibility for profit deviations; (2) explain unplanned profit results; and (3) identify what action should be taken in the future. Our illustration will use a manufacturing operation, but the same analysis can be performed for all business activities such as products sold in a retail store, services offered by a bank, and houses built by a contractor.

GENERAL APPROACH TO PROFIT VARIANCE ANALYSIS

Objective 3: Separating variable and fixed costs for the analysis

There are many different approaches to **profit variance analysis.** One of the most effective approaches to use is a contribution margin income statement approach in which the analysis is divided into two parts:

1. The factors that are involved with the calculation of the contribution margin, and
2. The fixed costs incurred during a given period.

Variable and fixed costs must be treated separately in profit variance analysis because sales volume has a different effect on each type of cost behavior. Although costs are incurred for the manufacturing, selling, and administrative functions, the most important aspect of the cost performance for profit variance analysis is the way each cost responds to changes in sales volume. The profit variance analysis approach based on a contribution margin income statement used in this chapter is diagrammed in Figure 12-1.

A variable cost incurred to produce or sell a product will rise or fall in total amount as more or fewer units are sold. In contrast, the total amount of a fixed cost will remain constant regardless of how many units are sold as long as the firm operates within the *relevant range.* Also, recall that the variable costs incurred to produce and sell products are subtracted from sales revenue to compute the contribution margin. The fixed costs do not affect the amount of the contribution margin because they are subtracted from it as period costs to determine net income. Consequently, the variable costs reported on the income statement are affected by two types of change: (1) a change in the unit cost of producing or selling a product because of different amounts of such cost elements as materials, labor, variable manufacturing overhead, or sales commissions; and (2) a change in the sales volume that increases or decreases the total variable costs proportionately. Note that the other three factors listed above that can contribute to a profit variance—sales volume, selling price, and sales mix—also will affect the amount of contribution margin reported on a given income statement.

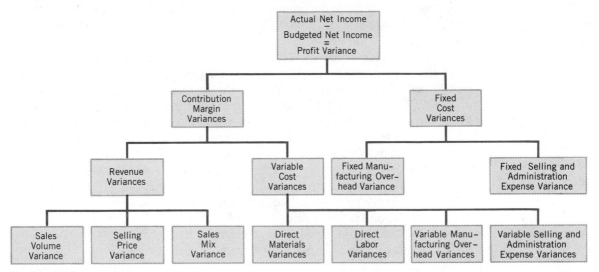

Figure 12-1
Summary of Variance Analysis

Contribution margin variance analysis can be performed to evaluate differences in the amount of actual contribution margin reported and the amount planned in the master budget for the period. The fixed costs are evaluated separately from the variable costs included in the contribution margin variance analysis to complete the explanation of the sources of a profit variance. The actual fixed costs shown as period costs on an income statement are compared with the amounts budgeted when the profit plan was prepared. Since sales volume does not affect the fixed costs, the variance analysis needed for them is much simpler than the procedures required for the variable costs evaluated with contribution margin variance analysis.

The algebraic summation of the four variances computed with contribution margin variance analysis and any variances associated with the fixed costs of a period equals the profit variance of the same period. Essentially the same analysis involved with contribution margin variance analysis can be used to explain differences in gross profit as an *alternative way* to evaluate profit deviations. In addition, contribution margin variance analysis is a valuable tool for evaluating the profitability performance of segments of the business such as departments, divisions, sales territories, and plants. As such, contribution margin variance analysis can be an important phase of segment performance evaluation, which is a subject covered in the next chapter.

CONTRIBUTION MARGIN
VARIANCE ANALYSIS — SINGLE PRODUCT

To illustrate the use of contribution margin variance analysis, we will use the 1987 operating performance of the J&J Company. Our coverage of contribution margin variance analysis begins by assuming that the J&J Company only produces and sells a single product, a pair of downhill skis sold to sporting goods stores throughout the country. The single-product situation eliminates the possibility of a sales mix influence on profits, a complication we will intro-

Objective 4:
Use of contribution margin variance analysis with a single product

duce later. The income statement in Figure 12-2 shows a comparison of the budgeted and actual contribution margins for the 1987 performance of the J&J Company.

Figure 12-2 shows that the J&J Company's actual net income before tax is $134,400—$365,600 lower than the $500,000 budgeted. In addition, the actual contribution margin is only $3,254,400 compared with a budgeted amount of $3,600,000, for an unfavorable variance of $345,600. The objective of contribution margin variance analysis is identifying the sources of the $345,600 unfavorable variance. The variance column of the report in Figure 12-2 does not reveal the detailed information needed to explain the contribution margin variance, although we can see that the company sold more units than it planned in the budget. Actual sales volume in units consists of 45,200 pairs of skis, while 45,000 pairs were budgeted. Since sales mix is not a contributing factor with the one-product situation, we know that differences in sales volume, selling price, and variable costs are the factors that must be examined to explain the unfavorable $345,600 contribution margin variance.

Remember that we want to consider one factor at a time while holding each of the other factors constant to perform contribution margin variance analysis. Let's begin by using the following analysis to identify the budgeted and actual unit selling prices, variable costs, and contribution margins that were used to prepare the comparative income statements shown in Figure 12-2:

Objective 5: Distinguishing between a sales volume variance, selling price variance, and variable cost variance

	Budget		**Actual**	
Selling price	($9,000,000/45,000) =	$200	($8,814,000/45,200) =	$195
Variable costs – production	($4,950,000/45,000) =	110	($5,062,400/45,200) =	112
Variable costs – selling	($450,000/45,000) =	10	($497,200/45,200) =	11
Contribution margin	($3,600,000/45,000) =	$ 80	($3,254,400/45,200) =	$ 72

Next, this information is used to identify the three sources of the $345,600 unfavorable contribution margin variance—sales volume, selling price, and the variable costs incurred to produce and sell the products.

SALES VOLUME VARIANCE

A **sales volume variance** is incurred when the actual number of units sold differs from the units planned during the budgeting process. Causes of sales volume variances include:

1. Price changes
2. The action of a competitor that increases its share of the market
3. An economic downturn
4. An ineffective marketing effort
5. The inability of the production function to produce enough units to fill the sales orders obtained by the sales department
6. A general decline in sales for the industry involved

Note that either the marketing department or the production function may be responsible for a sales volume variance depending on the specific cause found during the investigation of this type of variance. The sales volume variance is computed as:

J&J COMPANY
Income Statement — Budget versus Actual
Year Ended December 31, 1987

	Budget	Actual	Variance
Sales — units	45,000	45,200	200 F
Sales — dollars	$9,000,000	$8,814,000	$186,000 U
Variable cost of goods sold	4,950,000	5,062,400	112,400 U
Variable selling and administrative expenses	450,000	497,200	47,200 U
Contribution margin	3,600,000	3,254,400	345,600 U
Fixed costs:			
Manufacturing	2,250,000	2,280,000	30,000 U
Selling	310,000	304,000	6,000 F
Administrative	540,000	536,000	4,000 F
Total fixed costs	3,100,000	3,120,000	20,000 U
Net income before tax	$ 500,000	$ 134,400	$365,600 U

U indicates an unfavorable variance
F indicates a favorable variance

Figure 12-2

$$\text{Sales volume variance} = (\text{Actual sales units} - \text{Budgeted sales units}) \times \text{Budgeted contribution margin per unit}$$

The budgeted contribution margin is used to eliminate any effect of the actual selling price or actual costs. That is, the budgeted selling price less the budgeted variable costs equals the budgeted contribution margin with the selling price and variable costs held constant at budgeted amounts. The number of units sold, or sales volume, is allowed to vary between the actual sales units and the budgeted sales units. The difference between the two measures of sales volume is multiplied by the constant, the budgeted contribution margin.

In the case of the J&J Company, the budgeted contribution margin per pair of skis for 1987 is $80 because that amount would have been earned if the actual selling price and actual variable costs had been the same as those planned. The actual units sold are 45,200 compared with the 45,000 units budgeted. Consequently, the sales volume variance can be calculated as:

$$\text{Sales volume variance} = (45,200 - 45,000) \times \$80$$
$$= 200 \times \$80$$
$$= \$16,000 \text{ Favorable}$$

The sales volume variance is favorable because the company actually sold 200 more pairs of skis than it had planned.

SELLING PRICE VARIANCE

A **selling price variance** is the result of selling an actual number of units during a given period at an actual price that is *different* from the planned price. Causes of selling price variances include:

1. Unplanned price discounts
2. Reaction to competition
3. Using a different marketing channel such as an independent distributorship
4. Opening a new marketing territory
5. A change in management's pricing policy
6. Λ weak economy

The formula for computing a selling price variance is:

$$\begin{matrix} \text{Selling} \\ \text{price} \\ \text{variance} \end{matrix} = (\text{Actual selling price} - \text{Budgeted selling price}) \times \begin{matrix} \text{Actual} \\ \text{units} \\ \text{sold} \end{matrix}$$

The budgeted selling price for each pair of skis is $200 ($9,000,000/45,000), but the actual selling price is only $195 per pair ($8,814,000/45,200). The selling price variance is unfavorable and is computed by multiplying the difference of $5 per pair of skis by the 45,200 pairs actually sold as follows:

$$\begin{aligned} \text{Selling price variance} &= (\$195 - \$200) \times 45{,}200 \\ &= (\$5) \times 45{,}200 \\ &= \$226{,}000 \text{ Unfavorable} \end{aligned}$$

The result is an unfavorable selling price variance of $226,000. Note that we use the actual sales volume instead of the budgeted number of units because volume must be held constant and the price deviation occurred for the actual units sold. This large selling price variance should be investigated to determine if a better pricing structure can be achieved in the future. For example, the manager in charge of the marketing function may discover that unnecessarily high price discounts have been granted to certain customers by sales representatives, and the discounts can be reduced without any significant effect on the number of units sold.

VARIABLE COST VARIANCE

A **variable cost variance** arises when the actual variable costs needed to produce or sell a product differ from those planned. Common causes of variable cost variances are:

1. An inefficient use of direct materials
2. Low productivity from direct labor
3. Departures from planned maintenance costs budgeted as variable manufacturing overhead
4. Excessive spending for advertising
5. Less promotional cost than the amount planned
6. Higher actual sales commissions than those planned

For learning purposes, we can think of a variable cost variance as being the reverse of a selling price variance because sales revenue is added on the income statement and a cost is subtracted. When the actual variable cost per unit exceeds the amount planned, an unfavorable variable cost variance is incurred for each unit actually sold. In contrast, an actual variable cost per unit that is less than the amount planned produces a favorable variable cost variance. Note that these are opposite outcomes from the results we saw earlier with a selling price variance. The variable cost variance can be computed as:

$$\begin{matrix} \text{Variable} \\ \text{cost} \\ \text{variance} \end{matrix} = (\text{Actual costs per unit} - \text{Budgeted costs per unit}) \times \begin{matrix} \text{Actual} \\ \text{units} \\ \text{sold} \end{matrix}$$

The budgeted variable production costs for the J&J Company's 1987 performance are $110 per pair of skis ($4,950,000/45,000), whereas the budgeted variable selling costs are $10 ($450,000/45,000) for each pair. However, the actual results indicate that a variable production cost per unit of $112 ($5,062,400/45,200) and a variable selling cost of $11 per unit ($497,200/45,200) are incurred. Both variable cost variances are unfavorable and are computed as:

$$\begin{aligned} \text{Variable cost variance – production} &= (\$112 - \$110) \times 45,200 \\ &= \$2 \times 45,200 \\ &= \$90,400 \text{ Unfavorable} \\ \text{Variable cost variance – selling} &= (\$11 - \$10) \times 45,200 \\ &= \$1 \times 45,200 \\ &= \$45,200 \text{ Unfavorable} \\ \text{Total variable cost variance} &= \$90,400 \text{ Unfavorable} + \$45,200 \text{ Unfavorable} \\ &= \$135,600 \text{ Unfavorable} \end{aligned}$$

SUMMARY OF VARIANCES

Remember that the actual contribution margin for the J&J Company in 1987 is $345,600 less than the amount budgeted. The firm's management should be provided with a report such as the one shown in Figure 12-3 which summarizes the various variances as the sources of the unfavorable contribution margin variance. The selling price variance and the two variable cost variances should be investigated further to determine

1. What caused them and
2. What can be done to improve the company's profits in the future.

Figure 12-3

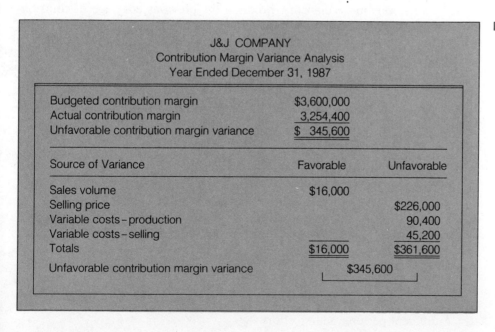

J&J COMPANY Contribution Margin Variance Analysis Year Ended December 31, 1987		
Budgeted contribution margin	$3,600,000	
Actual contribution margin	3,254,400	
Unfavorable contribution margin variance	$ 345,600	
Source of Variance	Favorable	Unfavorable
Sales volume	$16,000	
Selling price		$226,000
Variable costs – production		90,400
Variable costs – selling		45,200
Totals	$16,000	$361,600
Unfavorable contribution margin variance	$345,600	

FIXED COST VARIANCE ANALYSIS

Objective 6:
Performing fixed
cost variance
analysis

The profit variance analysis for the J&J Company can be completed with fixed cost **variance analysis** by comparing the actual fixed costs incurred for the manufacturing, selling, and administrative functions with those planned during the budgeting process. To do so, we should list the budgeted and actual amounts for the individual fixed cost items by business function. We assume that this comparative information has been obtained from the firm's accounting system and budgeting records, and that the results are shown in Figure 12-4 as a performance report prepared for management.

The company's major problem with the fixed costs is salaries, which are unfavorable in all three categories—manufacturing, selling, and administrative. Significant **fixed cost variances** should be investigated to determine if future savings can be found.

RECONCILING ACTUAL AND BUDGETED NET INCOME

When the variance results of the contribution margin analysis and fixed costs are combined, we have identified all of the sources of the total difference between the 1987 actual net income before tax and the amount budgeted for the year. Recall from Figure 12-2 that the budgeted net income before tax for 1987 is $500,000, and the actual amount is only $134,400, for an unfavorable variance of $365,600. The $345,600 unfavorable contribution margin variance plus the $20,000 unfavorable fixed cost variance is equal to the $365,600 difference between the budgeted and actual net income before tax. These results can be summarized in a report prepared for management such as the one shown in Figure 12-5.

CONTRIBUTION MARGIN
VARIANCE ANALYSIS—MULTIPLE PRODUCTS

Objective 7:
Introducing the
impact of sales
mix

When a firm sells more than one product, the previous coverage of contribution margin variance analysis must be extended to include the possibility of a fourth type of variance—a sales mix variance. In addition, each type of product sold is considered when the sales volume variance, selling price variance, and variable cost variance are computed. We discussed the impact of sales mix when we examined cost-volume-profit relationships in Chapter 6. Many of the same considerations apply to a sales mix variance as it affects the contribution margin variance.

A **sales mix variance** is the result of actually selling relative quantities of products that are different from those planned. Businesses usually sell products with different contribution margins so a *consumer shift* from one combination of products to another mix will have an impact on a firm's profitability. Profit improvements result from a shift from less profitable products to those with higher contribution margins; conversely, profit reductions occur when the change is to more products with lower contribution margins even if the same number of units are sold before and after the change. Common causes of a sales mix variance, which is normally the responsibility of the marketing function, are:

1. Changes in consumer tastes and attitudes
2. A different personal selling effort

Figure 12-4

J&J COMPANY
Fixed Cost Variance Analysis
Year Ended December 31, 1987

	Budget	Actual	Variance
Manufacturing:			
Salaries	$1,120,000	$1,170,000	$50,000 U
Supplies	65,000	58,000	7,000 F
Utilities	540,000	524,000	16,000 F
Depreciation	515,000	515,000	-0-
Other	10,000	13,000	3,000 U
Total	2,250,000	2,280,000	30,000 U
Selling:			
Salaries	160,000	165,000	5,000 U
Promotion	85,000	79,000	6,000 F
Travel	35,000	31,000	4,000 F
Depreciation	25,000	25,000	-0-
Other	5,000	4,000	1,000 F
Total	310,000	304,000	6,000 F
Administrative:			
Salaries	415,000	418,000	3,000 U
Insurance	26,000	24,000	2,000 F
Property taxes	17,000	17,000	-0-
Utilities	15,000	11,000	4,000 F
Depreciation	60,000	60,000	-0-
Other	7,000	6,000	1,000 F
Total	540,000	536,000	4,000 F
Total fixed costs	$3,100,000	$3,120,000	$20,000 U

U indicates an unfavorable variance
F indicates a favorable variance

Figure 12-5

J&J COMPANY
Profit Variance Analysis Summary
Year Ended December 31, 1987

Budgeted net income before tax (Figure 12-2)	$500,000
Actual net income before tax (Figure 12-2)	134,400
Total profit variance	$365,600 U
Sources of profit variance:	
Contribution margin variance analysis (Figure 12-3)	$345,600 U
Fixed cost variance analysis (Figure 12-4)	20,000 U
Total profit variance	$365,600 U

U indicates an unfavorable variance

3. The impact of advertising and promotional spending
4. Change of pricing policy
5. An economic downturn that causes customers to purchase less expensive products
6. High-profit products that are at an advanced stage of their life cycle and no longer as popular with customers

To be able to evaluate the effect of a change from one sales mix to another, managers must be able to isolate the direct impact on profits of such a change without any influence from differing sales volume, selling price, and variable cost results. A favorable sales mix variance occurs when either: (1) the actual sales of a product with a high contribution margin are greater than the same product's budgeted sales or (2) the actual sales of a product with a low contribution margin are less than that product's budgeted sales. In contrast, an unfavorable sales mix variance arises when either: (1) the actual sales of a product with a high contribution margin are less than the same product's budgeted sales or (2) the actual sales of a product with a low contribution margin exceed the budgeted sales of that product.

To illustrate how we can extend contribution margin variance analysis to consider more than one product, let's change the facts presented earlier for the J&J Company. Assume that the firm produces two products, downhill skis and cross-country skis. The revenue and variable cost data for the downhill skis are the same as they were before, and the cross-country skis have the following budgeted contribution margin data:

	Per Pair of Cross-country Skis
Selling price	$120
Variable production costs	84
Variable selling costs	6
Total variable costs	90
Contribution margin – $ amount	$ 30
Contribution margin – % of selling price	25

Remember that each pair of downhill skis has a budgeted selling price of $200, budgeted variable costs of $120, and a budgeted contribution margin of $80 or 40% of sales ($80/$200). Consequently, the downhill skis are more profitable than the cross-country skis because the contribution margins as percentages of sales are 40% and 25%, respectively. Naturally, the firm would like to sell as many pairs of downhill skis as possible to earn high profits. A shift in the *relative number* of downhill skis to cross-country skis will reduce profits, and management should be able to evaluate the economic impact of this change. Assume that the J&J Company has prepared the budgeted contribution margin performance information for 1988 shown in Figure 12-6 as an important part of its overall profit planning. Figure 12-7 shows the actual contribution margin performance for the J&J Company that was recorded during 1988.

We can extract actual unit selling price and cost data from the income statement that will be used in the contribution margin variance analysis for the two-product situation as follows:

	Downhill Skis	Cross-country Skis
Actual selling price	$7,410,000/38,000 = $195.	$7,616,000/64,000 = $119.
Actual variable production costs	$4,256,000/38,000 = $112.	$5,568,000/64,000 = $87.
Actual variable selling costs	$418,000/38,000 = $11.	$296,000/64,000 = $4.625

Figure 12-6

J&J COMPANY
Budgeted Contribution Margin Performance
Year Ended December 31, 1988

	Downhill Skis	Cross-country Skis	Total
Sales-units	40,000	60,000	100,000
Sales-dollars	$8,000,000	$7,200,000	$15,200,000
Variable production costs	4,400,000	5,040,000	9,440,000
Variable selling costs	400,000	360,000	760,000
Total variable costs	4,800,000	5,400,000	10,200,000
Contribution margin	$3,200,000	$1,800,000	$ 5,000,000

Note that in Figure 12-7 the actual contribution earned during 1988 is only $4,488,000 compared with the budgeted amount of $5 million (Figure 12-6). Since two products are involved, the $512,000 unfavorable contribution margin variance potentially is caused by a sales mix variance as well as the other three variances we observed in the one-product situation. The computations involved with the sales volume variance, selling price variance, and variable cost variance are essentially the same for a two-product case as they are in a one-product situation. However, the effects of sales mix and sales volume must

Figure 12-7

J&J COMPANY
Actual Contribution Margin Performance
Year Ended December 31, 1988

	Downhill Skis	Cross-country Skis	Total
Sales – units	38,000	64,000	102,000
Sales – dollars	$7,410,000	$7,616,000	$15,026,000
Variable production costs	4,256,000	5,568,000	9,824,000
Variable selling costs	418,000	296,000	714,000
Total variable costs	4,674,000	5,864,000	10,538,000
Contribution margin	$2,736,000	$1,752,000	$ 4,488,000

be separated. In addition, the calculations needed for the sales mix variance must be introduced if all of the sources of the $512,000 unfavorable contribution margin variance for the J&J Company are to be examined.

SALES MIX VARIANCE

Remember that the sales volume variance results from selling more or less units than planned. The sales mix variance results from selling a different proportion of units than that planned. More than one technique is available to distinguish between these two variances because of their close interrelationship (both involve changes in the number of units sold). We will use a popular way to compute the two variances, but we should point out that other equally accepted approaches are available. Figure 12-6 shows that the J&J Company expects its total sales of 100,000 units to be divided into 40,000 pairs of downhill skis and 60,000 pairs of cross-country skis. Thus, the sales mix is 40% downhill skis and 60% cross-country skis. Note too that the budgeted sales of 100,000 units should result in a total contribution margin of $5 million or an average contribution margin per unit sold of $50 ($5,000,000/100,000).

This budgeted average contribution margin per unit is needed to compute the sales mix variance because it permits the selling prices and variable costs to be held constant at the budgeted amounts. Remember that the other three factors—sales volume, selling price, and variable costs—should be held constant when a sales mix variance is calculated. As long as the relative quantities of downhill skis and cross-country skis are sold with the 40%–60% relationship, the average contribution margin per unit will be $50 without changes in selling prices or variable costs. If the sales mix changes from the 40%–60% relationship, the average contribution margin per unit also will change even if unit selling prices and unit variable costs remain the same. If the change in mix is to more downhill skis or fewer cross-country skis, the average contribution margin per unit will increase because the contribution margin for the downhill skis is greater than the margin for the cross-country skis (40% versus 25%). In contrast, when the change in mix is to more cross-country skis or fewer downhill skis, the average contribution margin per unit will be lower than $50.

The sales mix variance for each product is computed as:

$$\text{Sales mix variance} = (\text{Actual sales units} - \text{Budgeted sales units}) \times (\text{Budgeted contribution margin per unit} - \text{Budgeted average contribution margin per unit})$$

With this equation, total sales volume for both products combined, selling prices, and variable costs are held constant. The $50 budgeted average contribution margin per unit is the contribution margin that would have been earned with a 40%–60% mix and no selling price or variable cost variances. The budgeted contribution margin per unit is the amount that should have been earned for each of the two products—downhill skis and cross-country skis—regardless of the sales mix involved.

Thus, the second part of the sales mix variance equation (budgeted contribution margin per unit less budgeted average contribution margin per unit) represents the relative profitability of each product compared with the average profitability of the sales mix planned. The contribution margin of downhill skis is higher than average ($80 versus $50), whereas the budgeted contribution margin of cross-country skis is lower than average ($30 versus $50). If more units of the most profitable product (downhill skis) are sold than the number of units included in the planned sales mix, the sales mix variance will be favorable. In contrast, actual unit sales of the product with a below-average contribution margin (cross-country skis) that exceed the number of units contained in the planned sales mix results in an unfavorable sales mix variance.

The first part of the sales mix variance equation (actual sales units less budgeted sales units) considers the change in the actual number of units of each product sold compared with the number that should have been sold with the planned sales mix. The equation can be used to compute the sales mix variances for each of the two products, which together represent the total sales mix variance, as follows:

Downhill skis

$$
\begin{aligned}
\text{Sales mix variance} &= (38{,}000 - 40{,}000) \times (\$80 - \$50) \\
&= (2{,}000) \times \$30 \\
&= \$60{,}000 \text{ Unfavorable}
\end{aligned}
$$

Cross-country skis

$$
\begin{aligned}
\text{Sales mix variance} &= (64{,}000 - 60{,}000) \times (\$30 - \$50) \\
&= 4{,}000 \times (\$20) \\
&= \$80{,}000 \text{ Unfavorable} \\
\text{Total sales mix variance} &= \$60{,}000 \text{ Unfavorable} + \$80{,}000 \text{ Unfavorable} \\
&= \$140{,}000 \text{ Unfavorable}
\end{aligned}
$$

Both of the sales mix variances are unfavorable because the company sold fewer units of the high-profit product (downhill skis) than planned and more units of the low-profit product (cross-country skis) than expected. Each of the 2,000 pairs of downhill skis below budgeted sales cost the firm $30, for a total unfavorable variance of $60,000. The increase of 4,000 pairs of cross-country skis over the number budgeted, while favorable for sales volume, was unfavorable to the sales mix and resulted in a variance of $80,000 (4,000 × $20). The $20 is the unfavorable difference between the $30 contribution margin from a pair of cross-country skis and the average contribution margin of $50 for the two products. The $140,000 unfavorable sales mix variance should be considered carefully by management to evaluate ways to improve the sales mix by increasing the relative quantity of downhill skis sold in the future.

SALES VOLUME VARIANCE

The computations required for a sales volume variance with more than one product are somewhat different from the procedures used when only one product is involved. This is due to the effect of the sales mix. As we have just seen, a sales mix variance is the result of selling a different combination of products than the mix planned. In other words, it is a measure of the impact of an increase or decrease in the relative number of products sold. In contrast, a sales volume variance measures the effect of a change in the total units of both products combined on the contribution margin. For example, the J&J Company planned to sell 100,000 units but actually sold 102,000.

We know from the sales mix variance analysis that the increase in the units sold occurred with a low-profit product so the mix implications are unfavorable. Based on physical quantity, however, higher actual sales than budgeted are favorable because they generate additional revenue. Since the sales mix and sales volume are so closely related, the impact of the two factors must be separated in contribution margin variance analysis. We can do this by considering the budgeted average contribution margin from the planned sales mix as the contribution margin expected from additional sales units when the sales mix is held constant. The budgeted average contribution margin also holds constant the selling prices and variable costs at budgeted amounts so we can evaluate the influence of sales volume only. The sales volume variance in a multiple product situation can be computed as follows:

$$\text{Sales volume variance} = (\text{Actual sales units} - \text{Budgeted sales units}) \times \text{Budgeted average contribution margin per unit}$$

The sales volume variance for the J&J Company in 1988 is favorable because the actual units sold exceeded the budgeted amount by 2,000, resulting in a favorable variance of $100,000 that is computed as:

$$
\begin{aligned}
\text{Sales volume variance} &= (102{,}000 - 100{,}000) \times \$50 \\
&= \quad\quad 2{,}000 \quad\quad \times \$50 \\
&= \$100{,}000 \text{ Favorable}
\end{aligned}
$$

Alternatively, a sales volume variance for each product could be calculated and added algebraically to determine the total sales volume variance as shown here:

Downhill skis

$$
\begin{aligned}
\text{Sales volume variance} &= (38{,}000 - 40{,}000) \times \$50 \\
&= \quad\quad (2{,}000) \quad\quad \times \$50 \\
&= \$100{,}000 \text{ Unfavorable}
\end{aligned}
$$

Cross-country skis

$$
\begin{aligned}
\text{Sales volume variance} &= (64{,}000 - 60{,}000) \times \$50 \\
&= \quad\quad 4{,}000 \quad\quad \times \$50 \\
&= \$200{,}000 \text{ Favorable}
\end{aligned}
$$

$$
\begin{aligned}
\text{Total sales volume variance} &= \$100{,}000 \text{ Unfavorable} + \$200{,}000 \text{ Favorable} \\
&= \$100{,}000 \text{ Favorable}
\end{aligned}
$$

SELLING PRICE VARIANCE

We can calculate the selling price variance for each of the products by applying the same formula introduced earlier in the single-product situation as:

$$\text{Selling price variance} = (\text{Actual selling price} - \text{Budgeted selling price}) \times \text{Actual units sold}$$

Downhill skis

$$
\begin{aligned}
&= (\$195 - \$200) \times 38{,}000 \\
&= \quad\quad (\$5) \quad\quad \times 38{,}000 \\
&= \$190{,}000 \text{ Unfavorable}
\end{aligned}
$$

Cross-country skis

$$
\begin{aligned}
&= (\$119 - \$120) \times 64{,}000 \\
&= \quad\quad (\$1) \quad\quad \times 64{,}000 \\
&= \$64{,}000 \text{ Unfavorable}
\end{aligned}
$$

$$
\begin{aligned}
\text{Total selling price variance} &= \$190{,}000 \text{ Unfavorable} + \$64{,}000 \text{ Unfavorable} \\
&= \$254{,}000 \text{ Unfavorable}
\end{aligned}
$$

VARIABLE COST VARIANCE

The variable cost variance formula introduced with the single-product situation can also be used to compute the variable cost variances for the two products of the J&J Company. Recall that the following equation is used:

$$\begin{array}{c}\text{Variable} \\ \text{cost} \\ \text{variance}\end{array} = (\text{Actual costs per unit} - \text{Budgeted costs per unit}) \times \begin{array}{c}\text{Actual} \\ \text{units} \\ \text{sold}\end{array}$$

Variable cost variance – production costs

Downhill skis	$= (\$112 - \$110) \times 38,000$	
	$= \quad \$2 \quad \times 38,000$	
	$= \$76,000$ Unfavorable	
Cross-country skis	$= (\$87 - \$84) \times 64,000$	
	$= \quad \$3 \quad \times 64,000$	
	$= \$192,000$ Unfavorable	

Total variable cost
variance – production costs $= \$76,000$ Unfavorable $+ \$192,000$ Unfavorable
$= \$268,000$ Unfavorable

Variable cost variance – selling costs

Downhill skis	$= (\$11 - \$10) \times 38,000$
	$= \quad \$1 \quad \times 38,000$
	$= \$38,000$ Unfavorable
Cross-country skis	$= (\$4.625 - \$6) \times 64,000$
	$= \quad (\$1.375) \quad \times 64,000$
	$= \$88,000$ Favorable

Total variable cost
variance – selling costs $\quad = \$38,000$ Unfavorable $+ \$88,000$ Favorable
$= \$50,000$ Favorable

Total variable cost
variance $\quad = \$268,000$ Unfavorable $+ \$50,000$ Favorable
$= \$218,000$ Unfavorable

SUMMARY OF VARIANCES

Remember that the actual contribution margin from the two products for the J&J Company is $512,000 less than the amount planned ($5,000,000 less $4,488,000). A complete analysis of the contribution margin deviation can be shown in a management report such as the one presented in Figure 12-8. The variance analysis information shows management what went wrong in the firm's contribution margin performance and must be corrected for future profit improvements.

**Objective 8:
Reporting profit
variances to
management**

CONTRIBUTION MARGIN VARIANCE ANALYSIS WITH STANDARD COSTS

When a firm uses standard costs to prepare the budget, the variance analysis discussed in Chapters 10 and 11 can be combined with contribution margin variance analysis. This combination provides a detailed breakdown of any total variable production cost variance. Remember that there are six different types of standard cost variances for the *variable* manufacturing costs incurred in the production function. These six variances are:

**Objective 9:
Combining con-
tribution margin
variances with
standard cost
variances**

1. Materials price variance
2. Materials quantity variance
3. Labor rate variance
4. Labor efficiency variance
5. Overhead spending variance
6. Overhead efficiency variance

Figure 12-8

J&J COMPANY		
Contribution Margin Variance Analysis		
Year Ended December 31, 1988		
Budgeted contribution margin		$5,000,000
Actual contribution margin		4,488,000
Unfavorable contribution margin variance		$ 512,000
Source of Variance	Favorable	Unfavorable
Sales mix:		
Downhill skis		$ 60,000
Cross-country skis		80,000
Sales volume:		
Downhill skis		100,000
Cross-country skis	$200,000	
Selling price:		
Downhill skis		190,000
Cross-country skis		64,000
Variable costs – production:		
Downhill skis		76,000
Cross-country skis		192,000
Variable costs – selling:		
Downhill skis		38,000
Cross-country skis	88,000	
Totals	$288,000	$800,000
Unfavorable contribution margin variance	$512,000	

Since our analysis is based on an income statement with a contribution margin format, the standard cost variances associated with fixed manufacturing overhead *do not* have to be considered. In this type of analysis, fixed manufacturing overhead is treated as a *period cost* instead of being charged to the products produced. We discussed this treatment in Chapter 5, which compared absorption costing and variable costing. To prepare the master budget, standard quantities of the variable production costs are multiplied by their respective unit standard prices or rates to compute the amounts estimated for each type of cost. Any difference between the budgeted costs and the actual costs incurred can be explained with the related standard cost variances. In aggregate, such variances will equal the variable production cost variance we computed earlier as a total amount with contribution margin variance analysis.

To illustrate how the combination of contribution margin variance analysis and standard costs is used, let's consider the case of the Azad Chemical Company, which produces and sells a single industrial cleaning fluid called "Renewzit." The firm uses standard costs to prepare its annual budget and based its 1987 projected production performance on the following estimates. (We assume all selling and administrative expenses are fixed in this illustration).

Production and sales in gallons		500,000
Budgeted selling price per gallon	×	$12
Budgeted sales in dollars		$6,000,000
Variable production costs per gallon:		
Direct materials (2 pounds @ $1.50 each)		$3
Direct labor (1/2 hour @ $8 per hour)		4
Variable manufacturing		
overhead (1/2 hour @ $2 per hour)		1
Total variable production costs per gallon		$8

During 1987, the Azad Chemical Company actually produced and sold 510,000 gallons of Renewzit with the following selling price and variable cost results:

Actual selling price per gallon	$11.50
Actual variable production costs:	
Direct materials purchased and used	
(1,122,000 pounds @ $1.60 each)	$1,795,200
Direct labor costs (280,500 hours @ $8.20 per hour)	2,300,100
Variable manufacturing overhead	586,500
Total actual variable production costs	$4,681,800

We can compute the actual unit costs for each cost element by dividing the totals shown above by the 510,000 gallons produced:

Direct materials	($1,795,200/510,000) = $3.52 per gallon
Direct labor	($2,300,100/510,000) = $4.51 per gallon
Variable manufacturing overhead ($586,500/510,000) = $1.15 per gallon	

Comparative reports for the firm's 1987 budgeted and actual contribution margin performance are shown in Figure 12-9. Note that the actual contribution margin is $1,183,200 compared with the budgeted contribution margin of $2 million, for an unfavorable variance of $816,800.

Since the Azad Chemical Company only sells one product, there is not any sales mix influence on the contribution margin. By calculating the sales volume variance, selling price variance, and the six standard cost variances for the variable production costs, we should be able to identify the sources of the unfavorable $816,800 contribution margin variance.

SALES VOLUME VARIANCE

A favorable sales volume variance was incurred by the Azad Chemical Company because the actual gallons sold (510,000) are 10,000 gallons more than those budgeted (500,000). The additional gallons caused both sales revenue and

AZAD CHEMICAL COMPANY
Contribution Margin Performance Report—Budget versus Actual
Year Ended December 31, 1987

		Budget		Actual
Sales–units		500,000		510,000
Sales–dollars	(500,000 × $12)	$6,000,000	(510,000 × $11.50)	$5,865,000
Variable cost of goods sold:				
Direct materials	(500,000 × $3)	1,500,000	(510,000 × $3.52)	1,795,200
Direct labor	(500,000 × $4)	2,000,000	(510,000 × $4.51)	2,300,100
Variable manufacturing				
overhead	(500,000 × $1)	500,000	(510,000 × $1.15)	586,500
Total	(500,000 × $8)	4,000,000	(510,000 × $9.18)	4,681,800
Contribution margin		$2,000,000		$1,183,200
Unfavorable variance			$816,800	

Figure 12-9

variable cost of goods sold to increase proportionately. The net effect is a higher dollar amount of contribution margin. The budgeted contribution margin per unit was $4 ($2,000,000/500,000), and the favorable sales volume variance is 10,000 gallons times $4, or $40,000.

SELLING PRICE VARIANCE

The budgeted selling price is $12 per gallon, but the actual selling price is only $11.50 per gallon. Thus, the selling price variance is unfavorable and is computed by multiplying the price difference of $.50 per gallon by the 510,000 gallons actually sold. The result is an unfavorable selling price variance of $255,000.

DIRECT MATERIALS VARIANCES

Remember that a direct materials variance can arise from either price or quantity sources. The actual price paid by the Azad Company during 1987 for direct materials was $1.60 per pound compared with a standard price of $1.50. The direct materials purchased and used amounted to 1,122,000 pounds, so the unfavorable materials price variance is $112,200 (1,122,000 times $.10). In producing the 510,000 gallons of Renewzit, the company should have used 1,020,000 pounds of direct materials (510,000 gallons times 2 pounds per gallon of finished product) instead of the 1,122,000 pounds actually recorded. The difference between the 1,122,000 actual pounds and the standard quantity allowed (1,020,000) is 102,000 pounds, which can be multiplied by the standard price of $1.50 to calculate the unfavorable materials quantity variance of $153,000. Consequently, the total materials variance is unfavorable and amounts to $265,200 ($112,200 + $153,000).

DIRECT LABOR VARIANCES

The total direct labor variance must be divided into its rate and efficiency components. An actual direct labor rate of $8.20 was incurred compared with the standard rate of $8. The $.20 difference is multiplied by the 280,500 actual direct labor hours recorded to determine the unfavorable labor rate variance of $56,100.

In addition, the 280,500 actual direct labor hours recorded exceed the 255,000 standard hours allowed (510,000 gallons of output times the standard of 1/2 hour per gallon) by 25,500 hours. The inefficient labor utilization results in an unfavorable labor efficiency variance of $204,000 (25,500 excessive hours times the standard labor rate of $8). As a result, the total unfavorable direct labor variance is $260,100 for the Azad Chemical Company ($56,100 + $204,000).

VARIABLE MANUFACTURING OVERHEAD VARIANCES

Two types of variable manufacturing overhead variances (spending and efficiency) can be computed for the company's 1987 performance. Remember from Chapter 11 that we calculate an overhead spending variance by comparing the actual variable manufacturing overhead with the variable portion of the flexible budget for the actual direct labor hours worked. An overhead efficiency variance is the difference between the variable manufacturing overhead budgeted for the actual direct labor hours worked (280,500 hours) and the amount budgeted for the standard direct labor hours allowed (255,000 hours). The variable manufacturing overhead rate per direct labor hour is $2. Thus, the spending and efficiency variances are computed as follows:

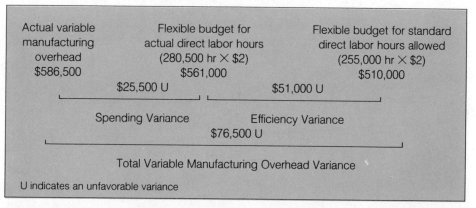

Actual variable manufacturing overhead $586,500	Flexible budget for actual direct labor hours (280,500 hr × $2) $561,000	Flexible budget for standard direct labor hours allowed (255,000 hr × $2) $510,000
	$25,500 U	$51,000 U
	Spending Variance	Efficiency Variance
	$76,500 U	
	Total Variable Manufacturing Overhead Variance	

U indicates an unfavorable variance

We can see that the unfavorable total variable manufacturing overhead variance amounts to $76,500, divided into an unfavorable spending variance of $25,500 and an unfavorable efficiency variance of $51,000. Note the important relationship of the six variances computed with the standard costs and the single variance we called a variable production cost variance earlier. If the direct materials variances ($265,200 unfavorable), direct labor variances ($260,100 unfavorable), and variable manufacturing overhead variances ($76,500 unfavorable) are totaled, the result is an unfavorable total variable production cost variance of $601,800.

In earlier illustrations, the variable production cost variance was computed by multiplying the difference between the actual costs per unit and the budgeted costs per unit times the number of actual units sold. Figure 12-9 shows that the actual total variable production costs per unit are $9.18 and the budgeted cost per unit is $8, for a difference of $1.18. If we multiply the $1.18 times the 510,000 gallons actually sold, the result is the same variance of $601,800 determined earlier by adding the various standard cost variances. These same results must occur because the standard costs were used originally in the preparation of the firm's budget.

SUMMARY OF VARIANCES

The actual contribution margin for the Azad Chemical Company is $1,183,200 compared with a budgeted contribution margin of $2 million. Thus, the unfavorable contribution margin variance is $816,800. We have identified a sales volume variance, a selling price variance, and six standard cost variances in the previous analysis. The algebraic summation of these variances should equal the unfavorable $816,800 contribution margin variance. (Remember that the amount of raw materials purchased equaled those used so none of the materials price variance is associated with the units left in the ending inventory.) The related variance information should (1) provide the company's management with a detailed understanding of why this phase of the profit plan was not achieved and (2) indicate what areas should be investigated further. The variances would be reported to management as shown in Figure 12-10.

Figure 12-10

AZAD CHEMICAL COMPANY
Contribution Margin Variance Analysis
Year Ended December 31, 1987

Budgeted contribution margin	$2,000,000
Actual contribution margin	1,183,200
Unfavorable contribution margin variance	$ 816,800

Source of Variance	Favorable	Unfavorable
Sales volume	$40,000	
Selling price		$255,000
Direct materials:		
Price		112,200
Quantity		153,000
Direct labor:		
Rate		56,100
Efficiency		204,000
Variable overhead:		
Spending		25,500
Efficiency		51,000
Totals	$40,000	$856,800
Unfavorable contribution margin variance	$816,800	

SUMMARY

Profit variance analysis is an important part of managerial accounting because it enables management to identify the sources of deviations from a planned profit performance. A profit variance is the difference between the *actual net income earned* and the *net income planned* for the same period. The five factors contributing to net income results—sales volume, selling price, sales mix, variable costs, and fixed costs—must be evaluated independently to perform profit variance analysis.

A useful approach to profit variance analysis is to separate the factors affecting the contribution margin from the fixed costs of a given period. When a single product is being considered, contribution margin variance analysis is used to compute the sales volume variance, selling price variance, and variable cost variance. The algebraic summation of these three variances is equal to the difference between the actual contribution margin and the budgeted contribution margin.

When a firm sells more than one product, a sales mix variance also must be considered because of the relative quantities of the different products sold. The fixed costs incurred for the manufacturing, selling, and administrative functions are evaluated by comparing the actual amounts for a given period with the budgeted amounts. By combining the contribution margin variance analysis with the fixed cost variance analysis, the sources of a profit variance can be identified for further investigation by the managers responsible for the various related activities.

Contribution margin variance analysis can be combined with standard cost variances to provide a detailed breakdown of the differences between actual and budgeted variable production costs. When this approach is taken, a materials price variance, materials quantity variance, labor rate variance, labor efficiency variance, variable manufacturing overhead spending variance, and variable manufacturing overhead efficiency variance are computed. The standard cost variances related to the fixed manufacturing overhead are omitted from the analysis because the fixed costs are treated as period costs in the contribution margin approach to the income statement.

GLOSSARY

CONTRIBUTION MARGIN VARIANCE ANALYSIS. A technique used to evaluate the sources of the difference between the actual contribution margin for a given period and the contribution margin budgeted for the same period or one for a previous period (p. 449).
FIXED COST VARIANCE. The difference between the actual fixed costs incurred for the manufacturing, selling, and administrative functions during a particular period and the fixed costs budgeted for the same period (p. 454).
FIXED COST VARIANCE ANALYSIS. A technique used to evaluate the actual fixed cost performance compared with the budgeted fixed costs (p. 454).
PROFIT VARIANCE. The difference between the actual net income earned and the planned net income for the same period (p. 446).
PROFIT VARIANCE ANALYSIS. A technique used to evaluate differences between actual and planned net income (p. 448).

SALES MIX VARIANCE. A variance affecting contribution margin that is caused by actual relative quantities of multiple products that are different from those planned (p.454).

SALES VOLUME VARIANCE. A variance affecting contribution margin that results from actually selling more or less total units than the amount planned (p.450).

SELLING PRICE VARIANCE. A variance affecting contribution margin that occurs when the actual selling price is different from the planned selling price (p.451).

VARIABLE COST VARIANCE. A variance affecting contribution margin that arises whenever the actual variable costs incurred to produce or sell a product are not the same as the variable costs planned (p.452).

DISCUSSION QUESTIONS

1. Identify the major sources of a profit variance. Why is this so essential to management?
2. Why is cost behavior important in performing profit variance analysis?
3. Explain the basic steps involved in the general approach to profit variance analysis that is discussed in this chapter.
4. How is a sales volume variance computed in a single-product situation?
5. How is a selling price variance calculated in a single-product case?
6. How is a variable cost variance computed in a single-product situation?
7. What is meant by an unfavorable contribution margin variance? What does it consist of?
8. How are fixed costs treated in profit variance analysis?
9. Are low fixed costs indicative of a good cost structure that will lead to good profit results?
10. "Profits are the result of the marketplace and management must accept what is there." Do you agree? Explain.
11. Indicate why an increased sales volume in units sold is not always a way to earn higher profits.
12. The controller of the Gobdel Company recently said: "A decrease in a variable cost is the same as one in a fixed cost as far as the impact on profits." Do you agree? Explain.
13. Why is a sales mix variance important? How is it computed?
14. You recently overheard the following comment: "I can't understand how our profits are below those planned when our sales volume in units is up and all selling prices and costs are exactly as we predicted." How could this happen? Explain.
15. How are standard costs combined with profit variance analysis to provide useful management information?
16. Explain how the variable cost variance can be further broken down when standard cost information is available.
17. Why is it impossible for a firm to incur an overhead capacity variance when variable costing is used?
18. The president of the Cohen Company is reviewing the firm's most recent financial results and is alarmed by the disappointing profit performance.

Based on the budget, the company planned to sell 50,000 units at a price of $10 with variable costs of $6 per unit. The actual accounting records show that 52,000 units were sold at a price of $9 with variable costs of $7 per unit. The president had been watching sales units and was pleased that they were above the budgeted amount. He does not understand why profit was not up accordingly. Identify the following variances for the president: contribution margin, sales volume, selling price, and variable cost.

EXERCISES

Exercise 12-1 Basic Contribution Margin Variance Analysis
The president of the Carter Company has just finished reviewing her firm's income statement for the quarter just ended and is disturbed by the profit results involved. Her main concern is the significant difference between the budgeted contribution margin and the one actually incurred. The company sells one product. A summary of the profit results follows:

	Budget	Actual
Sales – units	14,400	15,000
Sales – dollars	$146,880	$144,000
Variable costs	86,400	93,000
Contribution margin	$ 60,480	$ 51,000

Required:
Compute the three variances that are the sources of the contribution margin variance for the quarter.

Exercise 12-2 Basic Contribution Margin Variance Analysis
The Schultz Company's operating results for September and October included the following:

	September	October
Sales	$280,000	$241,200
Variable costs	196,000	187,600
Contribution margin	$ 84,000	$ 53,600

The firm's accountant has determined that variable costs per unit of a single product sold were the same in both months and that the company sold 14,000 units in September.

Required:
A. Explain the difference in contribution margin between the two months by computing the related variances.
B. Identify possible causes for each of the variances in part A.

Exercise 12-3 Basic Profit Plan Variance Analysis
The Rogers Company has just finished its first year of operation. The president had been pleased because sales volume for the company's single product has exceeded the amount budgeted. However, he is now alarmed because the firm's accountant has prepared the following income statement, which shows significantly lower net income than that budgeted:

ROGERS COMPANY
Income Statement
Year Ended December 31, 1987

	Budgeted	Actual
Sales:		
30,000 units at $10	$300,000	
32,000 units at $9.50		$304,000
Variable costs	180,000	195,200
Contribution margin	120,000	108,800
Fixed costs	80,000	86,000
Net income	$ 40,000	$ 22,800

Required:
Compute all variances related to the company's performance to explain the difference between budgeted and actual net incomes.

Exercise 12-4 Using Contribution Margin Variance Analysis to Evaluate Change

The Fendley Company produces a gear that is sold to various motorcycle manufacturers. Summarized income statements for the past two years are as follows:

	1986	1987
Sales	$500,000	$600,000
Variable costs	400,000	450,000
Contribution margin	$100,000	$150,000

During 1986 and 1987, the firm sold 200,000 gears and 250,000 gears, respectively.

Required:
Calculate the effect of changes in selling price, sales volume, and variable costs for 1987 compared with 1986.

Exercise 12-5 Analyzing a Contribution Margin Variance

The Hill Company produces a precision instrument used to measure voltage. The firm's controller is trying to evaluate why the 1987 actual contribution margin earned by the firm was substantially less than the amount budgeted. The company's annual income statement shows the following:

HILL COMPANY
Partial Income Statement
Year Ended December 31, 1987

	Budgeted	Actual
Sales	$400,000	$360,000
Variable costs	250,000	270,000
Contribution margin	$150,000	$ 90,000

The controller is particularly concerned about these profit results because the actual selling price was $10 higher than budgeted, or $60 per unit.

Required:
Compute the following:

1. Selling price variance
2. Sales volume variance
3. Variable cost variance

Exercise 12-6 Basic Contribution Margin Variance Analysis

The president of the Howard Company has received the following information concerning her firm's actual contribution margin earned compared with the amount budgeted:

HOWARD COMPANY
Partial Income Statement
Month Ended July 31, 1987

	Dollars		
	Budgeted	Actual	Difference
Sales	$800,000	$840,000	$ 40,000
Variable costs	520,000	490,000	(30,000)
Contribution margin	$280,000	$350,000	$ 70,000
Unit selling price	$10	$12	

Required:
Explain with profit variance analysis why the actual contribution margin was more than the budgeted contribution margin for July.

Exercise 12-7 Use of Contribution Margin Variance Analysis

The Mansen Company has prepared the following income statement information showing the actual contribution margin earned from the sales of the company's only product as compared with the budgeted performance:

	Budget	Actual
Sales – units	5,200	5,100
Sales – dollars	$468,000	$453,900
Variable costs	260,000	244,800
Contribution margin	$208,000	$209,100

Required:
Compute the selling price variance, sales volume variance, and variable cost variance.

Exercise 12-8 Analyzing Profit Variances

The Helm Company's controller is evaluating the profit performance of her firm compared with the budgeted target, as shown on the next page:

HELM COMPANY
Income Statement
Year Ended December 31, 1987

	Budgeted	Actual	Variance
Sales	$960,000	$1,049,200	$89,200 F
Variable costs	576,000	653,600	77,600 U
Contribution margin	384,000	395,600	11,600 F
Fixed costs	210,000	215,600	5,600 U
Net income	$174,000	$ 180,000	$ 6,000 F

The controller has determined that the firm had budgeted to sell 8,000 units of its single product and had incurred a favorable sales volume variance of $28,800 during 1987.

Required:
A. How many units were actually sold during 1987?
B. Reconcile the difference between budgeted and actual net income for 1987 by determining all of the variances involved.

Exercise 12-9 Contribution Margin Variance Analysis with Two Products

The Foster Company produces two products—a standard model and a deluxe model. The actual and budgeted data for the firm's 1987 contribution margin performance is shown below:

	Standard Model		Deluxe Model	
	Per Unit	Number of Units	Per Unit	Number of Units
Budgeted sales	$15	75,000	$20	25,000
Budgeted variable costs	10	75,000	14	25,000
Actual sales	13	80,000	18	20,000
Actual variable costs	11	80,000	13	20,000

Required:
A. Determine the contribution margin variance for 1987.
B. Compute all variances underlying the difference between the actual contribution margin and budgeted contribution margin for 1987.

Exercise 12-10 Contribution Margin Variance Analysis with Two Products

The Marsh Company produces two products, A and B. The following facts were recorded for the production and sale of the two products during 1987:

	Budgeted	Actual
Product A		
Sales – units	60,000	65,000
Sales – dollars	$300,000	$331,500
Variable costs	180,000	201,500
Product B		
Sales – units	40,000	38,000
Sales – dollars	$320,000	$269,800
Variable costs	160,000	163,400

Required:

A. Was the actual contribution margin higher or lower than the amount budgeted? How much?
B. Explain the difference in budgeted contribution margin and actual contribution margin by computing the variances involved.

PROBLEMS

Problem 12-1 **Analysis of Contribution Margin Difference**
The Garcia Company, which only produces and sells one product, recently completed its first year of operation. Eldon Garcia, the firm's president, was pleased to observe that sales volume in units were ahead of projections. However, he is now alarmed to see the profit results shown on the following income statement:

GARCIA COMPANY
Income Statement
Year Ended December 31, 1987

	Budgeted	Actual
Sales – units	90,000	95,000
Sales – dollars	$1,080,000	$1,092,500
Variable costs	756,000	826,500
Contribution margin	324,000	266,000
Fixed costs	174,000	192,000
Net income	$ 150,000	$ 74,000

Required:
Compute all variances contributing to the difference between budgeted and actual net incomes.

Problem 12-2 **Contribution Margin Variance Analysis with One Product**
The Flax Company produces and sells a single product. The firm's 1987 income statement showed the following:

Sales (90,000 units)	$774,000
Variable costs	450,000
Contribution margin	$324,000

The company currently is preparing a budgeted income statement for 1988. Sales units are expected to increase 10% with an average selling price of $8.80 per unit. Variable costs per unit are expected to increase 6%.

Required:
A. Determine the budgeted contribution margin in dollars for 1988.
B. Explain why the budgeted contribution margin computed in part A is different from the $324,000 earned in 1987 by computing:

1. Selling price variance
2. Sales volume variance
3. Variable cost variance

Problem 12-3 Profit Variance Analysis with Incomplete Data
The controller of the Reid Company is trying to determine why the firm's actual profit results for June, 1987 deviated significantly from those budgeted. To do so, he has prepared the following income statement and collected the related facts.

REID COMPANY
Income Statement
Month Ended June 30, 1987

Sales (5,400 units)	$31,320
Variable costs	23,760
Contribution margin	7,560
Fixed costs	5,200
Net income	$ 2,360
Profit variance	$ 4,640 Unfavorable
Variable cost variance	2,160 Unfavorable
Budgeted sales in units	6,000
Budgeted contribution margin per unit	$ 2

Required:
Compute all variances necessary to explain the unfavorable profit variance.

Problem 12-4 Contribution Margin Variance Analysis with Two Products
The Walsh Company produces and sells two types of microcomputer—standard and portable. The firm's budgeted contribution margins for 1987 were computed as follows:

	Standard	Portable
Sales–units	10,000	6,000
Sales–dollars	$8,000,000	$5,400,000
Variable costs	4,800,000	3,348,000
Contribution margin	$3,200,000	$2,052,000

The actual sales results for 1987 showed the following:

	Standard	Portable
Sales–units	11,000	7,000
Sales–dollars	$8,470,000	$6,370,000
Variable costs	5,500,000	3,990,000
Contribution margin	$2,970,000	$2,380,000

Required:
Compute the following:

1. Sales volume variances
2. Selling price variances
3. Sales mix variances
4. Cost variances

Problem 12-5 Profit Variance Analysis with Two Products

The Watch-Out Company produces and sells two models of radar detectors, regular and pocket-size. The firm's 1987 budget showed the following projections:

	Regular	Pocket-Size	Total
Sales – units	10,000	6,000	16,000
Sales – dollars	$3,000,000	$2,160,000	$5,160,000
Variable costs	1,200,000	864,000	2,064,000
Contribution margin	1,800,000	1,296,000	3,096,000
Fixed costs:			
Manufacturing			1,324,000
Selling			368,000
Administrative			888,000
Net income			$ 516,000

An accountant in the controller's department prepared the income statement shown next after the year 1987 had ended:

	Regular	Pocket-Size	Total
Sales – units	11,000	5,500	16,500
Sales – dollars	$3,190,000	$1,958,000	$5,148,000
Variable costs	1,375,000	781,000	2,156,000
Contribution margin	1,815,000	1,177,000	2,992,000
Fixed costs:			
Manufacturing			1,356,000
Selling			374,000
Administrative			902,000
Net income			$ 360,000

Required:
A. What is the profit variance for 1987?
B. Compute the following variances to explain the difference between budgeted and actual net incomes:
   1. Sales volume variances
   2. Selling price variances
   3. Sales mix variances
   4. Variable cost variances
   5. Fixed cost variances
C. Identify possible causes for each of the variances computed in part B.

Problem 12-6 Profit Variance Analysis with Three Products

The Lakeview Marina sells three kinds of boats: powerboats, fishing boats, and sailboats. The marina manager is currently evaluating the business' financial performance for 1987 to determine why the planned net income was not achieved. He is particularly concerned about the contribution margin earned compared with the amount budgeted. The following data have been collected:

	Sales Units	Budgeted Sales Dollars	Budgeted Cost of Sales	Budgeted Contribution Margin
Powerboats	100	$1,200,000	$680,000	$520,000
Fishing boats	300	1,200,000	900,000	300,000
Sailboats	200	400,000	320,000	80,000

	Sales Units	**Actual** Sales Dollars	Cost of Sales	Contribution Margin
Powerboats	80	$ 976,000	$560,000	$416,000
Fishing boats	310	1,178,000	930,000	248,000
Sailboats	240	420,000	388,800	31,200

Required:
Compute the following variances:

1. Selling price variances
2. Sales volume variances
3. Sales mix variances
4. Cost variance

Problem 12-7 Contribution Margin Variance Analysis with Two Products
The All-Sports Company produces and sells two types of artificial turf used primarily for football and baseball fields. For 1987, the firm budgeted sales of 100,000 rolls of high-grade turf and 150,000 rolls of medium-grade turf. The budgeted income statement showed the following:

	High-Grade	Medium-Grade	Total
Sales	$10,000,000	$10,500,000	$20,500,000
Variable costs	6,000,000	7,350,000	13,350,000
Contribution margin	4,000,000	3,150,000	7,150,000
Fixed costs			5,650,000
Net income			$ 1,500,000

The president of the firm has just received the income statement shown next and is disappointed with the actual net income earned. He had been carefully watching sales and was pleased to observe that they were higher than those forecast. 97,000 rolls of high-grade turf were sold along with 160,000 rolls of medium-grade turf. He notes that most of the deviation between planned and actual profits involved the financial items leading to the contribution margin. He wants your help in taking the analysis further.

	High-Grade	Medium-Grade	Total
Sales	$9,700,000	$10,720,000	$20,420,000
Variable costs	5,820,000	7,840,000	13,660,000
Contribution margin	3,880,000	2,880,000	6,760,000
Fixed costs			5,655,000
Net income			$ 1,105,000

Required:
Calculate the following:

1. Selling price variances
2. Sales volume variances
3. Sales mix variances
4. Variable cost variances

Problem 12-8 Contribution Margin Variance Analysis with Standard Costs
The Mitchell Company operates a standard cost system to plan and control costs for its single product. During 1987, the firm planned to produce and sell 40,000 units with the following budgeted income statement:

MITCHELL COMPANY
Budgeted Income Statement
Year Ending December 31, 1987

Sales		$2,000,000
Variable cost of goods sold		1,280,000
Contribution margin		720,000
Fixed costs:		
Manufacturing	$320,000	
Selling	120,000	
Administrative	110,000	550,000
Net income		$ 170,000

An analysis of the standard variable costs required to produce one unit indicates:

Direct materials:	4 lb at $3 per lb	$12
Direct labor:	2 hr at $8 per hr	16
Variable overhead:	2 hr at $2 per hr	4
Total		$32

During 1987, the following actual costs were recorded:

Direct materials purchased and used:	170,000 lb at	$ 527,000
Direct labor:	83,500 hr at	684,700
Variable overhead:		171,175
Total		$1,382,875

The firm's actual income statement for 1987 is shown next.

MITCHELL COMPANY
Income Statement
Year Ended December 31, 1987

Sales (42,000 units)		$2,016,000
Variable cost of goods sold		1,382,875
Contribution margin		633,125
Fixed costs:		
Manufacturing	$326,000	
Selling	122,000	
Administrative	114,000	562,000
Net income		$ 71,125

Required:
A. Compute the contribution margin variance for 1987.
B. Compute the profit variance for 1987.
C. Compute the following to explain the profit variance calculated in part B.
   1. Selling price variance
   2. Sales volume variance

3. Direct materials variances
4. Direct labor variances
5. Variable manufacturing overhead variances
6. Fixed cost variances

Problem 12-9 Contribution Margin Variance Analysis with Standard Costs

The Bronze Company produces and sells a specialized, high-priced type of suntan lotion. During 1987, the company projected that it would sell 105,000 bottles of lotion at $12 each. A standard cost system is used by the company with the following standard costs per bottle:

Direct materials (12 oz at $.25 each)	$3.00
Direct labor (.2 hr at $12 each)	2.40
Variable overhead (.2 hr at $3 each)	.60
Total	$6.00

The budgeted and actual income statements have been prepared by the firm's accountant as follows:

BRONZE COMPANY
Income Statement
Year Ended December 31, 1987

	Budgeted	Actual	Variance
Sales	$1,260,000	$1,265,000	$ 5,000 F
Variable cost of goods sold	630,000	718,200	88,200 U
Contribution margin	630,000	546,800	83,200 U
Fixed costs:			
Manufacturing	210,000	216,000	6,000 U
Selling	120,000	122,000	2,000 U
Administrative	160,000	168,000	8,000 U
Total	490,000	506,000	16,000 U
Net income	$ 140,000	$ 40,800	$99,200 U

The actual variable costs incurred by the company in the production and sale of 110,000 bottles are divided as follows:

Direct materials purchased and used:	1,340,000 oz at $.28 each
Direct labor:	22,800 hr at $12 each
Variable manufacturing overhead:	?

Required:
Compute the following variances to explain why the firm's actual net income was $99,200 lower than the amount budgeted:

1. Selling price variance
2. Sales volume variance
3. Variable production cost variance
4. Direct materials variances
5. Direct labor variances

6. Variable overhead variances
7. Fixed cost variances

Problem 12-10 Contribution Margin Variance Analysis with Standard Costs and Two Products

The Shelby Company produces and sells two products, RX7 and RX8. A standard cost system is used to control costs with the following standards applicable to the firm's 1987 operation:

RX7

Direct materials:	4 lb at $1 each	$ 4
Direct labor:	6 hr at $9 each	54
Variable overhead:	6 hr at $2 each	12
Total		$70

RX8

Direct materials:	5 lb at $1.20 each	$ 6
Direct labor:	7 hr at $9 each	63
Variable overhead:	7 hr at $2 each	14
Total		$83

During 1987, the company planned to produce and sell 90,000 units of RX7 and 60,000 units of RX8 with the following budgeted income statement:

	RX7	RX8	Total
Sales	$9,000,000	$7,500,000	$16,500,000
Variable cost of sales	6,300,000	4,980,000	11,280,000
Contribution margin	2,700,000	2,520,000	5,220,000
Fixed costs:			
Manufacturing			3,140,000
Selling			860,000
Administrative			420,000
Net income			$ 800,000

The actual costs recorded for the production and sales of 94,000 units of RX7 and 58,000 units of RX8 included:

RX7

Direct materials purchased and used:	380,000 lb at $1.10 each
Direct labor:	566,000 hr at $9.20 each
Variable overhead:	$1,173,120

RX8

Direct materials purchased and used:	296,000 lb at $1.25 each
Direct labor:	410,000 hr at $9.20 each
Variable overhead:	$844,480

The actual income statement reported by the firm showed the following:

	RX7	RX8	Total
Sales	$9,212,000	$7,250,000	$16,462,000
Variable cost of sales	6,798,320	4,986,480	11,784,800
Contribution margin	2,413,680	2,263,520	4,677,200
Fixed costs:			
Manufacturing			3,148,000
Selling			868,000
Administrative			429,000
Net income			$ 232,200

Required:

Compute the following variances to explain the difference between the firm's actual and budgeted net income:

1. Selling price variances
2. Sales volume variances
3. Sales mix variances
4. Direct materials variances
5. Direct labor variances
6. Variable overhead variances
7. Fixed cost variances

13

ACCOUNTING FOR DECENTRALIZED OPERATIONS

CHAPTER OVERVIEW AND OBJECTIVES

This chapter discusses how managerial accounting techniques are used in decentralized operations. After studying this chapter, you should be able to:

1. Explain the major characteristics of a decentralized operation.
2. Identify the benefits and limitations of decentralization.
3. Describe the nature and role of responsibility accounting in a decentralized operation.
4. Distinguish between cost centers, profit centers, and investment centers.
5. Realize how allocated costs should be treated for performance evaluation purposes.
6. Prepare and evaluate a segmented income statement with a contribution report format.
7. Recognize how return on investment (ROI) analysis is used to evaluate profit performance.
8. Determine how residual income (RI) analysis is used to evaluate profit performance.
9. Explain the importance of intrafirm transfer pricing in a decentralized organization.
10. Discuss three approaches to transfer pricing—cost-based, market-based, and negotiated market-based.

USE OF DECENTRALIZATION

In Chapter 1, we identified the organizing function of the management process as the development of the structure or capacity within which managers work to achieve a firm's goals. Ideally, the organizational structure that is created will facilitate the achievement of the business's goals while assuring that the employees are properly directed and motivated. The design of an effective organizational structure has two major considerations: (1) The grouping of work activities and employees as identifiable segments of the firm and (2) the choice between centralized or decentralized authority for the managers of the various segments selected.

Business segmentation, that is, the division of work into specialized units, enables a firm to accomplish more than it otherwise could. Departments, divisions, sales territories, plants, and branches are typical business segments within a firm. This grouping of activities is usually accomplished on the basis of one or more of the following:

1. Business functions
2. Products
3. Customers
4. Geographical territories

In a functional grouping, the business is organized according to its major business functions such as accounting, finance, marketing, production, and personnel. Segmentation by products combines all activities needed to design, produce, finance, and market a product or product line.

If a firm deals with significantly different customers, these customers may provide the basis for segmentation. For example, an aerospace manufacturer may have one division serving military customers and another serving non-military customers. In segmentation by geographical territories, the segments are identified with the regions of the country or world for which they are responsible.

The segmentation approach that is chosen depends on a given firm's *operating conditions and environment*. The main concern should be how the firm can best achieve the coordination and communication between the segments that are needed to attain the goals of the business as a whole. A particular firm may use more than one approach for different phases of its operation.

Objective 1: Identifying the key characteristics of decentralized operations

Another important consideration in the structuring of a business organization is deciding whether to select centralized authority, decentralized authority, or some combination of the two. With centralized authority, top management performs most of the decision making and seeks to retain control over the entire operation. In contrast, **decentralized authority** is based on a delegation of authority downward throughout the organization to managers who have a great deal of autonomy and participate actively in the decision-making process. The managers to whom authority is delegated are responsible for their segments' performances and are accountable to their superiors for results.

Consequently, we have four key terms in the implementation of decentralized authority:

1. Delegation
2. Authority
3. Responsibility
4. Accountability

Delegation is the downward distribution of job assignments and corresponding decision-making power to managers in an organization. **Authority** is the right to make the decisions necessary to perform the assigned tasks. **Responsibility** is the obligation on the part of the managers receiving the authority to attain the desired results. **Accountability** is the measure of how well the results are accomplished, and it is fulfilled through periodic performance reports that show the managers who delegated the authority what has happened.

Note that authority and responsibility should be *equal* because it would not be reasonable to hold a manager responsible for something he or she is not authorized to do. Also, responsibility is never delegated since the ultimate responsibility for the assigned job activities resides with the manager delegating authority for them. He or she must be sure that the subordinate managers perform their assignments efficiently and effectively.

Completely centralized authority is largely obsolete today because of the size and complexity of most business organizations. The managers at the top simply do not have the expertise, information, or time to make the wide range of decisions concerning personnel, production, marketing, and financial matters correctly and on a timely basis. As a result, most businesses have adopted some form of decentralized authority that is compatible with their internal and external conditions. For example, General Electric Company's 1981 annual report summarized the firm's use of decentralized authority as:

> *The call for GE employees to assume full responsibility for the decisions they make on behalf of you (the stockholders) and the company. It means moving more decision-making power to the operations—to managers who know their markets best.*

The general movement to decentralized authority has created the need for managerial accounting techniques that measure the performance of *both* the individual segments of an oganization and the firm as a whole. A decentralized organization is more difficult to coordinate than one with centralized authority simply because there are more people involved in the decision-making process. Even though the various segments are somewhat autonomous, their actions still must be coordinated to ensure that they are in the best interests of the firm's overall goals. This coordinated effort was identified as *goal congruence* in Chapter 8 where we explained the unifying effect of budgeting. We now need to consider other managerial accounting techniques that can be combined with budgeting for effective control of a decentralized operation. So that you can understand the need for these additional managerial accounting techniques, we will next consider the benefits and limitations of decentralization.

BENEFITS AND LIMITATIONS OF DECENTRALIZATION

A trade-off between the benefits and limitations of decentralization will determine how effectively this type of authority will work for a given business. Some companies use a mix of centralized and decentralized authority in order to achieve a balance between these benefits and limitations. For example, General Motors Corporation uses centralized planning along with decentralized production operations.

Objective 2: Understanding the benefits and limitations of decentralization

BENEFITS OF DECENTRALIZATION

The major benefits of decentralization are:

1. *Better decision making* is achieved at the operating level because the man-

agers involved have more reliable information concerning current local conditions than top-level managers.

2. Top managers are *relieved of the detail work* associated with the day-to-day operations and can concentrate on long-term planning and decision making.

3. Individual segment managers have *greater incentive* to perform well because they are stimulated by the opportunity to operate a semiautonomous business.

4. Since the managers of the various segments are deeply involved with decision making and are fully responsible for their results, they receive *better training* that prepares them for advancement in the organization.

5. *Performance measurement is more effective* because individual effort as well as group effort is evaluated.

6. Decentralization may be the *only effective way* to cope with an organization's size because work activities are divided into units that are small enough to stay in contact with their environment and respond to changes on a timely basis.

LIMITATIONS OF DECENTRALIZATION

The limitations of decentralization are particularly important for managerial accounting because they can have a significant impact on the way managerial accounting applications are developed for a particular organization. The major limitations of decentralization are:

1. *Additional accounting costs* are incurred to accumulate and report the information concerning the performance of the various operating segments as well as the firm as a whole. In essence, the accounting system itself is segmented to make available the detailed information that is needed.

2. A *duplication of effort* resulting in inefficiencies may result from decentralization as the various segments require separate staff and service functions that otherwise could be centralized to serve multiple segments.

3. Valid performance measurement that is fair to all segments *may be difficult to achieve* because of the use of common resources and operating differences. Added pressure will be placed on a clear distinction between what is controllable by the segment managers and what is uncontrollable. In addition, difficulties with an equitable pricing policy for transfers of products or services between segments often arise.

4. *Costly mistakes* may occur if the segment managers aren't adequately trained and skilled for their decision-making responsibilities. A more experienced top management may not make these same mistakes.

5. Concern about individual performance evaluation may cause segment managers to make decisions that *are not in the firm's best interests.* For example, a segment may choose to purchase inventory from an outside supplier when another segment of the firm produces the same product. As a result, less total profit may be earned by the firm.

6. Coordinating operations *will be much more difficult* for top management because decision making is dispersed throughout the organization.

MANAGERIAL ACCOUNTING IMPLICATIONS OF DECENTRALIZATION

The choice of business segments depends on such factors as an organization's size, nature of the business activities involved, management philosophy, and geographical dispersion. For example, as shown in Figure 13-1, a franchised automobile dealership might be segmented into six departments:

1. New car sales
2. Used car sales
3. Leasing
4. Repair shop
5. Body shop
6. Parts

Even service firms divide their activities into well-defined segments. An accounting firm typically is structured into departments for auditing, management services, and tax work.

Once the choice of specific business segments is made, a segment manager is assigned to each of them. Assuming decentralized authority is used, each segment manager is given the authority to make decisions and take whatever action is necessary to achieve the goals of his or her particular segment. In turn, the segment manager is held both *responsible* for the segment's performance and *accountable* through periodic performance reports that are prepared in detail for the segment manager and in summary form for higher levels of management.

Ideally, both efficiency and effectiveness measures will be used to evaluate each segment's performance. This means that resource inputs, product or service outputs, and the segment's goals will be considered in the evaluation process whenever possible. To evaluate a segment's performance, the accounting system must be designed so that detailed information for each segment is available. This segment information is only made available to external sources in summary form since complete disclosure would be valuable to competitors.[1] Instead, the detailed information is for management's use in planning activities for each segment, allocating scarce resources, evaluating actual performance, and taking corrective action whenever necessary to improve the efficiency and effectiveness of future operations.

RESPONSIBILITY ACCOUNTING DEFINED

Responsibility accounting is an important managerial accounting topic that provides much of the personalized information needed to manage the segments of a business. In essence, responsibility accounting requires each manager to *participate* in the development of financial plans for his or her segment and *provides timely performance reports* that compare actual results with those planned. When responsibility accounting is combined with the budgeting pro-

Objective 3:
Use of responsibility accounting

---

[1] As mentioned in Chapter 1, certain financial information about the operating segments of diversified companies must be reported publicly to comply with Statement of Financial Accounting Standards No. 14 ("Financial Reporting for Segments of a Business Enterprise") issued by the Financial Accounting Standards Board.

Figure 13-1
Automobile Dealership Organizational Chart

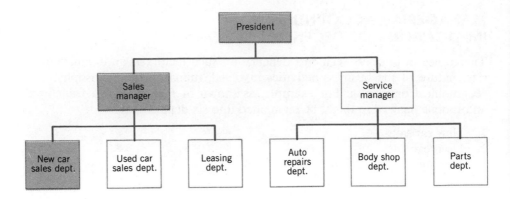

cess discussed in Chapter 8, the combination provides managers with an effective means of planning and controlling a firm's performance.

Responsibility accounting works well for all kinds of decentralized operations regardless of whether the segments are based on business functions, products, customers, or geographical territories. The responsibility accounting system is a *subset* of the firm's general accounting system. It is used to accumulate performance information by segment and to report the results to the responsible managers. As such, a responsibility accounting system must be tailored to meet the specific needs and operating conditions of a given firm so that performance reporting for all financial items considered is accomplished by centers of responsibility (the segments of the business) within the organization.

All persons involved with the design, implementation, and operation of a responsibility accounting system must completely understand both the assignment of authority and responsibility in the organization as well as the network of accountability. This understanding is necessary to ensure that the right kind of responsibility centers are utilized and that the performance evaluation and reporting are meaningful.

FEATURES OF RESPONSIBILITY ACCOUNTING

The following are the most essential features of responsibility accounting:

1. Best choice of responsibility centers
2. Correct matching of accounting system and organization
3. Emphasis on controllability
4. Use of participative management
5. Relevant performance reporting
6. Application of management by exception

Choice of Responsibility Centers

Objective 4:
Distinguishing between the different types of responsibility center

A **responsibility center** is a business segment, such as a department, that can be established as a cost center, a profit center, or an investment center, with the proper control focus as follows:

Type of Responsibility Center	Control Focus
Cost center	Cost performance
Profit center	Profit performance
Investment center	Return on investment performance

Many large firms have all three types of responsibility center. The choice between the three types depends on the answer to the question "What aspect of the financial performance is to be controlled?" If the only concern is the costs incurred in a particular department, for example, that segment will be defined as a cost center. A segment's size is not the determining factor in the choice of responsibility center. Instead, the choice is made on the basis of *what constitutes the financial performance to be evaluated* in a given center.

Cost Centers. Cost centers are the most frequently used type of responsibility center because so many business segments do not have revenue responsibilities. A cost center can be small or large depending on the activities involved. For example, a retailing firm's accounting department could be established as a separate small cost center or as part of a large cost center consisting of the company's entire administrative function. A large cost center such as a manufacturing plant may be further divided into many cost centers such as the fabricating department, testing department, and assembly department.

Performance evaluation with a cost center emphasizes efficiency measures to assure that the operating results of a given period are achieved with the minimum possible cost. This efficiency is evaluated with performance reports that show the actual costs of operating the center compared with the budgeted costs that represent an acceptable efficiency level. A manufacturing operation often will use standard costs for the efficiency measures reported for its cost centers.

Profit Centers. A profit center exists when revenues as well as costs can be traced to the business segment. A sales department of a retail store can be organized as a profit center since earnings from the segment's activities can be measured. A profit measure such as segment income or contribution margin is used to evaluate the earnings performance of a profit center.

Profit center managers are often responsible for both the production and sale of the products involved. Efficiency and effectiveness measures should be considered when evaluating a profit center since its manager is responsible for revenue and cost performances.

Some profit centers are classified as artificial centers because they mainly sell their output within the firm's organization. The selling price involved with sales to other segments of the same organization is called a transfer price. This price may not accurately reflect what the same products would sell for on the open market. The use of an artificial profit center provides a profit incentive to the manager responsible for its performance even though the results usually are not the same as they would be with outside sales. The Delco Electronics Division of General Motors Corporation is an example of a business segment selling a significant part of its output to other segments within the same organization since Delco provides radios for GM automobiles. The choice of a reasonable transfer price has a major impact on the reliability of performance evaluation for an artificial profit center. We will discuss transfer pricing later in this chapter.

Investment Centers. The most complete form of responsibility center is an investment center. Here, the manager in charge is held responsible for the return on the resources used by the segment. In this case, the manager of an investment center is accountable for the *revenues, costs,* and *operating assets* with the goal of achieving a satisfactory return on investment. A department store operated by a chain store organization is an example of an investment center as long as the store manager can control all the financial factors contributing to return on investment measurement.

An investment center manager has extensive authority for such actions as purchasing fixed assets, establishing credit terms, determining appropriate inventory levels, and setting selling prices. The manager is responsible for earning acceptable profits and for selecting the operating assets required for the profit results. Efficiency and effectiveness measures are used to evaluate the performance of an investment center with primary attention directed toward the actual return on investment achieved compared with the budgeted return on investment.

Return on investment analysis is considered later in this chapter and is defined as some measure of income divided by the investment in operating assets required to earn the income. Like any investment, high returns indicate good performance by an investment center. The most beneficial feature of an investment center is that it usually represents the ultimate in autonomy. As a result, it offers the center manager the opportunity and incentive to achieve satisfactory return on investment results as though the person is in charge of his or her own company.

Matching Accounting System with Organization

Once the choice between the different responsibility centers has been made for a particular firm's organizational structure, the accounting system, as an integral part of the total *management information system,* must be designed to accumulate financial data for each responsibility center. This is accomplished through added digits in the coding system used for the chart of accounts that identify a financial item not only by its nature (e.g., direct labor) but also by the responsibility center in which the item is incurred (e.g., a specific production department). For example, account number 410-12 could be used to record direct labor in a particular cost center. The 410 designates that direct labor is involved and the 12 indicates the cost center in which the cost is incurred. The type of responsibility center determines how many accounts must be given the added designation to identify the source of responsibility involved.

The added designations would be used most extensively in an investment center since its revenues, costs, and operating assets must be identified and accounted for separately from those of other centers. The segmentation of the accounting system provides the firm with the capability to accumulate reliable financial data with which individual performances can be measured as well as the performance of the business as a whole.

Controllability Focus

In the evaluation of their responsibility centers' financial performances, managers should be held accountable for only the financial items over which they *have* control. At their level of management, they must be able to regulate — or at least significantly influence — all costs, revenues, or invested resources classified as being controllable during a given accounting period. This means that the managers responsible for controllable costs, revenues, or invested resources can make decisions that will influence the actual amounts of the items incurred during the reporting period involved. The two key dimensions of controllability, therefore, are the *specific level of management* and *the given time period.*

For example, a controllable cost is one that can be authorized by a particular manager during a specified time period. The manager of a sales department in a retail store usually can control the labor costs of the department but cannot influence the real estate taxes paid on the building occupied by the store. Therefore, this manager would be held accountable for labor costs, but not for property taxes.

Many costs present serious problems when management must decide which ones are controllable and thus should be accounted for in responsibility reports prepared for managers. If the time period involved is long enough, all costs can be changed and could potentially be classified as being controllable. However, responsibility accounting is mostly short-term oriented with periodic reports prepared for intervals such as months, quarters, and years.

As the time period shortens, fewer costs will be controllable. Therefore, we must be careful to distinguish between those costs that are controllable for the reporting period and those that are uncontrollable. For example, if top management decides to increase its firm's production capacity at a particular plant (operated as a profit center), the resulting increase in depreciation expense is controllable at the point of the decision and at the top management level. When the added capacity is being utilized, the related depreciation expense is not controllable by the plant manager who can do nothing about the amount of the depreciation or the decision to expand the capacity in the first place.

A given manager's freedom to make decisions about costs will be determined by the amount of authority he or she is delegated by higher management. These same factors that influence the firm's definition of controllable costs will have the same effect on controllability for revenues and operating assets.

Participative Management

The managers accountable for the performance of the responsibility centers should actively participate in the development of the planned financial performance, which is expressed in the form of a *budget*. We mentioned the importance of management participation in the Chapter 8 coverage of the master budget. When managers prepare their own estimates, the goals become self-imposed instead of being established by higher management. This approach should motivate managers to do everything possible to achieve the planned performance and is an important part of management by objective.

With management by objective, each manager responsible for a business segment participates with the managers to whom he or she is accountable in defining segment goals that are compatible with the overall organizational goals. The segment goals then become the responsibility of the segment manager who is accountable for their accomplishment. The financial goals are formulated in the master budget, and the responsibility accounting system reports how well the segment is achieving its financial goals.

Performance Reporting

The manager of a responsibility center is evaluated with performance reports that show the financial items for which that manager is responsible. The reporting phase of responsibility accounting is based on the premise that the assignment of authority and responsibility flows from *top to bottom* in an organization while accountability flows from *bottom to top*. Consequently, the performance reports start at the lowest level of management and build upward, with the managers receiving information concerning their own performance as well as that of any other manager under their supervision.

Figure 13-2 shows a partial version of a responsibility reporting system used to control the operating expenses of cost centers in the automobile dealership shown in Figure 13-1. Cost centers have been established at three levels of management: department manager, sales or service manager, and the president of the firm. For illustrative purposes, we have restricted our attention to the shaded area of Figure 13-1, although all segments would be included in a real-life situation. Also, we could easily expand on this simplified illustration by using profit centers instead of cost centers.

As the performance information flows from bottom to top, it is cumulative and less detailed. At the top of the organization, the president is responsible for one large cost center representing the entire business. In turn, the overall cost center is further divided into cost centers as subunits for the major areas of business activity and management authority–responsibility relationships. The expected operating expenses are shown in the Budget column, and the actual results are presented in the Actual column. The variances shown in the right-hand column are the differences between the expected and actual results.

When responsibility accounting is applied in a manufacturing firm, the standard cost variances discussed in Chapters 10 and 11 are included in the reports prepared for the responsible managers. Note the important linkages between the levels of management in Figure 13-2. The detailed information concerning the controllable costs in the new cars department is summarized as total performance results that are included in the report prepared for the next level of management—the sales manager's office. In addition, summary results for all other departments accountable to the sales manager are shown in this report.

Figure 13-2

	Budget	Actual	Variance
President's Report:			
President's office	$ 12,800	$ 13,900	$ 1,100 U
Sales departments	102,900	112,370	9,470 U
Service departments	92,500	98,600	6,100 U
Total	208,200	224,870	16,670 U
Sales Manager's Report:			
Sales manager's office	9,500	9,900	400 U
New car sales department	56,600	61,970	5,370 U
Used car sales department	28,200	32,100	3,900 U
Leasing department	8,600	8,400	200 F
Total	102,900	112,370	9,470 U
New Car Sales Manager's Report:			
Sales salaries	18,200	19,800	1,600 U
Advertising	20,000	23,200	3,200 U
Utilities	4,400	4,850	450 U
Insurance	3,200	3,200	—
Rent	10,000	10,000	—
Other	800	920	120 U
Total	$ 56,600	$ 61,970	$ 5,370 U

The same approach is used to prepare the president's report, which consists of summary information for the two cost centers directly below the president, the sales manager's office and the service manager's office as well as the performance results for the president's office. Detail is reduced as we move up through the organization because higher-level managers are mainly concerned with problem areas, not the entire performance below them. When a summary report such as the one shown for the sales manager reveals a significant variance from the planned performance, the president can request the detailed reports supporting the deviation. This approach eliminates the need for higher management to waste time evaluating reports that indicate that the related performance is in control when compared with the company's goals.

Management by Exception

Significant variances between the planned and actual performance of each responsibility center are emphasized in the performance reports so their causes can be determined and corrective action taken whenever necessary (or adaptive action if the goals are considered unrealistic given current information). This application of management by exception is intended to identify a situation that is likely to be out of control without the need to evaluate all results.

For example, in the automobile dealership illustration, the unfavorable variances would be investigated to explain why the actual expenses reported are $16,670 higher than expected. The president can ask for the detailed copies of the performance reports from all levels of the organization showing significant total variances and can trace the deviations downward through the performance reports to identify their sources so that corrective action can be taken to improve future profitability. In turn, each responsible manager can do the same thing for his or her activities.

BEWARE OF COST ALLOCATION

Our discussion of responsibility accounting has stressed the importance of holding managers accountable for controllable costs only. However, we also must recognize that cost allocation is a popular practice because the typical organization incurs a number of *common costs that cannot be traced to a single segment* of the business. These indirect costs must instead be assigned to the segments on a basis that management believes best approximates the benefits the segments will receive from the common costs. This was mentioned in Chapter 3 and will be discussed in more detail in Chapter 14.

Examples of indirect costs for production departments in a manufacturing firm are the costs of service departments such as maintenance, cost accounting, engineering, and purchasing. As segments of the firm, these service departments can be established as responsibility centers, and their costs can be controlled with responsibility accounting procedures. When the service department costs are allocated to production departments to measure the total cost of producing products, the concept of controllability *should not be passed along* with the allocation process. The same is true for other costs that are common to the entire organization such as rent, insurance, and utilities.

Although the primary goal with cost allocation is to select an allocation method that *best* identifies the segments to which the costs are assigned as the causes for incurring the indirect costs, this goal is rarely attained. In many

Objective 5: Limitations of cost allocations for responsibility accounting cases, the results of cost allocation are arbitrary and inconsistent for various segments as well as for different time periods.

We must keep the use of cost allocation in proper perspective: different costs are used for different purposes. When we want full costing information such as the use of absorption costing for total product cost measurement, allocated costs must be considered. This full costing approach is required by generally accepted accounting principles and certain contractual requirements. In contrast, if we are evaluating management performance with responsibility accounting, allocated costs should be ignored. The amount of cost allocated to a segment depends on the formula used for the allocation process rather than the decision making of the manager responsible for the segment.

The direct costs of a business segment are the only costs that are potentially controllable by the segment manager. In turn, each direct cost must be carefully evaluated to determine whether the two issues associated with controllability, level of management and specific time period, indicate that a controllable direct cost is involved. As a result of this analysis, significant differences between the costs included in various financial reports are found, depending on the purpose of a particular report. The reports prepared for performance evaluation of cost centers, profit centers, and investment centers should not show any allocated costs as being controllable by the managers responsible for the centers.

SEGMENTED INCOME STATEMENT WITH A CONTRIBUTION REPORT FORMAT

Objective 6: Using a segmented income statement

Managers of profit centers or investment centers require more detailed information about their centers' earnings performances than that contained in an income statement prepared for the firm as a whole. Such managers must regularly evaluate the sales volume, selling prices, sales mix, and cost performance of their segments as semiautonomous businesses. The focus of the evaluation is on both (1) a segment's contribution to the firm's profits and (2) the performance of the segment manager as measured by the controllable financial items involved. A **segmented income statement** with a contribution report format is used to provide this detailed information about the segments' earnings performances. This type of income statement is an extension of the income statement with a contribution margin format introduced in Chapter 5. Three important cost classifications are used to prepare a segmented income statement:

1. Variable costs separated from fixed costs
2. Direct costs separated from indirect costs
3. Controllable costs separated from uncontrollable costs

A segmented income statement for the Johnson Manufacturing Company's 1987 operating performance is presented in Figure 13-3. Note that the company is organized into three divisions — Tools Division, Hardware Division, and Paint Division — that are operated as investment centers. The firm's products are sold to hardware stores located throughout the country. The top management of the company has delegated the authority to make all the decisions necessary to operate the divisions as semiautonomous units to the division managers. The segmented income statement is one of many reports used to

Figure 13-3

JOHNSON MANUFACTURING COMPANY
Segmented Income Statement — Contribution Report Format
Year Ended December 31, 1987

	Tools Division	Hardware Division	Paint Division	Total Firm
Sales	$700,000	$900,000	$500,000	$2,100,000
Variable costs:				
Manufacturing	350,000	355,500	285,000	990,500
Selling	14,000	22,500	15,000	51,500
Total	364,000	378,000	300,000	1,042,000
Contribution margin	336,000	522,000	200,000	1,058,000
Controllable fixed costs:				
Manufacturing salaries	56,000	168,000	56,600	280,600
Selling salaries	76,080	117,920	32,400	226,400
Sales promotion	18,600	24,200	16,200	59,000
Total	150,680	310,120	105,200	566,000
Controllable income	185,320	211,880	94,800	492,000
Uncontrollable fixed costs:				
Depreciation	42,000	63,000	32,000	137,000
Property taxes	3,320	4,880	2,800	11,000
Total	45,320	67,880	34,800	148,000
Segment income	140,000	144,000	60,000	344,000
Common fixed costs:				
Building occupancy				25,300
Insurance				14,600
Advertising				16,500
Administrative				80,500
Other				2,100
Total				139,000
Net income before tax				$ 205,000

evaluate the performance of the divisions to see how effectively division managers are fulfilling their responsibilities. Four important measures of operating performance are included in the segmented income statement:

1. Contribution margin
2. Controllable income
3. Segment income
4. Net income before tax for the firm as a whole

Each of these measures has a different meaning and is used for a different purpose in evaluating profit performance. To be able to prepare a segmented income statement such as the one in Figure 13-3, a firm must maintain detailed records of each segment's revenues and costs with its accounting system. Depending on how a given firm is segmented, the same approach can be taken for products, plants, customers, or sales territories. Let's examine the most essential features of a segmented income statement with a contribution report format.

CONTRIBUTION MARGIN

The first measure of profit performance is the contribution margin for each division and for the firm as a whole. The contribution margin is an important performance measure because it shows the effect on income of changes in sales volume (number of units sold). The availability of the contribution margin information enables a division manager to easily calculate the impact of an increase or decrease in sales by multiplying the contribution margin percentage by the related change in sales. Consequently, the first advantage of a segmented income statement is that it emphasizes cost behavior for each segment. We can determine the contribution margin for each division by subtracting all of that division's variable costs (manufacturing and selling) from its sales.

CONTROLLABLE INCOME

The second important performance measure is the controllable income for each segment and for the firm as a whole. To determine the **controllable income** for each division, we must distinguish between controllable costs and uncontrollable costs. All of the variable costs incurred by the divisions of the Johnson Manufacturing Company are assumed to be controllable. The contribution margin less the controllable fixed costs is equal to the controllable income. This measure, in turn, is an indicator of how well a segment manager is fulfilling his or her responsibility for the segment's profit results. As such, the information is essential for the application of responsibility accounting discussed earlier.

Three of the fixed costs—manufacturing salaries, selling salaries, and sales promotion—are classified as controllable fixed costs because they are direct costs for the divisions, and the division managers have the discretion to change the amounts involved. Even if a fixed cost can be traced to a specific division, it cannot be considered in the calculation of controllable income if it does not fit the definition of a controllable cost. As a result, the second performance measure, controllable income, provides valuable information for evaluating how well division managers are managing their segments' controllable profit variables in making a contribution to the firm's overall earnings.

SEGMENT INCOME

The next performance measure included in the segmented income statement is **segment income,** which is controllable income less the uncontrollable fixed costs that can be traced as direct costs to the divisions. These fixed costs are uncontrollable because they are committed costs, not discretionary ones, even though they are direct costs. Many managers believe that segment income is the best indicator of *long-term profitability* for a business segment because it is based on all revenues and costs directly traceable to the related segment.

The Johnson Manufacturing Company classifies two fixed costs as being direct costs for the divisions, but uncontrollable by the division managers: (1) depreciation and (2) property taxes that are related to the inventory. In the long run, each division must be able to cover all its direct costs in order to make a contribution to the company's overall profit performance, so segment income is an important measure that management must watch carefully.

NET INCOME BEFORE TAX

The final performance measure is the only one of the four measures that reflects all revenues and costs. Until the net income before tax is computed for the firm as a whole, no attempt is made to identify the operating results as the traditional net income measure we are accustomed to seeing on income statements. Even then, net income is not traced to the divisions as operating segments. We want to avoid cost allocations for performance evaluation because of the arbitrary results mentioned earlier. All common fixed costs are accounted for and combined in the Total Firm column of the segmented income statement.

Given the objective of an income statement such as the one shown in Figure 13-3, it would serve no useful purpose to attempt to allocate the five common fixed cost items—building occupancy (costs such as rent and utilities), insurance, advertising, administrative, and other—since the division managers cannot do anything about them. Their total amount is simply subtracted from the total segment income for the firm to determine the net income before tax. This is a measure of the overall earnings performance in a traditional accounting sense, but has no direct bearing on the performance evaluation of the divisions as investment centers.

The use of the four performance measures gives management a complete picture of what contributed to the overall profitability of the firm and should provide useful information for making decisions about which divisions to expand through resource allocations in the future. Profit performance variability, responsibility performance evaluation, segment profitability, and the firm's total earnings all are disclosed in the one income statement.

RETURN ON INVESTMENT ANALYSIS

Return on investment (ROI) analysis is an important managerial accounting technique that can be used to evaluate the relative profitability of a firm, an investment center, or a manager responsible for an investment center. The main advantage of ROI analysis compared with other profitability measures is that it relates an earnings performance to the investment in resources needed to achieve the earnings. In general, we would expect a business with a large amount of assets to earn more than one with a small amount of assets. Therefore, absolute amounts of income are not always accurate measures of how effectively the related resources are being managed. For example, one business may be earning $25,000 while using $100,000 of assets, whereas another business may be earning $25,000 on a $500,000 asset base.

Objective 7: Applying ROI analysis

The general formula for ROI analysis is:

$$ROI = \frac{Income}{Investment}$$

As we saw earlier in the discussion of a segmented income statement, there are different measures of the income performance for different aspects of a business (the firm as a whole, a segment of the business, or the manager responsible for a segment). Therefore, different measures of income performance are used for the numerator of the ROI formula depending on what is being evaluated. The same is true for the definition of the investment in assets required for the earnings performance (the denominator of the ROI formula). The following is a list of the different measures of income and investment used for the three performances that can be evaluated with ROI analysis:

Performance Being Measured	Definition of Income	Definition of Investment
Firm as a whole	Net operating income – usually defined as income before interest and taxes	The average amount of operating assets used productively during the period
Investment center	Segment income	The average amount of operating assets directly used by the segment
Investment center manager	Controllable income	The average amount of operating assets under the control of the segment manager

When the firm as a whole is evaluated with ROI analysis, net operating income is usually defined as income before interest expense and taxes. The interest expense is eliminated because it is considered a return to creditors for the funds they have contributed to the business. Segment income is used to measure the performance of an investment center because it includes all income statement items directly incurred by the segment. The uncontrollable costs are eliminated with the use of controllable income when the performance of the manager responsible for an investment center is being evaluated.

The average amount of operating assets is used in the calculation of ROI to reflect changes in asset balances that take place during the period. All productive assets—cash, accounts receivable, inventories, and plant assets—are included as operating assets.

EXPANSION OF ROI FORMULA

An expanded version of the ROI formula presented earlier is:

$$\text{ROI} = \text{Margin earned} \times \text{Turnover of assets}$$

$$= \frac{\text{Income}}{\text{Sales}} \times \frac{\text{Sales}}{\text{Investment}}$$

The expanded version of the ROI formula is preferred by most managers because it emphasizes the fact that return on investment is actually a function of two variables: **margin earned** (income/sales) and **turnover of assets** (sales/investment). To achieve a desired ROI, management must control both variables. ROI can be improved by:

1. Increasing sales or
2. Reducing costs or
3. Decreasing the investment in assets.

To illustrate how ROI analysis works, let's consider its application in the Johnson Manufacturing Company case using the segmented income statement information presented in Figure 13-3. Assume that top management of the company wants to determine the ROI for each of the three divisions operated as investment centers. The segment incomes shown in Figure 13-3 provide the measures of income used in the analysis. In addition, management has deter-mined that the following amounts of operating assets can be directly traced to the three investment centers:

	Tools Division	Hardware Division	Paint Division
Operating assets directly used in 1987	$625,000	$750,000	$500,000

The ROI for each of the three divisions is computed with the following anal-ysis:

		Tools Division	Hardware Division	Paint Division
Segment income – Figure 13-3	(a)	$140,000	$144,000	$ 60,000
Sales	(b)	700,000	900,000	500,000
Operating assets	(c)	625,000	750,000	500,000
Margin earned	(a/b = d)	20%	16%	12%
Turnover of assets	(b/c = e)	1.12 times	1.2 times	1.0 times
ROI	(d × e)	22.4%	19.2%	12%

The Tools Division has the highest ROI of 22.4%. The Hardware Division and the Paint Division have ROIs of 19.2% and 12%, respectively. This ROI information will be valuable to management in seeking future profit improve-ments and determining which segment to expand. Remember that profitability improvements can be considered by evaluating the impact of (1) increased sales, (2) reduced costs, or (3) decreased investment in assets. To do so, assume that management is not satisfied with the 12% ROI of the Paint Division and wants to evaluate ways to improve the segment's margin earned or its turnover of assets. We will consider each alternative independently for illustrative pur-poses, although they normally would be evaluated concurrently in a real life business situation.

Impact of Increasing Sales

The impact of sales increases on ROI can be evaluated using a contribution margin approach since only the variable costs increase with the change pro-vided the business remains within the relevant range of operation. If added fixed costs are necessary to increase the firm's capacity, they will also affect the margin earned on the increased sales.

Assume that the manager of the Paint Division plans to enter a new market-ing territory with an expected sales increase of $50,000 during the next year. Figure 13-3 shows that the Paint Division's contribution margin is 40% ($200,000/$500,000). Thus, the manager concludes that the increased sales of $50,000 should result in an incremental contribution margin of $20,000 ($50,000 × 40%). No additional operating assets will be required to serve the new territory. The total sales with the change are projected at $550,000 ($500,000 + $50,000) and the revised segment income should be $80,000 ($60,000 + $20,000). The planned ROI for the division during the next year is:

$$\text{ROI} = \text{Margin earned} \times \text{Turnover of assets}$$

$$= \frac{\$80,000}{\$550,000} \times \frac{\$550,000}{\$500,000}$$

$$= 14.545\% \times 1.1$$

$$= 16\%$$

Consequently, the division expects to improve its ROI from 12% to 16% by increasing sales from $500,000 to $550,000. The margin earned would increase from 12% to 14.545%, and the turnover of assets would rise from 1.0 times to 1.1 times because of the proposed sales increase.

Impact of Decreasing Costs

The manager of the Paint Division is considering several changes in the production process that should decrease the division's variable manufacturing costs from $285,000 to $245,000. Segment income will be increased by the $40,000 cost savings since sales will not be affected by the change and will remain at $500,000. The investment in assets also will be unchanged at $500,000. If the cost savings of $40,000 are achieved, divisional ROI for the next year is:

$$\text{ROI} = \text{Margin earned} \times \text{Turnover of assets}$$
$$= \frac{\$100,000}{\$500,000} \times \frac{\$500,000}{\$500,000}$$
$$= 20\% \times 1.0$$
$$= 20\%$$

Although the asset turnover remains at 1.0 times, the $40,000 cost reduction will increase the margin earned from 12% to 20%, thus raising the ROI to 20% —an improvement over the 12% performance of the current year.

Impact of Decreasing Operating Assets

Traditionally, managers are more concerned with income statement items than they are with balance sheet items because of the emphasis on income statement performance measures such as profit margins and earnings per share. Consequently, they are accustomed to periodic evaluation of selling prices, sales volume, sales mix, and costs, but not the most effective combination of assets that should be maintained to support the income performance. Some managers are inclined to increase the asset base of the business any time it potentially will increase sales without really justifying the decision on the basis of a sufficient amount of increased profit from the added investment. Apparently, they hope that any excess assets will somehow remain hidden on the balance sheet without ever affecting the all-important income statement.

A major benefit of ROI analysis is that it forces managers to be prudent in their selection and utilization of operating assets and to consider the important profitability linkage between the balance sheet and the income statement. In many cases, businesses are forced to look at their operating assets to see if they can be reduced because that is the only way ROI can be improved. If the operation is efficient, costs may be as low as possible and any further cost reductions may impair the segment's ability to perform. Competition and the marketplace may prevent the segment from raising selling prices, increasing the units of product sold, or changing to a better sales mix so higher sales cannot be attained by one of these changes. A close inspection of the operating assets often reveals such opportunities as the following for reducing the investment in the resources needed to support the segment's activities:

1. Reduce cash balances to the absolute minimum amount needed to support the operation. A thorough analysis of the cash receipts and cash disburse-

ments often will indicate that idle cash is being maintained unnecessarily or the flow of cash is not efficiently managed.

2. Shorten the collection period required for accounts receivable. A tighter credit policy and more attention to overdue accounts often will reduce accounts receivable without affecting sales.

3. Decrease inventories by increasing turnover, stocking smaller amounts, and timing the acquisitions more carefully so they arrive only when needed. A "just in time" approach to inventory management has become popular in recent years. In such cases, inventory arrives just in time to be used in production instead of being carried in stock. Sometimes, inventory can be shipped directly from a supplier to the customer in a merchandising firm so the item does not have to be stocked.

4. Evaluate the effect of leasing fixed assets instead of owning them.

5. Determine whether all fixed assets are being used productively. If some of them are not, see if they can be sold for a reasonable residual value.

We assume that the manager of the Paint Division has considered several possibilities for reducing operating assets and has concluded that they can be decreased from $500,000 to $400,000 without any significant effect on sales or segment income (the assets to be eliminated are not depreciable). ROI with the $100,000 reduction in operating assets would be:

$$\text{ROI} = \text{Margin earned} \times \text{Turnover of assets}$$

$$= \frac{\$60,000}{\$500,000} \times \frac{\$500,000}{\$400,000}$$

$$= 12\% \times 1.25$$

$$= 15\%$$

If the operating assets are reduced by $100,000, ROI will increase from 12% to 15% even though the profit margin remains 12%. The increased ROI is the result of a better turnover of the assets.

RESIDUAL INCOME ANALYSIS

An alternative to ROI analysis for evaluating profit performance is **residual income (RI) analysis.** Residual income is the amount of income earned in excess of a certain minimum return on the investment in operating assets required. The minimum rate of return used to compute RI should not be less than a firm's *cost of capital,* which is its cost of obtaining funds in the form of debt and owners' equity as explained in Chapter 9.

Residual income is computed as follows:

$$\text{RI} = \text{Income} - (\text{Investment in operating assets} \times \text{Required ROI})$$

When the RI is positive, the income from an investment in operating assets is greater than the firm's required ROI and, therefore, the investment is attractive. A negative RI indicates that an investment's return is inadequate to satisfy the minimum amount required by management. When residual income is used to evaluate performance, the objective is to maximize the amount of residual income instead of the return on investment. Residual income analysis has an advantage over ROI analysis because it prevents the possibility of a segment manager rejecting an opportunity to earn a return on investment acceptable to the firm as a whole, but below the ROI of his or her investment center. For

Objective 8:
Applying RI
analysis

example, assume that top management of the Johnson Manufacturing Company has decided that a minimum ROI of 15% is acceptable. Since the Tools Division has an ROI of 22.4%, its manager would be inclined to reject an opportunity to earn 17% from a new product line that the company is considering, even though the 17% is acceptable to the firm, because the division's ROI would be reduced with the investment.

In contrast, the residual income approach would charge the division manager only 15% so all projects with a return in excess of 15% will be attractive. To illustrate the difference between ROI analysis and RI analysis, assume that the new product line will require additional operating assets of $200,000 in order to earn the 17% return, with segment income of $34,000 ($200,000 × 17%). If ROI analysis is used, the Tools Division's ROI will decline from 22.4% to 21.1% even though the project will earn a profit higher than the minimum amount required by the firm and thus will benefit the business as a whole. The decrease in ROI that would discourage the division manager from accepting the project because of the negative effect on the division's performance evaluation can be shown as:

	Present Situation	New Product Line	Proposed Situation
Segment income	$140,000	$ 34,000	$174,000
Investment in operating assets	$625,000	$200,000	$825,000
Return on investment	22.4%	17%	21.1%

With RI analysis, the objective is to maximize a dollar amount instead of a percentage, so any investment offering a positive residual income will be attractive to a segment manager. We can see how this works for the Tools Division in the following analysis:

	Current Situation	New Product Line	Proposed Situation
Investment in operating assets (a)	$625,000	$200,000	$825,000
Minimum return (a) × 15% = (b)	93,750	30,000	123,750
Segment income (c)	140,000	34,000	174,000
Residual income (c) − (b)	$ 46,250	$ 4,000	$ 50,250

The residual income for the division would be increased by $4,000 with the addition of the new product line. The use of RI as a performance evaluation tool would encourage the manager of the Tools Division to make the investment because it is good for the division as well as the firm as a whole. Note that although the residual income from the investment is only $4,000, the incremental segment income involved is $34,000.

The biggest limitation of the RI approach is that it is difficult to compare the performance of business segments of different sizes since the larger segments will have more residual income than the smaller ones. Nevertheless, it is an important performance evaluation technique that can be used as an alternative to ROI analysis and other measurement techniques. It is particularly helpful in evaluating the future profits from new projects compared with a firm's minimum profitability requirements.

**Objective 9:
Importance of
intrafirm transfer
pricing**

INTRAFIRM TRANSFER PRICING

One of the most important and complicated decisions made in decentralized businesses is the choice of reasonable prices for products or services transferred from one segment of the organization to another. **Transfer pricing** refers to the prices charged by one segment of a decentralized firm for products and services transferred to another segment. For example, the Delco Electronics Division of General Motors Corporation provides radios for the Oldsmobile Division. The key question is, "What prices should be charged for such intrafirm transfers?"

Since both the buyer and the seller are members of the same organization, the transactions are not as independent as they would be with external sources. Nevertheless, when intrafirm transfers of products or services are made, part of the revenue of one segment becomes part of the cost of another segment. The transfer price involved has a significant impact on the profits reported by both segments. Consider the profit goals of the parties directly or indirectly involved with an intrafirm transfer of products or services:

1. The manager of the selling segment will want to receive the highest possible selling price to make his or her profit performance look good.
2. The manager of the buying segment will want to pay the lowest possible price so that segment's profit results will be favorably affected.
3. Top management will want transfers between the segments to occur if it is more profitable to do so than having the buying segment acquire the products or services from outside sources. This will ensure that the firm's own operating capacity is used and that the overall profit of the firm will be the highest possible.

These three basic profit goals are not always congruent, and their achievement depends on how effectively the firm implements transfer pricing strategies.

There are three general approaches to intrafirm pricing decisions: *cost-based prices, market-based prices,* and *negotiated market-based prices.* We will illustrate the basic concept of each approach with a hypothetical situation and then discuss the three approaches in more detail. The Microcomputer Company is an integrated manufacturer of microcomputers sold to retail stores throughout the country. The term "integrated" means that the company produces the major components used for the finished product, a microcomputer. One division of the firm produces a silicon chip that is used as the microprocessor needed for each computer. Another division assembles all the components involved with a microcomputer, tests the final product, and prepares it for shipment to a customer. Each division is organized as an investment center, and ROI analysis is used to evaluate the performance of the divisions as semiautonomous businesses.

If the transfer is based on cost, the Chips Division will not show a profit, so this will distort the segmented earnings of the two divisions by transferring all the profit to the Assembly Division. The total earnings of the firm will be unaffected by the use of the cost method as long as the Assembly Division buys all its chips from the Chips Division. Cost is measurable with a good managerial accounting system, although it may be subject to disagreement about definitions. But what is market? If the Chips Division only produces for the Assembly Department, its manager will not know exactly how much the chips could be sold for to outside sources.

However, if we can determine a reasonable estimate of market, this approach will enable the Chips Division to earn a profit and facilitate performance evaluation with ROI analysis. At this point, we often need to consider negotiated market prices because the buyer and the seller may have to agree on what is a fair price for both parties, given such factors as the seller's cost structure, the seller's operating capacity utilization, and alternative sources of supply for the buyer. Top management may provide assistance in this negotiation process, but should not interfere with the investment center autonomy involved. Let's consider each of the three approaches to transfer pricing more completely.

COST-BASED TRANSFER PRICES

Objective 10: Identifying the three approaches to transfer pricing

The most basic form of transfer price is the transferring segment's cost, which we used in the illustration of process costing in Chapter 4. There, the Finishing Department was charged for the full cost of the products transferred from the Blending Department. When the segment transferring products or services is operated as a cost center, a **cost-based pricing** policy is sound because no attempt is made to measure revenue and profit. In other cases, the absence of an established market price may force a firm to use some variation of cost such as cost plus a certain markup. However, the complications of different costs for different purposes that we have observed throughout the coverage of managerial accounting also prevail in transfer pricing. Even if a firm decides that a cost-based transfer pricing policy is best, it must select from the many definitions of cost to determine those costs to be included in the price charged by the transferring segment. Some combination of actual cost, standard cost, full (absorption) cost, and variable cost can be used to define the cost base used for transfer pricing.

A major potential problem with cost-based pricing is that the selling segment may have no incentive to efficiently control costs when these costs are automatically passed on to the buying segment without the true test of an outside market. To prevent this from happening, actual costs should not be used to establish transfer prices. Instead, *standard costs* should be utilized whenever they are available, and, if they are not, *budgeted costs* should be applied. The use of the cost targets should provide the manager of the selling segment with an incentive to control costs because any inefficiency will not be passed on to the buyer and will remain the responsibility of the selling segment's manager.

The use of full cost or variable cost depends on how much of the unit product cost management wants covered by the transfer price. If only variable costs are considered, the results will be discouraging to the selling segment since it always will show a loss from the fixed costs that are ignored. Even as a cost center, this can create motivational problems for the selling segment's manager who is forced to accept not only a profitless transaction but also a selling price that is lower than the segment's total operating costs. As a result, full costs are usually considered. However, the problem with this approach is that the amount transferred *appears to be a variable cost* to the buying segment. This, in turn, can result in bad decisions on the part of the buying segment's manager that lead to reduced profits for the firm as a whole.

To illustrate, assume the Selling Division of a given company produces a major component that is needed by the firm's Buying Division for the production of a finished product. The manager of the Selling Division proposes to base the transfer price on full cost plus a 20% markup. The proposed transfer price is based on the following data collected by the Selling Division's accountant:

Variable costs	$ 80
Fixed costs	120
20% markup on total cost ($200 × 20%)	40
Transfer price	$240

The Buying Division estimates that additional variable costs of $560 will be required to complete the finished product, so its total cost would be $800 ($240 + $560) if the transfer price is accepted. However, the Buying Division's manager refuses to accept the $240 price because the final product sells for only $780 and the manager does not want to incur a loss of $20 per unit (selling price of $780 less total costs of $800). In addition, an outside supplier has offered to provide the component at a price of $200. Assume that the Selling Division cannot sell the component to another buyer or use the related operating capacity in any other way. If this outside offer is accepted by the Buying Division because the two managers will not compromise their positions, the result is lower profit for the firm as a whole, as shown in the following differential analysis:

	Purchase from Selling Division	Purchase from Outside Source
Selling price–finished product	$780	$780
Variable costs–Selling Division	80	
Variable costs–Buying Division	560	560
Price paid to outside source		200
Contribution margin	$140	$ 20

We can see that the firm's contribution margin per unit will be $120 lower if the component is purchased from the outside source. The $120 is the difference between the variable costs of the Selling Division and the outside price ($80 compared with $200). The fixed costs of the Selling Division will remain constant regardless of whether or not the transfer is made, so they are irrelevant for this decision. These results, which are potentially detrimental to the firm as a whole, are typical of full cost-based transfer pricing. Thus, the approach must be used carefully. As we will see later, the important issue concerning costs for all transfer pricing decisions is that the manager of the selling segment should always be able to accurately distinguish between the segment's fixed and variable costs associated with the products or services being transferred. In addition, a more complete analysis of the effect of costs on transfer pricing than the one shown above will require a consideration of the alternative uses of the selling segment's operating capacity (the opportunity cost concept).

MARKET-BASED TRANSFER PRICES

If a readily identifiable market exists for the products or services transferred, a **market-based transfer price** is generally considered the best approach for transfer pricing. This approach is consistent with the basic goal of giving segment managers the authority to operate semiautonomous businesses (profit or investment centers) by buying and selling on their own.

Performance evaluation is facilitated with market-based transfer prices because the results are compatible with those that would have been attained from outside transactions. In theory, the buying segment should not be expected to pay more or less in an internal transfer than it would for a purchase from an outside source. At the same time, the selling segment should not be expected to earn more or less revenue from an internal transfer than it would in a sale to a customer who is external to the seller's firm. To be fair to the buyer, the market price may have to be adjusted for certain cost savings associated with intrafirm transfers such as sales commissions and advertising expenses.

If all intrafirm transfers could be based on an accurate comparison of how comparable sales would be priced in the open market, the subject of transfer pricing would be easier to manage. Unfortunately, this doesn't always happen, and a strict definition of market prices does not work in many cases because of such limiting conditions as:

1. Many intrafirm transfers involve intermediate products that do not have a well-defined price in the open market since they are partially completed products and are not sold at that stage.
2. Imperfect information about reliable market prices prevents their use because management's time would be totally consumed just trying to gather good pricing information.
3. Product differences in nature, quality, quantity, credit terms, and delivery schedules make comparisons difficult, if not impossible.
4. At times, firms use distress prices in the marketplace to get rid of excess or obsolete inventory, and these temporarily low prices should not be used as a basis for regular transfer prices.

Despite these limitations, a market-based transfer pricing policy is important to an understanding of the total ramifications of transfer pricing. The following key steps should be followed when a firm uses a market-based transfer pricing approach:

1. Establish a reliable retrieval system to constantly monitor market prices and report changes as they occur.
2. The buying segment should purchase products and services internally as long as the conditions are comparable with outside purchase opportunities. In addition to the same price, this includes delivery schedules and quality control.
3. If the selling segment does not meet all of these conditions offered by outside competition, the buying segment should be authorized to purchase outside its firm.
4. The selling segment should be free to reject internal business that is not as profitable as outside sales and sell to external sources.
5. Distribute or otherwise make available throughout the organization reliable managerial accounting information to be used in evaluating what is profitable for the selling segment, the buying segment, and the firm as a whole.
6. Establish an impartial group of managers to consider disagreements between buying and selling segments over transfer prices and to offer solutions that are equitable for both parties. In many firms, these recommendations from the impartial group are binding on the managers of the buying and selling segments.

NEGOTIATED MARKET-BASED TRANSFER PRICES

Even when reliable market prices are not available, essentially the same benefits of a market-based transfer pricing approach can be obtained with **nego-**

tiated market prices. This means that the buying segment and the selling segment discuss the situation as though they "are" the market to find a price that they both agree is fair. Both parties should represent their segments as if they were unrelated firmwise and explain the justification for any specific price they may have in mind. Such factors as the costs involved, alternative outside sales opportunities of the selling segment, the impact of added volume for the seller given its operating capacity, purchase options of the buyer, and the effect of the transaction on total firm profits should be discussed openly. This approach is an extension of the authority given them to manage a profit or investment center.

If the buyer and seller are not able to agree on an equitable price, each should have the freedom to terminate the negotiating process and do business elsewhere if possible. Again, an impartial group of managers should be available to help settle disputes as long as their actions are not detrimental to the spirit of autonomy that is associated with the operation of a profit or investment center. Some firms even use an impartial and fair form of arbitration to settle disputes that arise when a buying segment and a selling segment negotiate transfer prices. The biggest problem with negotiated market-based prices is the time-consuming process involved because the unique features of each case must be considered carefully and repeat business in the future often requires substantial revision of the prices agreed on earlier due to changes that have occurred in the interim.

USING A GENERAL RULE FOR TRANSFER PRICING

We can see from the previous discussion that (1) transfer pricing problems can be quite complex and that (2) there is not a theoretically correct solution for all situations. Although we have suggested that market-based transfer prices are generally best, we also pointed out that this approach is limited by such factors as the absence of comparable market prices, imperfect information about market conditions, and differences in the products involved. In all cases, the managers of the segments involved must use good judgment about what is fair for the buyer and the seller as well as what is in the best interests of the entire firm. A complete understanding of the cost structure of the segments and the incremental impact of the costs and revenues associated with a transfer pricing decision is essential.

We conclude our discussion of transfer pricing by considering a general rule that segment managers can use as a *starting point* in the process of determining prices that are justifiable as being equitable to the buyer, the seller, and the firm as a whole. This general rule, which is based on the differential analysis introduced in Chapter 7, only provides a useful starting point without all of the facts and considerations that ultimately are involved in transfer pricing decisions.

The general rule is that a *transfer price should be no less than the unit variable cost of the products or services being transferred plus the contribution margin per unit that is lost by the selling segment from sales to outside sources because of a decision to sell internally.* Note that the contribution margin given up is the opportunity cost of making an internal sale since it is a measure of the profit foregone from external sales. The following equation represents this minimum transfer pricing rule:

$$\text{Minimum transfer price} = \text{Variable cost per unit} + \begin{array}{c}\text{Contribution margin}\\\text{per unit lost on}\\\text{outside sales}\end{array}$$

The amount of the lost contribution margin depends on the *production capacity utilization* of the selling segment. If the segment is already operating at full capacity to satisfy external demand, some outside business will have to be eliminated. Thus, the opportunity cost (foregone profit) is the contribution margin associated with the lost sales. The result will be a transfer price that is equal to the market price of the products or services switched from outside to inside sales (variable costs + contribution margin = selling price). In contrast, if the selling segment has enough excess capacity to provide the products or services for intrafirm transfers without giving up outside sales, the opportunity cost is zero and the minimum transfer price is equal to the unit variable costs involved.

The general rule precludes the possibility of the selling segment accepting a transfer price that results in an opportunity cost that is greater than the contribution margin earned from an internal sale. Note that the use of this general rule makes the selling segment indifferent to whether a sale is made to internal or external sources; the resulting contribution margin will be the same in either case.

Many firms use the rule as a starting point in establishing a ceiling and a floor for the eventual transfer price selected after a more complete analysis of the specific conditions involved. That is, the highest selling price would be the price to outside sources (the market price in most cases), and the lowest price would be the selling segment's variable costs, a price that would enable the segment to use idle capacity but not cover all costs. Any price above this floor will improve the performance of the selling segment.

To illustrate how the general rule is applied, let's reconsider the situation introduced earlier with the Buying Division of a firm that uses a component in its production process that can be purchased from the Selling Division of the same company or from an outside supplier. Recall that the Selling Division's variable costs for the component are $80 per unit and the fixed costs $120 per unit. The Buying Division needs $560 additional variable costs to complete the finished product involved. Assume further that the Selling Division sells the same component to outside sources at a normal selling price of $240. The Selling Division can produce 2,000 components each month, whereas the Buying Division only needs 1,000 units per month. If the Selling Division can sell all 2,000 components to outside sources, the transfer price for every unit diverted to the Buying Division, using the general rule, is $240 because:

$$\text{Minimum transfer price} = \text{Variable cost per unit} + \begin{array}{c} \text{Contribution margin} \\ \text{per unit lost on} \\ \text{outside sales} \end{array}$$

$$= \quad \$80 \quad + \quad \$160$$
$$= \quad \$240$$

What would happen if a transfer price of $220 is established? The Selling Division would have $20,000 less contribution margin (1,000 units × the lost contribution margin per unit of $20). The result would be lower profits for the firm as a whole, which is a situation that often is called **suboptimization** because the overall profitability is less than it could have been with a better decision. If the Buying Division can find a price lower than $240 per component, it should accept the lower price and let the Selling Division sell all its output to external sources. An outside price higher than $240 should be rejected because the firm would be more profitable with the transfer of components from the Selling Division to the Buying Division at the $240 price.

If the Selling Division can only sell 1,000 units externally, the floor price would be $80 since there would be no lost contribution margin on outside sales, shown as follows:

$$\text{Minimum transfer price} = \text{Variable cost per unit} + \begin{array}{c} \text{Contribution margin} \\ \text{per unit lost on} \\ \text{outside sales} \end{array}$$

$$= \quad \$80 \quad + \quad \$0$$
$$= \quad \$80$$

Consequently, any transfer price above the $80 minimum will improve the performance of the Selling Division even if it does not cover all the Selling Division's costs or produce a profit. Although unlikely, an outside price lower than $80 obviously would be attractive to the Buying Division and would be below the Selling Division's variable costs so it would be accepted. These ceiling and floor guidelines can provide a useful starting point for the managers involved in the search for a reasonable transfer price. You should note that this decision is a make or buy decision similar to those discussed in Chapter 7.

SUMMARY

Business organizations are structured with well-defined groupings of work activities and employees as identifiable segments. Decentralized authority usually is used to disperse decision making throughout the organization to achieve better performance and relieve top management of the detail work involved with the day-to-day operations. Decentralization can also provide better motivation and training for the segment managers whose performance is regularly evaluated to monitor their contribution to the firm's overall operating results. A decentralized performance reporting function requires more sophisticated accounting than that needed for the firm as a whole.

Responsibility accounting is an important part of decentralized performance evaluation because it segments the accounting system and provides the personalized information needed to manage the segments of a business. A choice must be made between cost centers, profit centers, and investment centers in the operation of a responsibility accounting system. The accounting system is tailored to the segments of the organization so that reliable performance data can be collected, summarized, and reported to management on a segment-by-segment basis. Only controllable financial items should be considered in the performance evaluation process. The segment managers should actively participate in the development of the financial plans for their segments. Performance reports are prepared periodically to compare the actual and planned performances with a focus on any significant variances that are evaluated using management by exception.

A segmented income statement with a contribution report format can be used to evaluate different aspects of a firm's profit performance. This type of income statement shows the contribution margin, controllable income, and segment income for each segment without any allocated costs included.

Return on investment (ROI) analysis is used to evaluate the profit performance of a firm as a whole, a segment of the business, or the manager of the segment. This technique relates income performance to the investment in the operating assets needed to earn the income. In some cases, residual income (RI) analysis is a better measure of performance than ROI analysis because it involves a dollar amount of residual income instead of a percentage measure.

Intrafirm transfer pricing is one of the most difficult aspects of a decentralized operation. Products or services transferred from one segment to another typically are priced on the basis of cost, market, or negotiated market. A market-based transfer price is generally considered the best approach, but cannot be used in many cases because the market price is not well defined.

GLOSSARY

ACCOUNTABILITY. The measure of how successfully assigned operating results are accomplished in a decentralized organization (p.483).

AUTHORITY. The right to make the decisions necessary to perform assigned tasks in a decentralized organization (p.482).

BUSINESS SEGMENTATION. The division of an organization's work into specialized units (p.482).

CONTROLLABLE INCOME. Segment revenues less all variable and fixed costs controllable by the segment manager (p.494).

COST-BASED TRANSFER PRICING. A transfer price that is based on some form of the selling segment's costs (p.502).

COST CENTER. A responsibility center in which only controllable costs are considered with no concern for revenues or invested assets (p.487).

DECENTRALIZATION. The structuring of an organization into well-defined segments with a delegation of decision-making authority downward throughout the organization (p.482).

DELEGATION. The downward distribution of job assignments and corresponding decision-making power to managers in an organization (p.482).

INVESTMENT CENTER. A responsibility center in which the controllable revenues, costs, and investment in operating assets are considered in evaluating its performance (p.487).

MARGIN EARNED. One of the two components of ROI analysis that is computed by dividing some measure of income by sales (p.496).

MARKET-BASED TRANSFER PRICING. A transfer price that is based on essentially the same amount the selling segment of a firm would receive from an outside sale (p.503).

NEGOTIATED MARKET-BASED TRANSFER PRICING. A transfer price agreed on by both a selling segment and a buying segment of the same firm who act as though they represent a market in their negotiations (p.504).

PROFIT CENTER. A responsibility center in which both controllable revenues and costs are considered in the evaluation of the center's performance (p.487).

RESIDUAL INCOME (RI) ANALYSIS. An evaluation of the amount of income earned in excess of a certain minimum return on the investment in operating assets (p.499).

RESPONSIBILITY. The obligation on the part of managers to whom authority is delegated to attain the desired results (p.482).

RESPONSIBILITY ACCOUNTING. A specialized form of accounting used to evaluate the financial performance of responsibility centers (p.485).

RESPONSIBILITY CENTER. A business segment organized as a cost center, a profit center, or an investment center so responsibility accounting can be performed (p.486).

RETURN ON INVESTMENT (ROI) ANALYSIS. A technique used to evaluate profitability by multiplying the margin earned times the turnover of assets. Alternatively, income can be divided by the investment in operating assets (p.495).

SEGMENTED INCOME STATEMENT. An income statement that shows the contribution margin, controllable income, and segment income for each of an organization's segments as well as the net income for the firm as a whole (p.492).

SEGMENT INCOME. The revenues of a business segment less its direct variable and fixed costs (p.494).

SUBOPTIMIZATION. A potentially adverse effect of transfer pricing that occurs when the overall profitability of a firm is less than it could have been with a better pricing decision (p.506).

TRANSFER PRICE. The price used to transfer products or services between segments of the same firm (p.501).

TURNOVER OF ASSETS. One of the two components of ROI analysis that is computed by dividing sales by the investment in assets required to achieve the sales (p.496).

DISCUSSION QUESTIONS

1. What are the two most important considerations facing management in the design of an effective organizational structure?
2. How are the segments of a business established?
3. Distinguish between centralized and decentralized authority. Explain the main features of decentralized authority.
4. Why is some form of decentralized authority likely in today's business world? What are the major benefits of decentralization? The major limitations?
5. What is meant by responsibility accounting? Define a responsibility center.
6. Compare the use of a cost center, a profit center, and an investment center. Give an example of each.
7. Explain how information flows through a responsibility accounting system.
8. Identify the main features of responsibility accounting. How does responsibility accounting relate to decentralization?
9. How are participative management and management by exception utilized in responsibility accounting?
10. "The biggest problem with responsibility accounting is the negative impact of allocated costs." Do you agree? Explain.

11. What is meant by a segmented income statement? What are its major components and how are they used?
12. Distinguish between contribution margin, controllable income, and segment income.
13. Differentiate between a direct cost and a common cost in the development of a segmented income statement. How is each type of cost treated?
14. How is return on investment computed? Why is it beneficial to consider the margin earned and the turnover of assets?
15. What is meant by net operating income? Is this the same as the net income reported in an annual report?
16. If a firm is not satisfied with the return on investment of a particular segment, what steps can be taken to improve it?
17. "It is ridiculous to even think about reducing operating assets as a way to improve ROI. You increase profits by increasing operating assets." Do you agree? Explain.
18. What is the major limitation of ROI analysis when it is applied to segments of a business?
19. Explain the term "residual income." Why is it sometimes a better performance measure than ROI?
20. The Scott Company operates two investment centers, the Western Division with operating assets of $20,000,000 and the Eastern Division with operating assets of $2,000,000. Can residual income analysis be used to compare the performance of the two divisions? Explain.
21. What is meant by the term "intrafirm transfer pricing"? Why is this item so important to management?
22. What are the three basic approaches to transfer pricing that are available to management? Explain the major limitations of each.
23. Why are cost-based transfer prices used so often? What is meant by "cost" in this form of transfer price?
24. If the market price for a product or service can be determined, why is it typically the best approach to transfer pricing?
25. What are the main steps followed in the application of market-based transfer prices?
26. Why are negotiated market-based transfer prices often the most realistic form of transfer pricing?
27. If segment managers are given complete freedom in setting transfer prices, how can the results be detrimental to the profitability of the entire firm? Explain the basic rule that can be used as a starting point in the development of transfer prices to avoid the danger of suboptimization.

Exercises

Exercise 13-1 Use of a Segmented Income Statement

The Long Company operates two divisions—the Container Division and the Paper Division. Income statement information for the past month is as follows:

| | Division | | Total |
	Container	Paper	Company
Sales	$300,000	$450,000	$750,000
Variable costs	180,000	315,000	495,000
Contribution margin	120,000	135,000	255,000
Direct fixed expenses	40,000	80,000	120,000
Controllable income	80,000	55,000	135,000
Allocated fixed cost	30,000	40,000	70,000
Segment income	50,000	15,000	65,000
Unallocated fixed costs			35,000
Net income			$ 30,000

Required:

A. By how much would the firm's net income increase if Container Division's sales increase by $20,000?

B. By how much would Paper Division's sales have to increase for the firm's total segment income to rise by $12,000?

Exercise 13-2 Basics of a Segmented Income Statement

The O'Bannon Company's top management is concerned about segment prof-itability and has decided to prepare segmented income statements for its five divisions. As a first step, the firm wants to develop such an income statement for its Welding Machine Division based on the data below:

Revenue from sales	$450,000
Allocated home office costs	86,000
Fixed overhead direct to the division—$66,000 of which is controllable by the division manager	120,000
Variable costs for the division	234,000
Reported segment net income	10,000

Required:

A. Prepare a segmented income statement for the Welding Machine Division.

B. Is the segment income reported in part A different than the $10,000 shown above? Why?

C. What is the best responsibility accounting measure of performance in part A?

D. Explain the difference between controllable income and segment income.

Exercise 13-3 Fundamentals of Responsibility Accounting

Dan Stone, president of a franchised automobile dealership, is explaining how departmental accounting is applied to the firm's two operating departments — Parts and Service and Automobile Sales. He summarizes the accounting treat-ment by stating, "The Parts and Services Department is operated as a cost center, whereas the Automobile Sales Department is considered a profit center."

Required:

Evaluate the firm's treatment of the two departments. Do you see any potential problems with this approach? Would you suggest any changes?

Exercise 13-4 Cost Allocation Based on Ability to Pay

The Sell-Low Variety Store allocates indirect operating expenses to its three departments on the basis of sales. In 1986, the following allocations were made:

	Dep't A	Dep't B	Dep't C	Total
Sales	$600,000	$480,000	$120,000	$1,200,000
Indirect operating expenses	288,000	230,400	57,600	576,000

Assume that in 1987 Departments A and B have sales of $600,000 and $480,000, respectively, but Department C's sales increase to $360,000 because of the popularity of a new product line. Assume further that the total indirect operating expenses of $576,000 remain the same in 1987.

Required:

A. Determine the allocation of indirect operating expenses in 1987, using the same approach taken in 1986.
B. Are the results of part A logical for an equitable allocation of indirect operating expenses?

Exercise 13-5 Use of ROI Analysis

You have been asked to compare the operating performance of three companies in the same industry, summarized with incomplete information as follows:

	Company A	Company B	Company C
Sales	$2,000,000	$1,200,000	—
Net income	200,000	120,000	—
Investment in assets	1,000,000	—	3,000,000
Margin earned	—	—	8%
Turnover of assets	—	—	2
ROI	—	12%	—

Required:

A. Fill in the blanks above to provide the additional information about each company.
B. Based on the facts given, which company has been the most successful?

Exercise 13-6 ROI versus RI Analysis

The Data Processing Equipment Division of the Bucklew Company recently reported a segment margin (income) of $900,000 for the year based on an investment in assets of $4 million. In January of the current year, the division manager is considering a major investment of $2 million that will increase the segment margin by $350,000 annually.

Required:

A. What was the division's ROI for the previous year?
B. If ROI analysis is used to evaluate division performance, is the division manager likely to accept the new investment assuming the firm's minimum ROI is 15%? Would the investment be accepted if RI analysis is used?
C. Would the evaluation in part A be appropriate for the performance of the division manager as well as the division?

Exercise 13-7 Evaluating Profitability Performance

The Grace Company operates four departments. The company has gathered the following departmental data:

Department	Sales	Cost of Goods Sold	Operating Expenses	Operating Assets Beginning Balance	Ending Balance
1	$ 80,000	$ 60,000	$ 6,000	$ 60,000	$ 80,000
2	36,000	14,000	9,400	88,000	80,000
3	600,000	500,000	78,000	360,000	520,000
4	500,000	300,000	110,400	500,000	620,000

Required:
A. Rank the four departments on the basis of return on investment.
B. Assume that the company requires a minimum return on the average investment in operating assets of 10%. What is the residual income of each department?

Exercise 13-8 Evaluating Profitability Performance

The Fly-Right Company, an overnight package delivery service, wants to maintain a 20% before-tax return on the average investment in operating assets. The operating assets totaled $900,000 on January 1 and are estimated to be $940,000 on December 31. The company anticipates that it will deliver 60,000 packages during the next calendar year. The variable costs per package average $5, and total fixed costs are budgeted to be $200,000.

Required:
A. What should the company charge to deliver a package in order to achieve its goal?
B. If the company actually delivers 56,000 packages at the price determined in part A, what is the firm's actual rate of return on its average investment in operating assets?
C. If the company actually delivers 58,000 packages at a delivery price of $11.20 per package, what is the company's residual income, assuming a minimum acceptable return on assets of 15%?

Exercise 13-9 Using ROI and RI Analysis

The Millet Company has compiled the following budgeted data for next year's operations:

	Account Balance on 1/1	Account Balance on 12/31
Cash	$ 20,000	$ 50,000
Accounts receivable	50,000	70,000
Inventory	90,000	100,000
Plant and equipment	160,000	140,000
Accounts payable	40,000	60,000
Total fixed costs	$100,000	
Variable costs per unit	10	
Estimated volume	20,000 units	

Required:
A. If the company wants to earn net income at the estimated volume that is a 15% before-tax return on its average investment in operating assets, what should the selling price per unit be?
B. If the company actually produces and sells 18,000 units at the price com-

puted in part A, what is the firm's actual rate of return on its average investment in operating assets?

C. If the company actually sells 24,000 units at a selling price of $17 per unit, what is the company's residual income, assuming a minimum acceptable return on assets of 12%?

Exercise 13-10 Evaluating Change with ROI Analysis

The president of the Darrow Company is very concerned about the Household Goods Division's return on investment. He recently met with the division manager and requested that certain changes be considered to hopefully improve the division's ROI. For the past year, the Household Goods Division reported the following:

Segment income	$ 100,000
Segment sales	2,000,000
Operating assets used	800,000

Required:
A. Determine the division's margin earned, asset turnover, and ROI for the previous year.
B. Evaluate the effect on the division's ROI of each of the following changes independently:
1. Reducing variable costs by $10,000 with no change in sales or assets.
2. Reducing operating assets used by $175,000 with no change in sales or costs.
3. Implementing a promotional campaign that will increase sales by $200,000 and the segment income by $32,000. Assets used will not be affected.

Exercise 13-11 Company Profits and Transfer Pricing

The Automotive Division of Higley Company normally puchases its parts from the firm's Components Division. The Automotive Division manager has just been informed that the Components Division is increasing the price of a particular gear from $100 to $110. The Automotive Division manager immediately placed phone calls to three outside suppliers who informed him that their prices for the same product are still $100 and will remain unchanged.

The Components Division manager has explained that the price increase is necessary because of inflation, and the following data represent the costs associated with supplying 10,000 units annually to the Automotive Division:

Variable costs per gear	$95
Fixed costs per gear	10

The Components Division manager has determined that no alternative uses of the production capacity utilized for the 10,000 gears are available.

Required:
A. Will the company as a whole be more profitable if the Automotive Division buys the gears from an outside supplier at $100 each?
B. Suppose an outside supplier offers to sell the gears to the Automotive Division for $92 each. Should the offer be accepted?
C. Suppose the Components Division can use the production capacity to produce an alternative product that will be sold to an external customer at a

contribution margin of $15,000. Should this be done instead of producing the 10,000 gears for the Automotive Division?

Exercise 13-12 Basic Conflict with Transfer Pricing

The Seaver Company's Southeastern Division produces a single product that it sells to external sources at $30 each. The total cost required to produce the product, based on absorption costing, is $24, determined as follows:

Variable production costs per unit	$18
Fixed production costs per unit	6

The $6 per-unit fixed costs are determined by dividing the total fixed manu-facturing costs of $600,000 by the 100,000 units produced annually. The Southeastern Division can produce as many as 120,000 units annually. The Southwestern Division of the firm has offered to purchase 18,000 units of the product from the Southeastern Division at a price of $24 plus the transporta-tion costs involved. The manager of the Southeastern Division has refused the offer.

Required:
Is the Southeastern Division manager correct in declining the offer? Why?

Exercise 13-13 Floor/Ceiling for Transfer Pricing

Three independent cases showing relevant information for the Selling Division and Buying Division of the same firm are shown below. In each case, the Sell-ing Division produces a product that can be sold to outside customers or to the Buying Division.

Selling Division	Case 1	Case 2	Case 3
Production capacity (units)	60,000	400,000	200,000
Units that can be sold to outside customers	60,000	340,000	200,000
Regular market price	$ 200	$ 80	$ 100
Variable costs per unit	120	50	70
Fixed costs per unit–based on total			
production capacity	40	10	15
Buying Division			
Units required annually	10,000	40,000	20,000
Purchase price from external source	$ 210	$ 72	$ 98

Required:
A. Based on the information above, determine whether the Buying Division should purchase the products from the Selling Division or from an exter-nal source in each case.
B. Assume in Case 2 that the Buying Division offers to purchase 40,000 units at $60 each from the Selling Division but the offer is refused. Determine the impact on the firm's profits.
C. Assume in Case 2 that the Selling Division currently is selling 380,000 units to outside customers. How would the Selling Division determine the selling price for the 40,000 units required by the Buying Division? Under what circumstances should the Buying Division go outside for one-half of its requirements?
D. Assume in Case 3 that the Selling Division can reduce its variable selling expenses by $7 per unit for each product sold internally. Would this change your answer to part A?

PROBLEMS

Problem 13-1 Preparing a Segmented Income Statement

Bocknik Enterprises showed an operating loss in 1987. The president insists on determining which of the firm's three products is the source of the loss. Total company data as well as individual product information is as follows:

Sales	$1,000,000
Less variable costs	565,000
Contribution margin	435,000
Less fixed costs	450,000
Net income (loss)	$ (15,000)

	Product 1	**Product 2**	**Product 3**
Sales	$300,000	$200,000	$500,000
Contribution margin ratio	30%	60%	45%
Direct fixed costs	$120,000	$ 70,000	$180,000

Required:
Prepare an income statement segmented by products.

Problem 13-2 Income Measures within a Company

New Car Sales is one of four divisions which combine to create the total operations of Hack's Motors. Sales for April, 1987 totaled $625,000 based on the sale of 55 cars during the period. Variable cost of goods sold was $400,000. In addition, the sales force is on a commission-only basis and earned an average of $1,100 per sale. The office staff has total monthly salaries of $61,500. Occasional advertising through local television, radio, and newspapers costs a total of $24,000 per month. The office building and car lot have six years of $8,000 monthly depreciation remaining. Taxes on this property total $1,200 per month.

Required:
Using the above information, calculate:

1. Contribution margin
2. Controllable income and
3. Segment income for the New Car Sales Division of Hack's Motors.

Problem 13-3 Distinguishing Between Controllable and Uncontrollable Costs

Michael Johnson has just completed his first month as manager of the Region 6 Division of Hartco Industries. His superiors are holding him responsible for all costs incurred by and allocated to the Region 6 Division. The costs include:

1. $2,500 monthly depreciation of the plant and warehouse buildings.
2. $7,800 for secretarial salaries.
3. $1,200 for cost accounting services allocated based on the number of employees in each division.
4. Property taxes of $600 on the buildings occupied by the division.
5. $900 in advertising renewable on a monthly basis.

Required:
Within the framework of responsibility accounting, for which of the above costs should Michael Johnson be held accountable?

Problem 13-4 Responsibility for Costs and Loss of Production

Northeastern Manufacturing Company's production process is highly technical. High quality for its products and its workers is essential. Several divisions of the firm provide parts to the Final Production Division. The high-quality workers necessary in each division are valuable resources. The labor market is such that workers can be more demanding than in many other production areas.

The Tool and Die Division has recently been experiencing skyrocketing labor costs. In order to improve its financial performance, the division manager has begun hiring apprentices rather than experienced workers. Apprentices can be hired at $4 per hour less than the experienced workers. This cost savings will improve the segment income for the Tool and Die Division.

The Final Production Division requires 2,200 units per month from the Tool and Die Division in order to operate at full capacity. All units produced can be sold.

The apprentices in the Tool and Die Division are unable to produce units at the same rate as experienced workers. With the apprentices as part of the work force, the Tool and Die Division is only able to produce 1,500 units per month. This, in turn, has caused a slowdown in final production.

The Sales Division is experiencing a decrease in revenues. The availability of 700 fewer units per month has decreased the division's revenues by $18,200 each month. Operating income for Sales has decreased by $9,000 monthly.

The Final Production Division has laid off workers in reaction to the slowdown. This cost savings has eliminated most of the variable costs associated with the lost units of production. Because of the fixed costs, the Final Production Division is showing a decrease in operating income of $3,000 per month.

The Tool and Die Division is pleased with the situation. The apprentices have saved considerable costs, in spite of the lower production rate. The operating income of this division has increased by approximately $13,000 per month.

Required:

As corporate vice president, how would you analyze the present situation, keeping in mind that division managers' compensation is largely influenced by a bonus plan based on operating income?

Problem 13-5 Use of Responsibility Accounting

Andrews Automobiles, Inc. is a franchised dealership operating in the Midwest. In recent years, the firm has experienced unsatisfactory profit results because of slumping sales in the area. At the suggestion of the firm's CPA, responsibility accounting was implemented at the beginning of 1987. The following departments were organized as profit centers.

1. New Car Sales
2. Used Car Sales
3. Service – Mechanical
4. Service – Body Shop
5. Parts and Accessories

Monthly reports are prepared showing the profit results of each of the five departments. On April 20, 1987, the Parts and Accessories manager and the Used Car Sales manager have demanded a meeting with the firm's president, Bill Andrews, to discuss the way responsibility accounting is being applied. In particular, they are protesting two policies that currently are in effect.

1. The Parts and Accessories Department must transfer all parts and accessories to other departments internally at their original invoice cost.
2. The Used Car Sales Department is charged the full dollar amount allowed by the New Car Sales Department on a used car traded in for a new car. In many cases, this amount exceeds the ultimate selling price of the used car. The Used Car Sales manager tells the president about a recent case that is typical. A 1981 model automobile with a wholesale market value of $4,800 was traded in on a new car with a list price of $12,240 and a dealer cost of $9,792. An allowance of $6,528 was given on the used car to promote the deal, and the customer paid cash of $5,712. Consequently, a profit of $2,448 ($6,528 + $5,712 − $9,792) was recognized by the New Car Sales Department. The retail market value of the used car was $5,520, and it was sold at that price two weeks later. Since the Used Car Sales Department was charged $6,528 when the used car was added to inventory, it incurred a loss of $1,008 on the ultimate sale.

Both managers (Parts and Accessories as well as Used Car Sales) are upset by what they consider unfair practices and a violation of the basic premise of responsibility accounting as it was originally explained to them.

Required:
A. Do you agree or disagree with the two managers?
B. What would you do to improve the situation, if anything?
C. Why is your answer to part B important to Mr. Andrews, as well as to the other two managers?

Problem 13-6 Expanded Version of the ROI Formula
Jackson Manufacturing Company recently provided the following information:

Sales	$250,000
Fixed costs	95,000
Variable costs	100,000
Operating assets	156,250

Required:
Calculate Jackson Manufacturing Company's:

1. Margin earned
2. Turnover of assets
3. Return on investment

Problem 13-7 Calculating ROI
Harper Real Estate Company has three main divisions: Residential Sales, Commercial Sales, and Property Management. For the sales divisions, the major variable cost is incurred for commissions to the sales force. Property Management pays no commissions. Because the Property Management Division requires a much smaller staff, the assets used in its operation are significantly less.

	Residential Sales	Commercial Sales	Property Management
Revenues	$400,000	$300,000	$150,000
Variable costs	180,000	120,000	30,000
Fixed costs	160,000	60,000	45,000
Operating assets	320,000	400,000	200,000

Required:
A. Calculate the ROI for each of the three divisions.
B. The management of Harper Real Estate Company cannot agree on which division is most profitable. Some managers say the Residential Sales Division brings in the most revenue, and is, therefore, the most important. Others say the Commercial Sales Division's superior net income makes it the most profitable. Which of the three divisions is most profitable? Why?

Problem 13-8 Performing ROI Analysis with Changes
The following income statement is provided by Berkley, Inc.:

Sales	$2,000,000
Less variable expenses	1,200,000
Contribution margin	800,000
Less fixed expenses	640,000
Operating income	$ 160,000

Berkley's average operating assets were $1 million during the period.

Required:
A. Use the ROI formula to compute the firm's return on investment for the period.
B. For each of the following independent situations, indicate whether the margin earned and turnover of assets will increase, decrease, or be unaffected as a result of the events described. Then compute the new ROI figure.
1. Sales increase by $200,000.
2. By using less expensive raw materials, a cost savings of $20,000 per period can be realized.
3. The company issues bonds and uses the proceeds to buy $250,000 in equipment.
4. An improvement in inventory control procedures has allowed the inventory level to be reduced by $200,000.

Problem 13-9 Performing ROI Analysis
The president of Bartlett Company believes that the firm's return on investment must be improved. Each of the firm's three upper level managers has suggested a different strategy for improvement. The following information is available:

Sales	$642,000
Net operating income	57,780
Average operating assets	321,000

Required:
A. Compute Bartlett's present ROI.
B. For each of the following suggestions, recompute the ROI.
1. Manager X suggests an advertising campaign which would cost $35,000 per year but is expected to increase sales by 9% and net operating income to $69,978.
2. Manager Y suggests that the introduction of computers leased for $28,422 annually would reduce the costs now incurred by 10%.

3. Manager Z thinks there is enough unused equipment that operating assets can be reduced by $53,500.

Problem 13-10 Understanding How Change Affects ROI

The following data have been gathered from Harris Corporation's financial records for the operations during 1987:

Sales	$850,000
Contribution margin	552,500
Fixed costs	425,000
Average operating assets	680,000

Required:
A. Using the available information, calculate Harris Corporation's:
1. Margin earned
2. Turnover of assets
3. Return on investment
B. Recalculate the three ratios required in Part A, assuming that Harris projects a 10% increase in sales.
C. If Harris Corporation could reduce its total variable costs by $17,000, how would the amounts of the three measures in part A change?
D. One Harris Corporation executive has proposed a plan which would reduce the average operating assets by $25,000. Recalculate the margin earned, turnover of assets, and ROI if this change could be made. *Note:* Parts B, C, and D are to be considered independently.

Problem 13-11 ROI and Residual Income Analysis Compared

Information about three different firms' operations for 1987 is given below:

	Company A	Company B	Company C
Sales	$1,000,000	800,000	600,000
Operating income	90,000	18,000	30,000
Investment in operating assets	600,000	200,000	150,000
Minimum return required	18%	12%	15%

Required:
A. Compute the residual income for each company.
B. Compute the ROI for each company.
C. All three companies have been offered an investment opportunity with a 16.5% rate of return. If the companies rely on ROI analysis, which one(s) will make the investment? If residual income analysis is used instead, will any of the results be different?

Problem 13-12 Use of Residual Income Analysis

Hopkins Incorporated relies on the residual income analysis method when making investment decisions. Management has determined the minimum acceptable return to be 13%. Three possible investments are available. Information about these opportunities is as follows:

	Investment A	Investment B	Investment C
Additional operating assets required	$65,000	$100,000	$400,000
Expected additional income	11,050	12,500	56,000

Required:

A. Using residual income analysis, which investment will be the first choice of the Hopkins management?

B. Is the investment chosen in part A the most profitable one of the three? Explain.

Problem 13-13 Basic Transfer Pricing Considerations

Modern Productions, Incorporated wants to make its operations more efficient. All divisions are producing and selling at capacity. No intracompany transfers have as yet been made. Division 1 feels that its operations could be made more efficient if the units produced by Division 2 could be purchased by Division 1. Division 2 provided this information about its products:

Variable cost per unit	$12
Fixed cost per unit	14
Contribution margin per unit	17

Required:

Provide three transfer prices which could be considered by Modern Productions Incorporated. Are any of the three the best?

Problem 13-14 Basics of Transfer Pricing

Masterworks, Inc. has four divisions. Traditionally, each division has worked autonomously, with no intrafirm transfers because the divisions have all produced at full capacity and been successful selling their units to outside sources. Division A provides the following information about its operations:

Variable costs per unit produced	$3.25
Fixed costs per unit produced	4.60
Contribution margin per unit	7.90

Required:

Suggest three possible transfer prices for the Division A units. If intrafirm transfers begin, which of these three prices would least change the firm's net income as compared to what has been reported in the past?

Problem 13-15 Use of Negotiated-Market Transfer Prices

Parsons Industries is a manufacturing firm with two major divisions. Division 2 is interested in buying units from Division 1. The two managers involved seem unable to agree on a reasonable transfer price.

Division 1 currently produces and sells 67,000 units to outside buyers. It is operating below its productive capacity of 70,000 units. Financial records show a selling price of $9 per unit, variable costs of $2.10 per unit, and fixed costs of $3.25 per unit.

The manager of Division 2 suggests that the transfer price should be set equal to the variable cost per unit. He would like to buy 10,000 units for a total cost of $21,000. Division 1 would like the transfer price to be equal to the selling price of $9 per unit for a total cost of $90,000.

Required:

Assume that the managers of the two divisions are unable to compromise on the transfer price issue. You are called in as an unbiased arbitrator. In this case, what would your beginning point of negotiation be? Would you begin with the low price suggested by the Division 2 manager, the high price proposed by Division 1, or something else?

Problem 13-16 Use of the Basic Transfer Pricing Formula

Harper Industries has a Widget Division that produces and sells a standard widget as follows:

Production capacity in units	150,000
Selling price to outside customers	$27
Variable costs per unit	14
Fixed costs per unit (based on capacity)	8

The firm has a Deluxe Products Division which could use the widgets in its production process. Currently, the Deluxe Products Division purchases 22,000 widgets per year from an outside supplier at a unit cost of $25.

Required:
For each of the following independent situations, determine the transfer price using the floor/ceiling formula discussed in this chapter:

1. The Widget Division expects to sell 110,000 units to its outside customers.
2. There is an excess demand for the standard widget. The Widget Division can sell all it can produce to outside customers.
3. Again, the Widget Division finds that it can sell all units that can be produced. By avoiding selling costs, $2 in variable expenses can be eliminated on intracompany sales.

Problem 13-17 Selling Division's Capacity Utilization and Transfer Pricing

During 1986, the Component Division of Music Makers, Inc. sold 42,000 units to outside buyers for a total revenue of $1,575,000. Variable costs totaled $367,500. Another division of Music Makers has approached the Component Division about the possibility of an intrafirm transfer of 20,000 units during 1987.

Required:
Determine the minimum transfer price to be considered under each of the following independent situations:

1. The market remains strong; all units could be sold to outside buyers.
2. A new competitor in the market has cut Component Division's expected sales by 50% of the units sold in 1986.
3. Component division has the capacity to produce up to 50,000 units. The market of outside buyers is expected to maintain its 1986 level.

PART 5

CONSIDERATION OF SPECIALIZED MANAGERIAL ACCOUNTING TOPICS

14

COST ALLOCATION: A CLOSER LOOK

CHAPTER OVERVIEW AND OBJECTIVES

This chapter expands on the previous coverage of cost allocation and explains how it should be used by a business. After studying this chapter, you should be able to:

1. Describé why cost allocation is necessary when the full cost of producing a product, offering a service, or operating a segment of a business must be computed.
2. Explain what cost objectives, cost pools, and cost allocation bases are.
3. Recognize when separate departmental rates should be used to apply manufacturing overhead to products instead of using a single plantwide rate.
4. Distinguish between direct departmental overhead costs, indirect departmental overhead costs, and service department costs.
5. Define three cost allocation bases—usage, activity, and capacity.
6. Discuss the problems associated with inequitable cost allocations.
7. List the basic steps involved with service department cost allocation.
8. Describe how three service department cost allocation methods—direct, step, and reciprocal—are used.
9. Explain why a dual cost allocation base is necessary for certain service department costs.
10. Differentiate between actual and budget performance data in selecting cost allocation bases.
11. Outline the major steps involved with the cost allocations needed to compute departmental overhead rates.
12. Prepare a cost allocation schedule that provides the information needed to calculate predetermined departmental overhead rates.

Objective 1:
Proper use of cost allocation

WHY COST ALLOCATION IS NEEDED

In Chapter 3, we introduced cost allocation as a fundamental step in product costing when a full costing (absorption costing) approach is used. The full cost of a product is the total of all costs directly traceable to the product plus a fair share of the indirect costs needed for its production. A full costing approach also can be taken to accumulate the costs of a service provided by a firm or those incurred to operate a segment of a business. Although cost allocation is necessary for full costing, we have emphasized that it can have serious limitations and should not be used in many managerial accounting applications (e.g., segment performance evaluation when the segment manager cannot control the allocated costs). The most important consideration with cost allocation is knowing when it is appropriate and when it should be disregarded. Remember that there are different costs for different purposes, and this important point dictates that cost allocation should only be used in certain situations.

For many managerial decisions, we need a definition of cost that is a departure from full cost because of the purpose for which we are using the information. If we are considering a special order to produce a certain number of products with what otherwise would be unused capacity, we are mainly concerned with the relevant costs involved. If we are evaluating the financial performance of a cost center manager, we should only focus on the costs that are controllable by the segment manager. In other managerial accounting applications, however, our definition of cost broadens to a more complete or full cost coverage.

Full cost information is used for external financial reporting because generally accepted accounting principles require full costs for inventory valuation and income determination purposes. Long-term selling prices should be established on the basis of full costs if a firm is to earn satisfactory profits. Many businesses have to justify the prices they charge with accurate full cost information, including:

1. A hospital that is reimbursed for health care services by an insurance company.
2. A defense contractor producing a product for the federal government at a cost-plus price.
3. A utility requesting a rate increase from a regulatory authority.
4. A university proposing to conduct a research project with funding from a governmental agency.

All of these pricing decisions require cost allocation to determine full costs for the activities involved because many of the related costs are indirect to the work being performed.

To assist you in developing a perspective of the need for cost allocation, assume that your school is considering a tuition fee increase for the next academic year and wants to base the new fees on the full cost of providing classroom instruction. The direct costs of teaching, such as instructors' salaries, are only a part of the overall costs needed to operate the school. Additional considerations are the costs associated with such activities as secretarial support, student services, academic advising, the library, central administrative functions, the bursar's office, the physical plant, computer services, and the registrar's office. Although these activities are only indirectly related to classroom instruction, they are indispensable for the operation of the academic process. Consequently, their costs must be included in the full cost of providing the credit hours that are being priced. Since the indirect cost cannot be traced to the classroom performance, they must be allocated on some reasonable basis to credit hours so that the school can approximate the full cost of instruction.

The same situation exists in most business organizations because indirect costs are incurred and must be considered in order to develop full cost information. Nevertheless, the managers of these organizations must be prepared to remove the cost allocations from the financial information used in many managerial decision-making functions for which the allocations are not intended. In this chapter, we consider the fundamental features of cost allocation, but continue to emphasize that the concepts and procedures involved are primarily used to determine the full costs of some business activity. At times, a secondary benefit of a correct use of cost allocation is that it makes an organization's segment managers more cost conscious concerning the support services they receive. This often encourages the managers to control their requests for other departments' costs (e.g., those of a computer operation providing data processing services).

COST OBJECTIVES, COST POOLS, AND COST ALLOCATION BASES

Objective 2: Defining cost objectives, cost pools, and cost allocation bases

In general, cost allocation consists of three fundamental considerations:

1. Identifying the cost objectives to which indirect costs will be allocated. A **cost objective** is any activity for which separate cost measurement is performed. Examples are a product, service, project, department, or division. Note that some of these cost objectives are the output of a business, whereas others are segments of the organization. The cost objective chosen is the independent variable in the allocation process.

2. Determining the cost pools that are to be assigned to specific cost objectives. A **cost pool** is simply an amount to be allocated during a given period. It can consist of two types of costs: (1) a cost that is indirect to any single cost objective because it is incurred for the common benefit of more than one cost objective (e.g., the rent on a building occupied by several departments) or (2) the total costs needed to operate a service department such as a purchasing function. A cost pool—the dependent variable in the allocation process—can consist of a single cost item or several similar items that are grouped so they can be allocated together.

3. Selecting a **cost allocation base** for each cost pool–cost objective relationship that provides the best linkage between the incurrence of the dependent variable (cost pool) and the performance of the independent variable (cost objective). Since the indirect costs involved cannot be traced to the cost objectives, the cost allocation base selected for each case ideally should be considered the best measure of the way the performance of the cost objective causes the incurrence of the related cost pool. Unfortunately, we are unable to define an accurate cause-and-effect relationship in many cases. Instead, we must use the best estimate of the benefits received by the cost objective from the cost pool. Examples of cost allocation bases are direct labor hours, direct labor cost, machine hours, number of employees, square footage occupied, and purchase orders processed.

Objective 3: Departmental overhead rates versus a plant-wide rate

USE OF PREDETERMINED DEPARTMENTAL OVERHEAD RATES

Reliable cost allocation is particularly important when the predetermined overhead rate utilized to apply manufacturing overhead to products is developed on a departmental basis. In earlier chapters, we used a single predetermined overhead rate throughout the production operation to apply manufacturing overhead to the products on a perpetual basis. The use of a single rate, often called a **plantwide overhead rate** or blanket rate, provides satisfactory overhead application results in small firms that do not divide their production operation into specialized departments. Most firms use more than one department in the production process, however, and the various departments may have significant cost and production differences that require multiple **departmental overhead rates** instead of a single plantwide rate.

The use of departmental rates enables management to recognize the way different products require different amounts of manufacturing overhead as they move through the various departments. For example, one department may be highly automated with little labor input required, so machine hours will provide the best matching of the department's overhead costs to the products being produced. Another department may be labor intensive, and direct labor hours will be the most accurate basis for applying overhead. Other complicating factors are that some departments have higher overhead costs than others and certain products require differing amounts of production time in the various departments.

In such cases, a plantwide rate can produce *inaccurate* product cost results by *averaging out* the cost and production differences between departments without any consideration of the way the products being produced actually require the overhead costs. The result of an excessive amount of averaging with a plantwide rate can be inequitable applications of overhead to the various products. To illustrate the significant product costing differences between a plantwide rate and departmental rates that can occur, consider the case of the Diverse Company that operates two departments, Machining and Assembly, and works on two jobs, 101 and 102, during a given period.

The budgeted annual manufacturing overhead, budgeted direct labor hours, and direct labor requirements for each job are shown in Figure 14-1. If departmental overhead rates are developed, $50 per direct labor hour and $10 per direct labor hour would be applied to each job worked on in the Machining Department and Assembly Department, respectively. The plantwide rate is $30 per direct labor hour, regardless of the department involved, based on the assumption that equal amounts of time will be spent on a given job by the various departments.

Note that the same amount of overhead ($24,000) is applied to the two jobs with the plantwide rate because each job required 800 direct labor hours. However, this is not equitable treatment since Job 101 requires 600 hours in the Machining Department, which has much higher manufacturing overhead costs than the Assembly Department ($500,000 versus $100,000), whereas the same job only consumed 200 hours in the Assembly Department. In contrast, Job 102 used only 300 hours in the Machining Department and 500 hours in the Assembly Department, so it should have been assigned less overhead than Job 101.

If we use a single rate of $30 per direct labor hour, we are not taking into consideration the important relationships between the labor time requirement of each job and the manufacturing overhead costs of the two departments. The departmental overhead rates provide a better matching of the capacity utilization of each of the two departments because of the operating differences involved. Job 101 is charged with overhead amounting to $32,000, whereas Job 102 only absorbs $20,000. This difference in the amount of overhead applied is consistent with the utilization of the two departments' capacity in the produc-

Figure 14-1

		Machining Department	Assembly Department	Plantwide
DIVERSE COMPANY				
Comparison of Departmental Overhead Rates and a Plantwide Rate				
Budgeted annual manufacturing overhead	(a)	$500,000	$100,000	$600,000
Budgeted direct labor hours	(b)	10,000	10,000	20,000
Departmental overhead rates:				
Per direct labor hour	(a/b)	$ 50	$ 10	
Plantwide overhead rate:				
Per direct labor hour	(a/b)			$ 30
Job 101 requirements:				
Direct labor hours		600	200	800
Job 102 requirements:				
Direct labor hours		300	500	800
Overhead application:	Job 101		Job 102	
Departmental rates:				
Machining	(600 × $50)	$30,000	(300 × $50)	$15,000
Assembly	(200 × $10)	2,000	(500 × $10)	5,000
Total		$32,000		$20,000
Plantwide rate	(800 × $30)	$24,000	(800 × $30)	$24,000
Difference in overhead application		$ 8,000		$ (4,000)

tion of the two jobs, thus providing a better matching of the overhead costs and the products produced. When we compare the results with the plantwide rate and those with departmental rates, Job 101 is undercharged by $8,000, whereas Job 102 is overcharged by $4,000.

Objective 4: Identifying different types of overhead costs

To develop departmental overhead rates, we must consider three types of manufacturing overhead:

1. **The manufacturing overhead cost items that can be directly traced to the departments organized as cost objectives.** Note that these costs are direct costs for the departments, but they are indirect to the products or services involved. An example of such a cost item is a department manager's salary.
2. **Indirect departmental costs that are incurred for the common benefit of multiple cost objectives, including the production departments for which we are developing overhead rates.** Examples are rent, depreciation, and utilities incurred as building occupancy expenditures. At times, these common costs are incurred for the benefit of manufacturing, selling, and administrative functions, so they must be allocated to all three activities on some reasonable basis.
3. **The overhead costs that are directly or indirectly associated with the service departments providing support to the production departments.** Examples of such services are maintenance, data processing, quality control, factory office, and purchasing. Again, to utilize a full cost approach for the

departmental overhead rates, the service department costs must be allocated to the production departments. If the service departments were not available, the production departments would have to provide the related services themselves or procure them from outside sources. Consequently, the production departments must include a reasonable portion of the service department costs in the departmental overhead rates used to value finished products at full cost.

DIFFERENT COST ALLOCATION BASES

The base chosen to allocate the indirect manufacturing costs grouped as a cost pool to a cost objective such as a particular production department usually is one of three types:

1. Usage
2. Activity
3. Capacity

Objective 5: Use of different types of cost allocation bases

Remember that whenever practical our primary objective is to establish a cause-and-effect relationship between a cost pool and a cost objective. If this relationship cannot be determined, we want to estimate as accurately as possible the benefits that will be received by the cost objective from the cost pool. Usage is a measure of the amount of a cost pool consumed by a cost objective. Thus, it often provides the best allocation base. For example, a maintenance department's costs may be charged to the various production departments on the basis of the maintenance services performed for each of them.

There are two basic problems with usage as a cost allocation base:

1. The utilization of many indirect manufacturing costs cannot be directly measured on any reliable basis, and any attempt to do so would only be a rough estimate. Examples are rent on a building occupied by several departments, a plant manager's salary, and a personnel department.
2. The usage of service department costs involves both a measure of the quantity of a given service that is performed and a rate that is charged for the service. For example, how much is to be charged for each maintenance hour performed for a given production department? If the rate is based on the actual costs incurred by the maintenance department, inefficiencies of that department may be passed on to the production departments without any concern for cost control on the part of the maintenance department manager. This can be a significant problem when the production department managers are forced to use internal service departments and cannot seek competitive bids from outside sources.

Cost allocation for support rendered by a service department on the basis of usage is an example of transfer pricing for an intrafirm service performance. The basic concepts and procedures concerning transfer pricing that we discussed in the previous chapter will be applicable.

When usage cannot be determined reliably, some measure of activity may provide a reasonably accurate cost allocation base. An activity measure is considered an indicator of the amount of a cost pool needed to support the volume of work performed by a cost objective. For example, the costs of operating a personnel department performing such services as employee hiring, training, payroll records, aptitude testing, performance evaluation, and promotion can be allocated to the production departments on the basis of the number of employees in each department. Cost allocation based on an activity measure is most effective when variations in a significant portion of a service department's costs are the result of changes in the level of activity being considered. Regression analysis, discussed in Chapter 5, can be used to evaluate the validity of a certain activity measure as a causal factor for the costs involved.

The third type of cost allocation base is a measure of the **capacity** provided by a cost pool to cost objectives. A capacity approach is founded on the premise that the amount of a cost pool is basically fixed regardless of the usage requested or volume of activity experienced by the cost objectives. In other words, the amount of cost will support all levels of activity unless the cost pool itself is increased or decreased, thereby changing the fixed amount of support capacity it can provide. An example is building occupancy costs (rent, janitorial, property taxes, insurance, and utilities) that are allocated on the basis of the number of square feet occupied by several departments. Regardless of the volume of activity performed by the various departments, they will be allocated a share of the building occupancy costs proportionate to the square feet occupied. Examples of typical cost allocation bases are shown in Figure 14-2.

AVOIDING INEQUITABLE COST ALLOCATION BASES

**Objective 6:
Problems with
inequitable cost
allocation bases**

Any cost allocation base that produces results that are inequitable to different segments of the business should be avoided. Such inequitable cost allocation bases often adversely affect management's attitude toward the entire cost allocation process. Two approaches that are sometimes used in the business world —equality and ability to pay—can have a *negative behavioral impact* on management so they should be avoided unless they happen to provide good approximations of cause and effect or benefits received.

Equality simply means that each cost objective involved with a particular allocation is assigned the same amount. If this base is used without any justification, the results will be unfair and detrimental to management's support of cost allocation in general. Thus, an equality base should only be used when it provides a reasonably good approximation of the way the related cost is used by the various cost objectives. For example, a retail store manager may divide his or her time equally between four sales departments operated by the store. In that case, it would be fair to allocate one fourth of the store manager's salary to each of the departments if the goal is to determine the full cost of operating the departments as semiautonomous businesses.

An **ability-to-pay approach** is based on the *illogical assumption* that the most successful segments of a business should be charged with the largest amounts of indirect costs. This approach can lead to undesirable results. An example of an ability-to-pay approach is the use of sales revenue to allocate costs. In most cases, sales revenue as a cost allocation base is inaccurate because there is no causal relationship between the sales revenue and the indirect cost involved. The basic problem with using sales revenue to allocate an indirect cost is that the relative amounts allocated largely depend on the performance of the *other* segments of the business. To illustrate this problem, assume that the Pointe Variety Store operates three departments—Hardware, Tools, and Paint. The

Figure 14-2

Allocated Costs and Their Cost Allocation Bases

Indirect Departmental Costs	Cost Allocation Bases
Building occupancy	Square footage
Company airplane	Miles flown
Employee fringe benefits	Payroll dollars, hours worked
Plant manager's salary	Number of employees, payroll dollars
Power	Machine hours
Supplies	Hours worked, direct materials used
Telephone	Number of phones, number of calls
Workmen's compensation insurance	Payroll dollars

Service Department	Cost Allocation Bases
Cafeteria	Number of employees
Cost accounting	Hours worked
Data processing	Computer time used
Engineering	Service hours rendered, hours worked
Factory office	Number of employees, hours worked
Maintenance	Service hours rendered
Materials handling	Services rendered, direct materials cost
Medical facilities	Services rendered, number of employees
Personnel	Number of employees
Purchasing	Direct materials cost, orders placed
Quality control	Units produced, direct labor hours

store's annual rent is $240,000, and management has decided to allocate the rent on the basis of departmental sales revenue. In 1986, the departmental sales revenue and related rent allocations are as follows:

Department	Hardware	Tools	Paint	Total
1986 sales revenue	$1,000,000	$800,000	$200,000	$2,000,000
% of total	50%	40%	10%	100%
Rent allocation based on % of total sales revenue:				
$240,000 × 50%	$ 120,000			
$240,000 × 40%		$ 96,000		
$240,000 × 10%			$ 24,000	

Assume that the Paint Department increases its 1987 sales revenue to $700,000, while the other two departments have the same sales revenue they experienced in 1986. The rent allocation schedule shown next would be used in

1987 and would be highly inequitable to the Paint Department, which is penalized by its good sales performance relative to the other two departments.

Department	Hardware	Tools	Paint	Total
1987 sales revenue	$1,000,000	$800,000	$700,000	$2,500,000
% of total	40%	32%	28%	100%
Rent allocation based on				
% of total sales revenue:				
$240,000 × 40%	$ 96,000			
$240,000 × 32%		$ 76,800		
$240,000 × 28%			$ 67,200	

Note that the inequity to the Paint Department in 1987 is the result of its sales increasing from $200,000 to $700,000 while the other two departments experienced constant sales from the previous year. As a result, the Paint Department is charged with 28% of the annual rent in 1987, or $67,200, compared with only 10%, or $24,000, in 1986. In contrast, the constant sales of the other two departments reduce their allocations because the rent assigned to the Hardware Department decreases from 50% to 40% ($120,000 to $96,000), and the amount charged to the Tools Department declines from 40% to 32% ($96,000 to $76,800).

COST ALLOCATION METHODS FOR SERVICE DEPARTMENTS

Objective 7: Steps needed to allocate service department costs

The allocation of service department costs involves four steps:

1. Preparing a manufacturing overhead flexible budget for each service department.
2. Selecting appropriate cost allocation bases for the various service departments.
3. Choosing a **cost allocation method** for ordering the sequence in which the service department costs are to be distributed to other departments.
4. Allocating the service department costs using the costs allocation bases and cost allocation method identified earlier.

In addition to choosing a cost allocation base for each service department, we must also decide on the order in which the service department costs will be assigned to other departments. This ordering or sequencing process is based on a service department cost allocation method, which is used along with the cost allocation bases chosen. A service department cost allocation method must be considered because many service departments serve both production departments and other service departments.

The basic question involved with the choice of a service department allocation method is "How much do we want to consider the manner in which the various service departments serve each other?" Potential answers are "not at all," "partially," and "completely." To illustrate the importance of this question, assume that the Flip Company operates two service departments, Factory Office and Purchasing, and two production departments, Wiring and Assembly. In Chapter 3, we discussed how service departments support the production departments and how their costs are included in the cost of the products worked on in the production departments. Therefore, we know that the costs incurred within the Factory Office Department and the Purchasing Department must be allocated to the Wiring Department and to the Assembly Department if we want to calculate the full costs of operating the two production departments and the products they produce. However, many service departments also support other service departments, and the way we recognize these relationships affects the amount of cost ultimately assigned to each production department.

In our illustration, the Factory Office Department provides such services as payroll, accounting, and personnel for the Purchasing Department as well as the two production departments. In addition, the Purchasing Department is responsible for buying supplies and equipment for the Factory Office Department while providing similar services for the production departments.

Three methods are available for ordering the assignment of service department costs to other departments:

1. Direct method
2. Step method
3. Reciprocal method

A choice between the three methods is made based on our answer to the earlier question concerning how much we want to recognize the ways the different service departments serve each other.

**Objective 8:
Sequencing of
service depart-
ment cost alloca-
tions**

DIRECT METHOD

The **direct method** is the simplest of the three methods to use because the costs of a given service department are not assigned to any other service department. Instead, the various service departments' costs are only allocated to the production departments. In general, the direct method is the least accurate cost allocation method because it completely ignores the interrelationships between service departments. Nevertheless, the direct method is widely used so we need to know how to apply it.

Let's illustrate how the direct method is used by continuing the Flip Company case with the following facts:

Service Department	Budgeted Manufacturing Overhead Costs	Allocation Base
Factory Office	$180,000	Number of employees
Purchasing	$90,000	Direct materials cost

Department	Number of Employees	Direct Materials Cost
Factory Office	15	—
Purchasing	10	—
Wiring	60	$400,000
Assembly	30	$100,000

Figure 14-3 shows the allocation of the two service departments' costs with the direct method. The budgeted manufacturing costs of the two production departments are $620,000 for the Wiring Department and $380,000 for the Assembly Department. With the direct method, we allocate the budgeted costs of the Factory Office Department and the Purchasing Department straight to the two production departments without any concern for services performed by the service departments for each other.

Figure 14-3

		FLIP COMPANY		
	Service Department Cost Allocation — Direct Method			

Department	Factory Office	Purchasing	Wiring	Assembly
Manufacturing overhead				
before allocation	$180,000	$90,000	$620,000	$380,000
Allocate Factory Office				
Department costs	(180,000)			
$180,000 × 66.7%			120,000	
$180,000 × 33.3%				60,000
Allocate Purchasing				
Department costs		(90,000)		
$90,000 × 80%			72,000	
$90,000 × 20%				18,000
Total production				
department costs			$812,000	$458,000

The allocation bases used are (1) number of employees for the Factory Office Department and (2) direct materials cost for the Purchasing Department. The Wiring Department employs 60 people, and 30 people are employed in the Assembly Department, for a total of 90 employees. Thus, 66.7% (60/90) of the Factory Office Department's budgeted costs are allocated to the Wiring Department and 33.3% (30/90) to the Assembly Department. The $500,000 total direct materials cost is divided into $400,000 for the Wiring Department and $100,000 for the Assembly Department. As a result, 80% ($400,000/$500,000) of the Purchasing Department's budgeted costs are assigned to the Wiring Department and 20% ($100,000/$500,000) to the Assembly Department.

Because the direct method is being used, service department costs totaling $192,000 are allocated to the Wiring Department ($120,000 from the Factory Office Department and $72,000 from the Purchasing Department). In addition, costs amounting to $78,000 are allocated to the Assembly Department ($60,000 from the Factory Office Department and $18,000 from the Purchasing Department). After the cost allocation process is completed, the two production departments, Wiring and Assembly, have total costs of $812,000 and $458,000, respectively, to apply to the products produced during the year.

STEP METHOD

With the **step method,** a limited number of relationships between service departments are considered. This means that the costs of some, but not all, of the service departments are distributed to other service departments. The allocation process is sequential and consists of one-way distributions to specific service departments according to a specified order. That is, the first service department chosen for allocation has its costs distributed to every other service and production department it supports. When the costs of a second service department are allocated, they are assigned to every department supported except the service department chosen in the first step. This process is repeated using the general rule that once a given service department's costs have been allocated, no costs are allocated back to that department. Thus, there will be as many steps in the allocation process as there are service departments.

There are several different rules used to identify the sequencing for allocation with the step method. We will illustrate the one that starts with the service department that provides the greatest amount of support to other service departments. Then, the service department that provides the second greatest amount of support to other service departments is selected next, and so forth. The process ends when the costs of the service department that provides the least amount of support to other service departments are distributed.

Let's use the above example to illustrate this process. We assume that the Factory Office Department provides more support to the Purchasing Department than it would receive from the Purchasing Department because of the nature of the services involved. This often happens because the Factory Office Department does not use raw materials. Therefore, the Factory Office Department's costs would be considered in the *first step* of the allocation process. These costs would be allocated to the Purchasing Department, Wiring Department, and Assembly Department using the number of employees in the three departments as the allocation base.

As a *second step,* the budgeted direct overhead costs for the Purchasing Department plus the portion of the Factory Office Department's costs allocated in step one to the Purchasing Department are distributed to the two production departments. This step allocation process is shown in Figure 14-4. Note that the denominator for the cost allocation base used for the Factory Office Department's costs changes with the step method from the one used earlier with the direct method. The total number of employees in the Purchasing Department (10), Wiring Department (60), and Assembly Department (30) is 100. Thus, 10% of the Factory Office Department's costs are assigned to the Pur-

Figure 14-4

FLIP COMPANY
Service Department Cost Allocation — Step Method

Department	Factory Office	Purchasing	Wiring	Assembly
Manufacturing overhead before allocation	$180,000	$ 90,000	$620,000	$380,000
Allocate Factory Office Department costs	(180,000)			
$180,000 × 10%		18,000		
$180,000 × 60%			108,000	
$180,000 × 30%				54,000
Allocate Purchasing Department costs		(108,000)		
$108,000 × 80%			86,400	
$108,000 × 20%				21,600
Total production department costs			$814,400	$455,600

chasing Department, 60% to the Wiring Department, and 30% to the Assembly Department. The resulting cost allocations are shown in Figure 14-4. The $18,000 cost allocation from the Factory Office Department is added to the Purchasing Department's own costs of $90,000 for a total cost of $108,000 that is then distributed between the two production departments on the basis of their 80%–20% usage of direct materials cost. The final result of the two-step process is the determination of the full costs of operating both production departments, amounting to $814,400 for the Wiring Department and $455,600 for the Assembly Department.

Note the differences in the cost allocation results with the two methods. When we used the direct method, the Wiring Department was allocated service department costs totaling $192,000 and the Assembly Department received total costs of $78,000. The step method resulted in allocated service department costs of $194,400 for the Wiring Department and $75,600 for the Assembly Department.

In many cases, the increased accuracy with the step method is worth the extra costs associated with it. Some businesses are forced to use the step method because of its potentially better accuracy compared with the direct method. An example is a hospital allocating service department costs to patient care for insurance reimbursement purposes according to a step method formula. The improved accuracy of the step method over the direct method is the result of partially considering the relationships between the service departments. Unless the step method is required, each firm should decide between the two methods on the basis of cost/benefit analysis—a measurement we rely on so often in deciding between different managerial accounting applications.

RECIPROCAL METHOD

The third cost allocation method is called the **reciprocal method** (or cross-allocation method) because it recognizes all interdepartmental relationships between the service departments. Remember that the interdepartment services recognized with the step method were one way only because we considered how one service center served a second service center but ignored any reciprocal relationship involving support provided by the second service department to the first.

When these reciprocal relationships have an important impact on the amount of costs allocated, the reciprocal method can be used to provide better accuracy. Its use also eliminates the possibility of choosing the wrong sequence with the step method. A complete description of the reciprocal method will be deferred to a cost accounting text because of certain complexities associated with the topic and the likelihood that the increased precision associated with it often will not justify the added costs involved. Application of this method requires the simultaneous solution of a series of linear equations that recognize the interactions between the various service departments.

USE OF A DUAL COST ALLOCATION BASE

Objective 9: Need for a dual cost allocation base in some cases

The cost behavior patterns of some service departments require the use of a **dual cost allocation base**—one part for variable costs and the other for fixed costs. A dual base may be needed for the same reason we discussed earlier in the Pointe Variety Store example (page 532) when we discussed the potential weakness of using sales dollars to allocate costs. If the fixed costs of a service department are assigned to other departments on some variable basis such as expected usage of the related service, inequities often arise because the amount allocated to one department is influenced by what happens in other departments.

The fixed costs of a service department are a measure of the capacity available in that department, not a measure of the incremental costs needed to perform a certain service. The fixed costs will be incurred whether or not the service is performed. The fixed cost structure of a service department is established when management decides what the long-term needs of the other departments will be for the service involved. When a responsibility accounting approach is taken, the managers of the departments using the related service should participate in determining how much capacity is required to meet their long-term needs. The result is often called the *peak capacity* of the service department.

Once this capacity is set, it becomes a fixed cost that cannot be changed easily. If the cost is spread among the departments using the service on the basis of usage or activity, inequities are likely. For example, if a given production department decides to save money by reducing the amount of service requested, more of the fixed costs involved with the service will have to be allocated to other departments even if their usage is constant. This situation is complicated by the fact that the managers of the other departments will have no control over the costs involved, which can lead to bitter disputes between managers.

To illustrate how these inequities can occur, let's consider the case of the Chapman Company's Computer Department. The Computer Department provides data processing services for three production departments—Machining, Wiring, and Assembly. Most of the Computer Department's costs are fixed because they consist of such items as equipment depreciation computed on a straight-line basis, building occupancy, a department manager's salary, and computer programmers' salaries. The variable cost items are supplies, electricity, and computer operators' hourly wages. The Computer Department's 1986 budget for its direct operating costs can be summarized on the basis of cost behavior as follows:

Budgeted variable costs	$ 50,000
Budgeted fixed costs	350,000
Budgeted total costs	$400,000

The department's variable costs are related to the number of hours the computer is operated to perform various data processing services for the three production departments. Assume that the firm's policy is to allocate the total costs of the Computer Department to the production departments on the basis of the relative number of computer hours they require. Figure 14-5 shows the budgeted hours of computer time for the three production departments and the resulting Computer Department cost allocations for 1986.

Assume that the manager of the Machining Department decides to reduce budgeted costs for 1987 by consolidating departmental reports, thus decreasing the computer time required from 1,000 hours to 600 hours. The other two production departments plan to use the same number of computer hours as they did in 1986. What is the projected impact on the Computer Department's budgeted costs for 1987? We know that a reduction of the volume of any activity will only affect the related variable costs. Thus, the 25% reduction of total

Figure 14-5

CHAPMAN COMPANY
Computer Department Cost Allocation Schedule — Single Base
Year Ending December 31, 1986

Department	Machining	Wiring	Assembly	Total
Computer hours budgeted	1,000	600	400	2,000
Relative use of computer services	1,000/2,000 50%	600/2,000 30%	400/2,000 20%	2,000/2,000 100%
Allocation of Computer Department's $400,000 operating costs:				
$400,000 × 50%	$200,000			
$400,000 × 30%		$120,000		
$400,000 × 20%			$80,000	

computer hours (2,000 hours versus 1,600 hours) resulting from the Machining Department manager's decision to eliminate 400 computer hours will not produce a proportionate decrease in the total operating costs of the Computer Department.

The budgeted variable costs for the Computer Department in 1986 are $50,000, and 2,000 computer hours are projected. The variable cost rate is $25 per hour ($50,000/2,000), but the $350,000 budgeted fixed costs would have been the same for any level of activity during 1986. Assume that the Computer Department's 1986 budgeted cost structure remains the same for 1987. We can determine the budgeted operating costs for the Computer Department in 1987 as follows:

$$\text{Budgeted total operating costs} = \$25 \ (1,600 \text{ hours}) + \$350,000$$
$$= \$390,000$$

Therefore, the reduction of 400 computer hours will only decrease the budgeted operating costs of the Computer Department by $10,000 ($400,000 to $390,000). If we allocate the $390,000 costs in 1987 based on budgeted usage, the results will be inequitable to the Wiring Department and the Assembly Department since they will have to bear a much higher portion of the fixed costs involved even though they will use the same number of computer hours as they did in 1986. These results are shown in Figure 14-6.

Note what has happened in the cost allocations for 1987. An attempt to achieve a cost reduction with an interdepartmental service obviously does not result in a complete cost savings for the entire firm as it would with the purchase of the same service from an outside source. The decision of the Machining Department manager to reduce the computer hours required simply has shifted fixed costs to the other two production departments. In 1986, the Machining Department was allocated 50% of the $350,000 fixed costs, whereas it only was assigned 37.5% in 1987.

As a result, the fixed costs allocated to the Machining Department decreased by $43,750 [($350,000) (50%) − ($350,000) (37.5%)], and that same amount is

Figure 14-6

CHAPMAN COMPANY
Computer Department Cost Allocation Schedule — Single Base
Year Ending December 31, 1987

Department	Machining	Wiring	Assembly	Total
Computer hours budgeted	600	600	400	1,600
Relative use of computer services	600/1,600 37.5%	600/1,600 37.5%	400/1,600 25%	1,600/1,600 100%
Allocation of Computer Department's $390,000 operating costs:				
$390,000 × 37.5%	$146,250			
$390,000 × 37.5%		$146,250		
$390,000 × 25%			$97,500	

simply shifted to the other two departments. Thus, the Wiring Department and the Assembly Department must absorb additional costs of $26,250 and $17,500, respectively, or a total of $43,750 in 1987 for the same services they received in 1986. This would happen even though there are no cost increases in the Computer Department. An increased percentage of the fixed costs is allocated to the Wiring Department in 1987 (37.5% versus 30% in 1986), and 25% is assigned to the Assembly Department (versus 20% in 1986). These increases take place even though their computer utilization is the same in both years.

A dual cost allocation base can be used in such cases to avoid the inequities associated with the single base we have just illustrated. The fixed portion of the dual base would be established when the operating capacity of the Computer Department is developed to meet the long-term needs of the three production departments. When such resources as computer equipment, software, floor space, and people are acquired, the amounts chosen are based on the service needs of the Computer Department's users, the production departments.

Once the capacity is established, the production departments are committed to their share of the capacity regardless of their subsequent utilization decisions because the fixed costs involved will remain constant for all activity levels. The dual allocation base approach will encourage individual department managers to use the capacity to which they are committed since they will be charged for it anyway. The variable cost portion of the dual cost allocation base in this case would be computer hours as a measure of production department usage.

To illustrate the application of a dual cost allocation base for the Computer Department's services, assume that when the department was organized, its resource base was developed to provide the same number of hours of service to the three production departments as those identified earlier for the 1986 budget. Consequently, 1,000 hours or 50% of the capacity is needed for the Machining Department, 600 hours or 30% for the Wiring Department, and 400 hours or 20% for the Assembly Department. These amounts represent the maximum computer capacity available to all three departments and is based on their peak needs. Regardless of the number of computer hours requested by one of the departments in a given year, these percentages will be used to allocate the budgeted fixed costs of the Computer Department. Thus, the fixed portion of the dual allocation base assigns fixed costs in lump sum amounts that are based on the predetermined long-term needs of the production departments. The variable costs would be charged to the three departments at the rate of $25 per computer hour. Figure 14-7 shows the effect of using the dual cost allocation base to assign the Computer Department's operating costs to the production departments in 1986 and 1987.

When the dual cost allocation base is used, the cost allocations in 1987 are much more equitable than they are with the single-base approach. The Machining Department manager's decision to reduce the required computer hours lowers just the variable costs assigned to that department. Only the variable costs of the Computer Department can actually be decreased without reducing the department's capacity.

Since the Machining Department committed itself to 50% of the Computer Department's capacity, one half of the fixed costs are allocated to the Machining Department despite the reduced demand for computer time. The other two production departments also are assigned their share of the capacity costs to which they are committed. The $43,750 cost allocation associated with the inequitable results of using the single base in Figure 14-6 is assigned to the Ma-

Figure 14-7

CHAPMAN COMPANY
Computer Department Cost Allocation Schedule—Dual Base
Years Ending December 31, 1986 and 1987

Department	Machining	Wiring	Assembly	Total
1986 Allocations				
Variable costs allocated with $25 per hour rate	(1,000 hours × $25) $ 25,000	(600 hours × $25) $ 15,000	(400 hours × $25) $10,000	(2,000 hours × $25) $ 50,000
Fixed costs totaling $350,000 allocated with capacity	50% $175,000	30% $105,000	20% $70,000	100% $350,000
Total Computer Department's costs allocated	$200,000	$120,000	$80,000	$400,000
1987 Allocations				
Variable costs allocated with $25 per hour rate	(600 hours × $25) $ 15,000	(600 hours × $25) $ 15,000	(400 hours × $25) $10,000	(1,600 hours × $25) $ 40,000
Fixed costs totaling $350,000 allocated with capacity	50% $175,000	30% $105,000	20% $70,000	100% $350,000
Total Computer Department's costs allocated	$190,000	$120,000	$80,000	$390,000

chining Department when the dual cost allocation base is applied. We can see this $43,750 difference by comparing the costs assigned to the Machining Department with the single base ($146,250) to the costs distributed with the dual base ($190,000). As a result, we have achieved cost allocations with the dual base that are more equitable to all three producing departments because they reflect management's agreement about the size of the capacity needed in the Computer Department as well as the budgeted usage of the capacity.

SHOULD ACTUAL PERFORMANCE RESULTS BE USED IN COST ALLOCATION?

In the previous discussion of cost allocation, we were concerned with allocations that were made at the beginning of an accounting period in order to determine the full costs of an operating performance throughout the period. Consequently, we only used budgeted performance data for the allocation process. Some businesses wait until an accounting period is over before they perform cost allocations. However, this approach usually is inferior to allocations made at the beginning of the period because the related information is not available to management as the operating performance occurs.

Objective 10: Use of actual or budgeted performance data

When the end-of-the-period approach is used, management must decide whether to allocate actual or budgeted costs to the different segments of the firm. For example, should the actual costs incurred by a Maintenance Department during a period just ended be used or should management allocate the costs budgeted for that department's performance even though the actual costs are known? *The answer in most cases is that the budgeted costs should be allocated.* If the actual costs were used, any inefficiencies in the Maintenance Department would be passed on to the other departments. The result of this type of allocation would be detrimental to the departments receiving the maintenance services and would not provide an adequate incentive to the Maintenance Department manager to control costs. Any unfavorable variance between the actual and budgeted costs would be lost in the cost allocation process.

One adjustment to the way budgeted costs are allocated at the end of the period compared with those distributed at the beginning of the period would be for the *quantities (or amounts)* of service considered. Remember that cost allocations made at the beginning of the period are computed on the basis of:

Total cost allocated = Budgeted quantities of service × Budgeted rate

When the allocations are performed at the end of the period, the actual quantities of service should be used instead of the budgeted quantities. This change will provide information about potential inefficiencies indicated by differences between actual and planned performance. As such, the costs involved with allocations made at the end of a period would be calculated as:

Total cost allocated = Actual quantities of service × Budgeted rate

To illustrate the difference between the two approaches, let's return to the example presented earlier for the Computer Department cost allocation using a dual base. Since the allocations were made at the beginning of the year, the variable costs were assigned on the basis of the budgeted quantities of service and the budgeted rate per hour. For example, the Wiring Department was charged with variable costs as follows:

$$\text{Total cost allocated} = 600 \text{ hours} \times \$25 \text{ per hour}$$
$$= \$15,000$$

Suppose that the firm waited until the year ended to make its cost allocations, and that the Wiring Department actually used 625 computer hours during the year. In that case, the actual hours recorded should be used for the allocation since the Wiring Department exceeded its planned hours. Accordingly, the cost allocation would be determined as:

$$\text{Total cost allocated} = 625 \text{ hours} \times \$25$$
$$= \$15,625$$

As a result of the difference between the use of actual and budgeted computer hours, the Wiring Department would be charged $15,625 versus $15,000. This difference is caused by the fact that the department used 25 more hours than expected. The reason for this difference should be investigated to see if the extra hours were necessary.

COMPREHENSIVE ILLUSTRATION OF COST ALLOCATION

As a final illustration of cost allocation, let's see if we can apply what we have learned by considering how departmental overhead rates are computed for full costing (absorption costing) purposes by the Mulhap Company. The firm operates two service departments, Factory Office and Maintenance, and two production departments, Mill Room and Finishing. The *step method* is used to allocate the service department costs beginning with the Factory Office Department. Building occupancy costs and the plant manager's salary are *common costs* that must be allocated to the four departments as indirect departmental overhead. The cost allocation process used by the company is diagrammed in Figure 14-8.

Objective 11:
Key steps needed for cost allocation and departmental overhead rates

The major steps needed by the Mulhap Company to perform the cost allocations and to compute the predetermined overhead rate for each of the production departments can be summarized as follows:

1. Prepare flexible budgets for the service departments and the production de-

Figure 14-8
Cost Allocation
Process

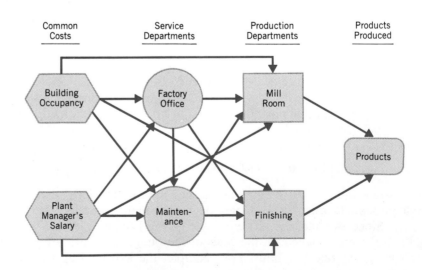

partments showing their direct manufacturing overhead on the basis of cost behavior.

2. Identify all indirect departmental overhead costs that are incurred for the common benefit of the various departments.
3. Select a cost allocation base for each indirect departmental cost and every service department cost to be allocated. Allocate variable costs and fixed costs separately whenever necessary.
4. Choose a cost allocation method for the service departments to establish the sequencing of their distribution.
5. Prepare a cost allocation schedule that shows the calculations made during the allocation process.
6. Once all costs have been allocated, complete the schedule by calculating the predetermined departmental overhead rates needed for full costing in the production departments.

To perform the cost allocations needed for the Mulhap Company at the beginning of 1987, assume that the following data are available:

Objective 12: Preparing a cost allocation schedule

Summarized Budget Data for 1987

Manufacturing Overhead	Budgeted Amount	Cost Allocation Base
Building occupancy	$360,000	Square footage
Plant manager's salary	60,000	Departmental payroll
Factory Office Department:		
Fixed overhead costs	120,000	Number of employees
Maintenance Department:		
Variable overhead costs	80,000	Budgeted maintenance hours
Fixed overhead costs	60,000	Capacity commitment %
Mill Room Department:		
Variable overhead costs	60,000	
Fixed overhead costs	410,595	
Finishing Department:		
Variable overhead costs	90,000	
Fixed overhead costs	229,405	

Item	Factory Office	Maintenance	Mill Room	Finishing	Total
Square footage	6,000	4,000	60,000	30,000	100,000
%	6	4	60	30	100
Dept. payroll	$50,000	$150,000	$300,000	$500,000	$1,000,000
%	5	15	30	50	100
Number of employees	*	5	15	20	40
%		12.5	37.5	50	100
Maintenance hours	*	*	6,000	2,000	8,000
%			75	25	100
Direct labor hours	None	None	20,000	30,000	50,000
%			40	60	100
Maintenance capacity commitment %	None	None	80	20	100

* Not needed for the allocation process so they are omitted.

Given these data, we are ready to proceed with the cost allocation process needed for the 1987 budgeted performance of the Mulhap Company. Figure 14-9 shows the cost allocations that lead to the predetermined departmental overhead rates for the Mill Room Department and the Finishing Department.

MULHAP COMPANY
Cost Allocation Schedule
Year Ending December 31, 1987

	Service		Production	
	Factory Office	Maintenance	Mill Room	Finishing
Direct overhead costs:				
Variable	–0–	$ 80,000	$ 60,000	$ 90,000
Fixed	$120,000	60,000	410,595	229,405
Total	$120,000	$140,000	$470,595	$319,405
Allocate Building Occupancy costs:				
$360,000 × 6%	21,600			
× 4%		14,400		
× 60%			216,000	
× 30%				108,000
Allocate Plant Manager's salary:				
$60,000 × 5%	3,000			
× 15%		9,000		
× 30%			18,000	
× 50%				30,000
Allocate Factory Office costs:	$144,600			
	(144,600)			
$144,600 × 12.5%		18,075		
× 37.5%			54,225	
× 50%				72,300
Allocate Maintenance costs:		181,475		
Variable costs		(80,000)		
6,000 maintenance hours × $10*			60,000	
2,000 maintenance hours × $10				20,000
Fixed costs		(101,475)		
$101,475 × 80%			81,180	
× 20%				20,295
Total budgeted production department overhead costs (1)			$900,000	$570,000
Budgeted direct labor hours (2)			20,000	30,000
Predetermined departmental overhead rate per direct labor hour (1)/(2)			$45	$19

* Maintenance Department variable cost rate: (Budgeted variable costs/Budgeted maintenance hours) ($80,000/8,000 hours) = $10 per hour

Figure 14-9

The first step in the preparation of the cost allocation schedule is to insert the direct overhead costs for each department as shown in Figure 14-9.

There are two indirect departmental overhead costs (building occupancy and the plant manager's salary). These costs must be allocated first because they will be assigned to all four departments as common costs. The $360,000 building occupancy costs are distributed based on the square footage occupied by the four departments. As a result, 6%, 4%, 60%, and 30%, respectively, of the total building occupancy costs are assigned to the Factory Office Department, Maintenance Department, Mill Room Department, and Finishing Department. The same approach is taken with the plant manager's salary based on the relative amounts of the departmental payrolls. We assume that the payroll costs are reasonably close approximations of the time devoted by the plant manager to the various departments.

Remember that the step method is used for the cost allocation process in Figure 14-9. The Factory Office Department provides the greatest amount of service to other departments so it is the first service department whose costs are allocated. The Maintenance Department does not perform much work for the Factory Office Department. The number of employees provides the base for allocating the Factory Office Department costs to the other three departments. Five employees work in the Maintenance Department, 15 are in the Mill Room Department, and 20 are in the Finishing Department so the denominator of the cost allocation base is 40 (5 + 15 + 20). Consequently, the percentages used to distribute the Factory Office Department costs are 12.5% (5/40), 37.5% (15/40), and 50% (20/40). Note that we ignore the number of employees in the Factory Office Department because we are not allocating any costs to it. Once we have finished with the Factory Office Department cost allocation, the total costs assigned directly and indirectly to the Maintenance Department can be distributed.

A dual allocation base is chosen for the Maintenance Department's costs because of the fixed costs that might be distributed inequitably with a single base. The variable costs associated with the maintenance services are assigned on the basis of budgeted maintenance hours for each of the production departments, and the fixed costs involved are allocated using the capacity percentages to which the production departments committed themselves when the Maintenance Department was organized. The Mill Room Department is committed to utilizing 80% of the maintenance capacity in the long run, and the Finishing Department needs the other 20%.

The total fixed costs of the Maintenance Department, including the allocated costs, are $101,475, so the Mill Room Department is assigned $81,180 ($101,475 × 80%) and the Finishing Department $20,295 ($101,475 × 20%). During 1987, we expect the Mill Room Department to use 6,000 maintenance hours and the Finishing Department 2,000 hours for a total of 8,000 budgeted hours. Thus, we want to assign 75% of the variable maintenance costs to the Mill Room Department and the other 25% to the Finishing Department. We do this by charging each of the two departments on the basis of a variable cost rate, determined as follows:

$$\text{Variable Maintenance Department rate} = \frac{\text{Budgeted variable Maintenance Department costs}}{\text{Budgeted maintenance hours}}$$

$$= \frac{\$80,000}{8,000}$$

$$= \$10 \text{ per hour}$$

For each maintenance hour budgeted for a production department, $10 is charged to cover the variable costs. The Mill Room Department is allocated $60,000 (6,000 hours × $10 or $80,000 × 75%) at the beginning of the year and the Finishing Department $20,000 (2,000 hours $\times$ $10 or $80,000 $\times$ 25%). As a result, the total Maintenance Department costs distributed to the two production departments are $141,180 ($81,180 + $60,000) to the Mill Room Department and $40,295 ($20,295 + $20,000) to the Finishing Department.

After we finish allocating the Maintenance Department costs, the costs assigned directly and indirectly to the two production departments are added to estimate the full overhead cost of operating the departments. In turn, the expected total departmental costs can be used to compute the predetermined overhead rates that are used to apply manufacturing overhead on a full costing basis to the products as they are worked on in the two departments. Note that the *direct overhead costs* traced to the two production departments during the budgeting process are $470,595 for the Mill Room Department and $319,405 for the Finishing Department.

During the cost allocation process, we assigned additional costs of $429,405 ($216,000 + $18,000 + $54,225 + $60,000 + $81,180) to the Mill Room Department so the total manufacturing overhead costs considered in computing the predetermined departmental overhead rate are $900,000 ($470,595 + $429,405). Indirect departmental costs and service department costs amounting to $250,595 ($108,000 + $30,000 + $72,300 + $20,000 + $20,595) were distributed to the Finishing Department and can be added to the direct departmental overhead costs of $319,405 to determine the total manufacturing overhead costs needed to operate the Finishing Department, or $570,000. Direct labor hours are used in both production departments as the denominators of the predetermined departmental overhead rate calculations. The Milling Department's overhead rate is $45 per direct labor hour ($900,000/20,000 hours), whereas the overhead rate in the Finishing Department is $19 ($570,000/30,000 hours).

As the various products pass through the two production departments, $45 per hour will be charged to the products for every hour recorded during their production in the Mill Room Department; $19 per direct labor hour will be applied to the products for each hour spent on them in the Finishing Department. Since the two overhead rates are based on all overhead costs incurred by the departments directly or indirectly in the production process, the result is a full costing approach to the manufacturing overhead phase of product costing. The direct labor cost and direct materials cost recorded during the production operation also would be traced to the products produced with either job order costing or process costing to complete the procedures needed to accumulate full product costs.

SUMMARY

Cost allocation is a managerial accounting technique that must be used carefully. A full cost approach to product costing depends on reliable cost allocation because a fair share of indirect departmental overhead costs and service department costs must be included in the cost of finished inventory. The same approach can be used to determine the cost of performing a service or operating a segment of a business. On a limited basis, cost allocations may have a control feature because they make the managers of the segments receiving services aware of the costs involved instead of treating them as free goods.

Three items must be considered in any cost allocation: the cost objective involved, the cost pool to be allocated, and the most reliable cost allocation base available. The cost allocation base provides the linkage between the cost pool (a group of homogeneous cost items) and the cost objective (an activity for which separate cost measurement is considered). Whenever possible, a specific cost allocation base should be chosen because it represents a close approximation of the way the performance of a cost objective causes the incurrence of the related cost pool. In many cases, however, this cause-and-effect relationship cannot be determined, and the best estimate of the benefits received from the costs involved is used instead.

Cost allocation is particularly important when predetermined departmental overhead rates are utilized instead of a plantwide rate. To compute a departmental overhead rate, we need to know the direct overhead traceable to the department as well as the indirect costs allocated to it. There are three general types of cost allocation bases: *usage, activity,* and *capacity.* Normally, usage is the most accurate type because it is a measure of the amount of a cost pool that is consumed by a cost objective.

Inequitable cost allocations based on equality or ability to pay should be avoided because the results can be detrimental and can lead to disagreements among the managers of the various segments of a business. Sales revenue is an example of an ability-to-pay approach that is often misused.

In addition to cost allocation bases, a cost allocation method is needed for service department costs. A cost allocation method provides the basis for determining the order in which the service department costs are to be allocated. The choice between three methods—direct, step, and reciprocal—depends on how many interrelationships between the service departments we want to recognize. At times, a dual cost allocation base is necessary to distinguish between the treatment of a service department's fixed and variable costs.

If cost allocations are performed at the end of an accounting period, budgeted costs still should be used instead of actual costs to prevent inefficiencies from being lost in the allocation process. However, such end-of-the-period allocations should involve actual quantities of service provided instead of budgeted quantities.

GLOSSARY

ABILITY-TO-PAY COST ALLOCATION BASE. A cost allocation approach based on the assumption that the most successful segments of a business should be charged with the largest amounts of indirect costs (p.532).

ACTIVITY COST ALLOCATION BASE. A cost allocation base involving some measure of a cost objective's activity that requires a certain level of support from a cost pool (p.531).

CAPACITY COST ALLOCATION BASE. A cost allocation base that considers the operating capacity of a cost pool available to a cost objective (p.532).

COST ALLOCATION BASE. The means chosen to link a cost pool to a cost objective (p.528).

COST ALLOCATION METHOD. The sequencing process used to determine how service department costs are allocated to other departments (p.534).

COST OBJECTIVE. Any activity for which separate cost measurement is performed (p. 528).

COST POOL. A group of homogeneous costs that are to be allocated to more than one cost objective (p. 528).

DEPARTMENTAL OVERHEAD RATE. A predetermined overhead rate established for each department (p. 529).

DIRECT METHOD. The cost allocation method that does not recognize any interrelationships between the service departments since their costs are charged directly to the production departments (p. 535).

DUAL COST ALLOCATION BASE. The allocation of a service department's costs on the basis of a separation between the variable costs and fixed costs involved (p. 538).

EQUALITY COST ALLOCATION BASE. The distribution of costs equally among cost objectives regardless of how the costs are utilized (p. 532).

FULL COST. The direct costs traceable to a cost objective plus a fair share of all indirect costs required to support the cost objective (p. 526).

PLANTWIDE OVERHEAD RATE. A single predetermined overhead rate used to apply manufacturing overhead throughout the production operation (p. 529).

RECIPROCAL METHOD. The cost allocation method that recognizes all interrelationships between service departments (p. 538).

STEP METHOD. The cost allocation method that recognizes some of the relationships between service departments but does so on a one-way basis only (p. 536).

USAGE COST ALLOCATION BASE. A cost allocation base that is a measure of the amount of a cost pool utilized by a cost objective (p. 531).

DISCUSSION QUESTIONS

1. What is the primary use of cost allocation? A secondary use?
2. Distinguish between a cost objective, a cost pool, and a cost allocation base.
3. What is a cost objective? Give an example.
4. What is a cost pool? Give an example. Identify the two types of costs that can make up a cost pool.
5. Explain the basic objective involved with the selection of a cost allocation base.
6. Why are departmental predetermined overhead rates usually better than a single plantwide rate?
7. Identify the three types of manufacturing overhead that must be considered in the development of a departmental overhead rate.
8. "In this modern age of automation, machine hours are more likely to provide the best denominator for a predetermined overhead rate." Do you agree?
9. What is the most important factor in the choice of activity measure for the application of manufacturing overhead within a specific department?
10. Give three examples of cost allocation bases and explain why they might be appropriate.

11. What are the three general types of cost allocation bases? When would each type be appropriate?
12. What is meant by cost allocation based on equality? Ability to pay?
13. "In order to save time and money, the most logical way to allocate costs is to use ability to pay because this reflects activity in a simplistic manner." Do you agree? Explain.
14. Why is sales volume a potentially dangerous way to allocate costs?
15. Why is a flexible budget used to determine the service department costs that are later allocated?
16. Identify the three basic cost allocation methods used for service department costs.
17. Why is the step method sometimes better than the direct method in the allocation of service department costs?
18. "A step cost allocation method is always preferable." Do you agree? Explain.
19. Explain what is meant by a dual allocation base. What is the basic purpose of one?
20. Are actual performance results ever used in cost allocation?

EXERCISES

Exercise 14-1   Departmental Rates for Manufacturing Overhead

The Bander Company uses departmental overhead rates to apply manufacturing overhead in its two production departments according to the following budgeted data:

	Department A	Department B
Machine hours	12,600	—
Direct labor cost	—	$348,480
Manufacturing overhead	$340,200	$906,048

Job 106 was recently completed by the firm using 840 machine hours in Department A and direct labor cost of $8,200 in Department B.

Required:
A. How much manufacturing overhead was applied to Job 106?
B. Why would departmental overhead rates be better than a plantwide rate for the Bander Company?

Exercise 14-2   Use of Departmental Overhead Rates

The annual budget for the Francis Company showed the following estimated production data:

	Assembly Department	Finishing Department
Direct labor cost	$ 111,600	$1,746,000
Machine hours	135,000	1,650
Manufacturing overhead	$1,620,000	$2,095,200

The Assembly Department is highly automated with a sophisticated robotics system. In contrast, the Finishing Department is primarily manual labor with little automation.

Required:
A. What would be the best basis to use for manufacturing overhead application in each department?
B. What would be the predetermined overhead rate for each department?
C. Job 714 requires the following:

	Assembly Department	Finishing Department
Direct labor cost	$2,700	$69,840
Machine hours	5,400	66

Calculate the difference in the manufacturing overhead applied to Job 714 if a plantwide overhead rate based on direct labor cost had been used versus the departmental rates in part B.

Exercise 14-3 Basic Cost Allocation

Allocate the $100,000 of indirect costs incurred by IUB Company this year based on: (1) square feet, (2) payroll, and (3) hours worked.

	Department A	Department B	Department C
Square feet	9,000	7,000	4,000
Payroll	$300,000	$200,000	$500,000
Hours worked	10,000	20,000	10,000

Exercise 14-4 Using an Ability-to-Pay Cost Allocation Method

Western Transport allocates all common costs to its various divisions. The problems associated with tracing these costs to the individual divisions led the company to allocate the costs based on the total revenue of each division. The following allocations were made in 1986:

Division	Revenue (Millions)	Costs (Millions)
A	$ 60.00	$10.91
B	30.00	5.45
C	20.00	3.64
Totals	$110.00	$20.00

For 1987, total common costs remained unchanged. Neither Division A nor Division B was able to increase their respective revenues, and Division C saw its revenues drop by 50%. In 1988, the results were the same for Divisions A and B, but Division C tripled its revenues from 1987.

Required:
A. Allocate the costs for 1987 and 1988 using division revenues.
B. What are the indications of the results in part A?

Exercise 14-5 Cost Allocation and Sales Revenue

Eromnek Company has three product lines, each of which is the responsibility of a different manager. The managers are evaluated based on the pretax income their products generate. The following monthly income statement data are provided:

(in 000s)	Product 1	Product 2	Product 3	Total
Sales	$2,000	$1,200	$1,200	$4,400
Direct variable costs	1,080	360	225	1,665
Allocated fixed costs	682	409	409	1,500
Income	$ 238	$ 431	$ 566	$1,235

The product line 1 manager believes that unit sales will drop from 120,000 to 80,000 if the price per unit is increased to $20. The change will not affect sales for the other products or variable costs per unit. Fixed costs are allocated by sales revenue.

Required:
A. Will the price increase benefit the firm?
B. Will it benefit the manager?
C. Evaluate how the firm is allocating its fixed costs.

Exercise 14-6 Evaluation of Cost Allocation

Maloy Metalworking allocates maintenance costs based on the maintenance hours required by each production department. The following data are available for July and August of 1987:

	Shaping	Finishing	Fabricating	Total
July				
Maintenance hours	2,000	5,000	3,000	10,000
Costs allocated	$20,400	$51,000	$30,600	$102,000
August				
Maintenance hours	2,000	4,000	2,000	8,000
Costs allocated	?	?	?	$ 92,000

Maintenance costs have a fixed component of $52,000 and a variable component of $5 an hour.

Required:
A. Allocate the costs for August using Maloy's method.
B. Based on your results in part A and July's allocations, evaluate this method.

Exercise 14-7 Use of the Direct Method for Service Department Costs

Schrimper Fisheries has three service departments and two production departments. You have gathered the following information:

	Service Department			Production Department	
	1	2	3	4	5
Direct overhead costs	$67,000	$57,000	$36,000	$50,000	$90,000
Square feet occupied	15,000	10,000	4,000	20,000	46,000
Number of employees	30	20	40	480	280
Machine hours	—	—	—	8,000	12,000

Costs are to be allocated on the following bases: Department 1—square feet; Department 2—number of employees; and Department 3—machine hours. There is no distinction made between fixed and variable costs in the service departments.

Required:
Determine the necessary cost allocations using the direct method. (Round your answers to the nearest $1.)

Exercise 14-8 Use of the Step Method for Service Department Costs

Refer to Exercise 14-7. Allocate the service department costs using the step method of allocation. Allocate Department 1 first, Department 2 second, and Department 3 third. (Round your answers to the nearest $1.)

Exercise 14-9 Use of a Dual Cost Allocation Method

The firm of Davis, Dawson, and Deffenbaugh, CPAs provides its own computer services for its Audit and Tax Departments. Based upon projected capacity, the Audit Department should use 2,000 computer hours per month and the Tax Department 3,000 computer hours per month. The budgeted monthly costs of the firm's computer services include $7,000 of fixed costs and $3,000 of variable costs.

Required:
A. Determine the allocation of budgeted computer services cost for both departments.
B. Determine the proper monthly allocation if the Tax Department decides to lower its computer usage by 500 hours per month for the summer.
C. What will happen if a dual cost allocation base isn't used in part B?

Exercise 14-10 Use of Dual Cost Allocation Rates

Wrap Bauxite's Transportation Department delivers ore from the firm's mining operations to its east and west processing plants. The department was organized to handle up to 120,000 tons per year for the east plant and 80,000 tons per year for the west plant. Budgeted Transportation Department costs at this activity level total $540,000 ($0.45 variable costs per ton and $450,000 of fixed costs). Next year's budget calls for the department to deliver 110,000 tons to the east plant and 60,000 tons to the west plant.

Required:
A. Determine the amount of transportation costs that should be allocated to each plant at the beginning of next year.
B. Compute overhead application rates for the transportation services charged to each plant.

Exercise 14-11 Use of Budgeted or Actual Amounts for Cost Allocation

The R.J. Morris Tobacco Company operates an exercise facility for its employees. The variable costs of the facility are allocated to other departments based on the number of employees per department. You have collected the following data for 1987:

	Budgeted	Actual
Exercise facility variable costs (per employee)	$50	$55
Number of employees by department:		
Maintenance	40	42
Production 1	400	396
Production 2	1,400	1,408
Production 3	600	590

Required:
Allocate the costs of the exercise facility at the end of 1987 in order to compare budgeted and actual performance.

Exercise 14-12 Effect of Cost Allocation on Cost Reimbursement

General Hospital's Medical and Surgical Departments are treated as profit centers, while its Admissions and Records Departments are treated as cost centers whose service costs are allocated to the profit centers based on the following schedule:

| | | Profit Center | |
	Costs	Medical	Surgical
Admissions Department	$400,000	60%	40%
Records Department	$500,000	25%	75%

Insurance company reimbursements for patients cover 35% of total Medical Department costs and 85% of the Surgical Department costs. To illustrate how the reimbursements are computed, the hospital would receive $220,000 to cover its admission costs, calculated as follows:

Medical reimbursements:	$400,000 × .6 × .35 = $ 84,000
Surgical reimbursements:	$400,000 × .4 × .85 = 136,000
Total admissions costs	$220,000

General Hospital is considering changing some procedures which would increase records costs by $15,000 and decrease admissions costs by $10,000.

Required:

Calculate the hospital's current costs and reimbursememts and compare them to its projected costs and reimbursements if the changes are made. Should the changes be made?

PROBLEMS

Problem 14-1 Plantwide Overhead Rate versus Departmental Overhead Rates

The Beral Company produces two products: X and Y. During its first year of operation, the firm used a plantwide rate to apply manufacturing overhead based on the following:

$$\frac{\text{Budgeted manufacturing overhead}}{\text{Budgeted direct labor hours}} \quad \frac{\$380,000}{200,000} = \$1.90$$

Two production departments are used to produce X and Y with departmental manufacturing overhead and direct labor budgeted for the year as:

| | Budgeted Overhead | Budgeted Direct Labor Hours | Direct Labor Required | |
			Product X	Product Y
Department A	$280,000	100,000	3 hours	1 hour
Department B	100,000	100,000	1 hour	3 hours

During the first year, the firm actually produced the 25,000 units budgeted for both Product X and Product Y according to the budgeted production requirements. Annual sales were 21,000 units of Product X and 20,000 units of Product Y.

Required:

A. How much manufacturing overhead was charged to the units sold using the firm's application method?

B. How much manufacturing overhead would have been charged to the units sold using departmental overhead rates?

C. What would be the difference in the valuation of the ending inventories with the two methods in parts A and B?

Problem 14-2 Use of Plantwide Overhead Rate or Departmental Rates

The Fun-Time Company produces gag items for use by practical jokers. The firm's plant has three manufacturing departments, M1, M2, and Assembly. Management, in trying to decide how to apply manufacturing overhead to its products, chose to look at three products—whoopee cushions, joy buzzers, and exploding cigars—to use in evaluating possible application rates. Budgeted manufacturing overhead is $450,000 — $170,000 for Department M1, $180,000 for Department M2, and $100,000 for the Assembly Department. Departments M1 and M2 both have direct labor budgets of 2,500 hours. Budgeted direct labor hours for the Assembly Department are 4,000. Each product requires the following amounts of direct labor in the three departments:

	Direct Labor Hours		
	M1	**M2**	**Assembly**
Whoopee cushions	500	200	300
Joy buzzers	400	500	100
Exploding cigars	100	300	600

Required:

A. Allocate manufacturing overhead based on a plantwide rate.

B. Allocate manufacturing overhead by departmental rates.

C. Which method would you choose? Why?

Problem 14-3 Basic Cost Allocation Techniques

The Fix-It Company manufactures automotive replacement parts. Mr. Hunt, manager of the company's new southeastern plant, wants you to help him allocate the following indirect costs to the Plant Office, Production, and Assembly departments:

Item	Cost
Building occupancy	$4,000,000
Power for machinery	2,000,000
Plant manager's salary	50,000
Employee fringe benefits	3,500,000

The following information has been gathered:

Department	Square Footage	Budgeted Payroll	Budgeted Machine Hours
Plant Office	1,000	$1,050,000*	—
Production	35,000	$6,300,000	700,000
Assembly	14,000	$3,150,000	300,000

* Excluding plant manager's salary

Required:

Prepare a schedule for Mr. Hunt that shows the cost allocations you would make based upon the information given.

Problem 14-4 Cost Allocation and Departmental Overhead Rates

Fit-Rite Boots, Inc. has collected the following information based on the normal operating capacities of the firm's Factory Office and its two production departments, Curing and Leatherworking:

Direct labor cost: Curing–$50,000; Leatherworking–$200,000

Floor space occupied: Factory Office–10%; Curing–20%; Leatherworking–70%

Overhead costs traceable to departments: Factory Office–$45,000; Curing–$47,000; Leatherworking–$103,000

Indirect costs not traceable to departments: Building occupancy–$10,000

Mr. Roy, the firm's controller, has provided the following additional information:

1. Factory office costs should be allocated to the production departments based on direct labor costs.
2. The Curing Department operates with a 40-hour week. Each of the four machines used will be idle approximately 330 hours a year for holidays, vacations, and other unavoidable machinery downtime.

Required:
A. Determine the overhead costs required directly or indirectly to operate the two production departments.
B. Develop departmental overhead rates using:
   1. Machine hours for the Curing Department
   2. Direct labor cost for the Leatherworking Department

Problem 14-5 Analysis of Cost Allocation Methods

Several managers of the Clements Company have expressed their concerns about problems associated with the firm's current cost allocation methods. Identify the changes that would help accomplish the objectives stated by the managers for each situation listed below:

1. There is concern that the firm's computer services are not being utilized enough. Computer costs (90% of which are fixed) are allocated using a transfer price of $80 per hour. The firm wants to encourage department managers to utilize these services.
2. The firm's Consulting Department costs have been increasing rapidly in recent years because of heavy demand from the production department managers. These costs have not been allocated to the departments in order to encourage use of the services. These costs are fixed, but discretionary. There is concern that the services are being overused.
3. Maintenance costs (both fixed and variable) are allocated on an hourly rate to each department based on actual hours of maintenance service provided. There is some concern that the managers are requesting emergency work only and are ignoring the use of preventive maintenance, thus leading to losses in production time because of breakdowns. Managers have been complaining that the maintenance cost allocation rate is too high.

Problem 14-6 Analysis of Service Department Cost Allocation

The McGinn Company operates two service departments and three production departments. Service department costs are allocated with the direct method. Budgeted activity data are presented below:

	Service		Production		
Costs	**1**	**2**	**1**	**2**	**3**
Direct costs:	$30,000	$33,000	$56,000	$ 90,500	$71,000
Service dept. allocations:					
Service one			5,000	15,000	10,000
Service two			13,860	7,920	11,220
Production department totals			$74,860	$113,420	$92,220
Allocation bases:					
Direct labor hours	2,000	3,000	5,000	15,000	10,000
Direct labor costs	$10,000	$ 9,000	$21,000	$ 49,000	$30,000
Machine hours	—	—	21,000	12,000	17,000

Required:

A. What basis is used to allocate costs for departments service one and two?
B. Calculate the difference in the costs allocated from service one to production one using:
   1. Direct labor hours versus direct labor cost.
   2. Direct labor hours versus machine hours.
   3. Which is the better measure to use, direct labor hours or machine hours? Give your reasons for your answer.

Problem 14-7 Use of the Step Method for Service Department Cost Allocation
Refer to Problem 14-6. Assume that service one costs are allocated based on direct labor hours and service two costs are allocated based on direct labor costs.

Required:

A. Use the step method to allocate costs in each of the following situations:
   1. Service one costs should be allocated first
   2. Service two costs should be allocated first
B. How would you decide which service department costs to allocate first if you were:
   1. Production one's manager
   2. The company controller

Problem 14-8 Use of a Dual Allocation Rate
The Morin Company operates three departments: Tooling, Machining, and Maintenance. The Maintenance Department's budgeted costs are $90,000 per month plus $.40 per machine hour, and the department can provide 250,000 machine hours of service per month, based on budgeted capacities of 160,000 hours for the Tooling Department and 90,000 hours for the Machining Department. The Tooling Department estimates it will use 130,000 machine hours of service in July, whereas the Machining Department projects it will use 70,000 machine hours.

Required:

A. Allocate maintenance costs to each department at the beginning of July, using a dual allocation rate.

B. Actual results for July show that that Maintenance Department's fixed costs were $95,000 and variable costs totaled $68,000. A labor strike resulted in the Tooling Department working only 80,000 machine hours during the month. The Machining Department recorded 70,000 actual machine hours. Allocate the Maintenance Department costs to each production department using a dual allocation rate assuming the cost allocation is performed at the end of the month.

C. What would happen if all the Maintenance Department's total costs in part B were allocated based on actual machine hours? Comment on this allocation method.

Problem 14-9 Actual versus Budgeted Amounts in Cost Allocations

The Athletic Trophy Company's Power Department supplies the electrical needs for the rest of the firm's departments. The company's controller has developed the following information:

Power Dept.'s budgeted costs for 1987: $165,000 ($145,000 in fixed costs)

Power Dept.'s actual costs for 1987: $175,000 ($150,000 in fixed costs)

Kilowatt Hours	Service		Production		
	Design	Maintenance	Machining	Finishing	Total
Budgeted for 1987	10,000	40,000	170,000	100,000	320,000
Used in 1987	12,000	34,000	150,000	84,000	280,000
Peak period needs	20,000	60,000	200,000	120,000	400,000

Variable and fixed costs are allocated separately with a dual rate.

Required:

A. How much of the Power Department's costs will be allocated to each department assuming the allocation is performed at the beginning of 1987?

B. Would your answer to part A change if the allocation is performed at the end of 1987?

Problem 14-10 Allocating Computer Service Costs

Ms. Osborne, manager of Division 1, and your firm's controller, Mr. Peacey, are meeting with you to discuss Ms. Osborne's complaint regarding Division 1's allocated computer costs for October. She wants to know why her division was charged more for computer service in October than it was in September although it actually used less computer services in the second month. Mr. Peacey has accumulated the data listed below:

	Total	Division 1	Division 2	Division 3
Peak requirements:				
Computer hours	20,000	8,400	2,800	8,800
% of total	100%	42%	14%	44%
September results:				
Computer hours	18,000	7,200	2,160	8,640
% of total	100%	40%	12%	48%
Cost assigned	$100,000	$40,000	$12,000	$48,000
October results:				
Computer hours	15,000	6,900	2,400	5,700
% of total	100%	46%	16%	38%
Cost assigned	$ 97,000	$44,620	$15,520	$36,860

Mr. Peacey explains that the large amounts of fixed costs needed for the computer services have to be accounted for regardless of the actual services used by any department. The computer services were developed with enough capacity to handle every division's peak requirements, and these costs must be absorbed somewhere. Since Division 1 used a greater share of the total computer time in October than it did in September, it was allocated more of the costs. Ms. Osborne still cannot understand why she should be charged more for using the computer less.

Required:
A. Comment on Ms. Osborne's complaint.
B. Determine the monthly fixed and variable costs for the computer services.
C. Properly reallocate computer service costs for September and October using a dual rate approach.

Problem 14-11 Cost Allocation Analysis
Jayhawk Industries has supplied you with the following data:

1. Department overhead costs consist of: Occupancy costs; Office Department; Maintenance Department; Production Department 1; and Production Department 2.
2. Normal capacity in each production department: 100,000 direct labor hours.*

3.

	Fixed	Variable
Occupancy costs	$110,000/yr	—
Office Department	$ 88,000/yr	—
Maintenance Department	$ 9,600/yr	$.60 per repair hour
Department 1	$106,400/yr	$.42 per direct labor hour
Department 2	$104,000/yr	$.18 per direct labor hour

* At normal capacity, scheduled repair hours: Department 1–2,200 hours; Department 2– 2,800 hours.

4. Costs are allocated as: (a) Occupancy costs–Office Department–10%, Department 1–42%, Department 2–48% (Maintenance floor space is very small); (b) Office Department costs by direct labor hours (no allocation to Maintenance); (c) Maintenance costs by repair hours.

Required:
A. Prepare a budget showing the overhead costs traceable to each department at normal operating capacity on the basis of cost behavior.
B. Allocate the service department costs and compute a predetermined overhead application rate per direct labor hour for each of the production departments.
C. Repeat Part A, assuming operations are at 80% of normal capacity and repair hours vary directly with direct labor hours.

Problem 14-12 Service Department Allocation and Overhead Application Rates
Peachtree Greeting Cards has two production departments (1 and 2) and two service departments (Housekeeping and Factory Office). Budgeted indirect manufacturing costs are applied based on budgeted direct labor cost. You have collected the following budgeted operating data, representing operations at normal capacity:

Payroll:	Housekeeping	$ 20,000
	Factory Office	180,000
	Dep't 1 (all direct labor)	600,000
	Dep't 2 (all direct labor)	400,000
Supplies:	Housekeeping	10,000
	Factory Office	4,000
	Dep't 1	12,000
	Dep't 2	14,000
Power:	Dep't 1	12,000
	Dep't 2	8,000
Heating:	Housekeeping	20,000
Other overhead:	Housekeeping	58,000
	Factory Office	6,000
	Dep't 1	34,000
	Dep't 2	12,000

Other Data:	Factory Office	Dep't 1	Dep't 2
Area occupied (sq. ft)	100	500	400

Required:

Prepare a cost allocation schedule and determine the overhead application rate for each production department using:

1. The direct method
2. The step method with the Housekeeping Department allocated first

Problem 14-13 Cost Allocation and Overhead Rates

You have determined the following information for the Holtz Production Company for the coming year:

Item of Overhead Cost	Budgeted Amount	Allocation Basis
Rent	$400,000	Square feet
Plant manager's salary	80,000	Department payroll
Office Department's fixed costs	140,000	Employees per department
Maintenance Department:		
Variable costs	90,000	Budgeted maintenance hours
Fixed costs	70,000	Normal capacity
Curing Department:		
Variable costs	40,000	
Fixed costs	320,000	
Shaping Department:		
Variable costs	60,000	
Fixed costs	480,000	
Finishing Department		
Variable costs	80,000	
Fixed costs	240,000	

The Office Department, Maintenance Department, Curing Department, Shaping Department, and Finishing Department utilize the following areas in square feet: 5,000, 2,000, 33,000, 35,000, and 25,000, respectively. In the same departmental order, department payrolls are: $50,000, $80,000, $320,000, $340,000, and $210,000 for 4, 4, 16, 17, and 13 employees, respectively. The Curing Department is committed to 3,000 maintenance hours; the Shaping Department to 5,000 maintenance hours; and the Finishing Department to 2,000 maintenance hours. Direct labor hours (at normal capacity) for each of these three departments will be: 20,000 for the Curing Department, 20,000 for the Shaping Department, and 30,000 for the Finishing Department.

Required:

Perform the necessary cost allocations and determine (1) the variable Maintenance Department rate and (2) the overhead application rates for the three producing departments. Allocate the Office Department's costs first.

Problem 14-14 Developing Different Overhead Application Rates

Bid-Rite Company is trying to determine the correct way to account for its manufacturing overhead costs. Actual manufacturing overhead costs have always been allocated to jobs at the end of each month, thus making it difficult to estimate prices to quote on new jobs. The firm's president is convinced that the company is operated efficiently, yet the jobs are continually either under- or overbid. The president believes that the problem results from the way the company accounts for manufacturing overhead. The firm's controller tells the president that total actual manufacturing overhead is allocated based on the actual direct labor hours for a month. However, the hourly manufacturing overhead rates fluctuate dramatically from month to month. The following information is provided from the firm's records of the previous year:

Prior Year's Overhead Costs (At Normal Capacity)

Indirect labor	$ 18,000
Plant manager's salary	40,000
Clerical salaries	14,000
Social security taxes	17,000
Workmen's compensation	3,200
Manufacturing supplies	3,600
Office supplies	2,400
Rent	4,800
Heat	12,000
Electricity	7,200
Depreciation	56,000
Insurance and property taxes on machinery	3,800
Machinery maintenance	10,000
Total	$192,000

Payroll Analysis

	Dep't 1	Dep't 2	Other	Total
Direct labor cost	$250,000	$70,000	—	$320,000
Indirect labor cost	10,000	8,000	—	18,000
Plant manager's salary	—	—	40,000	40,000
Clerical salaries	—	—	14,000	14,000

Other Information

	Dep't 1	Dep't 2
Floor space (sq. ft)	14,000	6,000
Employees	60	20
Direct labor hours	96,000	24,000
Machine hours	44,000	6,000
Depreciable asset cost	$540,000	$20,000
Annual depreciation rate	10%	10%

The amount of time spent by the plant manager in each department is related to the number of employees per department. Clerical salaries and office supplies consumed tend to vary with direct labor hours.

Manufacturing supplies directly used: Dep't 1 – $1,600; Dep't 2 – $2,000

Electricity is used 25% for lights, 75% for machinery

Power for machinery usage and machinery maintenance varies with machine hours

Required:

A. Is the president right in believing that how they account for overhead is the problem? Explain.

B. Allocate overhead costs between Departments 1 and 2.

C. Develop three overhead application rates that the firm could use based on different production activity measures.

15

QUANTITATIVE METHODS AND MANAGERIAL ACCOUNTING

CHAPTER OVERVIEW AND OBJECTIVES

This chapter describes several quantitative methods that are often used in managerial accounting applications. After studying this chapter, you should be able to:

1. Recognize why quantitative methods are important in managerial accounting.
2. Explain why decision making under uncertainty is inevitable and how risk analysis is used.
3. Calculate and use the expected value of the outcomes of a decision as well as the related standard deviation.
4. Realize how a payoff table is utilized in decision making and how to determine the value of perfect information.
5. Develop a statistical cost control chart using sampling techniques.
6. Explain how a fixed order quantity model is used to manage inventory.
7. Identify the main considerations of the order quantity decision in inventory management.
8. Discuss the major issues associated with the reorder point decision in inventory management.
9. Recognize why the ABC method is an important part of inventory planning and control.
10. List the basic features and applications of linear programming.
11. Construct a graphic linear programming model.
12. Realize how shadow prices are used to evaluate the profitability of capacity expansion.
13. Describe the main features and benefits of the Program Evaluation and Review Technique (PERT).

14. Develop a PERT network.
15. Formulate a linear programming problem with the simplex method and interpret the optimal solution. (Appendix to the chapter.)

USE OF QUANTITATIVE METHODS IN MANAGERIAL ACCOUNTING

In Chapter 1, we pointed out that an important feature of managerial accounting is its frequent interaction with other disciplines (including mathematics, statistics, and operations research). Until now, we have been using quantitative methods founded on relatively simple mathematics (e.g., cost-volume-profit analysis, high-low method of cost behavior determination, differential analysis, capital budgeting techniques, and profit variance analysis). This chapter describes how certain **quantitative methods** requiring more advanced mathematical and statistical techniques can be used in managerial accounting.

Using more sophisticated quantitative methods enables decision makers to better understand and handle the increasingly complex factors involved with many business problems. As the problems facing management become more complicated, managers must rely on more sophisticated decision-making approaches. When we apply a quantitative method, we build a model that is representative of the real-world conditions facing us in the decision-making process. We must be certain that the model developed is realistic, cost-effective, and based on accurate information. The managerial accountant's role in the model-building process is twofold:

1. The quantitative methods require a significant amount of relevant data (e.g., revenues, costs, and operating statistics) that must be provided by the managerial accountant. Thus, the managerial accountant must have a basic understanding of quantitative methods to determine what data are relevant.
2. The quantitative methods are useful for many managerial accounting functions involving planning, controlling, and decision making so an understanding of the methods enables the managerial accountant to be more effective in his or her own area.

The more sophisticated quantitative methods have been developed within the discipline of operations research (also called management science, decision science, and quantitative modeling). Since entire textbooks have been written about operations research, our attention will be restricted to a few quantitative methods that are particularly useful in managerial accounting. In addition, we will only consider these topics at a level requiring a basic proficiency in mathematics and statistics. Our goal here is only to introduce you to the use of the quantitative methods in managerial accounting. Let's begin the study of quantitative methods by examining decision making under uncertainty.

Objective 1:
Importance of quantitative methods

PART I UNCERTAINTY AS A FACTOR IN DECISION MAKING

Uncertainty is a condition of reality in today's business world since managerial decision making is future oriented. **Uncertainty** is defined as the possibility that

Objective 2:
Applying risk analysis to uncertainty

the actual future outcome from a decision may be different than the expected outcome. If we could predict the future with complete certainty, wrong decisions would only result from careless thinking or the failure to consider all relevant information. Unfortunately, certainty is rarely the case because the future is unknown when managers make decisions about such factors as:

1. Employment levels
2. Sales demand
3. Return on investments
4. Inventory purchases
5. Production schedules
6. Equipment replacement
7. Consumer reaction to a new product line

As an example of decision making under uncertainty, assume that we are attempting to forecast sales for the next budget period. We saw in Chapter 8 that a reliable sales forecast is crucial for an accurate budgeting application because almost all aspects of the budget depend on it. At the same time, the actual sales forecast will be influenced by market conditions and economic factors that are uncertain at the time the budget is being prepared. Suppose that we have reduced our expectations about the sales forecast to three possible outcomes—$1 million, $1.2 million, or $1.5 million. Which sales level should we choose as the foundation of the budgeting process? If we choose the wrong sales forecast, the entire budgeting process will be subject to costly errors that may adversely affect the profitability of the business.

USING RISK ANALYSIS TO MANAGE UNCERTAINTY

To manage uncertainty, decision makers can apply **risk analysis,** which involves assigning probabilities to the various outcomes possible. The **probability** of a particular outcome is the relative likelihood of it happening. As such, the probability of an outcome occurring is expressed as an index number between zero and one; a probability of .5 assigned to a particular outcome means that this outcome will occur approximately 50 times out of 100. For example, the probability of obtaining a head when flipping a fair coin is .5 because two equally likely outcomes (heads or tails) can occur.

Probabilities can be established on an objective basis or a subjective basis. When the decision involved is repetitive (e.g., inventory ordering), objective probabilities can be determined from either the analysis of historical data or the use of a theoretical probability distribution such as the normal distribution (a bell-shaped curve). Since many business decisions are nonrepetitive (e.g., a plant expansion), however, subjective probabilities often must be used because management cannot rely on previous experience to assess probabilities objectively.

The subjective form of probability involves the personal belief of the decision maker based on judgment, similar experiences, and an analysis of current operating conditions. This type of probability assessment is subjective because different managers may assign different probabilities to the same situation based on their personal beliefs.

Assume that we have considered the three sales projections mentioned above and have concluded that the following are realistic relative likelihoods of their occurrences during the next budget period:

Sales Forecast	Probability
$1,000,000	.2
1,200,000	.5
1,500,000	.3
All three sales levels	1.0

A basic feature of probability is that the relative likelihoods of the various outcomes must sum to one. This condition is satisfied for the three sales outcomes—distributed as .2 for sales of $1 million, .5 for sales of $1.2 million, and .3 for sales of $1.5 million. This case is an example of a discrete probability distribution because a specified number of sales outcomes (three in this case) are being considered. If the discrete approach is not realistic because an infinite number of outcomes are possible, a continuous probability distribution involving a range of outcomes may be used (e.g., a normal distribution).

Using these three probability assessments, we can determine the expected value of the sales forecast decision. The **expected value** is often used to make a decision because it is the best estimate for the possible outcomes. This is because the expected value is a measure of central tendency (location) that best characterizes or summarizes the probability distribution assigned to the outcomes. It is determined by summing the products of the outcomes multiplied by their respective probabilities. As such, the expected value is nothing more than the arithmetic mean using a weighted average approach with the probabilities applied as the weights.

Mathematically, the expected value (defined as $\bar{x}$) is computed as:

$$\bar{x} = \sum_{i=1}^{n} x_i p_i$$

where:

x_i = the various outcomes that may occur
p_i = the probabilities of the outcomes
n = the number of outcomes possible

Objective 3: Use of an expected value and a standard deviation

In the sales forecasting illustration, we can compute the expected value of sales as:

$$\bar{x} = \$1,000,000\,(.2) + \$1,200,000\,(.5) + \$1,500,000\,(.3)$$
$$= \$200,000 + \$600,000 + \$450,000$$
$$= \$1,250,000$$

The $1,250,000 expected value would represent a statistically reliable estimate of sales, given the probabilities assigned to the various outcomes. Since a single estimate for sales is usually selected to initiate the budgeting process, the expected value for sales is a logical target since it will occur on the average. As such, the expected value approach is a valuable tool when the decision maker faces uncertainty concerning future events.

To provide additional information about the extent of the risk involved with the use of expected value as a representative measure of the outcomes possible, we also can determine the amount of dispersion or spread around the expected value. The expected value will be the best estimate of the outcomes possible when the spread around it is minimal. In other words, the expected value is most reliable as an estimate when it is essentially the same as the different outcomes that may occur. The **standard deviation** (identified as "s") is the most commonly used measure of dispersion. It is the square root of the average of the squared deviations of the outcomes possible from their expected value, calculated as:

$$s = \sqrt{\sum_{i=1}^{n} (x_i - \bar{x})^2 \, p_i}$$

The standard deviation is used as an absolute measure of the risk associated with the dispersion around the expected value. A large standard deviation can signify high risk because the spread around the central tendency will be great, thus reducing the reliability of the expected value as being representative of the different outcomes possible. To illustrate what we mean by risk from the effect of dispersion, consider the following two sets of numbers, each of which has an expected value of 15. Set one consists of numbers 14, 15, and 16. Set two is comprised of numbers 5, 15, and 25.

If we use the mean of 15 to represent the first set, we would expect it to be an accurate representation of the three numbers because of the tight spread around the mean. In contrast, significant risk is associated with the use of a mean of 15 to represent the second set because the other two values are so different from the average value. Thus, dispersion as well as central tendency must be considered in making decisions under uncertainty. In the sales forecasting illustration, the standard deviation is computed as:

$$s = [(\$1,000,000 - \$1,250,000)^2(.2) + (\$1,200,000 - \$1,250,000)^2(.5)$$
$$+ (\$1,500,000 - \$1,250,000)^2(.3)]^{1/2}$$
$$= [(-250,000)^2(.2) + (-50,000^2(.5) + (250,000)^2(.3)]^{1/2}$$
$$= (\$325,000,000,000)^{1/2}$$
$$= \$180,278$$

What does the \$180,278 standard deviation tell us? It is a statistical measure of how wide the spread or dispersion is between the three sales estimates and their average. Suppose we have a second forecast with three sales estimates, an expected value of \$1,250,000, and a standard deviation of \$350,000. The larger standard deviation with the second forecast means it is more risky than the first forecast because greater dispersion is involved. Thus, the general rule with the standard deviation is that the larger it is, the greater the risk that the actual outcome will differ from the expected value.

If different expected values are involved in a decision-making situation, their relative risks cannot be evaluated by simply comparing their standard deviations. This problem can be overcome, however, by combining the expected value and the standard deviation to compute the coefficient of variation (defined as "v"). The **coefficient of variation** describes the degree of relative dispersion or spread from the expected value so it can be used to compare the risk associated with more than one set of outcomes. The coefficient of variation is computed as:

$$v = s/\bar{x}$$

When the coefficient of variation is near zero, we can be relatively certain that the actual outcome will be close to the expected value. As the coefficient of variation increases, the risk associated with the expected value as an estimate also rises because the dispersion around the central tendency is significant. In our illustration, the coefficient of variation is calculated as:

$$v = \$180,278/\$1,250,000$$
$$= .144$$

Since v is quite small, the expected value of $1,250,000 has a relatively low degree of risk as an estimate of sales for the next budget period.

USE OF A PAYOFF TABLE

The concept of expected value can be extended to the use of a payoff table that shows the profits or cost reductions associated with various combinations of the courses of action being considered by a decision maker and the outcomes that may occur. To illustrate, assume we are trying to decide whether we should expand a firm's production capacity so more finished products can be produced next year. At the present time, the firm's annual profit can range from $100,000 in a weak market to $300,000 in a strong market. The additional capacity will require significantly higher fixed costs that will be incurred regardless of the consumer demand for our products. If we knew for certain that the market demand for the products would be strong (resulting in a profit of $500,000), we would be justified in spending the additional money because of the increased profits involved. However, a weak market demand would lead to operating losses of $100,000 since the increased fixed costs would not be offset by higher sales volume.

Objective 4:
Evaluating payoff tables

A payoff table such as the one shown below can be constructed to show the profits associated with the courses of action and the various outcomes (often called states of nature) that can occur. The different profit estimates shown in the payoff table are based on relevant managerial accounting data. Each row of the payoff table represents a course of action being considered. The first row refers to the choice of expanding capacity and the second row consists of the choice of maintaining the existing capacity. The two columns represent the two possible outcomes—weak market and strong market.

The expected value of each course of action depends on the probability of each outcome occurring. Assume that we have compiled a great deal of information about the market conditions and have concluded that there is a 30% chance of a weak market and a 70% chance of a strong market, given a summary of economic forecasts made within and outside our firm.

		Outcomes	
		Weak Market	Strong Market
Probability of occurrence		.3	.7
Courses of Action	Expand capacity	($100,000)	$500,000
	Maintain capacity	$100,000	$300,000

The expected values of the two courses of action are calculated as:

$\bar{x}$ (Expand capacity) $= -\$100,000 \,(.3) + \$500,000 \,(.7)$
$\qquad = \$320,000$
$\bar{x}$ (Maintain capacity) $= \$100,000 \,(.3) + \$300,000 \,(.7)$
$\qquad = \$240,000$

Thus, we would be wise to expand the capacity because the expected payoff of that decision is $80,000 more ($320,000 − $240,000) than the alternative of keeping the existing capacity.

DETERMINING THE EXPECTED VALUE OF PERFECT INFORMATION

The payoff table analysis can be extended to estimate how much we should pay for additional information that will enable us to more accurately predict which outcome will occur. If we had perfect information, we would know which of the outcomes will occur and be able to make the right decision. That is, we would convert uncertainty to certainty with the perfect information. However, accumulating information is costly, and we must make sure that we do not pay too much for it. Although perfect information usually is not available, it does represent the most information we would be willing to buy because any additional information would be irrelevant. The amount we would be willing to pay for perfect information is called the expected value of perfect information. This amount defines the upper limit on how much we should pay for any additional information. The expected value of perfect information is calculated as:

Expected value with perfect information
− Expected value with existing information
= Expected value of perfect information

In the capacity expansion situation, a marketing research firm might be hired to study the market conditions more completely than we are able to on our own. Suppose that the marketing research firm can obtain perfect information that would guarantee a correct decision because we would know which outcome will occur. Note from the payoff table above that perfect information would tell us to maintain existing capacity in a weak market (earning a profit of $100,000) and expand capacity in a strong market (earning a profit of $500,000). Assuming the same probabilities of these two outcomes (30% and 70%), the expected value of perfect information can be calculated as:

$$\bar{x} \text{ (with perfect information)} = \$100,000\,(.3) + \$500,000\,(.7) = \$380,000$$
$$\bar{x} \text{ (with existing information as computed earlier)} = \underline{\$320,000}$$
$$\bar{x} \text{ (of perfect information)} = \underline{\$\ 60,000}$$

Consequently, the difference between the expected value with perfect information ($380,000) and the expected value with the existing information calculated earlier ($320,000) is the expected value of perfect information or $60,000. We should not pay more than the $60,000 for any additional information because it would not be worth the additional costs. If the cost of additional information is less than $60,000, we would have to estimate how much the information would benefit us in assessing the probabilities of the outcomes possible. Techniques are available to evaluate the value of imperfect information but they are beyond the scope of this textbook.

PART II APPLYING STATISTICAL COST CONTROL

**Objective 5:
Using statistical
cost control**

In Chapter 10, we introduced the concept of a control chart that can be used to monitor the significance of standard cost variances. Management judgment was used to establish the upper and lower limits of the control chart. Now, however, we will briefly examine how statistical techniques provide a more formalized basis for setting the control limits. Our objective in statistical cost control is to statistically differentiate between random and nonrandom fluctuations instead of relying on management judgment to do so.

Remember from Chapter 10 that random fluctuations are the result of chance and are *not* controllable by management. In contrast, nonrandom fluctuations require management attention because they are abnormal and should be investigated to see if they can be corrected. The random fluctuations can be statistically isolated within the upper control limit and the lower control limit of a control chart. The advantage of the statistical approach is that it eliminates the need for management judgment and potentially arbitrary decision rules about what is a significant variance.

The upper and lower control limits of a statistical cost control chart are developed using random samples drawn from the cost performance involved. This approach is especially useful when we are utilizing a standard cost system based on attainable standards. Each standard can be thought of as an expected value because some of the actual cost results are expected to be above and some to be below the standard. We need to know two things about each of the samples drawn:

1. The mean or expected value and
2. The amount of dispersion around the mean.

Even when small samples of four or five outcomes are selected, the Central Limit Theorem, a statistical concept, tells us that the **sample means** will be approximately normally distributed (in the form of a bell-shaped curve). Larger samples may produce an even closer fit to the normal probability distribution but may not be worth the extra cost involved. The use of the normal distribution is fundamental to statistical control because it provides the basis for setting the control limits, which define the range of random fluctuations from the average cost involved.

This approach avoids the arbitrary rules associated with management judgment in separating random and nonrandom variances. To illustrate how statistical cost control can be used, we will use $\bar{x}$ to define the mean of an individual sample and $\bar{\bar{x}}$ as the overall sample mean (the average of the individual sample means). It can be shown that the following relationships between an overall sample mean value and the related standard deviation approximately define the corresponding areas of a normal distribution:

$$\bar{\bar{x}} \pm 1s = 68\% \text{ of the area under a normal curve}$$
$$\bar{\bar{x}} \pm 2s = 95\% \text{ of the area under a normal curve}$$
$$\bar{\bar{x}} \pm 3s = 99.7\% \text{ of the area under a normal curve}$$

Since sample means in general are normally distributed, we will expect 997 observations out of 1,000 to fall within the area represented by the overall sample mean $\bar{\bar{x}}$ (as the best estimate of the population mean) plus or minus three sample standard deviations. In other words, only three of the 1,000 sample means would be expected to fall outside this range because of random behavior. Thus, with upper and lower control limits at three standard deviations from the overall average of the sample means on a control chart, a sample mean outside the control limits is highly unlikely to be the result of random fluctuations.

The calculations involved with s, the sample standard deviation, are very tedious but can be avoided by using the sample range (r) as a substitute. The **sample range** provides a satisfactory estimate of the amount of dispersion involved when small samples are selected. The range is simply the difference between the highest and lowest values obtained in a given sample. To use the range, we need a way to relate it to the sample standard deviation for the determination of control chart limits. Fortunately, tables that provide the information needed to convert from a certain number of sample standard deviations to an average range are readily available in statistical textbooks. For example, the factors required to set the control limits of three standard deviations for samples of various sizes are:

Sample Size	Factor
4	.73
5	.58
6	.48
7	.42

Assume that we have selected a sample size of five and control limits of plus or minus three standard deviations for statistical cost control. Our control limits are established as:

$$\text{Upper limit} = \bar{\bar{x}} + .58 \text{ (average range)}$$
$$\text{Lower limit} = \bar{\bar{x}} - .58 \text{ (average range)}$$

In other words, the control limits are based on the overall mean of the samples selected plus or minus their average range ($\bar{r}$) multiplied by the factor required for a sample of five. When these limits are used, we would expect 99.7% of the sample means related to the actual cost performance to fall within the limits. Therefore, if we find one that is outside the control limits, it is a signal that the variance involved is likely to be significant because an out-of-control state is indicated.

Let's see if we can apply what we have learned by developing a simple cost control chart for a company that has established what it considers to be an attainable standard of about 8 hours (the expected value of the labor performance) for each unit of output produced. The firm sets the control limits at three standard deviations, and we have selected four samples with five outcomes of the actual labor performance in each sample. The sample results, along with their sample means and sample ranges, are shown in Figure 15-1.

The overall sample mean of the samples is computed by summing the sample means and dividing the total by four. The average range is determined by adding the four ranges and dividing by four. We can establish the upper and lower limits for a control chart by combining the overall sample mean and average range with the factor required for a sample size of five as follows:

Figure 15-1
Sample Data for Hours Worked per Unit of Output

Sample	Outcomes of Direct Labor Hours per Product					Sample Mean	Sample Range
	1	2	3	4	5		
1	7.1	8.4	8.6	7.9	8.1	8.02	1.5
2	8.3	7.6	7.8	8.2	7.2	7.82	1.1
3	8.9	7.7	7.9	8.7	8.3	8.30	1.2
4	7.9	8.1	8.3	8.7	8.2	8.24	.8
Overall sample mean ($\bar{\bar{x}}$)						8.10	
Average range ($\bar{r}$)							1.15

$$\text{Upper limit} = 8.1 + .58\,(1.15) = 8.77$$
$$\text{Lower limit} = 8.1 - .58\,(1.15) = 7.43$$

These control limits can be used to establish the statistical cost control chart shown in Figure 15-2. By plotting the four sample means on the chart, we see that they are within the control limits. Thus, we conclude that the labor time required to produce the products is in control and the only variation is caused by random fluctuations that are uncontrollable by management.

PART III INVENTORY MANAGEMENT

BASIC CONSIDERATIONS OF INVENTORY MANAGEMENT

One of the most difficult problems facing the management of a merchandising or manufacturing firm is *effectively planning and controlling inventory.* Even a service operation such as a hospital must determine what kind of supplies inventory to maintain and how much of it is necessary. In many businesses, inventory is by far the largest investment in current assets, so it will have a significant impact on the earnings performance. The dependence on external sources at the input (supplier) and output (customer) ends of the inventory flow complicates inventory management. Uncertain consumer demand, unreliable suppliers, competition, obsolescence, limited working capital, strikes, and transportation problems are factors that significantly affect the inventory policy of a business.

The major objective of effective inventory management is determining and maintaining an optimal amount of inventory at all times. Too much inventory can result in unnecessary inventory carrying costs (e.g., insurance, handling, taxes, opportunity cost for the funds invested, and obsolescence). Conversely, an inventory level that is too low can lead to lost sales, production schedule disruptions, lost quantity discounts, and extra transportation charges. As a result, the optimal inventory level is between the extremes of too much and too little inventory. The many complicating factors related to the two extremes can quickly overwhelm inventory decision making based on judgment, experience, or trial-and-error procedures—thus resulting in costly mistakes for the business. More sophisticated inventory management techniques in the form of quantitative methods often are used to systematically evaluate the factors and conditions facing the decision maker. Next, we will examine the basic features of one of the most commonly used inventory management techniques called a fixed order quantity model.

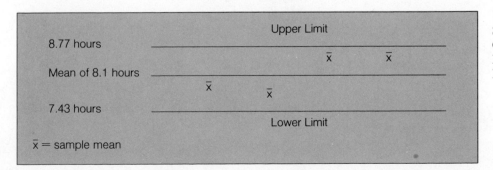

Figure 15-2
Statistical Cost
Control Chart for
Direct Labor
Hours

FUNDAMENTAL FEATURES
OF A FIXED ORDER QUANTITY MODEL

**Objective 6:
Managing
inventory with a
fixed order
quantity model**

Two basic decisions must be made with a fixed order quantity model:

1. How much inventory should a firm order with each order?
2. When should the order be placed?

An order may be placed to purchase the inventory from an outside supplier or to be manufactured by a firm's own production operation.

The first question is answered by determining the **economic order quantity (EOQ)**, which is the order size that will result in minimum total annual costs for the inventory involved. Once the EOQ is computed, that same amount is selected every time the firm places an order.

The second question is answered by computing the reorder point (RP), which is an adequate amount of inventory that should be on hand to satisfy the consumer demand for the related products until the new order is received. The time period between the placement of an order and the receipt of the related inventory is called the lead time. Consequently, the inventory ordering process with a fixed order quantity model operates in the following way. Once the stock of inventory declines to the RP, an order amounting to the EOQ is immediately placed. During the lead time, the firm uses the inventory included in the RP to satisfy consumer demand. Theoretically, as the firm is about to run out of the RP inventory, the latest order is filled and enough inventory is available until the next RP. The inventory ordering process with a fixed order quantity model is shown schematically in Figure 15-3.

ECONOMIC ORDER QUANTITY DECISION

**Objective 7:
Considerations of
an order quantity
decision**

What costs must be minimized in the EOQ decision? In general, the total costs associated with the inventory can be expressed as:

Total acquisition cost + Total ordering cost + Total carrying cost

The total acquisition cost is simply the number of units acquired (purchased or produced) multiplied by their unit cost. Unless quantity discounts are involved (a possibility we defer to more advanced study), the total acquisition cost will not be affected by the size of the order selected. That is, a certain number of units are required each year, and their total acquisition cost will be

Figure 15-3
Inventory Ordering
Process

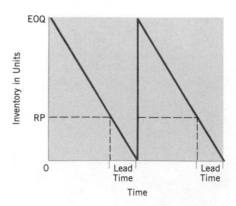

the same whether they are acquired in one order or in several orders placed during the year. Thus, the acquisition costs of the inventory are irrelevant to the choice of order size.

The two relevant costs for purposes of determining EOQ are (1) the total ordering costs and (2) the total carrying costs. The ordering costs include such incremental costs as the clerical costs needed to prepare and implement a purchase order or production order, setup costs associated with a related production process, costs incurred to receive and inspect the inventory, and data processing costs required to record the transactions. The ordering cost function will increase with the number of orders placed.

The carrying costs are those costs incurred because a firm maintains inventory balances. The opportunity cost of the funds invested in inventory, interest charges, storage space rent, taxes, handling charges, obsolescence, and insurance are examples of carrying costs. As the inventory level increases, the total carrying costs also increase.

Note that the two relevant costs, ordering and carrying, move in opposite directions. If large inventories are maintained, ordering costs will be low because the firm will seldom order. However, the carrying costs will be high because of the large inventory balances. If low inventory balances are maintained with a relatively small carrying cost, the firm will have to order frequently so the order costs will be large. We can visualize the trade-off between carrying costs and ordering costs in Figure 15-4.

As a result of this trade-off, we must carefully consider both of these relevant costs for a specific case and select an EOQ with the minimal total annual inventory costs. Once the ordering costs and carrying costs are identified, EOQ formulas are available for different operating conditions. The most basic case involves several limiting assumptions such as:

1. No quantity discounts.
2. The inventory is used at a relatively constant rate.
3. Demand for the inventory can be accurately estimated.
4. The entire inventory order is received at the same time.

The total cost function for the ordering and carrying costs is established as:

$$TC = D/Q \, (A) + Q/2 \, (I)$$

where:

TC = the total annual costs of ordering and carrying the inventory
D = annual demand
Q = order quantity
A = order cost per order
I = annual cost of carrying one unit of inventory

The annual demand for the inventory (D) divided by the order quantity selected (Q) is equal to the number of times orders are placed each year. If this result is multiplied by the cost per order, the result is the total ordering costs for the annual period. Since we assume that the inventory is used at a constant rate, the average inventory on hand at any time is $Q/2$. When we multiply the average inventory by the annual cost of carrying one unit of inventory, the total annual carrying costs are determined.

To minimize the total annual costs associated with the inventory decision, the point at which the total cost function is at its minimum (as presented in

Figure 15-4
Inventory Cost
Functions

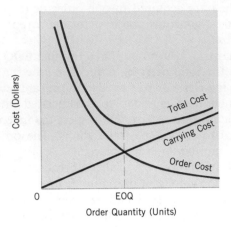

Figure 15-4) must be found. It can be shown with differential calculus that the minimum point on the cost function defining EOQ is:

$$EOQ = \sqrt{\frac{2DA}{I}}$$

To illustrate the use of this formula to determine an EOQ, assume the following facts:

$$D = 1,000 \text{ units of inventory}$$
$$A = \$8.10 \text{ per order}$$
$$I = \$2.00 \text{ per unit of inventory}$$
$$EOQ = \sqrt{\frac{2\,(1,000)\,(\$8.10)}{\$2}} = \sqrt{8,100} = 90 \text{ units}$$

If carrying costs are changed to $.50 in this case, EOQ is:

$$EOQ = \sqrt{\frac{2\,(1,000)\,(\$8.10)}{\$.50}} = \sqrt{32,400} = 180 \text{ units}$$

Assume instead that the ordering costs are $2.50 and the carrying costs are $2 with annual demand remaining at 1,000 units. EOQ is computed as:

$$EOQ = \sqrt{\frac{2\,(1,000)\,(\$2.50)}{\$2}} = \sqrt{2,500} = 50 \text{ units}$$

Thus, we can see that with an assumed demand of 1,000 units, the EOQ decision depends on the relationship between the ordering costs and the carrying costs. If the ordering costs are high relative to the carrying costs, large amounts should be ordered. In contrast, if the carrying costs are high compared with the ordering costs, a firm should order often to minimize the carrying costs. In the basic EOQ model used here, the EOQ point occurs where the ordering costs are equal to the carrying costs (see Figure 15-4).

REORDER POINT DECISION

**Objective 8:
Considerations of
a reorder point
decision**

The second major decision that must be made with the fixed order quantity model involves the right time to place an order—that is, the **reorder point (RP).** If instantaneous supply were always available, the reorder point would not be a critical factor. The decision maker would simply initiate the receipt of the EOQ by ordering from a supplier as the existing stock is exhausted. This ideal situation seldom exists in today's business world, and careful consideration must be given to the length of time (called the **lead time**) required between the placement of an order and the receipt of the related inventory. Customer demand during the lead time must be critically analyzed so the firm will have a satisfactory supply of inventory on hand when the order is placed.

Our coverage of the reorder point decision assumes that the lead time involved with different orders is constant instead of fluctuating. This is an important assumption because customer demand during lead time is treated as a variable that changes from order to order. If the lead time is also allowed to be a variable, we would have two closely related variables that would have to be estimated concurrently with a simulation technique. This complication does not arise when the lead time is held constant — a reasonable assumption for many businesses that have predictable delivery schedules. Otherwise, the interaction between lead time and customer demand must be simulated. Two factors must be considered in determining the reorder point:

1. An estimate of customer demand during lead time, and
2. The amount of safety stock kept on hand when the order is placed in case the actual demand exceeds the estimate.

Safety stock is simply the reorder point we choose less our best estimate of customer demand during lead time.

In establishing the reorder point, we must accept the fact that a business seldom operates with a highly predictable demand for its products during a specific period. This issue was discussed in Chapter 8 when we mentioned the difficulties associated with sales forecasting. Numerous uncontrollable variables such as consumer behavior, general economic conditions, competition, and technology greatly hinder management's ability to predict accurately the amount of inventory that will be demanded during lead time. The uncertainty involved, however, can be changed to a case of risk by assigning a probability distribution to the demand during lead time.

The arithmetic mean has certain statistical properties that enable us to call it a maximum likelihood estimator under most conditions. This simply means that it is the *best estimator* of several related values with which we are concerned. Thus, in the reorder point decision, the mean customer demand during lead time will be used as the estimate of the actual usage later experienced.

Since the actual usage will exceed the central tendency much of the time (some of the actual results will be above the mean while others will be below it), a safety feature — called safety stock — must be added to reduce the possibility of running out of inventory if actual usage exceeds the average amount forecast. There are a number of ways to determine the best amount of safety stock. The basic issue with the choice of a safety stock level is the same one we must consider with inventory in general. That is, carrying safety stock costs money, and we do not want to keep any more inventory than we have to. Ideally, the best safety stock level is the one for which the cost of carrying an additional unit is equal to the expected cost of stocking out of a unit.

This analysis requires a significant amount of relevant cost data that may be difficult to accumulate so many firms use a probabilistic approach to establishing a satisfactory safety stock level. Management simply estimates how often the firm can afford to stockout without formally assigning costs to that possibility. The probability of a stockout is dependent on the probability distribution that is applied to the customer demand during lead time. This probability distribution may be based on past performance data (called an empirical distribution) or the assumption that demand during lead time will approximate some theoretical distribution such as a normal function.

To illustrate how probabilities can be used to establish a proper level of safety stock, assume that (1) a sample of data was taken from the last 30 times we ordered and (2) the actual demand during lead time occurred with the frequencies shown in the second column of Figure 15-5. Assume further that a sample size of 30 is sufficient, but statistical methods are available to determine how large the sample should be. Note that the actual demand ranged from a low of 50 units to a high of 57 units. The frequencies refer to the number of times we experienced each of the actual usages.

The third column of Figure 15-5 shows the relative frequencies for each demand level. The relative frequency of a given demand is its frequency divided by the sample size of 30. As such, the relative frequency is the probability of a given demand occurring. For example, the probability of an actual demand of 50 units is 4/30 since we have experienced that demand four times out of the 30 times sampled. We can convert the relative frequencies into cumulative frequencies as shown in the fourth column. The cumulative frequency of a given demand level is the total relative frequencies of all actual usages that are less than or equal to the demand level we are considering. For example, the cumulative frequency of a demand of 55 units is 27/30, or the sum of the relative frequencies of usages of 50, 51, 52, 53, 54, and 55. Thus, the probability of an actual demand of 55 or less is .9 (27/30). These cumulative frequencies will be used to establish probabilistic limits for safety stock.

Given our sample of 30 orders, the mean demand can be computed as our estimate of actual usage during the lead time related to the next order we will place. Using the formula for expected value we introduced earlier, the mean demand is computed as:

$$\bar{x} = \sum_{i=1}^{8} x_i p_i$$

$$\bar{x} = 50 \,(4/30) + 51 \,(3/30) + 52 \,(3/30) + 53 \,(8/30) + 54 \,(7/30)$$
$$+ \, 55 \,(2/30) + 56 \,(2/30) + 57 \,(1/30)$$
$$= 53$$

Figure 15-5
Analysis of Actual
Demand During
Lead Time

Actual Demand in Units Ordered	Frequency	Relative Frequency	Cumulative Frequency
50	4	4/30	4/30
51	3	3/30	7/30
52	3	3/30	10/30
53	8	8/30	18/30
54	7	7/30	25/30
55	2	2/30	27/30
56	2	2/30	29/30
57	1	1/30	30/30
Totals	30	30/30	

The mean demand during lead time is 53 units so this is used as the best estimate of demand each time an order is placed. The final step is determining the amount of safety stock that should be on hand when an order is placed. If we decide not to carry any safety stock, the reorder point—the mean demand — is 53. Figure 15-5 shows that we would expect to stockout 12 out of every 30 times we order (40% of the time). The reason is that the cumulative frequency of 53 units is 18/30 so 30/30 less 18/30 is equal to 12/30—the probability of actual demand exceeding the mean.

It is unlikely that management would be willing to accept such a high likelihood of stocking out, but how much risk would management be willing to take? There is no simple answer to this question because management philosophies, industry conditions, and customer attitudes all dictate different policies concerning the risk of a stockout. If management wants to be certain a stockout will not occur, the reorder point should be 57 units. This means that four units of safety stock would be maintained (the reorder point less the mean demand of 53 units). By reducing the safety stock below four units, the chance of stocking out is increased accordingly.

The probabilistic approach gives management the opportunity to select the risk level with which it is comfortable. For example, if management decides that stocking out 10% of the time is acceptable, the reorder point would be established at 55 units with two units of safety stock. The probabilistic approach can be extended to a more complete analysis by evaluating the cost of carrying a unit of safety stock and the cost of a stockout.

USE OF THE ABC METHOD

As we have seen, the use of an inventory method such as the fixed order quantity model requires a significant amount of management time and managerial accounting information in order to be effective for a particular inventory item. Many firms stock thousands of inventory items so an attempt to perform this sophisticated analysis for each item would be too time consuming and too costly. This problem can be overcome by adopting a policy with which more control is exercised over the most expensive inventory items. The **ABC method,** which is used to classify inventory into cost categories according to the average annual usage multiplied by the related unit price, is an example of this approach.

Class A items are the *highest-dollar* category made up of few items and high prices. Most firms find that a small number of items (10% or less) account for a significant portion of the total inventory investment (80% or more). Class A items must be controlled effectively with a sophisticated approach, such as a fixed order quantity model, because of their relative importance.

Class B items are the *intermediate-dollar* category. Class C items are a large percentage of the total items but a *small percentage* of the total inventory investment. The Class B items would be given less attention than the Class A items in the inventory decision making, and the Class C items would receive the least amount of managerial concern because there are so many of them and their dollar amounts are insignificant. If necessary, other categories (D, E, and so on) can be added to provide a more effective classification of a particular firm's inventory. Computer programs are readily available to furnish the data processing capability required to divide the total inventory into an ABC breakdown. An example of an ABC approach is shown in Figure 15-6.

Objective 9: Importance of ABC method

Figure 15-6
ABC Inventory
Classification

Category	Number of Items	% of Total	Cost*	% of Total Cost
A	2,000	10	$ 81,000	81
B	5,000	25	11,000	11
C	13,000	65	8,000	8
Totals	20,000	100	$100,000	100

* (average usage × unit price)

PART IV LINEAR PROGRAMMING

DESCRIPTION OF LINEAR PROGRAMMING

Objective 10:
Basics of linear
programming

Linear programming (L.P.) is a mathematical technique used to determine the best allocation of scarce resources. Examples of the many ways L.P. is used in businesses are:

1. Determining the best product mix.
2. Developing production schedules.
3. Choosing optimal purchasing arrangements.
4. Dividing an advertising budget among the various media.
5. Selecting the best transportation routes for products produced in multiple plants.
6. Identifying the size of the most efficient labor force.
7. Making resource allocations during the master budgeting process.

To facilitate the discussion of linear programming in this chapter, we will restrict our attention to its application in product mix decisions, which is one of its most common uses. In Chapter 7, we saw that scarce resources and other limiting factors must be considered carefully when we determine the most profitable product mix. These limitations are called constraints in an L.P. model, and management tries to maximize their utilization. When multiple products and multiple constraints are being evaluated, linear programming provides a systematic way to deal with the complexities involved.

Four common characteristics must prevail to have a problem that is solvable with linear programming:

1. The problem must have an **objective function** (what the firm wants to accomplish) that can be maximized or minimized.
2. The problem must involve multiple variables (e.g., products) that might be chosen.
3. The problem must have constraints that are considered simultaneously.
4. All relationships involved must be linear.

As such, a linear programming model consists of maximizing or minimizing a linear objective function subject to a series of **linear inequalities** (representing the constraints). In developing a reliable linear programming application, we must carefully define the type of managerial accounting information that is required. The objective function is usually expressed as either the maximization of the contribution margin or the minimization of the variable costs involved. In most cases, fixed costs are irrelevant since they are unavoidable costs in decisions concerning resource allocations. That is, the fixed costs are ignored because they will not change regardless of what decision is made concerning a specific resource allocation. Therefore, the cost behavior analysis discussed in Chapter 5 is a fundamental part of developing a linear programming model.

GRAPHIC METHOD OF LINEAR PROGRAMMING

Relatively simple linear programming applications can be performed either graphically or mathematically. A **graphic solution** is really only feasible when two variables are being considered because we need an axis on a graph for each variable, thus limiting our analysis to two-dimensional space for all practical purposes. It is possible, but impractical, to develop a three-dimensional graph because few people can draw in three-dimensional space. When more than two variables are involved, a mathematical form of linear programming, called the simplex method, is utilized. This method (1) avoids the limitations of two-dimensional space and (2) provides a systematic way to determine an optimal solution to an L.P. problem. The **simplex method,** which is based on matrix algebra, is discussed in the appendix at the end of this chapter. The graphic method will be illustrated below.

Objective 11: Constructing a graphic linear programming model

Assume that the Calc-Right Company produces two types of electronic calculators, a Deluxe model that has memory and a Standard model without memory. The firm operates two production departments, the Wiring Department and the Assembly Department. Management of the Calc-Right Company wants to know the optimal mix of Deluxe and Standard calculators, given the following facts:

	Deluxe Calculator	Standard Calculator
Contribution margin per unit	$16	$12
	Wiring Department	**Assembly Department**
Production utilization in hours:		
Deluxe model	8	4
Standard model	4	6
Total hours available	12,000	8,400

Our task is to determine the number of Deluxe models and the number of Standard models that will utilize the 12,000 hours available in the Wiring Department and the 8,400 hours in the Assembly Department in a way that produces the maximum total contribution margin from the two products. These available hours are the company's scarce resources. Mathematically, the problem can be stated as:

$$\text{Maximize } Z = \$16D + \$12S \quad (1)$$

subject to:

$$8D + 4S \leq 12{,}000 \quad (2)$$
$$4D + 6S \leq 8{,}400 \quad (3)$$
$$D \geq 0 \quad (4)$$
$$S \geq 0 \quad (5)$$

where:

Z = the total contribution margin
D = units of the Deluxe model
S = units of the Standard model

Equation (1) is the objective function we want to accomplish. That is, we want to maximize the total contribution margin represented by \$16 for each Deluxe model and \$12 for each Standard model. Inequalities (2)–(5) are the constraints within which we must achieve the objective function. Eight hours of Wiring Department time are required for one Deluxe model (D) and four hours are needed for a Standard model (S). To finish the products, four hours of Assembly Department time are needed for a Deluxe model and six hours for a Standard model. Inequalities (4) and (5) simply restrict the production to zero or positive values since it would not be possible to produce negative units. As we will see later, these two inequalities are not actually plotted on a graphic linear programming model. Once we know the algebraic relationships for the objective function and the constraints, the optimal solution for the product mix decision can be determined graphically as shown in Figure 15-7 with the following steps:

1. Assign a product to each axis of the graph (any order will work; we have used D on the vertical axis and S on the horizontal axis).
2. Plot the two constraint inequalities as solid lines on the graph. The easiest way to do this is to treat the constraints as equalities and find the end points of the related lines (set one variable equal to zero and find the axis value for the second variable; then set the second variable equal to zero and find the axis value for the first variable). The end points for the two inequalities, (2) and (3), of the Calc-Right Company are computed as follows:

Inequality
(2)   If D is 0, $S = 12{,}000/4 = 3{,}000$ units (the end point on the S axis)
        If S is 0, $D = 12{,}000/8 = 1{,}500$ units (the end point on the D axis)
(3)   If D is 0, $S = 8{,}400/6 = 1{,}400$ units (the end point on the S axis)
        If S is 0, $D = 8{,}400/4 = 2{,}100$ units (the end point on the D axis)

3. Determine the **area of a feasible solution** that satisfies both constraint inequalities (the shaded area in Figure 15-7). Any solution to the product mix decision must be found within the shaded area because we do not have the capacity to produce product mix combinations outside it.
4. Plot the objective function as a dotted line on the graph. The easiest way to do this is to substitute a dollar value for Z that can be divided evenly by the two product contribution margins (\$16 and \$12) in the objective function equation. For example, we have used \$9,600 for the first dotted line in Figure 15-7 with end points determined as:

$$\$9{,}600 = \$16D + \$12S$$
$$D = 600$$
$$S = 800$$

5. Use a ruler to plot a second dotted line that is parallel to the line drawn in step 4 and also touches the furthest outside point of the shaded area's perimeter. This point, which occurs at point B in Figure 15-7, is the optimal solution in this case. The optimal solution is always at a point on the outside perimeter of the area of a feasible solution because our objective is to

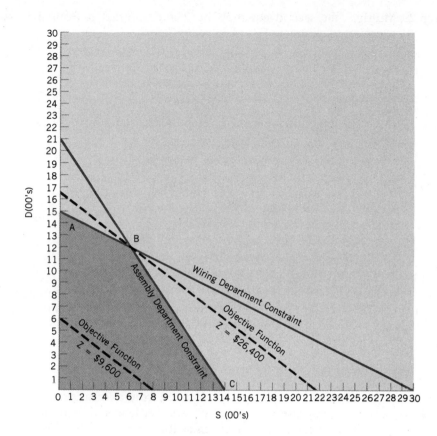

Figure 15-7
Linear
Programming—
Graphic Solution
(With Production
Constraints)

maximize the total contribution margin. In other words, the optimal solution occurs where the highest objective function line touches the outside perimeter of the shaded area. As long as the slope of the objective function is not the same as the slope of one of the constraint inequalities, we will have a single optimal solution at an axis point or an intersection of *constraint inequalities* (called *corner points*). If the slope of the objective function happens to be the same as that of a constraint inequality, we will have a number of optimal solutions along the related constraint inequality. This occurs when different combinations of products have the same total contribution margin.

6. Test the corner points (A, B, and C) of the area of a feasible solution to determine the related total contribution margin and prove that we have an optimal solution in step 5. The two constraint inequalities must be solved as simultaneous linear equations (just change the inequality signs to equality signs) to find the values for D and S at point B. The total contribution margins for the three points are computed as follows:

$$\text{Point A} \quad (D = 1,500) \quad 1,500 \, (\$16) = \$24,000$$
$$\text{Point C} \quad (S = 1,400) \quad 1,400 \, (\$12) = \$16,800$$
$$\text{Point B} -$$

Step 1 Identify the linear equations involved.

$$8D + 4S = 12,000$$
$$4D + 6S = 8,400$$

Step 2 Multiply the second equation by 2 and subtract it from the first equation to eliminate D and solve for S.

$$
\begin{array}{rl}
8D + & 4S = 12{,}000 \\
-\underline{8D + 12S} = \underline{16{,}800} \\
0D - & 8S = -4{,}800 \\
S = & 600
\end{array}
$$

Step 3 Insert S = 600 into the first equation of step 1 and solve for D.

$$
\begin{array}{rl}
8D + 4(600) = 12{,}000 \\
D = 1{,}200
\end{array}
$$

Step 4 Determine the total contribution margin for point B.

$$
\begin{array}{lll}
D = 1{,}200 & 1{,}200\ (\$16) = \$19{,}200 \\
S = \ \ 600 & \ \ 600\ (\$12) = \underline{\ \ \ 7{,}200} \\
& & \$26{,}400
\end{array}
$$

Consequently, the optimal solution is 1,200 units of the Deluxe model and 600 units of the Standard model with a total contribution margin of $26,400. Note that no other solution results in a total contribution margin as high as $26,400. Keep in mind, however, that the optimal solution will not always be found at the intersection of the constraint inequalities.

ROLE OF SHADOW PRICING

**Objective 12:
Applying the
shadow pricing
concept**

Additional important information can be obtained from a linear programming model. Management may also want to know whether it would be profitable to add to the capacity of a scarce resource such as the hours available for production in the Wiring Department. This profitability can be measured by the additional contribution margin that could be earned from the increased capacity, which is called the **shadow price** of the given scarce resource. A shadow price is the opportunity cost of not adding to the capacity because it is the contribution margin lost with that decision. If the shadow price exceeds the cost of the related expansion of capacity, it would be profitable to make the additional investment in the scarce resource. Therefore, shadow prices provide valuable information for management in making capacity decisions.

Shadow prices can be easily computed with the graphic approach to linear programming by:

1. Assuming a certain amount of additional capacity for a scarce resource.
2. Finding the total contribution margin with the increased capacity.
3. Subtracting the amount in part 2 from the total contribution margin with the original lower capacity level. The difference between the two total contribution margins is the related shadow price.

Let's illustrate the shadow pricing concept with the Calc-Right Company example. Assume that management wants to know the amount of contribution margin that could be earned by adding one hour of additional capacity in the Wiring Department. The easiest way to determine a shadow price with the graphic method is to hypothetically add several hours so the results can be visualized (as compared with a small increment of only one hour). For example, let's examine the optimal solution, as measured by total contribution margin, if we add 400 hours to the 12,000 hours of existing capacity of the department as shown in Figure 15-8. Note that the only change is in the constraint inequality for the Wiring Department where the 12,000 becomes 12,400. The optimal solution to the revised model is still found at point B in the following way:

Point A (D = 1,550) 1,550 ($16) = $24,800
Point C (S = 1,400) 1,400 ($12) = $16,800
Point B−   8D + 4S = 12,400
            4D + 6S = 8,400

Multiplying the second equation by 2 and subtracting it from the first equation:

$$
\begin{array}{r}
8D +\ 4S =\ \ 12{,}400 \\
-\ \underline{8D + 12S =\ \ 16{,}800} \\
\overline{0D -\ 8S = -\ 4{,}400} \\
S =\ \ \ \ \ \ 550
\end{array}
$$

8D + 4(550) = 12,400
        D = 1,275

(D = 1,275) 1,275 ($16) = $20,400
(S =   550)   550 ($12) = $ 6,600
                          $27,000

Consequently, the total contribution margin with the 400 additional hours of capacity in the Wiring Department is $27,000, or $600 more than we originally had with 12,000 hours. The contribution margin that can be earned with one additional hour of capacity is $1.50, computed as:

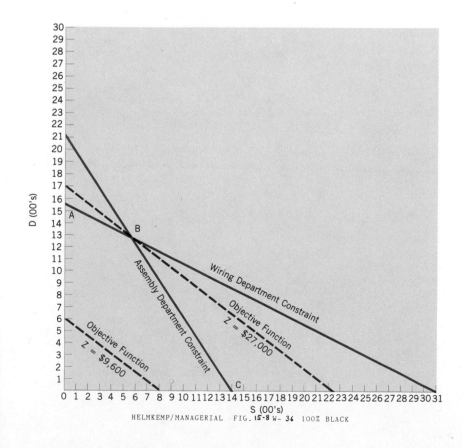

Figure 15-8
Linear
Programming—
Graphic Solution
(With Additional
Capacity Evalua-
tion)

HELMKEMP/MANAGERIAL   FIG. 15-8 W- 36   100% BLACK

Total contribution margin with the additional 400 hours (previous page)	$27,000
Total contribution margin with 12,000 hours (original solution)	− 26,400
Shadow price or opportunity cost of additional capacity	$ 600
Divided by the number of additional hours	400
Shadow price per hour of capacity	= $ 1.50

Therefore, it would be profitable for the firm to add to the capacity of the Wiring Department as long as the cost of doing so is less than $1.50 per hour and sufficient demand for the products exists.

INTRODUCTION OF A MARKETING CONSTRAINT

Often, the market will impose a constraint on the firm's ability to sell the number of units of a certain product. The constraint may be in the form of a maximum number of units or a minimum number of units. For example, the maximum number of units is simply the largest amount the market can absorb in a given period. These marketing constraints also can be handled effectively with linear programming. To do so, a constraint inequality is added for each relevant market condition to the model along with any production constraint inequalities. Assume that the Calc-Right Company has reason to believe that at most 500 Standard models can be sold. We would add another constraint inequality as follows and plot it on the graph as shown in Figure 15-9.

$$S \leq 500$$

Figure 15-9
Linear
Programming—
Graphic Solution
(With Production
and Marketing
Constraints)

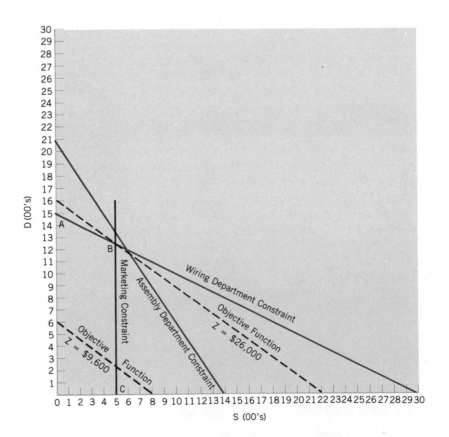

Note that our area of a feasible solution has been further restricted compared with the one we considered in Figure 15-7. The optimal solution without the marketing constraint was 1,200 Deluxe models and 600 Standard models. However, we now cannot sell the 600 Standard models so it would not be economically feasible to produce them. As such, the optimal solution shown in Figure 15-9 is point B, consisting of the 500 units of the Standard model and 1,250 units of the Deluxe model, computed as:

$$8D + 4S = 12,000$$
$$S = 500$$

Multiplying the second equation by four to solve for D:

$$8D + 4S = 12,000$$
$$- \underline{4S = 2,000}$$
$$8D + 0S = 10,000$$
$$D = 1,250$$
$$S = 500$$

Note also that the addition of the marketing constraint makes the Assembly Department production constraint ineffective or redundant because it does not influence the area of a feasible solution. The total contribution margin with a new optimal solution is $26,000 computed as:

Point A	(D = 1,500)	1,500 ($16) = $24,000
Point B	(D = 1,250)	1,250 ($16) = $20,000
	(S = 500)	500 ($12) = $ 6,000
		$26,000
Point C	(S = 500)	500 ($12) = $ 6,000

As a result of the marketing constraint, the contribution margin is lowered by $400 (from $26,400 in the original solution to the $26,000 shown above). The reason is we cannot reach the 600 units of the Standard model that are needed for the solution that optimizes the use of the production capacity.

PART V PROGRAM EVALUATION AND REVIEW TECHNIQUE (PERT)

BASIC CONCEPTS OF NETWORK ANALYSIS

A business decision maker often is concerned with projects involving numerous interrelated steps that must be performed in a sequential or parallel pattern. Construction of a building, performance of a research and development project, installation of computer equipment, new product development, the master budgeting process, and the implementation of a new accounting system are examples in which the decision maker must carefully consider multidimensional factors. **Program Evaluation and Review Technique (PERT)** provides a systematic procedure for planning and controlling such large-scale projects.

Objective 13:
Importance of a
PERT network

The objective in developing a PERT model is to diagram a network that represents the events and activities involved in the project under consideration. An event represents a stage of project accomplishment as of a given point in time. An activity is the action such as a work process or waiting time required to progress from one event to another. For example, if we are applying PERT to the master budgeting process, an event would be the completion of the sales

Objective 14:
Developing a
PERT network

forecast needed to prepare the sales budget, and one forecasting activity performed could be a marketing research study of consumer demand.

The primary concern in a PERT network is what is defined as the **critical path,** that is, the sequence of activities that must be performed within the estimated time to avoid a delay in the total project. As such, the critical path is the sequence of activities from the beginning of a project to its end with the longest completion time. Both time and costs can be included in a PERT network although we will only consider a time approach. The application of PERT, which is illustrated in Figure 15-10, consists of the following basic steps:

1. The development of the network showing the interrelationships between the events and the activities. The events in the network are shown as circles or rectangles in the network; the activities are shown as arrows. The network is structured by recognizing the beginning of the related project as event 1 and identifying the activities that must be performed to progress to the final event (the completion of the project that is often called the objective event). Alternatively, a backward approach may be used to reverse the process by beginning with the final event.

    In determining each event, we must ask three questions: (a) What events and activities must be accomplished before this event can occur? (b) What events and activities cannot be accomplished until this event occurs? (c) What events and activities can be undertaken concurrently with this event?
2. The estimation of the time requirements for the various activities.
3. The identification of the critical path on the network as well as the paths that have slack time. The critical path is the sequence of activities with the least amount of slack (slack is the amount of time an event can be delayed without affecting the completion time of the project).
4. The reduction of the critical path whenever possible to improve the overall project performance.

To illustrate the application of PERT, assume that the simplified network shown in Figure 15-10 is representative of the interrelationships of the events and activities we are concerned with.

USE OF PROBABILISTIC TIME ESTIMATES

One of the most important features of PERT is that time is built into the model on a probabilistic basis. After the network is established to the satisfaction of the decision maker, the individual or group responsible for each of the activities must determine the proper amounts for three time estimates:

1. **Optimistic Time** (o). The time the activity should take under perfect circumstances. It is so unlikely that we assume that it should only occur about one time out of 100.

Figure 15-10
PERT Network

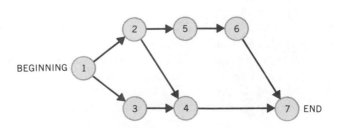

2. **Pessimistic Time (p).** The longest time period that could possibly be necessary under the most adverse operating conditions (excluding acts of God). Once again, this outcome is highly unlikely and the assumption is that it should only prevail in about one out of 100 cases.
3. **Most Likely Time (m).** The decision maker's projection of the most likely time required. If the activity were repeated numerous times, we would expect this outcome to occur most frequently.

In most PERT applications, we assume that a Beta probability distribution (a specific type of theoretical probability distribution) is a realistic description of the time required for the activities. It can be shown that a reasonably accurate approximation for the mean (identified as t_e) of a Beta probability distribution is:

$$t_e = \frac{o + 4m + p}{6}$$

We will use the mean as the best measure available for the central tendency of a probability distribution for each of the activity times involved based on the three time estimates—optimistic, pessimistic, and most likely. This approach is better than only considering the most likely time estimate because the extreme conditions (optimistic and pessimistic) are included. One of the unique features of a Beta probability distribution is that its specific shape is determined by the relationship of its mean and standard deviation. Although we will not consider the role of the standard deviation in this basic coverage of PERT, you should know that it provides useful information for assessing the risk associated with the activity time estimates involved.

Let's assume that the three relevant time estimates for each of the eight activities included in Figure 15-10 have been prepared by management as shown in Figure 15-11. We also have calculated the mean for each activity and the results are presented in Figure 15-11. To define a given activity, we use the event preceding it and the event succeeding it in numerical sequence.

We can now superimpose the expected times for each of the activities of the network as shown in Figure 15-12. The next step is to determine the critical path on the network as well as those paths that currently possess slack. The earliest date each event can be expected to occur is used for the calculation of the critical path. This period, defined as the earliest expected date (T_E), is computed as the summation of the individual t_e's on the longest path from the start

Activity	o	m	p	t_e
1–2	6	10	26	12
1–3	2	4	30	8
2–5	12	14	16	14
2–4	4	8	24	10
3–4	4	10	28	12
5–6	8	12	16	12
4–7	10	18	26	18
6–7	2	4	6	4

Figure 15-11
Activity Time in Weeks

Figure 15-12

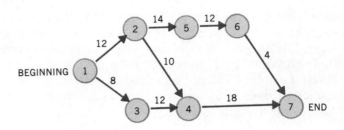

of the project to a given event. To determine T_E for a given event, we calculate t_e for all possible paths leading to the event we are considering and then select the longest path. For example, T_E for event 4 would be 22 weeks. Two paths are possible, 1-2-4 or 1-3-4, but the former is *longer* so it becomes T_E. We follow the same steps for each event in the network to obtain the results shown in Figure 15-13.

The next step in the computation of the critical path and slack paths is to determine the latest allowable time (T_L) for each event, which is the time period that will not create a delay in completing the project. If this time period is achieved for all events, the total project will be accomplished on time. We must assign a completion date to the final event before we calculate the various T_L's. The completion date may be established on the basis of (1) a contractural agreement, (2) management's goal, or (3) the beginning of a succeeding project. Thus, the date we select may be later than, prior to, or equal to the earliest expected time (T_E) for the project.

For illustrative purposes, we assume that $T_L = T_E = 42$ weeks. To calculate the T_L's for the events, we reverse the order of the process used for the T_E's. That is, we work backward through the network and calculate the T_L values by subtracting the summation of expected times (t_e's) for the activities on the longest path connecting the final event to a given event from the latest allowable time for completing the project. For example, given the project completion time of 42 weeks, T_L for event 2 would be 12 weeks [choosing the path with the longest time accumulation, we have $(42 - 4 - 12 - 14 = 12)$]. The same approach has been used to compute the other T_L values that are presented in Figure 15-14.

We can now determine the critical path, which is our main concern because on it we do not have any spare time or slack in meeting the overall completion date, from the network shown in Figure 15-14. We can compute slack for any event as $T_L - T_E$ since this represents the difference between the latest allowable time and the earliest expected time. Whenever the difference is 0, there is no slack for the related event. For example, the slack in event 4 would be two

Figure 15-13

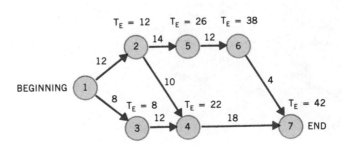

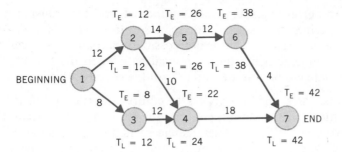

Figure 15-14

weeks, whereas that of event 5 would be 0. A complete listing of the slack values for the various events is shown in Figure 15-15.

Figure 15-15 shows that the critical path, which represents potential trouble spots because of the lack of spare time, is the sequence 1-2-5-6-7. The critical path always is the sequence of events that contains the greatest negative, least positive, or zero amounts of slack. In this case, the critical path contains zero slack because we originally set $T_L = T_E$. If T_L had been greater than T_E, we would have had the least amount of positive slack on the critical path. In contrast, if T_L had been less than T_E, the critical path would have contained the greatest amount of negative slack. The determination of slack in all cases provides the basis for a reliable evaluation of the relative-time importance of the various activities included in a project.

Once the critical path is known, we can select from three alternatives to minimize the problem of the time constraints involved:

1. Certain portions of the work on the critical path may be *eliminated*. In some cases, remedial tasks are not absolutely necessary and may be discarded to reduce the required time.
2. *Parallel action* may be possible instead of executing a planned sequential process. For example, the design of the second stage of a project would not normally begin until the testing of the first phase results is completed. In certain cases, however, both of these activities can be accomplished concurrently to save time. The possibility of wasted effort through necessary redesign must be closely evaluated if this alternative is selected.
3. The problem with the critical path may be reduced by applying *additional resources* to the related activities. Since slack time is available on other

Event	Slack ($T_L - T_E$)	Critical Path ($T_L - T_E = 0$)
2	0	x
3	4	
5	0	x
4	2	
6	0	x
7	0	x

Figure 15-15
Determination of
Event Slack and the
Critical Path

paths, resources (e.g., personnel, equipment, and materials) may be shifted from activities on a slack path to the critical path without any loss of project time. If such a shift is not possible, additional resources may be acquired for the activities on the critical path when the benefits from them are estimated to be commensurate with the costs involved.

In all three cases, the objective is to control the time problems associated with the critical path because it contains the least amount of spare time in the network. As such, PERT enables management to diagram the activities and events involved with a complex project and to anticipate problem areas before they develop.

SUMMARY

Quantitative methods are important managerial accounting tools based on mathematical and statistical techniques. A quantitative method is a model that is developed as being representative of the real world conditions facing a decision maker. Since uncertainty is a condition of reality in the business world, we must often rely on risk analysis using probabilities to evaluate future outcomes. The expected value and the related standard deviation provide useful information when probabilistic assessments are made. A payoff table can be constructed to probabilistically evaluate the outcomes of a given decision. Statistical cost control is performed by using statistical sampling techniques to construct a control chart. Sample means are used to distinguish between random and nonrandom fluctuations so management can decide which cost results require further investigation.

A fixed order quantity model provides an effective way to determine the most economical order quantity and the best reorder point in the management of inventory. The order quantity is chosen as a trade-off between the ordering costs and the carrying costs associated with the inventory. The reorder point is calculated as the mean demand during lead time plus a desired amount of safety stock. Many firms rely on the ABC method to classify inventory items on the basis of their relative investment so management can decide how much attention they deserve.

Linear programming is a mathematical technique used to determine the optimal utilization of scarce resources. To do so, an objective function is maximized or minimized subject to certain important constraints facing the decision maker. When two variables are being evaluated, a graphic form of linear programming can be used to determine the optimal solution to a specific problem. Shadow pricing is an important extension of linear programming that assists management in assessing the profitability of capacity expansion.

The Program Evaluation and Review Technique (PERT) enables management to effectively plan and control projects involving numerous interrelated steps. A network is developed to identify the pattern of activities and events that must be considered. Probabilistic time estimates based on the optimistic time, pessimistic time, and most likely time are developed for each activity that is to be performed. The critical path and the slack paths are evaluated to determine if the project can be finished on time and if any time reductions are possible.

APPENDIX: USE OF THE SIMPLEX METHOD

BASIC CONSIDERATIONS WITH THE SIMPLEX METHOD

The simplex method is an iterative process based on matrix algebra that systematically evaluates potential solutions to a linear programming problem until the optimal solution is found. The term "iterative process" means that it is repetitive; that is, the computational routine involved is repeated step by step until the optimal solution is identified. A major benefit of the simplex method is that each time the computations are performed, a better solution is found than the time before. Thus, we are guaranteed of always moving closer to the optimal solution.

Objective 15: Evaluating the basics of the simplex method

The simplex method has three major advantages over the graphic method:

1. It can handle any number of variables (e.g., products) instead of being restricted to two (or at most three) variables;
2. It can be easily programmed for computer processing to eliminate the tedious mathematical procedures that are otherwise involved; and
3. It provides important management information such as shadow prices directly from the model itself instead of requiring separate computations as we did with the graphic method.

Since computer programs are so readily available for a simplex method application, we will concentrate on the main factors involved in its problem formulation and in the interpretation of an optimal solution. We will defer many of the mathematical steps needed to move from one iteration to another one to a more advanced coverage of the simplex method. To illustrate the features of the simplex method, we will continue to use the information presented earlier in the chapter for the application of the graphic method in the Calc-Right Company case.

PROBLEM FORMULATION WITH THE SIMPLEX METHOD

The initial consideration of the problem formulation stage of the simplex method is identical to that of the graphic method. We want to identify the objective function as a linear equation and the subject-to constraints as linear inequalities. Recall that the objective function and constraints for the Calc-Right Company case are:

$$\text{Maximize } Z = 16D + 12S$$

subject to:

$$8D + 4S \leq 12{,}000$$
$$4D + 6D \leq 8{,}400$$
$$D \geq 0$$
$$S \geq 0$$

where:

Z = the total contribution margin in the objective function
D = units of a Deluxe model
S = units of a Standard model

The next step in the simplex method is to convert the production constraint inequalities into equalities (equations). These equalities are required for the algebraic procedures involved. (We do not have to make this conversion for the nonnegative constraints for D and S because they only serve as assumptions of the simplex procedure.) The conversion of the production constraint inequalities to equalities is accomplished with the addition of what are called slack variables (call them X and Y) to the two production constraints. A slack variable is nothing more than a measure of unused capacity that is added so we don't have to work with inequalities. Since the slack variables represent unused capacity, they would have a zero contribution margin when they are added to the objective function as follows:

$$\text{Maximize } Z = 16D + 12S + 0X + 0Y$$

subject to:

$$8D + 4S + X = 12{,}000$$
$$4D + 6S + Y = 8{,}400$$

To see how each of the slack variables represents unused capacity, assume that the firm chose not to produce any real products D or S. In that case, X would be 12,000 or the entire capacity of the Wiring Department and Y would be 8,400 or the entire capacity of the Assembly Department. The capacity of both departments is unused as indicated by the slack variables. In the initial setup of the simplex method, the first solution consists of slack only to give us a starting point that is consistent in all problems. Note that this is the origin of a graphic method application since no real products are produced when the entire capacity is unused. A simplex tableau, which is a matrix arrangement that provides a systematic accounting of the simplex procedures, is shown in Figure 15-16 with the problem formulation as the starting point of the simplex method application. Let's evaluate the key features of the tableau to see how it is constructed.

The Z row is nothing more than the objective function we want to maximize. D, S, X, and Y are the variables we are considering with only D and S representing real products. Note that just below the term "Mix" we present X and Y, the two slack variables. The variables in the mix position will always represent the solution for a given iteration. As we stated earlier, the initial solution consists of the two slack variables only. There will always be the same number of variables in a solution as there are equations in the tableau.

The two production capacities within which the firm must operate are shown in the Capacity column. In subsequent solutions, the production amounts selected for the real products will be shown in the same Capacity column. The

Figure 15-16
Initial Set-Up of
Simplex Tableau
for the Calc-Right
Company

Z		16	12	0	0	
	Mix	D	S	X	Y	Capacity
0	X	8	4	1	0	12,000
0	Y	4	6	0	1	8,400
	C	0	0	0	0	
	Z–C	16	12	0	0	

figures under D, S, X, and Y are nothing more than the values (called coefficients) required to produce each of the variables from the original equations. We can see that the initial mix does not produce a profit because a zero contribution is indicated for each of the slack variables (under the Z). We are now ready to evaluate other solutions to see if there is a better one. In effect, we are starting at the origin of a graphic method application and searching mathematically around the perimeter of the area of a feasible solution to find the product mix with the highest contribution margin.

The letter C refers to the cost of introducing a new variable into the solution mix. What would be the cost of adding one unit of D to the mix? The answer is 0 because we would lose eight units of X (slack with a contribution margin of $0) and four units of Y (slack with a contribution margin of $0). In other words, we are substituting a real product for slack time so that move would not cost anything. The same is true for S because one unit of it would replace four units of X and six units of Y, resulting in a cost of $0 since only slack time is eliminated. If we add one unit of a slack variable, we also must eliminate one unit of the same variable because of the one-to-one substitution shown in the tableau. This makes sense because the entire production capacity is unused in the initial tableau.

As a result of this analysis, we can say that the simplex tableau shows the rates of substitution between the variables in a given solution and the new variables that might be added. Our next step is to evaluate the opportunity cost of not having a variable in the solution $(Z - C)$. One additional unit of D will earn a profit of $16 ($16 − $0), and one additional unit of S will result in a profit of $12 ($12 − $0). The opportunity cost of each of the two slack variables is $0 ($0 − $0) because they do not produce any contribution margin. Since D has the highest opportunity cost, it should be added to the solution mix. Next, we must determine the maximum number of Deluxe models that can be introduced. We do so by considering the production requirements for D compared with the production constraints in the Wiring Department and the Assembly Department to see which one is the biggest constraint as follows:

Wiring Department constraint   — 12,000/8 = 1,500 units
Assembly Department constraint—   8,400/4 = 2,100 units

Therefore, 1,500 units of D are the maximum number we can introduce because the Wiring Department does not have enough capacity to add any more than that. To proceed to the second iteration, we would add the 1,500 units of D, thus replacing all the slack time available in the Wiring Department so X = 0 and X is dropped from the solution mix.

How much slack would be left in the Assembly Department after D is added? This question can be answered by comparing the total capacity in the Assembly Department with the amount needed to produce 1,500 units of D as follows:

	Hours
Total Assembly Department capacity	8,400
Capacity needed for 1,500 units of D (1,500 × 4)	6,000
Remaining capacity	2,400

The 1,500 units of D are multiplied by four because it takes four hours of Assembly Department time to produce one unit of D. To find the optimal solution to the problem, we would continue this analysis using a matrix algebra technique to change the values of the simplex tableau as we alter the solution mix until we arrive at the optimal answer. The simplex tableau with the optimal solution to the Cal-Right Company's product mix decision will be considered next so we can evaluate what kind of information the tableau provides.

INTERPRETATION OF OPTIMAL SOLUTION TABLEAU

Since we can rely on a computer program to take us efficiently and reliably from the problem formulation to the optimal solution, the interpretation of the final results is important to us in understanding the optimal solution and related information. The simplex tableau containing the optimal solution to the Calc-Right Company product mix decision is shown in Figure 15-17.

The optimal solution shown in Figure 15-17 is 1,200 units of D and 600 units of S. The total contribution margin involved can easily be determined by multiplying these quantities by the individual contribution margins of $16 and $12 for D and S, respectively. The result is a total contribution margin of $26,400, the same amount determined earlier with the graphic method.

How do we know that we have an optimal solution in Figure 15-17? The reason is that the $Z - C$ row tells us that there are no marginal gains to be found because the values are either 0 or negative. In other words, the introduction of a new variable to the solution mix would not be profitable because of the opportunity costs involved. The values shown in the D-S rows and D-S-X-Y columns represent the final rates of substitution that would prevail if we altered the optimal solution.

EXTENSION TO SHADOW PRICING

Shadow prices can be determined directly from the final simplex tableau. Remember from the graphic solution to this same problem shown earlier in this chapter that we calculated a shadow price of $1.50 per hour for the Wiring Department. Note in Figure 15-17 that $Z - C$ for X, the slack capacity of the Wiring Department, is $-1\frac{1}{2}$. If we were to introduce one unit of X into the solution, profits would be reduced by $1.50. If we had started with one hour less in the Wiring Department, our profits would be decreased by the same $1.50. Consequently, this line of reasoning tells us that if the capacity of the Wiring Department is increased by one hour, the total contribution margin will rise by $1.50, which is the shadow price involved.

As we can see in the final simplex tableau, the shadow price for the Assembly Department is $1 per hour. Thus, the addition of one hour of capacity in that department would increase profits by $1. Since no slack was included in the solution mix, we know that the capacity of both departments was fully utilized.

Figure 15-17
Simplex Tableau with Optimal Solution for the Calc-Right Company

	Mix	16 D	12 S	0 X	0 Y	Capacity
Z		16	12	0	0	
16	D	1	0	3/16	−1/8	1,200
12	S	0	1	−1/8	1/4	600
	C	16	12	1 1/2	1	
	Z − C	0	0	−1 1/2	−1	

Thus, if we want to produce more units than those included in the optimal solution, additional capacity will be required in both departments.

GLOSSARY

ABC METHOD. A technique used to classify inventory items on the basis of their relative investment (p. 579).

AREA OF A FEASIBLE SOLUTION. The area of a graphic linear programming model within which the optimal solution is found (p. 582).

CARRYING COSTS. Such incremental costs as the opportunity cost of funds invested in inventory, interest charges, storage space, insurance, and taxes incurred because a firm maintains inventory balances (p. 575).

COEFFICIENT OF VARIATION. An indicator of risk that is calculated by dividing the expected value into the related standard deviation (p. 568).

CONSTRAINT INEQUALITIES. Linear inequalities formalizing the constraints within which an optimal linear programming solution must be found (p. 580).

CRITICAL PATH. The sequence of activities from the beginning of a PERT network to its end with the longest completion time and minimal amount of spare time (p. 588).

ECONOMIC ORDER QUANTITY (EOQ). The best amount of inventory to order because it optimizes the trade-off between the related ordering costs and carrying costs (p. 574).

EXPECTED VALUE. The arithmetic mean using a weighted average approach with probabilities applied as the weights (p. 567).

GRAPHIC LINEAR PROGRAMMING. The visual display of the equations and inequalities involved in a linear programming problem that can be described with two-dimensional space (p. 581).

LEAD TIME. The time period between placing an inventory order and receiving it (p. 577).

LINEAR PROGRAMMING (L.P.). A mathematical technique used to determine the best allocation of scarce resources (p. 580).

MOST LIKELY TIME. The amount of time that should be required for a given activity in a PERT network more frequently than any other estimate (p. 589).

OBJECTIVE FUNCTION. An equation that describes what is to be maximized or minimized in a linear programming application (p. 580).

OPTIMISTIC TIME. The least amount of time a given activity in a PERT network could require (p. 588).

ORDERING COSTS. Incremental costs incurred to prepare, process, and record an inventory order (p. 575).

PESSIMISTIC TIME. The greatest amount of time a given activity in a PERT network could require (p. 589).

PROBABILITY. The relative likelihood of a given outcome occurring (p. 566).

PROGRAM EVALUATION AND REVIEW TECHNIQUE (PERT). A quantitative method used to plan and control projects with numerous interrelated steps (p. 587).

QUANTITATIVE METHOD. A model developed with mathematics and/or statistics to assist management in making effective decisions (p. 565).

REORDER POINT (RP). The measure of when an inventory order should be placed (p. 576).

RISK ANALYSIS. A probabilistic assessment of the outcomes possible in a particular decision (p. 566).

SAFETY STOCK. The amount of inventory maintained in excess of the expected demand during lead time when an inventory order is placed (p. 577).

SAMPLE MEAN. The average of the values chosen for a given sample (p. 571).

SAMPLE RANGE. The difference between the highest and lowest values of a sample (p. 571).

SHADOW PRICE. The opportunity cost of not adding to capacity that is determined with linear programming (p. 584).

SIMPLEX METHOD. A form of linear programming based on matrix algebra that optimizes an objective function subject to a series of constraints (p. 581).

STANDARD DEVIATION. A measure of the dispersion or spread around the expected value of several numbers (p. 568).

UNCERTAINTY. The possibility that the actual outcomes from a decision may be different than the expected outcomes (p. 565).

DISCUSSION QUESTIONS

1. Why are quantitative methods based on advanced mathematics or statistics often required in managerial accounting applications?
2. What is meant by uncertainty? How can we handle uncertainty in decision making?
3. What is meant by risk assessment? Apply this concept to your personal life.
4. Explain what is meant by the term "probability." How is it used in decision making?
5. What is expected value and how can we measure the amount of risk associated with a particular expected value as an estimate?
6. What is the coefficient of variation? How is it used in decision making?
7. Explain how a payoff table can be used as an important managerial tool.
8. Why is the concept of perfect information important to management?
9. What is statistical cost control? How is it combined with standard costs?
10. Why is the premise of a normal probability distribution important in the application of cost control measures?
11. Distinguish between the order quantity decision and the reorder point decision in inventory management.
12. What is the primary objective of sound inventory management?
13. What is meant by a fixed order quantity model? What kind of cost information is required for such a model?
14. What is lead time in the determination of a reliable reorder point?
15. Differentiate between ordering costs and carrying costs in an EOQ inven-

tory decision. How do each of these costs behave as a function of order size?

16. What are the two important factors that must be considered in the evaluation of a proper reorder point?
17. What is meant by the term "safety stock"?
18. How is the demand during lead time determined in a reorder point decision?
19. Why is the ABC inventory method such an important concept in the management of inventories? Would it be possible to have an ABCD approach? Explain.
20. What is linear programming? Identify a typical business problem that could be solved with linear programming.
21. What common characteristics are necessary for an effective linear programming application?
22. What is an objective function in a linear programming model? How are fixed costs typically treated in the determination of an objective function?
23. What is the graphic method of linear programming? Why is this method for all practical purposes limited to two variables?
24. Explain what is meant by a shadow price. Why is this an important consideration?
25. How is PERT used in the business world?
26. Distinguish between an event and an activity in the development of a PERT network.
27. What is the critical path and why is this an important consideration for management?
28. Explain how a probabilistic approach is taken to identify the time required for the activities in a PERT network.
29. Distinguish between the earliest expected time and the latest allowable time in a PERT application.
30. Once the critical path has been identified in a PERT network, what are typical management steps that can be taken to control the time problems involved?

EXERCISES

Exercise 15-1 Use of Expected Value

The Dart Company has collected the following information concerning the sales demand for one of its products with a selling price of $10 per unit and variable costs of $6 per unit:

Number of Units	Probability of Sales Demand
10,000	.10
11,000	.15
12,000	.25
13,000	.40
14,000	.05
15,000	.05

Required:
Compute the expected contribution margin for the firm.

Exercise 15-2 Determining Expected Value of Costs

The owner of the Campus Donut Shop is evaluating the purchase of a new donut-making machine. Two models are available: (1) a standard model with which a donut can be made at a variable cost of $.03 and (2) a deluxe model with a variable cost of $.01 per donut. The standard model can be leased for $1,200 per month whereas the deluxe model will cost $3,600 monthly. The number of donuts sold by the shop each month ranges from 108,000 to 144,000 with the following relative frequencies:

Number of Donuts	Relative Frequency
108,000	.15
120,000	.20
132,000	.55
144,000	.10

Required:
Based on the expected value of the costs involved, which of the two machines should be leased?

Exercise 15-3 Evaluating Expected Value and Risk

The Mawn Company is evaluating the purchase of a new machine. The expected net cash flows from the machine and the probabilities of their occurences are as follows:

Net Cash Flows	Probability
$ 6,000	.2
8,000	.1
9,000	.3
11,500	.2
15,000	.2

Required:
A. Compute the expected value, standard deviation, and coefficient of variation for the net cash flows.
B. Evaluate the amount of risk associated with this investment.

Exercise 15-4 Use of a Payoff Table and Expected Values

The Produce-Rite Company produces a perishable product with variable costs of $4 and a selling price of $10. Unsold units must be thrown away at the end of each month. Based on the operating performance of the past 50 months, the firm projects the following monthly demand for the product and related relative frequencies:

Number of Units	Frequency
1,000	5
1,100	15
1,200	15
1,300	10
1,400	5
	50

Because of the nature of the production process, the product must be manufactured in batches of 100 units.

Required:

A. Prepare a payoff table showing the actions management can take and the outcomes possible.
B. Based on the expected values of the payoff table, how many units should be produced?
C. What is the expected value of perfect information for the company?

Exercise 15-5 Risk Assessment and a Payoff Table

The sales manager of the Video Game Company is trying to evaluate which new electronic game to introduce next year—golf or baseball. The selling price of the golf game is significantly more than that of the baseball game. The sales manager believes that the state of next year's economy will have a major impact on the choice between the two products because of the different selling prices. Accordingly, he has developed the following probabilities for two possible economic outcomes:

Outcome	Probability
Strong	.6
Weak	.4

The total net cash flows expected from the two games for each economic outcome are:

	Strong	Weak
Golf	$180,000	$20,000
Baseball	90,000	60,000

Required:

A. Develop a payoff table for the choice between the electronic games.
B. Which game has the highest expected value of its net cash flows?
C. Which of the two games has the highest amount of risk as measured by the coefficient of variation?

Exercise 15-6 Use of a Statistical Control Chart

The Terry Company is evaluating the use of a standard cost system. The firm has recently experienced significant difficulties with labor costs. As part of the investigation of labor cost standards, the controller has sampled the hours required to assemble the components used for one of the firm's products, a stereo sound system. The sample data were collected for five finished products daily over a 10-day period as follows:

| | **Hours Required for Each Product** | | | | |
| | Sampled | | | | |
Day/Product	1	2	3	4	5
1	2	3	3	2	4
2	2	3	3	3	2
3	3	4	5	3	3
4	5	2	3	3	4
5	4	5	3	4	4
6	4	2	3	4	3
7	5	4	3	4	3
8	2	4	5	3	3
9	3	6	5	4	4
10	3	3	4	4	3

Required:

A. Calculate the overall sample mean and average range for the controller's sample data.

B. Define the upper and lower control limits based on three standard deviations.

C. Develop a control chart with three standard deviations and plot the sample results.

D. Are the labor hours sampled within the acceptable control limits?

Exercise 15-7   Basic Inventory Ordering Decision

The Sperry Company wants to determine the optimal order size for its major inventory item. The firm's accountant has collected the following facts:

Units required each year	30,000
Unit carrying cost per year	$ 600
Cost of placing an order	400

Required:

A. Calculate the firm's economic order quantity.

B. What will be the total annual ordering costs and carrying costs for the inventory?

Exercise 15-8   Using EOQ Analysis

The Hunt Company produces 10,000 blades annually for its lawn trimmer division. The blades are produced evenly throughout the year. The setup cost for a given production run for the blades is $40 and the cost incurred to carry one blade in inventory for the year is $.20.

Required:

A. What is the firm's EOQ for the blades?

B. How many times should the company produce the blades during the year?

C. What will be the total annual setup (ordering) costs and carrying costs for the inventory?

Exercise 15-9   Using EOQ Analysis

Cooper Electronics buys the radios installed in the sound systems produced by the firm. The radios cost $50 each. There is also a $100 fixed cost for each shipment of radios. Cooper Electronics expects to use 48,020 radios this year and estimates that the funds invested in inventory cost 20% annually.

Required:

A. Compute the firm's economic order quantity.

B. How many times each year will the firm order radios?

C. What will be the total annual ordering costs and carrying costs for the inventory?

Exercise 15-10   Determining the Proper Reorder Point

The Volter Company is attempting to determine the most effective time to reorder inventory. The lead time involved is one week and the firm wants to have enough safety stock available so the chance of stocking out is no more than 5%. The company's controller has examined the inventory records and has compiled the following information regarding inventory usage during lead time:

Usage During Lead Time	Frequency Quantity Was Used
60	3
61	6
62	8
63	60
64	13
65	7
66	3

Required:

Determine the best reorder point for the firm.

Exercise 15-11   Using the Graphic Method of L.P.

The Isbell Company produces two types of air filters—standard and deluxe. The contribution margins of the two products are:

Standard—$20

Deluxe—30

The air filters are produced in two departments—Cutting and Assembly. The monthly capacities in hours of the two departments and the production requirements for the products are as follows:

Department/Product	Standard	Deluxe	Hours Available
Cutting	.4 hours	1.2 hours	600
Assembly	.8 hours	.4 hours	400

Required:

A. How many units of each type of air filter should be produced to maximize the total contribution margin?
B. How much of the firm's production capacity is utilized with the solution in part A?
C. Calculate the shadow price for one additional hour of Assembly Department capacity by considering the economic impact of 40 more hours.

Exercise 15-12   Consideration of a Marketing Constraint

Refer to Exercise 15-11. Suppose only 240 standard air filters can be sold each month by the Isbell Company.

Required:

Determine the optimal mix of standard and deluxe air filters with the additional constraint imposed by the market. What is the total contribution margin from this solution?

Exercise 15-13   Product Mix Decision and Linear Programming

The Windler Company produces two products—A and B. The firm's budget shows the following for the two products:

Product	A	B
Sellling price	$25	$28
Variable costs	10	17
Allocated fixed costs	8	10

Both products require raw materials X and Y, which are available in limited supply. The production requirements and limitations are:

	A	B	Total Available
X	2 lb	1 lb	4,000 lb
Y	2 lb	3 lb	6,000 lb

Required:

A. Determine the optimal mix of Products A and B.

B. Assume that at most 1,000 units of Product A can be sold because of market conditions. How would this constraint affect the solution in part A?

Exercise 15-14 Developing a PERT Network

The Wells Painting Company has been asked to bid on a painting project. Bill Wells has determined that the project would consist of the following steps and required times:

Step	Description	Time
1	Move materials and equipment to job site	5 hours
2	Build scaffold and remove old paint	3 hours
3	At the same time step 2 is performed, blend paint and prepare brushes	1.5 hours
4	Paint surface	6 hours
5	Remove scaffold	1.5 hours
6	At the same time step 5 is performed, complete cleanup	1 hour
7	Return materials and equipment to shop	2 hours

Required:

A. Develop the PERT network for the painting project.

B. What is the earliest expected time (T_E) for the project?

C. Identify the critical path for the project.

Exercise 15-15 Use of a PERT Network

The Plan-Well Company wants to use a PERT network to perform a particular construction project. The firm's controller has developed the following estimates for the project:

Job Activity	Predecessor Job(s)	Estimated Days o	m	p
A	None	5	7	9
B	A	1	2	3
C	B	2	3	4
D	B	6	10	14
E	A	2	3	4
F	C	3	6	9
G	D	4	8	12
H	E	1	2	3
I	F, G	3	5	7
J	I, H	2	4	6

Required:

A. Compute the T_E for each activity.

B. Draw the PERT network for the project.

C. Determine T_E for each event.

D. Determine T_L for each event assuming T_L for the project is equal to the total T_E.

E. Determine the critical path for the network.

Exercise 15-16 Problem Formulation with the Simplex Method — Appendix (CPA)

The Ball Company manufactures three types of lamps which are labeled A, B, and C. Each lamp is processed in two departments, I and II. Total labor hours available per day for departments I and II are 400 and 600, respectively. No additional labor is available. Time requirements and contribution margin per unit for each lamp type are:

Labor Hours Required In:	Lamp A	Lamp B	Lamp C
Department I	2	3	1
Department II	4	2	3
Contribution margin per lamp	$5	$4	$3

Required:

A. Formulate the problem in simplex method form and develop the initial simplex tableau.

B. Which type of lamp would be introduced into the simplex solution mix from the initial tableau in part A? Why? How many units of the lamp type selected can be introduced?

Exercise 15-17 Interpretation of Optimal Solution with Simplex Method — Appendix (CPA)

A simplex solution for a linear programming profit maximization problem is shown below:

Mix	X1	X2	X3	S1	S2	Capacity
X1	1	0	4	3	−7	50
X2	0	1	−2	−6	2	60
Z−C	0	0	−5	−1	−9	

Assume that X1, X2, and X3 represent products. S1 is the slack variable related to the square feet (in thousands) of warehouse capacity and S2 is the slack variable concerning labor hours (in hundreds).

Required:

A. How many units of X1, X2, and X3 should be produced to maximize profits?

B. How much would the firm be willing to pay for 1,000 additional square feet of warehouse space? For 100 labor hours?

C. If the firm were able to obtain 200 labor hours, would the optimal solution change? Explain.

PROBLEMS

Problem 15-1 Use of Expected Value

The Josh Company is beginning to prepare its annual budget. In order to select the best forecast of sales demand in units, the firm's sales manager has developed the following relationships between selling prices and demand, along with the related probabilities:

Selling Price	Sales Demand in Units			
	10,000	11,000	12,000	13,000
$50	0%	20%	50%	30%
51	10%	25%	40%	25%
52	20%	30%	30%	20%
53	30%	50%	10%	10%
54	40%	40%	20%	0%

Required:
A. Compute the expected sales revenue for each selling price.
B. Identify which sales price should be selected to maximize the expected total sales revenue.

Problem 15-2   Use of Expected Value Analysis

The Avery Company produces a chemical product, XL4, which deteriorates and must be thrown away if it is not sold by the end of the month during which it is produced. The total variable cost of one unit of XL4 is $50 and its selling price is $80 per unit. The company can purchase the same chemical product from a competing company for $80 per unit plus $10 freight per unit. Management has estimated that failure to fill orders would result in the loss of 80% of customers placing orders for the chemical.

Avery has manufactured and sold the product for the past 20 months. Demand for the product has been irregular and at present there is no consistent sales trend. During the past 20 months, sales have been as follows:

Units Sold per Month	Number of Months
8,000	5
9,000	12
10,000	3

Required:
A. Compute the probability of sales of product XL4 of 8,000, 9,000, or 10,000 units in any month.
B. Compute the expected contribution margin if 9,000 units of product XL4 were ordered and either 8,000, 9,000, or 10,000 units were manufactured in that same month (with additional units, if necessary, being purchased).
C. Compute the average monthly contribution margin the company can expect if 9,000 units of product XL4 are produced every month and all sales orders are filled.

Problem 15-3   Evaluating Expected Costs and Their Risk

The Ness Container Company is considering the acquisition of a new packaging machine. After considerable analysis using capital budgeting techniques, two alternatives with equally acceptable returns have been identified. The firm's controller now wants to use expected value analysis to further differentiate between the two machines. To do so, she has developed the following per-unit cost information for a product produced with each machine and the related probabilities of their occurrence:

Machine A		Machine B	
Unit Cost	Probability	Unit Cost	Probability
$50	.20	$48	.10
51	.40	52	.60
54	.20	56	.20
56	.20	60	.10

Required:
A. Compute the expected cost per unit with each machine.
B. Evaluate the risk associated with each machine by calculating the standard deviation and coefficient of variation.

Problem 15-4 Use of Expected Value and Payoff Table

The Williams Florist orders and sells batches of fresh-cut specialized flowers. Weekly orders are placed in some denomination of 50 batches and the demand for the flowers is irregular from week to week. The store manager estimates the following probabilities for demand based on past performance and current market conditions:

Demand in Batches	Probability of Occurrence
500	.1
450	.5
400	.3
350	.1

The average cost of a batch of flowers is $12 with an average selling price of $20. Flowers unsold at the end of a week must be thrown away because of their condition.

Required:
A. Develop a payoff table for the decision concerning how many flowers to order each week.
B. If the store orders 450 batches each week, what are the expected profits?
C. If the store orders 500 batches each week, what are the expected profits?
D. What amount should be ordered weekly to maximize expected profits?
E. What is the expected value of perfect information for the florist?

Problem 15-5 Use of Statistical Cost Control

The Bever Company has decided to apply statistical cost control to its manufacturing labor performance. Increasing labor costs have significantly reduced the profitability of the firm's most popular product, a video player used primarily for educational purposes, in recent months. The firm's controller has carefully evaluated historical data and has determined that the average number of labor hours required to assemble a video player have been approximately 22.

During each of the past 10 days, the controller sampled the assembly labor performance and accumulated the following data:

			Hours Required		
Day/Sample	1	2	3	4	5
1	21	21	21.5	20.5	21
2	27	26	26	28	28
3	21	19	20	23	22
4	22	21	20	21	23
5	24	19	20	21	21
6	20	20.5	21	21.5	22
7	32	26	27	28	26
8	21	22	21	21	20
9	21	20	22	21	22
10	20	21	22	21	22

Required:

A. Develop a statistical control chart with upper and lower limits set at three standard deviations.

B. Based on your analysis in part A, should the company be concerned about its assembly labor performance?

C. Suppose the overall mean in the 10-day sample had been 26 hours. How would you advise the company?

Problem 15-6 Calculation and Evaluation of EOQ

The Thornton Company uses an EOQ model to order a chemical liquid used for its swimming pool maintenance product. Last year, the firm purchased and used 10,000 gallons of the chemical. The price paid was $15 per gallon and the cost of placing an order was $48.60. The carrying cost for the chemical is 18%.

During the preparation of this coming year's budget, the firm estimates that a 42% increase in the sales volume (in units) of the swimming pool maintenance product will take place. All costs are expected to be the same as last year.

Required:

A. Determine last year's EOQ for the firm.

B. How many times did the firm place orders for the chemical last year?

C. What were the firm's total annual costs of ordering and carrying the inventory last year?

D. If the firm had ordered 500 gallons each time, what would the total annual costs of ordering and carrying the inventory have been? If 700 gallons had been ordered each time?

E. If the firm uses last year's EOQ for ordering the chemical during the coming year, what would the total annual costs of ordering and carrying the inventory be?

F. Calculate the firm's EOQ for the coming year.

Problem 15-7 Calculating EOQ and RP

The Snider Company purchases ball bearings from an outside supplier at $40 per batch. Total annual production requirements are 6,400 batches. Production occurs evenly throughout the year. Order costs are $100 per order and annual carrying costs are 20%. The company faces a lead time of one week for an order. The Snider Company operates 50 weeks per year and wants to maintain a safety stock of 60 batches each time an order is placed.

Required:

A.   Calculate the firm's EOQ.
B.   Determine the total annual costs of ordering and carrying the inventory.
C.   Calculate the firm's reorder point.

Problem 15-8   Using Stockout Probabilities for Safety Stock

The Lynch Company estimates that each stockout of a popular product will cost the firm $80 because of customer dissatisfaction and lost sales in the future. The carrying cost for each unit of safety stock is $2. The product is ordered five times per year, and management has assessed the following probabilities of running out of stock with four safety stock levels:

Safety Stock Level	Probability of Stocking Out
50	.40
60	.20
70	.10
100	.05

The company wants to carry enough safety stock to minimize the combination of the expected cost of stocking out and the annual cost of carrying the safety stock.

Required:

Use an expected value approach to determine the best safety level for the company.

Problem 15-9   Product Mix and the Graphic Method

The Compton Manufacturing Company produces two products, X and Y, in its two departments—Machining and Assembly. The production requirements in hours for each product and the total hours available in the two departments are:

Department/Product	Hours Required		Total Hours Available
	X	Y	
Machining	2	3	600
Assembly	2.5	2.5	625

The financial data for the two products are:

	X	Y
Selling price	$100	$120
Variable costs	60	50
Fixed costs allocated	12	10

Required:

A.   Determine the best product mix using the graphic method of linear programming.
B.   Assume that only 150 units of product Y can be sold. Does this constraint change the optimal product mix?
C.   Refer to the optimal solution of part A. Is all of the firm's production capacity used to produce that product mix?

Problem 15-10 Using the Graphic Method of L.P.

The Stay-Cool Company produces and sells two types of ice-making machines — a commercial model and a residential model. Each machine is worked on in two production departments, Fabrication and Finishing. The production requirements in hours for the products and the total capacity in hours for the two departments are:

	Commercial Model	Residential Model	Total Hours Available
Fabrication	20	10	10,000
Finishing	30	10	12,750

The contribution margins for the two products are:

Commercial model	$60
Residential model	40

Required:

A. Determine the best mix of ice-making machines using the graphic method of linear programming.
B. Assume that the contribution margins are $82 and $40 for the commercial model and residential model, respectively. Would your answer regarding the best product mix change?
C. Suppose that only 600 residential models can be sold. Would your answer to part A change?

Problem 15-11 Use of Shadow Prices

Refer to Problem 15-10. Assume again that the contribution margins for the commercial model and residential model are $60 and $40, respectively.

Required:

A. Use the shadow pricing concept to compute how much the Stay-Cool Company would be willing to pay for one additional hour of Fabricating Department capacity.
B. Assume that instead of adding to the capacity of the Fabricating Department, the firm is interested in increasing the hours available in the Finishing Department. Should 200 hours be added in that department?

Problem 15-12 Use of Linear Programming (CPA)

Select the best answer to each of the following questions.

1. Boaz Co. manufactures two models, medium (X) and large (Y). The contribution margin expected is $24 for the medium model and $40 for the large model. The medium model is processed two hours in the machining department and four hours in the polishing department. The large model is processed three hours in the machining department and six hours in the polishing department. If total contribution margin is to be maximized, using linear programming, how would the objective function be expressed?
   a. 24X(2 + 4) + 40Y(3 + 6)
   b. 24X + 40Y
   c. 6X + 10Y
   d. 5X + 10Y

2. Johnson, Inc., manufactures product X and product Y, which are processed as follows:

	Type A Machine	Type B Machine
Product X	6 hours	4 hours
Product Y	9 hours	5 hours

The contribution margin is $12 for product X and $7 for product Y. The available time daily for processing the two products is 120 hours for machine Type A and 80 hours for machine Type B. How would the restriction (constraint) for machine Type B be expressed?

a. $4X + 5Y$
b. $4X + 5Y \leq 80$
c. $6X + 9Y \leq 120$
d. $12X + 7Y$

3. The Hale Company manufactures products A and B, each of which requires two processes, polishing, and grinding. The contribution margin is $3 for Product A and $4 for Product B. The graph below shows the maximum number of units of each product that may be processed in the two departments.

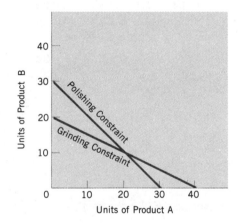

Considering the constraints (restrictions) on processing, which combination of Products A and B maximizes the total contribution margin?

a. 0 units of A and 20 units of B
b. 20 units of A and 10 units of B
c. 30 units of A and 0 units of B
d. 40 units of A and 0 units of B

4. In a system of equations for a linear programming model, what can be done to equalize an inequality such as $3X + 2Y \leq 15$?

a. Nothing
b. Add a slack variable
c. Add a tableau
d. Multiply each element by -1

5. When using the graphic method of solving a linear programming problem, the optimal solution will always be at:

    a. Minimum value of X

    b. X and Y intercept

    c. A corner point described by the feasible area

    d. Point of interception

6. The use of the graphic method as a means for solving linear programming problems:

    a. Can be used when there are more than two restrictions (constraints)

    b. Is basically limited to situations where there are two restrictions (constraints)

    c. Is limited to situations where there is one restriction (constraint)

    d. Cannot be used if there are any restrictions (constraints)

Problem 15-13 Evaluating an L.P. Problem Formulation (CMA)

Leastan Company manufactures a line of carpeting which includes a commercial carpet and a residential carpet. Two grades of fiber (heavy duty and regular) are used in manufacturing both types of carpeting. The mix of the two grades of fiber differs in each type of carpeting with the commercial grade using a greater amount of heavy duty fiber.

Leastan will introduce a new line of carpeting in two months to replace the current line. The present fiber in stock will not be used in the new line. Management wants to exhaust the present stock of regular and heavy duty fiber during the last month of production. Data regarding the current line of commercial and residential carpeting are presented next:

	Commercial	Residential
Selling price per roll	$1,000	$800
Production specifications per roll of carpet:		
Heavy duty fiber	80 lb	40 lb
Regular fiber	20 lb	40 lb
Direct labor hours	15 hours	15 hours
Standard cost per roll of carpet:		
Heavy duty fiber ($3/lb)	$ 240	$ 120
Regular fiber ($2/lb)	40	80
Direct labor ($10/direct labor hour)	150	150
Variable manufacturing overhead (60% of direct labor cost)	90	90
Fixed manufacturing overhead (120% of direct labor cost)	180	180
Total standard cost per roll	$ 700	$ 620

Leastan has 42,000 pounds of heavy duty fiber and 24,000 pounds of regular fiber in stock. All fiber not used in the manufacture of the present types of carpeting during the last month of production can be sold as scrap at $.25 a pound. Sufficient demand exists for the present line of carpeting so that all quantities produced can be sold.

There are a maximum of 10,500 direct labor hours available during the month. The labor force can work on either type of carpeting.

Required:

A. Calculate the number of rolls of commercial carpet and residential carpet Leastan Company must manufacture during the last month of production to exhaust completely the heavy duty and regular fiber still in stock.

B. Can Leastan Company manufacture these quantities of commercial and residential carpeting during the last month of production? Explain your answer.

C. A member of Leastan Company's cost accounting staff has stated that linear programming should be used to determine the number of rolls of commercial and residential carpeting to manufacture during the last month of production.

1. Explain why linear programming should be used in this application.

2. Formulate the objective and constraint functions so that this application can be solved by linear programming.

Problem 15-14 Evaluating an L.P. Problem Formulation (CMA)

The Elon Co. manufactures two industrial products—X-10 which sells for $90 a unit and Y-12 which sells for $85 a unit. Each product is processed through both of the company's manufacturing departments. The limited availability of labor, materials, and equipment capacity has restricted the ability of the firm to meet the demand for its products. The production department believes that linear programming can be used to routinize the production schedule for the two products.

The following data are available to the production department:

	Amount Required per Unit	
	X-10	Y-12
Direct materials: Weekly supply is limited to 1,800 pounds at $12 per pound	4 lb	2 lb
Direct labor:		
Department 1—Weekly supply limited to 10 people at 40 hours each at an hourly cost of $6	⅔ hour	1 hour
Department 2—Weekly supply limited to 15 people at 40 hours each at an hourly rate of $8	1¼ hours	1 hour
Machine time:		
Department 1—Weekly capacity limited to 250 hours	½ hour	½ hour
Department 2—Weekly capacity limited to 300 hours	0 hours	1 hour

The overhead costs for Elon are accumulated on a plantwide basis. The overhead is assigned to products on the basis of the number of direct labor hours required to manufacture the product. This base is appropriate for overhead assignment because most of the variable overhead costs vary as a function of labor time. The estimated overhead cost per direct labor hour is:

Variable overhead cost	$ 6
Fixed overhead cost	6
Total overhead cost per direct labor hour	$12

The production department formulated the following equations for the linear programming statement of the problem.

$$A = \text{number of units of X-10 to be produced}$$
$$B = \text{number of units of Y-12 to be produced}$$

Objective function to minimize costs:

$$\text{Minimize } Z = 85A + 62B$$

Constraints:
Materials

$$4A + 2B \leq 1,800 \text{ lb}$$

Department 1 labor

$$\tfrac{2}{3} A + 1B \leq 400 \text{ hours}$$

Department 2 labor

$$1\tfrac{1}{4} A + 1B \leq 600 \text{ hours}$$

Nonnegativity

$$A \geq 0, B \geq 0$$

Required:

A. The formulation of the linear programming equations as prepared by Elon Co.'s production department is incorrect. Explain what errors have been made in the formulation prepared by the production department.

B. Formulate and label the proper equations for the linear programming statement of Elon Co.'s production problem.

C. Explain how linear programming could help Elon Co. determine how much the firm would be willing to pay to increase the weekly supply of direct materials.

Problem 15-15 Use of a PERT Network

The Kost Company wants to develop a PERT network to manage a large-scale project. The following information has been developed for the various activities to be performed in the project:

Activity	Immediately Previous Activity	Days Required o	m	p
1	None	4	5	12
2	1	4	6	14
3	1	2	5	14
4	2	8	9	13
5	3	1	2	15
6	4, 5	2	5	8

Required:

A. Compute the expected time for each activity.

B. Develop the PERT network for the project.

C. Identify the critical path for the network.

Problem 15-16 Use of a PERT Network (CMA)

Crespi Construction Company uses critical path analysis in scheduling its projects. The following list of activities and the network diagram presented on the next page were prepared by Crespi for the Cherry Hill Apartment project prior to the start of work on the project:

Activity	Description of Activity	Estimated Time Required (in Weeks)
A	Site selection and land purchase	6
B	Survey	1
C	Excavation	3
D	Foundation	4
E	City water and sewage lines	8
F	Rough plumbing	8
G	Framing and roofing	6
H	Wiring	4
I	Interior walls	3
J	Plumbing fixtures	3
K	Exterior siding and painting	9
L	Landscaping	2

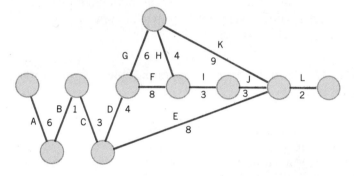

The Cherry Hill Apartment project is now in progress. An interim progress report indicates that the city water and sewage lines, rough plumbing, and wiring are all one-half complete and the exterior siding and painting have not yet begun.

Crespi will soon begin work on a building for the Echelon Savings Bank. Work on the building was started by another construction firm that has gone out of business. Crespi has agreed to complete the project. Crespi's schedule of activities and related expected completion times for the Echelon Savings Bank project are presented next:

Activity	Description of Activity	Predecessor Activity	Estimated Time Required (in Weeks)
A	Obtain on-site work permit	—	1
B	Repair damage done by vandals	A	4
C	Inspect construction materials left on site	A	1
D	Order and receive additional construction materials	C	2
E	Apply for waiver to add new materials	C	1
F	Obtain waiver to add new materials	E	1
G	Perform electrical work	B, D, F	4
H	Complete interior partitions	G	2

Required:

A. Define what is meant by "the critical path for a project."

B. Refer to the list of activities and the network diagram prepared for the Cherry Hill Apartment project prior to the start of the project.

    1. Identify the critical path by letters and determine the expected time in weeks for the project.

    2. Identify an activity that has slack time for this project and indicate the amount of slack time available for that activity.

C. Using the interim progress report for the Cherry Hill Apartment project, identify the critical path by letters and determine the expected number of weeks for the remainder of the project.

D. Refer to Crespi's schedule of activities and expected completion time for the work to be completed on the Echelon Savings Bank project.

    1. Identify the critical path by letters and determine the expected time in weeks for the project.

    2. Explain the effect on the critical path and expected time for the project if Crespi were not required to apply and obtain the waiver to add new materials.

Problem 15-17 Preparing an Initial Simplex Tableau — Appendix

Refer to Problem 15-14.

Required:

A. Develop the initial simplex tableau for the problem.

B. Which product should be introduced first into the initial solution? Why?

C. What is the maximum number of units of the product selected in part B that can be introduced?

D. How much capacity will be left for each constraint after the first product is introduced?

Problem 15-18 Simplex Method Solution Analysis — Appendix

The Denzer Company has used the simplex method to arrive at the following optimal solution to its product mix problem:

Mix	X1	X2	S1	S2	Capacity
X1	1	0	−5	3	250
X2	0	1	1	−1	140
Z−C	0	0	−5	−7	

Assume that X1 and X2 represent products produced and sold by the firm. S1 is in an equation concerning labor hours in Department 1, and S2 is in an equation concerning labor hours in Department 2.

Required:

A. How many units of X1 and X2 should be produced?

B. What is the opportunity cost of not adding 100 hours of capacity to Department 1? To Department 2?

16

ANALYSIS OF FINANCIAL STATEMENTS AND ACCOUNTING FOR CHANGING PRICES

CHAPTER OVERVIEW AND OBJECTIVES

This chapter contains two parts. Part I describes some of the techniques used to analyze a firm's financial statements. Part II examines the effect of changing prices on financial reporting. After studying this chapter, you should be able to:

1. Identify the objectives of financial statement analysis.
2. Recognize how to perform horizontal analysis, trend analysis, and vertical analysis.
3. Compute and use ratios to analyze a firm's profitability.
4. Compute and use ratios to analyze a firm's liquidity.
5. Compute and use ratios to analyze a firm's solvency.
6. List the limitations of financial statement analysis.
7. Explain the nature of inflation.
8. Differentiate between general price level changes and specific price changes.
9. Distinguish between constant dollar accounting and current value accounting.

PART I ANALYSIS OF FINANCIAL STATEMENTS

Managers and a number of external parties regularly use a firm's financial statements to evaluate the financial and operating performance of the business. In previous chapters, we have emphasized that decision makers are primarily concerned with historical financial statements as a basis for predicting the future. This chapter focuses on the basic techniques commonly employed by managers and various external parties to analyze a firm's balance sheet and income statement. These statements are emphasized here because they are a major source of financial data for decision makers to use in projecting future performance. In Chapter 17, we will consider a third statement, the statement of cash flows, which supplements the balance sheet and income statement.

SOURCES OF FINANCIAL INFORMATION

The firm's financial statements contained in the annual report are the end products of the accounting process. To report on the progress of a firm during the year, most publicly held firms also issue interim reports each quarter. (Recall that an interim report covers a period of less than 12 months.) Interim reports focus primarily on the income statement and contain summary data rather than a full set of financial statements. Still, they provide additional information for evaluating the financial position and the profitability of the firm's operations. Unlike the annual report, however, interim reports are unaudited reports. Annual and interim reports, with their accompanying schedules and explanatory notes, are a primary means by which management communicates information about the firm to interested parties.

A wealth of information is also available from other sources, however. Probably the most detailed information available on publicly held companies is contained in the reports that must be filed with the Securities and Exchange Commission (SEC). Financial advisory services, such as Moody's Investors Service and Standard and Poor's Corporation, also publish financial data for both public and privately owned companies. These are normally not as detailed as the SEC reports or the company reports. The advantage of advisory service reports is their accessibility, as they are available at most public and university libraries.

A comparison of the company under study with firms in a similar line of business and with industry norms is also useful. Industry data are available from a number of financial services. For example, Robert Morris Associates' *Annual Statement Studies* report income statement and balance sheet data and 16 financial ratios for many industries. Dun & Bradstreet publishes an *Industry Norms and Key Business Ratios* book, which contains typical balance sheets and income statements, and 14 selected financial ratios for over 800 different lines of business. The 14 ratios for the most recent year by industry groups are also published in a *Key Business Ratios* book by Dun & Bradstreet. Individual company and industry analyses are also available from stock brokerage firms. An abundance of useful information is also reported in various economic and financial newspapers and magazines such as the *Wall Street Journal, Forbes, Fortune, Business Week,* and *Barron's.*

In making comparisons with other companies, an analyst must recognize that the company under review may not be similar to other companies because of diversification into other product lines. Also, because of diversification, industry data may not clearly resemble the company under study. In such cases, the analyst attempts to identify the industry that the company best fits, and uses that industry's data and companies in that industry group for comparison.

THE NEED FOR ANALYTICAL TECHNIQUES

Information contained in the various sources of financial data is expressed primarily in monetary terms. When the absolute dollar amounts for most items reported in the financial statements are considered individually, they are generally of limited usefulness. Significant relationships may not be apparent from a review of absolute dollar amounts, because no indication is given whether a particular item is good or bad for a firm. For example, merely knowing that a company reported earnings of $100,000 for the current year is of limited use unless the amount is compared to other information, such as last year's earnings, the amount of funds invested, the current year's sales, the earnings of other companies in the same business, or some predetermined standard established by the analyst.

To simplify the identification of significant changes and relationships, the dollar amounts reported in the financial statements are frequently converted into percentages or ratios by the analyst. Some commonly recognized percentages are sometimes shown in supplementary schedules to the financial statements as part of the annual report. The analysis of relationships between dollar amounts of each item to some base amount is referred to as *horizontal analysis* and *vertical analysis. Ratio analysis* is the interpretation of the relationship between two items, such as current assets to current liabilities.

OBJECTIVES OF FINANCIAL STATEMENT ANALYSIS

Percentage analysis and ratio analysis have been developed to provide an efficient means by which an analyst can identify: (1) important relationships between items in the same statements; and (2) trends in financial data. Percentages and ratios simplify the evaluation of financial conditions and past operating performance.

Objective 1:
Identifying the
goals of financial
statement
analysis

The information is used primarily to forecast a firm's ability to pay its debts when due and to operate at a satisfactory profit level. However, because the analytical techniques are almost limitless—and so are the analysts' special interests and objectives—the choice of proper ratios and percentages must fit their purpose. For example, some financial data analysts are concerned with evaluating the firm's ability to meet its current obligations and still have sufficient cash left to carry out its other activities (i.e., the firm's liquidity as discussed in Chapter 8). The focus of this type of investigation is generally on the firm's current assets and current liabilities.

Other users, such as long-term creditors and stockholders, are also concerned with the firm's liquidity but, in addition, are interested in a firm's ability to pay its long-term obligations. This aspect of the analysis is concerned with the solvency of the firm. In a solvency analysis, the analyst assesses the financial structure of the firm and its prospects for operating at an earnings level adequate to provide sufficient cash for the payment of interest, dividends, and debt principal.

To serve as a basis for the discussion of percentage and ratio analysis, balance sheets and income statements for the Wesley Corporation during a two-year period are presented in the first two columns of Figures 16-1 and 16-2. In order to show the computations of ratios for two periods, a December 31, 1986 balance sheet is also included in Figure 16-1. The statements in Figures 16-1 and 16-2 are not in a format as they would appear in an annual report. For

WESLEY CORPORATION
Comparative Balance Sheets
December 31, 1988, 1987, and 1986
(000's omitted)

	Year Ended December 31			Change during the Year 1987–1988		Common Size Statements*	
	1988	1987	1986	Dollar Amount	Percent	1988	1987
Assets							
Current Assets:							
Cash	590	450	430	140	31.1	5.2	4.7
Marketable securities	570	660	690	(90)	(13.6)	5.1	6.9
Accounts receivable (net)	2,190	1,960	1,980	230	11.7	19.4	20.4
Inventory	3,040	2,680	2,790	360	13.4	27.0	27.9
Prepaid expenses	200	200	200	-0-	-0-	1.8	2.1
Total Current Assets	6,590	5,950	6,090	640	10.8	58.5	62.0
Long-term investments	600	750	750	(150)	(20.0)	5.3	7.8
Plant and equipment (net)	3,870	2,700	2,650	1,170	43.3	34.4	28.1
Other assets	200	200	200	-0-	-0-	1.8	2.1
Total Assets	11,260	9,600	9,690	1,660	17.3	100.0	100.0
Liabilities							
Current Liabilities:							
Notes payable	940	920	1,130	20	2.2	8.4	9.6
Accounts payable	1,570	1,370	1,550	200	14.6	13.9	14.3
Accrued expenses	160	160	160	-0-	-0-	1.4	1.6
Total Current Liabilities	2,670	2,450	2,840	220	9.0	23.7	25.5
Long-term liabilities — 11%	2,900	2,550	2,700	350	13.7	25.8	26.6
Total Liabilities	5,570	5,000	5,540	570	11.4	49.5	52.1
Stockholders' Equity							
Preferred stock, 10%	450	450	450	-0-	-0-	4.0	4.7
Common stock ($10 par value)	2,400	2,000	2,000	400	20.0	21.3	20.8
Additional paid-in capital	622	500	500	122	24.4	5.5	5.2
Retained earnings	2,218	1,650	1,200	568	34.4	19.7	17.2
Total Stockholders' Equity	5,690	4,600	4,150	1,090	23.7	50.5	47.9
Total Liabilities and Stockholders' Equity	11,260	9,600	9,690	1,660	17.3	100.0	100.0

* Computations are explained on page 623 .

Figure 16-1
Comparative Balance Sheets, Change during the Year, and Common Size Statements

example, the Change During the Year and the Common Size Statement columns are not part of the annual report presentation. These computations must be made by the analyst, as discussed later in this chapter.

It cannot be emphasized too strongly that, for financial statement analysis of an individual company to be useful, the relationships must be compared to other data or standards. Comparisons of the company under study may be made to industry averages, to the past performance of the company, and to the performance of individual companies in the same industry. (In the following discussion, rather than stating the need for comparison every time a particular analysis is performed, it will be assumed that this additional step is taken.)

PERCENTAGE ANALYSIS

HORIZONTAL ANALYSIS

An analysis of the change from year to year in individual financial statement items is called **horizontal analysis**. Horizontal analysis of the preceding year's financial statements is generally performed as a starting point for forecasting future performance. Most firms' annual reports include financial statements for the two most recent years **(comparative statements)**, and selected summary data for five to ten years.

In horizontal analysis, the individual items or groups of items on comparative financial statements are generally first placed side by side, as in the first columns of Figures 16-1 and 16-2. Because it is difficult to compare absolute dollar amounts, the difference between the dollar amount of one year and the next is computed in both dollar amount and percentage change. In computing the increase or decrease in dollar amount, the earlier year is used as the base year. The percentage change is computed by dividing the increase or decrease from the base year in dollars by the base year amount. For example, from 1987 to 1988 the Cash account of Wesley Corporation increased by $140,000, from $450,000 to $590,000 (Figure 16-1). The percentage change is 31.1%, computed as follows.

Objective 2: Performing horizontal, trend, and vertical analyses

$$\text{Percentage increase} = \frac{140,000}{450,000} = 31.1\%$$

A percentage change can only be computed when a positive amount is reported in the base year; the amount of change cannot be stated as a percentage if the item in the base year was reported as a negative or a zero amount.

A review of the percentage increases or decreases will reveal those items that showed the most significant change between the periods under study. Important and unusual changes, such as a significant percentage change in sales, should be investigated further by the analyst. The objectives of the investigation are:

1. To determine the cause of the change
2. To determine whether the change was favorable or unfavorable
3. To attempt to assess whether a trend is expected to continue

The analyst must also consider changes in other related items. For example, when reviewing the percentage changes in the balance sheet accounts included

WESLEY CORPORATION
Comparative Income Statements
For the Years Ended December 31, 1988 and 1987
(000 omitted)

	Year Ended December 31		Change during the Year		Common Size Statements	
	1988	1987	Dollar Amount	Percent	1988	1987
Sales	15,480	14,395	1,085	7.5	100.0	100.0
Less: Cost of goods sold	11,560	10,462	1,098	10.5	74.7	72.7
Gross profit on sales	3,920	3,933	(13)	(0.3)	25.3	27.3
Expenses:						
Selling expense	1,495	1,162	333	28.7	9.6	8.1
Administrative expense	895	984	(89)	(9.0)	5.8	6.8
Interest expense	415	370	45	12.2	2.7	2.6
Income tax expense	250	382	(132)	(34.6)	1.6	2.6
Total expenses	3,055	2,898	157	5.4	19.7	20.1
Net income	865	1,035	(170)	(16.4)	5.6	7.2
Preferred stock cash dividends	45	45	–0–	–0–	0.3	0.3
Net income available to common stockholders	820	990	(170)	(17.2)	5.3	6.9

Figure 16-2
Comparative Income Statements, Change during the Year, and Common Size Statements

in Figure 16-1, attention is directed to the change in plant and equipment because of the size of the change (43.3% increase). The cause of the change is an expansion in the firm's operations. In assessing whether the change is favorable or unfavorable, an analyst would seek further answers to such questions as: How is the added investment being financed? Is expansion going to cause severe cash flow problems? Are sales markets adequate to support the additional output? Answers to these questions, and announcements made by top management, will assist the analyst in determining whether further expansion is expected to continue. The analyst may look to the balance sheet, the income statement, the supplementary disclosures, and the statement of cash flows for additional data in answering these questions.

Sales in Figure 16-2 increased 7.5%, by itself a favorable trend. However, the rate of increase in cost of goods sold was 10.5%, and selling expenses increased by 28.7%. Thus, during the period the firm was unable to maintain its profit margin percentage (net income/sales). It appears that the increase in sales is at least partially the result of an increased sales effort. These items warrant further investigation by an analyst who is concerned with the profitability and long-term future of the firm. In this case, the analyst should try to determine whether inventory costs are continuing to increase, the extent of competitive pressures on the revenues of the firm, and the effect of the increased selling expenses on future sales.

TREND ANALYSIS

Trend analysis is commonly employed when financial data are presented for three or more years. In this analysis, the earliest period is the base period. Each financial statement item of the base year is set equal to 100. In subsequent years, statement items are stated as a percentage of their value in the base year by dividing the dollar amount in the succeeding year by the dollar amount in the base year. For example, assume that sales and net income were reported for the last five years as follows:

	(Base Year) 1984	1985	1986	1987	1988
Sales	1,000,000	1,050,000	1,120,000	1,150,000	1,220,000
Net income	200,000	206,000	218,000	222,000	232,000

It is clear that the dollar amounts of both sales and net income are increasing. However, the relationship between the change in sales and net income can be interpreted more easily if the changes are expressed in percentages by dividing the amount reported for each subsequent year by the base-year amount, thus producing:

	1984	1985	1986	1987	1988
Sales	100	105	112	115	122
Net income	100	103	109	111	116

Now it can be seen that net income is increasing more slowly than sales.

The relationship between sales and net income is only one trend that should be reviewed. The trend in other items should also be investigated, particularly since the level of net income is affected not only by sales, but also by the costs of the firm. In this case, it is possible that the firm's inventory costs are increasing faster than selling prices. Or the increase in sales may be the result of granting liberal credit terms, which are resulting in larger bad debt expenses. The point is that other related operating data must also be reviewed before drawing conclusions about the significance of one particular item. The overall objective is to evaluate various related trends and attempt to assess whether the trends can be expected to continue.

VERTICAL ANALYSIS

Horizontal analysis compares the proportional changes in a specific item from one period to the next. **Vertical analysis** involves restating the dollar amount of each item reported on an individual financial statement as a percentage of a specific item on the same statement. This specific item is referred to as the base amount. For example, on the balance sheet, individual components are stated as a percentage of total assets or total liabilities and stockholders' equity. On the income statement, net sales or total revenue are usually set equal to a base of 100%, with each income statement item expressed as a percentage of the base amount. Such statements are often called **common size statements** since all items are presented as a percentage of some common base amount.

Vertical analysis for Wesley Corporation is presented in the last two columns of Figures 16-1 and 16-2 (pages 620 and 622). Vertical analysis is useful for identifying the relative importance of items to the base used. For example, it can be readily observed that the cost of goods sold as a percentage of sales increased from 72.7% to 74.7%. Vertical analysis is also an important tool for comparing data to other standards such as the past performance of the firm, the current performance of competing firms, and averages developed for the industry in which the firm operates.

RATIO ANALYSIS

A financial statement ratio is computed by dividing the dollar amount of one item reported in the financial statements by the dollar amount of another item reported. The purpose is to express a relationship between two relevant items that is easy to interpret and compare with other information. For example, the relationship of current assets to current liabilities—called the current ratio—is of interest to most financial statement users. For a firm reporting current assets of $210,000 and current liabilities of $120,000, the current ratio is 1.75 ($210,000/$120,000). This means that the company has $1.75 in current assets for every $1 of its current liabilities.

The relationship could be converted to a percentage (175%) by multiplying the ratio by 100. In ratio form, or as a percentage, the relationship between the two items can be more easily compared to other standards, such as the current ratio of other companies, or industry-wide ratios.

Relevant relationships can exist between items in the same financial statement or between items reported in two different financial statements, so there are many ratios that can be computed. The analyst must give careful thought to which ratios best express the relationships relevant to the area of immediate concern. The analyst must keep in mind that a ratio shows a significant relationship that may have little importance when used alone. Consequently, to evaluate the adequacy of a certain relationship, the ratio should be compared to other standards, such as industry averages and the historical record of the company under study.

Ratios are classified according to their evaluation of a firm's *profitability, liquidity,* and *solvency.* Unless otherwise noted, the computations in the remainder of this chapter are based on the financial statements presented for Wesley Corporation in Figures 16-1 and 16-2. A summary of the ratios discussed in this chapter is presented in Figure 16-3.

RATIOS TO ANALYZE PROFITABILITY

Objective 3: Computing and using profitability ratios

Profitability analysis consists of tests used to evaluate a firm's earning performance during the year. The results are combined with other data to forecast the firm's potential earning power. Potential earning power is important to managers, creditors, and stockholders because, in the long run, the firm must earn a satisfactory income to survive. Potential earning power is also important to other parties, such as suppliers and labor unions, who are interested in maintaining a continuing relationship with a financially sound company. A firm's financial soundness depends on its future earning power.

Adequacy of income is measured in terms of the relationship between income and either total assets or common stockholders' equity, the relationship between income and sales, and the availability of income to common stockholders. If income appears to be inadequate, the next step is to determine whether the sales volume is too low. Are the cost of goods sold and/or other expenses too high? Is the investment in assets excessive in relation to the firm's sales? This same analysis was discussed in the ROI coverage in Chapter 13.

Ratio	Method of Calculation	Significance of Each Ratio
Profitability Ratios		
Return on total assets	$$\frac{\text{Net income} + \text{Interest expense (net of tax)}}{\text{Average total assets}}$$	Measures rate of return earned on total assets provided by both creditors and owners.
Return on common stockholders' equity	$$\frac{\text{Net income} - \text{Preferred stock cash dividend requirement}}{\text{Average common stockholders' equity}}$$	Measures rate of return earned on assets provided by owners.
Return on sales	$$\frac{\text{Net income}}{\text{Net sales}}$$	Measures net profitability of each dollar of sales.
Earnings per share	$$\frac{\text{Net income} - \text{Preferred stock cash dividend requirement}}{\text{Weighted average number of common shares outstanding}}$$	Measures net income earned on each share of common stock.
Price-earnings ratio	$$\frac{\text{Market price per share of common stock}}{\text{Earnings per share}}$$	Measures the amount investors are paying for a dollar of earnings.
Dividend yield	$$\frac{\text{Annual dividend per share of common stock}}{\text{Market price per share of common stock}}$$	Measures rate of return to stockholders based on current market price.
Dividend payout	$$\frac{\text{Total dividends to common stockholders}}{\text{Net income} - \text{Preferred stock cash dividend requirement}}$$	Measures the percentage of income paid out to common stockholders.
Liquidity Ratios		
Current ratio	$$\frac{\text{Current assets}}{\text{Current liabilities}}$$	A measure of short-term liquidity. Indicates the ability of a firm to meet its short-term debts from its current assets.
Quick ratio	$$\frac{\text{Cash} + \text{Marketable securities} + \text{Net receivables}}{\text{Current liabilities}}$$	A more rigorous measure of short-term liquidity. Indicates the ability of the firm to meet unexpected demands from the liquid current assets.
Receivable turnover	$$\frac{\text{Net sales}}{\text{Average receivable balance}}$$	Measures effectiveness of collections; used to evaluate whether receivable balance is excessive.
Inventory turnover	$$\frac{\text{Cost of goods sold}}{\text{Average inventory balance}}$$	Indicates the liquidity of inventory. Measures the number of times inventory was sold on the average during the period.
Solvency Ratios		
Debt to total assets	$$\frac{\text{Total liabilities}}{\text{Total assets}}$$	Measures percentage of assets provided by creditors and extent of using leverage.
Times interest earned	$$\frac{\text{Net income} + \text{Interest expense} + \text{Income tax expense}}{\text{Interest expense}}$$	Measures the ability of the firm to meet its interest payments out of current earnings.

Figure 16-3
Summary of Ratios

Rate of Return on Total Assets

Rate of return on total assets is a measure of how well management utilized all of the company's assets to generate income. The ratio is computed by dividing the sum of net income plus after-tax interest expense by average total assets for the year.

$$\text{Return on total assets} = \frac{\text{Net income} + \text{Interest expense (net of tax)}[1]}{\text{Average total assets}}$$

Interest expense (net of tax) is computed as:

$$\text{Interest expense} \times (1.0 - \text{Income tax rate})$$

Interest is added back to net income (it was deducted to derive net income) in the numerator to derive the total return earned on the total assets regardless of how they were financed. In other words, interest is a return to the creditors for the use of money to finance the acquisition of assets. Dividends paid to stockholders are not added back to net income because they were not an expense that was subtracted in computing net income. The net of tax interest expense is used, because that is the net cost to the firm for using borrowed funds. Since the interest is tax deductible, a tax savings results that is equal to the amount of interest times the tax rate (the tax shield concept).

Average total assets are used in the denominator because the income was produced by using the resources throughout the period. The sum of the beginning and ending total assets is divided by two to compute average total assets used during the period to produce the reported income. If sufficient information were available, a monthly or quarterly average would be preferred to minimize the effects of seasonal fluctuations.

The management of Wesley Corporation produced a return on average total assets of 11.40% in 1988 and 13.53% in 1987, as computed below assuming the tax rate was 22% and 27%, respectively.

1988	1987
$\dfrac{865 + 415\,(1.0 - .22)}{(9,600 + 11,260)/2} = 11.40\%$	$\dfrac{1,035 + 370\,(1.0 - .27)}{(9,690 + 9,600)/2} = 13.53\%$

During 1988, management produced approximately 11.4 cents in profit for every dollar of assets invested, compared with 13.5 cents for every dollar in 1987. The decrease is significant and results from decreased net income combined with an increased investment base. Such a decrease highlights the need for further investigation by the analyst.

Rate of Return on Common Stockholders' Equity

The return on total assets does not measure the return earned by management on the assets invested by the common stockholders. The return to the common

---

[1] There are variations in the way analysts compute the same ratios. For example, some analysts prefer to compute the return on total assets using one of the following alternatives for the numerator in the ratio:

1. Net income + Interest expense
2. Net income before interest expense and income taxes.
3. Net income

The various approaches to computing the same ratio points out the need for an analyst to exercise care when comparing ratios computed by different individuals.

stockholders may be greater or less than the return on total assets because of the firm's use of financial leverage. Financial leverage is the use of debt securities or other fixed-return securities, such as preferred stock, to earn a return greater than the interest or dividends paid to the creditors or preferred stockholders. If a firm is able to earn more on the borrowed funds than the fixed amount that must be paid to the creditors and preferred stockholders, the return to the common stockholders will be greater than the return on total assets. If the amount earned on the borrowed funds is less than the fixed interest and preferred stock dividends, the return to the common stockholders will be less than the return on total assets. The rate of return to common stockholders may be computed as:

$$\text{Return on common stockholders' equity} = \frac{\text{Net income} - \text{Preferred stock cash dividend requirement}}{\text{Average common stockholders' equity}}$$

The preferred dividend requirement is subtracted from net income to yield the portion of net income allocated to the common stockholders' equity. The denominator excludes the preferred stockholders' equity in the firm.

The computations for Wesley Corporation are shown here.

	December 31		
	1988	**1987**	**1986**
Common stock	$2,400	$2,000	$2,000
Additional paid-in capital	622	500	500
Retained earnings	2,218	1,650	1,200
Total common stockholders' equity	$5,240	$4,150	$3,700

$$\underline{1988} \qquad \qquad \underline{1987}$$

$$\frac{865 - 45}{(4,150 + 5,240)/2} = 17.47\% \qquad \frac{1,035 - 45}{(3,700 + 4,150)/2} = 25.22\%$$

Note that these rates are approximately 6% (17.47% − 11.40%) and 12% (25.22% − 13.53%) higher than the corresponding returns computed on total assets because the company earned a return on the assets financed by the creditors and preferred stockholders greater than the interest or dividends paid to them. In other words, the return earned on the total assets of 11.40% in 1988 and 13.53% in 1987 was greater than the net of tax fixed rates paid to the preferred stockholders and bondholders. The income earned in excess of the fixed amounts increases the common stockholders interest. However, the percentage decreased from 25.22% to 17.47%, a decrease worthy of further investigation.

Return on Sales

Return on sales—also called the profit margin—is calculated during a vertical analysis of the income statement. It reflects the portion of each dollar of sales that represents income. Return on sales is computed by dividing net income by net sales.

$$\text{Return on sales} = \frac{\text{Net Income}}{\text{Net sales}}$$

For Wesley Corporation, the rates are:

1988	1987
$\dfrac{865}{15,480} = 5.59\%$	$\dfrac{1,035}{14,395} = 7.19\%$

For 1988, each dollar of sales produced 5.59 cents in income. Consistent with the other rates computed, this ratio indicates a declining profitability trend for the firm. The rates should, of course, be compared to other standards to be more useful. If the return on sales for competing firms is 5%, for example, the 5.59% appears favorable. Even so, other data, such as increases in major expenses, should be investigated further because other problem areas or poor management practices could be discovered to explain the decline between the two years.

Earnings per Share

The earnings per share (EPS) of common stock is widely used in evaluating the performance of a firm. The ratio is commonly used to compile earnings data for the press and for statistical services. It is a widely publicized ratio, because it converts the absolute dollar amount of net income to a per share amount. That is, the EPS ratio is the amount of net income earned on one share of stock. It is computed as follows:

$$EPS = \frac{\text{Net income} - \text{Preferred stock cash dividend requirement}}{\text{Weighted average number of common shares outstanding}}$$

In the Wesley Corporation illustration, the calculations are:

1988	1987
$\dfrac{865 - 45}{240} = \$3.42$	$\dfrac{1,035 - 45}{200} = \$4.95$

The average number of common shares outstanding is computed on a weighted average basis. The weighted average is based on the number of months that the shares were outstanding. The average number of shares for 1987 and 1988 is computed on the assumption that there were 200,000 shares outstanding during all of 1987 and that 40,000 additional shares were issued at the beginning of 1988.

The EPS ratio means that for 1988 the firm earned $3.42 per share of common stock outstanding. Current generally accepted reporting standards require that EPS be disclosed in the face of the income statement.

The computation of EPS is much more complex than shown here, especially if a company has issued securities that are convertible into common stock. These complexities are discussed in detail in more advanced accounting courses.

Price-Earnings Ratio

The price-earnings ratio (P/E ratio) indicates how much investors are currently paying for each dollar of earnings. It enhances a statement user's ability to compare the market value of one common stock, relative to earnings, to that of other companies. It is computed by dividing the current market price of a share of common stock by the earnings per share.

$$P/E \text{ ratio} = \frac{\text{Market price per share of common stock}}{\text{Earnings per share}}$$

Assuming a market price of $40 per share for Wesley Corporation's common stock on December 31, 1988, the P/E ratio is:

$$\frac{40.00}{3.42} = 11.70 \text{ times}$$

The common stock of Wesley Corporation is said to be selling for 11.7 times its earnings.

Price-earnings ratios vary widely between industries since they represent investors' expectations about the future earnings power of a company. Thus, high P/E stocks are associated with companies with prospects of high earnings growth, whereas more stable firms have lower P/E stocks. For example, in the early part of 1985, companies associated with high-technology generally had a high P/E ratio, such as Apple Computer with a P/E ratio of approximately 30. On the other hand, companies in the auto industry had low P/E ratios. Ford Motor Company and General Motors, for example, had P/E ratios of three and six, respectively.

Dividend Yield

The dividend yield is normally computed by investors who are investing in common stock primarily for dividends, rather than for appreciation in the market price of the stock. The percentage yield indicates a rate of return on the dollars invested and permits easier comparison to returns from alternative investment opportunities. The dividend yield is computed as:

$$\text{Dividend yield} = \frac{\text{Annual dividend per share of common stock}}{\text{Market price per share of common stock}}$$

Cash dividends of $252,000 ($1.05 per share) were paid during 1988 to the common stockholders of Wesley Corporation.[2] Assuming a market price of $40 per share, the dividend yield is computed as follows:

$$\frac{1.05}{40.00} = 2.63\%$$

---

[2] The $252,000 can be verified as follows:

Retained earnings, 1/1/88 (Figure 16-1)		$1,650,000
Add: Net income (Figure 16-2)		865,000
Less: Cash dividends:		
Preferred stock	$ 45,000	
Common stock	252,000	(297,000)
Retained earnings, 12/31/88 (Figure 16-1)		$2,218,000

Dividends per share are computed as follows:

$$\text{Dividends per share} = \frac{\text{Dividends to common stockholders}}{\text{Number of common shares outstanding}}$$

$$= \frac{\$252,000}{240,000}$$

$$= \$1.05 \text{ per share}$$

Dividend Payout Ratio

Investors interested in dividend yields may also compute the percentage of common stock earnings distributed as dividends to the common stockholders each period. This ratio is referred to as the dividend payout ratio.

$$\text{Dividend payout ratio} = \frac{\text{Total dividends to common stockholders}}{\text{Net income} - \text{Preferred stock cash dividend requirement}}$$

For the Wesley Corporation, the 1988 ratio is:

$$\frac{252}{865 - 45} = 30.73\%$$

This ratio provides an investor with some insights into management's policy of distributing dividends as a percentage of net income available to the common stockholders. A low payout ratio would indicate that management is reinvesting earnings internally. Such a company would be desirable for someone interested in investing for growth in the market price of the shares. A company with a consistently high payout ratio would be of interest to an investor who depends on dividends as a source of current income (for example, a retired individual).

Some recent dividend payout percentages for selected companies are given in Figure 16-4. Over the years, the aggregate dividend payout ratio for U.S. corporations has averaged 40% to 60%.

RATIOS TO ANALYZE LIQUIDITY

Objective 4: Computing and using liquidity ratios

Liquidity—that is, the firm's ability to meet its short term obligations—is an important factor in financial statement analysis. After all, a firm that cannot meet its short-term obligations may be forced into bankruptcy and, therefore, will not have the opportunity to operate in the long run. The focus of this aspect of analysis is on working capital or some component of working capital.

Figure 16-4

Dividend Payout Ratio for Selected Companies	
Company	Dividend Payout Ratio (%)
Apple Computer, Inc.	–0–
Cincinnati Gas & Electric Company	73.9
Firestone Tire & Rubber Company	36.3
General Electric Company	42.1
General Motors Corporation	23.7
Holiday Inns, Inc.	25.2
K Mart Corporation	27.4
Levitz Furniture	17.3
McDonald's Corporation	16.9
Sperry	47.4

Source: Computed from annual reports by the author.

Current Ratio

Perhaps the most commonly used measure of a firm's liquidity is the current ratio, which is computed as:

$$\text{Current ratio} = \frac{\text{Current assets}}{\text{Current liabilities}}$$

The current ratio, a measure of the firm's liquidity, measures the creditors' margin of safety. It indicates the relationship of current assets to current liabilities on a dollar-per-dollar basis. A low ratio may indicate that the firm would be unable to meet its short-term debt in an emergency. A high ratio is considered favorable to creditors, but may indicate excessive investment in working capital items, such as holding slow-selling inventory, that may not be producing income for the firm.

Analysts often contend that the current ratio should be at least two to one. In other words, a firm should maintain $2 of current assets for every $1 of current liabilities. Although such a rule is one standard of comparison, it is arbitrary and subject to exceptions and numerous qualifications in the modern approach to statement analysis. Deviations from the 2:1 rule nevertheless indicate an area in which additional tests are needed to evaluate the firm's liquidity. For example, a firm with a ratio of 1:1 may have a difficult time meeting its short-term commitments. Therefore, to assess its liquidity, the quick ratio and turn-over ratios discussed below and the cash flow should be carefully investigated.

The current ratios for Wesley Corporation for 1988 and 1987 are:

1988	1987
$\dfrac{6,590}{2,670} = 2.47$	$\dfrac{5,950}{2,450} = 2.43$

Wesley Corporation shows a slight improvement in the relationship between current assets and current liabilities and, in the absence of other information, would be considered liquid, at least in the short run. However, a ratio of 2.4 or higher may signify excessive investments in current assets. That is, a high ratio may indicate that the company is holding too many assets that are not producing revenue.

Quick Ratio or Acid Test Ratio

One of the limitations of the current ratio is that it includes inventory and prepaid expenses in the numerator. However, these items are not as liquid as cash, marketable securities, notes receivable, or accounts receivable. In the normal course of business, inventories must first be sold, and then the cash collected, before cash is available. Also, most prepaid expenses, such as prepaid insurance and office supplies, are to be consumed and cannot be readily converted into cash. The quick or acid test ratio is often used to supplement the current ratio because it provides a more rigorous measure of liquidity. The quick ratio is computed by dividing the most liquid current assets by total current liabilities.

$$\text{Quick ratio} = \frac{\text{Cash} + \text{Marketable securities} + \text{Net receivables}}{\text{Current liabilities}}$$

The higher the ratio, the more liquid the firm is considered. A lower ratio may indicate that, in an emergency, the company would be unable to meet its immediate obligations.

The quick ratio for Wesley Corporation is computed:

	1988	**1987**
Cash	$ 590	$ 450
Marketable securities	570	660
Accounts receivable (net)	2,190	1,960
Total quick assets	$3,350	$3,070

1988	1987
$\dfrac{3,350}{2,670} = 1.25$	$\dfrac{3,070}{2,450} = 1.25$

A ratio of 1.25:1 in both years indicates that the firm is highly liquid. However, this observation is somewhat dependent on the collectibility of the receivables included in the numerator.

The current ratio and quick ratio are used to measure the adequacy of the firm's current assets to satisfy its current obligations as of the balance sheet date. However, these ratios ignore how long it takes for a firm to collect cash —an important aspect of the firm's liquidity. Since receivables and inventories normally make up a large percentage of a firm's current assets, the quick ratio and current ratio may be misleading if there is an extended interval between purchasing inventory, selling it, and collecting cash from the sale. Thus, the receivable turnover and inventory turnover ratios are two other measures of liquidity that are often used to yield additional information. These turnover ratios are sometimes called activity ratios.

Receivable Turnover

The receivable turnover ratio is a measure of how many times the average receivable balance was converted into cash during the year. It is also considered a measure of the efficiency of the firm's credit-granting and collection policies. It is computed as follows:

$$\text{Receivable turnover} = \frac{\text{Net sales}}{\text{Average receivable balance}}$$

The higher the receivable turnover ratio, the shorter the time period between recording a sale and collecting the cash. To be competitive, the firm's credit policies are influenced by industry practices. Comparison of this ratio to industry norms can reveal deviations from competitors' operating results.

In computing this ratio, credit sales should be used in the numerator whenever the amount is available. However, such information is normally not available in financial statements, so net sales is used as a substitute. An average of monthly receivable balances should be used in the denominator whenever possible. In the absence of monthly information, the year-end balance, an average of the beginning of the year and end of the year balances, or averages of quarterly balances are used in the calculation. The average of the receivable balances is used because net sales are earned over a period of time. Therefore, the denominator should approximate what the receivable balance was throughout the period. The computations for Wesley Corporation are:

1988	1987
$\dfrac{15,480}{(1,960 + 2,190)/2} = 7.46$	$\dfrac{14,395}{(1,980 + 1,960)/2} = 7.31$

Frequently, the receivable turnover is divided into 365 days to determine the average number of days it takes to collect receivables from sales on account.

1988	1987
$\dfrac{365 \text{ days}}{7.46} = 48.93 \text{ days}$	$\dfrac{365 \text{ days}}{7.31} = 49.93 \text{ days}$

During 1988, the corporation collected the average accounts receivable balance 7.46 times. Expressed another way, it took an average of 48.93 days to collect sales on account, an improvement of one day over 1987. These measures are particularly useful if one knows the credit terms granted by the firm. Assuming credit terms of 60 days, the average 49-day collection period provides some indication that the firm's credit policy is effective and that the firm probably is not burdened by excessive amounts of uncollectible accounts that have not been written off. A collection period significantly in excess of 60 days indicates a problem with either the granting of credit, collection policies, or both.

Inventory Turnover

The control of the amount invested in inventory is an important aspect of managing a business. The size of the investment in inventory and inventory turnover are dependent upon such factors as type of business and time of year. A grocery store has a higher turnover than an automobile dealership; the inventory level of a seasonal business is higher at certain times in the operating cycle than at others. The inventory turnover ratio is a measure of the adequacy of inventory and how efficiently it is being managed. The ratio is an expression of the number of times the average inventory balance was sold and then replaced during the year. The ratio is computed as follows:

$$\text{Inventory turnover} = \frac{\text{Cost of goods sold}}{\text{Average inventory balance}}$$

Cost of goods sold, rather than sales, is used in the numerator because (1) it is a measure of the cost of inventory sold during the year, and (2) the cost measure is consistent with the cost basis of the denominator. Ideally, an average of monthly inventory balances should be computed, but this information is generally not available to external parties in published reports. A quarterly average can be computed if quarterly interim reports are published by the firm.

The inventory turnover for Wesley Corporation based on the average of the beginning and ending balances is:

1988	1987
$\dfrac{11,560}{(2,680 + 3,040)/2} = 4.04$	$\dfrac{10,462}{(2,790 + 2,680)/2} = 3.83$

The average days per turnover can be computed by dividing 365 days by the turnover ratio:

1988	1987
$\dfrac{365 \text{ days}}{4.04} = 90.35 \text{ days}$	$\dfrac{365 \text{ days}}{3.83} = 95.30 \text{ days}$

The 1988 turnover ratio indicates that the average inventory was sold 4.04 times during the year as compared to 3.83 times in 1987. In terms of days, the firm held its inventory approximately 90 days in 1988 before it was sold, as compared to about 95 days in 1987.

The increased turnover in 1988 is generally considered a favorable trend. Inventory with a high turnover is less likely to become obsolete and decline in price before it is sold. A higher turnover also indicates greater liquidity, since the inventory will be converted into cash in a shorter period of time. However, given the nature of the firm's business, a very high turnover may indicate that the company is carrying insufficient inventory and is losing a significant amount of sales.

RATIOS TO ANALYZE SOLVENCY

Objective 5: Computing and using solvency ratios

A firm is using financial leverage whenever it finances a portion of its assets with a fixed charge security. Issuing bonds to finance the purchase of plant assets is an example of using financial leverage. Such debt securities commit the firm to making interest payments and repaying the principal on specified dates. If a firm fails to meet these commitments, the bondholders can force the firm into bankruptcy. Thus, borrowing increases the risk of default. The advantage to the common stockholders is that their return may be increased if the return earned on the funds borrowed is greater than the cost of the debt.

Several ratios are used to analyze the firm's ability to satisfy its long-term commitments and still have sufficient working capital left over to operate successfully. These ratios test the firm's **solvency.**

Debt to Total Assets

The percentage of total assets financed by creditors indicates the extent to which the firm uses debt financing. The ratio of debt to total assets, also called the debt ratio, is a measure of the relationship between total liabilities and total assets and is computed as follows:

$$\text{Debt to total assets} = \frac{\text{Total liabilities}^3}{\text{Total assets}}$$

A high debt to total assets ratio indicates a greater risk of default and less protection for the creditors. This percentage is important to long-term creditors and stockholders, since the creditors have a prior claim to assets in the event of liquidation — that is, the creditors must be paid in full before assets are distributed to stockholders. The greater the percentage of assets invested by stockholders, the greater the protection to the creditors.

For Wesley Corporation, the ratio is:

1988	1987
$\frac{5,570}{11,260} = 49.47\%$	$\frac{5,000}{9,600} = 52.08\%$

---

[3] Some analysts include preferred stock with the total debt rather than with equity on the basis that it has a preference to assets in liquidation and that it is often issued to obtain financial leverage for the common stockholders. Preferred stock is not included here because it does not have a maturity date and because dividends do not have to be paid.

Thus, for both years, approximately 50% of the assets were provided by the firm's creditors.

Because of the trade-off between increased risk for potentially greater returns to common stockholders, there is no percentage that is considered better than another. Other things being equal, firms with stable income can issue a greater percentage of debt than firms with volatile income. Stable income levels enable a statement user to better predict, from period to period, the level of debt costs that can be covered from cash generated by operations. Some selected examples of debt to total assets ratios computed from recent balance sheets are shown in Figure 16-5.

Times Interest Earned

The times interest earned ratio is an indication of the firm's ability to satisfy periodic interest payments from current earnings. The rough rule of thumb is that the company should earn three to four times its interest requirement. Since current interest charges are normally paid from funds provided by current operations, analysts frequently compute the relationship between earnings and interest.

$$\text{Times interest earned} = \frac{\text{Net income} + \text{Interest expense} + \text{Income tax expense}}{\text{Interest expense}}$$

Interest expense and income taxes are added back to net income in the numerator because the ratio is a measure of income available to pay the tax deductible interest charges.

For Wesley Corporation, the ratio is:

1988	1987
$\dfrac{865 + 415 + 250}{415} = 3.69$	$\dfrac{1,035 + 370 + 382}{370} = 4.83$

In 1987, earnings before interest and income taxes were 4.83 times interest expense. This ratio declined to 3.69 in 1988. The 1988 result is marginal but it

Figure 16-5

Debt to Total Assets Ratios for Selected Companies	
Company	Debt to Total Assets Ratio (%)
Apple Computer, Inc.	32.1
Circle K Corporation	60.8
Deere & Co.	61.3
Exxon	51.3
Ford Motor	67.8
General Electric	51.6
General Motors	54.6
RCA Corporation	66.8
Sperry	54.6
Standard Oil Company	51.6
Source: Computed from annual reports by author.	

still is an adequate coverage according to the rule of thumb. However, the result should be considered in relation to other trends in the company's financial status, especially the trend in this ratio, and in comparison with other standards, such as industry averages.

Objective 6:
Limitations of
financial state-
ment analysis

LIMITATIONS OF FINANCIAL STATEMENT ANALYSIS

The analytical techniques introduced in this chapter are useful for providing insights into the financial position and results of operations of a particular firm. Financial statement users must be most careful in interpreting trends and ratios computed from reported financial statements. Certain basic limitations and an explanation of each follow:

1. Financial analysis is performed on historical data primarily for the purpose of forecasting future performance. The historical relationships may not continue because of changes in: (1) the general state of the economy; (2) the business environment in which the firm must operate; and (3) the policies established by management.
2. The measurement base used in computing the analytical measures is historical cost. Failure to adjust for price changes may result in some computations providing misleading information on a trend basis and in any comparison between companies. For example, the return on total assets includes net income in the numerator, which is affected by the current year's sales and current operating expenses measured in current dollars. However, plant assets and inventory are measured in historical dollars—which are not adjusted to reflect current price levels. Thus, the ratio divides items primarily measured in current dollar amounts by a total measured primarily in terms of historical dollars. As discussed in Part II of this chapter, this limitation can be partially overcome by using price-level adjusted data reported as supplemental information by many firms.
3. Year-end data may not be typical of the firm's position during the year. Knowing that certain ratios are computed at year-end, management may improve a ratio by entering into certain types of transactions near the end of the year. For example, the current ratio can be improved by using cash to pay off short-term debt. To illustrate, assume that a firm reported current assets of $200,000 and current liabilities of $100,000 before paying $50,000 on accounts payable. The payment will increase the current ratio, as shown here:

	Before Payment	Payment	After Payment
Current assets	$200,000	$50,000	$150,000
Current liabilities	100,000	50,000	50,000

$$\text{Current ratio} = \frac{200,000}{100,000} = 2 \qquad \text{Current ratio} = \frac{150,000}{50,000} = 3$$

Also, a firm usually establishes a fiscal year-end that coincides with the low point of activity in its operating cycle. Therefore, account balances such as receivables, accounts payable, and inventory, may not be representative of the balances carried in these accounts during the year.

4. **Companies may not be comparable.** Data among companies may not provide meaningful comparisons because of factors such as the use of different accounting methods, the size of the companies, and the diversification of product lines—despite the fact that this chapter has emphasized such comparisons.

PART II EFFECTS OF INFLATION

In the United States, money (i.e., the dollar) is used as both a medium of exchange and as a measure of "real" value as determined by the amount of goods and services for which it can be exchanged. The amount of goods or services for which a dollar can be exchanged is called the **purchasing power** of the dollar. Although the price of some goods (for example, calculators, digital watches, and computers) has decreased in recent years, the economy of the United States and of most other countries has been characterized by significantly increasing prices of most goods and services. The general increase in prices results in **inflation,** which can be defined as a decrease in the purchasing power of the dollar or as an increase in the general price level. The general price level is the weighted average price of all goods and services in the economy.

Objective 7: Nature of inflation

Price changes are of two types: specific price changes and general price level changes. It is important to distinguish between these two types because they reflect quite different things.

1. **Specific price changes** are changes in the prices of individual goods or services such as bread, a computer, or medical services. The prices of specific items may increase or decrease from one period to another. In the current economy, for example, the prices of calculators and digital watches have been decreasing, while the prices of real estate and medical services have been increasing.
2. **General price level changes** are changes in the weighted average of all goods and services in the economy. A general price level change therefore represents a change in the value of money in all its uses. Specific price changes affect the general price level because the prices of specific goods and services constitute the items used to determine the general price level. Although the general price level may decrease (deflation), such a decrease is rare. It has occurred only once in the United States during the last 36 years—in 1949. The more common occurrence is inflation—that is, an increase in the general price level.

Objective 8: Differentiating between specific price changes and general price level changes

When the general price level increases, it takes more dollars to acquire a given amount of goods or services. Stated another way, the dollar buys a smaller amount of goods or services. The general price level is expressed in the form of an index number with a specific base year set equal to 100. Although agencies of the United States government publish several general price indexes, the most widely recognized is the *Consumer Price Index* (CPI), which is published monthly by the Bureau of Labor Statistics.

The CPI measures the average change in the prices of a "market basket" of goods and services purchased by families living in cities. The Financial Accounting Standards Board (FASB) recommends the use of the CPI to restate financial statements for general price level changes because it is readily available in the news media, timely, and produces results that are comparable to other general price indexes. A partial listing of the CPI and the yearly inflation rate are shown in Figure 16-6.

As can be seen in Figure 16-6, the general price level more than tripled from 1967 to 1985; that is, the 1985 dollar purchased less than one-third as much goods and services as the 1967 dollar. Stated another way, it would take $322.20 in 1985 to purchase the same goods and services that could have been purchased in 1967 for $100. Thus, there is an inverse relationship between changes in the purchasing power of the dollar and changes in the general price level index. The inflation rate is determined on the basis of the change in the average index for the year. Thus, for example, the inflation rate for 1985 is computed as $(322.2 - 311.1)/311.1 = 3.6\%$.

REPORTING THE EFFECTS OF INFLATION

As discussed in previous chapters, accountants prepare financial statements based on historical cost under the stable dollar assumption. These historical cost financial statements consist of aggregated amounts of dollars from different years. In each of these years, the dollar has a different purchasing power. As a result, the impact of inflation is difficult to assess by statement users. Because of the persistent nature of inflation, however, some accountants and users of

Figure 16-6

Consumer Price Index for all Urban Consumers			
Year	Average Index* (1967 = 100)	Year-End Index	Annual Average Inflation Rate
1967	100.0	101.6	
1968	104.2	106.4	4.2%
1969	109.8	112.9	5.4
1970	116.3	119.1	5.9
1971	121.3	123.1	4.3
1972	125.3	127.3	3.3
1973	133.1	138.5	6.2
1974	147.7	155.4	11.0
1975	161.2	166.3	9.1
1976	170.5	174.3	5.8
1977	181.5	186.1	6.5
1978	195.4	202.9	7.7
1979	217.4	229.9	11.3
1980	246.8	258.4	13.5
1981	272.3	281.5	10.3
1982	289.1	292.4	6.2
1983	298.4	303.5	3.2
1984	311.1	315.5	4.3
1985	322.2	327.4	3.6

* *Source:* U.S. Department of Labor, Bureau of Labor Statistics

financial information question the usefulness of the dollar measurements in the traditional historical cost statements. They disagree, however, on what should be done to make the financial statements more useful.

Although several approaches have been suggested, only two primary methods of reporting the effects of inflation have received relatively wide support: (1) constant dollar accounting (i.e., restating the historical cost financial statements for changes in the general price level); and (2) current value accounting (i.e., preparing the financial statements on the basis of current prices).

Objective 9:
Distinguishing
between constant
dollar accounting
and current value
accounting

CONSTANT DOLLAR ACCOUNTING

The objective of **constant dollar accounting** is to state all amounts in dollars of the same current purchasing power. To do this, the historical cost figures in the financial statements are converted—through the use of a general price level index such as the CPI—to the number of current dollars representing an equivalent amount of purchasing power. This is accomplished by multiplying the historical cost amounts by a fraction. The numerator of the fraction is the current general price level index number. The denominator is the general price level index number at the date the historical cost figure originated. For example, assume that land was purchased on December 31, 1975 for $100,000. The land would be restated to an equivalent number of end of 1985 dollars as follows:

$$\frac{\text{Current price index}}{\text{Historical cost price index}} \times \text{Historical cost} = \text{Restated cost}$$

$$\frac{327.4}{166.3} \times \$100,000 = \$196,873$$

If additional land were purchased on December 31, 1978 for $50,000, it would be converted to end of 1985 purchasing power dollars as:

$$\frac{327.4}{202.9} \times \$50,000 = \$80,680$$

Land would be reported on a 1985 constant dollar balance sheet at $277,553 ($196,873 + $80,680).

Restatement for general price level changes is not considered a departure from the historical cost principle because historical costs are merely restated. Thus, the restated amount for land of $277,553 does not represent the current market value of the land. The restatement does, however, represent a departure from the stable-dollar assumption.

Monetary Items

When preparing constant dollar financial statements, monetary and nonmonetary items must be separated because they are treated differently. **Monetary items** are those assets and liabilities that represent claims to receive or obligations to pay a fixed number of dollars. The number of dollars to be received or paid is fixed in amount, regardless of changes that may occur in the purchasing power of the dollar. Such items are already stated in terms of current purchasing power and, therefore do not need to be restated. Cash, accounts receivable, and notes receivable therefore are *monetary assets. Most liabilities are mone-*

tary because they represent obligations to pay fixed amounts of dollars. The principal nonmonetary liability is unearned service revenue.

Purchasing power gains and purchasing power losses result from holding monetary items over time. Holding monetary assets during a period of rising prices results in a loss in purchasing power since the value of money is falling. On the other hand, owing money (i.e., holding monetary liabilities) during a period of rising prices results in a purchasing power gain since the debts can be paid in the future with dollars of smaller purchasing power.

To illustrate a purchasing power loss, assume that Bray Company held $40,000 in cash throughout 1985. The loss in purchasing power would be:

Number of year-end dollars needed to maintain purchasing power:

$$\$40,000 \times \frac{327.4}{315.5} = \qquad \$41,509$$

Actual number of dollars held at year end	40,000
Purchasing power loss	$ 1,509

If Bray Company also held a $60,000 note payable throughout 1985, the gain in purchasing power would be:

Number of year-end dollars representing the same purchasing power as the amount owed at the beginning of the year:

$$\$60,000 \times \frac{327.4}{315.5} = \qquad \$62,263$$

Number of dollars actually owed	60,000
Purchasing power gain	$ 2,263

Nonmonetary Items

Nonmonetary items are those items that are not monetary in nature. Examples include inventory, plant assets, intangibles, service obligations, and stockholder's equity. Since these items do not represent claims to fixed amounts of cash, no purchasing power gain or loss results and the nonmonetary items must be restated in terms of constant dollars. By restating them, recognition is given to the effect of changes in the general price level from the time the items were originally acquired.

Constant Dollar Financial Statements

To illustrate the preparation of constant dollar financial statements, the following assumptions are made for Flint Company:

1. Restatement is based on the CPI (Figure 16-6).
2. Flint Company was formed on December 31, 1980. Capital stock was issued and all plant assets and land were acquired at that time. Plant and equipment items are depreciated by the straight-line depreciation method and have a 10-year remaining life with no residual value.
3. Ending inventory was acquired evenly throughout 1985; the average CPI for 1985 was 322.2 (Figure 16-6).
4. Beginning inventory of $100,000 was acquired evenly throughout 1984; the average CPI for 1984 was 311.1 (Figure 16-6).

5. A $50,000 cash dividend was paid on December 31, 1985.
6. Sales were made and other expenses (except for depreciation) were incurred evenly throughout the year.
7. Purchases were made evenly throughout the year.
8. The beginning constant dollar retained earnings balance is assumed to be $134,511.
9. The company began the year with monetary assets of $164,000 and monetary liabilities of $148,000. These amounts would be derived from the December 31, 1984 balance sheet.

Constant Dollar Balance Sheet. To illustrate the preparation of a constant dollar balance sheet, the historical cost balance sheet, restatement computations, and constant dollar balance sheet for Flint Company, adjusted to year-end dollars, are shown in Figure 16-7. Note that the monetary assets and liabilities are not restated. Nonmonetary assets and capital stock are restated on the basis of the current (1985) index over the index at the time the nonmonetary assets were acquired and capital stock issued (December 31, 1980). The restated retained earnings figure is an amount that is entered to bring the constant dollar balance sheet into balance.

Constant Dollar Combined Income and Retained Earnings Statement. A historical cost and constant dollar combined income and retained earnings statement for Flint Company is shown in Figure 16-8. It is as-

Figure 16-7
Constant Dollar Balance Sheet

FLINT COMPANY
Constant Dollar Balance Sheet
December 31, 1985

	Historical Cost	Restatement Factor	Constant Dollar
Assets			
Cash	$ 71,000	Monetary — not restated	$71,000
Accounts receivable	114,000	Monetary — not restated	114,000
Inventory	120,000	(327.4 / 322.2) × $120,000	121,937
Plant and equipment	300,000	(327.4 / 258.4) × $300,000	380,108
Accumulated depreciation	(150,000)	(327.4 / 258.4) × $150,000	(190,054)
Land	100,000	(327.4 / 258.4) × $100,000	126,703
Total	$555,000		$623,694
Liabilities			
Accounts payable	$ 79,000	Monetary — not restated	$ 79,000
Notes payable, due 1992	60,000	Monetary — not restated	60,000
Stockholders' Equity			
Capital stock	270,000	(327.4 / 258.4) × $270,000	342,098
Retained earnings	146,000	From Figure 16-8*	142,596
Total	$555,000		$623,694

* Also is the amount needed to balance liabilities and stockholders equity with total assets.

FLINT COMPANY
Constant Dollar Combined Income and Retained Earnings Statement
For the Year Ended December 31, 1985

	Historical Cost	Restatement Computation	Constant Dollar
Sales	$591,000	(327.4 / 322.2) × $591,000	$600,538
Cost of Goods Sold:			
Beginning inventory	100,000	(327.4 / 311.1) × $100,000	105,239
Purchases	381,000	(327.4 / 322.2) × $381,000	387,149
Goods available for sale	481,000		492,388
Less: Ending inventory	120,000	(327.4 / 322.2) × $120,000	121,937
Cost of goods sold	361,000		370,451
Depreciation	30,000	(327.4 / 258.4) × $30,000	38,010
Other expenses	130,000	(327.4 / 322.2) × $130,000	132,098
Total expenses	521,000		540,559
Net income	70,000		
Net income before purchasing power loss			59,979
Purchasing power loss		From Figure 16-9	(1,894)
Constant dollar net income			58,085
Beginning retained earnings balance	126,000	Assumed amount	134,511
	196,000		192,596
Less: Cash dividends	50,000	(327.4 / 327.4) × $50,000	50,000
Ending retained earnings balance	$146,000	To Figure 16-7	$142,596

Figure 16-8
Constant Dollar Combined Income and Retained Earnings Statement

sumed that sales were made and expenses, except for depreciation, were incurred evenly during the year. For a particular type of transaction that occurs continuously throughout the year, it is impractical to restate each individual transaction. Therefore, the average CPI for the year is used in the denominator to translate sales and other expenses to approximate the constant dollar amount that would have resulted had each transaction been restated. Cost of goods sold and depreciation expense are converted on the basis of the CPI that existed when the related assets were acquired. The cash dividend paid on December 31 is stated in terms of year-end dollars.

Computation of Purchasing Power Gain or Loss. In Figure 16-8 a purchasing power loss of $1,894 is reported in the constant dollar income statement. The purchasing power loss is computed in Figure 16-9. The first step is to identify net monetary items at the beginning and end of the period. Net monetary items are monetary assets less monetary liabilities. Flint Company started the period in a $16,000 net monetary asset position and ended the period with $46,000 in net monetary assets. Next, transactions that changed net monetary items are identified. The first column reconciles historical cost net

FLINT COMPANY
Computation of Purchasing Power Gain or Loss
For the Year Ended December 31, 1985

	Historical Cost	Restatement Factor	Constant Dollar
Beginning net monetary items*			
Cash and accounts receivable	$164,000		
Accounts and notes payable	148,000		
Net monetary assets	$ 16,000	(327.4 / 315.5) × $16,000	$ 16,603
Add: Transactions that increase net monetary items:			
Sales	591,000	(327.4 /322.2) × $591,000	600,538
	607,000		617,141
Less: Transactions that decrease net monetary items			
Purchases	381,000	(327.4 / 322.2) × $381,000	387,149
Other expenses	130,000	(327.4 / 322.2) × $130,000	132,098
Cash dividends	50,000	(327.4 / 327.4) × $50,000	50,000
	561,000		569,247
Net monetary items restated			47,894
Ending net monetary items*:			
Cash and receivables	185,000		
Accounts and notes payable	139,000		
Net monetary assets	46,000		
Less: Ending net monetary items — historical cost			46,000
Purchasing power loss (To Figure 16-8.)			$ 1,894

* Monetary items at the beginning of the period are the ending monetary items of the last period. Here the monetary items are assumed as given in No. 9 on page 641 . Ending monetary items are determined from the balance sheet in Figure 16-7.

Figure 16-9
Computation of Purchasing Power Gain or Loss

monetary items at the beginning of the year to the net monetary items at the end of the year. During the period, net monetary assets were increased $591,000 by sales (i.e., cash or accounts receivable were received) and decreased $561,000 by purchases of inventory, incurring other expenses, and the payment of cash dividends (i.e., cash paid or liabilities incurred).

The historical cost dollar amounts are then restated to constant dollars using the appropriate general price level restatement factor. Beginning net monetary items are restated to year-end constant dollars using the index on January 1 as the denominator in the restatement fraction. The denominator in the fraction to restate each type of transaction that changed the beginning net monetary items is the index at the date of the transaction. The net monetary items restated (constant dollar) are compared to the actual amount of ending net monetary items on hand to determine the purchasing power gain or loss.

The net monetary items restated amount shows that the company needed net monetary assets of $47,894 to maintain its purchasing power. Since its actual position was $46,000, the company had a loss in purchasing power of $1,894. The purchasing power loss resulted because Flint Company carried an excess of monetary assets over monetary liabilities throughout the year during which prices increased.

The need for constant dollar financial statements is an unsettled issue. Those who support their preparation argue that the stable dollar assumption does not reflect reality, particularly when inflation rates are high. They believe that the aggregation of dollars with different purchasing powers may mislead users of financial information and thereby cause poor decisions. In addition, they argue that the financial data in constant dollar financial statements are just as reliable and verifiable as historical cost data. Critics of constant dollar accounting argue that both historical cost and constant dollar financial statements are inadequate because they ignore real value changes. Consequently, most critics support the preparation of current value financial statements.

CURRENT VALUE ACCOUNTING

As explained earlier, constant dollar accounting does not depart from the historical cost concept. Rather, it merely restates historical costs in terms of the current purchasing power of money—that is, historical costs are adjusted only for general price level changes. **Current value accounting, (or current cost accounting),** however, is a departure from historical cost because it gives effect to specific price changes.

There are two basic concepts of current value: (1) **net realizable value** and (2) **current replacement cost (current cost).** Net realizable value is an exit value, an estimate of the amount an asset could be sold for in its present condition minus disposal costs. Current replacement cost is an entry value, an estimate of the amount that would have to be paid currently to acquire an asset in its present condition. It is generally referred to simply as current cost.

Proponents of current value accounting tend to support the use of current cost, rather than net realizable value, because (1) current costs are believed to be more objectively determinable by the use of current price lists of suppliers, prices in established markets for used assets, and specific price indexes, and (2) most assets are held for use rather than for direct sale. Thus, the current cost to replace an asset being used is considered more relevant than an estimate of its sales value as provided by net realizable value. In addition, the FASB encourages the disclosure of selected current cost information as discussed later in this chapter. Thus, the following discussion will concentrate on current cost accounting.

In the preparation of current cost financial statements, income activities are divided into two elements.

1. **Current operating income or loss.** Current operating income or loss is the difference between revenues and current cost of the assets sold or used at

the time of sale or use. Operating income is not recognized unless revenues exceed the cost to replace the assets sold or used to produce the revenue.

2. **Holding gains or losses.** Holding gains or losses are the changes in the current cost of assets held during the period.

Thus, the profit-making activities of the firm are recognized as resulting from the production and sale of a product (operating activities) and from holding assets during a period in which their prices increase or decrease.

To illustrate a holding gain or loss, assume that the land purchased by Flint Company for $100,000 in 1980 had a replacement cost of $153,000 and $170,000 on January 1 and December 31, 1985, respectively. A holding gain for 1985 of $17,000 is computed as follows.

Replacement cost – December 31	$170,000
Replacement cost – January 1	153,000
Holding gain	$ 17,000

Total holding gains of $53,000 ($153,000 – $100,000) would have been reported in prior years. In the historical cost accounting model, holding gains and losses are not recognized until confirmed by a transaction, the land is sold.

Realized and Unrealized Holding Gains or Losses

Holding gains and losses may be classified further into realized or unrealized categories.

Realized holding gains or losses relate to changes in the replacement cost of assets sold or used during the year.

Unrealized holding gains or losses relate to changes in the replacement cost of assets held at the balance sheet date.

For example, assume that a company purchased two units of inventory for $50 per unit. One unit was sold for $100 when its replacement cost was $70. The other unit was held at the end of the period, at which time its replacement cost was $80. Holding gains are computed as follows:

	Historical Cost	Current Cost	Holding Gain (Loss)
Cost of goods sold	$50	$70	$20 realized
Ending merchandise inventory	50	80	30 unrealized

Historical cost accounting would report a realized gross profit of $50 ($100 − $50) in the year of the sale, and an ending inventory of $50 in the year-end balance sheet. Current cost accounting would also report realized income of $50, but would separate it into operating income of $30 ($100 − $70) and a realized holding gain of $20. In addition, ending inventory of $80 would be reported in the balance sheet with an unrealized holding gain of $30 reported on the unit still held.

Reporting Realized and Unrealized Holding Gains or Losses

There has been considerable discussion regarding the appropriate reporting of holding gains and losses. Two methods that are commonly proposed are:

1. Including both realized and unrealized holding gains and losses in the income statement as an adjustment to current operating income, or
2. Including realized holding gains and losses in the income statement, but

reporting unrealized holding gains and losses in the stockholders' equity section of the balance sheet.

The first approach will be used in the illustration that follows and in the end of chapter material to this chapter. To illustrate the preparation of current cost financial statements, assume that the replacement cost of Flint Company's nonmonetary assets on December 31, 1985, and the replacement cost of goods sold at the time they were sold were as follows:

Inventory	$134,000
Plant and equipment (before depreciation)	360,000
Land	170,000
Cost of goods sold	388,000

Replacement cost of the plant and equipment at January 1, 1985, was $340,000. Plant and equipment items are depreciated by the straight-line method and have a 10-year useful life with no residual value.

The current cost balance sheet is shown in Figure 16-10. In the current cost balance sheet, monetary assets (cash and accounts receivable) and monetary liabilities (accounts and notes payable) are not changed from their historical amounts because they already reflect current values. Nonmonetary assets are reported at the current cost required to replace them in their present physical condition. In the case of the plant and equipment, the cost to replace the assets new is $360,000. At the end of 1985, the assets were one-half depreciated. Paid-in capital accounts are stated at their historical cost (see Figure 16-7) and retained earnings is computed as a balancing amount.

The current cost income statement for Flint Company is shown in Figure 16-11. In the current cost income statement, sales revenue is reported at current sales price and does not need to be restated. Some expenses are recorded at the time the goods or services are used to produce the revenue. Therefore, the historical costs of such expenses are a close approximation of their current cost. It is assumed that the current cost of the "other expenses" in the amount of $130,000 is equal to their historical costs. The current cost of some expenses at the time they are used or sold will differ from historical costs (primarily cost of goods sold and depreciation), and must be restated to their current cost. Cost of goods sold is computed by multiplying the number of units sold by the replacement cost of the units at the time of sale. Depreciation expense is determined by applying the depreciation methods used to the plant assets' replacement costs.

$$\text{Average current cost of plant and equipment} = \frac{\$340,000 + \$360,000}{2} = \$350,000$$

$$\text{Depreciation expense} = \frac{\$350,000}{\text{10-year useful life}} = \$35,000$$

By reporting current costs, each company recognizes the effect of the specific price changes that affect the resources used by that company. The holding gains and losses, both realized and unrealized, are included in the income statement in Figure 16-11. The amount of $73,000 is assumed. The computation is rather complex and is covered in more advanced accounting courses.

Figure 16-10

FLINT COMPANY
Current Cost Balance Sheet
December 31, 1985

Cash	$ 71,000
Accounts receivable	114,000
Inventory	134,000
Plant and equipment (net)	180,000
Land	170,000
Total Assets	$669,000
Accounts Payable	$ 79,000
Notes payable	60,000
Common stock	270,000
Retained earnings (balancing amount)	260,000
Total Equities	$669,000

Proponents of current cost accounting argue that current cost information is much more realistic than historical cost or constant dollar information—and therefore more useful. They also believe that a company has net earnings only if it has recovered the replacement cost of resources used, thereby permitting it to maintain its productive capacity. Critics of current cost accounting maintain that replacement costs are too subjective and difficult to verify and may therefore mislead decision-makers. In addition, they believe that the use of the last-in, first-out costing method to determine cost of goods sold and the use of accelerated depreciation methods are objective and verfiable and will result in reported earnings that approach those that would be reported under current cost accounting. Consequently, they argue, essentially the same earnings results could be obtained without departing from the historical cost basis.

The Financial Accounting Standards Board has been concerned with the re-

Figure 16-11

FLINT COMPANY
Current Cost Income Statement
For Year Ended December 31, 1985

Sales revenue		$591,000
Expenses:		
Cost of goods sold	$388,000	
Depreciation	35,000	
Other expenses	130,000	553,000
Current operating income		38,000
Holding gains and losses		73,000
Net income		$111,000

porting problems created by inflation. However, it has had difficulty reaching an agreement as to the proper solution. Each reporting basis—historical cost, constant dollar, and current cost—has its advantages and disadvantages. Because decision makers use financial information daily, a major change in the reporting basis has the potential of disrupting the decision making process and, therefore, the allocation of resources within the economy. In 1986, the FASB voted to cancel certain price level information requirements established in 1979. However, the Board encourages firms to report such information on a voluntary basis in supplemental schedules accompanying historical cost based financial statements.

SUMMARY

The first part of this chapter discussed three techniques—horizontal analysis, vertical analysis, and ratio analysis—that are commonly used in conducting an analysis of a firm's financial statements. The technique or techniques selected by an analyst depends upon the nature of the decision. For example, a short-term investor is normally interested in assessing the liquidity of a firm whereas a long-term investor usually analyzes a firm's solvency and profitability as well as its liquidity.

It was emphasized that the percentages and ratios computed for an individual firm should be compared to some other standards such as the historical record of the firm under study, the performance of other firms, or some standard established by the analyst. The limitations of using historical data based on historical cost to predict the performance of a firm must also be recognized.

The second part of the chapter discussed the effects of price changes on financial statements. Price changes are either specific or general. General price level changes are changes in the prices of a large sample of goods or services. A specific price change is the change in the price of a particular good or service, such as the sales price of a textbook. General price changes are recognized by restating historical cost data into constant dollar data as follows:

$$\frac{\text{Current price index}}{\text{Historical cost price index}} \times \text{Historical cost} = \text{Restated cost}$$

Specific price changes, usually measured in terms of replacement cost, are reflected in current cost financial statements.

GLOSSARY

COMMON SIZE STATEMENT. A financial statement in which the amount of each item reported in the statement is presented as a percentage of some specific base amount also reported in the same statement (p. 623).

COMPARATIVE STATEMENTS. Financial statements for the current year and prior years presented together to facilitate the analysis of changes in account balances (p. 621).

CONSTANT DOLLAR ACCOUNTING. The restatement of historical cost financial statements for changes in the general price level (p. 339).

CURRENT OPERATING INCOME (LOSS). Excess of current revenues over current costs needed to produce the revenues (p. 644).

CURRENT REPLACEMENT COST (CURRENT COST). The amount that would have to be paid currently to acquire an asset in its present condition (p. 644).

CURRENT VALUE ACCOUNTING (CURRENT COST ACCOUNTING). The preparation of financial statements on the basis of current costs (p. 644).

GENERAL PRICE LEVEL CHANGE. A change in the weighted average of the prices of all goods and services in the economy (p. 637).

HOLDING GAIN. A gain resulting from holding an asset when its replacement cost increases (p. 645).

HOLDING LOSS. A loss resulting from holding an asset when its replacement cost decreases (p. 645).

HORIZONTAL ANALYSIS. That part of an analysis based on the comparison of amounts reported for the same item in two or more comparative statements with an emphasis on the change from year to year (p. 621).

INFLATION. A decrease in purchasing power of money; also defined as an increase in the general price level (p. 637).

MONETARY ITEMS. Assets and liabilities that represent claims to fixed amounts of dollars established by contract or otherwise (p. 639).

NET MONETARY ITEMS. Monetary assets minus monetary liabilities (p. 642).

NET REALIZABLE VALUE. The amount an asset could be sold for less disposal costs (p. 644).

NONMONETARY ITEMS. All financial statement amounts that are not monetary in nature—that is, do not represent claims to fixed amounts of cash (p. 640).

PURCHASING POWER. The amount of goods or services for which a dollar can be exchanged (p. 637).

PURCHASING POWER GAIN. The gain from holding monetary liabilities during a period of rising prices (p. 640).

PURCHASING POWER LOSS. The loss from holding monetary assets during a period of rising prices (p. 640).

RATIO. Division of the amount reported for one financial statement item by the amount reported for another financial statement item. Ratio analysis is the evaluation of the relationship indicated by this division (p. 624).

REALIZED HOLDING GAIN OR LOSS. A gain or loss resulting from a change in the current cost of an asset sold during the period (p. 645).

SOLVENCY. A firm's ability to satisfy its long-term obligations (p. 634).

SPECIFIC PRICE CHANGE. A change in the price of a particular good or service (p. 637).

TREND ANALYSIS. That part of financial statement analysis involved with comparing the changes in a particular item over a series of years. In trend analysis, a base year is selected. Statement items in subsequent statements are expressed as a percentage of their value in the base year (p. 623).

UNREALIZED HOLDING GAIN OR LOSS. A gain or loss resulting from a change in the current cost of an asset held at the balance sheet date (p. 645).

VERTICAL ANALYSIS. That part of financial statement analysis in which the focus of the study is on the proportion of individual items expressed as a percentage of some specific item reported in the same statement (p. 623). (See·also *Common Size Statement*.)

DISCUSSION QUESTIONS

1. What is the objective of financial statement analysis?
2. Differentiate between horizontal analysis, trend analysis, and vertical analysis.
3. What is the importance of the base year when using trend analysis with percentages?
4. Explain what is meant by the term "common size statements."
5. What is the purpose of computing ratios?
6. Name and define the three financial aspects of a firm that are analyzed using ratio analysis.
7. Explain the significance of the following profitability ratios:
   a. Rate of return on total assets
   b. Rate of return on common stockholders' equity
   c. Earnings per share
   d. Price-earnings ratio
8. How are the current ratio and the quick ratio similar? How do they differ?
9. A firm's receivable turnover ratio declined from 14.3 in 1987 to 12.7 in 1988 to 10.4 in 1989. If the firm's credit terms are 30 days, what problems may be indicated by the ratios?
10. What risk does a company assume as the inventory turnover increases?
11. How could earnings per share decrease even though net income has increased from the previous year?
12. Why is the debt to total assets ratio of importance to a firm's management?
13. What are the limitations of financial statement analysis?
14. Which ratio will help to answer each of the following questions:
   a. How effective are the credit policies of the firm?
   b. How much confidence do investors have in the firm?
   c. Are the assets being used effectively?
   d. How is the firm being financed?
   e. Are the firm's current earnings sufficient to meet the annual interest payments?
15. Explain how the following alternative accounting principles will affect a company's reported earnings:
   a. Use of an accelerated depreciation method rather than straight-line depreciation.
   b. Use of LIFO rather than FIFO inventory valuation in a period of inflation.
   c. Use of the equity method rather than the cost method in accounting for long-term investments in equity securities.
16. What is meant by the phrase "purchasing power of the dollar?" How is it affected by inflation? By deflation?
17. Explain the difference between specific price changes and general price level changes.
18. Identify and briefly define the two primary methods used to report the effects of inflation.
19. Define monetary and nonmonetary items. Explain how purchasing power

gains and losses result from holding monetary items during a period of inflation.

20. Explain why monetary items are not restated when preparing a constant dollar balance sheet.

21. Explain why the current cost concept is preferred over net realizable value by proponents of current value accounting.

22. Explain how the current cost amount is calculated for cost of goods sold and depreciation expense.

EXERCISES

Exercise 16-1   Horizontal and Vertical Analysis — Income Statement

The 1987 and 1988 comparative income statements for Basin Corporation are shown below:

BASIN CORPORATION
Comparative Income Statements
For the Years Ended December 31, 1988 and 1987

	1988	1987
Sales	$800,000	$720,000
Cost of goods sold	480,000	396,000
Gross profit	320,000	324,000
Selling expenses	96,000	100,800
Administrative expenses	64,000	50,400
Interest expense	24,000	14,400
Income tax expense	47,600	55,440
Net Income	$ 88,400	$102,960
Earnings per share	$.442	$.515

Required:

A. Prepare common size income statements for 1988 and 1987.

B. Compute the dollar and percent change in each item from 1987 to 1988.

C. Comment on any significant changes from 1987 to 1988 revealed by the horizontal analysis. Can you determine whether the changes are favorable or unfavorable? Can you determine any trends from the data?

D. Comment on any significant changes from 1987 to 1988 revealed by the vertical analysis. Can you determine whether the changes are favorable or unfavorable? Can you determine any trends from the data?

Exercise 16-2   Horizontal and Vertical Analysis — Balance Sheet

The 1987 and 1988 condensed comparative balance sheets for Valley Corporation are shown next:

VALLEY CORPORATION
Balance Sheets
December 31, 1988 and 1987

	1988	1987
Assets:		
Current assets	$ 780,000	$ 720,000
Long-term investments	150,000	200,000
Plant and equipment (net)	2,200,000	1,680,000
Total Assets	$3,130,000	$2,600,000
Liabilities:		
Current liabilities	$ 310,000	$ 306,000
Long-term liabilities	1,300,000	1,160,000
Total Liabilities	1,610,000	1,466,000
Stockholders' Equity:		
Common stock	720,000	600,000
Additional paid-in capital in excess of par value	440,000	280,000
Retained earnings	360,000	254,000
Total Stockholders' Equity	1,520,000	1,134,000
Total Liabilities and Stockholders' Equity	$3,130,000	$2,600,000

Required:
A. Prepare common size balance sheets for 1988 and 1987.
B. Compute the dollar and percent change in each item from 1987 to 1988.
C. Comment on any significant changes from 1987 to 1988 revealed by the horizontal analysis. Can you determine whether the changes are favorable or unfavorable? Can you determine any trends from the data?
D. Comment on any significant changes from 1987 to 1988 revealed by the vertical analysis. Can you determine whether the changes are favorable or unfavorable? Can you determine any trends from the data?

Exercise 16-3 Trend Analysis

Burnside Company reported the following financial data over a five-year period:

	1985	1986	1987	1988	1989
Sales	$1,500,000	$1,591,200	$1,650,000	$1,614,600	$1,736,000
Gross profit	630,000	675,000	702,450	699,300	705,600
Operating expenses	405,000	437,400	453,600	447,930	451,300
Interest expense	40,000	44,000	44,000	44,000	50,000

Required:
A. Prepare a trend analysis of the data. Use the trend analysis to determine any favorable and unfavorable trends and any changes in the direction of any items over the five-year period.
B. What overall conclusion, if any, can be reached by an analysis of the trend analysis?

Exercise 16-4 Trend Analysis

Below are the 1985 through 1989 income statements of Farnsbook Corporation expressed in percentages using 1985 as the base year:

	1985	1986	1987	1988	1989
Sales	100%	108%	117%	126%	136%
Cost of goods sold	100	109	119	133	144
Selling expenses	100	106	112	122	133
Administrative expenses	100	110	121	133	146
Interest expense	100	114	130	136	139
Net Income	100	107	114	122	130

Required:

A. Determine the favorable and unfavorable trends in the items listed above. Determine also any changes in the direction of any item over the five-year period.

B. What overall conclusion can be reached by an analysis of the data presented above?

Exercise 16-5 Ratio Calculations

Match the ratio listed in the left-hand column to the methods of calculating the ratios listed in the right-hand column.

Ratio

1. Earnings per share
2. Quick ratio
3. Times interest earned
4. Price-earnings ratio
5. Debt to total assets
6. Current ratio
7. Return on sales
8. Inventory turnover
9. Dividend payout
10. Return on common stockholders' equity
11. Receivable turnover
12. Dividend yield
13. Return on total assets

A. $\dfrac{\text{Net Income} + \text{Interest expense (Net of tax)}}{\text{Average total assets}}$

B. $\dfrac{\text{Net Income} - \text{Preferred stock cash dividends}}{\text{Average common stockholders' equity}}$

C. $\dfrac{\text{Net Income} - \text{Preferred stock cash dividends}}{\text{Weighted average number of shares outstanding}}$

D. $\dfrac{\text{Market price per share of common stock}}{\text{Earnings per share}}$

E. $\dfrac{\text{Annual dividend per share of common stock}}{\text{Market price per share of common stock}}$

F. $\dfrac{\text{Total dividends to common stockholders}}{\text{Net Income} - \text{Preferred stock cash dividend requirement}}$

G. $\dfrac{\text{Current assets}}{\text{Current liabilities}}$

H. $\dfrac{\text{Cash} + \text{Marketable securities} + \text{Net receivables}}{\text{Current liabilities}}$

I. $\dfrac{\text{Net sales}}{\text{Average receivable balance}}$

J. $\dfrac{\text{Cost of goods sold}}{\text{Average inventory balance}}$

K. $\dfrac{\text{Total liabilities}}{\text{Total assets}}$

L. $\dfrac{\text{Net income} + \text{Interest expense} + \text{Income tax expense}}{\text{Interest expense}}$

M. $\dfrac{\text{Net income}}{\text{Net sales}}$

Exercise 16-6 **Ratio Significance**

Match the ratio listed in the left-hand column to the definition of its significance listed in the right-hand column.

Ratio	Significance
1. Debt to total assets	A. Measures rate of return earned on total assets provided by both creditors and owners.
2. Earnings per share	
3. Receivable turnover	
4. Current ratio	B. Measures rate of return earned on assets provided by owners.
5. Times interest earned	
6. Return on total assets	C. Measures net profitability of each dollar of sales.
7. Price-earnings ratio	
8. Return on common stockholders' equity	D. Measures net income earned on each share of common stock.
9. Dividend payout	E. Measures the amount investors are paying for a dollar of earnings.
10. Return on sales	
11. Quick ratio	F. Measures rate of return to stockholders based on current market price.
12. Dividend yield	
13. Inventory turnover	

G. Measures the percentage of income paid out to common stockholders.

H. A measure of short-term liquidity. Indicates the ability of a firm to meet its short-term debts from its current assets.

I. A more rigorous measure of short-term liquidity. Indicates the ability of the firm to meet unexpected demands from the liquid current assets.

J. Measures effectiveness of collections; used to evaluate whether receivable balance is excessive.

K. Indicates the liquidity of inventory. Measures the number of times inventory was sold on the average during the period.

L. Measures the percentage of assets provided by creditors and the extent of using leverage.

M. Measures the ability of the firm to meet its interest payments out of current earnings.

Exercise 16-7 **Profitability Analysis**

Brunson Corporation reported a net income of $1,520,000 for 1988. During the year, the company paid preferred stock cash dividends of $80,000 and common stock cash dividends of $800,000. Throughout the year, 600,000 shares of common stock were outstanding. The common stock is currently selling at $30 per share.

Required:
Compute the following ratios:

1. Earnings per share
2. Price-earnings ratio
3. Dividend yield
4. Dividend payout

Exercise 16-8 Liquidity Analysis

The following information was taken from the 1988 and 1987 financial statements of Gunderson Corporation:

	1988	1987
Cash	$ 60,000	$ 86,000
Marketable securities	150,000	132,000
Accounts receivable	144,000	126,000
Inventory	407,000	387,000
Prepaid expenses	18,000	30,000
Plant and equipment (net)	690,000	663,000
Accounts payable	390,000	360,000
Wages payable	25,000	20,000
Sales	1,680,000	1,662,000
Cost of goods sold	1,020,000	1,008,000

Required:
A. Compute the following items for 1988 and 1987:
  1. Current ratio
  2. Quick ratio
B. Compute the following items for 1988:
  1. Receivable-turnover ratio
  2. Average collection period of accounts receivable
  3. Inventory-turnover ratio
  4. Average days per inventory turnover
C. Comment on any potential problems indicated by these items.

Exercise 16-9 Profitability and Solvency Analysis

The following information is available for the Waller Corporation:

	1988	1987
Sales	$3,200,000	$2,940,000
Interest expense	138,000	142,000
Income tax expense	248,800	218,400
Net Income	292,000	256,000
Preferred dividends paid	18,000	18,000
Total assets	2,600,000	2,460,000
Total liabilities	1,460,000	1,620,000
Preferred stock	300,000	300,000
Common stock	526,000	498,000
Retained earnings	314,000	42,000
Tax rate	46%	46%

Required:
A. Compute the following ratios for 1988:
  1. Return on total assets
  2. Return on common stockholders' equity

   B. Compute the following ratios for 1988 and 1987:
1. Return on sales
2. Debt to total assets
3. Times interest earned

   C. Comment on any potential problems and/or improvements indicated by these ratios.

Exercise 16-10 Analysis of Two Companies

Financial data for two companies engaged in the same line of business is presented below for 1988:

	Ashton Company	Bishop Company
Sales (all on credit)	$2,400,000	$1,800,000
Total assets	1,200,000	600,000
Total liabilities	300,000	150,000
Average accounts receivable	300,000	150,000
Average inventory	360,000	210,000
Gross profit as a percentage of sales	40%	30%
Operating expenses as a percentage of sales	37%	25%
Net income as a percentage of sales	3%	5%

Required:
A. Compute the following items for each company (neither company has interest expense):
1. Net income
2. Return on total assets
3. Return on common stockholders' equity (no preferred stock)
4. Accounts receivable turnover
5. Inventory turnover

B. In which of the two companies would you buy stock? Explain your reasons.

Exercise 16-11 Constant Dollar Financial Statement Adjustments

Presented below are general price level indexes for specific dates or periods:

December 31, 1960	100	June 30, 1987	204
February 15, 1961	106	December 31, 1987	215
March 21, 1961	108	Average for 1987	206
May 1, 1976	169	June 19, 1988	220
September 23, 1980	190	December 31, 1988	233
December 31, 1983	197	Average for 1988	222

Presented below are transactions or accounts and their respective dates.

1. Cash on hand on December 31, 1988.
2. Equipment purchased on March 21, 1961.
3. Common stock issued on December 31, 1960.
4. Land purchased on February 15, 1961.
5. Preferred stock issued on September 23, 1980.
6. Accounts receivable balance on December 31, 1988.
7. Inventory (LIFO–accumulated evenly throughout 1987).
8. Depreciation expense for 1988 on equipment purchased on March 21, 1961.
9. Sales made during 1988.

10. Investment in common stocks purchased on May 1, 1976.
11. Accounts payable balance on December 31, 1988.
12. Bonds payable issued on December 31, 1983 maturing on December 31, 1999.
13. Purchases made during 1988.
14. Interest expense incurred evenly throughout 1988.
15. Allowance for Uncollectible Accounts balance on December 31, 1988.

Required:
Indicate what the numerator and denominator would be to adjust the above items for general price-level changes for presentation on the 1988 constant dollar financial statements. Sales are made and expenses were incurred evenly during 1988.

Exercise 16-12 **Purchasing Power Gain or Loss on Net Monetary Items**
On January 1, 1988, Lander Corporation has net monetary assets of $160,000. During 1988, the following transactions increased or decreased this balance:

1. Equipment was purchased on March 31, 1988 for $22,000 and $12,000 in cash dividends were paid on December 31.
2. Sales of $460,000 were made evenly throughout the period.
3. Purchases of $300,000 were made evenly throughout the period.
4. Selling expenses (excluding depreciation) of $80,000 were incurred evenly throughout the period.

Assume that the Consumer Price Index for all Urban Consumers was as follows for 1988:

January 1, 1988	110
March 31, 1988	115
Average for 1988	120
December 31, 1988	130

Required:
Compute the purchasing power gain or loss on the net monetary items for 1988.

Exercise 16-13 **Current Cost Income Statement**
Hull Corporation adopted a current cost accounting system in its first year of operation, 1988. At the beginning of 1988, the corporation purchased $72,000 of inventory, and at the end of the year inventory on hand was $43,200 on an historical cost basis and $68,400 on a current cost basis. At the time the inventory was sold, the current cost of the inventory was $39,600. Sales for the year were $90,000 and operating expenses, exclusive of depreciation were $26,300. Depreciation expense was $10,200 on an historical cost basis and $12,600 on a current cost basis. Holding gains totaled $42,000.

Required:
Prepare a current cost income statement for 1988 for Hull Corporation.

Exercise 16-14 **Current Cost Income Statement and Balance Sheet**
Beaton Company is considering the adoption of a current cost accounting system. Presented next is the company's balance sheet at the end of the first year of operations based on historical cost:

BEATON COMPANY
Balance Sheet
December 31, 1988

Cash	$ 75,000	Accounts payable	$ 57,000
Inventory	126,000	Common stock	150,000
Land	48,000	Retained earnings	42,000
	$249,000		$249,000

The following additional information is also available:

1. The cost of goods sold on an historical cost basis is $180,000; on a current cost basis it is $204,000.
2. No dividends were paid in 1988.
3. Ending inventory on a current cost basis is $148,000; land on a current cost basis is $72,000.
4. Operating expenses for 1988 were $90,000.
5. Sales for 1988 were $312,000.
6. Holding gains were $70,000.

Required:

A. Prepare an income statement for 1988 on:
   1. an historical cost basis.
   2. a current cost basis.
B. Prepare a balance sheet as of December 31, 1988 on a current cost basis.

PROBLEMS

Problem 16-1 Horizontal and Vertical Analysis

The 1987 and 1988 comparative income statements and balance sheets for Everett Corporation are shown next:

EVERETT CORPORATION
Comparative Income Statements
For the Years Ended December 31, 1988 and 1987

	1988	1987
Sales	$1,097,400	$930,000
Less: Cost of goods sold	466,395	372,000
Gross profit	631,005	558,000
Selling expenses	252,402	186,000
Administrative expenses	131,688	139,500
Interest expense	54,870	27,900
Income tax expense	82,305	93,000
Total expenses	521,265	446,400
Net Income	$ 109,740	$111,600
Earnings per share	$.937	$.956

EVERETT CORPORATION
Comparative Balance Sheets
December 31, 1988 and 1987

	1988	1987
Assets		
Current Assets		
Cash	$ 360,200	$ 330,500
Marketable securities	215,100	665,800
Accounts receivable (Net)	1,630,000	1,180,000
Inventory	1,997,600	1,313,900
Prepaid expenses	56,800	79,000
Total Current Assets	4,259,700	3,569,200
Long-term investments	300,300	637,800
Plant and equipment (Net)	5,930,000	3,880,000
Other assets	140,000	128,000
Total Assets	$10,630,000	$8,215,000
Liabilities		
Current Liabilities		
Accounts payable	$ 1,690,000	$1,230,800
Notes payable	1,200,000	600,000
Accrued expenses	510,000	360,000
Total Current Liabilities	3,400,000	2,190,800
Long-term Liabilities		
Bonds payable	2,000,000	500,000
Mortgage payable	1,206,260	1,529,200
Total Long-term Liabilities	3,206,260	2,029,200
Total Liabilities	6,606,260	4,220,000
Stockholders' Equity		
Preferred stock, 8%, $100 par value	200,000	200,000
Common stock, $10 par value	1,000,000	1,000,000
Additional paid-in capital in excess of par value	930,000	930,000
Retained earnings	1,893,740	1,865,000
Total Stockholders' Equity	4,023,740	3,995,000
Total Liabilities and Stockholders' Equity	$10,630,000	$8,215,000

Required:
A. Prepare common size financial statements for 1988 and 1987.
B. Compute the dollar and percent change for each financial statement item from 1987 to 1988.
C. Comment on any significant changes from 1987 to 1988 revealed by the horizontal analysis. Can you determine whether the changes are favorable or unfavorable? Can you determine any trends from the data?
D. Comment on any significant changes from 1987 to 1988 revealed by the vertical analysis. Can you determine whether the changes are favorable or unfavorable? Can you determine any trends from the data?

Problem 16-2 Ratio Analysis
Refer to the data in Problem 16-1.

Required:

Use the financial data presented in Problem 16-1 to answer the questions listed below:

1. Compute the average percentage markup on inventory cost for 1988 and 1987.
2. Compute the average income tax rate for 1988 and 1987.
3. Compute the return on sales for 1988 and 1987.
4. What percent of the total resources available to Everett Corporation were invested in plant and equipment in 1988 and 1987? Did the amount increase or decrease from 1987 to 1988?
5. Compute the debt to total assets ratios for 1988 and 1987. Do they look favorable or unfavorable? Explain.
6. Compute the times interest earned for 1988 and 1987. Does it look favorable or unfavorable? Explain.
7. Compute the 1988 return on common stockholders' equity.

Problem 16-3 Ratio Analysis
Refer to the data in Problem 16-1.

Required:

Use the financial data presented in Problem 16-1 to compute the ratios requested below:

1. Compute all ratios discussed in the chapter for 1988. Separate the ratios into the three categories: (1) profitability, (2) liquidity, and (3) solvency. The common stock's market value is $27 per share on December 31, 1988.
2. Comment on any ratios that point out abnormalities or possible danger signs.

Problem 16-4 Computation of Financial Statement Items Using Ratios
The information presented below relates to the Sterling Corporation for the year 1988:

Current assets, January 1, 1988	$100
Total assets, January 1, 1988	300
Long-term liabilities, January 1, 1988	100
Current ratio, January 1, 1988	2:1
Increase in working capital during 1988	$ 50
Net income as a % of ending total assets	25%
Total assets, December 31, 1988	$400
Noncurrent assets, December 31, 1988	250
Long-term liabilities, December 31, 1988	130
Debt to total assets, December 31, 1988	45%

Required:

Calculate each of the missing items requested below. (*Hint:* Reconstruct the balance sheets at the beginning and end of the year to start your solution.)

1. Current liabilities, January 1, 1988
2. Debt to total assets, January 1, 1988
3. Net income for 1988
4. Dividends declared during 1988
5. Current liabilities, December 31, 1988

Problem 16-5 **Effect of Transactions on Ratios**

The Oxford Corporation completed the transactions listed below in the left-hand column:

	Transaction	**Ratio**
1.	Retired bonds payable by issuing common stock.	Return on common stockholders' equity
2.	Purchased inventory on account.	Quick ratio.
3.	Sold inventory for cash.	Current ratio
4.	Issued additional shares of common stock for cash.	Debt to total assets
5.	Declared a cash dividend on common stock.	Dividend payout
6.	Paid the cash dividend declared in No. 5.	Dividend yield
7.	Wrote off an uncollectible account receivable to Allowance for Uncollectible Accounts.	Current ratio
8.	Collected an account receivable.	Receivable turnover
9.	Paid an account payable.	Return on total assets
10.	Sold obsolete inventory at cost.	Return on sales
11.	Issued a stock dividend on common stock.	Earnings per share
12.	Sold inventory on account.	Inventory turnover
13.	Purchased machinery on account.	Debt to total assets
14.	Retired bonds payable with cash.	Debt to total assets
15.	Issued common stock in exchange for land.	Return on common stockholders' equity
16.	Paid an account payable.	Quick ratio
17.	Declared a cash dividend on common stock.	Current ratio
18.	Sold inventory on account.	Quick ratio
19.	Collected an account receivable.	Current ratio
20.	Sold inventory for cash.	Receivable turnover
21.	Paid a cash dividend previously declared.	Current ratio
22.	Recorded accrued interest on notes payable.	Return on sales
23.	Issued bonds payable for cash.	Return on total assets
24.	Issued additional shares of stock for cash.	Earnings per share

Required:

State whether each transaction listed above would cause the ratio listed opposite it to increase, decrease, or remain unchanged.

Problem 16-6 **Financial Statement Analysis of Two Companies**

The 1988 financial statements of Cranswick and Dannenfelt Companies are presented below in summary form:

	Cranswick	**Dannenfelt**
BALANCE SHEET		
Cash	$ 75,000	$ 33,000
Accounts receivable (Net)	90,000	51,000
Inventory	240,000	60,000

Plant and equipment (Net)	375,000	900,000
Other assets	120,000	756,000
Total assets	$900,000	$1,800,000
Current liabilities	$270,000	$ 120,000
Long-term debt (10%)	150,000	180,000
Capital stock, par value $10	360,000	1,200,000
Additional paid-in capital	30,000	180,000
Retained earnings	90,000	120,000
Total liabilities and stockholders' equity	$900,000	$1,800,000

INCOME STATEMENT

Sales revenue (on credit)	$1,800,000-(1/3)	$2,700,000-(1/9)
Cost of goods sold	(1,050,000)	(1,350,000)
Expense (including interest and taxes)	(615,000)	(1,080,000)
Net Income	$ 135,000	$ 270,000

SELECTED INFORMATION FROM THE 1987 BALANCE SHEETS

Accounts receivable (Net)	$ 75,000	$ 57,000
Inventory	210,000	72,000
Long-term debt	150,000	180,000

OTHER RELEVANT FINANCIAL INFORMATION

Market price per share of common stock at end of 1988	$ 30	$ 18
Average income tax rate	30%	30%
Dividends declared and paid in 1988	$ 77,400	$ 451,200

Cranswick and Dannenfelt Companies are in the same line of business and directly compete with each other in a large metropolitan area. They each have been in operation for approximately 10 years, and each has experienced a relatively steady growth. The management styles of the two companies differ significantly. Dannenfelt is an extremely conservative company and Cranswick tends to be more progressive and risky in its activities. Cranswick Company has an annual audit performed by an independent CPA firm, but Dannenfelt does not.

Required:
A. Prepare a schedule that reflects a ratio analysis of each company. Compute as many of the ratios discussed in the chapter as possible. Use end of year balances as estimates of the average balances maintained throughout the year whenever necessary.
B. Prepare common size balance sheets and income statements for 1988 for both companies.
C. A friend of yours has decided to invest in either Cranswick or Dannenfelt Company and will purchase 15% of the common stock of the company she selects. Prepare a comparative evaluation of the ratio analyses you prepared in Requirement A, and any other information you consider important, to assist your friend in making a decision. She will pay the market price listed above. Also, give your recommendation regarding which stock you think she should purchase, stating your reasons for your choice.

Problem 16-7 Effect of Inventory Valuation Method on Ratio Analysis
Frank Company uses the FIFO method to cost its inventory and Cannon Company uses the LIFO method. The two companies are exactly alike except for the difference in the inventory costing methods used. Costs of inventory for

both companies have been rising steadily in recent years and each company has increased its inventory each year. Each company has paid its tax liability in full for the current year and for all previous years. Each company uses the same accounting methods for both financial reporting and income tax reporting.

Required:
For each ratio listed below, indicate which company will report the higher (or better) ratio. If it is not possible to determine from the information given above, state why.

1. Current ratio
2. Quick ratio
3. Inventory turnover
4. Debt to total assets
5. Return on common stockholders' equity
6. Earnings per share
7. Times interest earned
8. Return on sales

Problem 16-8 Limitations of Ratio Analysis

Carter Company and Darter Company both began operations on January 1, 1988. For illustrative purposes, assume that at that date their financial positions were identical and that their operations during 1988 were also identical. The only difference between the two companies is that they elected to use different accounting methods as shown below:

	Carter Company	Darter Company
Inventory valuation	FIFO	LIFO
Plant and equipment depreciation methods	Straight-line	Accelerated method

Financial statements for the two companies prepared at the end of 1988 are presented below:

	Carter Company	Darter Company
INCOME STATEMENT		
Revenues	$260,000	$260,000
Cost of goods sold	156,000	172,000
Gross profit	104,000	88,000
Operating expenses*	56,000	76,000
Net Income	$ 48,000	$ 12,000
BALANCE SHEET		
Cash	$ 32,000	$ 32,000
Accounts receivable	80,000	80,000
Inventories	56,000	40,000
Plant and equipment (net)	80,000	60,000
	$248,000	$212,000
Current liabilities	40,000	40,000
Long-term liabilities	60,000	60,000
Common stockholders' equity	148,000	112,000
	$248,000	$212,000

* Includes interest expense at $10,000. Depreciation expense was $20,000 for Carter and $40,000 for Darter. Income tax expense was $16,000 for Carter and $4,000 for Darter.

Required:

A.   Compute the following ratios for each company:
1.   Return on total assets
2.   Return on common stockholders' equity
3.   Return on sales
4.   Current ratio
5.   Receivable turnover
6.   Inventory turnover
7.   Debt to total assets

B.   Comment on the differences in the ratios caused by the two companies using different accounting methods.

Problem 16-9   Financial Statement Analysis of Two Companies

The 1988 financial statements of Mundell and Orden Companies are presented below in summary form:

	Mundell	Orden
BALANCE SHEET		
Cash	$ 40,000	$ 80,000
Accounts receivable (Net)	120,000	20,000
Inventory	240,000	60,000
Plant & equipment (Net)	1,000,000	300,000
Other assets	310,000	108,000
Total assets	$1,710,000	$568,000
Current liabilities	$ 200,000	$ 40,000
Long-term debt (10%)	400,000	100,000
Common stock, $10 par value	1,000,000	400,000
Additional paid-in capital in excess of par		
value	50,000	4,000
Retained earnings	60,000	24,000
Total liabilities and stockholders' equity	$1,710,000	$568,000
INCOME STATEMENT		
Sales revenue (on credit)	$1,800,000-(1/2)	$600,000-(1/3)
Cost of goods sold	(1,044,000)	(360,000)
Expenses (including interest and taxes)	(576,000)	(168,000)
Net Income	$ 180,000	$ 72,000
SELECTED INFORMATION FROM THE 1987 BALANCE SHEETS		
Accounts receivable (Net)	$ 80,000	$ 28,000
Long-term debt (10% interest rate)	400,000	100,000
Inventory	200,000	80,000
OTHER RELEVANT FINANCIAL INFORMATION		
Market price per share of common stock		
at end of 1988	$12.75	$10.50
Average income tax rate—1988	30%	20%
Dividends declared and paid in 1988	$80,000	$20,000
Income tax expense—1988	77,143	18,000

Mundell and Orden Companies operate in the same line of business and in the same state, but in different cities. Each company was founded 10 years ago. Both firms have an audit of their financial records by an independent Certified Public Accountant each year. Mundell is audited by one of the "Big 8" accounting firms, while Orden is audited by a local CPA firm located in the city where Orden is located. Both companies have received unqualified opinions for the last five years. Mundell Company wants to borrow $150,000 and Orden Company wants to borrow $60,000. The loans are two-year loans and will be used for "working capital purposes."

Required:

A. Prepare a schedule that reflects a ratio analysis of each company. Compute as many of the ratios discussed in the chapter as possible. Use end-of-year balances to approximate the average balances maintained throughout the year whenever necessary.

B. Prepare common size balance sheets and income statements for 1988 for both companies.

C. Assume you are the manager of the loan department of a bank located in one of the cities in the state where the two firms operate. You have been given the task of analyzing the situations of the two firms and recommending which loan is preferable. Based on the data given in the problem, and any other financial information you consider important, state your choice between the two companies for the loan and give your reasons.

Problem 16-10 Using Ratios to Analyze Financial Performance

Gentry Corporation commenced operations on January 2, 1986. Presented below is selected financial information from financial statements prepared at the end of the fiscal years (December 31) 1986, 1987, 1988, and 1989.

	1986	1987	1988	1989
Accounts receivable (Net) (credit terms, n/30)	$ 40,000	$ 50,000	$ 80,000	$110,000
Inventory	50,000	60,000	100,000	125,000
Net sales (3/4 on credit)	200,000	300,000	500,000	600,000
Cost of goods sold	130,000	180,000	320,000	400,000
Net Income (Loss)	(50,000)	30,000	70,000	50,000

Required:

A. Complete the tabulation format given below.

B. Evaluate the results of the first three related ratios identifying the favorable and unfavorable items. Give your recommendations to improve Gentry's performance.

C. Evaluate the results of the last four related ratios identifying the favorable and unfavorable items. Give your recommendations to improve Gentry's performance.

Items	1986	1987	1988	1989
1. Return on sales				
2. Gross profit % on sales				
3. Expenses as a percent of sales, excluding cost of goods sold				
4. Inventory turnover				
5. Day's supply in inventory				
6. Receivable turnover				
7. Average number of days to collect accounts receivable				

Problem 16-11 Financial Analysis Using Ratios

Below are several financial ratios for the Kellogg Company for the three years ended December 31, 1987, 1988, and 1989:

Ratio		1987	1988	1989
1.	Current ratio	4:1	3:1	1.5:1
2.	Accounts receivable turnover	9.5	7.8	4.7
3.	Inventory turnover	2.4	4.5	3.1
4.	Return on sales	16.8%	13.3%	9.9%
5.	Return on total assets	17.7%	14.9%	13.3%
6.	Return on common stockholders' equity	20.0%	23.1%	21.2%
7.	Debt to total assets	.138	.324	.343
8.	Times interest earned	17.7	5.2	4.5
9.	Earnings per share	$.40	$.60	$.70
	Additional Data:			
10.	Net income	$40,000	$60,000	$70,000
11.	Interest expense	4,000	24,000	36,000
12.	Tax rate	40%	40%	40%
13.	Total assets	$240,000	$500,000	$690,000
14.	No dividends were paid during the three-year period.			
15.	No stock was sold during the three-year period.			
16.	There is no preferred stock outstanding.			
17.	The data are based on a 360 day year.			
18.	Interest is computed at 10% on all liabilities.			

Required:

A. Using the data above, compute the following:
  1. Sales for 1987, 1988, and 1989
  2. Number of shares of common stock outstanding
  3. The increase in debt in 1988 and 1989
  4. The average number of days the accounts receivable were outstanding in 1987, 1988, and 1989

B. Based on the ratios given and computed in requirement A, evaluate Kellogg Company with respect to: liquidity, profitability, and solvency.

C. In your opinion, what are the two main problems facing Kellogg Company in the future? Be specific.

Problem 16-12 Constant Dollar Balance Sheet

Presented below is the December 31, 1988 historical cost post-closing trial balance for Upland Industries, Inc. The company began operations on January 2, 1988. General price level indexes for 1988 are given below.

January 2, 1988	200
February 1, 1988	205
September 1, 1988	215
December 31, 1988	220
Average for 1988	210

UPLAND INDUSTRIES, INC.
Post-Closing Trial Balance
December 31, 1988

Accounts	Debits	Credits
Cash	$ 63,000	
Accounts receivable (Net)	135,000	

Long-term investments in equity securities,		
purchased September 1, 1988	36,000	
Land, purchased February 1, 1988	45,000	
Equipment, purchased January 2, 1988	300,000	
Accumulated depreciation		$ 24,000
Accounts payable		54,000
Notes payable, dated January 2, 1988, due		
January 2, 1991		129,000
Common stock, no par, sold January 2, 1988		330,000
Retained earnings		42,000
Totals	$579,000	$579,000

A cash dividend of $15,000 was declared and paid on December 31, 1988.

Required:

A. Prepare a December 31, 1988 balance sheet on a constant dollar basis for Upland Industries, Inc.

B. Compute the 1988 constant dollar net income. How does this compare to the 1988 historical cost net income?

Problem 16-13 Current Cost Income Statement and Balance Sheet

Presented below are the 1988 income statement and balance sheet for the Goodburn Corporation prepared on an historical cost basis.

GOODBURN CORPORATION
Income Statement
For the Year Ended December 31, 1988

Sales		$1,182,000
Less: Cost of goods sold		722,000
Gross Profit		460,000
Operating expenses	$260,000	
Depreciation expense	60,000	320,000
Net Income		$ 140,000
Earnings per share		$1.40

GOODBURN CORPORATION
Balance Sheet
As of December 31, 1988

Assets	
Current assets:	
Cash	$ 144,000
Accounts receivable (Net)	228,000
Inventory	240,000
Total current assets	612,000

Property, plant and Equipment:			
Land		$180,000	
Plant & equipment	$444,000		
Less: Accumulated depr.	126,000	318,000	
Total property, plant & equipment			498,000
Total assets			$1,110,000
Liabilities			
Current liabilities:			
Accounts payable			$ 140,000
Wages payable			12,000
Accrued liabilities			6,000
Total current liabilities			158,000
Notes payable, due in 1993			120,000
Total liabilities			278,000
Stockholders' equity			
Common stock, no par, 100,000 shares, issued on June 1, 1980		540,000	
Retained earnings		292,000	
Total stockholders' equity			832,000
Total liabilities and stockholders' equity			$1,110,000

The following information relating to the replacement cost of Goodburn's assets and the 1988 expenses is available:

Inventory, December 31, 1988	$268,000
Plant and equipment (Net)	560,000*
Land	340,000
Cost of goods sold for 1988	806,000
Holding gains	130,000
Consumer Price Index for all Urban Consumers:	
June 1, 1980	183.6
December 31, 1986	268.3

* Plant and equipment items are depreciated by the straight-line method and have a ten-year remaining life.

Required:

Prepare a 1988 current cost income statement and balance sheet for Goodburn Corporation.

Problem 16-14 Constant Dollar and Current Cost Financial Statements

An income statement for the year ended December 31, 1988, and a balance sheet on December 31, 1988, for Darcy Company are presented here.

INCOME STATEMENT		
Net sales		$1,650,000
Cost of goods sold		1,205,000
Gross profit		445,000
Expenses:		
Depreciation	$ 38,000	
Other expenses	349,000	387,000
Net income		$ 58,000

BALANCE SHEET

Assets		Liabilities & Owners' Equity	
Cash	$125,000	Accounts payable	$151,000
Accounts receivable	175,000	Notes payable	200,000
Inventory	240,000	Common stock	300,000
Plant and equipment (net)	416,000	Retained earnings	305,000
Total	$956,000	Total	$956,000

Darcy Company was formed in 1978, at which time the common stock was issued and the plant and equipment were purchased. Inventory was purchased evenly throughout 1988, and sales were made and cost of goods sold and expenses (other than depreciation) were incurred evenly throughout the year. In addition:

1. Depreciation expense computed on the basis of the plant asset replacement costs is $75,000
2. The replacement cost of goods sold during 1988 was $1,205,000
3. A purchasing power gain of $15,500 was computed for 1988
4. The replacement cost of the December 31, 1988, inventory was $276,000
5. The replacement cost of plant and equipment on December 31, 1988, was $701,500
6. Assumed price indexes:

When the company was formed	145
December 31, 1988	200
Average for 1988	195

7. Holding gains were $36,000

Required:

A. Prepare a constant dollar and a current cost income statement for Darcy Company for the year ended December 31, 1988.
B. Prepare a constant dollar and a current cost balance sheet at December 31, 1988.

17

STATEMENT OF CASH FLOWS

OVERVIEW AND OBJECTIVES

This chapter discusses the preparation and uses of a statement of cash flows. When you have completed the chapter, you should be able to:

1. Explain the purpose and use of cash flow information.
2. Classify cash receipts and cash payments by operating, investing, and financing activities.
3. Identify the content and form of the statement of cash flows.
4. Describe the difference between the direct and indirect approach to reporting net cash flow from operating activities.
5. Explain how to report the effects of exchanges of noncash items.

A complete set of financial statements includes a balance sheet, an income statement, a retained earnings statement, and a statement of cash flows (SCF). Details of the first three statements are discussed in a financial accounting textbook, and the use of financial statements in general for managerial purposes has been discussed in earlier chapters of this book. In this chapter, we consider the statement of cash flows, an important tool for evaluating a firm's financial performance. This report is a useful statement for managers, investors, and creditors because it identifies the activities related to the receipts of cash and the purposes for which cash was used during a period.

BRIEF HISTORY OF THE DEVELOPMENT OF THE SCF

The operating, financing, and investing activities of a company are of considerable interest to users of financial statements because those activities change the financial position of a business. An analysis of comparative balance sheets for successive periods helps identify the total changes that have taken place in asset, liability, and owners' equity accounts, but does not give a clear explanation of what caused those changes. The income statement and retained earnings statement do give a partial explanation by showing a summary of the effects of operating activities, the amount of earnings distributed as dividends, and the amount of earnings retained for other uses. Neither statement, however, gives a full report of the sources (financing activities) nor the uses (investing activities) of financial resources.

For many years, the financing and investing activities of a firm were reported in a financial statement called a Statement of Changes in Financial Position (SCFP). That statement was used to report the sources and uses of financial resources (funds) for a specified time period. Funds were defined as either cash (or cash plus cash equivalents) or working capital. Firms were required to present a cash basis or working capital basis SCFP whenever financial statements purporting to present both financial position and results of operations were issued. Although most firms initially prepared their SCFP on a working capital basis, increasing requests for cash flow information by users of financial information produced a gradual shift from a working capital basis SCFP to a cash basis SCFP. The main reason for the switch to a cash basis SCFP was that a working capital basis often distorts the actual liquidity of a business. A firm pays bills with cash, not working capital. Increases in accounts receivable and inventory make a working capital focus look good, but both must be converted into cash before the firm has the money needed to pay off its obligations. Over time, the cash basis was used by a majority of firms as shown by surveys of 600 companies conducted by the American Institute of Certified Public Accountants.

	1985	1980
Number of Companies Reporting:		
Changes in working capital	220	541
Changes in cash	380	59
Total Companies	600	600

Because of the increased emphasis on the usefulness of cash flow information, the Financial Accounting Standards Board (FASB) has proposed replacing the SCFP with a **Statement of Cash Flows (SCF).** This requirement would be effective for financial statements for fiscal periods ending after June 30, 1987. Earlier application is encouraged and comparative financial statements for earlier periods must be restated.[1]

PURPOSE OF THE SCF

As stated by the FASB, "the primary purpose of a statement of cash flows is to provide information about the cash receipts and cash payments of an entity during a period."[2] The statement of cash flows also provides information about the investing and financing activities of the firm. Cash flow information, used with information contained in the other financial statements, should help managers, investors, creditors, and other users to assess:

**Objective 1:
Purpose and uses
of SCF**

1. The firm's ability to generate positive cash flows in the future;
2. The firm's ability to meet its obligations and pay dividends;
3. The firm's needs for external financing;
4. The reasons for differences between income and related cash receipts and payments; and

[1] Financial Accounting Standards Board, "Statement of Cash Flows," Proposed Statement of Financial Accounting Standards (Stamford, Conn., July 31, 1986).

[2] Ibid., par 4.

5. Both the cash and noncash aspects of the firm's investing and financing transactions during the period.

To provide information useful to financial statement users in making these assessments, the SCF should report the cash effects during a period related to operating activities, investing activities, and financing activities. In addition to providing information for use by external users, the SCF also provides important information for managers to utilize in planning and controlling operations.

CONCEPT OF CASH

In the preparation of the SCF, cash is defined as those items a bank would normally accept for deposit to the firm's checking account plus cash equivalents. Thus, cash flow statements should explain the change during the period in cash and cash equivalents. Investing cash in excess of immediate needs in short-term, highly liquid investments (**cash equivalents**)—such as treasury bills, commercial paper, and money market funds—is considered part of a firm's cash management rather than part of its operating, investing, and financing activities. Consequently, this temporary investment activity should not be reported in the statement of cash flows. In addition, gross amounts of both cash receipts and cash payments normally should be presented for each of the firm's operating, investing, and financing activities.

CLASSIFICATION WITHIN THE SCF

Objective 2: Classifications within the SCF

Classification in accounting facilitates the use of accounting information by grouping items with similar characteristics and separating items with different characteristics. In the statement of cash flows, cash receipts and payments are classified by business activities into three types—operating, investing, and financing. A basic description of each of these activities follows.

OPERATING ACTIVITIES

Operating activities involve the production or delivery of goods for sale and the providing of services. Cash flows from operating activities generally represent the effects of transactions that enter into the determination of net income. Cash inflows from operating activities include (1) collections from customers for the cash sale of goods and services or for accounts receivable, (2) interest receipts for loans made, and (3) dividend receipts from equity investments.

Cash outflows for operating activities result from cash payments to suppliers for the acquisition of inventory, to employees for services, to governments for taxes, to lenders for interest, and to other external parties for numerous types of expenses. The cash outflows may represent payments for goods and services acquired currently, or for the settlement of obligations incurred for goods or services charged to operations of prior periods.

INVESTING ACTIVITIES

Investing activities generally include those transactions involving (1) lending money and collecting the principal, and (2) acquiring and selling (a) securities that are not cash equivalents, and (b) productive assets that are expected to produce revenues over several periods. Cash inflows from investing activities include receipts from:

1. Principal repayments by borrowers (note that interest receipts on the loans are included in operating activities);
2. The sale of loans (receivables) made by the firm;
3. The sale of assets such as (a) debt or equity securities (other than cash equivalents), and (b) property, plant, and equipment.

Cash outflows for investing activities include:

1. Loans made or purchased by the firm; and
2. Payments to acquire assets such as (a) debt or equity securities (other than cash equivalents), and (b) property, plant, and equipment.

Cash inflows from the sale of loans, and cash outflows for loans made or purchased by the firm relate primarily to financial institutions such as finance companies and banks.

Financing Activities

Financing activities generally include obtaining resources (1) from owners and providing them with a return on and a return of their investment, and (2) from creditors and repaying the amounts borrowed or otherwise settling the obligation. (Again, note that interest payments are included in the statement as outflows from operating activities.)

Cash inflows from financing activities include:

1. Proceeds from the issuance of equity securities;
2. Proceeds from the issuance of bonds, mortgages, notes, and other short-term or long-term borrowings.

Cash outflows for financing activities result from:

1. The payment of dividends;
2. Outlays to repurchase the firm's shares of stock (to be retired or held as treasury stock); and
3. Outlays for repayments of amounts borrowed.

Most borrowing and repayment of amounts borrowed are financing activities. However, the settlement of liabilities, such as accrued expenses and accounts payable incurred to acquire inventory and supplies, is considered an operating activity.

The classification of some items depends upon the nature of the firm's operations. For example, there is a presumption that the acquisition and sale, or other disposal, of long-lived assets are investing activities. However, if long-lived assets are acquired or produced to be rented to others for a short period and then sold, the acquisition or production of those assets should be considered an operating activity. In addition, some gains and losses that are normally included in the income statement relate to investing or financing activities rather than to operating activities. For example, a gain or loss from the sale of plant assets or from the disposal of discontinued operations is generally a part of cash inflow from investing activities, and a gain or loss on the extinguishment of debt is generally part of a cash outflow from financing activities. Thus, considerable judgment must be exercised in the preparation of the SCF.

CONTENT AND FORM OF THE SCF

Objective 3:
Format of SCF

The SCF should report net cash provided or used by operating, investing, and financing activities as well as the aggregate effect of those flows on cash and cash equivalents during the period. Some flexibility is permitted in the form of the statement. For example, cash flow from operating activities might be presented either directly or indirectly, and investing and financing activities not involving cash payments or cash receipts may be presented in the body of the statement or in a separate schedule. These alternatives are discussed and illustrated later in this chapter.

CASH FLOW FROM OPERATING ACTIVITIES

As mentioned earlier, cash flow from operating activities may be reported either directly or indirectly.

Direct Method of Reporting Cash Flow from Operating Activities

Objective 4:
Direct vs.
indirect method

Under the **direct method,** major classes of operating revenues are shown as cash inflows from operations. For example, cash inflows may be reported for cash collected from customers and for cash received from interest and dividends. Conversely, cash payments for expenses are reported by major class such as cash paid to suppliers for goods and services, cash paid to employees, cash paid to creditors for interest, and cash paid to governments for taxes. The difference between the cash inflows from operations and cash payments for expenses represents the net cash flow from operating activities. The main advantage of the direct method is that it shows the operating cash receipts and payments. Knowledge of where operating cash came from and how cash was used in operations in past periods may be useful in estimating future cash flows.

To illustrate the direct method of presenting net cash flow from operating activities, assume that PMX Corporation's income statement for 1988 and selected comparative balance sheet data were as follows:

PMX CORPORATION
Income Statement
For the Year Ended December 31, 1988

Sales revenues		$694,000
Cost of goods sold		316,000
Gross profit on sales		378,000
Operating expenses:		
Advertising expense	$ 48,600	
Depreciation expense	69,300	
Insurance expense	4,200	
Repairs and maintenance expense	26,800	
Salaries and wages expense	112,600	
Total operating expenses		261,500
Net income before income tax		116,500
Income tax expense		21,000
Net income		$ 95,500

Selected comparative balance sheet data for 1988 and 1987 were:

	December 31	
	1988	1987
Accounts receivable	$169,400	$147,300
Inventory	101,600	109,500
Prepaid insurance	6,800	9,400
Accounts payable	74,200	81,600
Accrued salaries and wages payable	24,900	21,400
Accrued income taxes payable	9,300	–0–

In computing the amount of cash provided by operating activities, the normal approach is to convert the accrual basis net income to a cash basis income. To make this conversion, the relationship between the effect of operating transactions on accrual income and cash movements within the company must be considered. Thus, the different classes of accrual basis revenues are adjusted to show cash inflows from operations. For example, cash inflows may be reported for cash received from customers and for cash received from interest and dividends. Conversely, accrual basis expenses are adjusted to report cash outflows for various classes of expenses such as (1) cash paid to suppliers for inventory purchases; (2) cash paid to suppliers for other goods and services such as office supplies, advertising, and utilities; (3) cash paid to employees; (4) cash paid to creditors for interest; and (5) cash paid to the government for taxes. The difference between cash inflows from operations and cash outflows for expenses represents the net cash flow from operating activities. The conversion process is presented in the following sections.

Cash Received from Customers

Under accrual accounting, sales on account are recognized by a debit to Accounts Receivable and a credit to Sales at the time each sale is made. Under the cash basis, revenue is not recognized until cash is received. The conversion of accrual basis sales revenues to cash basis sales revenues may be done as follows:

$$\text{Accrual basis sales} \begin{Bmatrix} + \text{ beginning accounts receivable} \\ - \text{ ending accounts receivable} \end{Bmatrix} = \begin{array}{l} \text{Cash received} \\ \text{from customers} \end{array}$$

PMX Corporation's comparative balance sheet data show that accounts receivable on 12/31/87 and 12/31/88 were $147,300 and $169,400, respectively. Thus, cash received from customers is computed as shown here.

Accrual basis sales from the income statement	$694,000
Add: Beginning accounts receivable	147,300
Total cash collectible from customers	841,300
Less: Ending accounts receivable	169,400
Cash received from customers	$671,900

The beginning balance of accounts receivable is added to accrual basis sales. The total shows the amount of cash that could have been collected during the current period, including collections of sales recognized in prior years. The ending accounts receivable balance is subtracted because it represents sales that have not yet been collected. The result is cash collected from customers during the current period.

Cash Payments to Suppliers for Purchases

Under accrual accounting, purchases of merchandise on account are recognized when made by a debit to Inventory (in a perpetual system) and a credit to Accounts Payable. Under the cash basis, purchases are not recognized until cash is paid. Thus, to convert from accrual basis cost of goods sold to cash basis cost of goods sold, adjustments must be made for the changes during the year in inventory and in accounts payable as follows:

$$
\begin{matrix}
\text{Accrual basis} \\
\text{cost of} \\
\text{goods sold}
\end{matrix}
\left\{
\begin{matrix}
-\text{ beginning inventory} \\
+\text{ ending inventory}
\end{matrix}
\right\}
=
\begin{matrix}
\text{Accrual} \\
\text{basis} \\
\text{purchases}
\end{matrix}
$$

$$
\begin{matrix}
\text{Accrual} \\
\text{basis} \\
\text{purchases}
\end{matrix}
\left\{
\begin{matrix}
+\text{ beginning accounts payable} \\
-\text{ ending accounts payable}
\end{matrix}
\right\}
=
\begin{matrix}
\text{Cash paid} \\
\text{for} \\
\text{purchases}
\end{matrix}
$$

PMX Corporation's comparative balance sheet data show that on December 31,1987, and December 31, 1988, (1) inventory balances were $109,500 and $101,600, respectively, and (2) accounts payable balances were $81,600 and $74,200, respectively. Thus, cash paid to suppliers for purchases during 1988 can be computed as shown here.

Accrual basis cost of goods sold (from Income Statement)	$316,000
Less: Beginning inventory	(109,500)
Add: Ending inventory	101,600
Accrual basis purchases for the year	308,100
Add: Beginning accounts payable	81,600
Less: Ending accounts payable	(74,200)
Cash paid to suppliers for purchases	$315,500

The amount of purchases made during the year is computed first by deducting the beginning inventory balance from accrual basis cost of goods sold and adding the ending inventory balance to accrual basis cost of goods sold. After the amount of accrual basis purchases for the year is determined, the amount of cash paid to suppliers for purchases can be computed. This is done by adding beginning accounts payable (goods purchased last year but paid for during the current year) and deducting ending accounts payable (goods purchased this year but not yet paid for).

Cash Paid for Expenses

Under accrual accounting, expenses are recognized when resources are used to earn revenues. Some expenses are prepaid, some are paid during the current period as incurred, and some are accrued at the end of the period. Under the cash basis, expenses are recognized when they are paid for. The relationships between various expenses and cash payments depend upon the related changes in prepaid expenses and/or accrued expenses. Thus, the conversion of an accrual basis expense to a cash basis expense is made as follows:

$$\text{Accrual basis expenses} \begin{cases} - \text{ beginning prepaid expenses} \\ + \text{ ending prepaid expenses} \\ \qquad\qquad \text{or} \\ + \text{ beginning accrued expenses} \\ - \text{ ending accrued expenses} \end{cases} = \begin{matrix} \text{Cash payments} \\ \text{for} \\ \text{expenses} \end{matrix}$$

PMX Corporation's comparative balance sheet data show that the December 31, 1987, and December 31, 1988, balances in the Prepaid Insurance account were $9,400 and $6,800, respectively. Thus, the conversion of accrual basis insurance expense to cash basis insurance expense is:

Accrual basis insurance expense from income statement	$4,200
Less: Beginning prepaid insurance	(9,400)
Plus: Ending prepaid insurance	6,800
Cash paid for insurance	$1,600

Beginning prepaid insurance is deducted from accrual basis insurance expense to remove the amount paid for in prior years. Ending prepaid insurance is then added to show insurance paid for this year that will not be charged to insurance expense until later years.

Reference to the comparative balance sheet data of PMX Corporation shows liabilities for two accrued expenses: salaries and wages payable and income taxes payable. Accrued salaries and wages payable on December 31, 1987, and December 31, 1988, amounted to $21,400 and $24,900, respectively; the amounts of accrued income taxes payable on those dates were $-0- and $9,300, respectively. Thus, the conversion of accrual basis salaries and wages expense and income tax expense to cash basis expenses are made as shown here.

	Salaries and Wages Expense	Income Tax Expense
Accrual basis expense from the income statement	$112,600	$21,000
Add: Beginning accrued expense	21,400	-0-
Less: Ending accrued expense	(24,900)	(9,300)
Cash paid during the year	$109,100	$11,700

Beginning accrued expenses are added to accrual basis expenses, since they were paid for this year, even though they were recognized as expenses last year. Ending accrued expenses are then deducted, because they were charged to expenses this year but will not be paid for until next year.

Using the cash basis information determined in the preceding paragraphs, we can prepare the cash flow from operating activities section of the SCF by the direct method as shown in Figure 17-1. Note that the cash paid for advertising expense and for repairs and maintenance expense equals the amounts in the respective accounts, since there are no related prepaid or accrued amounts. In addition, fewer classes of expense payments might be used by grouping several of the expenses together as one item. For example, advertising, insurance, and repairs and maintenance might be grouped and listed as "cash paid to suppliers for other services."

A summary of the computation of cash flows from operating activities and the conversion of accrual basis income to cash basis income is presented in Figure 17-2.

Figure 17-1

PMX CORPORATION
Statement of Cash Flows
For the Year Ended December 31, 1988

Cash flow from operating activities:		
Cash received from customers		$671,900
Less cash paid:		
To suppliers for purchases	$315,500	
To employees for salaries and wages	109,100	
For insurance	1,600	
For advertising	48,600	
For repairs and maintenance	26,800	
For income taxes	11,700	
Total cash paid for operating activities		513,300
Net cash flow from operating activities		$158,600

Indirect Method of Reporting
Cash Flow from Operating Activities

Rather than showing the major classes of operating cash receipts and cash payments, the same amount of net cash flow from operating activities may be re-

Figure 17-2
Summary Computation of Cash Flows from Operating Activities

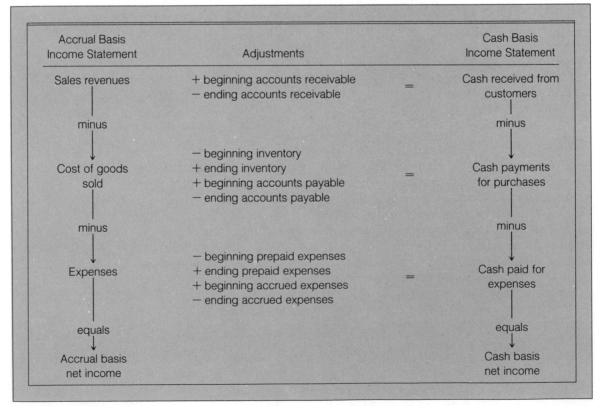

ported by the **indirect method.** This is done by removing from net income or adding back to net income the effects of all deferrals of past cash receipts and payments and all accruals of expected future cash receipts and payments. That is, accrual basis net income is adjusted to a cash basis net income by making adjustments to convert accrual net income to net cash flow from operating activities. Items that were deducted in arriving at accrual net income, such as expenses incurred but not yet paid, and expenses paid for in prior periods and expensed in the current period, like depreciation and amortization, are added back to accrual income. Items that were added in determining accrual net income, such as interest earned but not yet received and sales revenues recorded but not yet received, are deducted from accrual income. The main advantage of the indirect method is that it focuses attention on the differences between accrual basis net income and cash flow from operating activities. An understanding of the differences may be important to managers, investors, creditors, and others who wish to use assessments of income as an intermediate step in assessing future cash flows. Note that we used the indirect method to prepare the budgeted statement of cash flows in Chapter 8.

Analyzing Changes in Balance Sheet Accounts.

The amounts needed to adjust accrual basis net income to cash basis net income are normally determined by analyzing changes in balance sheet accounts that relate to items of revenue or expense during a period. The analysis of account changes is much the same as that discussed earlier when the direct method was used. For example, accounts receivable are recorded as accrual sales are made and reduced as cash is collected. Consequently, an increase in the Accounts Receivable account means that sales recorded during the period exceeded collections from customers by the amount of the increase (sales revenues recorded but not yet received). To adjust to a cash basis, the increase in accounts receivable is deducted from accrual net income on the SCF. Conversely, a decrease in accounts receivable during the period would have the reverse effect and, therefore, would be added to accrual basis net income on the SCF.

Changes in some other current assets, such as inventory and prepaid expenses, relate to expenses but have a similar effect on net income. For example, a decrease in the Inventory account during the period means that the firm sold more merchandise than it purchased. Thus, cost of goods sold is higher under accrual accounting than it would have been on a cash basis (expenses paid for in prior periods and expensed in the current period). As a result, the decrease in inventory is added back to accrual basis income on the SCF. Again, an increase in inventory would have the reverse effect and would, therefore, be deducted from accrual net income. A similar analysis can be applied to changes in prepaid expenses. For example, an increase in prepaid expenses means that the firm paid more cash than the amount of related expenses recognized (expenses paid for this period but not yet charged to an expense account). Thus, the increase is deducted to adjust accrual income to cash basis income on the SCF.

The amount of revenues and expenses recognized on an accrual basis also may be related to changes in liability accounts, particularly current liabilities. For example, accounts payable generally relate to the purchase of merchandise inventory. A decrease in the Accounts Payable account means that the firm paid for more purchases than it made during the period. As a result, cash paid for purchases is higher than purchases recorded on an accrual basis. To adjust accrual net income to cash net income, the decrease in accounts payable is deducted on the SCF. Of course, an increase in accounts payable would be added back on the statement.

Accrued liabilities (expenses) relate to the recognition of accrual basis expenses. For example, an increase in accrued salaries and wages payable means that more salaries and wages expense was recorded than was paid for during the period. The increase, therefore, is added back to accrual basis net income to convert to cash basis net income on the SCF. As before, a decrease in an accrued liability would have the opposite effect.

In addition to the items discussed before, expenses paid for in prior periods and related to long-term assets, such as depreciation, amortization, and depletion expenses, were deducted during the current period in computing accrual basis net income. Since no cash outlay was made in the current period, these expenses are added back to accrual basis net income on the SCF to adjust to cash basis net income.

An example of the indirect approach, based on the income statement and comparative balance sheet data presented earlier for PMX Corporation, is shown in Figure 17-3. The procedures used to adjust accrual basis net income to cash basis net income are summarized in Figure 17-4.

In addition to reporting cash flows from operating activities, the SCF reports, separately, the gross inflows and outflows of cash from investing activities and financing activities.

CASH FLOWS FROM INVESTING ACTIVITIES

As mentioned earlier, investing activities involve both outflows and inflows of cash from various types of transactions. Investing activities include (1) lending money and collecting on the loans, and (2) acquiring and selling, or otherwise disposing of, (a) securities that are not cash equivalents and (b) productive assets that are expected to generate revenue over a long period of time.

Cash outflows for investing activities are made primarily for the acquisition of productive assets (such as equipment and buildings), and for the purchase of

Figure 17-3

PMX CORPORATION Statement of Cash Flows For the Year Ended December 31, 1988	
Net income	$ 95,500
Adjustments to convert net income to net cash flow from operating activities:	
Increase in accounts receivable ($169,400 — $147,300)	(22,100)
Decrease in inventory ($101,600 — $109,500)	7,900
Decrease in prepaid insurance ($6,800 — $9,400)	2,600
Decrease in accounts payable ($74,200 — $81,600)	(7,400)
Increase in accrued salaries and wages payable ($24,900 — $21,400)	3,500
Increase in accrued income taxes payable ($9,300 — $0)	9,300
Depreciation expense	69,300
Net cash flow from operating activities	$158,600

Type of Account	Change in Balance During Current Year	Adjustment Required to Convert Accrual Basis Net Income to Cash Basis Net income
Current asset — other than cash and cash equivalents	Increase Decrease	Minus Plus
Current liability	Increase Decrease	Plus Minus
Depreciation/amortization expense	Increase	Plus
Gain on sale of long-term asset	Increase	Minus
Loss on sale of long-term asset	Increase	Plus

Figure 17-4
Conversion of accrual basis net income to cash basis net income

securities that are not cash equivalents. (Recall that short-term, highly liquid investments are considered a component of cash rather than cash investments.) Cash outflows for investing activities also includes loans made or purchased by the firm.

Cash inflows from investing activities result essentially from events opposite of those producing cash outflows for investing activities. Thus, cash inflows include receipts from the sale of productive assets (such as equipment and buildings), and from the sale of securities that are not cash equivalents. Cash inflows from investing activities also include receipts from loans by either principal repayments by borrowers or by the sale of loans made by the entity. Note that the related interest receipts are not treated as investing activities, but rather are included as interest revenue in operating activities.

Cash inflows and cash outflows should be shown individually by activity at their gross amounts. For example, the total receipts from the sale of productive assets during the period should be reported as a cash inflow, and the total payments for new productive assets should be reported as a cash outflow. An example of the cash flows from investing activities section of the SCF follows:

Cash flows from investing activities:	
Purchases of property, plant, and equipment	$(365,000)
Proceeds from the disposal of property, plant, and equipment	106,000
Purchases of investment securities	(235,000)
Proceeds from the sale of investment securities	68,000
Loans made	(55,000)
Collections on loans	42,000
Net cash used by investing activities	$(439,000)

CASH FLOWS FROM FINANCING ACTIVITIES

Financing activities involve both outflows and inflows of cash from various types of transactions for a firm. These activities generally include (1) obtaining resources from owners and providing them with a return on their investments as well as a return of their investments, and (2) obtaining resources from creditors and repaying the amounts borrowed or otherwise settling the obligations.

Cash inflows from financing activities include the proceeds received from the issuance of equity securities and from debt securities, such as bonds, notes, mortgages, and other short- or long-term borrowings. Cash outflows from financing activities generally represent events opposite of those producing cash inflows. Thus, cash outflows from financing activities include payments (1) for the reacquisition of the entity's equity securities (either for retirement or to be held as treasury stock); (2) dividend payments; and (3) repayments of amounts borrowed. Note that payments representing interest on borrowings are not included in financing activities, but are included as interest expense in operating activities.

As with investing activities, cash inflows and outflows from financing activities should be shown individually at their gross amounts. For example, the total receipts from long-term borrowing during the period should be shown separately from total payments to reduce long-term debt. An example of the cash flows from financing activities section of the SCF follows:

Cash flows from financing activities:	
Proceeds from short-term debt	$124,500
Payments to reduce short-term debt	(86,000)
Proceeds from issuing long-term debt	800,000
Payments to reduce long-term debt	(350,000)
Proceeds from issuing capital stock	500,000
Payments for the purchase of treasury stock	(240,000)
Cash dividends paid	(130,000)
Net cash provided by financing activities	$618,500

DIRECT EXCHANGE (NONCASH) TRANSACTIONS

Objective 5: Reporting direct exchange transactions

Firms sometimes engage in significant financing and investing transactions that do not directly affect cash, **called direct exchange (noncash) transactions,** such as the exchange of a long-term note payable or capital stock for a plant asset. In some cases, these transactions are completed by giving part cash (a down payment) and a debt or equity security for the remainder of the purchase price. Since the transactions represent a combination of investing activities (the acquisition of a plant asset) and financing activities (the issuance of debt or equity securities), accounting standards require that both types of transaction be disclosed.

Accountants and financial statements users disagree on the appropriate treatment of these joint transactions. Some believe that noncash transactions should be treated as cash flow equivalents and that they should be included in the body of the SCF. For example, the exchange of a firm's shares of common stock with a fair market value of $500,000 for a building would be included as both an investment transaction for the purchase of plant assets and as a financing transaction for the issuance of common stock. Although the net effect on cash flow is zero, both the investing and financing activity would be disclosed.

Other accountants and users believe that noncash transactions should be excluded from the body of the SCF and disclosed in a separate schedule. They believe that including them within the body of the statement complicates the statement and limits its usefulness in providing meaningful information about cash flows. This latter treatment is used later in this chapter because the SCF is easier to understand with it. As such, the cash portion of a combined cash and noncash transaction will be reported in the body of the SCF, with the noncash portion disclosed in a separate schedule. For example, assume the purchase of equipment with a cost of $350,000; the purchaser made a down payment of $100,000 and gave a two-year note payable for the remainder. The cash portion of the transaction ($100,000) would be included in the cash flows of investing activities as the purchase of plant assets, whereas the noncash portion ($250,000) would be disclosed in a separate schedule.

Other types of noncash transactions often engaged in by a firm include the conversion of debt securities into equity securities, and the acquisition of plant assets through capital leases. These transactions often involve little or no cash inflows and outflows in the period in which they occur, but generally have a significant effect on the future cash flows of a company. Examples of the treatment of these noncash transactions are included in the following section.

PREPARING THE SCF — AN EXTENDED ILLUSTRATION

The comparative balance sheets and statement of income and retained earnings of Apex Corporation presented in Figure 17-5 are used to illustrate the preparation of the SCF. During 1988, Apex Corporation entered into the following transactions that are relevant to the SCF:

1. A new wing was added to a building at a cost of $600,000 cash.
2. New equipment was purchased at a cost of $337,000; cash of $87,000 and a note payable for $250,000 that is due January 2, 1991, were given in exchange.
3. Equipment with a book value of $100,000 was sold for $92,000 cash.
4. Long-term stock investments were sold for $274,000.
5. Bonds payable of $150,000 were issued for cash at par.
6. An additional 30,000 shares of $5 par value common stock were issued for $259,500.
7. Cash dividends of $174,000 were declared and paid.

Reference to the comparative balance sheets shows that cash and cash equivalents increased by $164,000 ($482,000 − $318,000) during 1988. Thus, the SCF should show the operating, investing, and financing activities that caused the increase in cash and cash equivalents. A SCF, using the direct method of reporting cash flows from operating activities, is presented in Figure 17-6.

In Figure 17-6, cash flows from operating activities are presented with the direct method. In order to contrast the direct and indirect methods, Figure 17-7 presents the SCF of Apex Corporation with cash flows from operating activities determined with the indirect method.

SUMMARY

This chapter describes the preparation and uses of the statement of cash flows (SCF). The SCF is intended to provide users of financial statements with rele-

APEX CORPORATION
Comparative Balance Sheets

	December 31	
	1988	1987
Assets		
Current assets:		
Cash and cash equivalents	$ 482,000	$ 318,000
Accounts receivable (net)	246,500	189,000
Inventory	471,000	483,000
Prepaid expenses	54,000	21,000
Total current assets	1,253,500	1,011,000
Operating assets		
Buildings	1,800,000	1,200,000
Accumulated depreciation—buildings	(522,000)	(472,500)
Equipment	1,011,000	774,000
Accumulated depreciation—equipment	(400,500)	(348,000)
Land	350,000	350,000
Total operating assets	2,238,500	1,503,500
Long-term stock investments (at cost, which is less than market value)	250,000	400,000
Total assets	$3,742,000	$2,914,500
Liabilities and Stockholders' Equity		
Current liabilities:		
Accounts payable	$ 450,000	$ 478,500
Accrued expenses	31,500	24,000
Total current liabilities	481,500	502,500
Long-term liabilities:		
Notes payable, due January 2, 1991	250,000	–0–
Bonds payable, due July 1, 2001	900,000	750,000
Total long-term liabilities	1,150,000	750,000
Stockholders' equity:		
Common stock, $5 par value	975,000	825,000
Paid-in capital in excess of par value	448,500	339,000
Retained earnings	687,000	498,000
Total stockholders' equity	2,110,500	1,662,000
Total liabilities & stockholders' equity	$3,742,000	$2,914,500

Figure 17-5
Apex Corporation financial statements

vant information about the cash receipts and cash payments of a business during a specific period. The concept of cash used in the SCF is that of cash plus cash equivalents. Cash equivalents are investments in short-term, highly liquid securities that the firm intends to convert to cash as needed for normal operations. The statement also provides information about the investing and financing activities of the firm. This information, which is not readily available from the other financial statements, is important to users who are interested in projecting the future cash flows of the business.

The SCF classifies cash flows into three types of business activities: (1) oper-

APEX CORPORATION
Statement of Income and Retained Earnings
For the Year Ended December 31, 1988

Net sales		$6,930,000
Cost of goods sold		3,660,000
Gross profit		3,270,000
Operating expenses other than depreciation	$2,625,000	
Depreciation expense	102,000	
Total operating expenses		2,727,000
Operating income		543,000
Other revenues, gains, expenses, and losses:		
Dividends and interest revenue	36,000	
Gain on sale of investments	124,000	
Interest expense	(92,000)	
Loss on sale of equipment	(8,000)	
Net other revenues and gains		60,000
Net income before income tax		603,000
Income tax expense		240,000
Net income		363,000
Retained earnings, January 1		498,000
Total		861,000
Less: Cash dividends		174,000
Retained earnings, December 31		$ 687,000

Figure 17-5 **continued**

ating activities, (2) investing activities, and (3) financing activities. Operating activities involve the production or delivery of goods for sale or the providing of services. Cash flows from operating activities generally summarize the effects of transactions that enter into the determination of net income.

Gross cash inflows and gross cash outflows are reported separately for investing activities and financing activities. Investing activities generally include transactions involving (1) lending money and collecting on the loans, and (2) acquiring and selling (a) securities that are not cash equivalents, and (b) productive assets that are expected to produce revenues over several periods. The net effect on cash of the gross inflows and outflows from investing activities is reported as net cash received or used in investing activities. Financing activities generally include obtaining resources (1) from owners and providing them with a return of and a return on their investments, and (2) from creditors and repaying the amounts borrowed. Interest revenue and expense related to investing and financing activities are reported as a part of operating activities.

Net cash flow from operating activities may be reported by the direct method or the indirect method. With the direct method, major classes of operating revenues are shown as cash inflows from operations, and major classes of expenses are reported as cash outflows from operations. The difference between cash inflows and cash outflows from operations is reported as the net cash flow from operating activities.

Under the indirect method, net cash flow from operations is reported by adjusting accrual basis net income to cash basis net income. Accrual basis net

Figure 17-6
Statement of cash
flows—direct
method

APEX CORPORATION
Statement of Cash Flows
For the Year Ended December 31, 1988

Cash flows from operating activities:		
Cash received from customers (1)		$6,872,500
Cash received from interest and dividends		36,000
Cash provided by operating activities		6,908,500
Less cash paid:		
To suppliers for purchases (2)	$3,676,500	
To suppliers for operating expenses (3)	2,650,500	
For interest and taxes (4)	332,000	
Cash disbursed for operating activities		6,659,000
Net cash flow from operating activities		249,500
Cash flows from investing activities:		
Purchase of building and equipment (5)	(687,000)	
Proceeds from the sale of equipment	92,000	
Proceeds from the sale of investments	274,000	
Net cash used by investing activities		(321,000)
Cash flows from financing activities:		
Proceeds from issuing bonds payable	150,000	
Proceeds from issuing common stock	259,500	
Cash dividends paid	(174,000)	
Net cash provided by financing activities		235,500
Net increase in cash and cash equivalents		$ 164,000
(1) Beginning accounts receivable		$ 189,000
Plus: Sales		6,930,000
Less: Ending accounts receivable		(246,500)
Cash received from customers		$6,872,500
(2) Accrual basis cost of goods sold		$3,660,000
Less: Beginning inventory		(483,000)
Plus: Ending inventory		471,000
Plus: Beginning accounts payable		478,500
Less: Ending accounts payable		(450,000)
Cash paid to suppliers for purchases		$3,676,500
(3) Operating expenses other than depreciation		$2,625,000
Less: Beginning prepaid expenses		(21,000)
Plus: Ending prepaid expenses		54,000
Plus: Beginning accrued expenses		24,000
Less: Ending accrued expenses		(31,500)
Cash paid to suppliers for operating expenses		$2,650,500
(4) Interest expense		$ 92,000
Income tax expense		240,000
Cash paid for interest and taxes		$ 332,000
(5) Building addition		$ 600,000
Cash paid for equipment purchase		87,000
Cash payments for building and equipment		$ 687,000
Schedule of noncash investing and financing activities:		
Note payable given in exchange for equipment		$250,000

APEX CORPORATION
Statement of Cash Flows
For the Year Ended December 31, 1988

Net cash flow from operating activities:		
Net income		$363,000
Adjustments to convert net income to net cash flow from operating activities:		
Depreciation expense		102,000
Increase in accounts receivable ($246,500 — $189,000)		(57,500)
Decrease in inventory ($471,000 — $483,000)		12,000
Increase in prepaid expenses ($54,000 — $21,000)		(33,000)
Decrease in accounts payable ($450,000 — $478,500)		(28,500)
Increase in accrued expenses ($31,500 — $24,000)		7,500
Gain on sale of investments ($274,000 — $150,000)		(124,000)
Loss on sale of equipment ($92,000 — $100,000)		8,000
Net cash flow from operating activities		249,500
Cash flows from investing activities:		
Purchase of building and equipment	$(687,000)	
Proceeds from the sale of equipment	92,000	
Proceeds from the sale of long-term investments	274,000	
Net cash used by investing activities		(321,000)
Cash flows from financing activities:		
Proceeds from the issuance of bonds payable	150,000	
Proceeds from the issuance of common stock	259,500	
Cash dividends paid	(174,000)	
Net cash provided by financing activities		235,500
Net increase in cash		$164,000
Schedule of noncash investing and financing activities:		
Note payable given in exchange for equipment		$250,000

Figure 17-7
Statement of cash flows—indirect method

income is adjusted for noncash revenues, expenses, gains, and losses. Noncash items that were deducted in determining accrual basis net income are added back to calculate cash basis net income; conversely, noncash items that were added in determining accrual net income are deducted to compute cash basis net income. Direct exchange (noncash) transactions representing significant investing and financing activities may be reported either in the body of the SCF or in a separate schedule.

DEMONSTRATION PROBLEM

Weaver Brothers, Inc., a merchandising concern, was organized in 1983. Because it is located in a rapidly growing area, it has enjoyed rapid growth as well. Presented below are comparative balance sheets and a statement of income and retained earnings prepared on January 31, 1988, the end of Weaver Brother's fiscal year. Its statement of cash flows has not yet been prepared.

WEAVER BROTHERS, INC.
Comparative Balance Sheets

	January 31	
	1988	1987
Assets		
Current assets:		
Cash and marketable securities (at cost)	$ 334,000	$ 455,000
Accounts receivable (net)	523,000	385,000
Notes receivable	–0–	40,000
Interest receivable	–0–	2,000
Merchandise inventory	1,312,000	816,000
Prepaid expenses	67,000	46,000
Total current assets	2,236,000	1,744,000
Investments:		
Long-term investments in equity securities (at cost, which approximates market value)	30,000	185,000
Property, plant, and equipment:		
Land	40,000	40,000
Buildings	1,925,000	650,000
Accumulated depreciation—buildings	(152,000)	(85,000)
Equipment	1,040,000	415,000
Accumulated depreciation—equipment	(275,000)	(184,000)
Total property, plant, and equipment	2,578,000	836,000
Total assets	$4,844,000	$2,765,000
Liabilities and Stockholders' Equity		
Current liabilities:		
Notes payable	$ 220,000	$ 400,000
Accounts payable	415,000	280,000
Income taxes payable	41,000	64,000
Interest payable	12,000	26,000
Accrued expenses payable	65,000	143,000
Total current liabilities	753,000	913,000
Long-term liabilities:		
Notes payable, due August 31, 1991	700,000	300,000
Bonds payable, due June 30, 2007	800,000	–0–
Total long-term liabilities	1,500,000	300,000
Stockholders' equity:		
Common stock, $2 par value	900,000	600,000
Paid-in capital in excess of par value	950,000	500,000
Retained earnings	741,000	452,000
Total stockholders' equity	2,591,000	1,552,000
Total liabilities and stockholders' equity	$4,844,000	$2,765,000

WEAVER BROTHERS, INC.
Statement of Income and Retained Earnings
For the Year Ended January 31, 1988

Net sales revenues		$4,735,000
Cost of goods sold		2,246,600
Gross profit		2,488,400
Operating expenses other than depreciation	$1,747,400	
Depreciation expense	158,000	
Total operating expenses		1,905,400
Operating income		583,000
Other revenues, gains, expenses, and losses:		
Dividend and interest revenue	14,000	
Gain on sale of investments	27,000	
Interest expense	(69,000)	
Net other expense		28,000
Net income before income tax		555,000
Income tax expense		166,000
Net income		389,000
Retained earnings, February 1, 1987		452,000
Total		841,000
Less: Cash dividends paid		100,000
Retained earnings, January 31, 1988		$ 741,000

Additional information:

1. Long-term investments in equity securities with a cost of $155,000 were sold during the year for $182,000.
2. A new building was purchased during the year at a total cost of $1,275,000. A cash payment of $875,000 plus a long-term note payable for $400,000 was given to cover the cost of the purchase.
3. Additional equipment was purchased for $625,000 cash.
4. Bonds payable of $800,000 were issued for cash at par value.
5. An additional 150,000 shares of the $2 par value common stock were issued for $5 per share.
6. Cash dividends of $100,000 were declared and paid.

Required:
A. Prepare a cash flow statement for the year ended January 31, 1988, for Weaver Brothers, Inc. Use the direct method of presenting the net cash flow from operating activities.
B. Verify the amount of net cash flow from operating activities using the indirect method.

ANSWER TO DEMONSTRATION PROBLEM

A.

WEAVER BROTHERS, INC.
Statement of Cash Flows
For the Year Ended January 31, 1988

Cash flows from operating activities:		
Cash received from customers (1)		$4,637,000
Cash received from dividends and interest (2)		16,000
Cash provided by operating activities		4,653,000
Less cash paid:		
To suppliers for purchases (3)	$2,607,600	
To suppliers for operating expenses (4)	1,846,400	
To creditors for interest (5)	83,000	
To governments for taxes (6)	189,000	
Cash paid for operating activities		4,726,000
Net cash flow from operating activities		(73,000)
Cash flows from investing activities:		
Purchase of building and equipment	(1,500,000)	
Proceeds from the sale of investments	182,000	
Net cash used by investing activities		(1,318,000)
Cash flows from financing activities:		
Proceeds from issuing bonds payable	800,000	
Proceeds from issuing common stock	750,000	
Payments to settle short-term notes payable	(180,000)	
Cash dividends paid	(100,000)	
Net cash provided by financing activities		1,270,000
Net decrease in cash		$ 121,000
(1) Net sales revenue		$4,735,000
Add: Beginning accounts and notes receivable		425,000
Less: Ending accounts and notes receivable		(523,000)
Cash received from customers		$4,637,000
(2) Dividend and interest revenue		$ 14,000
Add: Beginning interest receivable		2,000
Less: Ending interest receivable		–0–
Cash received from dividends and interest		$ 16,000
(3) Cost of goods sold		$2,246,600
Less: Beginning merchandise inventory		(816,000)
Add: Ending merchandise inventory		1,312,000
Add: Beginning accounts payable		280,000
Less: Ending accounts payable		(415,000)
Cash paid to suppliers for purchases		$2,607,600
(4) Operating expenses other than depreciation		$1,747,400
Less: Beginning prepaid expenses		(46,000)
Add: Ending prepaid expenses		67,000
Add: Beginning accrued expenses payable		143,000
Less: Ending accrued expenses payable		(65,000)
Cash paid to suppliers for operating expenses		$1,846,400

(5) Interest expense	$ 69,000
Add: Beginning interest payable	26,000
Less: Ending interest payable	(12,000)
Cash paid to creditors for interest	$ 83,000
(6) Income tax expense	$ 166,000
Add: Beginning income taxes payable	64,000
Less: Ending income taxes payable	(41,000)
Cash paid to governments for taxes	$ 189,000
Schedule of noncash investing and financing activities:	
Note payable given in exchange for equipment	$ 400,000

B. Net cash flow from operating activities — indirect method

Net income	$389,000
Adjustments to convert net income to net cash flow from operating activities:	
Increase in accounts receivable ($523,000 — $385,000)	(138,000)
Decrease in notes and interest receivable ($0 — $42,000)	42,000
Increase in inventory ($1,312,000 — $816,000)	(496,000)
Increase in prepaid expenses ($67,000 — $46,000)	(21,000)
Increase in accounts payable ($415,000 — $280,000)	135,000
Decrease in income taxes payable ($41,000 — $64,000)	(23,000)
Decrease in interest payable ($12,000 — $26,000)	(14,000)
Decrease in accrued expenses payable ($65,000 — $143,000)	(78,000)
Depreciation expense	158,000
Gain on sale of investments ($182,000 — $155,000)	(27,000)
Net cash flow from operating activities	$(73,000)

GLOSSARY

CASH EQUIVALENTS. Short-term, highly liquid investments such as treasury bills. (p. 672).

DIRECT EXCHANGE (NONCASH) TRANSACTIONS. Transactions that represent joint investing and financing activities with no direct effect on cash, such as the exchange of common stock for a plant asset (p. 682).

DIRECT METHOD. A method of reporting cash flows from operating activities by which major classes of operating revenues and expenses are shown as cash inflows and cash outflows from operations (p. 674).

FINANCING ACTIVITIES. Activities involving the acquisition of resources from (1) owners and providing them with a return on and a return of their investments, and (2) creditors and repaying the amounts owed or otherwise settling the obligation (p. 673).

INDIRECT METHOD. A method of reporting cash flow from operating activities by which accrual basis net income is adjusted to cash basis net income by adding or subtracting noncash expenses, revenues, losses, and gains (p. 679).

INVESTING ACTIVITIES. Activities involving (1) lending money and collecting on the loans, and (2) acquiring and selling (a) securities that are not cash equivalents, and (b) productive assets that are expected to produce revenues over several periods (p. 672).

OPERATING ACTIVITIES. Activities involving the production or delivery of goods for sale and the providing of services (p. 672).

STATEMENT OF CASH FLOWS (SCF). A financial statement that reports cash receipts and cash payments for a firm for a specific time period (p. 671).

DISCUSSION QUESTIONS

1. What are the purposes of the statement of cash flows (SCF)?
2. What is the concept of cash used in the preparation of the SCF?
3. What are the three main parts of the SCF?
4. Explain what is meant by:
   a. Operating activities
   b. Investing activities
   c. Financing activities
5. List three examples of investing activities and three examples of financing activities.
6. What is the direct method of reporting cash flows from operating activities?
7. What is the indirect method of reporting cash flows from operating activities?
8. Do all revenues in the income statement represent an increase in cash? Explain.
9. Colin Company sold a piece of undeveloped land for $75,000 that had cost $50,000 five years ago. What effect does this transaction have on the current year's income statement? What effect does the transaction have on the current year's SCF?
10. Do all expenses on the income statement represent a decrease in cash? If not, identify some expenses that do not reduce cash during the current period.
11. A company reported a net loss of $40,000 on its income statement and a $20,000 positive net cash flow from operating activities. How could this happen?
12. Indicate how the following are computed from the information found in accrual basis financial statements:
    a. Cash received from customers
    b. Cash paid for purchases
    c. Cash paid for operating expenses
13. Total sales revenue for 1988 was $450,000, of which one-fourth was on account. The balances in Accounts Receivable were $22,000 at the end of 1988 and $34,000 at the end of 1987. How much cash was received from customers during 1988?
14. How are dividends paid and interest earned from investment activities treated on the SCF?
15. What are direct exchange (noncash) transactions? How are they treated on the SCF?
16. Give three examples of direct exchange (noncash) transactions.
17. Dee Company's fiscal year ends on December 31. Dee's board of directors declared a cash dividend on December 20 of the current year, payable on

January 15 to stockholders of record on December 31. What effect would the declaration of the dividend have on the SCF for the current year? What would be the effect on the SCF for the following year?

EXERCISES

Exercise 17-1 Conversion from Accrual Basis to Cash Basis
The following information was taken from the general ledger accounts of Cox Company, which uses the accrual basis of accounting:

	December 31	
	1988	1987
Accounts receivable	$ 46,700	$31,800
Inventory	39,000	42,100
Prepaid insurance	1,800	2,200
Accounts payable	28,600	30,400
Wages payable	2,600	3,800
Sales	105,600	
Cost of goods sold	58,900	
Operating expenses (including $19,000 depreciation expense)	35,400	

Required:
A. Compute:
  1. The amount of cash collected from customers during 1988.
  2. The amount of cash paid to suppliers for purchases during 1988.
  3. The amount of cash paid to suppliers for operating expenses during 1988.
B. Prepare a schedule to compute net cash flow from operating activities during 1988 using the direct method.

Exercise 17-2 Net Cash Flow from Operating Activities — Indirect Method
Assume the same information as given in Exercise 17-1.

Required:
Prepare the cash flow from operating activities section of the SCF using the indirect method.

Exercise 17-3 Net Cash Flow from Operating Activities — Indirect Method
Assume you are preparing a SCF and have the following information.

Net income (accrual basis)		$120,000
Depreciation expense	$54,000	_____
Decrease in accounts payable	8,500	_____
Amortization of goodwill	19,000	_____
Gain on sale of plant assets	16,900	_____
Increase in inventories	7,500	_____
Decrease in accounts receivable	15,000	_____
Net cash flow from operating activities		$_____

Required:
Prepare the cash flow from operating activities section of the SCF using the

indirect method by filling in the blanks above with positive or negative amounts.

Exercise 17-4 Computing Net Cash Flow from Operating Activities — Indirect Method

The following information was taken from the comparative financial statements of Baker Company, which were prepared on an accrual basis.

	December 31	
	1988	1987
Net sales	$392,000	$360,000
Cost of goods sold	164,000	142,000
Operating expenses (including depreciation expense of $28,000 each year)	148,000	140,000
Net income	80,000	78,000
Accounts receivable (net)	74,000	68,000
Inventory	52,000	60,000
Accounts payable	34,000	32,000
Wages payable	10,000	16,000

Required:

Prepare a schedule to compute the net cash flow from operating activities using the indirect method.

Exercise 17-5 Cash Flow from Operating Activities — Direct Method

An income statement and selected comparative balance sheet information for Brake Company follow:

BRAKE COMPANY
Income Statement
For the Year Ended June 30, 1988

Sales revenue		$467,200
Cost of goods sold		310,000
Gross profit		157,200
Operating expenses:		
Advertising expense	$16,400	
Depreciation expense	16,000	
Salaries and wages expense	44,000	
Utilities expense	29,600	
Total operating expenses		106,000
Net income before income tax		51,200
Income tax expense		10,100
Net income		$ 41,100

	June 30	
	1988	1987
Accounts receivable	$81,400	$89,600
Inventory	62,000	58,500
Accounts payable	29,400	22,700
Income taxes payable	3,200	5,600

Required:
Prepare the cash flow from operating activities section of the SCF for Brake Company for the year ended June 30, 1988, using the direct method.

Exercise 17-6 Cash Flow from Operating Activities — Indirect Method
Assume the same data as given in Exercise 17-5.

Required:
Prepare the cash flow from operating activities section of the SCF using the indirect method.

Exercise 17-7 Cash Flow from Operating Activities
Following are descriptions of changes in balance sheet accounts and other selected events for Favor Company:

1. Decrease in accounts receivable _____
2. Increase in inventory _____
3. Gain on sale of securities included in cash
    equivalents _____
4. Depreciation expense _____
5. Increase in accounts payable _____
6. Decrease in accrued expenses _____
7. Loss on sale of equipment _____
8. Cash dividends paid _____
9. Amortization of discount on bonds payable _____
10. Increase in interest receivable _____

Required:
Indicate whether each of the items should be added to (+) or subtracted from (−) net income using the indirect method of determining net cash flow from operating activities. If the item should be neither added nor subtracted, indicate this as NA.

Exercise 17-8 Cash Flow from Operating Activities
Following are three items that have an effect on the computation of cash flow from operating activities. None of these were specifically discussed or illustrated in the chapter, but you should be able to "reason" the appropriate treatment.

1. Earnings on a long-term investment in common stock accounted for by the equity method amounted to $36,000.
2. Premium amortization on a long-term investment in bonds amounted to $2,700.
3. Discount amortization on bonds payable amounted to $9,600.

Required:
Explain how each item is treated in the preparation of the cash flow from operations section of the SCF using the indirect method.

Exercise 17-9 Effect of Transactions on SCF
Following is a list of transactions completed by Ace Company during 1988:

	Transaction	(a) Section of SCF	(b) Amount	(c) Amount Added (+) or Deducted (−)
1.	Borrowed $25,000 with a six-month note payable	_____	_____	_____
2.	Accounts receivable decreased by $48,000 during the year	_____	_____	_____
3.	Sold for $18,000 a plant asset with a book value of $10,000	_____	_____	_____
4.	Issued common stock for cash, $80,000	_____	_____	_____
5.	Purchased a plant asset for $67,000, giving $17,000 cash and a $50,000 note payable	_____	_____	_____
6.	Exchanged 10,000 shares of common stock for land with a fair value of $85,000	_____	_____	_____
7.	Declared and paid a $30,000 dividend	_____	_____	_____
8.	Purchased treasury stock for $60,000 cash	_____	_____	_____
9.	Paid a long-term note payable of $100,000	_____	_____	_____
10.	Accounts payable decreased by $20,000 during the year	_____	_____	_____

Required:
For each transaction, indicate (1) the section (i.e., operating, investing, or financing) of the SCF in which the cash effect is reported (if the effect is not reported in any of the sections, place a NA on the line); (2) the amount; and (c) whether the amount is added (+) or deducted (−) in that section.

Exercise 17-10 Cash Flow from Investing Activities
The following transactions were undertaken by Smith, Inc., during 1988:

1. Sold for $87,000 used machinery with a book value of $64,000.
2. Issued capital stock for cash, $120,000.
3. Purchased land to be held for future expansion, $250,000.
4. Paid off a long-term $80,000 note payable plus interest of $7,500.
5. Purchased machinery, giving $30,000 cash and a two-year, 12% note payable for $100,000.
6. Purchased Smith, Inc., common stock to be held as treasury stock, paying $96,000.
7. Sold a long-term bond investment, with a book value of $96,000, for $102,000, including $4,000 accrued interest.
8. Purchased common stock of Duper Company to be held as a long-term investment, paying $190,000.

9. Issued bonds payable at par value for $400,000.
10. Declared and paid cash dividends of $70,000.
11. Purchased and retired 5,000 shares of Smith, Inc., $10 par value preferred stock for $57,000.

Required:
Prepare the net cash flow from investing activities section of the SCF.

Exercise 17-11 Cash Flow from Financing Activities
Refer to the transaction data given in Exercise 17-10.

Required:
Prepare the net cash flow from financing activities section of the SCF.

Exercise 17-12 Preparing a SCF
An income statement for the year ended December 31, 1988, and comparative balance sheets for 1988 and 1987 for Prince Company follow:

PRINCE COMPANY
Income Statement
For the Year Ended December 31, 1988

Sales revenue		$655,060
Cost of goods sold		291,400
Gross profit		363,660
Operating expenses:		
Advertising expense	$ 29,800	
Depreciation expense	26,880	
Salaries and wages expense	136,400	
Utilities expense	42,300	
Total operating expenses		235,380
Net income before income tax		128,280
Income tax expense		36,400
Net income		$ 91,880

PRINCE COMPANY
Comparative Balance Sheets

	December 31	
	1988	1987
Cash	$ 90,800	$ 40,320
Accounts receivable (net)	71,200	79,800
Inventory	312,000	268,000
Prepaid expenses	32,000	10,000
Plant assets	356,000	232,000
Accumulated depreciation — plant assets	(67,200)	(40,320)
Total assets	$794,800	$589,800
Accounts payable	$117,120	$110,000
Income taxes payable	21,200	12,800

Accrued salaries and wages payable	10,400	12,800
Long-term notes payable	56,000	80,000
Common stock, $5 par value	280,000	220,000
Paid-in capital in excess of par value	140,000	20,000
Retained earnings	170,080	134,200
Total liabilities and stockholders' equity	$794,800	$589,800

An inspection of the general ledger accounts produced the following additional information:

1. New equipment was purchased during the year for $124,000 cash.
2. A long-term note payable of $24,000 was paid off.
3. Twelve thousand shares of common stock were issued during the year at an issue price of $15 per share.
4. Cash dividends of $1 per share were declared and paid on outstanding shares, including those issued during the year.

Required:
Prepare a SCF. Use the indirect method of reporting net cash flow from operating activities.

PROBLEMS

Problem 17-1   Analyzing Transactions
Several transactions of Dameler Company follow:

1. Sold unissued common stock for cash _____
2. Borrowed money using a four-year note payable _____
3. Exchanged common stock for a building _____
4. Sold used machinery for cash equal to its book value _____
5. Sold securities classified as cash equivalents _____
6. Accrued interest payable increased during the year _____
7. Exchanged common stock for convertible bonds _____
8. Sold land for more than its book value _____
9. Sold treasury stock for more than its cost _____
10. Paid a long-term note payable _____
11. Depreciation expense was recorded for the year _____
12. Declared and paid a cash dividend _____
13. Sold long-term investments for less than book value _____
14. Merchandise inventory decreased during the year _____
15. Paid cash for new office furniture _____

Required:
For each of the transactions, indicate the section (operating, investing, or financing) of the SCF in which the cash effect of the transaction would be reported. If the transaction is not reported in the body of the statement, indicate so.

Problem 17-2   Preparing a SCF — Direct Method
Comparative balance sheet information for 1988 and 1987 and income statement data for 1988 for Seeley Company follow:

	1988	1987
Cash	$ 18,600	$ 22,400
Accounts receivable	26,900	25,200
Inventory	32,700	34,800
Property, plant, and equipment	68,000	50,000
Accumulated depreciation	(30,000)	(27,000)
Total assets	$116,200	$105,400
Accounts payable	$ 23,400	$ 22,100
Accrued expenses	12,900	13,900
Long-term note payable	10,000	-0-
Common stock	20,000	20,000
Retained earnings	49,900	49,400
Total liabilities and stockholders' equity	$116,200	$105,400
Sales	$ 98,700	
Cost of goods sold	56,600	
Gross profit	42,100	
Operating expenses including deprecia-		
tion	36,600	
Net income	$ 5,500	

Property, plant, and equipment assets were purchased during the year, but none were sold. Dividends were declared and paid during December of 1988.

Required:
Prepare a SCF for Seeley Company. Use the direct method of reporting net cash flow from operating activities. (*Hint:* You will need to analyze changes in balance sheet accounts to determine the effects of investing and financing activities.)

Problem 17-3 Preparing a SCF — Indirect Method
Comparative balance sheets for 1988 and 1987 and a 1988 income statement for Trimont Company follow:

	1988	1987
Cash	$ 34,400	$ 49,600
Accounts receivable (net)	67,600	60,800
Inventory	90,800	99,200
Property, plant, and equipment	232,000	160,000
Accumulated depreciation	(80,000)	(68,000)
Patents	24,000	28,000
Total assets	$368,800	$329,600
Accounts payable	$ 53,600	$ 48,400
Accrued expenses payable	2,600	7,600
Long-term notes payable	20,000	-0-
Long-term mortgage payable	33,000	36,000
Common stock	40,000	40,000
Retained earnings	219,600	197,600
Total liabilities and stockholders' equity	$368,800	$329,600
Sales	$354,800	
Cost of goods sold	226,400	
Gross profit	128,400	
Operating expenses (including deprecia-		
tion expense and patent amortization		
expense)	98,400	
Net income	$ 30,000	

Property, plant, and equipment assets were purchased during the year, but none were sold. Dividends were declared and paid in October 1988.

Required:
Prepare a SCF. Use the indirect method of reporting net cash flow from operating activities.

Problem 17-4 Preparing a SCF—Indirect Method

Andes Company had balance sheets on December 31, 1988 and 1987, as follows:

	1988	1987
Cash	$ 454,000	$ 201,600
Accounts receivable (net)	356,000	399,000
Inventory	1,560,000	1,340,000
Prepaid expenses	160,000	50,000
Property, plant, and equipment	1,780,000	1,160,000
Accumulated depreciation	(336,000)	(201,600)
Total assets	$3,974,000	$2,949,000
Short-term notes payable	$ 106,000	$ 64,000
Accounts payable	585,600	550,000
Accrued expenses payable	52,000	64,000
Long-term notes payable	280,000	400,000
Common stock, $5 par value	1,400,000	1,100,000
Paid-in capital in excess of par value	700,000	100,000
Retained earnings	850,400	671,000
Total liabilities and stockholders' equity	$3,974,000	$2,949,000

An investigation of the firm's 1988 income statement and the general ledger accounts produced the following information:

1. Net income for 1988 was $459,400.
2. Depreciation expense of $154,400 was recorded; a fully depreciated machine with a cost of $20,000 was discarded and its cost and accumulated depreciation were removed from the accounts.
3. New equipment costing $640,000 was purchased during the year with cash.
4. A long-term note payable of $120,000 was paid off.
5. Sixty thousand shares of common stock were issued during the year at a price of $15 per share.
6. Cash dividends of $1 per share were declared and paid on the outstanding common stock, including those issued during the year.

Required:
Prepare a SCF for Andes Company for the year ended December 31, 1988. Use the indirect method of reporting net cash flow from operating activities.

Problem 17-5 Preparing a SCF—Direct Method

Comparative balance sheets for 1988 and 1987 and the 1988 income statement for Siga Company follow:

	December 31	
	1988	1987
Cash	$ 75,600	$ 89,600
Accounts receivable (net)	73,500	63,000
Merchandise inventory	35,000	46,200

Property, plant, and equipment (net)	301,000	280,000
Patents	18,900	21,000
Total	$504,000	$499,800
Accounts payable	$ 63,000	$ 77,000
Accrued expenses payable	10,000	20,000
Income taxes payable	13,500	2,800
Long-term notes payable	15,000	50,000
Common stock, $5 par value	315,000	294,000
Retained earnings	87,500	56,000
Total	$504,000	$499,800
Sales revenue	$420,000	
Cost of goods sold	245,000	
Gross profit	175,000	
Expenses (includes depreciation of $28,000 and patent amortization of $2,100)	112,000	
Net income before income tax	63,000	
Income tax expense	14,000	
Net income	$ 49,000	

Additional information:

1. Property, plant, and equipment assets were purchased for $49,000 cash.
2. A $35,000 note payable was paid off during the year.
3. Common stock was sold for $21,000 cash.
4. Cash dividends of $17,500 were declared and paid.

Required:
Prepare a SCF for Siga Company for the year ended December 31, 1988. Use the direct method of reporting net cash flow from operating activities.

Problem 17-6   **Preparing a SCF—Direct Method**

Comparative balance sheets for 1988 and 1987 and the statement of income and retained earnings for the year ended December 31, 1988, for Mather Company follow:

	December 31	
	1988	1987
Current assets:		
Cash	$ 207,000	$ 268,000
Marketable securities, at cost	180,000	150,000
Accounts receivable (net)	585,000	515,000
Notes receivable	120,000	80,000
Interest receivable	8,000	4,000
Merchandise inventory	981,000	1,040,000
Prepaid expenses	41,000	78,000
Total current assets	2,122,000	2,135,000
Investments:		
Long-term investments in equity securities at cost, which is less than market value	450,000	420,000
Property, plant, and equipment:		
Land	500,000	400,000
Buildings	3,000,000	2,400,000
Accumulated depreciation—buildings	(1,420,000)	(1,100,000)
Equipment	1,550,000	1,200,000
Accumulated depreciation—equipment	(640,000)	(480,000)
Total property, plant, and equipment	2,990,000	2,420,000

Intangible assets:		
Patents	270,000	300,000
Total Assets	$5,832,000	$5,275,000
Current liabilities:		
Notes payable	$ 200,000	$ 600,000
Accounts payable	735,000	560,000
Income taxes payable	120,000	110,000
Interest payable	15,000	53,000
Salaries and wages payable	254,000	304,000
Total current liabilities	1,324,000	1,627,000
Long-term liabilities:		
Notes payable, due April 30, 1992	350,000	-0-
Bonds payable, due November 30, 1996	1,000,000	800,000
Mortgage note payable, due January 1, 1992	100,000	-0-
Total long-term liabilities	1,450,000	800,000
Stockholders' equity:		
Common stock, $2 par value	1,100,000	1,000,000
Paid-in capital in excess of par value	916,000	860,000
Retained earnings	1,042,000	988,000
Total stockholders' equity	3,058,000	2,848,000
Total Liabilities and Stockholders' Equity	$5,832,000	$5,275,000

Net sales		$10,240,000
Cost of goods sold		5,585,000
Gross profit		4,655,000
Operating expenses:		
Advertising expense	$ 306,000	
Amortization expense	30,000	
Depreciation expense	480,000	
Salaries and wages expense	1,894,000	
Other operating expenses	1,403,000	
Total operating expenses		4,113,000
Operating income		542,000
Other revenues, expenses, gains, and losses:		
Interest and dividend revenue	54,000	
Interest expense	(188,000)	
Loss on sale of investments	(60,000)	
Net other expenses and losses		(194,000)
Net income before income tax		348,000
Income tax expense		144,000
Net income		204,000
Retained earnings, January 1, 1988		988,000
Total		1,192,000
Less: Cash dividends		150,000
Retained earnings, December 31,1988		$ 1,042,000

Additional information:

1. Land was purchased during the year for $100,000. A long-term mortgage note was given for the entire purchase price.
2. A building was purchased for $600,000 cash.
3. Equipment was purchased at a total cost of $350,000. A note payable due April 30, 1992 was given for the entire purchase price.
4. Bonds payable of $200,000 were issued at par value for cash.

5. Long-term investments in equity securities with a cost of $210,000 were sold for $150,000. Additional long-term investments in equity securities were purchased at a cost of $240,000.
6. 50,000 shares of $2 par value common stock were issued for $156,000.

Required:
Prepare a SCF for Mather Company for the year ended December 31, 1988. Use the direct method of reporting net cash flow from operating activities.

Problem 17-7 Preparing a Statement of Cash Flows

The Lange Company experienced the following changes in balance sheet accounts during 1988:

	Change	
Account	Debit	Credit
Cash	$169,000	
Accounts receivable		$252,000
Inventory	168,000	
Plant assets	490,000	
Accumulated depreciation		126,000
Accounts payable	112,000	
Accrued expenses		42,000
Long-term debt	21,000	
Common stock		280,000
Retained earnings		260,000
Totals	$960,000	$960,000

The firm earned $316,000 during 1988 and paid cash dividends of $56,000. Fully depreciated plant assets that originally cost $6,000 were sold for their residual value of $1,000.

Required:
Prepare a statement of cash flows for 1988.

Problem 17-8 Evaluating Cash Flow Problems

The president of the Cash-Out Company just received copies of her firm's financial statements for 1988. She is concerned about the fact that the company earned record profits but is faced with a serious shortage of cash. Comparative balance sheets for 1987 and 1988 as well as the 1988 income statement are shown next.

CASH-OUT COMPANY
Income Statement
Year Ended December 31, 1988

Sales	$8,064,000
Cost of goods sold	4,620,000
Gross profit	3,444,000
Operating expenses	2,568,000
Net income	$ 876,000

CASH-OUT COMPANY
Balance Sheet
As of December 31, 1987 & 1988

	1988	1987
Assets		
Cash	$ 30,000	$ 456,000
Accounts receivable	1,188,000	1,032,000
Inventory	1,734,000	1,440,000
Plant assets (net)	4,620,000	4,044,000
Total	$7,572,000	$6,972,000
Liabilities and Stockholders' Equity		
Accounts payable	$ 228,000	$ 336,000
Accrued expenses	132,000	240,000
Long-term debt	2,700,000	2,640,000
Common stock	2,496,000	2,496,000
Retained earnings	2,016,000	1,260,000
Total	$7,572,000	$6,972,000

The president has asked the firm's controller to provide an explanation about why the cash balance has declined so much even though the company earned a net income of $876,000 with $180,000 of depreciation expense in 1988. Cash dividends of $120,000 were paid during 1988 because of the firm's high profits.

Required:
Prepare a statement of cash flows for 1988 that will assist the controller in explaining the firm's cash problems to the president.

Problem 17-9 Conversion of Accrual Basis to Cash Basis

The following account balances were taken from comparative trial balances of the Bengston Company as of December 31, 1987 and 1988:

	1988	1987
Accounts receivable	$228,000	$180,000
Interest receivable	600	840
Inventory	264,000	240,000
Prepaid supplies	2,160	1,200
Accounts payable (from purchases)	276,000	228,000
Accrued operating expenses	9,600	12,000
Sales	960,000	
Interest revenue	1,800	
Cost of goods sold	720,000	
Supplies expense	2,400	
Operating expenses	96,000	

Operating expenses include depreciation expense of $2,400 and amortization expense of $1,200.

Required:
Compute the following:

A.   Cash basis sales.

B. Cash paid for supplies during 1988.
C. Cash paid for inventory purchases during 1988.
D. Cash paid for operating expenses during 1988.
E. Interest income collected during 1988.
F. Net cash flow from operating activities during 1988 using the direct method.
G. Net cash flow from operating activities during 1988 using the indirect method.

Problem 17-10 Preparing a SCF — Indirect Method
Comparative balance sheets for 1987 and 1988 and the statement of income and retained earnings for 1988 for Litchfield Company follow:

LITCHFIELD COMPANY
Comparative Balance Sheet

	December 31	
	1988	1987
Current assets:		
Cash and cash equivalents	$ 568,000	$ 705,000
Accounts receivable (net)	871,300	812,700
Loans receivable	240,000	160,000
Interest receivable	18,000	10,000
Merchandise inventory	2,510,000	2,640,000
Prepaid expenses	117,000	197,000
Total current assets	4,324,300	4,524,700
Investments and funds:		
Long-term investments in equity securities (at cost, which is less than market value)	363,000	486,000
Bond sinking fund	485,000	350,000
Total investments and funds	848,000	836,000
Property, plant, and equipment:		
Land	500,000	420,000
Buildings	3,200,000	2,100,000
Accumulated depreciation — buildings	(1,165,000)	(945,000)
Equipment	2,420,000	1,650,000
Accumulated depreciation — equipment	(890,000)	(630,000)
Total property, plant, and equipment	4,065,000	2,595,000
Intangible assets:		
Patents	410,000	400,000
Trademarks	116,000	120,000
Total intangible assets	526,000	520,000
Total assets	$9,763,300	$8,475,700
Current liabilities:		
Short-term notes payable	$ 400,000	$1,200,000
Accounts payable	825,000	648,000
Income taxes payable	–0–	120,000
Interest payable	27,000	16,000
Salaries payable	63,000	77,000
Mortgage payable, current portion	8,000	–0–
Other accrued expenses	201,000	183,000
Total current liabilities	1,524,000	2,244,000

Long-term liabilities:		
Notes payable, due September 30, 1993	900,000	400,000
Bonds payable, due December 31, 2017	1,000,000	-0-
Mortgage payable	72,000	-0-
Total long-term liabilities	1,972,000	400,000
Stockholders' equity:		
Common stock, $10 par value	2,200,000	2,000,000
Paid-in capital in excess of par value	2,400,000	2,150,000
Retained earnings	1,867,300	2,081,700
Treasury stock, at cost	(200,000)	(400,000)
Total stockholders' equity	6,267,300	5,831,700
Total liabilities and stockholders' equity	$9,763,300	$8,475,700

LITCHFIELD COMPANY
Statement of Income and Retained Earnings
Year Ended December 31, 1988

Net sales		$15,158,000
Cost of goods sold		8,928,400
Gross profit		6,229,600
Operating expenses:		
Other than depreciation and amortization	$5,636,000	
Depreciation expense	530,000	
Amortization expense	44,000	
Total operating expenses		6,210,000
Operating income		19,600
Other revenues, expenses, gains, and losses:		
Gain on sale of investments	46,000	
Bond sinking fund revenue	35,000	
Loss on sale of equipment	(115,000)	
Net other expense and loss		(34,000)
Net loss		(14,400)
Retained earnings, January 1		2,081,700
Total		2,067,300
Less: Cash dividends paid		200,000
Retained earnings, December 31		$ 1,867,300

Additional information:

1. Land was purchased on July 1, 1988 for $80,000. A ten-year mortgage note was given for the entire purchase price. The mortgage is payable in ten equal annual payments of $8,000 plus interest on the unpaid balance. The annual payment is due each June 30.
2. A building was purchased for $1,100,000. Cash of $600,000 plus a long-term note payable of $500,000 was given in exchange.
3. Equipment was purchased for $1,070,000 cash.
4. Equipment with an original cost of $300,000 and accumulated depreciation of $50,000 was sold for $135,000 cash.

5. A patent was purchased for $50,000 cash.
6. Long-term investments in equity securities with a cost of $123,000 were sold for $169,000.
7. A $100,000 deposit was made to the bond sinking fund during 1988. In addition, the fund earned $35,000, which was debited to the bond sinking fund.
8. Bonds payable of $1,000,000 were issued for cash at par value.
9. An additional 20,000 shares of $10 par value common stock were issued for $18 per share.
10. Treasury stock costing $200,000 was sold for $290,000. The excess of the selling price over cost was credited to paid-in capital in excess of par value.
11. Cash dividends of $200,000 were declared and paid.
12. Depreciation expense was $220,000 on the building and $310,000 on the equipment. Amortization expense was $40,000 on patents and $4,000 on trademarks.
13. Loans made during the year amounted to $800,000, and loans receivable collected during the year were $720,000.
14. Cash paid to reduce short-term notes payable amounted to $800,000.

Required:
Prepare a SCF for Litchfield Company for the year ended December 31, 1988. Use the indirect method of reporting net cash flow from operating activities.

APPENDIX A
TIME VALUE OF MONEY

Interest is the payment made for the use of money. As such, interest is the measure of the time value of money. A dollar expected sometime in the future is not equivalent to a dollar held today, because of the time value of money. The dollar available today can be invested to earn interest, so it will increase in value to more than one dollar in the future. Consequently, we would rather receive a dollar now than receive the same amount in the future, even if we are certain of receiving it at the later date. Businesses often invest and borrow large sums of money, so the time value of money is an important topic. The dramatic increase in interest rates in recent years has had a corresponding impact on the time value of money. For example, the average interest rates on short-term bank loans between 1965 and 1970 ranged from 5% to 9%. By the middle part of the 1970s, the rate averaged as much as 14%. In the early 1980s, the interest on short-term bank loans exceeded 20% at times. While interest rates in the mid-1980s declined from their all-time highs, they still were double digit in many cases. We begin the examination of the time value of money with a discussion of simple and compound interest.

SIMPLE AND COMPOUND INTEREST

Simple interest is interest earned on an original amount invested (the ***principal***). The amount of principal and the interest payments remain the same from period to period, since interest is computed on the amount of principal only as:

Interest (in dollars) = Principal (in dollars) × Rate (% per year) × Time (in years)

To illustrate the computation of simple interest, assume that the Brown Supply Company sells merchandise in exchange for a $2,000 two-year note receivable, bearing simple interest of 12% per year. The amount of interest due Brown Supply Company at the end of two years is:

$$\text{Interest} = \text{Principal} \times \text{Rate} \times \text{Time}$$
$$= \$2,000 \times .12 \times 2$$
$$= \$480$$

Compound interest is interest earned on the original amount invested (principal) plus previously earned interest. As interest is earned during any period, it is added to the principal; interest is computed on the new balance (often called the compound amount) during the next period. Interest can be compounded in a number of ways, such as daily, monthly, quarterly, semiannually, or annually. As an illustration of compound interest, assume that the note receivable held by the Brown Supply Company is the same as that described earlier, except that the interest is compounded annually. The total interest for the two-year period can be computed.

(1) Year	(2) Beginning Balance	(3) Compound Interest [Column(2) × .12]	(4) Ending Balance
1	$2,000.00	$240.00	$2,240.00
2	2,240.00	268.80	2,508.80

In the second case, the total interest is $508.80, compared with the $480.00 computed earlier. The difference of $28.80 represents interest earned in the second year on the first year's interest ($240 × .12) and is the product of using compound, rather than simple, interest. In most cases involving the time value of money, compound interest is applicable, so we will consider only compound interest in the discussion that follows.

The time value of money is used in a wide variety of accounting applications, including the valuation of bonds, valuation of notes receivable or payable, determination of amounts to contribute to a pension plan, accounting for installment contracts, valuation of leases, and capital budgeting. Four cases must be considered in developing an understanding of the time value of money.

Case I	—Future value of a single amount
Case II	—Future value of an ordinary annuity
Case III	—Present value of a single amount
Case IV	—Present value of an ordinary annuity

CASE I (FUTURE VALUE OF A SINGLE AMOUNT)

As we have seen earlier, an amount of money invested today will have a higher future value than the original principal because of interest earned. The *future value of a single amount* invested today can be computed as follows.

$$FV = PV(1 + i)^n$$

where:

FV = Future value
PV = Present value of single amount invested (principal)
i = Interest rate per period
n = Number of periods

Schematically, the future value computation can be shown as:

Present value (principal invested) → Compounded at i interest rate for n periods → Future value (accumulated amount)

The interest rate is normally expressed as an annual rate. However, interest is often compounded more frequently—daily, monthly, quarterly, or semiannually. In such cases, the interest rate and number of periods must coincide with the compounding schedule. For example, if 12% per year interest is earned over a two-year period with quarterly compounding, the interest rate and number of periods used in the future value formula are 3% and eight, respectively. This means that the annual interest rate (12%) is divided by the number of times compounding takes place (4) within a year, giving 3%, and the number of years (2) is multiplied by the number of compounding periods (4), giving eight periods.

To illustrate the use of the future value formula with annual compounding, consider again the Brown Supply Company case with compound interest. The future value of the note receivable is found as follows.

$$FV = \$2,000 \ (1 + .12)^2$$
$$= \$2,508.80$$

As we see, the total amount due Brown Supply Company at maturity ($2,508.80) is the same as we computed earlier by adding the compound interest to the principal. If the note receivable involves quarterly compounding, we must revise the formula by dividing the 12% interest rate by four and multiplying two years by four as:

$$FV = \$2,000 \ (1 + .03)^8$$
$$= \$2,533.60$$

The amount of interest earned with quarterly compounding will be $24.80 more than it was with annual compounding. Note that the mathematics involved with the future value formula become more tedious as we increase the number of periods involved. Fortunately, tables have been developed for various combinations of interest rates and periods to avoid the necessity of using the formula each time a future value of a single amount of money must be computed. Table A-1 shows the future value of $1 for various interest rates and various periods.

Suppose we want to know how much a dollar invested today at 12% interest compounded annually will be worth 10 years from now. We simply find the amount (called a *factor*) in the 12% column and 10 periods row of Table A-1 — 3.1058. Thus, the dollar invested now will become approximately $3.11 in 10 years, because of the compound interest earned. Note that the left-hand column of Table A-1 (and the other tables discussed later) refers to periods instead of years. This enables us to use the table even if interest is compounded more frequently than once a year. As we noted earlier for such cases, the number of years is multiplied by the number of times compounding occurs to determine the number of periods that must be considered. In addition, an annual interest rate is divided by the number of compounding periods to convert it to the appropriate interest rate. For example, assume the dollar invested earlier will earn 12% interest compounded semiannually instead of annually. We need to multiply 10 years by 2 (20 periods) and divide 12% by 2 (6%) to determine the appropriate factor in Table A-1. The factor is 3.2071 — located in the 6% interest rate column and 20 periods row. Therefore, the dollar will grow to approximately $3.21 over the 10-year period. This same adjustment is required with the later tables whenever interest is compounded more frequently than once a year.

The factors in Table A-1 were determined by using the future value formula with a principal of $1. By multiplying a specific factor found in the table for the appropriate combination of interest rate and number of periods by the single amount of money involved, the future value of that amount can be calculated. To illustrate the use of Table A-1 when the amount involved is more than $1,

Periods	2%	3%	4%	5%	6%	8%	10%	12%	16%	20%
1	1.0200	1.0300	1.0400	1.0500	1.0600	1.0800	1.1000	1.1200	1.1600	1.2000
2	1.0404	1.0609	1.0816	1.1025	1.1236	1.1664	1.2100	1.2544	1.3456	1.4400
3	1.0612	1.0927	1.1249	1.1576	1.1910	1.2597	1.3310	1.4049	1.5609	1.7280
4	1.0824	1.1255	1.1699	1.2155	1.2625	1.3605	1.4641	1.5735	1.8106	2.0736
5	1.1041	1.1593	1.2167	1.2763	1.3382	1.4693	1.6105	1.7623	2.1003	2.4883
6	1.1262	1.1941	1.2653	1.3401	1.4185	1.5869	1.7716	1.9738	2.4364	2.9860
7	1.1487	1.2299	1.3159	1.4071	1.5036	1.7138	1.9487	2.2107	2.8262	3.5832
8	1.1717	1.2668	1.3686	1.4775	1.5938	1.8509	2.1436	2.4760	3.2784	4.2998
9	1.1951	1.3048	1.4233	1.5513	1.6895	1.9990	2.3579	2.7731	3.8030	5.1598
10	1.2190	1.3439	1.4802	1.6289	1.7908	2.1589	2.5937	3.1058	4.4114	6.1917
11	1.2434	1.3842	1.5395	1.7103	1.8983	2.3316	2.8531	3.4785	5.1173	7.4301
12	1.2682	1.4258	1.6010	1.7959	2.0122	2.5182	3.1384	3.8960	5.9360	8.9161
13	1.2936	1.4685	1.6651	1.8856	2.1329	2.7196	3.4523	4.3635	6.8858	10.6993
14	1.3195	1.5126	1.7317	1.9799	2.2609	2.9372	3.7975	4.8871	7.9875	12.8392
15	1.3459	1.5580	1.8009	2.0789	2.3966	3.1722	4.1772	5.4736	9.2655	15.4070
16	1.3728	1.6047	1.8730	2.1829	2.5404	3.4259	4.5950	6.1304	10.7480	18.4884
17	1.4002	1.6528	1.9479	2.2920	2.6928	3.7000	5.0545	6.8660	12.4677	22.1861
18	1.4282	1.7024	2.0258	2.4066	2.8543	3.9960	5.5599	7.6900	14.4625	26.6233
19	1.4568	1.7535	2.1068	2.5270	3.0256	4.3157	6.1159	8.6128	16.7765	31.9480
20	1.4859	1.8061	2.1911	2.6533	3.2071	4.6610	6.7275	9.6463	19.4608	38.3376
25	1.6406	2.0938	2.6658	3.3864	4.2919	6.8485	10.8347	17.0001	40.8742	95.3962
30	1.8114	2.4273	3.2434	4.3219	5.7435	10.0627	17.4494	29.9599	85.8499	237.3763

Table A-1
Future Value of $1

assume again that the two-year note receivable of Brown Supply Company has a 12% interest rate compounded annually. The factor in Table A-1 for 12% interest and two years is 1.2544, so the note's future value is:

$$FV = \$2,000 \,(1.2544)$$
$$= \$2,508.80$$

This is the same result we obtained earlier with the future value formula. If interest is compounded quarterly, the factor from the table is 1.2668 (3% and 8 periods), so the future value is:

$$FV = \$2,000 \,(1.2668)$$
$$= \$2,533.60$$

Again, the future value is the same as the one computed earlier with the formula approach.

CASE II (FUTURE VALUE OF AN ORDINARY ANNUITY)

In contrast to the single amount of money considered in Case I, an *annuity* consists of a series of payments over a specified number of periods, with compound interest on the payments. An *ordinary annuity* is a series of equal payments that occur at the end of each time period involved. Here we will consider only ordinary annuities and defer the subject of annuities due (in which the payments occur at the beginning of the time periods) to more advanced accounting courses.

The future value of an ordinary annuity is the sum of all payments, plus the compound interest accumulated on each. For example, if a business makes a deposit of $5,000 to a savings program at the end of three consecutive years, with each payment earning 12% interest compounded annually, the total amount accumulated over the three-year period is the future value of an ordinary annuity. One way to calculate the future value of the series of payments would be to treat each payment separately and determine the amount of interest earned.

(1) Year	(2) Beginning Balance	(3) Annual Interest [Column (2) × .12]	(4) Payment	(5) Ending Balance
1			$5,000	$ 5,000
2	$ 5,000	$ 600	5,000	10,600
3	10,600	1,272	5,000	16,872

It can be seen from these calculations that interest is earned for only two periods, even though three payments were made. As the number of payments increases, this approach obviously becomes more time consuming.

A formula can be used also to calculate the future value of an ordinary annuity. The formula is more complicated than the one used for the future value of a single amount, however, so it is not normally utilized. Instead, a table, such as Table A-2, is used, because it contains factors for various combinations of interest rates and number of periods as computed with a *future value of an ordinary annuity* formula when payments of $1 are involved.

To illustrate the use of Table A-2, consider again that the company makes three annual payments of $5,000 at the end of each year and earns 12% interest, compounded annually. The factor for 12% interest and three periods in Table A-2 is 3.3744. Since the factor represents the future value of three payments of $1 at 12% interest, it is used to determine the future value of the actual payments made as:

$$FV = \$5,000 \ (3.3744)$$
$$= \$16,872$$

This is the same answer we found earlier by treating each payment separately. The three payments of $5,000 each (total of $15,000) will increase in value to $16,872 over the three-year period. The difference between the $16,872 future value and the payments totaling $15,000 is interest amounting to $1,872. If semiannual payments of $2,500 had been involved during the three-year period, the appropriate factor from Table A-2 would be for six periods and 6%. Again, this adjustment is required because of semiannual compounding. The factor for six periods and 6% from Table A-2 is 6.9753, so the future value of the ordinary annuity is:

$$FV = \$2,500 \ (6.9753)$$
$$= \$17,438.25$$

As we see, the future value of $17,438.25 with semiannual compounding is higher than the $16,872.00 computed with annual compounding, because additional interest is earned.

Periods	2%	3%	4%	5%	6%	8%	10%	12%	16%	20%
1	1.0000	1.0000	1.0000	1.0000	1.0000	1.0000	1.0000	1.0000	1.0000	1.0000
2	2.0200	2.0300	2.0400	2.0500	2.0600	2.0800	2.1000	2.1200	2.1600	2.2000
3	3.0604	3.0909	3.1216	3.1525	3.1836	3.2464	3.3100	3.3744	3.5056	3.6400
4	4.1216	4.1836	4.2465	4.3101	4.3746	4.5061	4.6410	4.7793	5.0665	5.3680
5	5.2040	5.3091	5.4163	5.5256	5.6371	5.8666	6.1051	6.3528	6.8771	7.4416
6	6.3081	6.4684	6.6330	6.8019	6.9753	7.3359	7.7156	8.1152	8.9775	9.9299
7	7.4343	7.6625	7.8983	8.1420	8.3938	8.9228	9.4872	10.0890	11.4139	12.9159
8	8.5830	8.8923	9.2142	9.5491	9.8975	10.6366	11.4359	12.2997	14.2401	16.4991
9	9.7546	10.1591	10.5828	11.0266	11.4913	12.4876	13.5795	14.7757	17.5185	20.7989
10	10.9497	11.4639	12.0061	12.5779	13.1808	14.4866	15.9374	17.5487	21.3215	25.9587
11	12.1687	12.8078	13.4864	14.2068	14.9716	16.6455	18.5312	20.6546	25.7329	32.1504
12	13.4121	14.1920	15.0258	15.9171	16.8699	18.9771	21.3843	24.1331	30.8502	39.5805
13	14.6803	15.6178	16.6268	17.7130	18.8821	21.4953	24.5227	28.0291	36.7862	48.4966
14	15.9739	17.0863	18.2919	19.5986	21.0151	24.2149	27.9750	32.3926	43.6720	59.1959
15	17.2934	18.5989	20.0236	21.5786	23.2760	27.1521	31.7725	37.2797	51.6595	72.0351
16	18.6393	20.1569	21.8245	23.6575	25.6725	30.3243	35.9497	42.7533	60.9250	87.4421
17	20.0121	21.7616	23.6975	25.8404	28.2129	33.7502	40.5447	48.8837	71.6730	105.9306
18	21.4123	23.4144	25.6454	28.1324	30.9057	37.4502	45.5992	55.7497	84.1407	128.1167
19	22.8406	25.1169	27.6712	30.5390	33.7600	41.4463	51.1591	63.4397	98.6032	154.7400
20	24.2974	26.8704	29.7781	33.0660	36.7856	45.7620	57.2750	72.0524	115.3797	186.6880
25	32.0303	36.4593	41.6459	47.7271	54.8645	73.1059	98.3471	133.3339	249.2140	471.9811
30	40.5681	47.5754	56.0849	66.4388	79.0582	113.2832	164.4940	241.3327	530.3117	1181.8816

Table A-2
Future Value of an Ordinary Annuity of $1

CASE III (PRESENT VALUE OF A SINGLE AMOUNT)

In Case I, we were concerned with the determination of the future value of a single amount of money. Many accounting applications of the time value of money involve the reverse of the future value consideration, the concern with computing the present value of some future amount of money. As noted earlier, money held today is worth more than the same amount of money received in the future because of the time value of money. Consequently, the present value of a given amount to be received in the future will be less than the future value. To determine the present value of a specific future amount, the future value must be discounted with an appropriate discount (interest) rate to the present. Future value and present value have a reciprocal relationship, as can be seen by comparing the formulas for the future value and the present value of a single amount of money. Recall that the future value is computed as:

$$FV = PV (1 + i)^n$$

In contrast, the *present value of a single amount* of money is calculated as:

$$PV = \frac{FV}{(1 + i)^n}$$

where:

PV = present value
FV = future value of amount to be accumulated
 i = interest rate per period
 n = number of periods

Schematically, the present value computation can be shown as:

Present value   Discounted at i Future value
(amount to be ← interest rate   ← (amount to be
invested now)   for n periods   accumulated)

To illustrate the use of the present value of a single amount of money formula, consider again the note receivable held by Brown Supply Company. We determined earlier that the future value of the note was $2,508.80 when interest was compounded annually. By discounting the $2,508.80 for two years at 12%, we can determine its present value, which should be $2,000, as:

$$PV = \frac{\$2,508.80}{(1 + .12)^2}$$
$$= \$2,000.00$$

If the interest is compounded quarterly, we learned earlier that the future value of the note is $2,533.60. However, the present value of the note should remain at $2,000 when it is discounted for eight periods at 3% interest per period, or:

$$PV = \frac{\$2,533.60}{(1 + .03)^8}$$
$$= \$2,000.00$$

As another example of calculating the present value of a single amount of money, assume that the Holmes Company has a liability of $23,958, which must be paid in three years. The company wants to know how much it must invest today to have $23,958 in three years if the amount earns 10% interest, compounded annually. The amount to be invested would be determined as:

$$PV = \frac{\$23,958}{(1 + .10)^3}$$
$$= \$18,000$$

Consequently, the $18,000 (present value) will increase in value to $23,958 (future value) by the end of the third year, because interest amounting to $5,958 will be earned. Like the future value formulas, the math involved with the computation of present value with a formula can be tedious, so a table is normally used. Table A-3 shows factors for various combinations of interest rates and number of periods when the present value of $1 is computed. By multiplying an appropriate factor from the table by the single amount of money involved, its present value can be determined. For example, in the Brown Supply Company case with annual compounding, a value of .7972 is found in Table A-3 for 12% interest and two periods. Thus, the present value of the note receivable is:

$$PV = \$2,508.80 \,(.7972)$$
$$= \$2,000$$

With quarterly compounding, the value in Table A-3 is found for 3% interest and eight periods (.7894) and used as follows.

$$PV = \$2,533.60\ (.7894)$$
$$= \$2,000$$

Table A-3 can also be used to determine the amount that the Holmes Company must invest today to have $23,958 three years later with the same factors discussed earlier. The factor in Table A-3 for 10% interest and three periods is .7513, so the present value of $23,958 is:

$$PV = \$23,958\ (.7513)$$
$$= \$18,000$$

Note that each of the factors shown in Table A-3 for a particular combination of interest rates and number of periods is one divided by the corresponding factor found in Table A-1. This must be true because of the reciprocal relationship between the formulas for future value and present value of a single amount. For example, the factor in Table A-3 for 12% interest and two periods is .7972, which is the same as one divided by 1.2544 (Table A-1). Consequently, you can always determine the appropriate Table A-3 factor from Table A-1 and vice versa if both tables are not available.

CASE IV (PRESENT VALUE OF AN ORDINARY ANNUITY)

In Case II, we considered how to determine the future value of an ordinary annuity—a series of equal payments made at the end of each time period involved. Our final concern with the time value of money is the reverse of Case II—that is, the present value of a series of equal future payments representing an ordinary annuity. The present value of an ordinary annuity is the amount that would have to be invested today at a certain compound interest rate to enable the investor to receive the series of future payments over a specified period of time. Assume that the Briden Corporation has obligations of $6,000 that must be repaid at the end of each of the next three years, including the current one. The firm wants to know how much it would have to invest today to repay each of the obligations if the amount invested earns 10%, compounded annually. One way to determine the amount of the required investment would be to treat each $6,000 payment as a single amount. Each payment would be discounted to its present value (using Table A-3), and the results would be added to determine the total amount needed to be invested. If this approach is taken, the following calculations are necessary.

(1) Year	(2) Payment	(3) Factor (Table A-3 — 10%)	(4) Present Value [Column (2) × Column (3)]
1	$6,000	.9091	$ 5,454.60
2	6,000	.8264	4,958.40
3	6,000	.7513	4,507.80
Total present value			$14,920.80

Table A-3
Present Value of $1

Periods	2%	3%	4%	5%	6%	8%	10%	12%	13%	14%	15%	16%	17%	18%	19%	20%
1	0.9804	0.9709	0.9615	0.9524	0.9434	0.9259	0.9091	0.8929	0.8850	0.8772	0.8696	0.8621	0.8547	0.8475	0.8403	0.8333
2	0.9612	0.9426	0.9246	0.9070	0.8900	0.8573	0.8264	0.7972	0.7832	0.7695	0.7561	0.7432	0.7305	0.7182	0.7062	0.6944
3	0.9423	0.9151	0.8890	0.8638	0.8396	0.7938	0.7513	0.7118	0.6931	0.6750	0.6575	0.6407	0.6244	0.6086	0.5934	0.5787
4	0.9238	0.8885	0.8548	0.8227	0.7921	0.7350	0.6830	0.6355	0.6133	0.5921	0.5718	0.5523	0.5337	0.5158	0.4987	0.4823
5	0.9057	0.8626	0.8219	0.7835	0.7473	0.6806	0.6209	0.5674	0.5428	0.5194	0.4972	0.4761	0.4561	0.4371	0.4191	0.4019
6	0.8880	0.8375	0.7903	0.7462	0.7050	0.6302	0.5645	0.5066	0.4803	0.4556	0.4323	0.4104	0.3898	0.3704	0.3521	0.3349
7	0.8706	0.8131	0.7599	0.7107	0.6651	0.5835	0.5132	0.4523	0.4251	0.3996	0.3759	0.3538	0.3332	0.3139	0.2959	0.2791
8	0.8535	0.7894	0.7307	0.6768	0.6274	0.5403	0.4665	0.4039	0.3762	0.3506	0.3269	0.3050	0.2848	0.2660	0.2487	0.2326
9	0.8368	0.7664	0.7026	0.6446	0.5919	0.5002	0.4241	0.3606	0.3329	0.3075	0.2843	0.2630	0.2434	0.2255	0.2090	0.1938
10	0.8203	0.7441	0.6756	0.6139	0.5584	0.4632	0.3855	0.3220	0.2946	0.2697	0.2472	0.2267	0.2080	0.1911	0.1756	0.1615
11	0.8043	0.7224	0.6496	0.5847	0.5268	0.4289	0.3505	0.2875	0.2607	0.2366	0.2149	0.1954	0.1778	0.1619	0.1476	0.1346
12	0.7885	0.7014	0.6246	0.5568	0.4970	0.3971	0.3186	0.2567	0.2307	0.2076	0.1869	0.1685	0.1520	0.1372	0.1240	0.1122
13	0.7730	0.6810	0.6006	0.5303	0.4688	0.3677	0.2897	0.2292	0.2042	0.1821	0.1625	0.1452	0.1299	0.1163	0.1042	0.0935
14	0.7579	0.6611	0.5775	0.5051	0.4423	0.3405	0.2633	0.2046	0.1807	0.1597	0.1413	0.1252	0.1110	0.0986	0.0876	0.0779
15	0.7430	0.6419	0.5553	0.4810	0.4173	0.3152	0.2394	0.1827	0.1599	0.1401	0.1229	0.1079	0.0949	0.0835	0.0736	0.0649
16	0.7284	0.6232	0.5339	0.4581	0.3936	0.2919	0.2176	0.1631	0.1415	0.1229	0.1069	0.0930	0.0811	0.0708	0.0618	0.0541
17	0.7142	0.6050	0.5134	0.4363	0.3714	0.2703	0.1978	0.1456	0.1252	0.1078	0.0929	0.0802	0.0693	0.0600	0.0520	0.0451
18	0.7002	0.5874	0.4936	0.4155	0.3503	0.2502	0.1799	0.1300	0.1108	0.0946	0.0808	0.0691	0.0593	0.0508	0.0437	0.0376
19	0.6864	0.5703	0.4746	0.3957	0.3305	0.2317	0.1635	0.1161	0.0981	0.0830	0.0703	0.0596	0.0506	0.0431	0.0367	0.0313
20	0.6730	0.5537	0.4564	0.3769	0.3118	0.2145	0.1486	0.1037	0.0868	0.0728	0.0611	0.0514	0.0433	0.0365	0.0308	0.0261
25	0.6095	0.4776	0.3751	0.2953	0.2330	0.1460	0.0923	0.0588	0.0471	0.0378	0.0304	0.0245	0.0197	0.0160	0.0129	0.0105
30	0.5521	0.4120	0.3083	0.2314	0.1741	0.0994	0.0573	0.0334	0.0256	0.0196	0.0151	0.0116	0.0090	0.0070	0.0054	0.0042

The firm would have to invest $14,920.80 today to have the money available to make payments of $6,000 at the end of each of the next three years. If numerous payments are involved, this approach will obviously be quite time consuming. Since the $6,000 payments can be viewed as an annuity, an easier way to discount them to their present value is to use Table A-4. The factors in Table A-4 have been derived from a formula representing the *present value of an annuity of $1*. In the table, factors for various combinations of interest rates and number of periods are presented for the determination of the present value of an annuity of $1. Again, a given factor must be multiplied by the actual amount of each payment involved. The factor is 2.4869 for 10% and three periods. Therefore, the present value of the $6,000 payments can be calculated as:

$$PV = \$6,000 \ (2.4869)$$
$$= \$14,921.40$$

As we see, the results are essentially the same as those obtained by discounting each payment and adding the individual present values. If semiannual payments of $3,000 were made to satisfy the firm's obligations, the present value calculation would require an adjustment of the number of periods and the annual interest rate. Six periods (three years × 2) and an interest rate of 5% (10% ÷ 2) would be used to determine the factor of 5.0757 from Table A-4, and the present value of the annuity would be:

$$PV = \$3,000 \ (5.0757)$$
$$= \$15,227.10$$

Note that the present value with semiannual payments is more than it was with annual payments. The reason for this is that the amount invested will not have as much time to earn interest because payments are made every six months rather than at the end of the year.

EXERCISES

Exercise A-1 Compute Simple Interest
The Style Company has agreed to take a note receivable in exchange for an overdue account receivable from the Pay-Late Company. Simple interest, at 16%, is payable beginning March 1 (the date of the exchange) and the note receivable is for a three-year term. The amount of the note receivable is $4,000 and interest will be paid at the maturity of the note.

Required:
Calculate the amount of interest due at the end of three years.

Exercise A-2 Compute Compound Interest
Refer to Exercise A-1. How much interest would be due if compound interest were involved?

Exercise A-3 Compute the Future Value of a Single Amount
Using Table A-1, compute the following future values:

1. $10,000 invested at 12% for 5 years, compounded annually
2. $10,000 invested at 12% for 5 years, compounded semiannually
3. $10,000 invested at 12% for 5 years, compounded quarterly

Table A-4
Present Value of an Ordinary Annuity of $1

Periods	2%	3%	4%	5%	6%	8%	10%	12%	13%	14%	15%	16%	17%	18%	19%	20%
1	0.9804	0.9709	0.9615	0.9524	0.9434	0.9259	0.9091	0.8929	0.8850	0.8772	0.8696	0.8621	0.8547	0.8475	0.8403	0.8333
2	1.9416	1.9135	1.8861	1.8594	1.8334	1.7833	1.7355	1.6901	1.6681	1.6467	1.6257	1.6052	1.5852	1.5656	1.5465	1.5278
3	2.8839	2.8286	2.7751	2.7232	2.6730	2.5771	2.4869	2.4018	2.3612	2.3216	2.2832	2.2459	2.2096	2.1743	2.1399	2.1065
4	3.8077	3.7171	3.6299	3.5460	3.4651	3.3121	3.1699	3.0373	2.9745	2.9137	2.8550	2.7982	2.7432	2.6901	2.6386	2.5887
5	4.7135	4.5797	4.4518	4.3295	4.2124	3.9927	3.7908	3.6048	3.5172	3.4331	3.3522	3.2743	3.1993	3.1272	3.0576	2.9906
6	5.6014	5.4172	5.2421	5.0757	4.9173	4.6229	4.3553	4.1114	3.9975	3.8887	3.7845	3.6847	3.5892	3.4976	3.4098	3.3255
7	6.4720	6.2303	6.0021	5.7864	5.5824	5.2064	4.8684	4.5638	4.4226	4.2883	4.1604	4.0386	3.9224	3.8115	3.7057	3.6046
8	7.3255	7.0197	6.7327	6.4632	6.2098	5.7466	5.3349	4.9676	4.7988	4.6389	4.4873	4.3436	4.2072	4.0776	3.9544	3.8372
9	8.1622	7.7861	7.4353	7.1078	6.8017	6.2469	5.7590	5.3282	5.1317	4.9464	4.7716	4.6065	4.4506	4.3030	4.1633	4.0310
10	8.9826	8.5302	8.1109	7.7217	7.3601	6.7101	6.1446	5.6502	5.4262	5.2161	5.0188	4.8332	4.6586	4.4941	4.3389	4.1925
11	9.7868	9.2526	8.7605	8.3064	7.8869	7.1390	6.4951	5.9377	5.6869	5.4527	5.2337	5.0286	4.8364	4.6560	4.4865	4.3271
12	10.5753	9.9540	9.3851	8.8633	8.3838	7.5361	6.8137	6.1944	5.9176	5.6603	5.4206	5.1971	4.9884	4.7932	4.6105	4.4392
13	11.3484	10.6350	9.9856	9.3936	8.8527	7.9038	7.1034	6.4235	6.1218	5.8424	5.5831	5.3423	5.1183	4.9095	4.7147	4.5327
14	12.1062	11.2961	10.5631	9.8986	9.2950	8.2442	7.3667	6.6282	6.3025	6.0021	5.7245	5.4675	5.2293	5.0081	4.8023	4.6106
15	12.8493	11.9379	11.1184	10.3797	9.7122	8.5595	7.6061	6.8109	6.4624	6.1422	5.8474	5.5755	5.3242	5.0916	4.8759	4.6755
16	13.5777	12.5611	11.6523	10.8378	10.1059	8.8514	7.8237	6.9740	6.6039	6.2651	5.9542	5.6685	5.4053	5.1624	4.9377	4.7296
17	14.2919	13.1661	12.1657	11.2741	10.4773	9.1216	8.0216	7.1196	6.7291	6.3729	6.0472	5.7487	5.4746	5.2223	4.9897	4.7746
18	14.9920	13.7535	12.6593	11.6896	10.8276	9.3719	8.2014	7.2497	6.8399	6.4674	6.1280	5.8178	5.5339	5.2732	5.0333	4.8122
19	15.6785	14.3238	13.1339	12.0853	11.1581	9.6036	8.3649	7.3658	6.9380	6.5504	6.1982	5.8775	5.5845	5.3162	5.0700	4.8435
20	16.3514	14.8775	13.5903	12.4622	11.4699	9.8181	8.5136	7.4694	7.0248	6.6231	6.2593	5.9288	5.6278	5.3527	5.1009	4.8696
25	19.5235	17.4131	15.6221	14.0939	12.7834	10.6748	9.0770	7.8431	7.3300	6.8729	6.4641	6.0971	5.7662	5.4669	5.1952	4.9476
30	22.3965	19.6004	17.2920	15.3725	13.7648	11.2578	9.4269	8.0552	7.4957	7.0027	6.5660	6.1772	5.8294	5.5168	5.2347	4.9789

Exercise A-4 Compute the Future Value of a Single Amount

An investor wants to know how much a $5,000 investment made today will amount to in 15 years if it earns 10% interest, compounded annually.

Exercise A-5 Compute the Future Value of an Annuity

Using Table A-2, determine the following future values:

1. $10,000 invested at the end of each year for five years at 12%, compounded annually.
2. $5,000 invested at the end of each six months for five years at 12% per year, compounded semiannually.
3. $2,500 invested at the end of each three months for five years at 12% per year, compounded quarterly.

Exercise A-6 Compute the Future Value of an Annuity

An investor wants to know how much she will have if she makes annual payments of $5,000 at the end of the year for 10 years, assuming that the money will earn 10%.

Exercise A-7 Compute the Present Value of a Single Amount

Using Table A-3, determine the present values of the following situations:

1. $10,000 in five years at 12%, compounded annually.
2. $10,000 in five years at 12%, compounded semiannually.
3. $10,000 in five years at 12%, compounded quarterly.

Exercise A-8 Compute the Present Value of a Single Amount

Don Johnson wants to establish a college fund for his only daughter, who is currently eight years old. He wants to know how much he must invest today for it to accumulate to be $50,000 in 10 years at 10%. Ignore income taxes.

Exercise A-9 Compute the Present Value of an Annuity

Using Table A-4, compute the present values of the following situations:

1. $10,000 to be paid at the end of each year for five years, assuming 12% interest and annual compounding.
2. $5,000 to be paid at the end of each six months for five years, assuming 12% annual interest and semiannual compounding.
3. $2,500 to be paid at the end of each three months for five years, assuming 12% annual interest and quarterly compounding.

Exercise A-10 Compute the Present Value of an Annuity

An investor wants to receive $5,000 at the end of each year for the next five years (including the current year). How much must she invest today to achieve this objective, assuming that the money earns 10%?

PROBLEMS

Problem A-1 Computing the Future Value of $1

Patricia Powers wants to invest $10,000 for a five-year period and receive the largest amount of interest possible. A local bank has offered her 8% interest compounded quarterly and a savings and loan association has offered her 10% interest compounded annually.

Required:

Which of the two investments will provide Patricia with the most money at the end of the five-year period?

Problem A-2 **Calculating the Future Value of an Annuity**

The Bond Company recently issued bonds totaling $535,000, and must establish a fund with which the bonds will be repaid at the end of 20 years. Annual payments of $10,000 will be made to the fund at the end of each of 20 years. A local bank has agreed to pay the company 8% for each of the first 10 years and 10% for each of the second 10 years on all funds invested if the money is deposited in the bank.

Required:

Will Bond Company be able to accumulate enough money with this arrangement to retire the bonds at the end of 20 years?

Problem A-3 **Computing the Present Value of $1**

Bill Sarner, a vice president with the Brown Company, is retiring. Under the terms of his salary agreement, he has the option of receiving a $60,000 bonus now or a deferred bonus of $90,000 in five years.

Required:

Assuming that Mr. Sarner can earn 10% on his investments, which option should he choose? Ignore income taxes.

Problem A-4 **Computing the Present Value of an Annuity**

Anne Rogers is considering retirement at age 50. She has accumulated a significant amount of cash, which is currently invested in a bank money market fund. Her accountant estimates that Ms. Rogers will need $30,000 per year to live on, for the next 15 years, until she qualifies for social security and receives an inheritance from her uncle. Her banker has guaranteed an interest rate of 10% compounded annually.

Required:

A. How much must Anne Rogers invest now to be able to receive $30,000 annually for 15 years?

B. How much interest income will she receive during the 15 years?

Problem A-5 **Combining Future Value and Present Value**

Robert Eddy loaned his sister $12,000, so that she could buy a new car. In return, Eddy received a note due in four years, with interest at 8% compounded semiannually. After one year, Eddy found himself in need of cash. The sister could not repay the loan at the time, so Eddy discounted the note at the bank for cash at 12% compounded quarterly.

Required:

A. How much cash did Eddy receive from the bank?

B. Did Eddy have interest income or interest expense from the transaction?

INDEX

Numbers in **boldface color** refer to pages in the glossary.